DESKTOP
COMMUNICATIONS

RELATED TITLES OF INTEREST FROM WILEY:

IBM PS/2 User's Reference Manual, Held

IBM PS/2: A Business Perspective, *Revised Edition,* Hoskins

Local Area Networks: The Second Generation, Madron

LANS: Applications of IEEE/ANSI 802 Standards, Madron

DESKTOP COMMUNICATIONS

IBM® PC, PS/2®, and Compatibles

David A. Honig

Kenton A. Hoover

WILEY

John Wiley & Sons, Inc.
New York • Chichester • Brisbane • Toronto • Singapore

Library of Congress Cataloging-in-Publication Data
Honig, David A.
 Desktop communications: IBM PC, PS/2 & compatibles/David A. Honig, Kenton A. Hoover.

p. cm.
ISBN 0-471-60613-8

Printed in the United States of America
90 91 10 9 8 7 6 5 4 3 2 1

TRADEMARKS

ADM3a is a trademark of Lear Siegler, Inc.

Amiga is a registered trademark of Commodore-Amiga, Inc.

The following are trademarks or registered trademarks of Apple Computer, Inc.: Apple, AppleLink, AppleTalk, LaserWriter, LocalTalk, Macintosh, and ProDOS.

ARCNET is a registered trademark of the Datapoint Corporation.

AST is a registered trademark, and Six-Pak is a trademark, of AST Research, Inc.

Atari is a registered trademark of Atari Corporation.

AT&T and Touch-Tone are registered trademarks, and StarLAN is a trademark, of American Telephone and Telegraph, Inc.

AT&T Mail and UNIX are registered trademarks of AT&T Information Systems.

AutoKey/3270 is a trademark of CDI Systems, Inc.

Automenu is a registered trademark of Magee Enterprises, Inc.

Banyan is a registered trademark, and VINES, VINES/286, VINES/386, and CNS are trademarks, of Banyan Systems, Inc.

Black Box is a registered trademark of Black Box Corporation.

BLAST is a registered trademark of Communication Research Group, Inc.

Carbon Copy PLUS is a trademark of Meridian Technology, Inc.

Chairman is a trademark of Dynamic Microprocessor Associates.

CL/I is a registered trademark of Network Innovations, Inc., an Apple Computer company.

Codex and UDS are registered trademarks of Motorola, Inc.

Commix is a trademark of Infotron LAN Systems, Inc.

Commodore is a registered trademark of Commodore Electronics, Ltd.

CompuServe is a registered trademark of CompuServe, Inc., an H & R Block Company

ComputerLand is a registered trademark of ComputerLand, Inc.

Confer II is a trademark of Advertel Communications.

The Coordinator is a trademark of Action Technologies, Inc.

CP/M is a trademark of Digital Research, Inc.

Data General and Dasher are trademarks of Data General Corporation.

Datapac and Envoy are trademarks of Telecom Canada Ltd.

dBASE is a registered trademark of Ashton-Tate Corporation.

The following are trademarks or registered trademarks of Digital Communications Associates, Inc.: DCA, DART, CROSSTALK, Transporter, IRMA, IRMAcom, and CASL.

The following are trademarks of Digital Equipment Corporation: DEC, DDCMP, VAX, VT, VT100, VT220, VMS, and DECnet.

DESQview is a trademark of Quarterdeck Office Systems.

DIALOG is a registered trademark of Lockheed Corporation.

Dow Jones News/Retrieval Service is a trademark of Dow Jones & Company, Inc.

EasyLAN is a trademark of Server Technology, Inc.

EasyLink is a trademark of Western Union.

Excelan is a registered trademark of Excelan, Inc.

FANSI-CONSOLE is a trademark of Hersey Micro Consulting, Inc.

GEnie is a trademark, and Quick-Comm is a registered trademark of General Electric Corporation.

G/Net is a trademark of Gateway Communications, Inc.

The following are trademarks of Hayes Microcomputer Products, Inc.: Hayes, Smartcom II, Smartcom III, Smartmodem 1200, Smartmodem 1200B, V-series Smartmodem 9600, SCOPE, and Transet 1000.

Hewlett-Packard is a registered trademark of Hewlett-Packard Company.

Higgins is a trademark of Conetic Systems Inc.

HyperAccess is a registered trademark, and HyperProtocol is a trademark of Hilgraeve, Inc.

The following are trademarks or registered trademarks of International Business Machines Corporation: IBM, Personal Computer XT, XT, Personal Computer AT, AT, PC Jr, Personal Computer RT, RT, Personal System/2, PS/2, and PC-DOS; 3090, 3101, 3161, 3270, 3178, 3179, 3180, 3278, 3279, 3290, 3705, 3720, 3725, and 7171; Series/1, System/34, System/36, System/38, AS/400, and ES/9370; MVS/TSO, VM/CMS, OfficeVision, AIX, and VM/XA; NetView, DisplayWrite, PC Network, PROFS, Micro Channel Architecture, and Systems Application Architecture.

Infoswitch is a registered trademark of CNCD Communications Ltd.

Intel is a trademark of Intel, Inc.

ITT is a registered trademark of International Telephone and Telegraph, Inc.

Kermit is a trademark of Henson Associates, Inc.

LAP-LINK is a trademark of Traveling Software, Inc.

LEXIS is a registered trademark of Mead Data Central, Inc.

The following are registered trademarks of Lotus Development Corporation: Lotus, 1-2-3, Lotus Express, Lotus Signal, and Symphony.

MacLinkPlus/PC is a trademark of Dataviz, Inc.

Mail-Com is a trademark of Digisoft Computers, Inc.

MCI Mail is a service mark of MCI Communications Corporation.

Microcom is a registered trademark, and the following are trademarks, of Microcom, Inc.: MNP, Microcom Networking Protocol, Adaptive Packet Assembly, Data Phase Optimization, Universal Link Negotiation, and Statistical Duplexing.

The following are trademarks or registered trademarks of Microsoft Corporation: Microsoft, MS-DOS, Microsoft Windows, Windows/386, Word, Excel, Flight Simulator, and XENIX.

MIPS is a registered trademark of MIPS Computers, Inc.

MultiMate is a registered trademark of MultiMate International.

NeXT is a trademark of NeXT, Inc.

Norton Commander is a trademark of Peter Norton Computing, Inc.

Novell and NetWare are registered trademarks, and SFT is a trademark, of Novell, Inc.

OAG is a registered trademark of Dun and Bradstreet, Inc.

Omninet is a trademark of Corvus Systems, Inc.

OnTyme is a trademark of McDonnell Douglas Corporation.

PC Anywhere is a trademark of Dynamic Microprocessor Associates, Inc.

PCnet is a trademark of Orchid Technology.

PC-PLUS is a trademark of Alloy Computer Products, Inc.

PC-TALK is a trademark of The Headlands Press, Inc.

PC World is a trademark of PCW Communications, Inc.

PC-Write is a trademark of Quicksoft, Inc.

PC II is a trademark of Advanced Digital Corporation.

Persoft and SmarTerm are registered trademarks, and PDIP is a trademark of Persoft, Inc.

ProComm Plus is a registered trademark of Datastorm Technologies, Inc.

ProModem is a trademark of Prometheus Products, Inc.

Proteon is a registered trademark of Proteon, Inc.

Radio Shack is a registered trademark of Tandy Corporation.

The following are trademarks or registered trademarks of VM Personal Computing, Inc.: RELAY, RELAY Silver, RELAY Gold, and RELAY/3270.

SCRABBLE is a registered trademark of Selchow & Righter Company.

Sidekick is a registered trademark of Borland International.

SideTalk is a trademark of Lattice Corporation.

SMC is a registered trademark of Standard Microsystems Corporation.

The Sniffer is a trademark of Network General Corporation.

Softrans is a trademark of Softronics, Inc.

Software Digest is a registered trademark, and PC Digest is a trademark of National Software Testing Laboratories, Inc.

The Source is a registered trademark of SOURCE Telecomputing Corporation, a subsidiary of CompuServe, Inc.

SQZ! is a trademark of Turner Hall Publishing, a division of Symantec Corporation.

The following are trademarks or registered trademarks of Sun Microsystems, Inc.: Sun Microsystems, SunOS, Sun Workstation, TOPS, and NFS.

Tapestry is a trademark of Torus Systems.

Tektronix and PLOT-10 are trademarks of Tektronix, Inc.

Telenet and Telemail are registered trademarks of Telenet Communications Corporation, a US Sprint company.

Teletype is a trademark of Teletype Corporation.

Televideo and the model designations 912, 920, and 950 are trademarks of Televideo Systems, Inc.

Tempus-Link and Tempus-Access are registered trademarks, and Tempus-Share is a trademark, of MicroTempus, Inc.

Texas Instruments is a registered trademark of Texas Instruments, Inc.

TYMNET is a registered trademark, and X.PC is a trademark of TYMNET, Inc.

US Sprint is a registered trademark of US Sprint Communications Company.

VA3400 is a trademark of Racal-Vadic, Inc.

Westlaw is a registered trademark of West Publishing Company.

WordPerfect is a trademark of WordPerfect Corporation.

WordStar is a trademark of MicroPro Corporation.

XEROX and Diablo are registered trademarks, and Ethernet is a trademark, of XEROX Corporation.

YMODEM is a trademark of Omen Technology Incorporated.

The following are trademarks or registered trademarks of 3Com Corporation: 3Com, 3+, 3+Menus, 3+NetConnect, 3+Plus, 3+Remote, 3+Route, 3Server, 3Server3, 3+Share, 3+TurboShare, 3+3270, CIOSYS, and MultiConnect.

Contents

Introduction

The term *data processing* has traditionally identified the useful work done by computers. Personal computers, also called microcomputers, are fine data processors, and are also very good at *communications processing*. The first communications processing came into being when distant users needed access to the services of large computers. Later, computers began to communicate directly with each other, allowing users to take advantage of their combined resources. Once personal computers became popular, however, communications was suddenly no longer merely an adjunct to data processing; it had become an end in itself.

Today's microcomputers are involved in all kinds of communication, and perform the functions of many other devices. They communicate by telephone line, cable, and even radio. Portable models go everywhere, checking in with their home bases via international networks. Accordingly, communications software is now just as important as the "data-processing" application programs (word processing, database management, and spreadsheets) that once dominated the market.

In this book, we'll explore the many kinds of communication possible with PCs. Our presentation is limited to the IBM® PC, XT™, AT®, and PS/2®, along with compatible machines. When we use the term "PC" without qualification, we mean *any* representative of this class of computers. (The IBM PC *Jr*® and RT®, and their clones, are not considered.) If we need to discuss features of some individual machine, such as the AT, we'll say so. Occasionally, we'll refer to "the PC family" to identify all machines listed above *except* PS/2s.

The scope of this book is further limited to PCs running IBM's PC-DOS®, Microsoft®'s MS-DOS®, OS/2®(from either vendor), and other operating systems compatible with these. For most of our purposes, PC-DOS and MS-DOS are effectively identical, and will be referred to simply as DOS. Where there's a distinction to be made between MS-DOS and PC-DOS, or when we discuss features unique to OS/2, we'll explicitly name one of them. We assume that you have a basic working familiarity with one of these operating systems.

PC Desktop Communications

Integrating communications capabilities into a PC can be beneficial in two ways: the PC can add power to the communications, or the communications can add power to the PC. These two benefits may also coexist in the same setting.

To begin with, PCs can enhance both computer and non-computer communications. Suitably equipped PCs can replace various communication devices, and do their jobs much better. Thus, a PC can play the role of not only a telephone dialer or answering machine, but also a facsimile machine, weigher, or factory control station, not to mention almost any kind of terminal. The PC's versatility does not derive from processing power alone— a microprocessor can be added to an answering machine or, for that matter, a toaster, at little expense—but from its balance of programmability, disk storage capacity, and user interface, coupled with the availability of specialized plug-in hardware. We'll examine such PC role-playing in detail.

The obvious example of communication that adds power to the PC is a link between the PC and a host computer system, such as a mainframe. This allows the user to take advantage of the host's resources; it may also give the host valuable access to certain resources more easily attached to a PC, such as floppy disk drives. Once the PC user has established a "base camp" of communications with the mainframe, he or she may work with terminal-oriented applications, upload and download files, and perhaps harness other mainframe resources, such as its substantial disk storage, fast line printers, industry-standard tape drives, and, of course, zippy central processor. We'll explore not only how to hook your PC to another computer (mainframe, mini, or micro), but also how to make the two work together.

As we suggested above, we'll also discuss ways in which communications and PCs serve each other. Electronic mail is probably the best example. Although its growth has largely depended on personal computers, e-mail really constitutes communication among human beings, and it can be addictive. The authors have used electronic correspondence for over a decade; in years past, several people we know have even conducted long-distance romances with electronic love letters, apparently finding it much easier to express gooey sentiments by wire.

Types of Inter-Computer Communications

Our principal focus is *asynchronous data communications*, representing the world's de facto standard for communication between digital devices. With the simple and inexpensive additions of a modem and some communications software, a PC can tap into numerous "async" resources: public databases, electronic mail systems, bulletin boards, other PCs, and most host computer systems. Asynchronous communications is a flexible, and usually affordable, portal to a vast array of services and opportunities.

We'll also cover *synchronous communications*, which provides the most powerful means of access to IBM mainframes, certain other big computer systems, and many wide-area networks. Synchronous communications with PCs, in a typical corporate environment, is just as important as asynchronous, but is somewhat less interesting as a topic of study because it's much more cut-and-dried: ordinarily, a company buys a product to emulate a given synchronous terminal or implement a certain synchronous protocol, plugs it in, wires it up to a single host or network, and that's the end of that. Therefore, we'll devote somewhat less attention to synchronous communications.

Local area networks (LANs) represent the newest fashion in data communications, providing a means of interconnecting devices within a restricted area at relatively high speeds. LANs constitute such a complex and important subject that we could not hope to treat them exhaustively. Instead, we offer a thorough introduction to LAN technology and products, and refer you to other sources for coverage in more depth.

We also discuss many of the accessories designed to facilitate and optimize both synchronous and asynchronous communications. Such devices, which include line drivers, data compressors, and buffered modems, can help to solve compatibility problems, save money, and improve the speed and reliability of communications. Further, we provide information about accessories for, and alternatives to, LANs.

Organization and Presentation: Words to the Wise

The toughest part of designing this book was to decide on its organization—in particular, to determine the order in which to cover certain subjects. Discussions with various authors and lecturers have confirmed that no "natural," obvious sequence of topics exists where data communications are concerned. There are so many interdependencies among subject areas that any linear exposition must involve some forward references and gaps. Thus, as you follow us through the text, a bit of reflection and re-reading may prove helpful.

We also acknowledge that, although we provide cross-references from one section to another, we sometimes say the same thing in two or more places. Our intention is to make each chapter fairly self-contained: we'd rather repeat ourselves on occasion than assume that the reader has read, and can recall perfectly, all prior material.

Often, we illustrate a class of products with a representative sample, and such choices do, of course, constitute endorsements. The reader is advised, however, not to take our choices as dismissals of other options. For example, the products we discuss may be illustratively useful, but not the best of their kind. Furthermore, the relative merits of various products often change over time, and fine new products appear.

Last, a word about current events. We have tried to provide a useful balance of basic technical information, which is relatively stable, and information about the latest standards, products, and services, which is by nature ephemeral. Of course, we cannot hope to keep you fully abreast of the rapidly changing PC data-communications market—and since this morning's hot product might be this afternoon's industry joke, an uncritical enumeration of such offerings here would be neither useful nor responsible. For up-to-the-minute information, we urge interested readers to take advantage of the many excellent magazines and trade journals devoted to PCs and data communications, some of which are listed in Appendix I. Such publications can test and review the latest items as they appear and, equally important, put them in context with older offerings.

ACKNOWLEDGMENTS

We extend our special thanks to Lorien Phippeny for her help with certain illustrations.

We also thank the following for their invaluable assistance in preparing the manuscript for publication: Bob Abes, Ken Adair, Spencer T. Barton, Peter Carruthers, Frank da Cruz, Andrew Daecher, Red Fisher, Ed Gee, Robert Gillespie, Dr. Katherine Gottschalk, Carol Gould, Glen Hoag, John D. Hoag, Aphra B. Honig, Dr. Ken Lebensold, Toby Nixon, Richard Reich, Norman Rudnick, Sammy Sagarmudra, Steven Sheriff-Abern, Barbara Van Dyk, Peter Wagner, and Stan Worth.

Particular credit is due those at John Wiley & Sons who sweated out our numerous textual revisions: Ellen Greenberg, Ruth Greif, and Teri Zak.

Finally, our thanks to BAKA Industries, Inc. (Ithaca, New York) and University Computers, Inc (Chicago, Illinois) for technical and moral support.

1 THE BASICS OF DATA COMMUNICATIONS

FUNDAMENTAL CONCEPTS

This section introduces basic concepts of data communications, and defines some terms we will use repeatedly.

Any form of communication involves patterns: for example, patterns of ink on a printed page, electrical current variations in a wire, or vibrating air molecules. In order to communicate information, we must first agree on assigned meanings for particular patterns, and then find a way to transmit sequences of such patterns.

Data communications is the process of moving information among interconnected digital devices. Let us define *data* as information encoded in discrete symbols rather than in, say, the complex patterns of speech. These symbols will belong to well-defined sets, such as the set of characters that can be displayed on a PC screen. Each element of such a set is, in turn, expressed as a sequence of the two binary symbols 0 and 1. Computers, and other devices with which computers work, are manipulators of these binary symbols, commonly called *bits* (an abbreviation for "binary digits"). Data communications, then, is ultimately a matter of transporting bits from one place to another. In many cases, data are organized into units of *bytes* or *characters*, parcels of seven or eight bits, where each parcel is recognized by the communicating partners as a basic unit of information.

The paths between data-processing devices, such as PCs and printers, are called *communications channels* or *communications links*, and might involve electrical cable, telephone lines, microwave channels, or some combination of these. The devices themselves are usually called *stations*; when we need to distinguish their respective roles in the communications process, we refer to them as *transmitters* and *receivers*.

We'll simplify matters for now by concentrating on communications channels that merely connect one device to another, as shown in Figure 1.1. Of course, more than two devices may be linked together on a single channel, but that would be networking, which we'll get to later on.

A quick exercise: Without looking at the list below, jot down on paper all the questions you can think of about a communications channel.

Good Questions to Ask about a Communications Channel

- What medium (e.g., electrical wire, radio waves) is used?
- How is information carried on the medium?
- How can we be sure that transmitted information is understood?

FIGURE 1.1: The communications channel

- Can information be corrupted during transmission?
- Can anyone eavesdrop on the communication?
- Can information flow in both directions at the same time?
- How does information get onto the medium?
- How fast can information be sent?
- How far can information be sent? And at what cost?
- How do the transmitter and receiver coordinate the transfer of data?

We'll address each of these questions in this and the following two sections. We are not actually going to provide explicit answers to any question, since such answers are possible only for specific cases. Our purpose here is primarily to teach you how to think, and talk, about each issue.

What Medium is Used?

We tend to picture a communications medium as a pair of wires forming an electrical circuit. While most communications media do in fact consist of wires, such as coaxial cable or twisted pair, you may also encounter more exotic types, such as optical fibers, radio or microwave links, or laser beams. We must also consider one special, compound medium: a telephone connection. We will examine the properties and uses of each medium at appropriate points in the text.

How is Information Carried on the Medium?

We transfer information by creating patterns in the energy flow (electricity, radio waves, light, sound) through the medium. Such pattern creation is called *signaling*. Different forms of signaling are appropriate for different media. In a wire, for example, electrical current in one direction could indicate a binary 1, and in the other direction a binary 0. In principle, this is no different from some of the signaling methods human beings employ, such as waving good-bye, using sign language, or nodding the head.

   Data communications involves two classes of signaling: *digital* and *analog*. Digital signals are associated with devices that operate by *switching*—that is, by turning an electrical current (or some other form of energy) on and off. Computers are organized assemblies of such devices. Digital signals can take on only two values, and are represented graphically by square waves with right-angle corners (Figure 1.2a). One of the values is associated

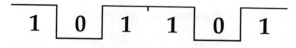

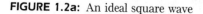

FIGURE 1.2a: An ideal square wave

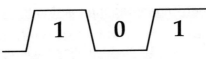

FIGURE 1.2b: Real square wave showing switching time

with a binary 0, the other with a binary 1. In practice, two different voltages are usually assigned to represent 0 and 1.

The representation of digital signals as perfect square waves is a bit idealistic, or, perhaps, a useful fiction. Any device capable of creating a truly square wave would have to be able to switch in zero time, that is, instantaneously. In reality, switching times may be a few billionths of a second, which means, in graphic terms, that the transitions would be sloping rather than vertical. This is indicated in Figure 1.2b, which provides a close-up view of a fragment of the wave.

Analog signals are associated with living things or physical objects. They are generated by something that moves in a continuous sweep, such as the cone of a loudspeaker reproducing a musical passage. Analog signals are represented graphically by sinusoidal waveforms (Figure 1.2c), where the value of the signal, or voltage, is continuously changing.

Digital signaling is natural to computers. Within the machine, all communication is digital; this is also the simplest means of intercomputer communication. Unfortunately, while computers always transmit and receive digital signals, it is often infeasible to carry signals between them in digital form. The sharp, clean square waves become rounded and fuzzy when carried over electrical wires. The longer the wire, the more the waveform is affected by this kind of distortion. *Capacitance* is the inherent property of electrical conductors that causes this problem.

The capacitance of any electrical communication line makes the line act as a *low-pass filter*, which preferentially passes low frequencies and inhibits high frequencies. Because of this effect, digital signals do not survive transmission over great distances as well as analog signals do. (Analog signals are also deleteriously affected by capacitance, but not to the same degree.) The longer the communication line, the more pronounced the problem becomes.

Along very long communication lines, then, we must either insert *repeaters* at intervals to regenerate the digital signal, or else convert signals from digital to analog form and back again. Further, the mainstay of long-distance communication, the telephone system, is engineered to carry human conversation, and thus gives us no choice but to use analog signals. Therefore, we must have devices to convert signals from digital to analog form and vice versa. *Modems*, the devices used for this purpose, will be covered in Chapter 3.

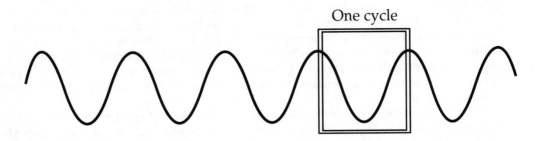

FIGURE 1.2c: Sinusoidal waveform

How Can We Be Sure That Transmitted Information Is Understood?

Communication of any kind is difficult without *standards* specifying a generally accepted way of communicating. Without them, computers made by two different manufacturers would have little chance of establishing a fruitful working relationship.

Consider the English language, which sometimes serves as a formal standard. For example, English is the international standard language for air traffic control. It is also fair to call the IBM PC itself a standard, not because it's made by IBM, but because of the huge industry it has spawned in add-ons, compatibles, and software.

We will examine many standards in the pages that follow. For now, we'll talk about how standards come into being and how they are used.

Formal technical standards are instituted by various organizations established for that purpose (see Appendix J). Many countries have national standards bodies; there are, for example, the American National Standards Institute (ANSI), the Canadian Standards Association, and the British Standards Institute. There are also international bodies such as the International Telegraph and Telephone Consultative Committee (CCITT) and the International Standards Organization (ISO). Each of the approximately 90 countries of the ISO is represented by its primary national standards body. ANSI fills that role in the case of the United States.

Standards are also set by professional and industry associations such as the Electronic Industries Association (EIA) and the Institute for Electrical and Electronic Engineers (IEEE). Then there are de facto standards, introduced by leading companies and ratified by the marketplace.

Numerous standards, both de facto and formal, are in common use for data communications: RS-232, Centronics, and IEEE-488 for interfaces; Bell 103 and 212A for modems; SNA/SDLC and X.25 for protocols; and ASCII and EBCDIC for character codes. Of the many standards relevant to PCs, the single most important is RS-232, possibly the most common standard in the computer world. Almost every computer built has RS-232 capability. If a machine can handle RS-232, it can talk directly or indirectly to almost any other. Another standard of fundamental importance is ASCII (American Standard Code for Information Interchange). This code, described in detail in Chapter 6, is shared by many computers, printers, and other text-oriented devices, and is the dominant system (of several in use) for representing characters as fixed patterns of bits. Most text handled by PCs— whether for processing, storage, or communication—is expressed in ASCII form. As we shall see, however, ASCII is not universal; IBM mainframes and certain other computers lean heavily on alternative systems for character representation.

It's tempting to think that standards should be rigid, precise prescriptions for How Things Should Be Done, but such is far from the truth. Standards are often presented as recommendations rather than rules, and are implemented in various ways by different manufacturers. They usually function as frameworks for product design—a state of affairs with both advantages and disadvantages. This flexibility frees the designer to use a subset of a given standard's specifications in order to reduce complexity and cost, or a superset to provide attractive extra features. However, this same freedom may also give rise to incompatibility.

The development of microchips has had a significant effect on standards. If a standard proves popular, it is likely to be incorporated in a chip or small set of chips. Such chips make it cheaper, and thus more inviting, for manufacturers to build the standard into a new machine. Thus, the popularity of certain standards tends to be self-reinforcing. A few years ago, computer engineers were fond of predicting: "Anything that is at all standard will eventually be put on a chip and cost $5 or less." Perhaps someday you'll be able to walk into the corner store and shell out $4.95 for an 800 MHz IBM PS/4 on a chip small enough to lose in a square yard of shag carpet.

Can Information Be Corrupted During Transmission?

Absolutely. Communication channels are hostile environments for information. What emerges at the receiving end may not be the same as what entered at the transmitting end, because the signal may be changed by both inherent effects of the medium and interference from external sources. Inherent effects will, for example, cause a signal to be attenuated with distance. Distorting electrical interference may come from such sources as fluorescent lights, arc welders, lightning, and even backfiring cars.

When a signal is mangled to the extent that an intended symbol resembles a different symbol or becomes unrecognizable altogether, we say that a *transmission error* has occurred. Ways to minimize the effects of such errors are discussed at several points in this book. The chief tools for dealing with transmission errors are *communication protocols*, the sets of rules and procedures that computers follow in order to manage data transfer and to conduct dialogues among themselves. In Chapters 7 and 8 we will study the need for protocols and examine many popular examples, including XMODEM, Kermit, and X.25.

Can Anyone Eavesdrop on the Communication?

Business competitors, disgruntled employees, unscrupulous agents of powers foreign and domestic, and skulking teenage meddlers all may want to eavesdrop on your communications. Anyone who wants to do so badly enough will find a way. We do not wish you to become paranoid, but we do suggest caution, with a bit of mild anxiety around the edges. We will return to the issue of security many times in later discussions.

Can Information Flow in Both Directions at the Same Time?

It depends on the type of channel. *Simplex, half-duplex, full-duplex,* and *multiplex* are terms used to describe the directional flow of data traffic, as shown in Figure 1.3. You'll rarely encounter the term *simplex*, which refers to a link on which data flow in one direction only, as from a PC to a printer. Simplex operation can thus be likened to traffic on a single-lane, one-way street. A full-duplex link carries two independent streams of traffic simultaneously in opposite directions (like a two-way street with a single lane going each way). A half-

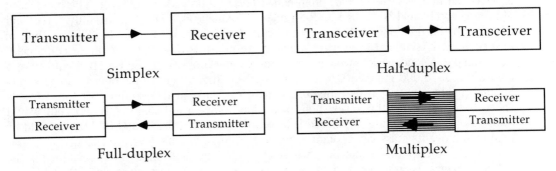

FIGURE 1.3: Plexes

duplex link allows a single stream of data whose direction can be reversed. This method, like a single-lane bridge set in a two-way street with access controlled by traffic lights, is sometimes referred to as *two-way alternate communications*. A multiplex link can handle several streams of traffic at the same time, either in one or two directions (like a multilane highway).

The expression *full-duplex* is redundant, in that *duplex* by itself means the same thing (and, in fact, is sometimes used for the purpose). *Full-duplex* is, nevertheless, the commonly used term, and serves to emphasize the distinction from half-duplex. Most PC communication links run in full-duplex mode, but some specialized links to old-fashioned devices still wheeze along in half-duplex. Actually, half-duplex makes a lot of sense for some purposes, but we'll get into that later.

We have defined these *-plex* terms here as they apply to communication links. They take on different shades of meaning in other contexts. In particular, *half-duplex* and *full-duplex* have come to be used in some technically incorrect and therefore misleading ways, about which we will warn you in due course.

HOW FAR? HOW FAST? HOW MUCH?

When we move data, several questions arise. How fast can data be transmitted? Over what distance? What will it cost? (And while we're at it, who's going to foot the bill?)

The "speed" of data transfer refers to the rate at which symbols can be passed across a link. Distance, the overall length of the link, is an important consideration since it may affect the degree of signal loss. Most of the limitations on data transfer speed and distance can be lifted through the use of more sophisticated technology, but this raises questions about the cost of communication. This section sets forth means of expressing communication rates, examines the effects of distance, and introduces the most important technologies applied.

Bandwidth and Data Rate

Bandwidth is a measure of a channel's capacity for carrying signals. It is expressed in different terms for analog and digital signals.

If you could "watch" an analog waveform pass by you, you could measure its *frequency* by counting the number of crests (or troughs) that rolled by in a given interval of time. Since the crests of electrical analog signals are usually much more closely spaced than those of ocean waves, many more pass by during the same interval. The frequency of an electrical signal is measured in *cycles per second*, often called *hertz* (abbreviated as "Hz"). The bandwidth of an analog channel is defined as the range of frequencies that it can usefully carry, and is equal to the difference between its lower and upper frequency limits. This method of measurement is similar to the way frequency response is described for audio equipment. For example, a loudspeaker with a frequency response of 40 to 18,000 Hz would have a bandwidth of 18,000 minus 40, or 17,960 Hz. Note that an electronic device can generally handle signals only within its range of frequencies. This speaker would probably struggle valiantly to reproduce the lowest note of a pipe organ, a gut-shaking 16 Hz, but would sound like it was croaking. If you fed it a recorded dog whistle, at 30,000 Hz, it would be unable to move its mass fast enough to make the signal audible (even to a dog).

A standard telephone connection, whose characteristics will concern us very much in the following pages, is engineered to carry frequencies between approximately 300 and 3,300

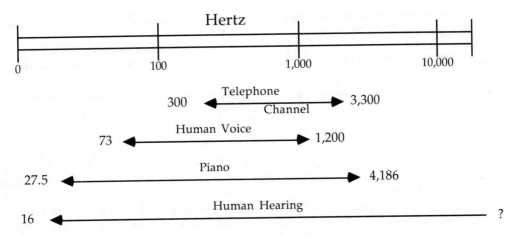

FIGURE 1.4: Bandwidth comparisons

Hz, just adequate to accommodate a human conversation. Such a connection is generically called a *voice-grade channel*. A lightning-fast calculation tells us that the *analog bandwidth* of such a line is 3,000 Hz. Figure 1.4 compares the bandwidth of a telephone connection, which is a signal carrier, with the bandwidths of two signal sources (the human voice and a piano) and one signal receiver (the human ear).

Properly speaking, bandwidth is strictly an analog measure. The capacity of a digital channel is expressed not in Hz but, quite directly, in the maximum number of bits that can be crammed through it in a second. "Digital bandwidth" is thus measured in bits per second (bps). For example, a fast channel may be specified as having a bandwidth of 10 million bits (10 megabits) per second, or 10 Mbps.

The complex mathematics of information theory determines that the digital capacity corresponding to the 3,000-Hz analog bandwidth of a telephone line is 30,000 bps (30 kilobits per second, or 30 kbps). The figure of 30 kbps for a telephone line is a theoretical maximum and far exceeds the speeds actually attained by affordable equipment. Research labs have, however, built modems that closely approach this limit.

A channel's *data rate*, also measured in bps, indicates the amount of data traffic it is actually set up to carry. Obviously, the data rate of a channel cannot exceed its bandwidth, but it can certainly be lower. Typical data rates for a standard telephone connection are 1,200 and 2,400 bps, that is, 1.2 and 2.4 kbps.

Data rate is often called *line speed*, or simply *speed*, although this usage is technically incorrect. While it's true that electrical current has a speed, in the sense of distance traveled per second, bits themselves do not. But it seems that almost everyone uses this word, so we'll sometimes call it speed as well. You may also have heard the term *baud* used as a measure of speed. This is a similar case: while baud is often incorrectly thought to be synonymous with bps, it is not. The subtle difference between the two terms will be discussed later.

Data communications in general involves speeds ranging from 50 bps to several hundred Mbps, but most PC data communications are conducted at speeds toward the low end of this range. As shown in Figure 1.5, a PC may communicate with a telex network at 50 bps, with another computer over a telephone line at 2,400 or 9,600 bps, or with another PC over a local area network (LAN) at 5 Mbps. (A LAN interconnects a group of devices in

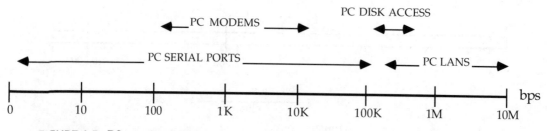

FIGURE 1.5: PC speed ranges

proximity to one another at very high speeds.) For comparison, typical rates for sustained data transfers between PCs and their fixed disk drives are as low as 150 Kbps, and rarely exceed 500 Kbps.

Note that a full-duplex link rated at 1,200 bps is actually capable of carrying 2,400 bps since, in principle, it can accommodate 1,200 bps in each direction. In practice, the full capacity of a channel can rarely be utilized in both directions simultaneously; most communications applications send far more data in one direction than the other at any given moment.

In case "bits per second" is a measure as vague to you as "furlongs per fortnight," let's compare bps rates to some other measures with which you may be familiar:

	100	1k	10k	100k	1M
Bits per second	100	1k	10k	100k	1M
Characters per hour	32k	360k	3.6M	36M	360M
Text pages per minute	0.1	1.2	12	120	1,200
Time to transmit one page of text	9 min	55 s	5 s	0.5 s	0.05 s

Speed Limits

In almost any data communications application, you want as much transmission speed as you can get, but there are always significant limiting factors. As indicated earlier, *speed* in this context refers not to rapidity of signals on the line but to *capacity*, the rate at which data can be fed into a device or through a channel. Imagine a bucket brigade, a line of people passing pails of water from a well to a burning building. The speed that we're concerned with here defines not the time it takes for a single bucket to travel from one end of the line to the other, but the amount of water that is transmitted in a given time. The two rates must be related, but not necessarily in a simple way. If buckets are passed very rapidly, for example, water may slosh out and be lost, resulting in a lower overall rate of water delivery than if buckets are passed at a moderate rate.

An absolute ceiling on transmission speed for PC communications is imposed by the maximum rate at which data can be pumped into or out of a PC. This ceiling cannot be precisely quantified because it varies with such circumstances as the model of PC and the location within it (diskette, fixed disk, memory) of the data to be moved. A useful range is 100 kbps to 2.5 Mbps, with typical rates tending toward the low end of the range. The ceiling rate could be regarded as the "effective bandwidth" of a PC.

Another limitation is the speed of the communications path, which may consist of many components, including junctions of transmission lines with different rate capabilities. The effective speed of a path can be no greater than the speed of its slowest component. If the transmission rate is not uniform throughout, a bottleneck forms at each junction where a high-capacity transmission line feeds a low-capacity one. This bottleneck must be alleviated with a *buffer*, a temporary storage place for data in transit, normally consisting of a block of memory. A buffer is somewhat like the waiting lounge at an airport where passengers arrive in low-capacity vehicles and must wait to board large-capacity airliners. *Buffering* is the process of managing such a storage area, and of shuffling data into and out of it. Since buffers have a finite capacity, the flow of data through a buffered channel must be controlled to eliminate any chance of buffer overflow; if this happens, the "spilled" data are lost.

Ports and Interfaces

People can communicate with their voices, bodies, ears, and eyes. PCs must use *ports* to link with the outside world. The two standard types found on PCs are the RS-232 serial port and the Centronics parallel port. The RS-232 serial port is the general-purpose communications workhorse of the PC and a primary topic of this book. The specialized parallel port is used almost exclusively for sending data to printers.

When two devices, say, a PC and a printer, are linked together, the ports that bind them, along with the connection between the two ports, constitute an *interface*, or point of interaction of independent systems. Strictly speaking, a port is only one component of an interface, but the two terms are often used interchangeably.

Low-speed communication, for most types of digital device that require it, is accomplished via RS-232 interfaces. Generally, RS-232 serves for communication at speeds up to 20 kbps, but, as we shall see, RS-232 ports in PCs may handle speeds as high as 115.2 kbps. RS-232 is the most "general-purpose" of all PC interfaces, in the sense that it facilitates communications with a multitude of different devices and, directly or indirectly, over any distance. Centronics, on the other hand, resembles RS-232 in being a low-speed interface, but is appropriate only for communication at very close quarters.

For communications at speeds greater than 115.2 kbps, PCs must be outfitted with yet another kind of port. General-purpose interfaces capable of high-speed operation, such as RS-422, are available for PCs, but where operation at speeds in the Mbps range is required, it is usually accomplished with special-purpose ports. Of such special purposes, the most significant to us are connections to local area networks (LANs).

Distance

No matter what kind of port the PC has, the emerging signal is good for transmission over only a short distance: a few feet in the case of Centronics, up to a few thousand feet with RS-232, and a few miles with the most generous of LANs. Some additional equipment is needed to prepare data for longer journeys. This need usually arises when one must conform to the signaling requirements of long-distance communication links—for example, modems to cater to telephone connections, or ground stations for private satellite channels. There is a middle ground, however, involving distances of a few miles, for which other solutions may be valuable. For example, if you have the wherewithal to lay a private cable, you can take advantage of special devices such as *line drivers*. These gadgets relay RS-232 data over distances up to a few miles. Figure 1.6 shows the distances reached by PCs coupled with various technologies.

With almost any kind of communication, you pay more to cover a greater distance. So it is with data communications—although, as with telephone calls, there may be small

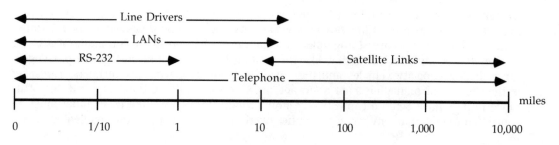

FIGURE 1.6: Distance ranges of various technologies

anomalies in the pricing structure due to regulatory and market factors. For any given range of distances, certain communication technologies are available, but, as shown in Figure 1.7, costs generally rise in close proportion to distance until some limit of each technology is reached, at which point costs for that method rise very quickly.

Multiplexing

The faster and more expensive a method of communication is, the greater is the incentive to share it. Figure 1.8 illustrates the range of speeds feasible for various kinds of communication. The facilities diagrammed toward the upper end of the scale are typically shared among a community of users.

Ordinary telephone lines are almost always used for single communications sessions. Leased telephone lines, which offer greater speeds, may either be dedicated to a single session at a time or have their bandwidth divided up among several sessions by devices called *multiplexers*. LANs normally carry multiple simultaneous sessions. Such shared use of communications channels requires that we distinguish between a physical connection and a logical connection. A *physical connection* is something, such as a cable, telephone connection, or radio circuit, that carries signals from one place to another. A *logical connection* is

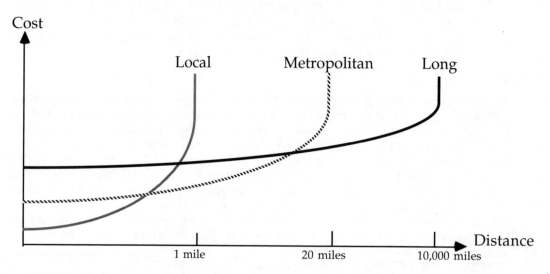

FIGURE 1.7: Cost versus distance graphs

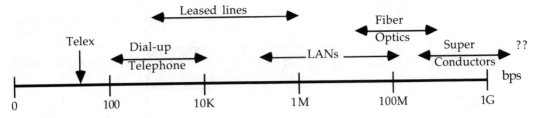

FIGURE 1.8: Speeds available with various kinds of communication

a stream of traffic between two processes; several such logical streams might be multiplexed onto a single physical connection.

The technique of multiplexing is very important and of increasing significance to PCs. Let's look for a moment at how multiplexing is accomplished. On analog circuits, we usually find *frequency division multiplexing (FDM)*, as illustrated in Figure 1.9a. Here, each stream of traffic is assigned its own frequency band, allocated in such a way that it does not encroach on any other stream. You may be familiar with the idea of FDM from television and radio: whether you receive television signals "off the air" or via cable, you tune to a certain channel that corresponds to the band of frequencies assigned to a particular station. Although the same method is used for cable and broadcast TV, the effect of FDM seems more striking with cable, which squeezes 40 or 50 stations onto a single circuit.

On a digital channel, multiplexing by frequency makes little sense. Instead, we normally encounter *time-division multiplexing (TDM)*, illustrated in Figure 1.9b. In this method, very brief intervals, or short "bursts" of time, are assigned in rotation to competing logical channels. Plain TDM works by simply assigning to each logical data stream fixed parcels of time at regular intervals. This method is very often inefficient because demand is not uniform: at any moment, some logical channels are likely to be busy and others idle. Apportioning time according to demand, a technique called *statistical TDM*, makes possible much more efficient and fair use of the communication link. This form of multiplexing requires a protocol to organize and identify the data belonging to each logical stream. Since they are not of immediate relevance to PC communications, we will not directly address such protocols in this book.

No matter what method of multiplexing is used, the effect is—or should be—to give each user the illusion that he, she, or it has exclusive use of a channel. LANs, for example, typically rely on TDM; each station on the network can have what appears to be an

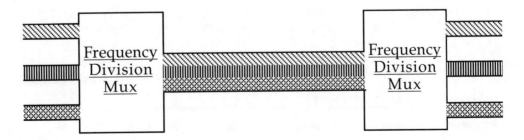

FIGURE 1.9a: Frequency division multiplexers

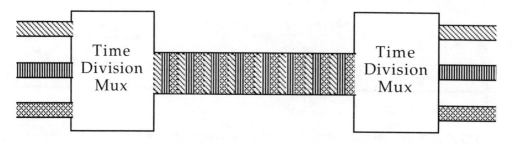

FIGURE 1.9b: Time division multiplexers

immediate and unrestricted dialogue with any other station, but in reality the bandwidth of the LAN cable is dynamically shared among dozens or hundreds of conversations taking place simultaneously among numerous stations.

SYNCHRONOUS AND ASYNCHRONOUS COMMUNICATIONS

The distinction between synchronous and asynchronous modes of data communications is addressed here because it is so basic to our discussion. A full grasp of the technical details is not essential, however, to understanding what follows. Those who are at all technically inclined are urged to read on. But if you are already overwhelmed with bps, bauds, and bandwidths, it is quite all right to skip to the next section.

Bit Timing and Coordination

The period of time required to transmit a bit is called, sensibly enough, a *bit time*. A little cogitation will show you that bit time is inversely proportional to line speed. Thus, for a line speed of 1,200 bps, a bit time is 1/1200 of a second. Each station on a communication link is supplied with a steady stream of timing signals at bit-time intervals, as shown in Figure 1.10.

The issue of *coordination* concerns the relationship between the timing pulses used by the transmitter and those employed by the receiver. (To appreciate the difficulties involved in coordination, imagine two people trying to play catch while wearing blindfolds and earplugs.) It should be evident that the pulses must occur at the same regular rate for each station, or no useful communication will be possible. The question is how to synchronize the two pulse trains. The following discussion somewhat simplifies the timing principles involved.

The transmitter can do its job simply enough: on receiving each "clock tick," it determines the value (0 or 1) of the next bit to be transmitted, selects the appropriate signal for that

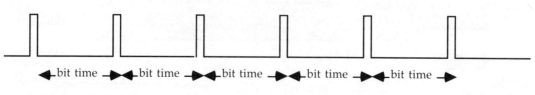

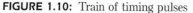

FIGURE 1.10: Train of timing pulses

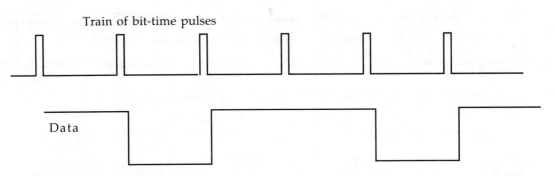

FIGURE 1.11: Transmitted bits

bit value, and "writes" that signal on the outgoing data line. Figure 1.11 shows how this would work for a simple square-wave data stream.

Receivers usually do their job by "reading" the signal on the input line once per bit time, and recording the result in a *shift register*—a piece of hardware in which bits can be queued up, that is, assembled in a linear formation, as if waiting for service. Such devices are pivotal in the complementary processes of *serializing* and *deserializing* bytes. If the line is read at a point close to the middle of each bit, then all will be well. If, however, the receiver checks the line close to the beginning or end of each bit, it reads the signal very close to the transition points, entailing a great risk of spurious readings. Figure 1.12 illustrates such a dicey situation. In practice, the danger is even greater than the diagram suggests, because the distortion that afflicts transmitted electrical signals is greatest at the transition points, rounding the corners and reducing definition.

Ideally, the timing pulses used by the receiver should be identical to those used by the transmitter, although the receiver will delay each bit-reading operation for half a bit time so that the reading will occur in the middle of a bit. The receiver and transmitter must therefore be coordinated so that, while data transfer is under way, the transmitter regularly writes a bit at one instant and the receiver regularly reads it (again ideally) half a bit time later. There are two common means of effecting this coordination: synchronous and asynchronous.

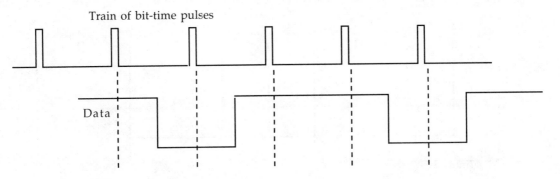

FIGURE 1.12: Received bits

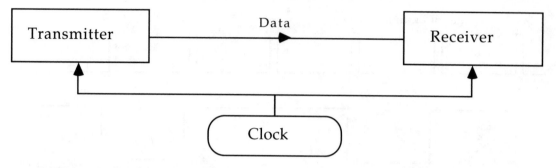

FIGURE 1.13: Synchronous operation

Synchronous Operation

Synchronous is defined as "occurring at the same rate and exactly together." In synchronous communication, the transmitter and receiver are locked in step by virtue of their sharing a single clock, or source of timing pulses, as shown in Figure 1.13.

This coordination scheme may seem so simple and effective as to obviate any alternative. The need for another method arises because synchronous operation entails substantial over-head (i.e., time consumed by non-productive operations) to carry the clock signals the length of the communications path. Synchronous communication could, in fact, be said to double the amount of information that must be moved: for each bit of data transferred, one data pulse and one timing pulse are required. The data and timing pulses may be sent on two separate wires, or the two kinds of information can be combined on a single wire. The latter method depends on a signaling scheme that guarantees that the signal will change every bit time even if the data value does not. This enables the receiver to detect the presence of a new bit by the *fact* that the signal changed, and to determine the value of that new bit by the *manner* of the change. Several such schemes have been devised, one of which, *biphase encoding*, is shown in Figure 1.14. Here, a signal transition occurs at every bit boundary; a 0-bit is indicated by a signal persisting for an entire bit time, a 1-bit by a signal that "flips" halfway through. The value of the signal in this scheme thus bears no relationship to the value of the data. Instead, each bit value is encoded in the number of signal transi-tions per bit time: no transition per bit time for a 0-bit, and one transition per bit time for a 1-bit.

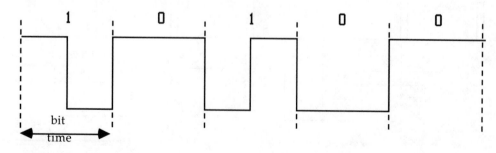

FIGURE 1.14: Biphase signaling

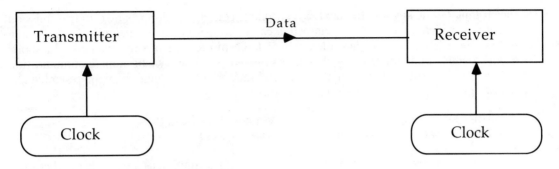

FIGURE 1.15: Asynchronous operation

Asynchronous Operation

Superficially, *asynchronous* means "without synchronization." In this context, the term does not mean that two devices have no coordination at all, but rather that they operate "without *established* coordination." In asynchronous communication, each station has its own independent clock, as shown in Figure 1.15.

The two clocks are not continuously locked in step, but instead are brought into synchronization for brief periods by a "trigger" signal that the transmitter injects into the data stream as a preface to each character. The two clocks must be accurate enough to keep pulsing in close synchronization for the duration of the character. Once the character is completed and the line is idle, the clocks may drift out of sync, to be resynchronized for the next character whenever it shows up. Thus, the transmitter and receiver are somewhat freewheeling, falling into synchronization transitorily as each character is transferred.

Since we're about to begin using them, this is a good time to observe that the common terms *sync* and *async* often refer to synchronous communications and asynchronous communications, respectively.

The distinction between sync and async operation in general can be illustrated by an analogy from the world of music. A symphony orchestra operates synchronously under the guidance of a conductor who, in addition to enforcing a certain interpretation of a piece, also serves as a common clock for the players. A string quartet, by contrast, normally operates asynchronously. In such a small group, each musician keeps time with a "mental metronome," as it were. The audible and visual cues received from the other players allow him or her to adjust the metronome to keep a common tempo.

Owing to the need to transfer timing information as well as data, synchronous communication hardware tends to be somewhat more complex and expensive than asynchronous. (This does not quite explain, however, why tickets for the Berlin Philharmonic cost so much more than those for the Kronos Quartet.) At any given bit rate, synchronous communication, when used to best advantage, is significantly more efficient than asynchronous, as we shall see below. That qualification, "when used to best advantage," is essential, because it's commonly and mistakenly supposed that synchronous communication is *invariably* more efficient than async.

Practical Differences

As we shall see, asynchronous communication is suited to traffic that consists of characters appearing at odd intervals, such as those originating at a keyboard with delays between the striking of one key and the next. Synchronous communication is suited to transmission patterns in which large blocks of characters can be transferred as single units. One example is the inter-PC transfer of disk files, where large blocks are readily available. In short, asynchronous communication is character-oriented, whereas synchronous communication is message-oriented. Patterns in the data streams of the two modes might resemble the following, where each dash represents idle time:

--T-h--i-s- -m--e-s-s-a--g-e -i----s- a-s--y-n-c-h--r-o-n--o-u-s--.--
--This message is -------synchronous with-------3 blocks.--

In asynchronous communication, each character is transmitted as a separate unit because, as noted above, synchronization must be independently established for each character. Since an async receiver can never know in advance when a character is going to arrive, each character is preceded by a trigger signal called a *start bit*. This bit serves both to alert the receiver to an imminent arrival and to bring the receiver into bit-synchronization for the duration of that character. Likewise, each character is followed by a *stop bit* that both confirms completion of the character and gives the receiver a moment to get ready for the next start bit. The start and stop bits are thus like an envelope that carries a character over the async link. Figure 1.16 illustrates a flow of characters bracketed by start and stop bits.

The advantages of async operation are technical simplicity and efficiency in handling single characters. Its great disadvantage lies in the overhead required for all those start and stop bits: in a typical situation, with eight-bit characters, this extra cost for "shipping and handling" is 25 percent. If characters occur at infrequent intervals, the overhead is immaterial because the time occupied on the line would otherwise have been unproductive. When many characters are to be sent in immediate succession, however, the enforced delays of two bit times between each pair of characters add up significantly.

On a synchronous data link, there are fixed time slots in which bits may be transmitted. No trigger is needed to synchronize the transmitter and receiver, but some flag is still required to mark the beginning of each character. That is, even given *bit*-synchronization, something is still needed to provide *byte*-synchronization. There is no technical reason why characters could not be transmitted over a synchronous link much as in the async case: start bits would alert the receiver that a character was about to appear, although stop bits would be redundant. The universal practice, however, is to send as many characters as can be mustered at a shot, with no gaps between them. A batch of characters sent in this manner is called a *block* or *message*. Each block is prefaced by a couple of special codes called *sync characters*. An idling synchronous receiver is constantly on the lookout for sync characters, which enable it to get into byte-synchronization with the transmitter.

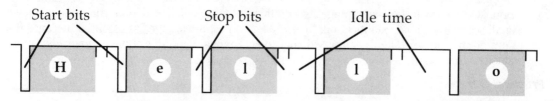

FIGURE 1.16: Asynchronous flow

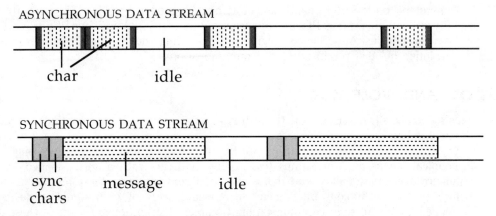

FIGURE 1.17: Asynchronous and synchronous data streams

The overhead for synchronous transmission, then, is fixed for whatever number of characters can be sent at once (as a block). If single data characters are transferred, each block will incur a 200 percent overhead for the sync characters. If data are sent, say, in 512-character blocks, then the overhead will be a mere 0.39 percent. The distinction is illustrated in Figure 1.17. Obviously, synchronous operation is better suited to conditions allowing the transfer of substantial blocks of data.

Moving data in an asynchronous environment is like shipping goods by truck on a highway. Synchronous traffic resembles freight trains on a rail line. If you imagine that a single truck or railroad car carries exactly one byte of data, you have a powerful model of the differences between sync and async.

When data messages are of indeterminable length, and when their minimum size is very small, trucking is definitely the better choice; it is inefficient and uneconomical to dispatch trains with small numbers of cars. When data messages are consistently long, either means of transportation would be satisfactory, although the railroad would always be somewhat more efficient.

While some devices can communicate either synchronously or asynchronously, any given link will be set up to operate in one mode or the other. For this reason, among others, the data communications user rarely has to choose between the two; the choice will almost always be dictated by the application and by the vendors of the equipment being interconnected.

Synchronous and Asynchronous Devices

Although the RS-232 standard includes specifications for both asynchronous and synchronous operation, most devices that use RS-232 interfaces, such as terminals, printers, plotters, and modems, are engineered for operation in only one of the two modes. Most serial printers and plotters, for example, are asynchronous. Synchronous terminals that support ASCII do exist, but anything that is generically dubbed "an ASCII terminal" is understood to be asynchronous. Modems come in both varieties. Old-fashioned Remote Job Entry (RJE) terminals are all synchronous; so are many interactive terminals made for mainframe environments, including those you see in most travel agencies.

Computers, on the other hand, are most often equipped with RS-232 ports that work equally well in either mode. PCs are an exception; most RS-232 ports for PCs are engineered for asynchronous use only. This is a significant limitation, one that has profoundly influenced the evolution of other products for PC communications.

HISTORY AND "ROLE MODELS"

This section briefly describes how the history of data communications continues to influence the field today.

Once data transmission moved beyond the use of voice, gestures, and messengers, such mechanical means as Aldis lamps (essentially spotlights with a spring-loaded Venetian-blind arrangement to allow coded flashing) and semaphore systems became important. Before modern technology intervened, an amazing array of such signaling devices was developed for line-of-sight communication. Complex distributions of some of these devices made possible the relaying of messages over greater distances. Indeed, a semaphore network covered the width of continental Europe in the early 1800s. What we might consider modern data communications started with the telegraph systems developed in the mid-1800s. The telegraph was the first means of sending information over an electrical circuit, making possible nearly instantaneous communication between very distant stations. Some elements of that technology are still seen in PC communications today.

The most successful of the early telegraph systems, generally credited to Samuel Morse, began operation in 1844. A skilled operator used a manual telegraph key to make and break an electrical connection to a distant buzzer. Data were sent in Morse code, still used today by amateur radio buffs. Ironically, some radio amateurs now use personal computers to generate and interpret Morse code for them.

The twentieth century saw the introduction of the *teletypewriter exchange (telex)*, with the teletypewriter displacing the telegraph key. Typists replaced key operators, and reception was automated by means of a printer. (Telex is also a trademark for certain communications products, mostly unrelated to telex.)

Because it uses variable-length sequences of dots and dashes to represent characters, Morse code is not appropriate for telex: teletypewriters were designed to use a fixed-length code of five bits per character. The telex code was called *Baudot* after the great telegraph pioneer Emile Baudot, who actually invented it to enable a number of key-telegraph operators to share a line. Thus, he originated what we call multiplexing. Characters were transmitted asynchronously at a rate of approximately 50 bps. This technology is the basis of the worldwide telex network that is still going strong after 50 years, with 250,000 terminals in the United States and over 1.8 million worldwide.

Many of the communications technologies used by today's computers, while far more advanced, evolved directly from telex machines and have much in common with them. Indeed, some IBM PC models are fully capable of connecting directly to a telex network.

Telex, Teletypes, and Current Loop

A telex system sends a text message from one teletypewriter to another at low speed and low cost. Dialogue is possible but awkward, since most systems are half-duplex.

In the old days, a teletypewriter transmitted a character as soon as the operator hit a key; the character could not be held back because there was no such thing as a RAM chip or even magnetic-core memory. Thus, there were arbitrary delays in the appearance of characters, depending on the typing pattern of the operator. This inefficient use of transmission time was eventually eliminated by the off-line preparation of messages on paper tape for subsequent rapid transmission, a practice that also allowed the sender to correct typing errors.

Signaling current, as distinct from AC operating power, is provided to a telex machine by the local exchange to which it is connected. The teletypewriter can signal only by allowing or interrupting this current flow. A call is initiated by closing the circuit to allow current flow, and it is terminated by interrupting the current for about a second. While a session is in progress, all signaling is accomplished by very brief current interruptions, each lasting no more than a tenth of a second.

When current is flowing, the line is said to be in *MARK* state. When current is interrupted, the line is in *SPACE*. MARK is used to send a binary 1 and SPACE to send a binary 0. These terms carry over to other areas of data communications, so that any signal used to represent binary 1 is called a MARK, and any used for binary 0 is called a SPACE.

Characteristics of Today's Terminals

In the 1960s, teletypewriters (called teletypes for short) were themselves used as primitive computer terminals. Teletype Corporation's models ASR 33 and ASR 35 were found plugged into early timesharing systems. These machines used the ASCII character set and ran at a blistering 10 characters per second. By today's standards they were horribly noisy and achingly slow, but their sluggishness was not so frustrating to people who were not accustomed to anything faster.

In the early 1970s, most teletypes were wheeled out to the graveyard and replaced by video display terminals (VDTs). These, the first terminals made expressly for computers, behaved very much like teletypes except that their output was displayed on cathode-ray tubes (CRTs) instead of on rolls of paper. Not surprisingly, they became known as "glass teletypes." The display was scrolled just as it would have been on paper, with the screen providing a window onto the last 24 lines or so of output. These glass teletypes offered only two significant new features—quiet operation and higher speeds—but that was enough to ensure their success.

Terminals have come a long way since then, but scrolled output, popular since the ancient Egyptians developed papyrus scrolls, survives. No PC owner would attempt to use a teletype as a console, although such would be possible with a very few primitive applications. DOS versions prior to 3.4 obliviously labored on with scrolling.

The Data Communications Model

In discussing a data communications session, it's useful to refer to a more or less classical model, as outlined here. Although this picture involves concrete items, such as terminals and host computers, we have deliberately made it abstract because the building blocks of specific examples can vary enormously.

Two digital devices are connected together in a manner that allows data to be passed back and forth between them. One device plays the role of a *terminal*, the other that of a *host*. A terminal is a character translator that incorporates an input device, normally a keyboard, and an output component, usually a screen or printer. (It may be unusual to think of a terminal as a translator, but its job can be characterized—pun inevitable—as that of translating key presses into character codes for transmission, and of converting received character codes into either tiny images on a screen or inky impressions on paper.) A host is a computer that plays host to terminal users, offering them data processing services. A terminal user establishes a session with the host which, in turn, makes available certain host services. The session is usually transitory, and so will be terminated at some point, normally by the user, once his or her work has been completed. When the session is over, the connection between the two devices may be severed.

The paradigm of data communications, which most readers will recognize, consists of a human being sitting at a dumb terminal, dialing a modem-telephone connection to a large computer, logging into its timesharing system, and running interactive applications on it. After some period, the user logs out, hangs up the phone, and goes for a cup of coffee.

Our model involves three components: user, terminal, and host, here identified as "roles." Traditionally, the user has been a human operator, the terminal a box with a screen and keyboard, and the host a mainframe or minicomputer. In a more generalized model, however, the roles may be played by any of several entities. The terminal may be an actual dumb terminal, or a computer emulating a terminal by virtue of a suitable program. The host must be a computer of some kind, but need not be a host in the traditional sense. For our purposes, the role of host can be played by any computer appropriately programmed to communicate with, and perform services for, a user. This definition of host encompasses PCs and other microcomputers equipped with suitable software. The services provided by the host may include the ability to run general application programs, or may be restricted to certain special functions such as file transfer, electronic mail, or access to databases. Finally, the user, while most often a human being, may be yet another program playing the equivalent role.

We will examine situations that closely follow this model. Typically, the user's PC will emulate a terminal in order to access the services of another computer, according to a conventional pattern. We'll also encounter examples in which communication patterns are constrained to conform to the model even though they don't really fit it. All larger computers have evolved to communicate primarily with terminals and to treat them, not inappropriately, as dumb, slow, and slavish. PCs have tended to respect this hierarchy and to play the role of terminals. There are two related reasons for this. First, such behavior has been perfectly adequate for the many instances in which a PC replaces a true terminal. Second, it has befitted the PCs, as the new kids on the block, to conform to the established order, rather than to expect mainframes to accept some new mode of communication for the benefit of these young upstarts. It has only slowly become apparent to IBM and other companies in a position to do something about it that a peer-to-peer relationship between PC and mainframe would better serve both partners in many applications.

Several factors, especially the emergence of LANs and IBM's recent extensions to its Systems Network Architecture (SNA), are slowly making it possible for PCs to link to other computers without pretending to be terminals.

PC COMMUNICATION RESOURCES

While it can play many valuable roles in desktop communications, the original PC was not intended to be a communications whiz. It was nevertheless designed to be easily expandable by means of add-in cards. For exotic modes of communication such as facsimile transmission, for which new hardware must be added anyway, the PC's inherent limitations in communications matter little. When it comes to more basic data communications functions, such as connecting to an IBM mainframe, a stock PC is sadly lacking in power. The PS/2 does represent a small step forward over its predecessors in this regard, and OS/2, especially in its Extended Edition, makes great leaps over DOS.

As previously noted, the standard types of interface provided on PCs for general use by DOS and by application programs are the RS-232 serial and the Centronics parallel. Many other types of interface are available, but they are installed in PCs only for special purposes and do not concern us in this section.

An Overview of RS-232

Later chapters will reveal, in gruesome detail, what RS-232 ports are made of and how they work; we'll also explore many of the realms of communications that can be entered through them. For now, let's take a superficial look at the ports themselves.

A PC's RS-232 port may be called any of several things: simply an RS-232 port, a *serial port*, an *asynchronous port*, or a *COM port*. "RS-232," its most definitive designation, identifies the port with the standard to which it is designed to conform. "Serial" (defined later) and "asynchronous" both relate to primary characteristics of the port. In the wider world of computing, plenty of ports are serial and/or asynchronous but do not conform to RS-232. When you encounter a PC port identified by either of these terms without further qualification, however, you can be certain it's RS-232.

COM is the term DOS and OS/2 use to identify RS-232 ports, just as they assign to other devices tags like "LPT" and "A." COM, as you can guess, is short for *communication.*

An RS-232 port is built onto a board inside the PC and includes a connector, which appears at the back of the PC, for external devices to plug into. If the board supplies only a serial port, it is called a *serial card* or *async adapter card*. An RS-232 port does not take up much room on a card, the connector being its bulkiest component; hence, it is common to find such a port on a multifunction card that includes other goodies, such as a clock or extra memory. In IBM's PS/2s and a few PC compatibles, an RS-232 port is incorporated on the motherboard. (The *motherboard* is the main internal circuit board, which carries the processor and other vital chips.) Some cards on the market provide multiple RS-232 ports.

The 25-pin connector shown in Figure 1.18, conventionally used with RS-232 ports, is called a *DB25*. A male DB25 connector on the back of a PC is almost certain to belong to a serial port. Serial adapters supplied by IBM for its ATs and XT286s use 9-pin *DE9s* instead; these save space without any loss of function, since IBM's implementation of RS-232 makes use of only nine wires anyway. Most laptop manufacturers also favor these smaller connectors.

IBM's architecture for the PC family allows installation of up to two serial ports. Some compatibles accommodate as many as four. Actually, you can easily install more than two on even a true IBM PC, but the usefulness of the extra ports may be limited. Many PCs come with one RS-232 port as standard equipment; on others, even one async port is an extra-cost option, an option most buyers will want.

PC-DOS identifies RS-232 ports as COM1, COM2, COM3, and COM4. (Versions prior to 3.3 supported only COM1 and COM2.) Normally, the first port installed is COM1, the second COM2, and so on, but you can assign them as you please. COM1 is given the alternative but rarely used name AUX, for *auxiliary.*

The PS/2 architecture supports a generous total of eight async ports. Only the first four are accessible under DOS 3.3; OS/2 allows the use of COM5 through COM8 as well.

Now you know where an RS-232 port comes from and how to address it politely, but how does it work? The most fundamental fact about RS-232 is that it's a *character interface,*

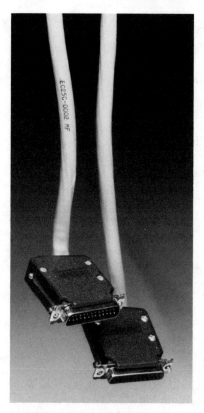

FIGURE 1.18: DB-25 Connections.
Reprinted with permission of Black Box Corporation,
Pittsburgh, PA. Copyright ©*1987.*
All rights reserved.

intended for linking up devices that handle data in units of characters rather than BIG BLOCKS OF BYTES. This makes it suitable for terminals, printers, modems, and plotters, but quite unsuitable for devices like disks and tapes.

RS-232 is also a "low-performance" interface, meaning not that the accuracy of transmission must be low, but that it serves for communication at low speeds and over short distances. In principle, RS-232 can be used at any speed up to 20 kbps, but in practice a small set of speeds is standard: 50, 110, 134.5, 300, 600, 1,200, 2,400, 4,800, 9,600, 14,400, and 19,200 bps (134.5 bps may seem to be an oddball rate, but it was once quite popular for typewriter-style terminals). In some cases, a serial port on a PC may be capable of running at speeds beyond those in the conventional set, e.g., 38.4, 57.6, and 115.2 kbps. Even the highest of these speeds is still "low-performance" compared to the Mbps rates common in interfaces for disks, tapes, and LANs.

Different digital devices deal with characters of different sizes. Characters are variously encoded in units of five, six, seven, or eight bits, and RS-232 is flexible enough to handle all of them (but only one size at a time). For most PC applications, 7- and 8-bit characters are used.

To sum up, RS-232 provides a standardized physical means of moving characters back and forth between two local devices at relatively low speeds. It is found on almost all computers, the vast majority of modems, and a great many terminals, plotters, and other character-oriented devices. While RS-232 is strictly a local interface, it plays a vital role in long-distance communications by hooking computers to the modems that handle the long-haul connections.

The Centronics Parallel Interface

Centronics Data Computer Corporation, which has been manufacturing printers for many years, created the Centronics parallel interface specifically for its own product line. The interface has long been an industry standard. A PC can support up to two parallel ports, known in DOS and OS/2 as LPT1 and LPT2.

The key difference between Centronics and RS-232 lies in the fact that Centronics is a *parallel interface*, while RS-232 is *serial*. A serial interface provides a single line for data moving in each direction (assuming full-duplex operation). Data bits must be transmitted serially, one after another. A parallel interface, on the other hand, has several (typically eight) data lines, allowing all the bits in a byte to travel simultaneously. The difference is illustrated in Figure 1.19. A parallel interface with eight data lines, like the Centronics, can transmit data eight times as fast as a serial one, but at the cost of seven additional pins and wires.

Parallel ports made for machines in the PC family are distinguished from those for PS/2s by the fact that they support data output only. This is because they were intended purely for interfacing with printers (you send data to a printer, but the latter doesn't send any data back). The Centronics interface does include special, nondata *control circuits* for the printer's use in signaling such status conditions as "not ready" and "out of paper."

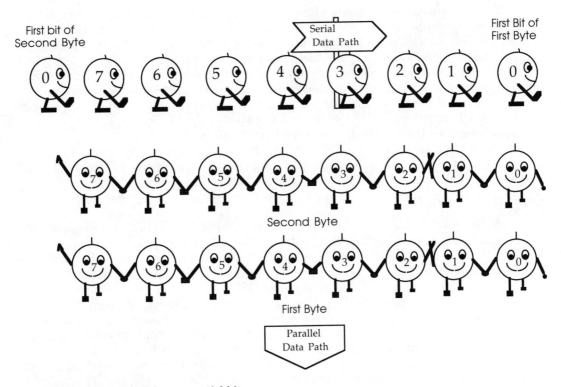

FIGURE 1.19: Parallel versus serial bits

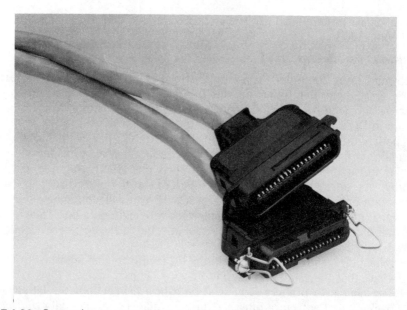

FIGURE 1.20: Centronics connectors. *Reprinted with permission of Black Box Corporation, Pittsburgh, PA. Copyright ©1987. All rights reserved.*

The standard connector specified for Centronics ports is the 36-pin design shown in Figure 1.20, which can be seen on parallel printers and on some non-IBM-type microcomputers. IBM, which hates to follow any standard it did not invent, has wired the PC's parallel port for a DB25 connector instead, and the compatibles have followed suit. This is unfortunate, because, if it weren't for this anomaly, one could safely assume almost any DB25 connector to be part of an RS-232 interface. IBM can justify the use of the smaller connector (with 25 pins instead of 36) by the fact that its machines implement only a subset of the Centronics standard. Fortunately, IBM has established a convention for PCs: serial ports, as mentioned above, use male DB25s; parallel ports use female DB25s.

More information about both the RS-232 and the Centronics interfaces is provided at relevant points in this book. Chapter 4 and Appendices A and B give full technical details, including pin configurations and circuit descriptions.

Instant DOS, Instant OS/2

So far we have discussed those hardware components of a stock PC that are important in communications. Now, we turn to the software. We will have frequent recourse to the terms *DOS, OS/2, BIOS,* and *driver*, to be only briefly defined here. Figure 1.21 illustrates their interrelationships. Later in this chapter, we'll provide more details about OS/2; for now, most of our remarks about DOS also apply to OS/2.

DOS, of course, stands for Disk Operating System. In general, an operating system is the most basic software, or set of instructions, used by a computer: it tells the machine how to operate. DOS also provides services to application programs; in particular, it gives them access to computer resources such as the disk drive(s), memory, keyboard, monitor, and processor. Before operating systems came into common use in the mid-1950s, every application had to incorporate code to control each needed resource, making applications both less consistent and more complex than they are today.

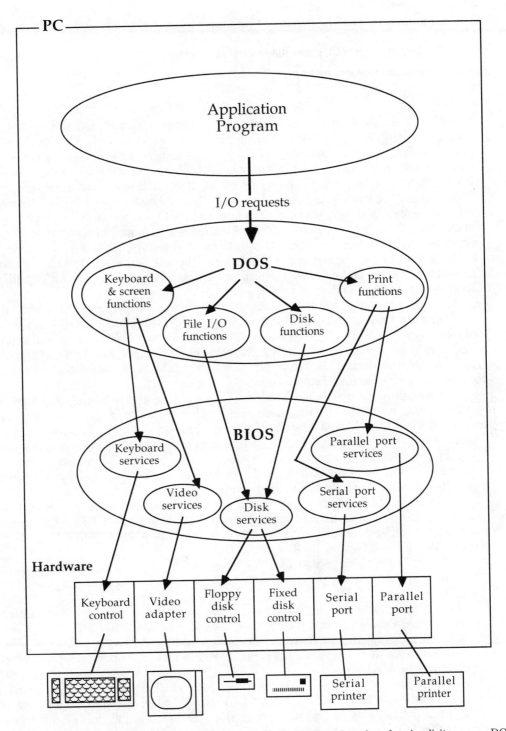

FIGURE 1.21: Role of DOS and the BIOS in managing PC I/O. (Note that, for simplicity, many DOS and BIOS components are not pictured.)

We can describe DOS by dividing it into three functional components:

An input/output (I/O) and file-system manager

A command processor

Very little else

In DOS, as in most operating systems, applications typically access the disk drives through the high-level *file system*, leaving most low-level details of I/O to be handled by device drivers, discussed below. As a file-system manager, DOS maintains collections of data in the form of files on disks. A *sector* is the basic unit of information that can be read from, or written onto, a disk. Each sector usually holds 512 bytes, but other sizes, ranging from 128 to 1,024 bytes, are sometimes used. From the standpoint of DOS, a disk is a mass of numbered sectors, where each data file is a list of sector locations. However, DOS allows the user to treat the disk as a set of named files arranged in a hierarchical fashion, typically organized into groups called *directories*. A directory, really a special kind of file, contains a list of files instead of a list of sectors. The fact that every directory is also a file makes possible the hierarchical organization of directories and subdirectories with which most readers will be familiar.

The DOS file system allows each application program to perform I/O operations (i.e., read from and write to disk drives) without implementing the complex code that keeps track of sector locations. Files can also be shared in simple fashion. For example, one application might put data in a file named RESULTS.RSN; the next application that comes along can find this data by reading the sector list called RESULTS.RSN, rather than searching the entire disk for the sectors themselves.

DOS also provides "device independence," allowing the user to address standard devices other than disks as if they, too, were files—with obvious restrictions (for example, the system will not let you "read" from a printer or "write" to a mouse). This approach enables users to redirect data from, say, a word processor to a printer, again without need for any special code within applications to support such activity. Particularly important for communications, users can also redirect I/O between applications and ports, or from one port to another, as we'll discuss in later chapters.

DOS's *command processor* is the program that puts the prompt on the screen (the infamous A>) and deals with the commands entered from the keyboard. The command processor provides utilities for such everyday chores as formatting disks (FORMAT), configuring ports (MODE), and backing up files (BACKUP).

The "very little else" portion of DOS takes care of such matters as keeping track of the time and date, loading programs, allocating memory to programs, and handling error conditions.

The operating system of a mainframe is more capable and supports many other, more elaborate functions, which may include multitasking, user validation and security, networking, virtual memory, and file-sharing. DOS is skeletal by comparison, but it's all a PC user really needs. As we'll see, OS/2 offers multitasking and networking support, which can certainly be nice to have.

Both the file-system manager and the "very little else" are packaged into the memory-resident portion of DOS, which is loaded into memory when you start up a PC, or reset it with Ctrl/Alt/Del. This portion of the operating system loads and runs all other programs and makes DOS services available to them.

The command processor is stored on a disk file called COMMAND.COM. This file is loaded and run when the operating system is started and, thereafter, each time any other program terminates. It may be considered the "default" program: in the absence of any other program, DOS makes sure that the command processor is running. (It is possible to use a processor other than COMMAND.COM if you wish; to learn how, read the chapter on "Configuring Your System" in your DOS manual.)

OS/2, the successor to DOS, is a *multitasking*, or *multi-application*, operating system. It allows several independent applications to be active, that is, loaded into memory and executing, at one time. Since a PC has but a single processor, only one program can be literally executing at any instant, but the processor is shared among all active programs in a way that makes them appear to be running concurrently. OS/2 includes a number of other features desirable in a multi-application system, such as means for programs to communicate with one another and to share the screen in an orderly fashion. Again, we'll return to OS/2 features later in this chapter.

The BIOS (Basic Input/Output System) consists of a set of programs stored in read-only memory (ROM) chips built onto the motherboard of the PC. (Like any program stored in ROM, the BIOS is technically called *firmware*.) The BIOS comprises the code that is run when the PC is started up, along with programs for low-level access to devices. The start-up code, called the Power-On Self Test (POST), determines what hardware is present in the machine, runs appropriate diagnostics on that hardware, and finally, if all is well, loads the operating system. The balance of the BIOS is code for accessing and manipulating standard devices, such as keyboard, screen, serial ports, printers, diskette drives, and fixed disk drives. Examples of BIOS services are writing a character to the screen, reading a character from a serial port, getting the status of a printer, and setting the real-time clock.

IBM's BIOS is a standard in the sense that its functions are uniform for all models in a given model group (PC, XT, AT, PS/2) and upward-compatible across model groups. Thus, any function implemented in an XT's BIOS will also be available in the PS/2 BIOS; the reverse, however, will not be true, since extra functions are added with each new BIOS generation. Listings of the BIOS programs for all models prior to the PS/2s are published in the relevant IBM Technical Reference Manuals. With the PS/2 line, IBM instituted a new policy of providing full documentation on BIOS services without supplying actual program listings. BIOS programs in clones differ from IBM's for reasons of copyright, but the imitations must be functionally identical to the original in order to be "IBM-compatible."

It is the uniformity of the BIOS that allows PC-DOS to run on any IBM-compatible computer, again subject to upward-compatibility restrictions. This effective standard enables IBM and other manufacturers to build machines using varying hardware components— dozens of makes of disk drive, countless distinct styles of keyboard from IBM alone, etc.— which all behave the same way.

"Well-behaved" application programs under DOS accomplish input and output by calling the operating system; the operating system in turn calls the BIOS, and the BIOS manipulates the actual hardware. For file I/O and keyboard input, the preceding sequence not only constitutes proper behavior but also is almost universally adopted; for other devices, such as serial ports, neither the BIOS nor DOS offers particularly snappy handling. This state of affairs has compelled many application programmers to bypass the BIOS and DOS altogether; most sophisticated programs address serial ports and video adapters directly.

Let's clarify this I/O management hierarchy with an example of reading some data from a file via DOS. The application calls the operating system, saying "read the next 20 bytes from file C:\123\APHRA.WK1" (assume that the application has already "opened" this file). DOS figures out where the appropriate bytes reside on the disk and calls the BIOS to "read sector 2,364 of disk number 2." The BIOS directs the disk drive to position its head(s) over the appropriate cylinder, select the head with which to read (if there's more than one), wait for the sector to come around under that head, and, finally, read the data. For more information about this process, we recommend *The Norton Disk Companion*, a booklet distributed with the famous Norton Utilities. In 27 pages it thoroughly explains the operation of PC disks, and it does so, amazingly, without a single illustration.

OS/2 works in a similar manner, with two notable exceptions. First, OS/2 is more self-contained; it makes little use of the BIOS. Second, it does not permit application programs to call the BIOS or to manipulate the hardware directly; programs are constrained to perform all I/O via OS/2 services. Since the selection of services made available to user programs by OS/2 is far richer than that provided by DOS, the latter restriction is not a significant handicap.

The business of managing a hardware device, and of directing data movement to and from it, is referred to as *driving* that device. A given device's driving program is called a *device driver*, or *driver* for short. DOS and OS/2 both consist largely of drivers, and, as with most operating systems, it is possible to add device drivers to them for nonstandard devices such as tape drives and RAM disks.

Not-so-fast OS/2

The preceding sketch will be sufficient for many readers. Here we provide some additional information about OS/2's development and features that will be helpful as background for topics to be covered in later chapters.

When the original IBM PC was being designed in 1981, Microsoft® was asked to develop DOS. IBM, which until that point had not manufactured microcomputers, rightly expected Microsoft's experience in the field to enhance market acceptance of the new machine, particularly in the nonbusiness community. The design of MS-DOS was based on earlier operating systems. In essence, Microsoft modified the older code to give DOS a closer resemblance to another of the company's products, XENIX®, a UNIX® derivative with which some readers may be familiar. Microsoft kept DOS relatively "modular" or "generic" (i.e., not tied to a particular machine) so that it could be adapted for use with other computers. One aspect of this modular design was that some low-level PC functions were incorporated into the BIOS instead of DOS itself, giving rise to the application-DOS-BIOS I/O management hierarchy cited above. This design decision has had a profound effect on certain PC-family applications, especially in the networking context. Further, due to a fundamental lack of compatibility with the BIOS, OS/2 applications tend to steer clear of it altogether, relying instead on OS/2's own services.

IBM and Microsoft again collaborated to create OS/2. Microsoft brought to the project the work it had already performed on enhancements for MS-DOS, along with its knowledge of operating-system development for small computers. IBM contributed its expertise in the area of connection to IBM mainframes, little of which, unfortunately, has manifested itself in OS/2 to date.

By adding multitasking capability, OS/2 corrected a major deficiency of DOS. We noted above that a multitasking operating system allows several tasks to run simultaneously in memory. For reasons that will become clear as we go along, it's useful to speak of these tasks as distinct *processes*; here, an application may be considered a process. (Note, however, that a computer running under a multitasking operating system, like OS/2, is very different from a *multiprocessing* computer, which is endowed with two or more *processors*.) Under multitasking, each process may gain access to system resources, such as files, memory, ports, and the processor, with little or no concern for any other processes running at the same time. Thus, OS/2, unlike DOS, allows a user to run several applications at once. For example, if a DOS user were running a spreadsheet and wished to start a word processor, she'd have to quit the spreadsheet, allowing DOS to free up any resources the application had been using—memory, disk files, and so on. Then, she would start the word processor, calling on DOS to begin loading the new application code into memory and executing its instructions. Under OS/2, however, both applications may be in memory at once, allowing the user to switch between them with a few quick keystrokes.

This sounds simple enough, but in fact it is not simple at all. For example, what if an application should "crash," ceasing to respond to user input? When this happens in a single-tasking, DOS environment, the PC usually requires rebooting, but under OS/2, other loaded applications can continue to run without interruption. How such wonders are actually accomplished is well beyond the scope of this book; readers who wish to pursue the issue further will find a text on OS/2 "internals" listed in Appendix I. Here, we'll focus on aspects of OS/2's design that are particularly important for communications.

The usefulness of a multitasking operating system is not limited to the tricks we've just described. Another of its virtues is its ability to support *interprocess communication*, meaning, in this context, communication among processes running in memory. Under a single-tasking operating system like DOS, "communication" among concurrent processes within a machine is, of course, not possible. Multitasking operating systems can perform *cooperative processing*, in which two or more separate processes work together to accomplish a task, passing intermediate results back and forth between them. OS/2 provides several methods of doing this, but the most important is the *pipe*, so called because it serves as a duct for data between two programs. A pipe is accessed somewhat like a file, and can be given a name in much the same way. One program writes to the pipe, and the other program reads from it. In many cases, data between the reader and writer are buffered, so that their respective output and input need not be synchronized.

Pipes have been part of DOS since the mid-1980s, but technical limitations prevented the early pipes from being much used. To begin with, they were a rather inflexible extension of the file system. Due to memory-management restrictions, DOS treated all writes to pipes as if they were writes to disk, stuffing everything into a special "PIPE" file. Under OS/2, which incorporates a mechanism to prevent what might be called "clogged pipes," pipes are instead maintained in system memory, which makes them a very fast means of interprocess communication. Second, while early DOS pipes were said to be "anonymous," OS/2 extends the facility to include *named pipes*, giving them a "handle" that can be grabbed by a potentially limitless number of different processes. Thus, a process running under OS/2 can either create a named pipe, much like creating a file, or use an existing named pipe, much like reading a file.

As a simple example, consider a user who wants to have his word processor collect some data, in the form of a table, from a spreadsheet program running at the same time. The word processor program creates a named pipe called, let's say, TABLEFORTWO, which will then be available for any process that wishes to write to it. The user tells the spreadsheet application to send out the data for inclusion in the word-processor document. The spreadsheet finds the named pipe TABLEFORTWO and writes the formatted table into it. At this point, the word processor, which has been waiting quietly in memory for something to appear in the pipe, springs back to life, inserts the table at the point in its open document where the user left the cursor, and *voila!* You have just seen cooperative processing at work.

Of course, this example involves two processes on the same computer—but OS/2 doesn't stop there. As mentioned above, both DOS and OS/2 have long had the important ability to redirect I/O in various ways, possibly sending it to destinations never envisioned by the writer of the relevant application software. Under plain DOS, this ability was cut off at the physical boundaries, so to speak, of the PC, so it wasn't possible to redirect data over a LAN. OS/2's named pipe enhancements permit I/O to be redirected even over a network. Named pipes provide a generic communications mechanism for use by applications programmers, in much the same way that the file system serves as a generic mechanism for I/O with printers and ports. Thus, if named pipes facilitate interprocess communication within a machine, then they also facilitate communication among processes running on multiple machines, so that cooperative processing, also called *distributed processing*, can be carried out over a network. This ability is used to implement most of the network interconnectivity for OS/2, as we'll discuss at length in Chapter 14.

We have omitted some further technical details of the pipe scheme that are not relevant to communications. The system is worthy of study, if only because its nomenclature is so vivid; if you're curious, for example, about how processes "spawn" each other, we urge you to consult other sources.

2 COMMUNICATION SERVICES

THE SWITCHED TELEPHONE SYSTEM

The services of the switched telephone system, also known as the *dial-up telephone network*, are provided to consumers by means of *subscriber lines*. Each such line consists of a pair of copper wires, called a *local loop*, that connects the customer's premises to a Central Office of the local telephone company. The local loop is also connected to a local distribution system within the customer's building, which extends the loop to a network of jacks into which telephones, answering machines, and modems can be plugged. Except in the rare case of a party line, each local loop serves a single telephone number. At the Central Office, the local loop is connected to a switching system, which, in turn, is connected to a hierarchical network of telephone systems covering the globe.

Note that a local loop is just a pair of wires. Because most telephone cables contain four conductors, some people mistakenly assume that four wires are involved. For normal single-line telephones, however, only two are actually used; the same pair of wires serves to carry conversation in both directions, as well as operating the ringer. The other pair may be used for back-up or for another line installed in the same building. The strands making up four-conductor cable are usually color-coded and paired off, red with green for one circuit, and yellow with black for the other.

A telephone number can be thought of as the address of a subscriber line in the network. We tend to think of people or companies as having telephone numbers, but in reality only local loops have such numbers. (In a limited sense, numbers do belong to individuals, following them around in the form of pagers, mobile telephones, and call-forwarding services.)

When you dial a number, the telephone system attempts to switch into place a temporary connection between your local loop and that of another subscriber—if you are lucky, the one whose number you dialed. If it fails, it proffers a rude tone or a recording in self-exoneration. (Many of these "recordings" are not artifacts of human speech at all, but are synthesized by a computer.) A completed connection may be routed through a series of switching centers; each center is usually connected to the next by a high-bandwidth *trunk* multiplexed to carry several simultaneous calls. The trunk itself might be an electrical cable, a radio link via communications satellite, or a microwave link.

Using the Telephone System for Data Transmission

When people first wanted to make digital devices communicate over long distances, they turned to the telephone system—because it was there. The telephone network was a huge communications infrastructure, reaching almost every corner of the world. But since the telephone network was engineered to carry speech rather than digital data signals, computers and terminals had to conform by converting their signals into something resembling a human voice. This gave rise to the all-important modem.

For some datacom applications, the telephone system is wonderfully convenient and economical; for others, it can be infuriatingly slow, frustratingly error-prone, or frightfully expensive. Let's consider its pros and cons.

The advantages of switched phone lines for data communications include:

Flexibility. You can dial from practically anywhere to practically anywhere else, usually (at least within a given country) with ease.

Cost. Equipment costs are low, most service charges are based on actual usage, and local calls are cheap. Long-distance calls may or may not be affordable, depending on the application.

Standardization. Although there are several different and incompatible modem types, it is generally easy to determine what you need and to get it working.

The disadvantages of dial-up systems are:

Low Speed. Life is easy if you want to run at 2,400 bps or less, and it is now possible to attain about 12,000 bps with some systems. But modem data transfer rates cannot be expected to rise much above this, and for more speed you must employ other, more costly means, such as leased lines.

High Cost. Long-distance charges are considerable, especially during the business day.

Errors. Transmission errors can affect data on any kind of communication link, but telephone connections are particularly susceptible. Perhaps the most irksome aspect of telephone lines is the enormous variation in transmission quality. In some areas of the country, you can run at 2,400 bps and rarely see an error. In others, running at even 1,200 bps may be difficult.

Nearly everyone has had an unacceptable connection during a voice call. Typical problems are static on the line, a second conversation in the background (never an interesting one), an echo, or just a weak signal. Such obtrusive problems can, of course, blight a data call, but modems are less tolerant than human beings, and data can also be destroyed by subtle effects we would never notice.

It is sometimes difficult to pin down the sources of errors. All manner of electrical effects are held culpable, including noise from telephone company equipment (especially with older switching systems), external interference (from numerous sources, such as transformers, generators, and other machinery), and crosstalk (i.e., interference from calls on adjacent cables). In addition, some cheaper modems perform less than optimal filtering of received signals. No doubt all of these are to blame in some circumstances.

Disconnections. A user may be plagued, over a period of a few weeks or months, by a rash of mysterious terminations of data calls. One moment the line is busy carrying data; the next moment it's dead. These disturbances are very trying, since it is difficult to track down the culprit. Some hosts are gracious enough to hold a disconnected session open for a few minutes, enabling the user to resume work if the connection is reestablished.

A similar problem can arise with the "call waiting" services popular today. The audible signal intended to alert the customer to a second call coming in can outrage a modem, prompting it to hang up. Manufacturers are aware of this danger, and design modems willing to overlook these breaches of etiquette; older modems, however, may lack such poise. Even if the call isn't disconnected, any data being transferred at the moment of intrusion are certain to be messed up. Telephone lines used heavily for data transmission should probably not have call waiting installed. In many areas, a feature called "selective call waiting" or "cancel call waiting" allows a subscriber to defeat the call waiting system for the duration of one outgoing call. This feature is discussed further in Chapter 3.

Bandwidth. We have already mentioned the standard bandwidth one should expect on a telephone line. Greater transmission speed requires greater bandwidth, just as increasing amounts of automobile traffic would require an increasingly wide road. Unfortunately, due to sneaky cost-cutting measures instituted by phone companies, infrequent servicing of equipment, and other problems, bandwidth is not always what it's supposed to be.

The most sophisticated high-speed modems can adapt to whatever bandwidth is available by reducing their operating speed to suit line conditions. For more primitive modems at the other extreme, almost any line, even intercontinental, should provide adequate bandwidth for 300-bps operation. Modems operating in the middle of the speed range, especially at 2,400 bps, may be caught short and fail to perform. In such cases a human being often must step in, either to select a lower speed or to redial in the hope of a better connection.

International communication by modem generally works well at 1,200 bps; making connections at higher speeds, however, tends to be difficult.

LEASED TELEPHONE LINES

For very heavy or continuous telephone use between two fixed locations, a *leased line* may be preferable to dial-up calling. A leased line is a permanent, direct link between two subscriber locations. To obtain one, you ask a phone company for a "private line" connecting the two points, for which you pay a fixed monthly fee. (The use of the term *private* here is a bit misleading: certainly the line is established for your exclusive use, but it is not "private" in the sense of being under your exclusive control—see below). A rough rule of thumb suggests that a leased line is cheaper than dial-up if you use it more than five hours a day, but many factors may affect actual cost.

Leased lines are usually obtained for use at some fixed speed, typically 9,600, 19,200, or 56,000 bps. The trendy line for the hard-core datacom enthusiast appears to be T1, running at 1.544 Mbps, and costing enough to cater to the Very Discriminating. The term *T1* is widely used to describe certain digital transmission facilities operating at this speed, but properly refers to the tariff established for such high-speed services.

Recent reports suggest that most T1 lines are not now being used at anything approaching their capacity. Nevertheless, there are always people who want more. Until recently, the fastest leased line, used for an inter-mainframe connection, ran at 8 Mbps. With optical fiber pushing transmission rates over 100 Mbps, however, 8 Mbps is beginning to seem sluggish, and many large corporations now want and get substantially faster links. Leased lines operating at very high speeds are normally used with multiplexers, which divide the bandwidth into several lower-speed channels for different data streams, i.e., separate logical connections.

Leased lines for lower speeds are constructed using the same components as dial-up lines, but bypass the Central Office switching systems. The permanent connections, isolated from noise generated by switching equipment, offer improved transmission quality. In addition, several technical enhancements allow leased lines to accommodate higher operating speeds than switched lines. Most important are the use of multiple local loops in tandem and the application of a process called *conditioning*, which improves the transmission quality of a local loop. Conditioning a communication line involves the addition of filtering devices that reduce certain kinds of distortion, hence permitting passage of a "cleaner" signal. Data transmission on analog leased lines also requires the use of modems.

Some advantages of leased lines over switched lines are:

Lower Cost. The cost saving associated with a leased line is usually, although not necessarily, the motivation for obtaining it in the first place. For some applications, only a leased line is acceptable, despite a possibly higher cost.

Speed. Higher speeds are ordinarily available.

Dedication. Once installed, a leased line is always there when you need it. There's never a busy signal or a wait to be connected—that is, almost never. One of the authors once worked at a large bank in New York City whose remote job entry (RJE) terminal was linked by a leased line to a computing service in the Midwest. At the start of work one morning he found the leased line lying there all dead. The telephone company, it turned out, had taken the liberty of borrowing it for another customer because the bank had not used it for several days. Service was restored in very short order.

Security. A leased line provides better security, because it cannot be "dialed up." It can still be tapped, however; security-conscious users will use data-encryption units.

The disadvantages of leased lines are:

Possibly Higher Cost. Few PC applications would justify the expense of a dedicated long-distance leased line. The use of a single channel on an already available multiplexed long-distance line—for example, where such a line has been leased by a large corporation—is another matter. For local connections, i.e., those made through a single Central Office, leased lines should definitely be considered; lines supporting rates up to 19,200 bps may be very reasonably priced.

Installation delays. You may have a long wait between order and delivery—up to a year, in some rare cases. On the other hand, with luck you may wait only days. In any case, plan well ahead.

Metallic Circuits

A leased line routed through a single telephone exchange can be set up as a *metallic circuit*, or *copper pair*, meaning that a continuous metal conductor connects the two line terminations. All-metal leased lines consist of local loops connected together at the Central Office, and can be used to a large extent as if they were private cables. Because the line is all metal and relatively short, digital signals can be sent directly, without a modem, thus affording greater speeds. In principle, any two locations served by the same telephone exchange can be connected in this fashion.

In contrast to metallic circuits, the transmission path of a switched telephone connection normally involves *transformers*, devices that block the passage of DC signals. These transformers, known as *hybrids*, constitute the interfaces between two-wire and four-wire circuits. Since digital signals have a DC character, the presence of hybrids represents one of several possible barriers to their passage over a regular telephone connection.

Another factor to consider is that local loops longer than about 18,000 feet often incorporate *loading coils*. These coils improve voice communication by counteracting the filtering effects of long wire runs, but unfortunately they make a modem's job harder. Metallic lines leased for data transmission will work better without loading coils; to order such a coilless line from your telephone company, cite AT&T® specification number 43401.

Special transmission devices called *line drivers*, used with metallic circuits, are described in Chapter 5.

Two-Wire and Four-Wire Lines

As noted above, a normal dial-up line appears in the customer site as two wires. Leased service, however, offers the option of a four-wire line in which two local loops are pressed into joint service. Not surprisingly, four wires can provide twice the transmission speed of two: one pair is used for each direction of data flow. In addition to the lure of extra speed, a four-wire line generally costs little more than a two-wire line. The cost disparity is relatively small because telephone lines between Central Offices are almost all four-wire to begin with. To upgrade from two- to four-wire leased service, the company need only add a bit more wire at each end, and nothing in the middle.

Leasing a line may be bewildering to customers with a little knowledge of data communications. A colleague of ours once requested a private line and was asked, "Half-duplex or full-duplex?" Puzzled, he replied, "Surely it's up to me how I use the line." "Nope," the supplier insisted, "we have half-duplex and full-duplex. Which do you want?" The problem stemmed from a misuse of terms, a common occurrence noted in Chapter 1. The supplier was being technically inaccurate in identifying a two-wire line as half-duplex, and a four-wire line as full-duplex. Although (in the absence of utter perversity) a four-wire line is always used for full-duplex communication, a two-wire line serves both modes equally well. The choice is the customer's and dictates the type of modem required.

Bypass

Hordes of competitors vie in the long-distance communication-services market: AT&T, the "alternate" long-distance telephone carriers, packet switching networks, etc. But access to any of these services is normally via local loops, dialed or leased. Quests for greater bandwidth, lower cost, or simply the avoidance of the local telephone company have led many organizations to seek substitutes for local loops. This pursuit has given rise to the watchword *bypass*.

Ordinarily, the local telephone company is granted exclusive right-of-way for communication lines; that is, only they may lay local loops over or under public thoroughfares. Some people in the business world have managed by various means to circumvent this regulation. For example, for short distances, say, between two buildings across the street from each other, a few companies have compensated local authorities to allow a private connection, or have surreptitiously run their cable through disused utility ducts. Very short line-of-sight connections, as between adjacent buildings, can sometimes be effected by light-based links, which have the advantage of being unregulated but which suffer seriously degraded performance in bad weather. For a more general case, such as establishing a direct link to a long-distance carrier, more formal solutions are available. Usually, however, they make economic sense only for high-speed requirements.

Radio is, in principle, an inviting medium for bypass, and a few products and services exploit it. Motorola, for example, has marketed a radio-based LAN. Radio has severe practical limitations, however, and should rarely be considered except for low-bandwidth mobile applications. The biggest problem with radio is congestion: there's little or no frequency space available for allocation to new services. Space may be found, however, for applications that involve only one-way broadcasting of data. Arrangements can sometimes be made to "hide" a low-speed data stream in the broadcast signal of a radio station. Lotus® uses this technique with its Signal® product for distributing stock market information.

Local microwave offers high bandwidth and is used for some wideband bypass connections to long-distance carriers. But even microwave channels are limited these days by heavy congestion.

Many local telephone companies are themselves offering bypass services, typically via optical fiber links. Fiber is both fast and reliable, but its availability tends to be restricted to areas of high commercial density. In some cases, local fiber loops may also tie into intercity fiber links, providing high-volume throughput independent of standard long-distance trunks.

Communications satellites offer the ultimate in bypass service, enabling a corporation to establish multiple long-haul links through a single supplier. The capacity and reliability of satellite communications are very high, but so is the cost. The user must not only rent a satellite channel (from a vendor such as RCA or Satellite Business Systems) but may also have to provide a costly ground station at each location. Although sharing a ground station with another company in the vicinity may substantially reduce the cost, a high-speed link to that station must then be implemented.

PACKET SWITCHING NETWORKS

A *packet switching network (PSN)* can be thought of as an alternate long-distance service engineered specifically for data transmission. Although private PSNs exist, we will limit ourselves to consideration of those available to the public, sometimes called public or packet data networks (PDNs), public switched packet data networks (PSPDNs), or value-added networks (VANs).

A PSN typically covers a large geographic area, often an entire country, and may extend internationally. It consists of minicomputers, one in each major city served, interconnected in a *distributed network* by high-speed leased lines typically running at 56 kbps. A distributed network is one in which the connections between *nodes*—the minicomputers—are not arranged in any fixed pattern. In principle, any node may be connected to any other; connections are made according to complex algorithms, which attempt to maximize the efficiency with which data are moved through the network. Figure 2.1 shows a small hypothetical PSN in the United States with a couple of active connections.

Data to be sent through a network are encapsulated in units called *packets*, which are passed from node to node until they reach their destinations. Packets are transferred on the store-and-forward principle: a packet is briefly stored by each of the nodes that handles it. The path through a network is error-free because the packets are transferred using error-correcting protocols.

PSNs are used primarily for terminal-to-host traffic and secondarily for host-to-host communication. Terminals and PCs usually access a network in transitory fashion via local dialed modem links. Hosts, on the other hand, must normally be connected to network nodes via leased lines. Such host hookups require the use of either some dedicated interface equipment or a specialized protocol. (X.25, an important international standard protocol designed for this purpose and supported by almost all commercial PSNs, is discussed in

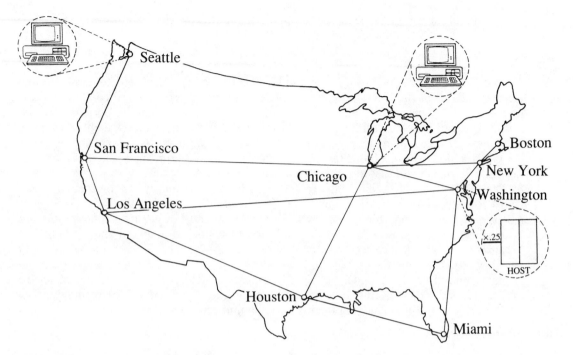

FIGURE 2.1: A hypothetical packet switch network

Chapter 8.) The major costs of PSN use are those associated with attaching and equipping a host, and the periodic charges levied by the PSN company.

Companies that offer computer services to widely distributed customer bases have been quick to exploit the potential of PSNs. Among them are electronic mail services and information utilities that market to the public, and insurance companies that must provide mainframe access to a dispersed community of agents. When such services are made available on a PSN, users located almost anywhere can gain access merely by placing a local telephone call into the network, which then completes the connection. Direct long-distance telephone connections, the conventional alternative, would be much more expensive for users and more hazardous for data. While these PSN uses are among the most important and most evident, there are many others, some of which are cited below.

A feature common to most commercial PSNs is a high degree of *connective redundancy*. The network is designed so that no single line loss can partition it; that is, no breakdown of a single link can sever any node from the rest of the network, because at least one alternate path exists between every pair of nodes. Thus, the inevitable occasional failure of a link should not affect customer traffic. The failure of a node is more serious, but only the customers attached to that node should suffer.

Most large countries have a single PSN run by the governmental postal, telephone and telegraph agency (PTT). The United States has several nationwide commercial networks. The two largest, Telenet® and TYMNET®, also have links to many foreign PSNs. PSNs covering smaller areas of the country are being developed by many of the local Bell operating companies. The leading Canadian services are Datapac™, run by Telecom Canada (a consortium of the country's telephone companies), and Infoswitch®, established by Canada's two major railroad companies.

History

The PSN concept was dreamed up in the late 1960s by the Advanced Research Projects Agency (ARPA) of the U.S. Department of Defense. ARPA's goal was to create a network that would allow researchers all over the country, and a few outside its borders, to share certain computing resources. There was increasing pressure to make available the super-computers for which so many government-sponsored researchers were clamoring. Even the Pentagon could have gone broke buying a megabuck, number-crunching behemoth for every defense-related lab and institute that needed one.

The result was ARPANET, also called DARPANET, primarily the brainchild of one Larry Roberts. This network began operation in 1970, expanded in the mid-seventies, and is still going strong today. ARPANET quickly spread beyond its military roots and is currently used by researchers of all kinds in universities throughout the land. In fact, because ARPANET lacked security, the defense establishment has since deployed new (and yet more expensive) networks.

Quite apart from its support of scientific research, ARPANET was in and of itself a fascinating and long-lived research project. A colleague of the authors spent many happy years working on it and enjoying the network community it spawned.

Why Switch Packets?

Let's dig a little more deeply into PSNs. Conceptually, PSN operation involves two mechanisms: the *communications subnet*, which attends to the transportation of packets from one point to another, and the *access system*, which is the interface for the network's users—hosts, PCs, and terminals. While these two elements of network operation are rather different, the work relevant to both is performed by the network nodes.

The access system manages the facilities that enable customers to hook into the net (local phone lines, modems, etc.). Every node is equipped with these facilities. For this purpose, each node functions as a *packet assembler/disassembler (PAD)*. The PAD takes the incoming data from its attached terminals, assembles them into packets, and then passes the packets on to the communications subnet. Similarly, when a packet arrives over the subnet for one of its terminals, the PAD extracts the data and sends them out on the appropriate line. Some users, such as X.25 hosts, supply data already in packetized form to the node. Another common scenario involves several terminals at a single location, all requiring network access. In such cases, it's usually better to connect the terminals by installing a PAD and using a single line to the local node, rather than running individual lines to the node for each terminal.

The access system will likely handle several modes of communication to suit different subscribers, e.g., asynchronous dial-up for ASCII terminals and PCs, synchronous dial-up for BiSync and SDLC terminals, dial-up X.25 for PADs, and leased-line X.25 for permanently connected hosts. Figure 2.2 illustrates a variety of users on a network. The system calls on the communications subnet to move the packetized data between nodes. The access system is very versatile, so it can cope with a heterogeneous assortment of customers. In contrast, the subnet is highly streamlined for pumping packets, the homogeneous units of traffic, through the network's arteries.

Packet switching is analogous to freight containerization in the shipping industry. The efficiencies engendered by standardized containers have, in the last two decades, revolu-

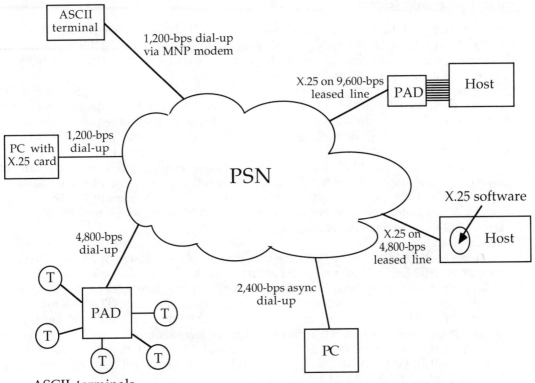

FIGURE 2.2: A variety of ways of accessing packet switch networks

tionized large-scale shipping. A shipper can fill containers with tennis balls, Taiwanese PC clones, or bottles of Scotch; the carrier moves them around with uniform equipment (the same cranes, trucks, ships, and so on); and the entire operation proceeds more quickly and smoothly than with older methods.

Telenet

To explore the practical aspects of PSN operation, let's consider one particular example, Telenet, in more detail. Telenet, the first commercial PSN, was started in 1972 by the engineering firm of Bolt, Beranek, and Newman, one of the primary contractors on ARPANET. Early development was somewhat shaky, and in 1979 Telenet was sold to GTE. Since then, it has grown strongly; Telenet Communications Corporation, now a US Sprint® company, has become the world's largest supplier of packet switching services and private data networks.

As of January 1989, Telenet was accessible by dialing from over 18,000 local telephone exchanges in the United States for asynchronous data transmission. Most of these access points supported 1,200- and 2,400-bps connections, with 2,400-bps service in about 150 cities. In addition, Telenet was accessible from 75 other countries, some through its own international extensions and others by arrangement with foreign PSNs.

A Sample Session with Telenet

PC users usually take advantage of PSNs by dialing their local node, via standard PC modems, and establishing terminal sessions with network hosts. Figure 2.3 lists a short but marvelously illustrative terminal session the authors conducted with Telenet in order to connect to CompuServe®, a "multipurpose electronic utility."

On connecting to Telenet, we are required (a) to type two carriage-returns, which the network node uses for auto-baud detection, i.e., to determine the data rate and other transmission characteristics of our terminal. Once the node knows the parameters, it (b) introduces itself and (c) gives us the identification code of the Telenet port to which we are connected (this information will come in handy if the port goes haywire). Telenet then (d) prompts us to tell it what kind of terminal we're using or emulating. The network does not distinguish particular models of terminal, but merely differentiates between video and hard-copy types. D1 is the rather obscure code to identify CRT terminals and PCs. Telenet now does its best to tailor output to our screen. Next, Telenet (e) gives us a prompt, the @, at which point we can enter commands.

Many commands are available in Telenet, but the most important is the one used to establish a connection to a host. This command consists of a C followed by a host address, in this case 202202 for CompuServe. (Host addresses are very much like telephone numbers; on Telenet, in fact, most begin with the three digits of the host's telephone area code.) Telenet tries to open a path between our terminal and CompuServe. The first connection attempt fails and Telenet (f) responds with the NETWORK OUTAGE message; there are many other types of connection failure, with corresponding messages. On our second attempt, we (g) clumsily mistype the host address and Telenet (h) complains that we have given it an ILLEGAL ADDRESS. All goes well on the third try, and the network (j) announces 202 202 CONNECTED.

At this point, we are transparently connected to the host. The connection is "transparent" in the sense that the network drops out of sight, leaving an apparently direct link to the host. We then (k, l) log in to CompuServe and do whatever we have to do. After completing the body of the session, we (m) log out of CompuServe; the host (n, o) gives us some statistics on the session and then sends a message to the network telling it to disconnect us. Telenet (p) cuts our connection to CompuServe and (q) issues another prompt, at which point we can either connect to another host or hang up.

PSN Features

PSNs usually support two types of connection: *virtual calls* and *permanent virtual circuits (PVCs)*. A virtual call, sometimes called a *switched virtual circuit*, is a temporary logical connection between two parties, as in the sample session above; analogous to a dialed telephone call, it is the most common type of PSN connection. A PVC is akin to a leased telephone line; once established for a customer, it is left permanently in place. Some large corporations use PVCs on PSNs as long-distance links in their own private networks.

Transparency, mentioned above, is another valuable feature of PSNs. Such a network can be installed between two communicating devices without either one needing to know the network is there. The only possible bleary spot on this apparently transparent link stems from the transmission delays inherent in such a store-and-forward scheme. PSNs are, nonetheless, sufficiently fast that the delays are likely to be imperceptible to a human operator, even on a cross-country link. In any event, one might argue that these minute

a) CR CR
b) TELENET
c) 415 218S

d) TERMINAL=d1

e) @c 202202

f) 202 202 LOCAL NETWORK OUTAGE 00 1F

g) @c 20202

h) ILLEGAL ADDRESS

i) @c 202202

j) 202 202 CONNECTED

k) User ID: 75776,660
l) Password:

```
┌─────────────────────────────────────────┐
│  Body of CompuServe session is omitted   │
└─────────────────────────────────────────┘
```

m) Enter choice ! bye

   Thank you for using CompuServe!

n) Off at 17:14 PST 16-Dec-87
o) Connect time = 0:01
p) 202 202 DISCONNECTED 00 40 00:00:00:43 30 12

q) @

FIGURE 2.3: A sample session with Telenet

delays are the price paid for reliable and economical data transportation. PSNs use terrestrial (i.e., overland) circuits for most connections; satellite channels are called into play for some but not all links. Therefore, despite the delays imposed by the store-and-forward mechanism, a PSN connection could well be faster than a direct telephone link that happens to be routed via satellite.

Some networks offer *dial-out* capability. This feature makes a PSN even more like a telephone service, and is particularly useful for PC-to-PC communication. A PC in one city can dial into its local PSN node and place a virtual call to a node in another city, where it is allocated a dial-out modem. Using that modem, it may dial any telephone number local to that node. The authors took advantage of such a facility while writing this book to transfer material (including this chapter) between Mr. Honig's computer in Chicago and Mr. Hoover's in San Francisco.

Advantages and Disadvantages of PSNs

The advantages of PSNs, as opposed to direct telephone connections, include:

Cost. PSN charges are based primarily on the amount of data transferred. Connect time is also likely to be a factor, but connect distance usually is not, except for international hookups. PSNs have varying fee structures, which may be negotiable for valued customers. Incidentally, many networks bill each host for all the network usage related to it; in turn, each host bills its users. Accounting would be a horrendous burden if the PSN company had to set up an account for, and bill, every user.

Services. "Value-added" services may be available. This could mean that the processing power inherent in the nodal minicomputers of a PSN are called upon to transform the data being transmitted. For example, protocol conversion (described in Chapter 12), as from asynchronous ASCII to IBM 3270 data stream, may be possible. Other common value-added services are electronic mail and conferencing (see Chapter 11).

Reliability. The connection between the terminal's local PSN node and the network host is generally error-free. However, the phone link between a PC and the local PSN node is subject to the usual transmission errors, and thus constitutes a weak link in the chain. Although PCs can in principle avail themselves of X.25 to circumvent this problem, in practice such implementation is troublesome, as X.25 is a synchronous protocol. Major PSN vendors, acknowledging the phone-link shortcoming, have recently begun to support asynchronous protocols whereby PCs and terminals can more easily gain reliable network access. Popular examples are X.PC, supported by TYMNET, and MNP®, supported by Telenet. We'll have more to say about these protocols in Chapter 8.

PSNs' main disadvantage is that they can make the use of protocols over the virtual connection between network users very risky. Problems may crop up, for example, if a PC and a host attempt to use a protocol to transfer a file across the net in a manner independent of any protocol used by the PSN itself. Such difficulties are a direct result of the net's inherent propagation delays. Many protocol implementations, designed on the assumption that the transmission path is nonstop, foul up when they do not receive messages within the very short periods expected. But a few protocols (discussed in later chapters), notably ZMODEM, have been designed with great attention to PSNs and are therefore prepared to deal with delays.

PBXS AND CENTREX

PBX stands for Private Branch eXchange. A PBX is an organization-internal telephone switching system. For a company that requires many lines at a single location and has a high percentage of inside office calls, a PBX is almost de rigueur. Models are available with as few as two lines and as many as thirty thousand. A typical small configuration is shown in Figure 2.4. Both PBXs and Central Office exchanges are commonly referred to simply as *switches.*

If you haven't encountered PBXs at work, you've probably used them in hotels, which may make you wonder what's so great about them. Here are a few answers:

- PBXs provide control over communication in a way that is largely independent of the telephone company.

- Since modern PBXs are computer-controlled, their vendors can offer all manner of fancy features, such as call forwarding, intercom, voice mail, and so on.

- Some PBXs can handle digital traffic and support intraoffice, point-to-point, serial links without modems.

- For internal connections, certain PBXs permit the multiplexing of data and voice over a single two-wire circuit.

Numerous variations on the term *PBX* exist. The name *Private Automatic Branch eXchange (PABX)* is sometimes used to distinguish automated PBXs from their manually-operated predecessors. A *Computerized Branch eXchange (CBX)* is controlled by a built-in microprocessor. A *digital*, or *voice-and-data*, PBX is one that handles digital, rather than analog, communication streams. (All digital PBXs are normally computerized,

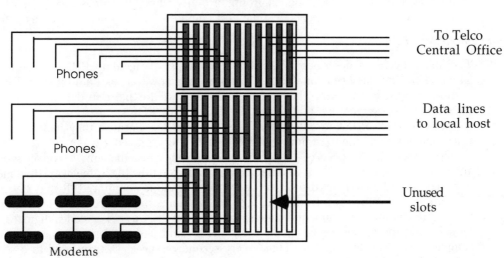

FIGURE 2.4: Example of a PBX setup

but CBXs are not necessarily digital, and their digital computers may serve solely to manage analog lines.) *Data* PBXs support data traffic only, not voice.

A PBX is basically a cabinet with numerous slots into which *line cards* (sometimes called *port cards*) are inserted; each telephone, or other connected device, may require either one or two cards, depending on the system architecture. Within the PBX cabinet, the cards are hooked to the switching system, which establishes the connections between them. The PBX vendor supplies different line cards to support different devices. Each device is connected to the PBX by twisted-pair wiring spanning up to perhaps 4,000 feet. The customer buys a PBX together with line cards for existing devices. Within the limitations of the cabinet, the system can expand to support new devices; the customer simply buys and installs additional line cards as needed. In some cases, additional cabinets can be installed to provide extra slots.

Almost any modern PBX will support standard Touch-Tone® telephones; indeed, they constitute the majority of phones attached to PBXs. Most will also support a range of other phones, including fancy models made especially for PBX use that often feature LCD panels, programmable buttons, and intercom speakers. Local loops to the telephone company Central Office, commonly known as *outside lines*, are connected through line cards in much the same way as internal lines. PBX vendors refer to these outside lines as *trunks*. This nomenclature is at odds with normal telephone parlance, in which *subscriber lines* are distinct from *interoffice trunks*.

You may wonder how a PBX can route to the appropriate extension a call coming in from the public telephone network. Incoming calls are routed through a special type of Central Office line called a *direct inward dial (DID)* trunk. DID trunks carry control signals informing the PBX of the last four digits of the dialed number. They may also be used for outgoing calls, although in some cases separate lines are designated for incoming and outgoing calls.

A concept fundamental to PBX operation is the *line group*. A number of lines serving the same function can be assigned to a group, which will have a telephone number of its own. Outside lines form such a group, usually addressed by the number 9. Dialing a 9 gets the first available line in the assigned group, or a busy signal if none is free. Similarly, a set of lines providing access to ports of some host computer is also often defined as a group.

Voice-and-Data PBXs

The above overview describes all existing PBX types. Voice-only PBXs can, of course, handle data that has been "analogized" by modems; however, as data-oriented PBXs are of more interest to PC users, they are the only kind we'll explore in detail. We'll consider the data-and-voice type first and then, briefly, data-only PBXs.

Data-and-voice PBXs are also known as digital PBXs because they handle all traffic, voice and data, in digitized form. Voice signals are digitized by devices called *codecs* (coders/decoders). A codec is the approximate inverse of a modem; it converts between analog voice signals and bits, digitizing speech in roughly the same way that music is digitized on audio compact discs. One codec per telephone is required. It may be supplied on a line card to support a traditional type of telephone, or be part of the telephone itself, as in more elaborate instruments made specifically for PBX use. The codec digitizes speech by sampling the analog signal 8,000 times per second and rendering a measure of each sample as an eight-bit number. Thus, every second of speech is translated to a sequence of 8,000 bytes. Multiplying 8,000 by 8, we see that a digital-PBX telephone requires a 64 kbps transmission channel.

Special adapters support PBX connections for digital devices such as computers and terminals. Adapters are certainly available for RS-232 interfaces, and some PBX vendors also offer adapters, in the form of plug-in cards, for PCs. RS-232 devices on PBXs normally operate at 19,200 bps. PCs equipped with suitable adapters can theoretically communicate at speeds up to 64 kbps, but, since some of this capacity is normally consumed by a protocol, effective data rates are limited to 56 kbps. The trend in PBX design is to support two full-duplex 64-kbps channels, plus one 16-kbps control channel, per four-wire circuit; normally, one data channel is used for voice, the other for data. The control, or *signaling*, channel carries dialed numbers for setting up calls and other *out-of-band signaling*—signals related to, but carried separately from, the conversation or other kind of data. Examples are codes generated by function buttons on fancy phones, display messages, and maintenance and diagnostic information. This three-channel arrangement follows standards being established for Integrated Services Digital Networks (ISDNs), the networks of tomorrow, whose mysteries are revealed later in this chapter.

PBXs manage their switching in various ways. Some switch packets of data, as described in the last section. Most digital PBXs, however, switch by time division multiplexing: each second, the PBX provides each connection with 8,000 opportunities, or time slots, in which a data byte can be passed from sender to receiver. (These *time* slots are not to be confused with the *card* slots mentioned earlier.) For example, suppose a PBX supports 256 concurrent connections. When party A makes a connection to party B, each is assigned a slot to read on and a slot to write on. Party A might get slot 21 to write on and slot 165 to read on; party B is then told to read on slot 21 and to write on slot 165. A mechanical analogy of this scheme is a wheel, rimmed with 256 paper clips numbered 1 to 256, turning at 3,000 revolutions per second. Line cards are positioned around the wheel. When a transmitter has a byte to send, it waits for its assigned paper clip to pass by and affixes the byte to (writes on) the clip. A receiver waits for its clip to come around and removes (reads) any byte attached to it.

PBX switching is performed by *dedicated logic*, i.e., by a special processor designed for that purpose and with nothing else to do. The PBX computer oversees, but is not directly involved in, the switching process. The computer's primary responsibilities are managing call setup and termination, providing call accounting, and supporting user features.

Blocking

An effect called *blocking*, which afflicts many older PBXs, renders a system incapable of managing simultaneous connections for all attached lines. A PBX might, for example, support 1,000 lines but have a capacity of only 256 connections; since any connection involves two lines, only about half of the PBX users may conduct calls at the same time. This may be tolerable when PBXs are used for voice only, although there are exceptions, as when telemarketing companies must keep most of their staff continuously on the phone. Digital PBXs usually experience much higher user demand, because data calls typically last longer than voice calls. The switching capacity of a *non-blocking* PBX matches its line capacity: all users can be communicating simultaneously. A non-blocking PBX does not, of course, reduce one's chances of getting an ordinary busy signal. It just guarantees that, if the desired line is, in fact, free, a connection will be established.

Most PBXs made today are *virtually non-blocking*. This splendid euphemism means that the PBX can handle simultaneous calls for a substantial majority of its lines, say 80 percent. With such a system, the chances of a given call being blocked are so slim as to be negligible for most practical purposes.

Using Modems with Digital PBXs

While digital PBXs facilitate internal data calls without modems, they do not obviate modems for external data calls. Modems can be used with these PBXs in two ways. Either they are placed on internal PBX lines, as on regular telephone lines, or the PBX can be supplied with a *modem pool*.

In the first case, a modem's analog signal must travel through the PBX. This presents no problem because a digital PBX can handle modem traffic perfectly well, treating it as if it were voice. It means, however, that data are converted to analog signals for the short trip from modem to PBX, redigitized for the journey through the switch, and then changed back to analog form for their excursion into the outside world.

In the second case, several modems (the pool) are installed on outside lines. When a PC, digitally connected to the PBX, makes an outside call, the PBX automatically selects a modem-equipped trunk. To the PBX, the modem pool is a line group, each line of which is equipped with a modem and linked to the telephone company's Central Office. Ordinarily, only 1,200-bps asynchronous modems are supported. Some PBXs further assist outside data connections by offering X.25 interfaces for packet switching networks.

PBX Features

If you were a PBX manufacturer, and you already had a computer sitting in your PBX, you'd probably be inclined to find useful tasks to keep it busy, in particular by adding more frills for your customers. The number of whizzo features available on PBXs is staggering, and, of course, most customers want all 150 of them even though they'll never use more than about a dozen. Features are selected and deselected for a given line by either entering special Touch-Tone sequences on the phone or pressing special function buttons, if provided. Some of the most popular features:

> *Call forwarding*, one of the PBX features also available to regular telephone sub-scribers, automatically transfers incoming calls to another line. Generally, PBX call forwarding can transfer calls only to other PBX lines, not to outside lines.

> *Last number redial*, with the press of a single button, redials the previously tried number.

> *Coverage path* programming reroutes incoming calls if your line is busy or you fail to pick up after a certain number of rings. Thus, if you are already tied up or temporarily away from your desk, your calls will bounce to another phone, where someone else can handle the call or (you hope) take a message for you. A coverage path is often more difficult to program than plain call forwarding. Several levels of coverage may be possible: if you're busy on a call, the secretary is out to lunch, and the receptionist is dallying with the Federal Express driver, an incoming call to your number can get shunted around so many times that the caller is bound to give up before being answered. Many large organizations seem to be handling their excess telephone traffic this way.

> *Send all* is a special case of call forwarding; it forwards all calls to the next party on the coverage path.

> *Call pickup* allows you to intercept on another line a call coming in to your number. For example, a friend of ours spends much of his working day in a lab separated

from his office by a passageway. When his office phone rings, he may be seen diving for the lab phone and stabbing in the code to intercept the call before it is automatically rerouted elsewhere along his coverage path.

Messaging features are included on many PBXs. Phones equipped with display panels can be used to display brief text messages. Such messages are stored by the PBX and retrieved individually by means of a code entered at the displaying phone. A step beyond this is *voice mail*, where the PBX acts as a centralized answering machine (with digital voice recording) for all its users.

The features described above primarily benefit voice users, but computers are not neglected. Features offered for data lines include *symbolic dialing, queuing* (lining up for service), and *menus.* Symbolic dialing allows a telephone number to be supplied to the PBX as an ASCII string. Queuing can be used on lines connecting to host ports. It allows callers to wait when all ports are busy, and to receive updated information on their positions in the queue. Menus present terminal users with a list of in-house services to which they can connect.

Another great benefit of PBXs is that telephone numbers, in the sense of subscriber addresses, can easily be reassigned from one line to another. Thus, when people change offices, they can retain their old numbers with little or no trouble. Also, individual phones can readily be restricted to certain types of calls. Phones in public areas, for example, can be programmed to allow internal calling only.

PBX Networks

Suppose a company is burdened with heavy telephone traffic among several large offices in scattered locations. If each office has a PBX, the company may elect to install leased lines interconnecting them. A set of analog lines would be adequate, but the T1 lines mentioned earlier are especially suited to this application. A T1 line comprises 24 64-kbps channels, ideal for a complement of interoffice links.

Some PBXs that accommodate such networking also support *feature transparency*, which makes the network appear to the user as a single virtual PBX. Such transparency implies, for example, that calls can be forwarded or "covered" from one PBX to another, a valuable feature for large organizations.

Leading suppliers of PBXs include AT&T, GTE, Mitel, Northern Telecom, and Rolm.

Centrex Systems

A Centrex system, functionally equivalent to a basic voice PBX, is a service leased from local telephone companies. Instead of having a private switch on your site, the telephone company leases you a part of its Central Office exchange. Centrex systems have some advantages over PBXs: they blend more seamlessly with the outside telephone network; their hardware receives regular, high-quality maintenance; they usually have battery backup to keep them operating in the event of a power failure; and the lessee incurs no capital cost. On the other hand, Centrex systems may not be expanded as easily as PBXs, and they also lack the PBX's wealth of features. For example, it is almost impossible to provide a Centrex system with voice mail.

Data PBXs

PBXs designed exclusively for switching data are frequently used to switch data paths between PCs and serial devices. An eight-port data PBX might, for example, host four PCs, two modems, and two serial printers. The modems and printers can be conveniently shared among the PC users, who can also transfer files among themselves by switching connections from one PC to another.

Data-only and data-and-voice PBXs are treated further in a section of Chapter 15 that compares local area networks with PBXs as systems for sharing data and devices among PCs.

INTEGRATED SERVICES DIGITAL NETWORKS

In the next 10 to 20 years, The Integrated Services Digital Network (ISDN) may supplant most of the communications networks we've come to know and hate. Traditional telephone systems, PSNs, and perhaps even cable-TV networks will wither away, to be replaced in our homes and offices by a super-sophisticated, all-purpose, multiplexed, high-speed digital "pipeline." The CCITT states that an ISDN "provides end-to-end digital connectivity to support a wide range of services, including voice and non-voice services, to which users have access by a limited set of standard multi-purpose user-network interfaces." (CCITT *Red Book* Fascicle III.5, Geneva 1985, p. 3.)

With the advent of ISDNs, all telecommunications will be effected digitally: telephones will conform to the new standard by digitizing voices, and modems will become white elephants (or doorstops). Basic ISDN service will provide the subscriber with connections capable of carrying 64 kbps; more and more kbps will simply be a matter of more and more k$. For a start, ISDNs can be expected to carry voice, facsimile, computer data, and telex traffic, as well as support remote meter reading and the monitoring of fire and burglar alarms. Eventually, these networks may also carry TV broadcasts (displacing cable TV), video conferencing, security information, and probably other things nobody's even thought of yet. Widespread implementation of this exciting and terrifying technology is still a decade or two away, but preliminary steps are already being taken.

The idea of ISDN was brought into the world in the early 1970s by the CCITT, which has slowly been developing a set of standards for such networks. The CCITT was motivated by the realization that data transmission requirements would continue to grow rapidly and, in the absence of a standard, would be met in many divergent and incompatible ways. The ISDN concept is to create a uniform worldwide network of digital pathways and digital switches capable of transporting any form of data that can be reduced to bits, essentially any kind of communication. The PSN concept was a significant step in the same direction for computer communication, and some PSN protocols will indeed be carried over to ISDNs. But ISDNs go much further, potentially integrating any and all communications services on a single standardized digital network—just as the name says.

Specifically, ISDNs promise:

- Pure end-to-end digital communications from anywhere to anywhere.
- An interface with worldwide standards for connectors, electrical signaling, and protocols.
- Compatibility with any and all types of communication, subject only to bandwidth limitations.
- Both circuit-switched connections (like dial-up telephone calls) and packet-switched connections (like those supplied by PSNs).

- Seamless integration among all networks whose suppliers follow the ISDN standards.
- The flexibility to allow devices to interface with the network in intelligent ways, accommodating computers, for example, as something more than expensive telephone dialers.

Although it's too early for any guarantees to be made, ISDNs will probably open the door to very fast call setups, a universal physical connector, and universal methods of addressing subscribers and accounting for network usage, perhaps with a debit card accepted by every public phone on Earth. We can expect a feast of value-added features, starting with those described for PBXs in the previous section.

As a practical matter, it is likely that existing networks, primarily the international telephone network, will slowly evolve into ISDNs. Private ISDNs will also appear; indeed, several multinational corporations are already building them. Presumably, even these private nets will have some point of contact with the public ISDN.

Only in the creation of some private networks will wholesale deployment of new equipment be called for. Converting North America's telephone system to ISDN is not such a Herculean labor as you might imagine: much Central Office switching equipment and high-speed interoffice trunk capacity is already digital. Telephone companies will certainly expend some time and effort in making their systems conform to ISDN standards, but to a large extent such conversion represents an evolutionary upgrade rather than a throw-out-and-replace operation. The next step will involve integrating large corporate customers' PBXs with revamped Central Office exchanges. Many PBX vendors are now building their products to ISDN standards—in many cases, even before those standards have been ratified by the CCITT. Since many PBX manufacturers also build Central Office switches, integration of the two should not prove too troublesome. From there, ISDNs will spread to small businesses in population centers, perhaps to residential lines, and so on. The exact pattern is difficult to predict, because it will be driven by customer demands, which, in turn, will be partly driven by marketing and advertising. Some rural telephone customers may not have access to ISDN in the foreseeable future.

Although it is appealing to speculate, many questions about ISDN must go unanswered. In the early days of its development, pioneers quipped that ISDN stood for "I Sure Don't kNow." Nowadays, they say: "I *Still* Don't kNow."

Standard Interfaces

ISDN depends on two fundamental interfaces: a *basic rate interface (BRI)* and a *primary rate interface (PRI)*. The BRI serves "standard terminal equipment" such as conventional telephones, computer terminals, and PCs. It provides one 16-kbps plus two 64-kbps channels on an existing local loop. The 16-kbps *D-channel* is used for control purposes, primarily managing the establishment of connections for the other two channels. Each 64-kbps *B-channel* can be used independently for network connections. For example, you could use them as two phone lines at one moment and, a minute later, have a phone conversation on one and transmit data on the other. Since a digitized voice signal requires a bandwidth of about 64 kbps, a voice call nicely fills up a B-channel.

The channel rates for a BRI add up to a total of 144 kbps. The actual raw bit rate of the interface is 192 kbps. The residual 48 kbps is taken up by the protocol that delivers the data across the interface and multiplexes the three channels.

Physically, the interface usually consists of three twisted pairs, two for signaling (one pair for each direction) and the third to supply power. This arrangement renders terminals potentially independent of local power feeds. Optical fiber will also be heavily used, and may eventually be more common than twisted pair.

It's undeniably a big step up from the approximately 19.2-kbps effective capacity of modem-bound local loops to the 192-kbps capacity required by ISDN. Squeezing that amount of information onto twisted pair is not easy (it was considered impossible only a few years ago), but over distances of about 1,000 meters or less, it can be done.

The PRI defines the connection between PBX and PBX, between PBX and Central Office, and between one Central Office and another. Somewhat similar to T1, it prescribes a bandwidth of either 1.544 or 2.048 Mbps, divided up into one 64-kbps signaling channel and some selection of data channels. A 1.544-Mbps primary interface would most often be split into 23 64-kbps data channels plus a 64-kbps control channel. It might otherwise, for example, be used for three 384-kbps data channels plus the 64-kbps control channel.

Also defined are 384-kbps, 1.536-Mbps, and 1.920-Mbps data channels, intended for such uses as fast facsimile, video teleconferencing, high-fidelity audio, and high-speed data communications.

ISDN Services

ISDNs provide two basic classes of service: *bearer services* and *teleservices*. In the case of bearer services, the network simply transports bits among users without concern for meaning. Two computers could use this low-level service for any data communication function, just as they would use a modem link or PSN connection. Teleservices are user-level services provided by a network itself. Familiar examples are voice telephony, Teletex (a modern version of telex), and facsimile transmission.

With ISDNs gradually taking over from the traditional phone system, the question of how customers on the old-style system will communicate with those on the new becomes very important. For voice, there's no problem. A typical voice call is frequently digitized today for at least some portion of its passage through the phone system. The codecs discussed earlier make voice ISDN compatibility a trivial concern. But what about data? How does the home PC with a 2,400-bps modem on an analog line communicate with the mainframe computer attached to an ISDN-style system? The general answer lies in the *communication resource*, a conversion component built into a PBX or Central Office switch. For example, a communication resource might translate between a 64-kbps ISDN data stream and the V.22 *bis* modem-signaling standard. The choice of which resources to provide is, however, entirely up to the ISDN vendor.

Preparing for ISDN

ISDNs may be just around the corner, but their imminence has not depressed the market for devices, such as modems, that exploit traditional networks. Still, some modem manufacturers, notably Hayes Microcomputer Products, are busily engaged in the development of ISDN-related items.

Will ISDNs make communication less expensive? They might, because, among other things, service providers can get more utility out of existing plant by following ISDN practices. On the other hand, since communication services, especially for data, will change so much with the coming of ISDNs, it's hard to compare what's available today with what one might expect tomorrow. In any event, ISDN, like most technical breakthroughs of the past 50 years, will undoubtedly become less expensive as the technology matures.

Can ISDNs live up to the rosy picture painted here? Will they prove to be a boon, or a debacle of compatibility and regulatory conflicts? We can hope that ISDNs will change the face of communication for the better, but it might be wise to pray, too. Much work is being done to develop standards for ISDNs, and many difficult areas remain. One area of possible concern is the lack of coordination among various developers. Another is that market pressures could hasten the adoption of an inadequate standard, as some have argued was the case with digital audio compact discs. On the positive side, it seems at least possible that the vast sums of money being invested in ISDN development will compel a high degree of integration and compatibility.

ISDN Protocols

To some readers, this section will be meaningless until they have read later chapters of this book. Nevertheless, for the sake of completeness, the protocols used with ISDNs are summarized here.

Raw data are passed over the user-to-network interface in a continuous sequence of 48-bit frames. Each frame includes two octets from each data channel, four bits from the signaling channel, and 12 bits used for synchronization or other nondata purposes. Thus, 36 bits in each 48-bit frame carry data; herein lies the difference between the raw 192-kbps rate and the 144-kbps effective rate.

Two protocols are employed on the signaling channel: *Q.931* and *LAPD*. Q.931 specifies procedures for setting up, maintaining, and clearing user connections, and includes messages such as:

SETUP	initiates a connection
CALL PROCeeding	tells the user that the network is attempting to establish the requested connection
ALERTing	indicates that the called user is being alerted (equivalent to a ring)
CONNect	indicates completion of a connection
RELease	indicates, or requests, call clearing
RELease **COM**plete	confirms disconnection

Since the signaling channel will be engaged only sporadically in call management, it is also possible to use it for a low-bit-rate data call.

LAPD is a variant of the link-access protocol of X.25. It serves to carry the Q.931 messages over the user-to-network interface, providing error control and flow control.

Intelligent devices enjoy considerable latitude in communicating over ISDN data channels. Over packet-mode connections, for example, they can make use of straight X.25, as currently employed with PSNs.

ISDN and Beyond

ISDNs hold the promise of speed and services that may seem luxurious compared to what we are accustomed to. But, all too quickly, we'll get used to them, and cry out for ever more bandwidth. In the mid- to late 1990s, we may see the introduction of *wideband* ISDNs operating at hundreds of megabits per second. This second-tier service will depend on replacing copper wire with optical fiber in local loops. Physical installation of optical-fiber cables is the easy part of the wideband upgrade; the hard part is switching lots of connections at such lightning speeds. Although superconductors might provide the answer, the replacement of all Central Office switches with new models built from superconductors would be a formidable task. But then, perhaps we can leapfrog fiber and install superconducting local loops running at gigabits per second.

Cable TV is a broadcast system; the cable carries a few dozen stations and you tune in the one you want. With gigabit-speed ISDNs, you would instead *dial* the station you wanted to view. Imagine lounging in your vacation cottage in Maine and hooking into KNBC in Los Angeles, or the BBC in London. If you need a snack (extremely likely), you call up Luigi's and have a video discussion about what kind of pizza they're going to deliver. Of course, the coming wonders in communications may transform habits of work as well as of leisure.

3

MODEMS

We need modems because they accommodate the essentially analog character of many of the communication facilities available to us, most notably the telephone system, engineered for human conversation. Digital computers, despite their pervasiveness, are still the aliens in this analog world, and modems are their interpreters. Although we treat modems here only in connection with PCs, they serve all kinds of digital devices, including terminals and big (and not-so-big) computers.

HOW MODEMS WORK

Modem is an abbreviation for "modulator/demodulator." To an engineer, *modulation* is the variation in the frequency or some other property of a *carrier* wave, such as radio, in accordance with a superimposed signal. The carrier transports the signal from one place to another, where *demodulation* retrieves the signal. The system is inherently analog.

The signal for modems consists of the patterns and symbols of communications mentioned in Chapter 1, particularly MARK, representing binary 1, and SPACE, representing binary 0. The simplest modem is a device that translates between digital MARK and analog MARK, and between digital SPACE and analog SPACE.

Modems normally work in pairs, as shown in Figure 3.1, shuttling data between two digital devices over an analog connection that typically involves a telephone line. You might envision a Rube Goldberg modem as a box that accepts digital square waves and uses a voice synthesizer to yell "One, one, zero, one, zero, zero, zero, one" into a telephone handset. A complementary box at the other end then retranslates the words "one" and "zero" into square waves. The operation of real modems is not too different from this model, except that modems use whistles—pure tones of fixed sound frequencies, created by modulating a sound-frequency carrier—instead of words. The whistle tones are easier than words to generate and recognize electronically.

Carriers and Sine Waves

The basic whistle, or carrier, modulated in the process of encoding data is a pure *sine wave*, a regular, smooth, continuous sweep of energy, as illustrated in Figure 1.2. The transmitting modem modulates the carrier, i.e., creates variations that encode the data being transferred. The receiving modem demodulates the signal, detecting the variations and reconstructing the original data. Figure 3.2 illustrates the three most important modulation methods: amplitude modulation (AM), frequency modulation (FM), and phase modulation (PM). Each technique manipulates a different property of the sine wave carrier. AM and

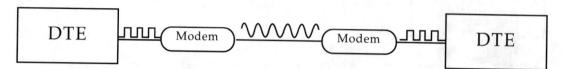

FIGURE 3.1: Modem pair in operation

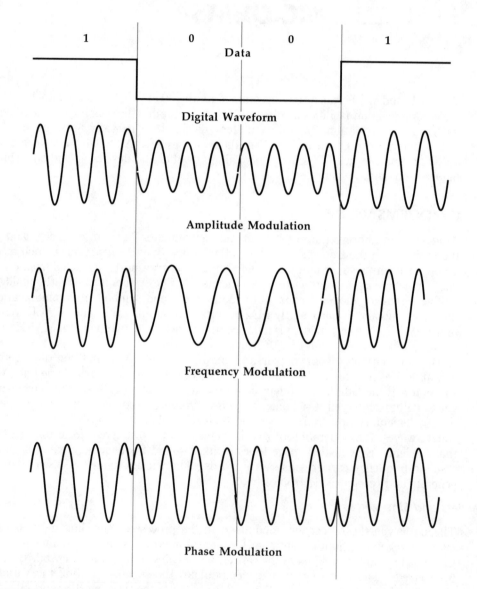

FIGURE 3.2: Modulation techniques

FM are common radio terms. The frequency to which you tune to bring in a desired radio station is that of its carrier. A demodulator circuit strips the audio signal from the radio frequency (RF) carrier and sends it along to the radio set's amplifier and loudspeaker.

Frequency Shift Keying

The simplest practical design for intermodem communication is to designate two different sound frequencies, i.e., whistles of two different pitches, as MARK and SPACE signals. The transmitting modem emits the frequency (analog MARK or SPACE) that corresponds to the state of its input (digital MARK or SPACE). The receiving modem "hears" one of the two analog signal tones and translates it into the digital MARK or SPACE understood by the computer. This method of encoding data, called *frequency shift keying (FSK)*, is used at low transmission speeds, as in the 300-bps modems commonly used with microcomputers before the advent of 1,200- and 2,400-bps models. The two tones that signal MARK and SPACE are the *symbols* the modem uses, in this case, for communicating information.

An analogy may make this clearer. At the sending end a person reads on a voltmeter the digital signal from his PC, and blows the appropriate MARK or SPACE whistle for each bit. At the receiving end a listener distinguishes between the whistle tones she hears and relays the signal to her PC by pressing one of two buttons to generate the appropriate MARK or SPACE voltage. If these people practiced all day, their PCs could probably communicate at about 2 bps.

Although FSK is both readily understood and cheaply implemented, it doesn't lend itself to full-duplex operation at transmission speeds much above 600 bps. This limit arises because the bandwidth of a telephone line does not permit wide separation between the MARK and SPACE frequencies, so the two do not "sound" very different. A transmitting modem would have no trouble switching between these frequencies at dizzying rates; the receiver, however, has a much more difficult job. It must distinguish between two fairly similar tones on a signal muddied by its journey through the phone system.

Raising the Speed Limit

There are three common approaches to engineering modems for higher speeds than those attainable with FSK.

The first is to increase the number of symbols used. A modem equipped to handle two symbols can transmit or receive only one bit at a time. Give it four symbols to work with, and it can transfer two bits at a time, because each of the four symbols can be identified with one of four possible two-bit combinations. For example, if we call the symbols A, B, C, and D, we can encode data thus:

A   00

B   01

C   10

D   11

To help you appreciate the efficiency gained by increasing the number of symbols, consider the various written forms in which an ASCII character (a sequence of seven bits) might be expressed. Using binary notation, 0 and 1, you need seven symbols. The job requires three if your symbols are the ten decimal digits, and only two if you choose hexadecimal (base-16) representation.

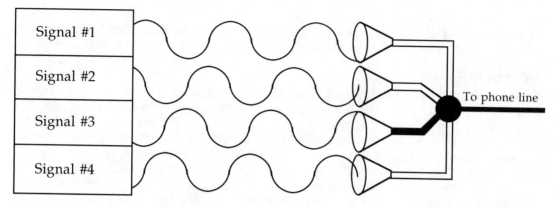

FIGURE 3.3: Selection of signals staggered by 90°-phase shifts

In the "human modems" analogy given earlier, the use of an increased number of symbols would require more whistles at the transmitter, and a receiver able to recognize the additional tones. The four two bit symbols could, in principle, be keyed by four different frequencies, amplitudes, or phase changes. Although our illustration of this technique involves frequency modulation, phase modulation would almost certainly be used in practice.

Phase modulation is, in itself, the second approach to raising modem data rates. The *phase* of a signal is the particular point it has reached in its cycle. Picture a sine wave as the path traced out by a point on the perimeter of a wheel rolling on a horizontal surface. The phase can be expressed as the angle, 0 to 360 degrees, through which the wheel has rotated since leaving its starting position. Zero and 360 degrees are the same, since the start and end of a cycle look identical. Now suppose we have a four-symbol modem (as in the example above) in which the symbols correspond to four changes of phase: 0, 90, 180, and 270 degrees. As shown in Figure 3.3, the modem's transmitting circuits are supplied with four signals of the same frequency, but staggered in phase by quarter-cycle (90-degree) increments. These four signals do not have a one-to-one correspondence with the four symbols. Rather, in order to transmit a given symbol, the modem selects whichever of these four signals has the appropriate phase *difference* with respect to the signal it is already sending. For example, assume that the bit-pair 01 is expressed by a 90-degree phase change. A transmitted sequence of 01s would then appear as a waveform that "skips" a quarter cycle at each symbol boundary. The modem generates this output by transmitting each of the four signals in turn, from #1 through #4 as depicted in Figure 3.3.

With phase modulation alone, modems can manage data rates of 1,200 and 2,400 bps. For still higher speeds, a combination of phase and amplitude modulation is used. Finally, many of the fastest modems, operating at 9,600 bps and above, take advantage of a third approach, *trellis encoding*, which essentially means modulating several independent carrier signals distributed across the voice-grade band. Extending the human-modem analogy, Trellis encoding would require several people transmitting and receiving simultaneously.

Additional technical details about the signaling habits of faster modems are provided in the third section of this chapter.

Bits per Second vs. Baud

This discussion of modem speeds is the perfect place to clarify the difference between *baud* and *bits per second*. The latter term is practically self-explanatory; it relates to individual

0s and 1s. *Baud*, a tribute to Emile Baudot, introduced earlier, refers to modulation rate. It is the measure of signaling speed, or symbols per second. For anything transmitting one bit at a time, such as a PC's serial port, bps and baud are identical. For a modem that groups bits together in composite symbols for transmission, the two rates differ. For example, the standard PC modem operating at 1,200 bps encodes two bits at a time. It therefore transmits 600 symbols each second, for a rate of 1,200 bps but 600 baud.

The use of the term *baud rate* is, strictly speaking, incorrect, since the word *baud* itself describes a rate, that of symbols per second. Unfortunately, language purists (including the authors) seem to be losing the battle, and it's probably futile to complain when people use *baud* interchangeably with *bps* or append the redundant "rate."

Other Aspects of Modem Design

While speed and modulation technique are a modem's most important characteristics, other design factors must also be considered—in particular, the following:

- Half-duplex or full-duplex operation
- Synchronous or asynchronous operation
- Tailoring to switched or to private lines

Let's look at the implications of these factors.

Full- vs. Half-duplex

The bottleneck in any communications setup is usually the telephone connection, if one is involved. Of course, you want the best performance, within the bounds of affordability, consonant with the demands of the application. Most modems used with PCs are full-duplex, and thus can transfer data simultaneously and independently in both directions. However, for the many applications requiring the unidirectional transfer of large amounts of information, a half-duplex modem may be preferable, since it can seize the entire bandwidth for whichever traffic direction is needed at any moment. A full-duplex modem, by holding open a channel in each direction at all times, inevitably wastes bandwidth.

A pair of half-duplex modems reverses the direction of data flow by a procedure called *turning the line around*. This involves three steps: (i) the transmitting modem turns its carrier off; (ii) the receiving modem detects the loss of carrier and turns its own carrier on, becoming a transmitter; and (iii) the first modem becomes a receiver and picks up the carrier from the other. This procedure is far from instantaneous, typically taking from 10 to 300 milliseconds, a period called the *turnaround time*. Thus, half-duplex modems may be unsuitable for interactive applications in which data are alternately spurting back and forth and possibly overlapping. But such is not always the case; many of the newest high-speed modems operate in half-duplex, yet can turn the line around so fast that they appear to be, and for many practical purposes may be treated as, full-duplex. The Hayes™ V-series Smartmodem 9600™ operates in this fashion, running in true full-duplex up to 2,400 bps, and in ping-pong half-duplex at 4,800 and 9,600 bps. Conclusion: for general applications, a full-duplex modem is a necessary compromise, but where a link is to be used solely for an inherently half-duplex application, such as one-way file transfer, a half-duplex modem may provide better performance.

Certain modems, designed for applications that involve a preponderance of data flow in one direction, are equipped with one high-speed channel and one low-speed channel. This is called *split-speed operation*. Consider, for example, the modems made for European use with videotex systems, which transmit 1,200 bps in one direction and 75 bps in the other. *Videotex services*, well known in Europe but not in America, send information, rendered in "pages" of low-resolution color graphics, from a database to dedicated (i.e., single-function) terminals in response to requests entered on small keypads. The videotex system typically provides information such as weather forecasts, sports results, airline schedules, and stock quotes, and is designed to be usable by anyone without training. Each query elicits the transmission of one page, and each page contains a menu enumerating other associated pages that may subsequently be requested. IBM and Sears introduced a videotex-like service to America in 1988 with their collaborative Trintex Prodigy[sm] system, which uses standard PC, rather than split-speed, modems.

In its Courier line, U.S. Robotics offers 9,600-bps modems that employ a split-speed design, transmitting at 9,600 bps in one direction and 300 bps in the other. The high- and low-speed channels switch directional duties according to traffic demands.

Synchronous vs. Asynchronous Modems

In a synchronous communications link, bits are timed by a single clock, normally located in the transmitting modem; the timing signals generated by the clock must be carried from end to end across the link. Every device involved in a synchronous link must have synchronous capability. Many computer systems, especially mainframes, are strongly oriented toward synchronous communication, and require the use of synchronous modems (usually at dial-up speeds of 2,400 and 4,800 bps, or over leased lines at 4,800, 7,200, and 9,600 bps). Roughly as many synchronous modems are designed for half-duplex operation as for full-duplex, and some are capable of both.

In contrast, each station on an asynchronous link has its own clock; the two clocks are brought into temporary synchronization by periodic trigger signals buried in the data. These clocks are an integral part of the I/O port of each station. PCs are better suited to asynchronous than to synchronous communication, and the marketplace offers a wide range of async modems for them, covering speeds from 110 bps up to 19,200 bps. Almost all are full-duplex and designed primarily for use on switched connections.

Switched Line vs. Private Line Modems

Any modem made for operation on switched lines can also be used on leased lines, but particular modem characteristics may take advantage of the higher transmission quality normally afforded by leased lines, especially the four-wire type. Certain modems are intended for operation on either line type, but with higher performance on leased lines. Other units are designed specifically for leased-line operation.

What Modems are Made of

A simplified block diagram of a modem is shown in Figure 3.4. The transmitter (or modulator) converts signals from digital to analog form, the receiver (or demodulator) from analog to digital. The *telephone line driver*, usually a chip within the modem, acts as an interface between the modem and the telephone line, just as the modem's RS-232 port is an interface with the PC. The telephone line driver conditions the analog output for transmission onto the phone line. The phone line itself is also electrically isolated from the modem circuitry by a transformer, which protects the line from stray DC voltages. All this care is taken to ensure that the signal making its way onto the line is well suited to the telephone system's electrical characteristics—the line impedance, for instance. Failure to do so (in particular,

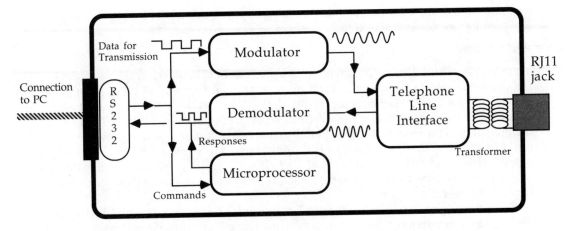

FIGURE 3.4: Block diagram of a modem

allowing DC voltages onto phone lines) might violate the dread Part 68 of the Federal Communications Commission (FCC) Rules and, worse, upset the phone company.

Echo Suppression

At one time or another, nearly everyone has been disturbed by an unpleasant echo on a long-distance voice call. This is not caused by faulty phone company equipment injecting an echo, but rather by the failure of a system designed to quash the echoes that naturally stray into such connections. Echoes are a fact of life in long-distance telephony where analog circuits are employed. On connections running longer than 1,500 miles or so, they are normally eliminated by devices called *echo suppressors*.

Echo suppressors do important work, but they operate by making the connection half-duplex. This effect is easily demonstrated. During a local call, both parties can talk simultaneously—wonderful for arguments. On a cross-country or overseas call, however, you will often find that only one party can talk at a time. This may be all right for people, but it's not much good for modems trying to conduct a full-duplex dialogue. To accommodate modems, phone companies equip long-distance lines with devices to turn off echo suppressors for the duration of a data call. To trigger the disabling of the suppressors, modems send a short tone of approximately 2,225 Hz (2,100 Hz in Europe) upon initial connection.

As more and more long-distance circuitry is converted to digital, the annoyances of these echos are diminishing. Since line quality and modernity are not yet uniform, however, echo suppression will continue to be important for the foreseeable future.

STANDARDS FOR PC MODEMS

Many standards have been established prescribing modulation techniques for various data rates in various environments, including, for example, a standard for asynchronous 1,200-bps full-duplex modems operating on U.S. switched lines, and another for 4,800-bps synchronous, half-duplex operation on leased lines. Two modems have little hope of communicating unless they follow a common standard. Fortunately, most modem products made today conform to one or more of them. Some of the newest and fastest PC modems, however, are exceptions; for example, there's a fair amount of behavioral variation among those designed for operation at 9,600 bps.

Bells and Whistles

Traditionally, Bell Labs, a division of American Telephone and Telegraph, established the standards for modem operation in the United States and Canada; all other manufacturers of modems for those markets complied. Until 1968, AT&T's manufacturing arm, the Western Electric Company, was the only modem maker in the United States. Through clever manipulation of the relevant tariffs, Ma Bell arranged that (a) only Bell-approved equipment could be attached to AT&T lines, and (b) only their own equipment was approved. The numerical titles of Bell standards (103, 212, 201, 208, etc.) were originally the model numbers of Western Electric modems, and were retained as designations for what later became the operating standards.

European modem manufacturers have largely conformed to standards set by the CCITT. Today, manufacturers for the North American market are turning increasingly to these international standards.

Another legacy of the days of tighter regulation is the *Data Access Arrangement (DAA)*. DAAs are AT&T-supplied devices that the company once required on the customer end of any telephone line to which "foreign" (i.e., non-Bell) equipment was attached. These devices served to protect the line from DC voltages and other potential hazards to the telephone system. Few newcomers to data communications are familiar with DAAs, but they still lurk in many installations.

The Bell 103A Standard

Now we'll consider a concrete example of the use of FSK, the Bell 103A-type modem. *Bell 103A* designates the standard for modem operation in North America at speeds not exceeding 300 bps. This is the simplest case of a real, practical modem. Although 300-bps operation is uncommon these days, many PC modems are able to run in the 103A mode.

Bell 103A prescribes FSK and dictates the exact frequencies to be used. Since it calls for full-duplex operation, a total of four frequencies, two for each direction of data flow, are needed. Frequencies are assigned in two bands, called the *low channel* and the *high*

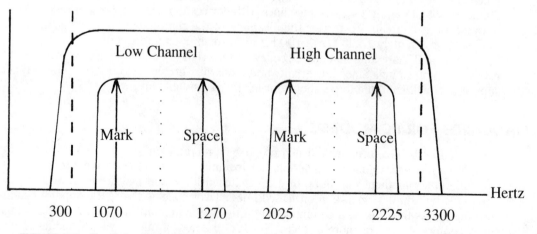

FIGURE 3.5: Graph for Bell 103 standard

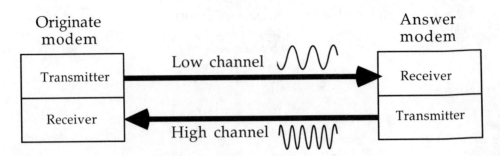

FIGURE 3.6: Assignment of channels with Bell 103 modems

channel, as shown in Figure 3.5. One modem transmits at 1,070 Hz and 1,270 Hz, the other at 2,025 Hz and 2,225 Hz.

Clearly, some convention must dictate which modem of a communicating pair will transmit on the high channel and which on the low channel. For this purpose, the modem initiating the call is dubbed the *originate modem,* and the unit at the receiving end is called the *answer modem.* According to Bell 103A, the originate modem transmits on the high channel, and the answer modem on the low channel, as shown in Figure 3.6.

Before personal computers came into being, most 103A-type modems were hard-wired either as originate or answer models. Terminal users bought originate units, and host computers were equipped with answer units. Except for a few models that sacrifice operational flexibility in favor of portability, almost all modems being built today can operate in either mode, and thus accommodate such contemporary practices as PCs calling other PCs.

Note how simple 103As are: they're just dumb signal translators (dumb enough to retail for as little as $30 each). They merely convert square waves into whistles and vice versa, caring nothing for how long a signal lasts, and knowing nothing about bits or bytes. All responsibility for timing is left to the PC or other device (terminal, printer, or plotter) the modem is working with.

If 103A-type modems are oblivious to bit timing, why are they are specified as 300-bps units? The answer is that this is the top speed they are expected to accommodate. The 103A standard covers operation up to this limit; as long as the transmitting and receiving stations are set to the same rate, a 103A system will handle 110 bps, 134.5 bps, or some peculiar rate such as 222.37 bps. In fact, this standard, like many, is conservative; in practice, well-made Bell 103A-standard modems are often used at 450 bps, but beyond thi the system quickly approaches the limits of FSK capability.

With suitable software, you could link two PCs equipped with 103A-type modems 1.76 bps, the lowest speed that PC serial ports can manage. At such a rate, the moden speaker, if left on, would let you discern each bit as it crawled by. Technically, both F 232 and Bell 103A support a data rate of even zero bps.

The 103A is the only modem whose operation we will examine in detail. This shoulc sufficient to give you a good general picture of how modems work.

The Bell 212A Standard

Most PC modems operate at 1,200 bps, following the *Bell 212A* standard. 212A prescribes a modulation scheme involving two-bit symbols and phase-shif

ing. Each transmitted symbol is encoded by one of four angles of phase shift, as follows:

Symbol	Phase Shift
00	90°
01	0°
10	180°
11	270°

The 212A standard also incorporates the 103A-standard mode for compatibility with older modems.

Although 212A provides specifications for modem operation with both synchronous and asynchronous terminals, most 212A-type modems made for the PC market have only asynchronous capability. This is not surprising, since a PC can't handle synchronous operation without special hardware. This is one of several cases in which modems are built, in the interest of practicality, to comply with only a subset of a standard.

While a 103A-type modem can operate over a range of speeds from zero to at least 300 bps, a 212A unit can't cope with substantial variation from 1,200 bps. For example, it cannot send data at 1,000 bps. This is because, at 1,200 bps, the modem operates internally as a synchronous device, in the manner described in the next section, "More About Modem Operation."

The predominance of the 212A standard has led several companies to offer the "guts" of such a modem in the form of a single, chip-like package (which actually incorporates three integrated circuits).

The Vadic VA3400™ Standard

Another 1,200-bps standard used in the United States, called *Vadic VA3400*, is held by a few diehards to be superior to Bell's. Bell was behindhand in establishing a 1,200-bps async standard, and Vadic scooped them. But while VA3400 enjoyed considerable popularity in its early days, it is incompatible with, and has been eclipsed by, 212A. The Vadic standard is little used today, and it's accommodated by few currently available modems. Many modems that implement Vadic also include Bell 212A; these are sometimes called "triple modems" because of their Vadic VA3400, Bell 212A, and Bell 103A compatibility.

CCITT V.22 bis

The introduction to North America of 2,400-bps PC modems marked a shift to acceptance of the international standards promulgated by the CCITT and used in most other parts of the world. (Bell offers no standard for async, full-duplex operation at 2,400 bps.) Like 212A, *V.22 bis* employs phase shift keying. *Bis*, by the way, is a French word meaning "again," or "second version." When used in reference to the standard, its pronunciation is usually Anglicized to rhyme with "kiss."

Most 2,400-bps modems incorporate 212A-type 1,200-bps operation to maintain compatibility with the huge population of the older species. Some also comply with the original CCITT V.22 (without *bis*) standard for 1,200 bps. Unlike 1,200-bps modems, however, many 2,400-bps models do not support the Bell 103A-type 300-bps mode; this is hardly tragic, as the popularity of such low speeds is waning rapidly.

Several reviewers have noted that 2,400-bps modems tend to perform somewhat better at 1,200 bps than do plain 1,200-bps-only units. This presumably results from the higher

circuit quality demanded by the increased data rate. Since the cheapest of the 2,400-bps units cost only a little more than 1,200-bps models, they may be a better buy even if the higher speed is not immediately required.

Be warned that, despite their adherence to international standards, V.22 *bis* modems built for the North American market may be incompatible with those intended for use elsewhere, due to the different requirements imposed by various phone systems. For example, there may be a mismatch in the tones used to disable echo suppressors.

Other Modem Standards

Appendix D lists the modem standards in vogue at this writing. A quick glance will show that Bell and CCITT standards address substantially similar data rates and other operating parameters. Each, for example, has its own standard for 0-to-300-bps async full-duplex switched use, one for 4,800-bps sync full-duplex private-line use, and so on. What's more, most of these corresponding pairs of standards employ the same modulation schemes. They differ considerably, however, in the details of their modulation methods, including such things as carrier frequencies and phase angles, meaning that true Bell-CCITT compatibility is practically nonexistent. One useful exception is the pair of standards for 1,200-bps async full-duplex dial-up use: 212A and V.22. While these are not identical, they are close enough that a 212A and a V.22 modem can often be coaxed into communicating with each other. This does not imply that a 212A-type modem will work in Europe. The 212A and V.22 modulation schemes may be compatible, but other technical characteristics are not.

Faster modems available for PCs, such as those for 9,600-bps operation, do not follow a single standard. Standards are not lacking—CCITT has specs for 4,800- and 9,600-bps units—but many manufacturers have chosen not to follow them. Getting modems to operate satisfactorily at these breakneck speeds is not easy, and some makers feel that they can do a better, or at least less expensive, job with proprietary designs than by adhering to established standards.

What You Hear from a Modem

When you place a data call with a speaker-equipped 1,200-bps PC modem, the speaker emits a brief burst of a pure tone followed by a sound best described as a "hash." The pure tone is the signal to disable the echo suppressors. The hash is the carrier, and it sounds that way because its phase is being forcibly changed 600 times per second, as dictated by the 212A standard. Why is the phase continually shifting if no data are being sent? Shouldn't the line be idle, i.e., in constant MARK, when the connection is first made? It turns out that 212A modems deliberately scramble all transmitted bits, including 1-bits sent while idling, to ensure that phase changes occur with most symbols. This method is adopted because, when phase changes are plentiful, it's easier for the receiving modem to stay in synchronization with the transmitter. The receiving modem unscrambles the bits to recreate the original data. This kind of scrambling, by the way, has no relevance to security.

Modems recognize one another by means of their carriers. Fortunately, every modem standard dictates the use of a distinct carrier frequency. It should be obvious that a modem equipped only for 1,200-bps operation has no hope of communicating with one equipped solely for 300 bps. However, they won't just whistle futilely at each other forever; after testing for a few seconds, they simply give up because they have failed to lock on to a compatible carrier.

This raises the question of how modems manage things when equipped to operate under more than one signaling standard. Suppose a 1,200-bps modem dials into a system capable of running at both 1,200 and 2,400 bps. How does the answering modem know which rate to use? It starts by "offering" to communicate at 2,400 bps, asserting the appropriate carrier for a couple of seconds. The originating modem does not recognize this carrier, and so fails to respond. The answering modem then tries again at 1,200 bps. This time the carrier is music to the calling modem's ears, and it responds in kind. Likewise, when a 2,400-bps modem dials into a 1,200-bps unit, it adjusts its speed downward to match.

This speed-switching behavior is governed by doctrines included in the 212A, V.22, and V.22 *bis* standards. However, each of these standards is self-contained, without explicit reference to any other. Hence, the 212A and V.22 *bis* standards do not clarify appropriate behavior for modems such as the typical U.S. 2,400-bps unit, which accommodates both. Fortunately, the standards and the examples given above point to a sensible strategy:

- An answering modem goes through its repertoire of data rates, starting with the highest and working downward until it receives a response.

- A calling modem, encountering a speed lower than it expects, adjusts itself to suit.

The adjustment technique suggested for the calling modem cannot be employed indiscriminately, because communications software may not be prepared for it. When a modem switches speed, the associated software must be alerted to the fact, so that it may change the speed of the serial port to match. The 212A standard calls for speed switching only by an answering modem: software designed for call answering normally accommodates this, but programs for call origination may not. There will always be a few cases in which human intervention is required to establish communications, despite the fact that the two modems involved share a signaling standard.

Standards Bearers

The modem standards we've been talking about so far might be called *modulation* or *signaling standards,* since they prescribe methods for coercing digital data into analog patterns. While they serve neatly to identify modems, these standards are by no means the only conventions observed by modem manufacturers. Here are the others:

- Standards for the interface between the modem and the information-processing device it serves. For PC modems, and indeed in a majority of other cases, this means RS-232. For PC-internal modems, those built on plug-in boards, other standards must also be adhered to: IBM's PC bus standard for PC/XT/AT-class machines, and Micro Channel™ Architecture for the PS/2 breed.

- A command language for the PC's use in sending dialing commands, etc., to the modem. This entails either following *the* standard, the Hayes Standard AT Command Set, or adopting a nonstandard language. (The Hayes command set is discussed in the fourth main section of this chapter.)

- The standards or regulations governing the modem's legal connection to the telephone system of the country in which it is to be used. The FCC is responsible for promulgating and enforcing such regulations in the United States.

MORE ABOUT MODEM OPERATION

This section deals especially with modem modulation methods, and is included for more technically oriented, or just plain curious, readers. If you are inclined to skip it, by all means go ahead to the next section.

It's amazingly difficult to dig up intelligible information on how modems really work. To begin with, consider the heart of a modem, the component that does the modulation and demodulation. Most modem makers don't build this part themselves but buy it ready-made, in the form of a little chip-like package, from one of a handful of manufacturers such as Cermetek, Fairchild, RCA, or Rockwell. In fact, the vast majority of makers buy all the standard modem components (RS-232 chips, microprocessor, phone-line interface, and modulator-demodulator), write a program for the microprocessor, solder the parts together, wrap the assembly in a nice package, put their label on it, and hustle it out the door. Oh, yes, and a few of them test it somewhere along the way. This helps to explain why relatively few people in the world truly understand modem operation, and even fewer can explain it in layman's terms. The authors do not claim to be among these rare modem experts, but we do wish to point out the strenuous search involved in culling even a few secrets of modem operation.

We'll start by examining more closely the two modulation methods given scant attention earlier.

Amplitude Modulation

Amplitude modulation (AM) involves varying the strength of the carrier—the vertical distance between peaks and troughs of the sine wave. (In electrical terms, this would be a variation in voltage.) In its crudest form, AM might entail transmitting a loud whistle for binary 1 and a soft whistle for binary 0. Telephone connections, however, are equipped with amplifiers to enable people to converse without having to shout. These amplifiers are *nonlinear*, i.e., boost to different degrees signals of differing original (unamplified) strengths. Such amplification distorts the relative levels within modulated data signals. Moreover, of all modulation methods, AM is the most sensitive to the effects of noise. For these reasons, it must be used with considerable care in modems; in fact, it is almost never used alone, but is valuable in combination with phase modulation.

Phase Modulation

Phase modulation involves varying the phase angle of the carrier, or "switching among phase angles," as it usually works in practice. This method is harder to describe because it has no clear parallels in human communication. The best analogy is perhaps that of changing step while walking. If two people walk exactly in step, left-right, left-right, they are "in phase." Out of step means "out of phase." If one person's left foot lands at the same instant as the other's right, the two are 180 degrees (half a cycle) out of phase. It's possible to be out of phase by any fraction of a cycle. Getting in step with a companion (if previously out), or deliberately getting out of step, requires executing a little skip to change phase. This is basically how phase modulation works: information is encoded by instantaneously skipping some portion of a cycle. For example, the transmitter could drop back half a cycle (180-degree phase shift) to encode binary 1. Binary 0 might then be encoded as no change of phase.

Phase modulation differs in one subtle but vital way from frequency or amplitude modulation. While walking alone, you can vary your pace (FM) or stamp your feet with varying degrees of loudness (AM), but you cannot be "270 degrees out of phase." You can be in or out of phase only with respect to something else. Also, frequency and amplitude can be held constant to express a given signal, but the intrinsic phase of an analog signal is, by definition, constantly changing. Therefore, communication using phase must rely on a phase difference between two signals. Fortunately, that can be the difference between the present phase of a carrier and its phase at a previous time. Thus, when phase modulation is used to key data, it is the *relative* change of phase between one symbol and the next that encodes a data value. This is called *differential phase shift keying (DPSK)*.

A Bit More

The use of symbols representing multiple-bit sequences was presented earlier as a key factor in increasing modem speed. We now consider in greater detail why this method works.

Suppose we wish to process bits at a brisk clip, say 20,000 bps. Our first impulse would probably be to increase the number of symbols transmitted per unit of time. Unfortunately, any data link imposes inflexible limits on symbol rate. Harry Nyquist, a Bell Labs researcher in the 1920s, defined the theoretical *Nyquist limit*, which states that a transmission system with a bandwidth of B Hz can carry no more than $2B$ symbols per second. This works out to about 6,000 symbols per second (baud) for a telephone line. In practice, the upper limit is generally rather less than B, or about 2,400 baud (not bps) for a telephone connection.

This limit can be shown to be intuitively reasonable. Consider the work done by the receiving modem. No matter what method of modulation is used, demodulation involves detecting changes in the *shape* of the incoming signal. Given that the signal is bent slightly out of shape merely by its journey through the phone system, the receiver needs time for extended observation in order to confidently identify each new shape as it is received. In fact, most demodulation schemes depend on measuring the time interval between successive *zero crossings* of the waveform. As illustrated in Figure 3.7, for DPSK, the maximum interval between zero crossings is a full cycle time. Hence, with a typical carrier frequency of only a couple of thousand Hz, a modem can process only a couple of thousand symbols per second.

Since the symbol rate itself is restricted to a modest level, the secret to high-speed modem communications is to use more symbols; the greater the number of symbols, the greater is the amount of information (i.e., number of bits) that can be packed into each one. The use of 2^n symbols permits the encoding of all permutations of n bits.

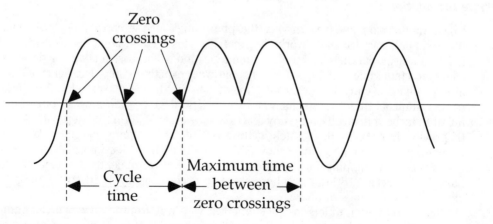

FIGURE 3.7: Zero crossings

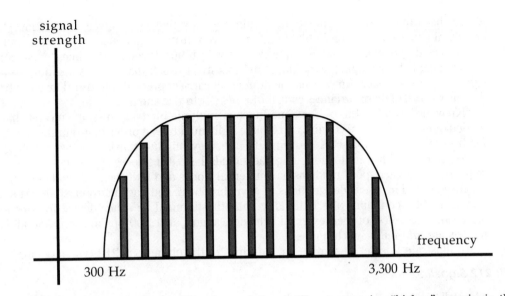

FIGURE 3.8: Multiple carriers in the voice-grade band. (The stronger, i.e., "higher," a carrier is, the more information it can encode.)

All very-high-speed modems achieve some part of their efficiency by transmitting more than one bit at a time. There are two ways to accomplish this: using a single carrier to convey multiple-bit symbols, or using several independent carriers.

The previously discussed 212A case is one example of the first method, where a single carrier is varied in four distinct ways. Specifically, with DPSK the phase can change by 0, 90, 180, or 270 degrees, each phase change representing a pair of bits, 01, 00, 10, or 11. These bit pairs are called *dibits*. Modulation schemes in use today encode not only bits and dibits, but also *tribits* and even *quadbits* — meaning, of course, packets of three and four bits, respectively. Encoding a tribit demands eight discrete symbols; a quadbit requires sixteen.

In trellis encoding, multiple carriers send several bits simultaneously. Suppose we select several carrier frequencies at well-spaced intervals across the telephone spectrum, as shown in Figure 3.8. Each carrier can be used independently to encode one or more bits at a time. This technique turns out to permit the highest modem speeds available today.

Carrying these ideas to a logical extreme, we can imagine a modem designed to encode 256 distinct symbols, each embodying an entire 8-bit byte. Such modems are said to be on engineers' drawing boards. The effect of this technology is to make parallel transmission possible on a single line.

Adding Complexity to Modems

Modems intended for higher-speed operation inevitably become more complex as they are made to accommodate increasingly sophisticated modulation techniques. This complexity manifests itself in two ways. First, a high-speed modem must adapt more closely to the transmission conditions of the link. Second, if such a modem is to encode more than one bit at a time, it must know what a bit actually is.

The transmission conditions of a dialed telephone connection, including noise level, distortion, and even usable bandwidth, not only vary considerably from one connection to another, but may also fluctuate within the duration of a given connection. Line-quality fluctuations are probably familiar to you from experience with voice calls. A sophisticated modem, trying to squeeze every last bps through the line, must continuously adapt to changing conditions by modifying such parameters as output level, signaling rate, and sometimes even the number of carriers pressed into use. The circuitry for dealing with all of these variances contributes heavily to size and price.

"Knowing" what a bit is, for simultaneous multiple-bit transmission, means that the modem must be able to recognize and isolate individual bits in order to group them together for transmission. Simple FSK modems do not; they blindly translate between digital and analog signals, oblivious to how long the signals last. Bit processing as described above requires that higher-speed modems have internal clocks and that their internal operation be synchronous. The usual designations of "synchronous" and "asynchronous" describe only how a modem communicates externally with the terminal or other device to which it is attached. Regardless of their external behavior, almost all 1,200-bps modems and all faster models are *internally* synchronous.

To illustrate this, let's examine the workings of the ubiquitous 212-type modem.

Bell 212 Signaling

The Bell 212A standard defines modem operation with both synchronous and asynchronous RS-232 interfaces, although, as already noted, most 212A modems sold for use with PCs support only asynchronous interfacing.

Between the PC and a synchronous modem, timing signals and data flow on two separate circuits in the interface. But how does a pair of synchronous modems manage to exchange the necessary timing signals, given that a single circuit must accommodate both data and timing information? Effectively, each symbol arriving at the receiving modem must differ from its immediate predecessor. For modem-to-modem use, we have two choices: either scramble the data, or use a modulation scheme that guarantees that each two successive symbols are different. Making successive symbols differ is easy with DPSK. For example, as shown in Figure 3.9, a binary 0 could be keyed by a phase shift of 120 degrees from the previous signal, and a binary 1 by a shift of 240 degrees, thus ensuring that the signal will change for every symbol even if the data value does not.

All 212A modems make use of the scrambling method. The symbol encoding the dibit 01 involves a phase change of zero degrees—equivalent to no change at all. This might seem to be at odds with the requirement that the signal change once per symbol time to enable the receiver to extract clock information. The solution is a *scrambler*, a device that subjects the transmitted data to a process of pseudo-randomization in a manner that ensures frequent symbol transitions. The receiver unscrambles the data to retrieve the original form. The scrambling algorithm developed by AT&T for 212s is most ingenious. It uses the encoded values of the bits in each character to parameterize the scrambling of the next few bytes. When even one symbol is corrupted by a transmission error, the unscrambler naturally starts churning out incorrect data. The algorithm design is such, however, that this spew of garbage persists for no more than a few characters; after that, scrambler and descrambler fall back into coordination. Scrambling has another beneficial effect: it prevents the continuous transmission of pure tones across telephone links. This is important because unscrambled signals could overload telephone-company amplifiers.

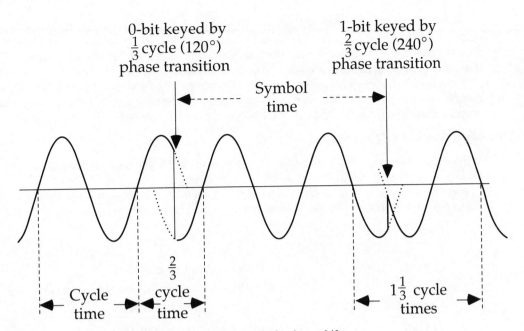

FIGURE 3.9: Keying bits by means of 120°- and 240°-phase shifts

OPTIONS WITH PC MODEMS

PC modems have four essential characteristics: they are asynchronous, full-duplex, designed for switched connections, and smart. The first three of these characteristics have already been described. Let's now consider what is meant by a smart, or intelligent, modem, and list its extra capabilities.

A *smart modem* is one whose built-in microprocessor enables it to bear up under the strain of dialing telephone, recognizing rings and busy signals, and so on. Such a modem interacts with the PC using a command-and-response language. The first smart modems came from a company called Bizcomp, but it was left to Hayes, a Bizcomp licensee, to put intelligent modems on the map.

Smartness is not limited to PC modems: many synchronous modems designed for mainframe networking also contain microprocessors. But smart synchronous modems use their intelligence not to respond to commands but to perform testing and diagnostic tasks, sometimes of a very sophisticated nature.

Auto Dial and Auto Answer

All but the cheapest PC modems feature *auto-dial* and *auto-answer* capabilities. Auto-dial modems—you guessed it—dial calls, usually with a choice of pulse (rotary dial) or Touch-Tone. Some offer what is called *adaptive dialing*: they try Touch-Tone for one digit and, if that doesn't work (the dial tone persists), fall back to pulse. An auto-answer modem can do the electronic equivalent of picking up a telephone handset to answer an incoming call. These two features allow one PC to call another in the middle of the night, when nobody is around, to exchange gossip. This is called *unattended operation*.

When the modem can dial calls, there's no need to have a telephone on the same line. For voice calls, of course, a telephone comes in handy; the PC, equipped with suitable software, can serve as an auto-dialer for it. Borland's popular Sidekick® is one of several software packages providing this feature.

Features in this category have become so commonplace that we tend to take them for granted. A few modems that lack auto-dial and auto-answer capabilities are still floating around; their users must manually dial hosts and take the line "off-hook" for incoming calls.

The Hayes Standard AT Command Set

While several command sets exist for PC modems, the Hayes set, introduced in 1981, has become the industry standard.

Here is an example of a short dialogue between a PC and a Hayes modem. Each command string sent by the PC is terminated by a carriage return.

From	Message	Comment
PC	ATZ	PC resets modem to its default state
Modem	OK	Command line executed
PC	ATDT452-9860	PC asks modem to dial the given number
Modem	CONNECT	Connection established

Modem enters its on-line mode, becoming transparent to data stream.

PC	+ + +	PC forces modem into command state
Modem	OK	Modem responds
PC	ATH	PC tells modem to hang up
Modem	OK	Modem confirms hang-up

Each command is represented by a letter and may be followed by a numeric parameter, e.g., a telephone number. A string of several commands may be sent to the modem, which will start executing them on receipt of a carriage return. Every command string must commence with AT to get the ATtention of the modem. The bit pattern representing this AT sequence, which varies according to the transmission speed and other factors, enables the modem to interpret correctly the PC's commands and, if the modem is capable of more than one transmission speed, to set the appropriate mode of operation for data transfer. In other contexts, this is called *auto-baud detection*.

The Z command causes the modem to reset itself to its *default state*, the setting or condition selected automatically, i.e., by default, if no other setting or condition is specified by the user. (When a modem is first turned on, it enters its default state.) This state effectively "defines" certain parameter settings, including the modem's responses to commands, whether it uses Touch-Tone or rotary dialing, and other matters of behavior.

The D command tells the modem to dial a call. T is a qualifier demanding Touch-Tone; P calls for pulse dialing. The modem ignores ordinary punctuation, such as hyphens and parentheses, within a phone number. Finally, H commands the modem to hang up the phone line.

The + + + string is not exactly a command; it is called an *escape sequence*. Once the modem has completed a connection, it enters *on-line mode*, and transmits all data from the PC over the phone line. If carrier is lost, or if the modem is turned off and then on again, the modem reverts to *command mode*; but some method is needed to force the modem out of on-line mode during use so that further commands can be issued without losing the connection. Also, although the escape sequence is unlikely to conflict with real data, some provision must be made to protect users who happen to transmit text that includes + + + sequences—for example, the text of this chapter. The modem provides this protection by recognizing the string as an escape only if idle periods of at least a second both precede and follow the + + +. Furthermore, modem commands are available to disable recognition of the escape sequence entirely or to modify the sequence so recognized. Modification may involve changing the operative character to something other than the plus sign or changing the length of the guard period bracketing the sequence. Further information about the escape sequence, along with a complete rundown on the Hayes command set, is given in Appendix C.

The Hayes command set, like its competitors, is designed for easy entry of keyboard commands, enabling smart modems to be used with dumb terminals. On a PC, a terminal emulator or similar program normally generates the modem commands, so the user scarcely needs to know them.

The Hayes standard is sometimes referred to as the "AT command set" because of the AT prefix on each command line. Some vendors probably prefer this designation to the name of their competitor. At least one has confusingly described its modem as "AT compatible." No matter what they call it, most modem makers now use the Hayes standard. Racal-Vadic, IBM, and a few others use their own commands, at least in some models; the mnemonics differ, but the functions are about the same. Some products offer more than one command language—usually the Hayes command set and a proprietary one.

The Electronics Industries Association (EIA), in collaboration with Hayes and other modem manufacturers, has been working on a national standard AT command set.

Stored Phone Numbers and Automatic Redial

Some modems offer such niceties as the ability to store telephone numbers and to redial a number automatically after encountering a busy signal. These may be valuable in modems to be used with dumb terminals, but for PCs they are useful only in modems equipped for synchronous operation. They are superfluous and almost certain to be wasted in async-only PC modems.

Software for asynchronous communications should be able to maintain dialing directories on PC files and perform automatic redialing at programmable intervals. These functions can invariably be handled with much greater flexibility by software than by a modem. Moreover, since no PC software directly supports such features in a modem, appropriate commands must be entered manually if a modem is to be used for such purposes.

Because modems operating in synchronous mode cannot accept commands, some tricks must be played to get them to dial connections. One option is to operate the modem asynchronously while placing a call and switch to synchronous operation once a connection is established. A second option, applicable to terminals capable of synchronous operation only, is to store a number in the modem, to be called automatically on an appropriate signal from the terminal.

Call Progress Monitoring

Telephone callers often yank the receiver off the hook and immediately start pounding buttons or tearing away at the dial, assuming the dial tone is present. The dial tone is one of those things we have come to expect will always be there, like water in the tap. It should not be taken for granted. When too many subscribers try to place calls at the same instant, an exchange can become overloaded, and a dial tone may not sound for several seconds after the receiver is picked up. During a power blackout in New York City a decade ago, telephones kept operating, thanks to their independent power source, but so many people began calling each other that the telephone system became fascinatingly lethargic.

A call made properly, after a dial tone is heard, is usually followed by a more or less brief pause, perhaps mottled with a few clicks; a series of rings; and then a voice, often shrouded by the raspy ambiance signifying an answering machine in action. If that's the case, you then hear the beep urging you to leave a message, and finally the hollow click that means you've been cut off in midsentence.

Now imagine a PC modem of vintage 1985 coping with a call, say, to a bulletin board system. The modem electronically goes off-hook and waits a second or two to be reasonably sure that a dial tone is present. It dials the number, and waits perhaps 30 seconds for a compatible modem to answer. As indicated in the previous chapter, the *only* tone the modem can recognize is the carrier of its kin. This limited procedure is surprisingly satisfactory in practice, and many smart modems work in this fashion. In most cases, the modem's inability to differentiate signals easily recognized by a human caller is compensated for by a built-in speaker, which facilitates *audible call-progress monitoring*. This enables the user to hear the sequence of tones on the line and to intervene when the modem reaches a wrong number or other impasse (possibly by diving for the phone and apologizing to the irate recipient of the call).

Audible call-progress monitoring can be very comforting for the user. Most modems support it, although there are exceptions, especially among the pared-down units designed for travelers. While it's useful to monitor the progress of a call up to the point of connection, listening to the furious racket of two conversing modems is not an appealing prospect. Convention dictates that the modem automatically mute the speaker shortly after carrier is detected, but Hayes' and many other modems offer a command to change speaker operation from this default setting. The alternate options are to leave the speaker either on or off at all times. The M2 command on Hayes-compatible models allows constant eavesdropping; try it at least once just to hear what goes on.

Fancier modems now include what is called simply *call progress monitoring*, meaning that they recognize the relevant tones all by themselves, rather than depending on the user's trained ear. On encountering a busy signal, such a modem knows enough to hang up and to send a code to the PC to tell the software what has happened. These modems also detect dial tones and rings, and some can even recognize a human voice. However, this feature monitoring does not altogether negate the value of a speaker, which is usually provided as well.

A modem's ability to detect a dial tone is important not so much for making an ordinary call, but for handling calls placed through PBXs and alternate long distance carriers. On these systems, it is often necessary to dial one number, wait for a secondary dial tone, and then dial another number. Less well-endowed modems can deal with such cases by means of pauses inserted into dialing strings. A familiar Hayes command string takes the form ATDP9,T5556789. The comma indicates a pause between the pulse-dialed 9, used to get an outside line from an older PBX or Centrex system, and the Touch-Tone dialing sequence sent to the telephone company exchange.

Modems with the comparatively rare feature called *visual call progress monitoring* have a small liquid crystal display (LCD) strip on the front panel that displays short text messages such as "RING" and "BUSY."

Call Waiting

On a line with call waiting installed, an active call may be interrupted by a beep lasting about half a second that announces another incoming call. The user can then switch back and forth between the two calls, keeping one party on hold while chatting with the other. As noted in Chapter 2, this feature can be a nuisance on a telephone line used for data calls.

The intrusion of another call is unlikely to be welcome during an active data call. For one thing, no modem recognizes the call-waiting signal. For another, if there's one thing a modem will not tolerate, it's being put on Hold. Some modems can be switched between "data" and "voice," but this is not much help, since both modems involved in the call would have to be placed in voice mode, which requires coordination by the users. For a third thing, the call-waiting beep may trample a few bytes of data or even cause the modem to disconnect.

For outgoing calls at least, these drawbacks may be a matter of no concern. Most telephone subscribers can take advantage of a feature called *selective call waiting* or *cancel call waiting*, which can defeat the call-waiting system for the duration of one outgoing call. The defeat is usually selected by dialing 1170 on a pulse-dial line or *70 on a Touch-Tone line before dialing the call itself. These combinations can easily be added to any modem dialing sequence. With a modem that understands the Hayes command set, a sequence of the form ATDT*70,555-1212 will do the job; the comma inserts a necessary pause. (Modems equipped for Touch-Tone can handle * and #.)

Call waiting, once defeated, is automatically reinstated when you hang up. However, without another service, called *three-way calling*, call waiting in most service areas can be defeated only for outgoing calls, not at all for incoming calls. Three-way calling allows the subscriber to add a third party to an existing conversation. That is, while one call between two parties is in progress, another number may be dialed, ordinarily to set up a conference call. However, the "other number" may just as well be the cancel-call-waiting code, which will have the desired effect regardless of whether the active call was incoming or originated by the subscriber. Unfortunately, the use of three-way calling to cancel call waiting on an incoming call may itself sufficiently disturb the modem that it will disconnect. It seems best to forgo call waiting on a line that must handle many incoming data calls.

Buffered Modems

A few PC modems offer a special feature: RAM chips that can store incoming data when the PC is unable to accept them. These *buffered modems* are particularly useful for receiving electronic mail, which can be stored while the PC is busy with other things, or even when it's turned off.

Several vendors sell add-on memories for their own modems.   The Prometheus ProModem™ line, for example, has optional, user-installable buffer cards with various quantities of memory. Also, outboard buffer boxes, such as Hayes' Transet™, should work with virtually any modem.

Programmable Modems

A highly sophisticated product, the *programmable modem*, amounts to a modem, communications package, clock, printer port, and some RAM (up to 1 Mbyte at least, often with battery back-up ensuring data survival if power is interrupted), all in one box no larger than that of a regular modem. Primarily used to deliver and receive messages and files without the aid of a computer, these devices are also known as *stand-alone modems*.

The user of these modems may, for example, program one to dial an electronic mail service at regular intervals to check for messages. When messages are found, the modem can download them, signal their presence by flashing a panel light or beeping, and, optionally, send them to a printer. The modem stores any downloaded material in its memory, which functions much like a RAM disk. Stand-alone modems can also handle protocol file transfers late at night, receive telex and TWX messages, and generally send or retrieve data without tying up a PC—an especially valuable capability when the called telephone number is chronically busy. Since such modems tend to be Hayes-compatible, they can function like any other PC modem when their special talents are not needed. Visionary Electronics of San Francisco has long sold a distinguished line of programmable modems.

INTERNAL, EXTERNAL AND ACOUSTIC MODEMS

We can divide PC modems into two types: *external* and *internal*. An external modem has its own cabinet and attaches to the PC with an RS-232 cable. An internal modem is built onto a board to be installed inside the PC's system unit. Many vendors offer both varieties. For example, Hayes' external Smartmodem 1200™ and internal Smartmodem 1200B™, suggested by Figures 3.10a and 3.10b, are functionally very similar.

It may sometimes be hard to choose between an internal and an external modem. Considering their comparative advantages may help.

Advantages of an External Modem

Mobility. It is easily shared among several computers simply by disconnecting the RS-232 cable from one machine and connecting it to another. Moreover, since it is compatible with any device equipped with an RS-232 interface, it can be

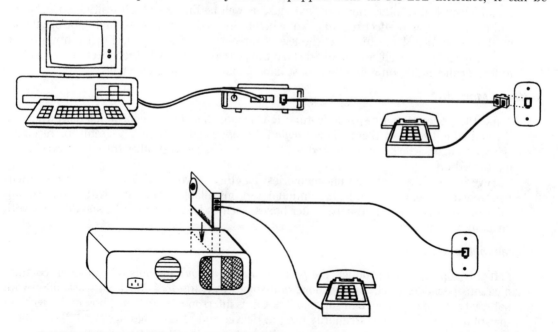

FIGURE 3.10a and b: Modem types and attachments

shared even by dissimilar machines including, presumably, many not yet built. An internal modem, on the other hand, is restricted to the type of computer for which it was designed; because it takes the form of a plug-in board, an internal unit made for the PC bus will not fit a PS/2 with the Micro Channel Architecture bus, and vice versa.

Slot Space; Power Source. It does not occupy a slot or consume PC power. Its self-sufficiency may be important because true IBM PCs and, to a lesser extent, XTs have notoriously inadequate power supplies; once you begin adding boards, you can easily run out of juice before running out of slots. (Internal modems built years ago were among the heaviest consumers of power. Modern units, fortunately, have very light electrical appetites.) A good rule of thumb is that a true PC can safely manage two high-power boards—for example, a hard disk card and a multifunction card, or a multifunction card and an accelerator board—in addition to the standard complement, but it would be on shaky ground with three. To be on the safe side, consider upgrading the power supply.

Status Display. External modems often have a set of light emitting diodes (LEDs) to indicate status. When a problem arises, the user can dig out the manual, learn what the lights signify, and use them for diagnosis.

Serviceability. It affords ready access to components for maintenance or repair.

Reset. Since it has its own on/off switch, an external modem can be reset simply by flicking it off and then back on.

Advantages of an Internal Modem

Port. It has a built-in COM port, so it does not tie up another in the PC. The built-in port, available only to the modem, can usually be configured as COM1, COM2, COM3, or COM4.

Cost. It is somewhat less expensive than the external modem, since it requires no cabinet or power supply.

Convenience. It is a good choice for AC-powered portable PCs. There's no extra box to be lugged around.

Physical security. It's less likely to be stolen than an external modem, which is easily detached and concealed. A thief would sooner take your whole machine than dig inside for a modem board.

Foolproofing. Internal modems are better for naive users. They may lose a month's work because they forgot to back up their files, or shove diskettes in the drive upside-down and wonder why all the files are backwards, but at least they don't have to worry about forgetting to switch on an internal modem.

Neatness. It requires no additional power cord or RS-232 cable, so it doesn't add to the usual behind-desk tangle.

The question sometimes arises: Should external modems be left turned on all the time? An even more important question is whether PCs should be kept constantly on. Many IBMers answer yes for PCs. The shock of switching transients is much more stressful to electronic circuits than is continuous use. The same is true of fixed disks. Firing up a disk until it is spinning at operating speed stresses both the motor and the disk; keeping it rotating involves negligible wear and tear. We recommend keeping PCs on all the time unless you are plagued with power line problems or uncertain ventilation. There is no consensus about switching external modems on and off, but modems tend to have congested circuits built into cramped, fanless housings, which suggests that they may overheat. A small survey of the authors and several colleagues indicates that this concern is valid. Those who leave external modems constantly on have sustained some serious losses, while those who turn them off while not in use have suffered no catastrophic failure. Of course, it's not practical to shut down modems that spend their working lives in answer mode serving bulletin boards and the like; the best advice is to keep them cool. At least one external modem is designed to turn on a PC, or other device to which it is connected, when it answers a phone call. This idea may have some merit, but a modem that is itself activated by the arrival of a call would be even better.

Acoustic Modems

A modem can be hooked up to a telephone line in two ways. Most modems, including all internal units, are directly wired to the line via a standard telephone jack (usually an RJ11C). An option for external modems is *acoustic coupling*, which involves cramming a standard telephone handset into a sort of padded cell. The mouthpiece sits next to a little speaker in the coupling, while the earpiece abuts a little microphone, as shown in Figure 3.10c. This method was used in many asynchronous modems ten or fifteen years ago, but fell out of fashion in the late seventies. With the proliferation of laptop PCs, acoustic modems are now making a minor comeback but will probably become obsolete again, as RJ 11C jacks are beginning to appear on airport pay telephones and in hotel rooms (see below). Acoustic coupling is crude and inevitably leads to low transmission reliability, so it should be used only where its convenience outweighs all other considerations. Vendors include Novation and Touchbase Design.

Hooking up an External Modem

An external modem, acoustic or otherwise, must be plugged into a COM port on the PC with a modem cable. Not all cables made to plug into serial ports are the same. A printer cable must not be used to connect a modem to the PC; it is configured differently and will not work.

What if all serial ports are already occupied? You can always buy another one, as outlined in Chapter 4. A serial port may also be shared, for example, by unplugging a printer when you wish to use the modem; not being able to print while communicating

FIGURE 3.10c: Modem types and attachments

probably won't be a great hardship. A serial switch box (discussed further in Chapter 5) makes sharing easier, achieving the same effect as unplugging one cable and plugging in another with the flick of a switch or click of a knob.

Modems for Laptops

Many laptop PCs are available with internal 1,200- or 300-bps modems as optional extras. To compete with these internal units, a new kind of miniaturized, low-speed external modem has appeared, weighing just a few ounces and small enough to fit in a pocket. They are designed to plug directly into a 25-pin serial port connector without an intervening cable, are fully self-contained, and are normally powered by a replaceable battery. Travelers with battery-operated laptops may prefer a pocket modem to an internal unit because the minimodem will not drain the computer's power reserves. Some models have optional acoustic coupling.

While intended primarily for owners of laptop PCs, and therefore restricted in features, pocket modems can be used with any type of personal computer. Although laptops have nine-pin serial ports, pocket modems are made with DB25 rather than DE9 connectors. A DE9 would permit direct connection to the computer but is not sturdy enough to support even the light weight of the modem. All mini-modem manufacturers supply 9-pin-to-25-pin conversion cables.

Can a laptop with pocket modem be connected to a cordless phone? Since cordless handsets generally lack modular jacks, an acoustic coupler will probably be needed. As long as the user stays still, and assuming that the handset does not have some unusual, coupler-defying shape, this might work. However, if the handset is moved around, the signal is likely to be momentarily weakened or distorted and the connection may be lost.

Rack-mount and Handset Modems

Hosts that use modems to support many dial-in lines generally use *rack-mountable* units. Each modem is built on a card that fits into a "cage" which, in turn, can be mounted in a standard 19"-wide equipment rack. One cage might house a couple of dozen modems. Rack-mounted modems are compactly housed and easily accessible for testing and replacement. In addition, overheating tends not to be a problem with rack-mounting, a big advantage because rack-mounted modems usually serve applications demanding continuous operation. Several PC modem manufacturers produce rack-mountable models, which should be considered for a PC being set up as a multiline bulletin board, or for other purposes requiring multiple modems.

Handset modems are an odd breed. They resemble ordinary external modems except that, instead of plugging directly into a line, they are connected between the telephone base and handset. This arrangement makes modem use on multiline telephones very easy, but it is pointless for single-line phones. Not surprisingly, handset modems are restricted to originating calls.

Using Modems in Hotel Rooms

Hooking modems into hotel phone systems can be frustrating. An almost insuperable problem is the relatively low connection quality provided by some hotels' PBXs. Further, the quality of phone lines varies widely from one part of the United States to another. The authors have encountered particularly bad connections in Texas, which a Houston hotelier jokingly blamed on seepage of crude oil into underground lines.

Many hotels have telephone systems built with the normal RJ11C jacks, making it easy to unplug the phone and connect the modem of a portable PC. An even better idea is to carry a *modular duplex jack*, sometimes called a *splitter*, which turns one RJ11C socket into two and allows the phone and modem to be plugged in simultaneously. (Radio Shack® has splitters, as well as the other gadgets mentioned below.) The only problem is that the wall jack is invariably located behind the bed or other piece of furniture thoughtfully bolted in place.

What do you do in a hotel with a nonmodular phone system? One end of the phone wire disappears into the instrument, the other into the wall. This problem persists even though some hotels catering to business people have begun providing telephones with extra jacks for the use of modem toters. In the absence of jacks, the trick is to buy a pair of leads with alligator clips on each end, and a "modular-to-spade line cord," which has an RJ11C plug on one end and four spade terminals on the other. Unscrew the base of the phone and identify the terminals of the incoming wires, usually located on a raised platform on the right-hand side as viewed from the front. (To be sure of having a screwdriver with which to open the phone, don't leave home without a multipurpose Swiss Army knife.) Plug the RJ11C jack into the modem and use the alligator leads to connect the red and green spade lugs on the adapter line cord to the red and green phone wires, respectively, being careful to avoid shorting them together. Beware of the black and yellow wires; they usually activate the light that flashes when the hotel has a message for you.

Disassembling a telephone requires removing the handset from its cradle, leaving the phone "off-hook." Before using the modem, hang up the phone by placing the handset on the hinged metal rack normally hidden by the plastic cradle.

A cautionary note: some travelers are rather cavalier about ripping telephone systems apart, knowing that their gear is FCC-approved and cannot damage the hotel's equipment. It is, in fact, far more likely that the phone system will damage the modem. Yet no matter how carefully the job is done, or how promptly the phone is restored to normal, in some places it is against the law to connect a foreign device directly to a private telephone system without first obtaining permission from its owner. We do not recommend breaking the law; ask for permission or carry an acoustic coupler.

A last suggestion is to dial long-distance data calls manually in case an operator comes on the line to ask for your room number. Perhaps someone will soon market a modem with a voice simulator to handle this chore.

SPECIAL PC MODEMS

Standards for 9,600-bps Modem Operation

There are two standards for 9,600-bps modem operation, both from the CCITT. *V.29* defines a half-duplex mode of operation used by Group III fax machines (see Chapter 11). *V.32* defines a full-duplex scheme with noise immunity slightly superior to that of V.29. Neither standard is ideal for PC modems. V.29 is appealing because it promises compatibility with the large installed base of Group III fax machines, but is limited in being half-duplex. V.32 would do a fine job but, for reasons set forth below, involves technology that is too costly for most PC users.

V.32 applies strictly to modems offering full-duplex operation at 9,600 bps. To achieve this high rate within the confines of telephone-line bandwidth, it calls for transmitting and receiving modems to signal using the same frequencies at the same time. This may seem impossible—like putting two-way traffic on a one-lane street—but it is merely very difficult. The difficulty arises from echoes and the need to remove from the received signal any echoed remnant of the transmitted signal. The required technology, called *echo-cancellation*, is not well developed, and modems that must employ it are necessarily expensive. For this reason, several manufacturers of high-speed PC modems have adopted compromise solutions, some of which are discussed below.

High-speed Modems

While modems operating at 1,200 and 2,400 bps still constitute the mainstream of the PC modem market, an increasing number of 4,800-bps, 9,600-bps, and even faster units have appeared in recent years. This high end of the market is changing so rapidly that we must direct you to computer magazines if you wish to keep abreast of new offerings. Here, we will simply summarize what to expect from high-speed modems and mention some areas of possible difficulty.

Standards

Many products sold in North America follow the CCITT's 9,600-bps standards only partially, if at all. As a result, there is little compatibility among different manufacturers' designs. The would-be user must clearly understand how such units will be employed. In many cases, these modems will be purchased in pairs or groups for closed communities of users.

Compatibility

All high-speed PC modems also operate at the lower speeds of 1,200 and 2,400 bps. Thus, although high-speed modems may not always be mutually compatible at their high speeds, they are totally compatible with all PC modems at the lower speeds.

Real-world Performance

Don't expect high-speed modems to perform consistently at their rated speed. Their specifications, not surprisingly, reflect operation under optimum conditions. In practice, performance is typically 20 to 30 percent less than spec—still a vast improvement over even 2,400-bps operation.

Fall-back

Because the quality of telephone connections varies so much, and because these modems operate close to the limit in squeezing the last few bps out of a line, it is important that they incorporate a *fall-back* mechanism. Fall-back, in this context, means adjusting operating speed to fit the ceiling imposed by the telephone connection. One measure of modem quality is the size of its fall-back decrement, smaller being better. On detecting a transmission impairment, some modems scale back the data rate by a few hundred bps at a time, while others immediately cut the speed by 50 percent. The first modems offer better performance, but the second group should be less expensive.

Error Control

Users of 1,200-bps modems may rarely witness communication errors, but errors become more frequent with increasing speeds, and an efficient means of correcting them becomes essential. Such error control is usually built into the high-speed modem itself instead of being effected, say, by PC software, and operates automatically when the modem establishes a connection with another, similarly equipped modem. We will examine techniques of recovery from transmission errors on communications lines later, in Chapter 7.

Mode of Operation

As we pointed out in the first section of this chapter, some high-speed modems do not operate in true full-duplex mode. Such modems are most often used for applications involving bulk data transfer, with nearly all traffic flowing in a single direction. Rather than wasting half the bandwidth of the telephone line on an unused channel, many of these modems transmit in half-duplex, while appearing to be full-duplex by virtue of their super-short turnaround times.

This duplicity gives rise to two observations. First, a 9,600-bps modem operating in the above manner is inherently only about twice as fast as a traditional 2,400-bps PC modem. Second, it would be nice if 1,200- and 2,400-bps modems could work in this fashion, but they can't.

Compression

Many of the fastest modems rely largely on techniques of data compression, to be studied in Chapter 9. As we shall see, the degree to which data can be compressed is a function of the nature of the data; the effectiveness of compression, and hence transmission speed, varies with content. Statistically random data, that is, without any predictable internal patterns, cannot be compressed at all.

Application

The efficiency of a high-speed modem varies considerably according to the patterns of data traffic. A unit shows to best advantage when performing tasks, such as file transfers, that pump data continuously across the connection. This, after all, is the kind of job for which these modems are designed.

Many host computers provide *input echoing* for attached terminals. This facility, to be dealt with fully in Chapter 6, causes every character transmitted to the host from the terminal to be echoed back so that it appears on the terminal's screen. Even with short turnaround times, half-duplex high-speed modems may be too slow for this echoing which, if it is to be comfortable for the user, should take no more than a fifth of a second. On the other hand, since most people cannot read at 9,600 bps (about 5,000 words per minute), running interactive terminal sessions at this speed may be overkill anyway. For either or both of these reasons, a user may well want to reserve top speed for file transfer and scale down to a more comfortable 2,400 bps for terminal use.

Design Compromises

Significantly, the specifications for the Hayes V-series 9600 modem mention the CCITT V.32 standard but do not claim compliance with it. This manufacturer made a sensible compromise in adopting the proven V.32 signaling method but using it in a restricted manner that is both affordable and sufficient for most PC applications. Essentially, Hayes implements the V.32 standard in a fast-turnaround half-duplex modem, obviating the costly echo cancelers needed for full-duplex operation.

Hayes does provide full-duplex V.32 modems for applications that need it (and users who can justify the cost), such as bridging remote LANs.

Security Modems

Security modems are designed with special features for access control. They are used primarily in an answering role for hosts with high security constraints, but a few models also have security features relevant to call origination. Security of data transmitted between modems is addressed by an entirely different class of products.

A security modem tends to be just like a standard PC modem with some extra intelligence or hardware. Several techniques are used to build security into modems, and a given product may employ one or more of them. The most common are:

Call-back. The modem maintains a list of valid users in memory. A user dialing in identifies herself by means of a standard username-and-password scheme. The modem then hangs up and calls the user back at the telephone number stored in the user profile. Nominally, this means that users can call in only from fixed locations; call-forwarding services can "fool" the system but not substantially compromise security. If a user needs to call in from several locations, a separate username can be provided for each one. To foil interception by sophisticated security-breakers, some models accept calls on one line and call back on another.

Passwords. A modem can incorporate its own username-and-password scheme. This option holds greatest promise for environments in which software-based security is weak or nonexistent. While such password protection is most important for incoming calls, some modems can also be set up to require a password for placing an outgoing call, which provides control not over an organization's top-secret computer files, but over its telephone bill. Some modems are so constituted that, if a caller enters a valid username but repeatedly gives incorrect passwords, the modem erases the true password from its table.

Secret keys. A modem can be designed so that it answers an incoming call but does not return carrier, i.e., start whistling, until it receives a particular character from the user. To a mischievous person dialing in, it would not be clear that a modem was even reached.

Lock and key. A modem may require a physical key to turn its power on.

Audit Trail. A modem can generate messages logging both valid and invalid access attempts.

Now let's look at a couple of products:

The Cermetek Security Modem offers four levels of access security: none; password validation only; password validation followed by callback on the same line; and password validation followed by callback on a separate line. In addition, it has a physical lock and key, and it outputs an audit trail. Codes can be stored for 25 users. It is compatible with the Hayes Smartmodem 1200.

Microframe's DATA LOCK & KEY™, for use in conjunction with existing modems, consists of two boxes: the DATA KEY, placed at the PC or terminal, and the DATA LOCK, placed at the host. Each box is inserted into the RS-232 connection between a device and its modem. The LOCK constantly monitors up to four phone lines, electronically isolating each from the host until the LOCK has communicated with a remote KEY. Each LOCK and KEY set is mated at the factory, and each box also has a physical lock and key for added safety. The LOCK can be programmed through a keypad to refuse communication with any lost KEY; moreover, if the LOCK hears from a KEY it "knows" to have been stolen, it sends that KEY an order to self-destruct.

A substantial school of thought maintains that security defenses should be implemented in software, not hardware. Anyone determined enough to break into a system may also be clever enough to circumvent any barriers erected in hardware alone. After all, hardware always behaves the same way; a cracker can learn the patterns of any particular device, or figure out which of the relatively few available products is being used, and find a loophole. Writing your own software allows you to take advantage of knowledge about each user and to exploit the element of randomness. You can even change the system every month or so. Enjoyable reading on this subject is *Out of the Inner Circle: A Hacker's Guide to Computer Security* by Bill "The Cracker" Landreth (Microsoft Press, 1985).

Other Kinds of Modems

In addition to PC modems, which are asynchronous units for general use with any kind of personal computer, there are other modem types for various speeds, applications, and environments. Here we list them and briefly describe their uses; many receive further treatment elsewhere in the book. All are relevant to our main concern, since representatives of each category might be attached to PCs for special applications.

Leased Line Modems

Leased telephone lines are capable of supporting high speeds, typically 50 to 100 percent greater than switched lines. Modems made to operate on leased lines are often faster variants of switched models.

Short Haul or Limited Distance Modems

Short haul modems are designed for use on customer-owned lines over distances up to about 25 miles. Strictly speaking, many are not modems at all, for they do not generate analog signals. They should be called "line drivers," but are called modems because their function is so similar. (Line drivers are discussed in Chapter 5.)

Data-and-Voice Modems

Data-and-voice modems, variously called "voice-over-data," "data-under-voice," or "simultaneous voice/data" modems, provide separate channels to allow both types of communication simultaneously. For example, such modems permit two people at different locations to transfer data and talk about the data at the same time without a second phone line. Their potential is even better illustrated by the connection of two PCs via a *remote package* (discussed in Chapter 10), which creates the illusion that a program running in one PC is also running in the other. Imagine two widely separated users discussing a spreadsheet; with a remote package, the display appears on both screens and can be altered by either user.

Simultaneous voice/data modems made for dial-up use have the serious but inevitable drawback of being incompatible with any other modems. To fit both data and voice channels onto a single voice-grade line, designers must resort to nonstandard modulation methods. Therefore, such products must be bought in pairs or larger quantities for closed communities of users. Another snag is that these modems must operate in half-duplex to provide even a data rate of 1,200 bps. This implies that software for them must be able to manipulate the modem control signals necessary to conduct a half-duplex dialogue; much PC software lacks this ability. Full-duplex operation is available at lower speeds, such as 300 bps.

These drawbacks of data-and-voice modems are of little concern to leased-line users. In that context, nonstandard modulation poses no problem, full-duplex operation is possible even at high data rates, and, most important, a great deal of money is saved by using one line instead of two. A friend of ours, who has such a setup between her home and her office, can take advantage of a relatively low-cost leased circuit because both locations are in the same telephone service area. The line accommodates a full-duplex 19.2-kbps data link along with a standard voice connection. When she's home, her secretary can forward calls to her without callers knowing that the transfer is taking place; she can also tie her home PC into her office network.

Coherent Communications Systems, a leading manufacturer of these modems, also makes data-and-voice multiplexers for leased lines.

Protocol Modems

Protocol modems, also called "error-correcting modems," have built-in drivers for some protocol. They are valuable in settings calling for an error-free connection to a device, such as a dumb terminal, that cannot itself drive a protocol.

Radio Modems

A few manufacturers offer modems that operate with radio waves rather than phone lines. Radio modems are made for short-distance communication, either within a building or over a line-of-sight link. They are of great value for mobile use. They also make data communications feasible in certain locations where telephone circuits are inadequate and cable installation would be very costly, as is the case in some old buildings. The speed of radio modems is usually between 1,200 and 2,400 bps. Vendors include DataRadio and Electronic Systems Technology.

Radio modems are also made for use with cellular (radio-based) telephone systems. Spectrum Cellular makes one called "The Bridge." Mobile data communication requires a special kind of modem that can recover from the "dropouts" occurring during hand-offs from cell to cell. The Bridge includes software for a special protocol and is made in 300- and 1,200-bps versions.

Multiport Modems

A *multiport modem* is one that incorporates a multiplexer. A pair of such modems divides the connection's data-carrying capacity among two or more sessions. They are used primarily on leased lines, typically for such purposes as connecting several branch-office terminals (say, three or four) to ports on a mainframe.

CRITERIA FOR SELECTING PC MODEMS

Here are some factors to consider before rushing to buy a general-purpose PC modem.

Quality and Price

Overall modem quality is a function of the components that go into it, engineering design, and quality control during manufacture. Quality deficiencies are most readily apparent on noisy telephone lines and certain long-distance connections, especially those of some alternative carriers. On long-distance links, noise may or may not be an issue, but other impairments, such as echoes and "phase jitter," will almost certainly be worse than on local calls.

If you are at all concerned about quality, a simple rule of thumb is to stay away from any modem that seems too cheap; a deal that appears too good to be true probably is. On the other hand, inexpensive off-brand models may be worthwhile bargains when your budget is tight and the application can tolerate an occasional error. If only local telephone lines are used, and the line quality in your area is reasonably good, such a model may well suffice.

Choosing a Hayes modem guarantees good performance, but any reputable brand, such as Okidata, Touchbase, or US Robotics, should serve well. Modems made by established manufacturers tend to be well engineered, to offer some of the most commonly desired features, and, most significantly, to be backed by both good technical support and a warranty that is actually enforceable.

While design and manufacturing quality are more important than most people recognize, it must be admitted that assessing quality can be difficult. And there's always a tradeoff among the Big Three: quality, features, and price.

In its December 1987 issue, *PC World* magazine reviewed eight "cheap" 1,200-bps external modems. The evaluations revealed remarkable differences and exposed significant flaws in every one, mainly in four areas: Hayes compatibility; overheating; ability to deal with transmission impairments; and quality control. The best in the group could be deemed reasonable purchases for budget-conscious users with undemanding applications, but one of the article's general conclusions was that, for serious business use, it's sensible to choose higher-priced, name-brand products.

Another tip is to look for units with such labels as AT&T, Codex®, Microcom®, Racal-Vadic, and UDS®, whose manufacturers furnish modems to other markets, especially for use with mainframes, where there is more insistence on high quality.

Internal and External Models

Do you want an internal or an external modem? Review the relative advantages listed earlier in the chapter. If this is not decisive, an external unit, by virtue of its greater flexibility, is likely to be a better choice.

When selecting an internal modem, pay attention to speed compatibility between the unit and your PC's bus. A PC's *bus speed*, quoted in megahertz, is not necessarily the same as its processor speed. As is true of any add-in board, the bus-interface circuitry on the modem card must be able to keep pace with the bus activity. Any internal modem can probably handle up to 8 MHz, but some may not be suitable for higher bus speeds.

Configuration and Features

What features do you need? Auto-answer and auto-dial have become almost universal, but a few bargain modems still lack these capabilities. Other fairly standard and useful features are self-test capability, an on-board speaker, call-progress monitoring, and, in the case of an external modem, status lights. More unusual features include multiline hook-up and good documentation (see below).

What loopback and diagnostic capabilities does the modem have? That is, how much can the modem help when—not if—things go wrong? For detailed information on this topic, see "Communications Troubleshooting" in Chapter 16.

Hayes Compatibility

Hayes compatibility involves two questions: Is the modem specified as "Hayes compatible"? If so, to what degree does the modem actually conform to the standard?

A Hayes-compatible modem provides access to vastly more software than would otherwise be available. Since Hayes and compatibles make up something like 90 percent of the PC modem market in North America, many software developers don't bother with anything else. Some software packages are designed to use the Hayes language but can be adapted by the user for non-Hayes commands. Then, of course, a very few programs are written specifically for non-Hayes models. Consider a non-Hayes-compatible modem only if you have some compelling reason to do so, and if you have a good idea of what software you'll be using with it.

The claim that a modem is Hayes-compatible may mean only that the unit is, say, 75 percent compatible with a Hayes Smartmodem of 1983 vintage. Although this is more likely to be an issue with a 1,200-bps modem than with a faster one, such semicompatibility at any rate leaves the modem far behind contemporary Hayes models, and it will be hobbled in two ways. First, it will not respond appropriately to certain newer AT commands, and may therefore prove incompatible with PC software expecting compliance with them. Second, the modem may lack important features associated with these commands. An example of such features is the W dialing-string modifier that tells the modem to wait for a second dial tone, a great convenience for modems dialing through PBXs and alternate long-distance services. True, almost any modem can handle pauses in a dialing string, indicated in the Hayes language by a comma, and these may suffice to make the modem wait for a second dial tone, but the W feature serves the purpose much more reliably.

While low-percentage compatibility with a Hayes antique is troublesome, it must be admitted that 100 percent imitation of Hayes' latest model far exceeds what is generally required of a modem. Most Hayes-oriented software is relatively undemanding and will work fine as long as the most important elements are in place.

Hayes compatibility implies more than just use of the Hayes command language. The unit should also have many of the same internal registers as the Hayes Smartmodems.

Other Compatibility Issues

Other compatibility-related questions may arise. Consider, for example, compatibility with your PBX, if you have one, with your telephone jacks, and, of course, with the modems of other systems you expect to contact.

Speed

If a particular speed is not dictated by the requirements of systems with which you're communicating, what speed should you choose? Probably nobody today would bother with a 300-bps modem. Although an enormous number of 1,200-bps models are in use, there is little reason now to buy a modem in this class. All 2,400-bps PC modems can communicate with the 1,200-bps type; the difference in price is minimal; more and more 2,400-bps services are available; and, as mentioned earlier, modems built for 2,400-bps tend to outperform 1,200-bps models at the lower speed.

The tough choice for many users, then, is between 2,400 and 9,600 bps. Most 9,600-bps modems can operate at 2,400 and 1,200 bps, so buying a 9,600-bps unit does not mean sacrificing the ability to talk to the slower types. But with whom can you communicate at 9,600 bps, bearing in mind that not all modems operate compatibly at that speed? It could well be argued that 2,400, or even 1,200, bps is fast enough for typical interactive applications. For transaction processing and file transfer, a higher speed will always be better, as long as connections are good. Even a fair number of long-distance connections may prove too poor for 2,400-bps performance.

On the whole, if you have an existing 1,200-bps modem, don't feel compelled to replace it with a faster unit unless you actually need or want the additional performance; your old modem will not become obsolete for many years. On the other hand, such a desire is understandable and, given recent advances in technology, not terribly expensive or difficult to fulfill. If you're establishing or renewing a system that calls for one or more modems, you'll probably want to stick to 2,400- or 9,600-bps units. At this writing, 9,600 bps is likely to make the most sense if you know you will actually be able to use this speed in the foreseeable future.

Freebies

Can you get some free software with the unit you buy? Plenty of modems, especially internal models for PCs, are sold with free communications packages. In some cases, these freebies rank among the best software products available. On the other hand, many "thrown-in" programs deserve to be thrown out. If you are given software of questionable quality, we suggest that you test it by loading it into your trash compactor.

Documentation

On balance, modem manuals are notoriously bad. Some are incomprehensible, and a few are so poorly printed as to be barely readable, even when the modem itself performs well. You may refer to the manual only occasionally, but when those occasions arise, typically when introducing a new piece of software or hardware, it's important that you be able to determine just what the modem can and cannot do. A data-communications crisis is no time to be confronted with an illegible, incomplete, or sloppily written manual.

Modem documentation should list the following fully and precisely, with diagrams where appropriate:

- Commands recognized and responses returned
- The meanings of all settings of all switches
- Cabling options and the expected behavior of RS-232 control circuits
- Diagnostic capabilities

Hayes has set a very high standard in documentation, and several other makers have striven to provide equally good manuals. But with so many manufacturers cutting corners in this area, the documentation for any prospective modem purchase deserves close scrutiny.

Modems as Toasters

Some modems in the *PC World* review cited above reached startling temperatures when left on for long periods. This is almost always more worrisome than actually dangerous, but dangerous all the same. Plenty of users have lost even name-brand modems, and occasionally other property carelessly left nearby, to modem overheating. When a metal-cased modem heats up, it's a matter for concern; when a plastic-cased unit reaches egg-frying temperatures, you're justified in wondering how soon it will melt. Try to get information about thermal characteristics from present owners of the modem you plan to buy. And, as suggested earlier, keep modems shut down, if you can, while not in use.

4 PC COMMUNICATIONS HARDWARE

In this chapter we figuratively take the lid off PC communications, and look more closely at the PC components summarized in Chapter 1.

We'll start by studying RS-232 with respect to the formal expression of the standard, and to its original purpose: that of connecting modems to terminals, computers, and like devices. As you may know, the PC's use of RS-232 has strayed from the standard, but it still incorporates much of the original design. Once we've covered the formal aspects of RS-232, we'll expand our investigation into RS-232's more practical application to PCs.

Finally, we'll discuss Centronics ports, special-purpose I/O ports, and cables.

THE RS-232 SERIAL PORT

Serial ports for PCs appear in various guises:

As standard equipment. The serial port is standard equipment on some computers, including PS/2s and many PC compatibles. Often, a parallel and a serial port are built onto a single internal board; sometimes the serial port is integrated into the motherboard, as is the case in the AT&T 6300s and IBM PS/2s.

As a serial adapter board. One or two serial ports may be built onto a printed circuit board, which the user plugs into a slot inside the PC. Since the components of a serial port take up little space, a board is rarely made for that purpose alone, but such boards are available. An example, with a single port, is shown in Figure 4.1.

As part of a multifunction board. Makers of hardware add-ons for PCs are scrambling to pack more and more functions onto a card. Integration of many functions, such as additional memory, ports, and clocks, onto single boards lowers the price of each function, making it economically feasible to cram ever more resources into a machine before it runs out of slots. A serial port is provided by many multifunction boards. The Six-Pak™ series from AST Research® is the most successful line.

Integrated with an internal modem. An internal modem combines the components of a serial port with those of a modem, dispensing with a connector. To a program, an internal modem is indistinguishable from a serial port because, in effect, that's exactly what it is. The only way a program could tell an internal from an external modem would be by detecting some aspect of behavior unique to a specific model.

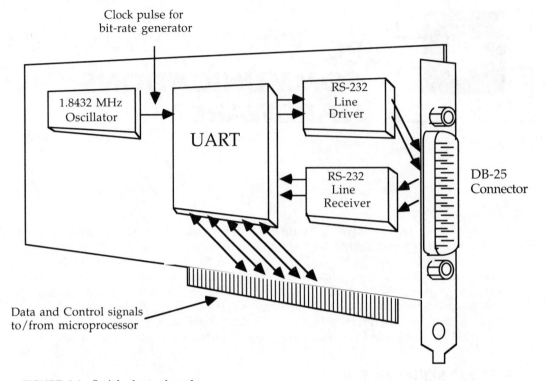

Clock pulse for
bit-rate generator

1.8432 MHz
Oscillator

UART

RS-232
Line
Driver

RS-232
Line
Receiver

DB-25
Connector

Data and Control signals
to/from microprocessor

FIGURE 4.1: Serial adapter board

On a multiport adapter. Some boards supply several, typically up to four, serial ports. They are made for such special purposes as networking and use with devices that permit the user to attach terminals to a PC in the hope of coaxing it to operate as a multi-user system.

PC ports and other attached devices, such as disk drives, keyboard, and video adapters, are connected to the processor, and to memory, by means of a *bus*, illustrated in Figure 4.2. The devices are identified and distinguished from each other by *I/O addresses*. The PC is like a small village with the bus as its main street. The I/O devices are houses, each with a

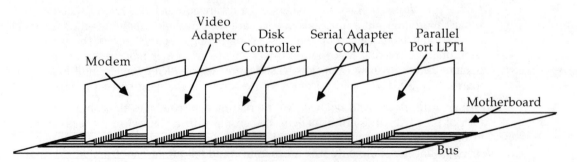

Video
Adapter   Disk   Serial Adapter   Parallel
Controller   COM1   Port LPT1

Modem

Motherboard

Bus

FIGURE 4.2: PC Bus structure

different number, lined up along the street. The bus is the common channel through which all internal communication flows. Even data exchange between the processor and memory travels on the bus, although, for greater efficiency, some 386-based PCs have a separate bus for this purpose. The processor sends instructions and data to I/O devices over the bus with addresses identifying the destinations. Every device is connected to the bus by a "gate" that "opens" only when it recognizes the device's address in the flow of information.

Interrupts

Before going on with our discussion of hardware, we should explain the *interrupt*, a mechanism vital to the operation of a computer's input/output system. An interrupt is a signal that diverts a processor's attention from one task to another, more important task. I/O devices often require service from a computer's processor at odd, unpredictable moments—for example, when a character happens to arrive at a serial port, when the user presses a key on the keyboard, or when a disk drive has properly positioned itself for a read or write operation. The processor may be churning away on an application program, or simply idling; the interrupt forces it to suspend its current activity and to execute the code that services the interrupting device. The amount of work involved in servicing an interrupt is usually small; it doesn't take much to read a character and stash it in a buffer, or to issue the next command in a sequence of I/O operations. Once the interrupt task has been completed, the computer resumes its previous activity, picking up where it left off.

People rely on interrupts in everyday life for similar purposes. The ring of a telephone, the knell of a door chime, and the clang of a fire alarm are signals that grab our attention and prompt us to drop what we're doing for a moment to respond to the call for action.

Software can drive an I/O device in either of two ways: by interrupts, or by *polling*. In polling, the device driver, the component of the operating system that manages the device, must periodically check the device to see if it requires service. If you were to turn off your telephone's ringer and pick up the handset every 30 seconds to learn if someone was calling you, that would be polling. Computers are more suited than people to polling (machines neither forget to poll nor get bored with it), but the technique tends to waste processor time when devices are idle. Software designed to use polling may be appropriate in some instances, but most device drivers on most computers depend wholly on interrupts.

Computers, including PCs, are designed with a fixed number of interrupt lines, i.e., hardware paths intended to carry interrupt signals to the processor. ATs and PS/2s have sixteen; plain PCs have eight. When an interrupt occurs, the interrupt hardware presents the processor with the "number of the interrupt," e.g., 1 to 8 for plain PCs, 1 to 16 for ATs. The processor uses the number to identify the device demanding attention. PCs and ATs normally allow only one active device per interrupt line, so such lines are often in short supply. On PS/2s each interrupt line can be shared among several active devices—a significant step forward in basic design. In effect, PCs can operate with only a limited number of devices simultaneously. PS/2s can, in principle, work with any number that can be physically attached. Because a PC serial port being used for communications, as opposed to a printer or plotter, is almost always interrupt-driven, interrupt restrictions are of great concern to us.

How Many Serial Ports Fit in a PC?

A fair question, but an awkward one to answer. For one thing, the question must be considered separately for PS/2s and original PCs. Even within the PC family, there are several possible answers:

As many as you can squeeze in.   Given the number of slots, the amount of power available, and the proper number of ports per card, it would seem that up to 32 could be crowded into an AT, but it would be a ghastly mess. There are no standards and only loose conventions for the assignment of I/O addresses and interrupt lines to ports beyond COM4.

The interrupt limitations of PC-family machines do not restrict the number of ports that can be installed, but they do impose a ceiling on the number that can be active at any moment, unless the ports are driven by special software.

Four.   If the conventions established by IBM are followed, four I/O addresses and interrupt request lines are mandated:

Device ID	I/O Address	Interrupt
COM1:	3F8	4
COM2:	2F8	3
COM3:	3E8	4
COM4:	2E8	3

Note that the two interrupt lines are doubly assigned. For the reasons cited above, this implies that only two of the four ports can be used simultaneously if interrupt-driven; moreover, those two must have different interrupt assignments. For example, COM1 could not be used simultaneously with COM3.

Two.   PC-DOS and IBM's BIOS can cope with only COM1 and COM2, although certain versions of MS-DOS handle four ports, as defined above. The two-port limit is effective for print operations managed by DOS, but, as we shall see, most communication programs shun the serial port services of DOS and the BIOS, and thus have fairly free rein. When it comes to software, it's safest to investigate any given product, but the ability to handle four ports is fairly common. Part of the code for IBM's BIOS (published in the technical reference manuals for each PC model group) was written to drive two serial ports, and part to handle four.

In practice, unless you know what you're doing and are prepared for trouble, you would be well advised not to venture beyond two ports. Even if your PC couples hardware and software for the operation of more than two ports, be careful about possible conflicts with other devices in your system. People occasionally have trouble using even a second COM port, since a few devices, such as certain mice, commandeer the interrupt line assigned to COM2.

How Many Ports Fit in a PS/2?

Again, it depends.

Eight, with qualifications.   IBM's architecture allows eight serial ports in a PS/2. Ports COM1 and COM2 are assigned as given above for PCs. COM3 to COM8 are assigned as follows:

Device ID	I/O Address	Interrupt
COM3:	3220	3
COM4:	3228	3
COM5:	4220	3

COM6:	4228	3
COM7:	5220	3
COM8:	5228	3

Four.   Versions of PC-DOS for PS/2s (3.3 and up) handle COM1 through COM4.

Eight.   OS/2 allows use of all eight ports.

Installing Serial Ports

Upon installation, a port must be *configured* to use a particular I/O address and interrupt line, which determine the COM number the port will assume in the system.

For the PC Family

Generally, serial ports are preset at the factory to operate as either COM1 or COM2. Prior to installation, decide whether the factory setting is appropriate and convenient. If it's not, you should be able to change the configuration to your choice of at least COM1 or COM2, and in some cases to COM3 or COM4 as well. This reconfiguration is usually accomplished by means of one or more shunts or DIP switches on the board. The instructions should tell you how to reset them. If a product is sold without literature describing its switches and jumpers, don't buy it.

For PS/2s

Serial ports are configured by software at the time of system initialization (boot-up). Part of the process of installing serial ports consists of creating a file listing the number of the slot in which the board is installed and the COM port numbers to be assigned to ports on that board.

Here are some important tips on configuring and installing ports. Most relate primarily to operation with DOS.

Sequence

You can configure COM ports in any order you like. For example, you could even skip COM1 and make COM2 the sole port in your system, and all but a very few, badly behaved pieces of software would run just fine. In the long run, however, configuring devices in numerical order will probably be less confusing.

Factory Settings

Some manufacturers, assuming that the user is likely to have a serial printer on COM1, suggest that their internal modems be installed as COM2 and preset their switches accordingly. If you do not already have a COM2 device, you can just follow the instructions, but you can also confidently ignore them and install the modem as COM1 if you prefer.

Conflicts

If you install two ports with the same I/O address, neither will be usable. Such installation is unlikely to harm the hardware, but there's no guarantee that it won't.

Software

The primary criteria for port configuration should be assignment in numerical order and adherence to the vendor's recommendations. In some cases, however, you must also consider compatibility between a port and the software that is to drive it, especially since, in most cases, only one program will be used with any given port. Not only must serial hardware be configured, but so must communications software.

Slots

In most cases, any slot will do for installing a serial board. But check the documentation for both PC and board for any contrary indication.

Toast

To avoid overheating, install an internal modem with the component side of the board adjacent to an empty slot, if there is one. Internal modems rank high in heat generation among common PC boards, so the more space for ventilation the better.

Power

Some PC power supplies, especially on older models, are notoriously feeble. In adding boards to a PC, then, you may run out of power before running out of slots. Since some internal modems consume considerable power, adding even one to a PC could overtax the supply. As a result, the PC would probably refuse to boot.

Oops!

The *Technical Reference Manual* for the IBM PC AT contains an error regarding the configuration options for the stock serial port. On page 3 of the *Serial/Parallel Adapter* section, the jumper settings in the illustration are reversed.

THE RS-232 STANDARD

We have been making sly references to RS-232 since Chapter 1. It is now time to present some facts about RS-232 and explain how it works. Appendix A summarizes the full standard.

The History and Purpose of RS-232

RS-232, strictly speaking, defines an interface between a DTE (piece of Data Terminal Equipment) and a DCE (piece of Data Circuit-terminating Equipment or, equivalently, Data Communications Equipment), as shown in Figure 4.3. DTE refers to anything *terminal with respect to data*, such as a terminal, a printer, or a computer—that is, a source and destination for data. A DCE is anything that *manages the communication of data*. Since the most common example of a DCE is a modem, the RS-232 standard, for our purposes, basically addresses the question of how to attach a modem to a PC.

RS-232 deals with three issues:

- Physical components, such as connectors and cables
- Electrical characteristics of signals sent across the interface
- Meanings of the signals

The standard was established in 1960 by the Electronics Industries Association (EIA). The version in use today is properly called EIA-232-D, the "D" suffix denoting the fourth (January 1987) revision. The previous revision, RS-232-C, was adopted in 1969 and reaffirmed

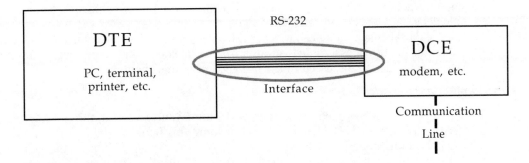

FIGURE 4.3: RS-232 Interface with DTE and DCE

in 1981. Since the C version held sway for so many years, references to it are still common. Also, since earlier versions of the standard had all but disappeared, RS-232-C was often called simply "RS-232," and the same thing appears to be happening with EIA-232-D.

RS-232 has become an international standard in the form of CCITT Recommendations V.24 (functional characteristics), V.28 (electrical), and ISO 2110 (mechanical). The CCITT standards, based on RS-232-C, incorporated a few other items, notably for diagnostic purposes. EIA-232-D brought the standard into line with the international recommendations, and updated the wording to reflect contemporary applications of the interface. Most C-dynasty implementations of RS-232, including that used with PCs, conform equally to the D revision. The U.S. military also has an RS-232-like standard called MIL-STD-188C.

RS-232 attempts to be all things to all modems, and thus is rather a mess. For example, it calls for 25 wires linking the DTE and DCE, but many of these lines are almost never used. It is conventional to use only a subset of 9 to 14 lines, and the standard itself recommends certain subsets for particular applications. For example, half-duplex operation over a two-wire point-to-point dedicated link calls for seven circuits; six are used for one-way transmission over a switched link. Except for the nine-pin connector on the AT and certain other models, IBM's RS-232 implementation for PCs conforms to one of these standard subsets.

Mechanical Characteristics

The mechanical section of an interface standard specifies how the two communicating devices are to be physically connected, with a socket on each device and a cable, with a plug on each end, to run between the sockets. Both plugs and sockets are properly called *connectors*. In a few cases, including some mini-modems, the DCE is physically very small, and may be plugged directly into a DTE without an intervening cable.

Prior to revision D, the RS-232 standard dictated that a 25-pin connector should be used, but neglected to mention what it should look like. Fortunately, the DB25 connector became a de facto standard, so widely accepted that it was often referred to, prematurely, as an "RS-232" or "EIA connector." Later, ISO 2110 formally adopted the DB25, and EIA-232-D followed suit.

Like most connectors, the DB25 comes in two genders: male (the one with pins) and female (the one with, uh, no pins). The standard states that the DTE should have a male socket and the DCE a female. This injunction is frequently ignored by manufacturers, but the consequences are minor. It just means that three varieties of cable are common: male-to-male, female-to-female, and male-to-female.

The standard is silent about cables, except to designate pin 1 of the connector as *shield*. At the DTE, this pin provides a route to ground when a shielded cable is employed. Conventions for RS-232 cabling are discussed in the last section of this chapter.

Functional Characteristics

Here we describe the intended use of each of the important circuits in the RS-232 interface. But first, a quick electricity lesson for those reading this book by the light of an oil lamp. The signal on an RS-232 line is expressed in terms of voltage. *Voltage* is the difference in electrical potential between two points that causes electrons to flow from one point to the other when they are linked by an electrical conductor. This flow is called a *current*. The concept of voltage is similar to that of pressure in a fluid. If a tube connects two points that have different levels of air pressure, for example, air molecules will flow to the point of lower pressure. Unlike pressure, however, voltage is purely relative; one thing has a voltage only in relation to another thing. To measure the voltage on a signal line, we must have a reference against which to do so. The reference is usually called a *ground*, after the ultimate reference point: the ground, whose potential is arbitrarily assigned the value of zero.

Now back to the standard. Interface circuits are classified in four groups: *ground, data, control,* and *timing*. The standard describes and names the circuits in each group; in many cases, only the initials of the names are used. The circuits are named from the standpoint of the DTE, reflecting the attitude that it is the more important of the two parties. The relevant pin assignments are shown in Figure 4.4.

Signal Ground serves as the ground reference for measuring signal voltages on all the signal wires.

Since the terms *DTE* and *DCE* may be unfamiliar and possibly a little confusing, in the following descriptions we will use, respectively, *terminal* and *modem* instead.

Data Circuits

Since RS-232 is a full-duplex interface, two wires are assigned to carry data, one for each direction. *Transmitted Data (TD)* runs from the terminal to the modem, *Received Data (RD)* from the modem to the terminal.

RS-232 Interface

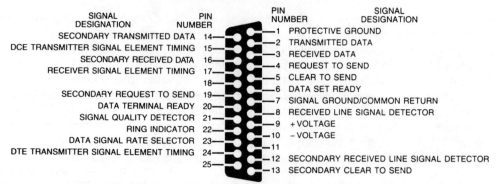

FIGURE 4.4: RS-232 pin assignments

Control Circuits

A control circuit carries an ON/OFF indication of some condition in the terminal or modem. Several alternative expressions reminiscent of flagpoles are sometimes used for the "on" and "off" conditions: circuits are said to be "high" and "low," "put up" and "put down," "asserted" and "dropped," and "raised" and "lowered."

DTE Ready (DTR) is raised by the terminal to let the modem know it is ready for business. DTR should be asserted at the start of a communication session and remain ON until the session is over. A terminal will normally assert DTR as long as the terminal itself is on. If DTR drops (is turned OFF) in the midst of a communication session, the modem may take offense and hang up the phone. Under RS-232-C, this circuit was named *Data Terminal Ready*.

DCE Ready is the modem's counterpart to DTR. In RS-232-C, it was called *Data Set Ready (DSR)*—a modem being a "data set" in obsolete terminology. DSR tells the terminal when the modem is turned on, connected to a communications channel, and ready to work. In the case of a modem on a dial-up line, "connected to a communications channel" means that it is "off-hook." Such a modem turns DSR on when it either answers an incoming call or starts dialing an outgoing one. A leased-line modem, in contrast, normally keeps this circuit high as long as the modem itself is powered on. There is no RS-232 signal that merely informs the terminal that the modem is on.

DTE Ready and DCE Ready were the only new names given to circuits in the D revision of RS-232. While they are much clearer than the old designations, it seems certain that the old ones will continue to be used. We shall stick with "Data Terminal Ready," "Data Set Ready," and the abbreviations "DTR" and "DSR" for the rest of the book.

The terminal raises *Request To Send (RTS)* to inform the modem that it wants to transmit data. Although many modems will not transmit unless they see this signal, it is essential only to a half-duplex unit, which must be told whether it is to transmit or receive at any given time.

Clear To Send (CTS) is intimately related to RTS. The modem turns CTS ON to indicate to the terminal that it is ready to transmit. In the case of a half-duplex modem, the state of CTS matches that of RTS after a delay of a few milliseconds, time which the modem needs to switch between its transmit and receive states.

Carrier Detect (CD), also called *Received Line Signal Detector (RLSD)*, or sometimes *Data Carrier Detect (DCD)*, tells the terminal whether or not the modem has established a usable connection. CD ON means that the modem is hearing a valid carrier from a remote modem, and implies that data transfer can proceed. The modem informs the terminal of the loss of a connection by turning CD OFF.

Ring Indicator (RI) is turned ON by the modem when it detects a ringing signal on its telephone line, thus alerting the terminal to an incoming call.

Timing Circuits

Timing circuits are used only for synchronous operation. *Transmission Signal Element Timing*, more commonly referred to as *Transmit Clock (TC)*, carries timing pulses from the modem to the terminal to synchronize the data passed on the TD circuit. Each time the signal on TC goes from OFF to ON, the terminal should present the next bit on TD. *Receiver Signal Element Timing*, colloquially called *Receive Clock (RC)*, does the analogous job for the received data stream: each time the RC signal goes from OFF to ON, the terminal should read the next bit on RD.

Of the 13 remaining lines, three are unassigned, two are reserved for modem testing, five are given over to a secondary channel, and three are special, infrequently used control lines of no concern here.

In sum, the behavior of the interface is fairly simple. Data flow from the terminal to the modem on TD and from the modem to the terminal on RD. In full-duplex operation, the two data streams flow simultaneously and independently. In asynchronous operation, the timing is done by the terminal, and the modem is oblivious to it. In synchronous operation, timing signals are normally generated by the modem, which brings the terminal into synchronization via the timing circuits.

Each of the control circuits, often called *modem control circuits*, conveys one ON/OFF condition either from the modem to the terminal or vice versa. The signal on such a line (its "state") should change comparatively rarely.

Imagine the modem as operated by an obedient little man, a telephone at his side and an assortment of communications machinery before him. DTR signals that the terminal needs him. He uses DSR to tell the terminal he is on duty and has a communication line available. TD provides the data he must send out over the phone line; he dutifully puts any data he receives from the remote modem onto RD.

If DTR is ON when the phone rings, he answers it; if DTR is OFF, he lets it ring and signals the terminal using RI. If the terminal, seeing the RI signal, decides to take the call, it raises DTR, cueing the operator to answer. When a connection has been established, either in or out, he first makes sure that a compatible operator is at the other end and then raises CD to tell the terminal that data flow may begin.

The terminal can tell him to hang up at any time by dropping DTR. If, on the other hand, the connection is lost because the remote operator hangs up or the telephone company makes one of its rare errors, the operator lets the terminal know by putting down CD.

Pinning Things Down

The Mechanical Characteristics section of the standard specifies the pin connections for each circuit. Figure 4.4 shows the pin assignments on a DB25 connector for the circuits discussed above.

RS-232 circuits are named in a confusing variety of ways. The nomenclature given above is the most popular. Alternatively, engineers often identify each circuit by its pin number in the standard 25-pin connector. The EIA standard uses two- or three-character labels (for example, AA and SBB), while the CCITT document goes in for mysterious numbers such as 101, 108.2, and 125. The labels and numbers are non-mnemonic and rarely encountered. They are listed in Appendix A, Table A.1, but we will avoid them here.

Electrical Characteristics

Electrically, RS-232 is simple. As shown in Figure 4.5, a positive voltage of $+3$ V to $+15$ V represents SPACE; a negative voltage of -3 V to -15 V represents MARK. (This should remind you of one of the signaling options in telex.) The transition region between -3 V and $+3$ V constitutes a grey area. In practice, values of $+12$ V and -12 V are usually used for transmission.

RS-232's electrical characteristics, with associated data and control circuit conditions, are:

Voltage	State	Data	Control
+	SPACE	0	ON
−	MARK	1	OFF

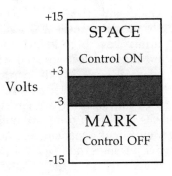

FIGURE 4.5: Electrical characteristics of RS-232

It might seem more logical to associate Data 0 with Control OFF, and Data 1 with Control ON, but that's not the way it is, so be on your guard.

The RS-232 standard calls for an interface design immune to electrical problems arising from open or short circuits. You should be able to unplug connectors during operation, patch one circuit to another, stick a metal screwdriver into the cluster of connector pins, or even connect all the wires in an interface together without causing anything to blow up. With a PC, you can certainly plug and unplug RS-232 cables when the machine is running, although it would be unwise to do so when data are flowing. Granted, one of the authors once managed to melt a pair of RS-232 line receiver chips, and cause blue smoke to billow from the back of a computer (not a PC), by playing with RS-232 connections, but for the most part RS-232 circuits may be interconnected with impunity. As we shall see later, there are many excellent reasons for making such interconnections.

Subsets

The simplest practical subset of RS-232 consists of two circuits, Signal Ground and either TD or RD, for a one-way link. ASCII terminals may be hard-wired to hosts with as few as three wires (Signal Ground, TD, and RD). Asynchronous ports for PCs use a nine-circuit subset.

Limitations and Liberties

RS-232 does have some serious limitations. For example, the standard specifies a data-rate ceiling of 20,000 bps. An RS-232 interface could go faster, doing everything else the same way, but, by definition, that would not be RS-232. In practice, the highest speed is usually 19,200 bps, simply because this is a standard rate, while 20,000 bps is not. Much of IBM's user documentation gives the impression that serial ports on PC-family machines can operate only at speeds up to 9,600 bps, and the manner in which versions of DOS prior to 3.3 manage COM ports does indeed impose that limit. But a program can bypass DOS, access a port directly, and drive it at rates up to 115,200 bps. One caveat: experience shows that, in a PC or XT, software may not readily keep pace with hardware at speeds greater than 19,200 bps. However, in an AT or PS/2 with adequate software, speeds of 57,600 and even 115,200 bps are feasible.

The RS-232 standard also restricts cable length, recommending a maximum of 50 feet (15 meters). A longer cable run, it states, is permissible if its total capacitance does not exceed 2,500 picofarads. Good cable today has a capacitance of about 12 picofarads per foot, implying usable lengths of slightly over 200 feet. This is overly conservative; RS-232 connections running half a mile have been known to work just fine. However, while RS-232 links longer than a few hundred feet are well worth trying, problems may crop up. Many factors may limit practical cable length, particularly the quality of the cable, the transmission speed, and the amount of electrical noise in the environment.

These limitations on speed and distance are largely irrelevant when using RS-232 for connecting modems. Modems used with a PC are unlikely to run faster than 19,200 bps, and why would you ever want to put a modem very far from the PC that's using it? When RS-232 is employed for other purposes, however, the limitations may be more of a problem. We will look into such matters later on in this chapter.

RS-232 AND PCS

Now we'll explore the use of RS-232 with PC COM ports and PC modems, taking IBM-supplied serial adapters and the Hayes Smartmodem 1200 as references. Remarks in this section also apply to most Hayes-compatible modems operating asynchronously.

The material presented here is relevant to ordinary PC asynchronous ports, but not to RS-232 ports made for synchronous connections or other special purposes. If you ever have to deal with such special applications, or with RS-232 on larger computers, you'll probably need to go strictly by the standard (and perhaps go buy the standard, available from the EIA).

Everyday use of RS-232 with PCs and PC modems has departed in some respects from the original standard. Some PC implementations use a DE9 instead of a DB25, with modified pin assignments; otherwise the standard is adhered to. Also, although data circuits are used in the original way, certain control circuits are used differently. Signal voltages, however, comply with the standard exactly; taking liberties here would be not only pointless but risky.

Most PCs have regular DB25 connectors, which is a bit wasteful given that only 9 of the 25 pins are actually used. Some manufacturers have substituted the smaller nine-pin DE9, illustrated in Figure 4.6. The DE9 is also used by IBM (and most clone makers) to hook monochrome monitors to their PCs.

The DE9 is frequently, if erroneously, referred to as a "DB9." It is one in a series of connectors named according to a "DXn" convention, in which D identifies the shape of the shell, X indicates size, and n gives the number of pins. It has become common practice, however, to prefix all D-shell connector names with "DB."

IBM originally used DB25s for PCs and XTs. They first used the DE9 on the AT, and continued its use with the XT 286 and Convertible. In the PS/2, they reverted to DB25s for the built-in serial ports, but supply add-on serial adapters with DE9 connectors.

Table 4.1 summarizes the RS-232 lines used by PCs. The first column lists the pin numbers for a DB25 connector. The second column gives the pin assignments used with IBM's DE9 connector. Note that the Receive Clock and Transmit Clock circuits described in the last section are absent here, because ordinary PC serial ports do not support the synchronous operation that demands timing circuits.

The DE9 connector makes a lot of sense, and has been adopted not only by IBM, but by some laptop manufacturers and a few others. There is one minor drawback: no standard exists for assigning DE9 pins to RS-232 circuits, and different vendors have chosen different

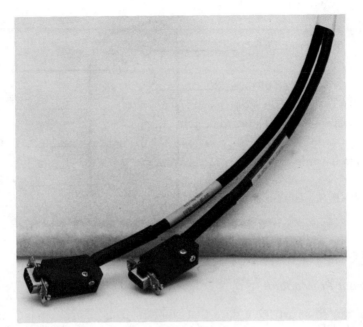

FIGURE 4.6: DE9 connectors. *Reprinted by permission of Black Box Corporation, Pittsburgh, PA. Copyright ©1987. All rights reserved.*

ways of doing so. Now that IBM has adopted the DE9, other companies are following its pin configuration.

Figure 4.7 shows the DE9 pin configuration and assignments used by IBM. For connecting a DB25 to a serial port equipped with a DE9, an adapter is available, consisting of a short cable with a DE9 on one end and a DB25 with standard pin assignments on the other. Since the adapter is normally used with RS-232 devices, the exact configuration of the DE9 pins is more or less academic.

TABLE 4.1: RS-232 interchange circuits as implemented for PCs

DB25	DE9			
Pin	Pin	Source	Abbrev.	Descriptive Name
2	3	PC	TD	Transmitted Data
3	2	Modem	RD	Received Data
4	7	PC	RTS	Request To Send
5	8	Modem	CTS	Clear To Send
6	6	Modem	DSR	Data Set Ready
7	5	—	—	Signal Ground
8	1	Modem	CD	Carrier Detect
20	4	PC	DTR	Data Terminal Ready
22	9	Modem	RI	Ring Indicator

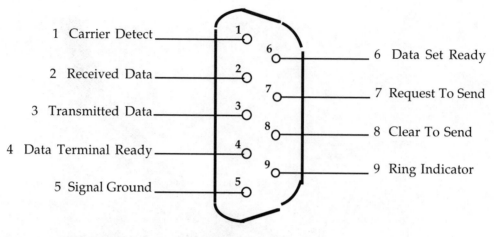

FIGURE 4.7: DE9 pin assignments (as used by IBM for RS-232)

The Truth about PC Modems

Modems are so smart these days that some modem control circuits have become largely redundant. A PC and its modem can communicate more effectively by means of the modem's command language than via control circuits. For example, since commands are used for practically everything else, a PC can tell the modem to hang up the phone much more easily by sending a brief command than by waggling DTR. Let's examine each control line as used in a PC-to-modem context.

Data Terminal Ready

Most PC communication packages, appropriately, turn DTR ON when they start up. PC modems largely treat DTR according to the standard, ignoring commands (and otherwise paying no attention to the PC) while DTR is OFF; if DTR drops during a communications session, the modem hangs up. Either a software or a modem hardware switch, however, can be set to make DTR appear permanently ON, so that the modem ignores a PC's real DTR signal. When this DTR override is selected, PC software can tell the modem to disconnect a call only by using a command.

Request To Send and Clear To Send

A regular PC modem totally ignores RTS, and constantly asserts CTS. As described in Chapter 8, however, certain error-correcting modems employ RTS and CTS for flow control.

Carrier Detect

The modem manipulates CD according to the standard unless optionally set to keep CD up all the time. With some modems, this option is switch-selected; others use a command (&C in the Hayes command set).

The need for such an option results from a discrepancy between the RS-232 standard and the requirements of smart modems. A DTE behaving strictly according to RS-232 rules should refuse to send data to the modem until CD comes ON. This originally made sense, because a dumb modem could do nothing with data until it had a connection by means of which to transmit them. But an intelligent, auto-answer, auto-dial modem is confronted with Catch-232: a connection can't be made at all unless the modem first receives some data—in this case, commands. A few older PC programs, following RS-232 conventions, do not send commands to the modem unless CD is ON. (This may also be true of some terminals.) A more sensible approach is for the software to ignore CD when sending modem commands, thus allowing this circuit to be used for its intended purpose of informing the DTE of the presence or absence of a remote connection.

Any communications software that answers incoming calls must depend on CD to serve its original purpose. When a dial-in caller disconnects, the modem drops CD—the only sure indication of call termination available to the software.

Data Set Ready

Ordinarily, the modem keeps DSR ON all the time. Some modems can be configured to manipulate DSR according to RS-232 rules, by means of the Hayes &S command. Few PC communication programs pay any attention to DSR, and most of those that do interpret it solely as an indicator of whether or not the modem is turned on.

Ring Indicator

PC modems used to answer calls are generally set up to do so automatically, rather than as a result of some action taken by the PC in response to an RI signal.

Smart Modems, Dumb Interfaces

If few RS-232 control circuits are important for use with smart modems and PCs, why was RS-232 designed this way? The reason is that the standard was developed nearly three decades ago, when modems were not exactly smart. In fact, they were exceedingly dumb. In those days, there were no microprocessors or even integrated circuits. An "intelligent" modem, had there been such a thing, would have tipped the scales at 98 pounds, cost about $20,000, and generated more heat than today's Chevrolet. To signal any condition to a dumb modem, you had to dedicate a line for the purpose. The same held true if you needed a modem to tell you anything.

Is RS-232 a tad obsolete? Yes. But that's not to say that it is bad. Although several proposed replacements are waiting in the wings, promising greater simplicity, speed, reliability, symmetry, and compatibility, RS-232 is simply so pervasive that it will be hard to shake. And it's certainly adequate, if far from ideal, for the low-performance applications with which it's associated. In short, RS-232 is likely to be around for some time to come because it is so common and so widely (if not always correctly) understood.

More about Smart Modems

Hayes modems use one or two RS-232 circuits in addition to those supported by PCs. Pin 12, unassigned by RS-232-C, is used as a High Speed Indicator; RS-232-D also specifically assigns pin 12 for this purpose. The Smartmodem 1200, for example, turns this circuit ON when establishing a call at 1,200 bps and OFF when operating in the range of 300 bps and below. The fact that pin 12 is not supported by the PC poses no problem, since the connection speed is also encoded in the responses sent by the modem, e.g., CONNECT 1200 and CONNECT 2400. The V-series Smartmodem 9600 uses pin 12 in combination with pin 23 to indicate its connection speed.

THE CENTRONICS PARALLEL PORT

Let's start by recapitulating what we learned about the Centronics parallel interface in Chapter 1.

- The key difference between Centronics and RS-232 is that Centronics is a parallel interface, transporting eight data bits (an entire byte) at a time on eight different circuits.

- A parallel interface lends itself to operation at higher data rates than a serial interface, but over considerably shorter distances.

- Parallel ports on PCs prior to the PS/2 series are limited to simplex operation, useful for little more than hooking up printers.

- IBM has established a convention of using DB25 connectors for parallel ports, rather than the standard 36-pin connectors usually seen on parallel printers.

- Cable length is limited to a few feet: 8 with comfort, 15 in an electrically quiet environment with a printer that's not too finicky, and 25 if you are very lucky.

- In principle, a parallel port is easier to use than a serial port, because it has no "operating parameters" to set.

- A PC can accommodate up to two Centronics ports, configured as LPT1 and LPT2. PC-DOS also recognizes the device name LPT3, but this appears to be a loose end, since the BIOS supports no third parallel port.

What follows is some basic technical information about the Centronics interface. Appendix B lists the I/O addresses assigned for parallel ports and gives pin assignments for both the standard Centronics connector and the DB25 connector used by IBM.

Operation of a Parallel Port

We have noted that, while RS-232 is the best known serial interface, it is by no means the only one. Similarly, Centronics is one of the best known but not the only parallel interface. Another celebrated example is the IEEE's 488, which has become the standard for interconnecting digital instruments and computers in laboratory environments. Hewlett-Packard® is the originator and strongest promoter of IEEE-488.

Parallel port hardware is simpler than that of a serial port because no circuitry for serializing and deserializing bits is required.

The key circuits in the Centronics interface are the eight assigned to the data bits, plus *Data Strobe, Acknowledge*, and *Busy*. We'll examine how these are used in the conventional arrangement of a computer driving a printer. The interface operates at a variable speed, governed by a *strobe pulse* rather than a clock pulse. A strobe pulse, which may appear at irregular intervals, is triggered by the operating system's printer driver each time it has a character ready on the data lines for the printer to read. The printer regulates the flow of data by means of the Busy and Acknowledge circuits; it indicates that it is ready to receive data (as opposed to being in an error, off-line, or other unsuitable condition) by asserting an appropriate signal on the Busy line, and pulses the Acknowledge line to confirm its receipt of each character.

The use of other circuits varies with implementation. IBM provides the printer with circuits for signaling that it is out of paper, notifying the PC of general I/O errors, and so on. Another special IBM circuit supplies electrical power at $+5$ V, which is neither used by the PC nor wired up to the DB25, but is handy for powering printer buffers and similar devices.) The IBM implementation, like most others, also includes a circuit to enable the printer to indicate whether or not it is "selected," i.e., in a state to receive data from the computer; when "unselected," it will accept manual commands for line feeds, form feeds, and the like.

The Centronics interface passes signals at the same voltage levels used in much PC circuitry—another reason it is simpler than an RS-232 interface, which boosts outputs to higher voltage levels. In the Centronics case, binary 1 is represented by $+5$ V, and binary 0 by zero V.

Parallel ports in the PS/2 series operate identically to those in the PC family, with the addition of an optional extended mode that allows bidirectional data transfer. Since the same data lines must be used for both input and output, two-way flow is half-duplex. The PS/2's ability to input data from a parallel port is harnessed in IBM's Data Migration Facility, which makes possible the speedy transfer of files from an older PC-family machine to a PS/2. Since a PC's parallel port allows output only, the Data Migration Facility does not support transfers in the other direction.

Overcoming Centronics' Distance Limitations

Gadgets are available to overcome the distance limitation inherent in Centronics interfaces, extending the range to several hundred feet. Most are simply parallel-to-serial converters, allowing you to use twisted pair to span the distance. Either two of these converters are used, one at each end (as shown in Figure 4.8a), or a serial port on the PC is linked to a single converter at the printer (Figure 4.8b). When using paired converters, look for a type designed for this purpose. Be sure that they are bidirectional (with respect to conversion, not data), and operate at a speed comparable to that of the parallel port (38.4 kbps is just right). Two well known converter sources are Integrated Marketing Corporation (INMAC) and Black Box Corporation.

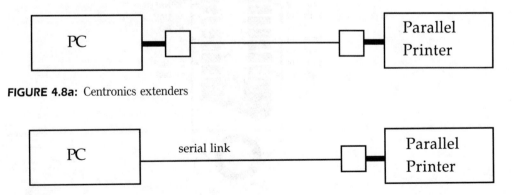

FIGURE 4.8a: Centronics extenders

FIGURE 4.8b: Serial to Centronics extension

SPECIAL-PURPOSE PORTS

Some other kinds of ports may be added to PCs for special purposes.

IEEE-488

IEEE-488, also known as the Hewlett-Packard Interface Bus (HPIB), or the General Purpose Interface Bus (GPIB), was developed by HP to interface electronic digital instruments with computers and with each other. It is commonly used in engineering laboratories, among other places. IEEE-488, like the Centronics interface, operates in a byte-parallel fashion; also, its 24-pin connector, illustrated in Figure 4.9, physically resembles the Centronics connector. The 24 circuits comprise eight data lines, eight control lines, and several grounds. Cable runs may extend as far as 20 meters, and data rates as high as 1 Mbps are possible.

Unlike RS-232 and Centronics, IEEE-488, as its aliases suggest, is a bus rather than an interface, and can interconnect up to 15 devices. Like buses internal to computers, IEEE-488 allows only one device at a time to transmit data; any number, however, can receive data simultaneously.

IEEE-488 ports for PCs are available from Black Box®, IO Tech, and National Instruments, among others. Some are cleverly designed to appear to the PC as Centronics ports. The benefit of this masquerade is that usually no special software is needed to drive an IEEE-488 port, as long as it is used solely for the output of data. The port is addressed

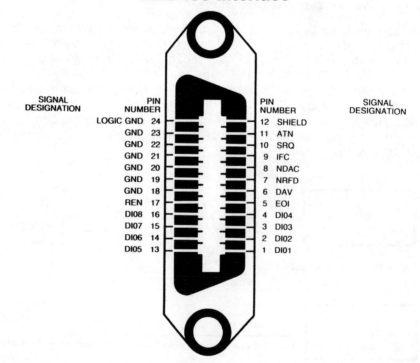

FIGURE 4.9: IEEE-488 pin assignments

as if it were a parallel printer—that is, as LPT1, LPT2, or LPT3. The many applications requiring only output capability might entail, for example, connection to one of Hewlett-Packard's excellent IEEE-488-equipped printers and plotters.

Auxiliary devices made for IEEE-488 include bus extenders, modems, print buffers, and RS-232/IEEE-488 converters.

Current Loop

A current loop interface, as indicated in Chapter 1, is important for telex communications. It is used primarily for interconnecting teletypes and teleprinters, occasionally for local hook-ups between async terminals and hosts, and infrequently for intercomputer links. There is no such thing as a "current loop interface to a modem." Typically used over telephone cable or similar connections, current loop can connect pairs of devices over distances up to a mile.

IBM-supplied serial ports made for PC and XT models can support a current loop interface as an alternative to RS-232. When the appropriate adapter card is configured for current loop, inputs and outputs are provided on four pins of the DB25 connector:

Pin	*Signal*
9	+ Transmit
11	− Transmit
18	+ Receive
25	− Receive

These pins were available because the RS-232-C standard left pins 11, 18, and 25 unassigned, and reserved pin 9 for modem testing. There is no standard connector for this interface.

The other interfaces discussed in this book are voltage-driven: the receiver senses voltages electronically. The current loop interface instead delivers current to energize comparatively crude electrical apparatus, such as an indicator lamp or the commutator in a teleprinter. (For a thorough description of commutator operation, see Ken Sherman's seminal *Data Communications: A User's Guide*, Reston Publishing, 1985, Second edition, pp. 68 ff.) The current supplied by a current loop varies with the receiver; 20 milliamps is common, but higher levels are sometimes needed. The voltage employed depends on distance: the longer the loop, the higher the voltage required. While 20 V may suffice for a couple of hundred feet, 90 V may be required for a half-mile of cable. This is not to say that you can put any desired voltage across a loop to furnish the current needed; high- and low-voltage systems are not generally compatible.

Most current loop interfaces employ start/stop signaling techniques, at rates of 150 bps or lower. People tend to associate such signaling with asynchronous RS-232 interfaces, but RS-232's use of the technique is, in fact, a carryover from current loop. The two common classes of current-loop design represent MARK and SPACE in different ways. On *polar working circuits*, current flows in one direction for MARK and in the other for SPACE; *neutral working loops* use current flow for MARK and zero current for SPACE.

Current loop, while old-fashioned, continues to find favor in many quarters. It is inexpensive to implement (as long as voltages remain moderate) and compatible with teletypes and other older equipment.

RS-422

In 1975 the EIA, acknowledging RS-232's deficiencies in speed and distance, proposed a replacement set of three new interface standards: RS-422, RS-423, and RS-449. RS-449 addressed mechanical and functional characteristics of the new interface, while RS-422 and RS-423 offered two alternatives for its electrical characteristics.

The new interface has had minor success, but has not caught on with personal-computer designers or users. It's easy to see why. With the admirable intention of developing a standard substantially more powerful than RS-232, the EIA regrettably squandered the opportunity to create a smaller and simpler replacement. RS-449 calls for a primary 37-pin connector and an optional, secondary 9-pin connector. One wag promptly dubbed the new standard "RS-Pincushion." *Sic transit gloria* standards body.

In 1987 the EIA introduced yet another interface standard, EIA-530, which is intended to gradually replace RS-449. EIA-530, described below, and several proprietary interfaces have incorporated RS-422 and/or RS-423, using other mechanical and functional specifications.

RS-423 offers low performance very similar to that of RS-232, and was included, in part, to provide a measure of interoperability with the older standard. RS-422 is the really interesting member of the pair, offering operation at speeds up to 10 Mbps and over distances as great as 4,000 feet—although not at the same time, unfortunately. At 10 Mbps, RS-422 will operate satisfactorily up to 40 feet, but the speed must be restricted to 100 kbps or less for the interface to handle 4,000-foot distances.

RS-422 achieves its high performance through the use of a *balanced line*, a method of electrical signaling significantly different from that used by RS-232 and RS-423, which employ an *unbalanced line*. Signals on an unbalanced line are transmitted in the form of voltages with respect to a ground. The problem with this scheme is that, although the Signal Ground line is normally grounded at both ends, these two grounds are not necessarily true earth grounds, and may have a voltage difference between them. This is especially likely when the devices at the ends of the line are powered by different AC electrical sources, called "feeders." A difference in voltage between the two devices causes a current to flow between them; the resulting voltage drop across the Signal Ground line biases the signal voltage, and may possibly shift it into the grey area between -3 V and $+3$ V. Any outside interference affecting the voltage on the signal line aggravates this effect, as illustrated in Figure 4.10.

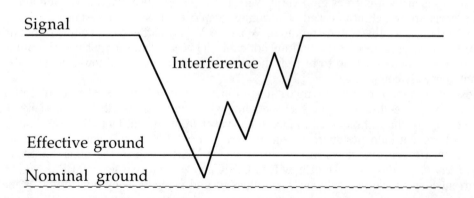

Figure 4.10: Effect of interference on an unbalanced line

A balanced line dispenses with grounds in favor of two signal wires for each circuit. Signals are then expressed as a voltage difference of varying polarity between the two wires. For example, wire A positive with respect to wire B can be used to signal MARK, and wire A negative with respect to wire B to indicate SPACE. The receiver reads the signal by detecting the voltage difference, subtracting the voltage on A from the voltage on B.

A balanced line has superior immunity to interference because a spurious voltage presumably affects both wires more or less equally, as shown in Figure 4.11. The voltages on both wires may change with respect to ground, but not with respect to each other, so the difference, and therefore the detected signal, remains unaltered.

An analogy to an unbalanced line would be a special water pipe, separate from the city water system, running between two houses. A data bit is a spurt of water transmitted from one house to the other. The value of the bit is encoded as the temperature of water in the pipe relative to the temperature of ordinary tap water. Temperature here corresponds to signal voltage, with tap water as the ground reference. A spurt colder than tap water represents a 0-bit; a spurt warmer than tap water is a 1-bit. Signal errors can arise if:

- The tap water is warmer in one house than in the other, equivalent to a difference in voltage between local grounds.

- The temperature of the spurt is altered in transit due to a hot or cold environment, equivalent to a biasing of the signal voltage by interference or a voltage drop along the line.

To operate in the same manner as a balanced line, we would instead use two special pipes. A spurt of water through pipe A that is warmer than a simultaneous spurt through pipe B represents a 1-bit; if the spurt in A is cooler than that in B, the bit is a 0. This system releases us from dependency upon the uncertain reference, tap water. Moreover, anything that

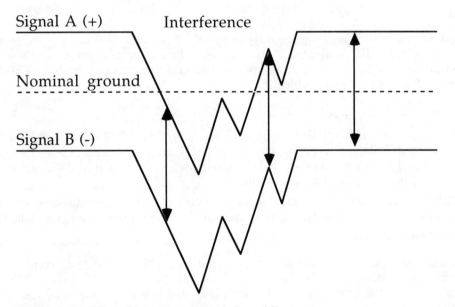

FIGURE 4.11: Effect of interference on a balanced line

warms or cools the two pipes is likely to affect the water flowing through them both equally, thus preserving the encoding.

RS-422 would be a good basis for a "medium-performance" communications interface, especially because appropriate driver chips are easily available. RS-422 is used in a number of personal-computer local area networks (LANs), which have relatively low performance. The Apple® Macintosh® also comes equipped with an RS-422 port, which allows it to tie into the 230.4-kbps AppleTalk® network.

The balanced-line technique is used in a number of communication products, such as line driver units (see Chapter 5), and in several other proposed replacements for RS-232. In these cases, the technique is not necessarily implemented according to RS-422 specifications.

Other Interfaces

Here are short introductions to some other personal-computer interfaces. We will also touch on several more LAN-specific interfaces later in the book.

Musical Instrument Digital Interface

MIDI is a serial bus used for interconnecting electronic musical instruments with computers and with each other. The relevant devices include synthesizers, samplers, and various signal manipulators. Although several vendors offer MIDI adapters for PCs, this interface is much more commonly used with Atari® and Macintosh machines, for which a greater variety of musical-instrument software is available.

Small Computer System Interface

SCSI is a parallel-bus system perhaps best known for its use in connecting fixed-disk drives to later models of the Macintosh. Since SCSI is a standard mass-storage interface, almost any disk drive can be found in a SCSI version.

EIA-530

Published in March 1987 as a suggested replacement for RS-449, EIA-530 is a conglomeration of RS-232, RS-422, and RS-423. It is intended for communication at speeds in the range of 20 kbps to 2 Mbps, and hence is not seen as a substitute for RS-232. EIA-530 includes the following three constituents:

Mechanical. Uses the ever-popular DB25.

Functional. Includes all the important circuits from RS-232: Transmitted Data, Received Data, DCE Ready, DTE Ready, Request To Send, Clear To Send, Received Line Signal Detect, and the three clock circuits. A trio of diagnostic circuits from EIA-232-D are also included.

Electrical. Implements the main interchange circuits (listed above) with balanced lines, following RS-422. The diagnostic circuits are built with unbalanced lines, following RS-423.

It's too early to make definite pronouncements, but EIA-530 may yet find acceptance in some quarters. It seems unlikely, however, that it will be adopted for PCs. It remains too unwieldy, and the Universal Physical Interface cited below is a far more promising alternative.

Universal Physical Interface

UPI has been suggested as an RS-232 replacement for smart devices. It employs a DE9 connector and four balanced lines, two for transfer in each direction. The lines are arranged symmetrically; that is, there is no distinction between DTE and DCE. One line of each pair is used for data, the other for control. Thus, if UPI were used as a PC-to-modem interface, modem commands and responses would flow over control lines conveniently segregated from data, and the need for RS-232-style single-function modem control circuits would be eliminated. UPI holds great promise as a successor to RS-232, but has yet to dislodge it from its pedestal.

CABLES

We now consider both garden-variety electrical cables, such as coaxial and twisted-pair cable, and more exotic types, such as optical fibers. First, here's a glossary of relevant terms:

The *gauge* of a wire is a measure of the conductor's cross-sectional area. Everywhere but in the United States, gauge units are called standard wire gauge (swg), often pronounced "swag." U.S. standards set forth exactly the same unit of measurement, but instead call it American wire gauge (awg). The smaller the gauge number, the thicker is the wire. Ordinary telephone wire, for example, is 22 gauge. Among other things, thicker cables (smaller gauge numbers) offer less *resistance* to electrical current. Resistance, measured in *ohms*, is the technical term for the opposition of an electrical conductor to the passage of current. It is the ratio of the voltage to the resulting current flow expressed in *amperes*. Electrical resistance is similar to a pipe's opposition to fluid flow. For example, if you blow with a constant pressure (the mechanical analog of voltage), it is harder to force a stream of air (current) through a narrow drinking straw (large gauge number) than through a wide pipe (small gauge number).

Table 4.2 relates sample awg numbers to cross-sectional areas in circular mils (a *mil* is a thousandth of an inch; a *circular mil* is the area of a circle one mil in diameter) and to electrical resistance per 1,000 feet of wire length. The temperature is specified because, for almost all metals used in wires, resistance rises as the metal becomes warmer.

The electrical conductor, most often copper, may be either a solid cylindrical wire or a bunch of very thin strands twisted together. The two types have different electrical qualities, and the stranded kind is physically more flexible.

Capacitance, briefly discussed in Chapter 1, is both a measure of capacity to store electricity and an inherent attribute of all electrical cables that stymies the clear flow of

TABLE 4.2: Sample standard wire gauges

AWG #	Area in circular mils	Ohms/1,000 ft at 20° C
0000	211,600	.0490
0	105,530	.0983
10	10,381	.9989
22	642	16.14
36	25	414.8

signals. As the signal voltage injected into a cable changes, the cable absorbs or releases some energy, like an electrical sponge, thereby slowing down the appearance of the signal at the receiver, altering its wave shape, and possibly messing up its phase or other attributes as well.

Cable capacitance is normally quoted in *picofarads per foot (pf/ft)*. A 50-foot run of a typical cable having a capacitance of 12 pf/ft presents a total capacitance of 600 pf. This measurement indicates the effect of a given cable on a signal of a given frequency. The lower the total capacitance, the higher the usable frequency will be. For digital signals, increased capacitance means more "rounding off" of the square-wave corners in transit.

Plenum refers to a chamber or conduit that is part of a habitable structure's air-moving system. The plenum of a building includes ventilation shafts and heating ducts, which tend to be inviting for cable runs. Running cables in plenum, however, usually involves meeting fire codes, which often dictate the use of cable specially designed for the purpose, or require the installation of metal cable ducts within the plenum. Special *plenum cables* have a fire-resistant outer jacket of Teflon or similar material. They are costlier than ordinary cables typically jacketed with a flammable plastic such as polyvinyl chloride (PVC).

Electromagnetic Interference or *Radio Frequency Interference, EMI/RFI*, refers to inter-ference in the electromagnetic spectrum, such as radio, TV, and X-rays. Many electronic devices, including PCs, can generate such interference. FCC regulations dictate maximum permissible levels of interference that microcomputers and similar devices may emit. The agency has recently complained that many imported PC clones exceed the EMI/RFI-generation limits. PCs are supposed to be FCC-certified, but many imported clones are apparently sold with false certifications.

EMI/RFI is what shielded cable protects your signals from. An acquaintance of ours lives in the Twin Peaks area of San Francisco, in the shadow of the city's TV and radio antennae. He picks up radio station KOIT on his modem. Rock music blares through the speaker when the modem is making a connection. Now, that's RFI. Curiously, it does not seem to cause data transmission errors.

Twisted Pair

A twisted pair (Figure 4.12a) consists of two conductors, usually copper wires, each covered by a (typically plastic) insulating jacket, and twisted together to form a cable. The twisting gives each wire equal exposure to any EMI noise source in the cable's vicinity, making it likely that the interference effects will cancel out. Such cables are also used for some of the electrical wiring in automobiles. Some cables contain *multiple twisted*

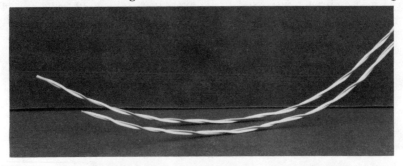

FIGURE 4.12a: Twisted pair cable. *Reprinted by permission of Black Box Corporation, Pittsburgh PA. Copyright ©1987. All rights reserved.*

pairs for use where one connection embraces several circuits. Often, especially in the case of multiple pairs, we find *shielded twisted pairs*, where each pair of wires is wrapped in an aluminized-mylar or aluminized-polyester foil shield.

Twisted-pair cable is cheap, flexible, and robust, and is used in a multitude of data communication applications. Its bandwidth is often quoted as a relatively low 10 Mbps, but recent reports suggest that the figure may actually be higher.

Multiconductor Cable

Multiconductor cable consists of multiple individual wires enclosed in a flexible PVC jacket, as shown in Figure 4.12b. The insulator of each strand is color-coded, as you'd expect. For more demanding applications, multiconductor cables are also available with shielding. Aluminized-plastic foil reduces high-frequency emissions; braided copper reduces low-frequency emissions. Multiconductor cables can be had with either or both of these shields.

Ribbon Cable

Ribbon cable (Figure 4.12c) consists of several conductors embedded in a flat insulating shell. It is cheaper than multiple twisted-pair, and is very flexible (it can even be folded). Furthermore, special D-series and Centronics connectors can be attached to ribbon cable by a snap-on mechanism, which involves much less fuss than the soldering or crimping required with other cable types. Ribbon is best suited to straight-through interconnects requiring a single connector type; the ease with which connectors can be attached makes this cable ideal for bus applications where many devices must be attached to a single cable. Ribbon is sold in standard configurations of 9, 15, 25, 36, 37, and 50 conductors.

Ribbon cable is often used for parallel-device hookups requiring Centronics connectors at both ends. For PC links to parallel printers, though, where a DB25 is needed at one end of the link, multiconductor cable is the rule.

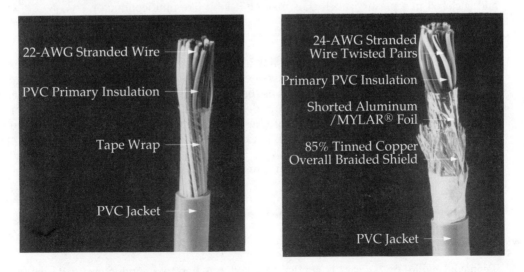

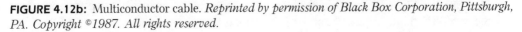

FIGURE 4.12b: Multiconductor cable. *Reprinted by permission of Black Box Corporation, Pittsburgh, PA. Copyright ©1987. All rights reserved.*

FIGURE 4.12c: Ribbon cable. *Reprinted by permission of Black Box Corporation, Pittsburgh, PA. Copyright ©1987. All rights reserved.*

While generally less sturdy than multiconductor cable, the ribbon type can easily be run under carpeting and through other constricted spaces. Inside the PC, ribbon is used for connecting the disk drives to their controllers. This particular cable is not shielded, but shielded versions are also made. At least one company offers ribbon cable rolled transversely and enclosed in a plastic jacket, thus making it look like multiconductor.

Coaxial Cable

Usually just called *coax*, coaxial cable, shown in Figure 4.12d, consists of a solid copper, or copper-clad steel, central conductor embedded in a thick insulator. This is surrounded by an electrical shield, which also functions as the second conductor and is, in turn, enclosed in an insulating jacket. The shield may be braided copper or solid aluminum, depending on the application. Of the many grades and varieties of coax, the best known are those employed for audio and video interconnects. Coax is expensive and has limited flexibility, but offers much better frequency performance (about a 300-Mps bandwidth) than the alternatives listed above. It is the standard cabling in some relatively high-performance LANs, including Ethernet.

Several standard grades of coaxial cable are available. The most common, RG 62 A/U, is used by IBM's 3270 series of equipment, among other applications.

Twinaxial Cable

Twinaxial cable, or *twinax*, is similar to coax, but has two conductors at its center, as illustrated in Figure 4.12e. It is used for local connections between IBM's System/36™ and System/38™ minicomputers and their terminals.

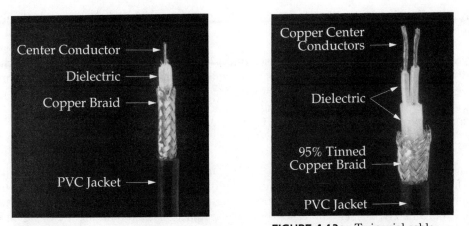

FIGURE 4.12d: Coaxial cable **FIGURE 4.12e:** Twinaxial cable

Optical Fibers

Optical fibers carry light waves modulated to carry data at rates in the hundreds of Mbps. The cables are built with, typically, one or two fine strands of glass wrapped in a web of tough plastic fibers to provide tensile strength, all enclosed in a PVC jacket, as shown in Figure 4.12f. Each conductor strand is composed of a central glass core surrounded by a *cladding* of glass with different optical properties. The light wave is carried through the core, and the cladding functions almost as a mirror to keep the wave within the core. In some newer types of optical fiber, the light conductors are made of plastic, rather than glass.

Optical-fiber cables have important advantages over electrical wires: their much smaller girth occupies far less space in cramped cable ducts; they are not susceptible to interference; and they emit no electromagnetic field. On the other hand, they are vastly more difficult than electrical cables to interconnect. Two optical fibers can be joined end-to-end only after careful polishing and alignment; then they must be fitted into a special connector. The construction of branching optical fiber cables poses even greater problems. For these reasons, fiber-optic links are typically used for point-to-point connections requiring high

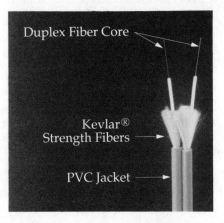

FIGURE 4.12f: Optical fiber cable. *Reprinted by permission of Black Box Corporation, Pittsburgh PA. Copyright © 1987. All rights reserved.*

bandwidth. Thanks to its complete freedom from radio emissions, optical cable lends itself to high-security applications, and certain military establishments have mandated that all new communication links be fiber-optic.

Prior to 1988, fiber-optic links were seldom used for PC communications except where security outweighed other considerations. Over the next few years, as installation becomes easier and less expensive, and as the demand for communication speed soars, many new applications may appear for this exciting technology. In particular, optical fiber will find widespread use as a connective medium for PC LANs.

Shielded vs. Unshielded Cables

The shield in a shielded cable serves two distinct but related purposes. First, it cuts down on radio-frequency (RF) emanations from the cable that might interfere with nearby electronic instruments (and incense the FCC). Second, it limits the effect of outside interference on the cable. Unfortunately, a shield increases the cable's capacitance, so that, all else being equal, unshielded cable can cover greater distances.

For signal integrity, shielded cable is generally preferable to unshielded, but unshielded cable is quite acceptable in environments not subject to high levels of electrical noise. For some devices, such as line drivers (Chapter 5), unshielded cable is preferred.

Classes of Cable

The National Fire Protection Association (NFPA) establishes regulations governing the manufacture of electrical equipment for use in the United States. After investigating the interaction of electrical cables and fires, the NFPA defined four distinct classes of cable for use in data communications:

CMP—for plenum and other air-handling spaces

CMR—for riser shafts

CM—for general use

CMX—for restricted use (exposed lengths shorter than 10 feet)

This classification system became effective on January 1, 1988, along with the NFPA's ruling that cable manufacturers must submit their products for testing to the Underwriters Laboratories (UL). New cable installations should comply strictly with NFPA requirements. State and local government agencies are charged with enforcing these codes, and a consumer's failure to follow them can result in fines and wasted effort, not to mention aggravated fire damage.

Connectors

Here's a quick rundown on connectors:

- Twisted-pair wires can be spliced by soldering their conductors together.
- Coaxial cables should always be joined with proper connectors; a T-shaped type facilitates cable "branches." Every connector interposed in a circuit, however, causes some deterioration of the signal, so continuous cable is often preferable.
- Devices can be hooked into coax without connectors by means of *vampire taps,* gadgets that allow a spike to be inserted through the braid and insulator, making contact with the central conductor.

■ Long coax runs should be terminated in a way that prevents reflections, ensuring that when a signal reaches the endpoint, it "dies" there, rather than being echoed back through the cable. Appropriate terminators, resembling single-ended connectors, are available from cable suppliers.

Cabling for RS-232

The ideal cable for RS-232 interconnects is a shielded multiconductor type. When such cables are made specifically for RS-232 applications, they commonly have 4, 7, 9, 12, 16, or 25 conductors. Each conductor is an insulated copper strand, and all conductors are wrapped together in an aluminized-mylar shield enclosed by an outer sheath of Teflon or PVC.

Ribbon cable may also be used for straight-through RS-232 applications when shielding is not desired.

A true anecdote about cables may be illuminating. Some scientists at a government research lab had occasion to use a supercomputer to create very detailed diagrams on a huge flat-bed plotter. Each plot took about ten hours—acceptable when everything went well. Often, however, a plot proceeded smoothly for the first seven or eight hours, only to go berserk as a result of program bugs or faulty input data. The researchers determined that it would be best to preview each plot on a graphics terminal before sending it to the plotter. Unfortunately, while the plotter was right next to the computer, the only available graphics terminal was housed in a building two-thirds of a mile away and, because of some obscure military regulation, could not be moved.

Feverishly searching for a solution, the scientists discovered an underground cable duct leading from the computer building to the home of the graphics terminal. Closer, and slightly grimier, inspection revealed a run of disused coax lurking in the duct. Unaware that the cable's electrical characteristics were totally incompatible with the transmission speed they planned to use, they set up a one-way RS-232 link, configured to run at 9,600 bps, using this cable (with a little spare telephone wire tacked on the end because the coax didn't quite reach). Miraculously, it worked.

It was fortunate indeed that the cable duct ran under an open meadow occupied only by grazing cows. Cows, after all, generate little or no electrical noise.

Further information about cables, specifically the IBM Cabling System, is presented in Chapter 14.

LOCAL SERIAL COMMUNICATIONS

RS-232 is probably both the most widely used and the least-standard standard in data communications. In this chapter, we see what's involved in using RS-232 to connect PCs to serial printers and other devices, explore available gadgetry, and present some case studies.

MODEM ELIMINATORS

Using RS-232 for a connection that does not involve a modem or other communications device amounts to establishing an interface between two DTEs. This method, called *direct connect*, may serve to hook one PC to another, a terminal or PC to a local host, or a PC to any serial device, such as a printer or plotter.

Direct connect interfacing is a little complicated, for several reasons. For one thing, RS-232 is an *asymmetric* interface, intended to connect a DTE and a DCE, which are configured rather differently. An RS-232 connection between DTEs requires an adapter known as a *modem eliminator*.

Second, not every device you'd expect to be a DTE is actually configured that way. For example, some microcomputers have an RS-232 port configured as a DCE to allow adapterless connection to a serial printer. This is certainly a convenience, but can easily cause confusion. On IBM PCs and compatibles, fortunately, most RS-232 ports are DTEs— but not all, so be careful.

Finally, the elimination of modems still leaves us with a load of modem control lines on our hands. It makes sense to use them for other purposes, such as flow control (see below). The problem is that no standard exists, so different computers and printers use different flow-control schemes.

Direct connect, then, is fraught with peril. Facilitating such an interface calls for some knowledge of RS-232, detailed documentation for the devices to be connected, and perhaps a few test instruments.

Flow Control Arrangements

PC printers are usually buffered, meaning that they have a few kilobytes of memory in which characters are stored between reception from the PC and actual printing. Printers are deliberately designed to receive characters faster than they can print them. This keeps printing smooth and efficient, but causes data to back up in the buffer. Therefore, a printer must be able to tell the PC to pause when the buffer is getting full, and to resume sending data when the buffer begins to empty again. This process is known as *flow control*. The *hardware flow control* method, supported by PCs, exploits unused RS-232 lines.

A printer operating under hardware flow control manipulates an RS-232 circuit to manage the data flow from the PC. The printer holds this line ON when ready to accept data, and turns it OFF when its buffer is stuffed. DTR is most often used for this purpose. Recall, however, that both the PC and the printer are nominally DTEs, and thus are sources for, rather than recipients of, DTR signals. The PC can hardly read the printer's DTR signal on its own DTR circuit; that would be like trying to hear with your mouth. The printer's flow-control signal must therefore be fed to some other circuit where the PC can see it. DOS expects a flow-control signal on DSR. In a page or two, we'll examine the adapters that make this possible.

An alternative method, called *software flow control,* relies on the ASCII characters Control-S and Control-Q, also called XOFF and XON, respectively. The printer sends the computer a Control-S character to suspend the flow and a Control-Q to restart it. Readers having experience with a PC running under DOS will be familiar with this mechanism: typing Control-S freezes the screen, after which any character (not necessarily Control-Q) restarts output. This technique is also used in many operating or timesharing systems to control output to terminals. It has the advantage of working over the data lines, which means that it will work on phone-modem links. Software flow control's disadvantages are its susceptibility to transmission errors and, in applications involving a printer, the necessity that the printer be equipped with a data transmitter, in most cases to send only two characters.

A few versions of MS-DOS support software flow control, although the bulk of the work is actually done by the BIOS. Only certain non-PC-compatible MS-DOS machines have this feature.

Many printers offer a choice of pins for hardware control, perhaps selected by a jumper. Some are capable of using either hardware or software flow control, selected by a switch. Again, DOS and OS/2 support only the hardware method.

Uses for Modem Eliminators

A modem eliminator, also called a *null modem,* replaces a pair of modems for a connection between two RS-232 devices configured as DTEs. This device would be aptly described as a "DTE-to-DTE adapter," but no one uses the term.

A modem eliminator must do three things:

1. Cross-connect the two data lines, so that a transmission by one device is received by the other.

2. Make any necessary cross-connection to provide a path for hardware flow-control signals. For PC-to-printer hookups, this means connecting the circuit that the printer uses for flow control to the PC's DSR line.

3. As much as possible, make it look to each device as if a modem were in place. Some communications software will not work unless it sees valid modem-control signals, particularly DSR, CTS, and CD. This could be important, for example, for file transfer over PC-to-PC links.

Figure 5.1 shows a wiring diagram for a modem eliminator to connect a PC to a serial printer using DTR for flow control. Many other configurations of modem eliminator are marketed to suit the needs of other DTE combinations.

Figure 5.2 is a photograph of a typical modem eliminator. We tend to think of modem eliminators as little boxes. These look like two back-to-back DB25 connectors and cost

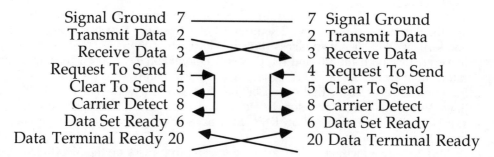

Signal Ground 7 ———————— 7 Signal Ground
Transmit Data 2 — 2 Transmit Data
Receive Data 3 — 3 Receive Data
Request To Send 4 — 4 Request To Send
Clear To Send 5 — 5 Clear To Send
Carrier Detect 8 — 8 Carrier Detect
Data Set Ready 6 — 6 Data Set Ready
Data Terminal Ready 20 — 20 Data Terminal Ready

FIGURE 5.1: Modem eliminator

between \$7.50 and \$40. Since all they do is reroute signals between circuits, they are very simple, contain no electronic components, and require no power.

In practice, modem eliminator boxes are less common than modem eliminator cables, also called *crossover cables*. These are nothing more than RS-232 cables with the necessary cross-wiring done internally. Ordinary types, without cross-connections, are known as *straight-through cables*.

Nomenclature may have unexpected importance. When a colleague of the authors bought his first PC, an IBM AT, he already owned a serial printer. He had a straight-through cable, so he figured he needed a modem eliminator to complete the connection. Unfortunately, he knew too much for his own good, and had a lot of trouble finding the right box. Radio Shack had a modem eliminator but with an inappropriate configuration. At ComputerLand®, the salespeople didn't know what he was talking about, and intimated that *he* didn't, either. He was puzzled. Surely lots of people needed to connect serial printers to PCs. How did they manage, knowing even less than he? What he needed, he eventually discovered, was a "serial printer cable for a PC," which has the appropriate crossovers and is readily available at any computer store. Moral: knowing what you need may not be nearly as important as knowing what the locals call it.

Remember, then, that a "PC modem cable" is of the straight-through variety, and different from a "serial printer cable for a PC," which is a modem eliminator cable. Don't try to interchange them.

FIGURE 5.2: Modem eliminator. *Reprinted with permission of Black Box Corporation, Pittsburgh, PA. Copyright ©1987. All rights reserved.*

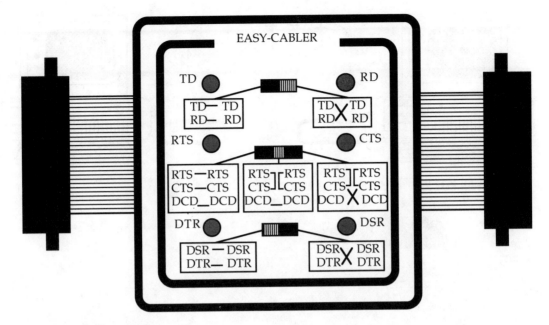

FIGURE 5.3: Easy-Cabler

Configuring Modem Eliminators

Making a direct RS-232 connection between pieces of equipment may call for some study to figure out which cross-connections are necessary. Several available tools can help, like the Easy-Cabler shown in Figure 5.3. This device makes it easy (hence the clever name) to run through the twelve wiring combinations most likely to work. This and similar gadgets are available from Black Box, Datacom Northwest, Inmac, and many other sources.

Once you've found the appropriate configuration, you can either look for a suitably configured modem eliminator or cable, order one built to spec, or build one yourself.

LINE DRIVERS AND LIMITED-DISTANCE MODEMS

Line Drivers

Suppose you want to connect a PC to a host in another building two miles away. Assume that the two buildings are already connected by an underground cable run, and that the connection must be made with RS-232 interfaces at both ends. How would you span the distance? Modems would do the trick, of course, but they'd be expensive and would limit the speed attainable. Fortunately, devices called RS-232 *line drivers*, or *Line Driver units (LDUs)*, are made especially for extending RS-232 beyond its usual reaches, up to perhaps 25 miles. Some are intended for use on customer-owned lines and others for local leased metallic-circuit telephone lines (copper pairs).

Figure 5.4 depicts line drivers as normally used in a point-to-point link, in matched pairs. Some models are also suitable for multipoint operation. Figure 5.5 shows a couple of LDUs.

LDUs resemble modems in that they are usually configured as DCEs, although some conveniently offer switch-selectable DTE or DCE operation. Indeed, many LDUs support full modem handshaking (i.e., they handle RS-232 control circuits just as a modem would).

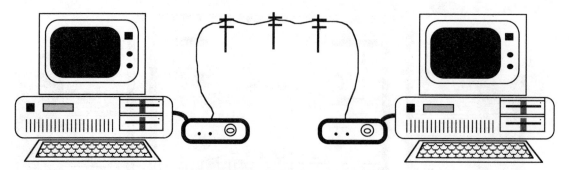

FIGURE 5.4: Line drivers in a point-to-point link

FIGURE 5.5a: Line driver unit. *Reprinted with permission of Black Box Corporation, Pittsburgh, PA. Copyright ©1987. All rights reserved.*

FIGURE 5.5b: Line driver unit. *Reprinted with permission of Black Box Corporation, Pittsburgh, PA. Copyright ©1987. All rights reserved.*

They can, of course, pass only data signals across the communication link, typically with a top speed of either 9,600 or 19,200 bps. Both asynchronous and synchronous types are sold. LDUs can operate over considerable distances with the balanced-line technique described in Chapter 4. Thus, bidirectional transfer normally requires four wires; a regular four-conductor telephone cable is likely to work admirably. Some LDUs, though, will even work on two-wire connections.

The range of a line driver is not fixed, but depends on both transmission speed and the quality (primarily the gauge) of the cable. The higher the data rate, the shorter is the distance that can reliably be covered. The relation of speed to distance for a typical line driver with a given cable type is:

Data rate, bps:	110	1,200	4,800	9,600	19,200
Distance, miles:	18	7.5	4.5	3.2	1.2

Speed and distance specifications for LDUs are normally quoted for an unshielded cable of some given gauge. As noted in Chapter 4, the extra capacitance of shielded cable severely restricts its performance.

An alternative to traditional LDUs are units designed to operate over fiber-optic connections. These do not generally provide much greater speed or distance, but the fiber medium does have some inherent advantages, such as improved security.

LDUs can often be used to advantage even over small distances. Suppose a company installs a PBX that outputs call-detail records through an RS-232 port. (Call-detail information consists of data about each call, similar to what shows up on a telephone bill.) The company wants to feed this call-detail output into a PC located a thousand feet away in order to generate a breakdown of long-distance charges for internal use. The distance is short enough that a straight RS-232 connection might serve, but long enough that its performance would be questionable. Moreover, the company wisely considers such a solution risky because of the sensitive nature of the data: an error in even a single bit could significantly affect the company's accounts. Other approaches might work, but an excellent solution is to install a pair of LDUs.

Although line drivers are not well known to most PC users, they are invaluable for certain applications. Universities, not surprisingly, make widespread use of them, as do some large business organizations.

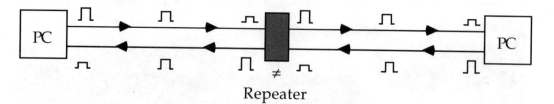

Repeater

FIGURE 5.6: Repeater

LDUs are sold by Black Box, Dynapac, Gandalf, Inmac, and RAD. The simplest async units cost less than $100 each; synchronous LDUs cost two or three times as much.

Repeaters

A *repeater,* also called a *booster,* can be inserted along a run of cable to boost signal strength. A repeater for RS-232 or Centronics links, costing about $100, consists of two ports back to back; each signal is received by one port and then retransmitted by the other. In this way, all the signals are regenerated as they pass through; if a signal has deteriorated (i.e., fallen to near zero voltage), it is boosted back to an acceptable level, as illustrated in Figure 5.6. (Figure 5.7 shows a Centronics repeater.) Thus, a repeater inserted at the midpoint of a cable run doubles a link's effective range. Because some repeaters are powered devices, installation may be awkward if the cable midpoint is far from an electrical outlet. LDUs are

FIGURE 5.7: Centronics repeater. *Reprinted with permission of Black Box Corporation, Pittsburgh, PA. Copyright ©1987. All rights reserved.*

generally the preferred way to extend range, but repeaters may be superior when control signals must be passed from end to end of a link.

Short-Haul, Limited-Distance, and Medium-Distance Modems

Short-haul, or *limited-distance modems (LDMs),* whose names are interchangeable, take over where line drivers leave off. They will drive customer-owned or all-metallic leased lines over distances of 20 to 30 miles. These are true modems in that they communicate using analog signals. Nonetheless, they offer cheaper and faster performance than regular modems, since they are not constrained by many of the limitations, such as voice-frequency bandwidth, of normal phone lines.

RS-232 LDUs are sometimes incorrectly referred to as short-haul or limited-distance modems. Line drivers communicate digitally, of course, and are not true modems. They do perform a similar function, however, and fit into communication links much as modems do.

Medium-distance modems go one step further than LDMs, so to speak, extending communication over the same circuits to distances of about 50 miles.

RS-232 GADGETS AND ACCESSORIES

Mail-order outfits like Black Box, Inmac, and Misco offer an amazing variety of accessories for RS-232. Here is a sampling.

Switch boxes allow several PCs to share a printer or modem, or allow a single PC to talk to any of several devices through one port. The simplest type of switch box, called an *ABC switch,* lets two devices (A and B) share, or be shared by, a third device (C), as shown in Figure 5.8. An *ABCD switch* connects any one device with up to three others, and so on. Manual switch boxes can be purchased for as little as $30, but high-quality units are priced at around $100 and up. For $400 to $800, a system can even be equipped with code-operated switches, "hands-off" models switched by special sequences of control characters

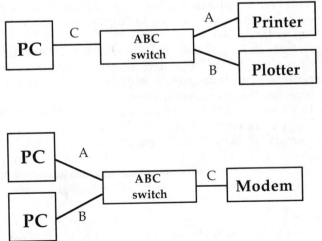

FIGURE 5.8: Switch boxes

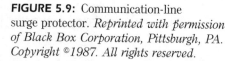

FIGURE 5.9: Communication-line surge protector. *Reprinted with permission of Black Box Corporation, Pittsburgh, PA. Copyright ©1987. All rights reserved.*

sent by the PC. Switch boxes are available to interconnect either serial or Centronics devices. When buying a switch box, give some thought to choosing a model with connectors whose genders are convenient for existing cables, if any.

Gender changers, also termed *gender matchers* and *gender menders*, enable you to plug together two identical connectors. Male-to-male and female-to-female types are available for about $10 each. "Gender canceller" would probably be a better name for such a device because, once it's in place, the genders of the connectors are not evident; the gender changer just mates two terminations of the same kind, making the entire connection symmetrical. Modem eliminators are sometimes erroneously advertised as gender changers; properly speaking, a gender changer has straight-through wiring.

Surge Protectors shield electronics from voltage surges on communication lines. One unit is shown in Figure 5.9. Surge sources include lightning, static, proximity to power lines, and, according to one broad-minded manufacturer, the detonation of thermonuclear devices. A surge protector is often a good idea not only because a big surge might burn out a circuit board or two, but also because small surges might degrade some component to the point of causing a subtle, intermittent, infuriating problem.

Surge protectors are available for both RS-232 lines and telephone lines. We particularly recommend phone line protectors for installations in areas subject to frequent electrical storms. Do not confuse the surge protectors discussed here with those used on power lines: their functions are much the same, but the devices are different.

Jumper Boxes consist of two back-to-back DB25s, with the wiring between the connectors left for the user to complete. The pins of each connector are brought out either to solder terminals or to patch pins. The jumper box is configured using jumper wires. Similar devices are available with a pair of Centronics connectors, or with one DB25 and one Centronics. They are useful for do-it-yourself modem eliminators, loopback adapters (to be described in the section on troubleshooting), and special-purpose devices. A typical jumper box is pictured in Figure 5.10.

Portable Buffers may be hard to find, but they occasionally come in handy. Such a device comprises an RS-232 port, a few kilobytes of RAM, and a battery. You can feed data into a portable buffer from one RS-232 device, unplug it, and attach it to another RS-232 device,

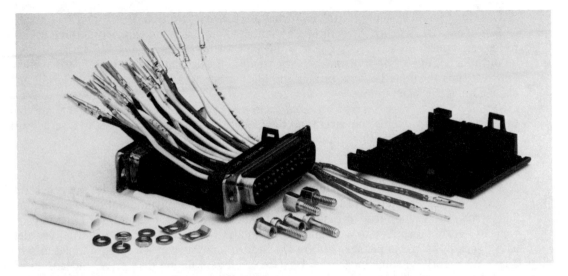

FIGURE 5.10: Jumper box. *Reprinted with permission of Black Box Corporation, Pittsburgh, PA. Copyright ©1987. All rights reserved.*

which then reads the stored data. Floppy disks are clearly preferable for carrying data between devices, but compatible floppy drives are often unavailable. This clever idea seems to have originated with the U.S. military, which built portable buffers to transfer data between ground-based computers and those on aircraft. Note that you cannot use a regular printer buffer for this purpose, because stored data are lost when you unplug the power cord.

Print buffers assist the PC user by acting as "reservoirs" for print files. Installed on either a serial or parallel connection between PC and printer, a buffer accepts data at high speed from the computer, then parcels it out little by little to the printer. This does nothing for the printer, but can greatly reduce the time a PC is tied up spitting out a print file. It's true that printers usually have their own internal buffers, but these tend to be small, typically just a few hundred bytes. External print buffers often accommodate 64 or 256 kilobytes, enough for most documents.

Work can be found for print buffers in other contexts, too—sometimes very creatively. Suppose you want to connect a serial printer to a PC over a telephone-modem link. Unless the printer is very fast, flow control is likely to be a obstacle: PCs accept only hardware flow control from printers, and such flow-control signals cannot be passed over a modem link. A print buffer between the printer and its modem should not only resolve the flow-control problem but also eliminate idle time on the telephone link. A buffered modem would be an equally acceptable solution.

Parallel/serial interface converters convert an RS-232 data stream into a Centronics parallel data stream, or vice versa, thus permitting a parallel printer to be connected to a serial port, or a serial printer to a Centronics port.

Case Study #1

Mr. Sergio Soppresso, a novice PC user, has an office containing a PC AT, a serial printer, a modem, and a plotter. The AT has both a standard Centronics port and one serial port. How can Mr. Soppresso connect all these devices so that any one is available for immediate use without continual switching of cables?

Of several possible solutions, the following are the most fruitful:

Install an ABCD switch. This three-way switch allows Sergio to connect all three devices to his serial port and access any one at a time.

Install a second serial port and an ABC switch. By dedicating one port to the modem and switching the other between printer and plotter, Serge can telecommunicate, print, and chew gum at the same time.

Install a parallel-to-serial converter and a second serial port. Now the printer is connected to the parallel port via the converter, and the modem and plotter are treated to a serial port apiece. This is essentially the solution Mr. Soppresso adopted.

Case Study #2

A company has bought an automated weighing system consisting of a scale connected to a PC. The PC will generate records of items weighed and send the data out of its serial port. The system designers intended that a printer be attached to the serial port, but the users want to feed the records into a second PC for analysis. The weigher PC must be regarded as a "black box": it can neither perform the needed analysis nor be reprogrammed to send its weight reports to some more useful device, such as a floppy disk drive. Indeed, all we can take for granted about this PC is that it runs DOS.

The problem is a weighty one, because the analysis PC is used for other purposes and cannot just sit idly waiting for data to arrive. It is already decided that a pair of LDUs will link the two PCs. How can we manage matters so that the second PC need not be dedicated?

One idea is to allow the second PC to send flow control information to the first. However, this is not a straightforward solution because, normally, only data can be passed between LDUs. This would appear to preclude the use of hardware flow control, the only flow-control method supported by DOS.

Conceivably, a flow-control converter might translate the PC's hardware signals into Control-S and Control-Q characters, easily transported by the LDUs, but such converters exist only for big computers, and carry appropriately hefty price tags.

One rather clever solution takes advantage of the fact that data will flow in only one direction, and uses the other data path to carry hardware flow-control signals. We could program the second PC to send such signals by manipulating its DTR line. We could then make a couple of jumper boxes, one to feed the DTR into the TD pin of one LDU, the other to feed the RD of the other LDU into the DSR input of the weighing PC. This rather complicated set of interconnections may make more sense with the aid of the first diagram in Figure 5.11. Assuming that the LDUs can handle noncharacter signaling, this might seem promising. It is likely, however, that the data are not buffered in the weighing PC, in which case bottling up its output might prevent any further weighing operations from being carried out.

The best solution is to put a buffer in the link; a regular printer buffer would probably do the job. The weighing PC's data can be stored there, and the other PC can unload the buffer at its leisure (the "buffer buffet" concept). Of course, the chosen buffer must be big enough for the job.

SETTING COM PORT PARAMETERS

Using a serial printer with a PC is about as straightforward as cutting your own hair. It can be done, but the obstacles involved constitute an argument for using a parallel printer instead.

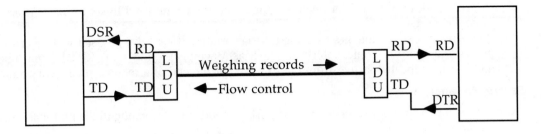

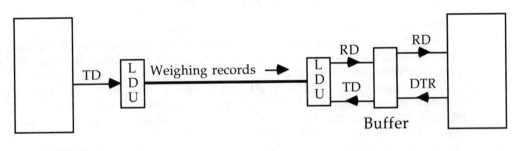

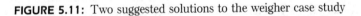

FIGURE 5.11: Two suggested solutions to the weigher case study

It turns out that, once the wiring is figured out, the main problem with connecting serial printers to PCs is setting the ports up correctly. This is mostly a matter of dealing with, or getting around, the operating system.

Serial Printers

It's debatable whether hooking printers to PCs is truly a matter of data communications. Certainly, most datacom books do not address the issue. The subject is included here because people need a great deal of guidance with it, and because it is intimately related to communications.

The PC printer market includes both serial printers, which connect to RS-232 ports, and parallel printers, which connect to Centronics ports. Both DOS and OS/2 are more oriented to parallel printers, but it can be quite reasonable to use either or both types. Here are some factors to consider when choosing between parallel and serial printers:

A printer's performance and output quality are in no way affected by the type of interface it uses. These characteristics, elaboration of which is beyond the scope of this book, must be considered on a model-by-model basis. Not many printers will operate with both interfaces; of the few that will, some have a port of each type built in, while others have one port standard and the other as an installable option.

The parallel printer offers several advantages: Fewer devices usually compete for parallel than for serial ports; data sent to a parallel printer need not be serialized for transmission, so printing ties up the PC for a shorter time; and there's no need to set up parameters for a parallel port.

There are two advantages to using a serial printer: It can also be used with microcomputers that lack Centronics interfaces (such as Macintoshes and some CP/M™ machines); and it can be located farther from the PC, even at the end of a modem-phone connection.

Setting Parameters

Before any PC program can use a COM port, the port must be configured with the following parameters:

- Data rate (110, 300, 1,200, 2,400, etc., bps)
- Parity option (odd, even, or none)
- Number of data bits per character (5, 6, 7, or 8)
- Number of stop bits per character (1, 1.5, or 2)

Parallel ports, by contrast, require no such programming.

When a COM port is used for a modem connection, any application program that makes use of the modem, such as a communications package, will itself take care of programming the port. In these cases, the user normally must provide the requisite parameters at some point. When, on the other hand, a COM port is used with a printer, no matter whether printing is effected by means of the operating system's PRINT command or directly from within application programs, the operating parameters for the port must be established in advance via the operating system's MODE command.

The MODE command must be the most confusing in DOS. It does several unrelated things; its syntax is hard to remember; its default parameter values are not what most people would expect, let alone choose; and some clone makers with customized versions of MS-DOS have extended its functions to include such niceties as the selection of processor speed when two or more clock rates are offered. At any rate, one of MODE's many talents is setting COM port parameters. Here's an example of the MODE command used to set COM1 to transmit eight-bit characters with one stop bit for a 1,200-bps serial printer operating without parity:

    MODE COM1:1200,N,8,1,P

The first argument, which identifies the port to be configured, must be COM1: or COM2:. This is immediately followed by the data rate; your choices here are limited to 110, 150, 300, 600, 1,200, 2,400, 4,800, or 9,600 bps. (The MODE command processor supplied with DOS version 3.3 extends the range of port arguments to include COM3: and COM4:, and the speed options to include 19,200 bps.) Next comes the parity option: "N" for no parity, "E" for even, or "O" for odd. (Parity is discussed in detail in the next chapter.) If this parameter is omitted, DOS will select even parity; it's a good idea always to include an argument for clarity. The fourth parameter, number of data bits per character, may be 7 (the default value) or 8. Fifth comes the number of stop bits, 1 or 2; the default value is 1 except when the speed is 110 bps, in which case it is 2. The final argument is either a "P" or is omitted; this parameter does not affect the operation of the port itself, but rather alerts DOS to the fact that a printer is attached to the port. To be precise, this "P" tells DOS to expect hardware flow control on the port, and thus not to get upset if the attached device sometimes conveys its preoccupation with data by lowering Clear To Send or Data Set Ready.

You must consult the printer manual to determine which values should be selected for these parameters. When using a printer, always include the final P. If the DOS MODE command sequence described above doesn't seem to be working, check the manual for your particular DOS version.

For the purpose of sending it data, the printer is identified by the "name" of the port to which it is connected. DOS provides a device pseudonym, PRN, to identify the default printer, so that printer may be used without a port specification. (The PRINT command gives you the option of specifying a port, but many application programs will send a print stream only to the default printer.) The fact that PRN is always equated with LPT1, however, makes the pseudonym seem superfluous. If you wish to use as your default printer one connected to a parallel port, that printer *must* be attached to LPT1. If the default printer is serially connected, you must change the meaning of PRN by using another mode of the MODE command, such as:

MODE LPT1 = COM1

This redirects to COM1 any data a program sends to PRN (or to LPT1). Using this form, you can redirect references to an LPT port to any COM port. If you redirect LPT1, PRN will be automatically redirected along with it. Typing MODE PRN = COM1 might seem to be a simpler and clearer way to handle this, but doing so will just get you an error message. The philosophy appears to be that COM*n* identifies a port, but implies nothing about what is connected to it; LPT*n*, on the other hand, identifies a printer.

Since the port setup information is lost when a PC is turned off or RESET, the appropriate MODE commands must be given each time DOS is started (i.e., each time you boot the system). Such commands therefore belong in the AUTOEXEC.BAT file. If a COM port is shared between a printer and, say, a modem, whether by manually switching connectors or via a switch box, you must be careful to re-enter MODE commands as needed. After one such device has been used, then, the appropriate MODE COM command must be repeated to reconfigure the port.

Should the need arise, how can you hook up a printer at a speed not supported by MODE? (You will get an error complaint if your MODE command specifies a data rate not found on the "approved" list.) Some laser printers, for instance, can connect at 19,200 bps but, as noted earlier, this rate is not supported by early versions of DOS. If no solution is provided by the printer vendor, the best option is to find some public-domain software to do the job. One such program, called COMMODE, will set a COM port to any speed of which the hardware is capable.

6 ASCII TERMINALS AND THEIR EMULATION

The first communication application of PCs was that of emulating asynchronous terminals. The PC emulates, or mimics, a terminal so that the PC can replace the physical terminal for the purpose of connecting to a host. In this context, a *terminal* is a device that can be connected to a separate computer (the host), allowing a human being to interact with programs running in the host. We'll focus on the kind generally known as "ASCII terminals" or "asynchronous terminals," that operate asynchronously using the ASCII character set.

Beyond the scope of this chapter are many synchronous terminals, such as those in IBM's 3270 family (the most important to us) and special-purpose types, such as point-of-sale (POS) terminals. On the surface, synchronous terminals may appear very similar to the async variety, but under the hood they are quite different. We'll cover the 3270 type in Chapter 12.

ASYNCHRONOUS TERMINALS

There are dozens of different terminal types in use today. They vary in such attributes as screen size (24 lines by 80 columns being most common), keyboard layout, degree of screen control, character and block-mode options, and user interface. *Video Display Terminals (VDTs)* display their output on screens, while *hard-copy terminals* resemble typewriters. We shall concern ourselves solely with VDTs, not only because hard-copy terminals are rather rare these days, but also because PCs are not known for emulating them.

The best known async terminals are the DEC™ VT100™ and IBM 3101. Some other important specimens are the Lear Siegler ADM-3a®, the DEC VT52 and VT200 series, the Tektronix™ 4010, and the Televideo™ 900 series.

Characteristics of Async Terminals

As VDTs evolved from the old "glass teletypes," many features have appeared that we consider standard today:

- *A variety of operating features* are now offered on async terminals, including several line speeds (e.g., 110, 300, and 1,200 bps) and numerous options for parity and echoing (to be discussed later). Selections were originally made with switches, but keyboard commands are now more usual.

- *Screen control,* which evolved to take advantage of the inherent capabilities of a video display, encompasses several features. The most common are *cursor addressing* (moving the cursor to a selected position on the screen), control over display attributes (making characters blink, for example, or vary in brightness), and the insertion or deletion of lines and characters. The development of screen control paved the way for such applications as spreadsheet programs and full-screen text editors.

- *Graphics capabilities* have been incorporated into some terminals, facilitating the display of charts, graphs, and line drawings. All terminals now have microprocessors and memory, providing what is laughingly known as *intelligence*. This jazzes up the user interface and makes *local editing* possible. To set line speed, parity, and the like, the user can enter a setup mode and select options from a menu presented on the screen, rather than with hardware switches. Local editing permits data to be entered and changed locally, usually by the line or screenful, before being sent off to the host.

Uses for Terminals

The most important uses for terminals, and for PCs emulating terminals, are:
Connecting to timesharing systems or terminal-oriented applications on hosts. Strictly speaking, a *timesharing system* is one that hosts multiple users, doling out slices of computer time to each in round-robin fashion. Despite this sharing, each user appears to have sole access to the host. The term is more commonly used to identify a shared operating or suboperating system that supports interactive computing facilities for terminal users, as opposed, for example, to off-line job processing. Many hosts, including most minicomputers and some non-IBM mainframes, are designed primarily to interact with such terminals. Connection to IBM mainframes is possible, but the number of services available may be very limited. Such hosts are more often accessed via synchronous terminals, as discussed further in Chapter 12.

Accessing information utilities. Terminals provide access to many information sources, including public databases, bulletin boards, and multipurpose systems such as CompuServe.

Dialing into electronic mail services. Available services include MCI Mail and EasyLink™.

THE ASCII AND PC CHARACTER SETS

Here we consider the ASCII character set, and the extended version used by PCs. ASCII, pronounced "ASSkey," stands for American National Standard Code for Information Interchange. It comes to us courtesy of ANSI, the American National Standards Institute, which adopted it in 1963. The standard was based on character codes used well before that time in the Teletype™ Model 33, and is found intact in terminals made today. The version of ASCII in current use was defined by the ANSI X3.4 document, issued in 1977, and is also recognized as International Alphabet #5 (IA5).

ASCII is one of two character codes widely used by computers, the other being EBCDIC ("EBsidik"), or Extended Binary-Coded Decimal Interchange Code. EBCDIC is strongly associated with its inventor, IBM, which uses the code in almost all its products except PCs. Although a few other computer manufacturers also use EBCDIC, most minicomputers and all microcomputers rely on ASCII. Other obscure character sets, including *correspondence code* and *display code*, have been used in the past, but are now rare and irrelevant to PCs.

The character code associated with a given computer is mostly a matter of convention. With most machines, little or nothing inherent in the processor itself dictates the use of any particular code. Rather, the character set is established in the software created to run on the computer, and in the terminals and printers made to connect to it. If you wanted to be truly perverse, you could connect an EBCDIC terminal to a PC—assuming the terminal used RS-232—and write software to process text in EBCDIC.

A character code like ASCII or EBCDIC prescribes a method of representing characters so that they can be processed by computers. Most of us think of characters in graphic terms, such as the shapes that make up the letters and punctuation marks printed on this page. We distinguish characters by appearance, and have a remarkable facility for doing so. Computers, on the other hand, can deal only with bits, and need a way of encoding characters in bit form.

In addition to letters and numbers, a useful character set for a computer includes carriage return, backspace, and tabulation characters for controlling the printing and display of text. On a typewriter, these are best thought of as *functions*, but to a computer they are characters like any other. To construct a character code, you would select all the characters you deemed necessary, arrange them in some useful sequence (letters in alphabetical order, and so on), and then assign to them consecutive identification numbers beginning with zero. Inside the computer, each character is identified by its number.

The Seven-Bit Code

ASCII is a "seven-bit code": each character is represented by a unique sequence of seven bits. Seven bits provide space for 2^7, or 128, encoded characters, the total number in the ASCII set. (EBCDIC is an eight-bit code, with space for 256 characters, but since some sequences are unassigned, the number of characters is smaller than 256.) The full and official ASCII table, which can probably be found in more appendices of more books and manuals than anything else on earth, is faithfully reproduced in Appendix E.

ASCII's seven-bit codes turn out to be a bit of a nuisance. Most computers, and certainly all PCs, are designed to handle data in eight-bit bytes: memory is organized in bytes, processors manipulate data in bytes or multiples of bytes, and communication hardware tends to send and receive data eight bits at a time. Dealing with ASCII means being confronted with seven-bit quantities rattling around in eight-bit parcels. The obvious way to handle this is to use the "low," or rightmost, seven bits of each byte to hold an ASCII code and leave the "high," leftmost, eighth bit free for other purposes, as shown in Figure 6.1.

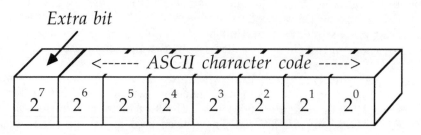

FIGURE 6.1: Seven-bit ASCII Code in an eight-bit field

Three things can be done with the eighth bit:

Nothing. Either ignore it altogether or set it always to zero. Transmitting (as opposed to storing or processing) ASCII data may then mean sending only seven bits for each character, thereby reducing transmission load. This waste of a bit may seem a bit of a waste, but it's often the best choice.

Use it to Extend the Character Set. Establish a convention whereby a 0 value for the eighth bit indicates that the low seven bits should be interpreted as ASCII; if the eighth bit instead has a 1 value, the low seven bits represent a character in some extended set. In other words, use character codes 0 to 127 for ASCII, and codes 128 to 255 for additional characters. IBM takes advantage of this scheme in its PC, adding 128 extra characters and defining the 256-character list as the "IBM PC Character Set." The extra codes represent letters with accent marks, Greek letters, some special symbols, and characters used for drawing block graphics on the PC screen. Although many PC manuals include tables of this character set, few such tables define the keystrokes used to generate certain control characters, so this information is given in Appendix E.

Use It for Parity During Transmission. Parity, a primitive means of error detection in some hosts, is little more than a cumbersome and inefficient relic, at least for PCs. However, it is still important enough to be discussed in a later section of this chapter.

You may have nothing to say about how the eighth bit is used, but if you do have a choice, here are some suggestions. Never use parity unless forced to do so by some host. For communication between PCs, the extended character set is likely to be valuable, although it requires transmitting full eight-bit data. For communicating with other ASCII systems, transmit data in seven-bit form, if possible.

A new eight-bit ASCII standard is in the works but, despite having been promised for several years, it has not yet materialized. Therefore, its impact on PCs, if any, remains to be seen.

PCs and ASCII

As we have said, the PC is basically an ASCII machine, but it doubles the size of the regular code set to accommodate a variety of other characters. Some of these are used to draw boxes, lines, and windows on the PC screen; some provide accented letters and the like for foreign languages; and others are useful for mathematical documents. The extra characters do not have corresponding keys on the standard PC keyboard. Each of the various foreign keyboards sold by IBM in other lands, however, does include keys for a relevant selection of these special codes.

The PC keyboard can generate much more than merely ASCII characters. The function keys, the cursor-control keys, and all key combinations involving Alt generate inputs that can be interpreted by programs, but these inputs are not characters; they have no character codes associated with them and cannot be stored in files.

HOW ASCII TERMINALS WORK

Now we delve into the grubby details of terminal operation and describe how characters are actually transmitted and received. The mechanisms described here, *start bits* and *stop bits*, are the underpinnings of all asynchronous communication.

Start and Stop Bits

Figure 6.2 illustrates, on an oscilloscope screen, what happens when a key is depressed on the keyboard of a terminal. An oscilloscope captures the waveform of the signal voltage on a wire and presents a snapshot, or *trace*, covering a fraction of a second. The duration of the trace depends on the line speed; at 1,200 bps, each bit lasts 1/1200th of a second, or 83.3 milliseconds. Our diagram depicts the transmission of a single character, the letter P.

Ten bits appear: seven for the ASCII code, called the *data bits*, plus an initial start bit, a final stop bit, and the extra eighth data bit. The ASCII table in Appendix E lists the binary code for P as 1010000. Since a bit voltage below the dashed line represents a MARK state (binary 1), and a voltage above the line represents SPACE (binary 0), the character sequence, read from left to right, seems to disagree with the ASCII code. This is because the bits for each character are transmitted in what most people perceive as *reverse order*. The low bit, the 0 on the far right of the code, is transmitted first, and so on through the high bit on the far left.

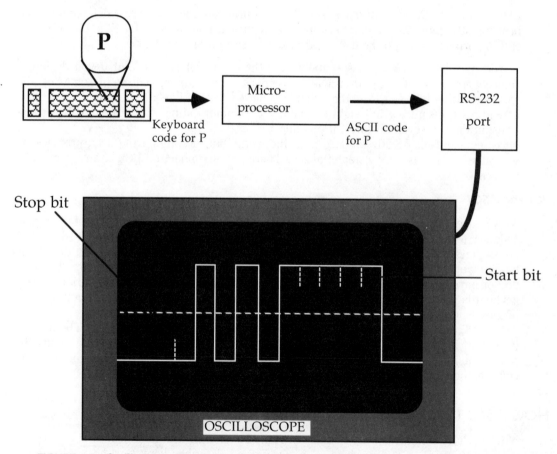

FIGURE 6.2: Oscilloscope picture of character sent by terminal

It's important to recognize that a total of three line conditions must be represented: in addition to 1s and 0s while data are being sent, there is also an idle condition during which no data are being sent. Thus we have three conditions (0-bit, 1-bit, idle) but only two states (MARK, SPACE) with which to express those conditions. It happens that MARK is usually used to represent the idle condition. This reflects telex-terminal requirements: as noted in Chapter 1, with telex, the session is terminated if SPACE is asserted for a long period of time.

Our depiction of SPACE at the top of the trace (positive voltage) and MARK at the bottom (negative voltage) follows RS-232 conventions. Illustrations of this kind drawn the other way around (i.e., reversing the voltage relationship) are equally valid, because what count are the comparative voltage conditions on the line.

Since a character may appear at any time, its beginning must be flagged in some way; otherwise, the receiver cannot distinguish between idle MARK and MARK representing a binary 1. The start bit, a bit-time of SPACE transmitted immediately before the first data bit, serves this purpose, signaling to the receiver that a character is arriving. Without a start bit, a character consisting of all 1s, for example, would be "invisible."

The stop bit that follows the last data bit is a bit-time's worth of MARK, which ensures a minimum gap between one character and the next. This allows the receiver time to reset and prepare for the next start bit. While a single stop bit is most common, some devices may require more than one; slow mechanical devices such as teletypes, for example, often require two. Standard numbers of stop bits are 1, 1 1/2, and 2. If the idea of a half-bit seems strange, remember that a bit in this context is only a unit interval of time. The sequence of one or more stop bits following a character is sometimes called a *stop element*—a better term, perhaps, since it allows no confusion between timing units and data bits.

The system we have been discussing is often called *start/stop communication*, and for practical purposes it is synonymous with asynchronous communication.

Framing Errors

We've seen how start and stop bits "frame" a character. The transmitter frames each outgoing character between a start and a stop bit; the receiver's job is to detect the frames and extract the correct data bits from them. Transmission errors, which can generate spurious bits and wipe out real bits, may wreak havoc with the receiver's perception of the correct framing.

A *framing error* is reported by receiving hardware when a stop bit is not detected when expected. Such an error can occur in three ways, illustrated in Figure 6.3. In (a), a spurious signal on an idle line is interpreted by the receiver as a start bit, and happens to be closely followed by a real transmitted character so positioned that one of its 0-bits (a SPACE) shows up when the receiver is expecting a stop bit (MARK). This misunderstanding is highlighted by the shaded area. In (b), the true start bit of a transmitted character is wiped out, and the receiver misinterprets a later 0-valued data bit as the start bit (left shaded area). If the line remains idle for a moment after the character is received, an incorrect character will be read. If the line is not idle, but another character quickly follows, then some 0-bit in the second character may be misinterpreted as the stop bit of the first (right shaded area), again resulting in error. In (c), the true stop bit of a character, shown as the drop to MARK, is messed up by a spurious signal, causing the line to drift into SPACE at the time MARK should appear. The line does fall to MARK afterward, but by then the damage has been done.

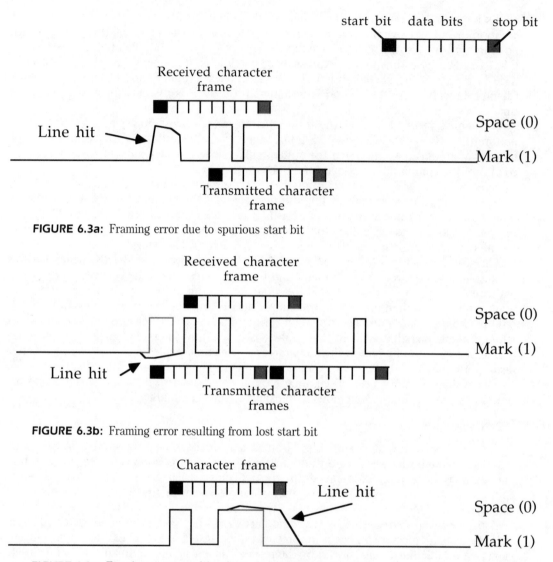

FIGURE 6.3a: Framing error due to spurious start bit

FIGURE 6.3b: Framing error resulting from lost start bit

FIGURE 6.3c: Framing error resulting from destruction of stop bit

When a framing error occurs, the associated character is usually discarded because it is suspect. It is sound practice for software to report framing errors to the user by means of a suitable diagnostic message, but most PC software packages simply ignore them.

It should be evident from the foregoing that errors producing "phantom" start bits can result in the undetected reception of spurious characters, as illustrated in Figure 6.4.

Characters per Second

Line speed normally specifies how many bits can be transmitted per second. To convert from bit rate to character rate, simply divide the line speed by the number of bits needed

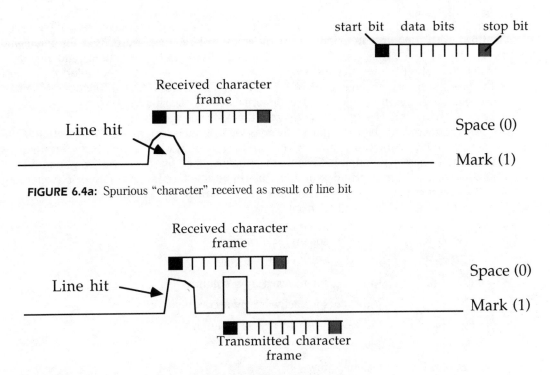

FIGURE 6.4a: Spurious "character" received as result of line bit

FIGURE 6.4b: Spurious character mixed up with real character

for each character, usually 10 (assuming 8 data bits, 1 start bit, and 1 stop bit). Hence, 1,200 bps corresponds to 120 *characters per second (cps)*. The 110-bps speed, however, most often translates to 10 cps, because it is used with mechanical equipment requiring 1 start and 2 stop bits, for a total of 11 bits per character. Bear in mind that character rates represent maximum capacity; in practice, idle time between keystrokes, and while the host is either awaiting input or busy with processing, reduces the actual character rate below this maximum.

BREAK

The BREAK key found on most terminals transmits a control signal rather than an ASCII character. Generally, SPACE is transmitted as long as this key is held down. The receiver recognizes BREAK when it sees SPACE for a period longer than a *character time*, defined as bit time multiplied by character size. Hosts often interpret BREAK as an interrupt signal. This is essential on half-duplex systems, being the only way the user can get a signal through to the host while the host is transmitting.

ANSI X3.64

The ASCII character set was originally developed for hard-copy terminals. It contains only a few basic *format effectors* : carriage return (CR), linefeed (LF), vertical tab (VT), horizontal tab (HT), formfeed (FF), and backspace (BS). When it comes to displaying text on screens, these are grossly inadequate.

The ANSI X3.64 standard expands ASCII by adding 132 character sequences, each identified with a control function. Since these control sequences are used for managing the display of text on screens, they are sent only from host to terminal, and not from terminal to host. (The one exception is the X3.64 character sequence that informs the host of the position of the terminal's cursor.) Control sequences cover such functions as cursor addressing, creating blinking or reverse video fields, and clearing the screen.

Each X3.64 character sequence starts with the ASCII escape character (ESC), a code that ASCII's designers had the foresight to reserve for just such a purpose, i.e., escaping from the normal interpretation of character codes. Hosts treat ESCs received from terminals as single control characters, often with some meaning ascribed by the operating system. When a host sends an ESC *to* a terminal, on the other hand, the terminal recognizes it as marking an X3.64 sequence and interprets the subsequent character(s) accordingly.

Here are some choice examples from X3.64:

<ESC>[nA	Move cursor up by n rows
<ESC>[nB	Move cursor down by n rows
<ESC>[nC	Move cursor forward by n columns
<ESC>[nD	Move cursor backward by n columns
<ESC>[$m;n$H	Position cursor to row m, column n
<ESC>[nL	Insert n lines
<ESC>[nM	Delete n lines
<ESC>[nP	Delete n characters
<ESC>[4m	Underscore
<ESC>[5m	Slow blink
<ESC>[7m	Reverse image

Some of these sequences include integer parameters. For example, <ESC>[3;72H moves the cursor to row 3, column 72. (X3.64 numbers all rows and columns upwards beginning with 1. Some other systems, such as the video functions in the PC BIOS, number them from 0.) To appreciate the value of X3.64, imagine having to write a spreadsheet program, or design a full-screen editor, for a terminal that doesn't accommodate it.

Since X3.64 includes some very esoteric functions, it would be unreasonable to expect every terminal to use the entire standard. Most terminal vendors implement only some subset.

Among the files furnished with PC-DOS is one called ANSI.SYS. This user-installable PC-screen driver, for a subset of X3.64, translates certain *function sequences* into the internal commands used by the PC. It may be tempting to use ANSI.SYS in making a terminal emulator for the PC because it saves a lot of work, and some products do indeed rely upon it. However, since ANSI.SYS includes only a very small portion of the X3.64 standard, and is rather slow into the bargain, most software developers prefer to write their own code to handle X3.64. Hersey Micro Consulting offers an excellent product called FANSI-CONSOLE™, which can be used in place of ANSI.SYS. FANSI-CONSOLE implements nearly the entire X3.64 standard, and performs some other neat tricks as well.

The first escape sequence (Esc [2 J) clears the entire screen.
Hence these first two sentences do not appear on the formatted
screen. Esc[2J
Esc[01;10HEsc[m At the top we have a message in plain text
Esc[03;10HEsc[mEsc[1m Here we see high intensity!!!
Esc[05;10HEsc[mEsc[3m How about some italics?
Esc[07;10HEsc[mEsc[4m Let's underscore the value of ANSI X3.64
Esc[09;10HEsc[mEsc[5m This line would blink on a screen
Esc[11;10HEsc[mEsc[7m This appears in reverse video
Esc[m

At the top we have a message in plain text

Here we see high intensity!!!

How about some italics?

Let's underscore the value of ANSI X3.64

This line would blink on a screen

This appears in reverse video

FIGURE 6.5: ANSI X3.64 data stream "before and after"

ANSI.SYS is described fully in Chapter 2 of the IBM DOS Technical Reference Manual.
Some versions of MS-DOS also come with the ANSI.SYS file; in other versions, this driver
is preinstalled, so it's there whether you like it or not.

Figure 6.5 shows two sample screen displays. The first was received with terminal emulation turned off, so that the ANSI sequences are displayed literally (the ESC
character is printed as "Esc"). The second is the same screen seen through a VT100
emulator.

PARITY AND ECHOPLEX

What kind of error control exists for asynchronous terminals? Originally, there wasn't any. If characters were damaged in transit, it was too bad. Teletypewriters sent messages to be read by human beings, capable of tolerating a rEmarkablenumber3 of errors}i before deciding that a message is K^r4::b*. The technology of the old days wasn't up to correcting errors anyway.

In telex systems, messages are often seen with an occasional garbled character. Concerned users handle this simply by repeating sensitive data and spelling out numerals.

Errors are more of a problem in messages for computer consumption. The only way to obtain a reliably error-free connection between a real terminal and a host is to install error-correcting modems (discussed in later chapters) at both ends. Short of that, two detection techniques, parity and echoplex, can help a little. Despite numerous flaws, they have been ruthlessly piggybacked onto terminal technology. Both take advantage of "holes" in the transmission stream to insert some redundant information, permitting certain errors to be found. Parity, used in this way, is frequently a nuisance. The ubiquitous echoplex rarely hurts, but it also is not uniformly helpful.

Parity for Communications

When terminal and host correspond in pure seven-bit ASCII, it may be possible to transmit full eight-bit bytes and use the eighth bit for the form of error control called *parity*. The transmitter sets the eighth bit of every byte to record some information about the seven-bit ASCII code, which the receiver can verify. Two parity variants are used, *odd* and *even*. We will describe odd parity; even parity works analogously.

With odd parity, the eighth bit of a transmitted character, called the *parity bit*, is varied so that the total number of binary 1s in the byte is always odd. If the ASCII code already contains an odd number of binary 1s, the parity bit is set to 0; otherwise it is set to 1. For example:

			ASCII code with odd parity	
	7-bit ASCII code			
Character	Hex	Binary	Hex	Binary
A	41	1000001	C1	11000001
B	42	1000010	C2	11000010
C	43	1000011	43	01000011
D	44	1000100	C4	11000100
E	45	1000101	45	01000101

What would it mean if a computer received a code of C3 (11000011 in binary)? This byte has four 1s, an even number. A transmitter operating under odd parity should never send such a code, so the receiver properly regards this as an error.

It is easy to see that parity will detect any error affecting a single bit. There are two possible error cases:

A 0 gets turned into a 1, so an extra binary 1 is received.
A 1 gets turned into a 0, so one binary 1 too few is received.

In either case the number of 1s is changed by one, changing the total from odd to even. Similarly, it is evident that parity will fail to detect any error which changes two bits, because in all possible error cases the total number of 1s will remain odd. In fact, one can reason inductively that parity, whether odd or even, detects all errors affecting an odd number of bits, and fails to detect any errors affecting an even number of bits, within a byte. Conclusion: Parity reveals only about half of all errors.

Parity is normally handled by hardware. The communications interface is told which parity mode to use, and it sets and checks bits accordingly.

Parity, in this context, is strictly a means of detecting errors, and offers no help in correcting them. It also leaves open the question of how users should be informed of the presence of errors. Because of these problems, and its poor performance in finding errors, many people feel that parity is more trouble than it's worth. These people are known as "parity poopers." (To be fair, we should point out that this much-maligned technique would help eliminate approximately half of the bogus characters detailed in our discussion of Figures 6.3(a) and (b) above.)

Many of parity's detractors would probably be surprised to learn that it was originally implemented in this context for a somewhat different purpose: as a means of obtaining statistics about the occurrence of errors. Even if the method disclosed only half the errors present on a given line, it gave data-center managers information about relative line quality and helped them determine which lines were in need of service.

Other Uses of Parity

Character-level parity, as employed by ASCII terminals, is of questionable value. In other communication contexts, parity is quite beneficial. Some communication protocols use "two-dimensional" parity for detecting errors. In this scheme, shown in Figure 6.6, not only does each character contain a parity bit ("vertical"), as just described, but a succession of characters is followed by a check character containing a "longitudinal," or "horizontal," parity bit for each character bit position. This system is used, for example, by IBM's Bisync protocol when transmitting ASCII data. It detects any error affecting only one character in such a message, no matter how many bits are damaged. In addition, two-dimensional parity

```
H   e   l   l   o   _   t   h   e   r   e
0   0   0   0   0   0   0   0   0   0   0   1
1   1   1   1   1   0   1   1   1   1   1   1
0   1   1   1   1   1   1   1   1   1   1   1   Longitudinal
0   0   0   0   0   0   1   0   0   1   0   1   Redundancy
1   0   1   1   1   0   0   1   0   0   0   0   Check (LRC)
0   1   1   1   1   0   1   0   1   0   1   0
0   0   0   0   1   0   0   0   0   1   0   1
0   1   0   0   1   0   0   0   1   0   1   1
1   1   1   1   1   0   1   0   1   1   1
```

Vertical Redundancy Check (VRC)

FIGURE 6.6: Two-dimensional use of parity

will expose a sizeable majority of errors affecting two or more characters. Damage to data is corrected by the retransmission of any message in which an error is found.

Parity is also enormously valuable in detecting errors in the *memory* of many computers, including IBM PCs (but excluding many compatibles). Each byte of PC memory is composed of nine "cells" in which binary values are stored; eight cells hold data bits, and the ninth holds a parity bit. Each cell of a given byte resides in a separate RAM chip, which explains why memory chips must always be added in multiples of nine. Parity-generating hardware in the PC's memory controller sets the parity bit when a value is written to main memory; special sensing hardware checks the parity when the byte is read.

When a memory chip fails, usually only a single bit (in each affected byte) is compromised. Typically, the broken bit becomes "stuck," meaning that it persists in reading out as the same value, no matter what is written into it. If the value stored into a byte happens to involve "writing" the stuck value onto a broken bit, the byte is read correctly. If, on the other hand, the value as written should set the broken bit to the inverse of its stuck value, then a parity error will be detected on a subsequent read. The parity check of memory functions only as a tip-off that something is amiss; any failure can be verified by a diagnostic program that alternately writes and reads the same byte.

Echoplex

When you are typing at a terminal, you normally expect that each character you strike will appear on the screen. It is instructive to consider how the displayed character gets there. The obvious method, called *local echo*, is to make the terminal display the character directly. However, in a valuable alternative method, called *echoplex*, the host first receives and then echoes the character, and the echo is displayed on the terminal screen, as shown in Figure 6.7a. If the character is damaged on its way to the host, the damaged version winds up on the screen. The user can spot this and take steps to correct it, perhaps by backspacing and retyping the affected character.

A third possibility is to instruct the local modem to echo the character. This would reveal any errors appearing between the terminal and its modem, but errors on this link should be most unlikely.

Echoplex has its merits, but its potential flaws are legion. Here are a few:

- First, what if the character arrives intact at the host, is echoed, and then is mangled on the way back? Damage is just as likely to occur on the return trip as it is on the way up. Fortunately, about the worst that could happen here is that the operator would have to make a few needless corrections.

- Second, what happens when errors involve "significant" characters? For example, a letter gets turned into a carriage return, a backspace into a number, or a simple request for HELP into a LAUNCH MISSILE command on a submarine on maneuvers in the Azores. Echoplex does not help, but neither does it make things any worse.

- Third, echoplex depends for its effectiveness on human visual acuity and/or vigilance. Data-entry clerks, whose cerebral cortices have generally been reduced to spaghetti by overexposure to CRTs, tend to pay little attention to feedback.

- Fourth (and by no means last), what about the delay? Granted, this is usually imperceptible to a human operator; even on a coast-to-coast link the echo takes only about 70 ms to appear, assuming the host echoes immediately. When echoing

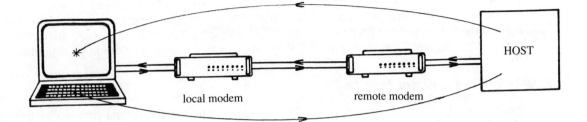

FIGURE 6.7a: Echoplex (remote echoing)

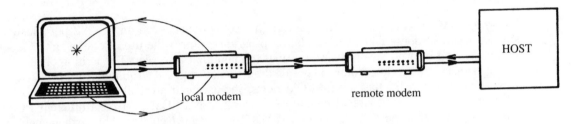

FIGURE 6.7b: Echoing by local modem

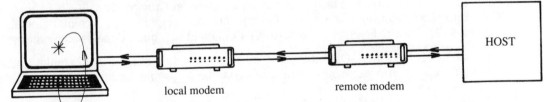

FIGURE 6.7c: Echoing by terminal

is handled by hardware or dedicated software, as is most often the case, the response is essentially instantaneous; it is slower if echoing is handled by the operating system, the timesharing system, or the particular application. Echoplex really hurts in communication over a satellite link, where the delay is an uncomfortable 650 ms or so.

In spite of all these snags, echoplex is a valuable technique. When terminals are to be operated by human beings, and no better option for error control seems imminent, echoplex should certainly be considered. Two important exceptions are communication via satellite and communication over links that charge the user according to the amount of data transmitted rather than the time it takes.

Echoplex is also a handy diagnostic aid in setting up a connection. If the host echoes characters correctly, you know you've selected the right transmission parameters. Garbled characters may provide clues to incorrect speed or parity.

PC PRODUCTS FOR TERMINAL EMULATION

PCs have no trouble emulating asynchronous terminals, because they have all the necessary hardware: screen, keyboard, and RS-232 port. Only a simple program is needed to tie everything together. Nevertheless, commercially available terminal emulators are hefty, expensive programs. The reason is that they offer many features in addition to emulation itself.

What a Terminal Emulator Must Do

Emulation capability may be the most obvious and vital part of a terminal emulator, but it is often a small part. There are four features you should expect in a commercial product:

Terminal Emulation Proper. The program makes the PC look and behave like the terminal it emulates. Primarily, this entails providing the necessary screen and keyboard functions—for example, implementing whatever subset of the ANSI X3.64 standard the emulated terminal requires.

Driving a COM Port. A PC emulating a terminal communicates via an RS-232 port, just as a real terminal does. Thus, the emulation program requires the use of one of the PC's COM ports, and incorporates software routines to make that possible. (The writing of such routines can be tricky; like bomb disposal, drag racing, and cat grooming, it's best left to experts.) When a PC has several COM ports, the user can normally tell the emulator which one to use. A few terminal emulators can even use a COM port on a different PC connected to the first via a LAN such as IBM's Token-Ring Network. This arrangement allows a community of users to share direct connections to hosts or a small pool of modems.

Ordering Modems About. Most PC modems today are "smart": their microprocessors enable them to perform useful tasks like dialing numbers and answering calls. PCs communicate with these modems using a set of commands and responses. A terminal emulator should handle at least the Hayes Standard AT Command Set, and perhaps some others.

Providing a User Interface. Often the most substantial portion of a terminal emulator, the user interface may provide menus, commands, on-line help, and facilities for automating terminal sessions.

Appendix C of the *IBM BASIC Reference* lists a 50-line BASIC program for an operationally viable, but skeletal, terminal emulator.

Additional Features of Terminal Emulators

Here is a sampling of special features found in better terminal emulation programs for PCs. A comprehensive list would run on for many pages.

Dialing Directory. Most terminal emulators allow users to maintain a sophisticated dialing directory containing one entry for each frequently contacted host. Each entry holds information such as host name, telephone number, line speed, and other communication parameters. The directory information should be sufficient to enable the terminal emulator to establish a connection to a host either specified by name (in a "connect" command) or selected from a menu. Often, programs can handle even complex connections, such as those made via alternate long-distance carriers or PSNs and those involving hosts with more than one telephone number (if the first number dialed is busy, a second is tried). Figure 6.8 shows a sample dialing-directory entry.

Host name: **Whizzo Chocolate Co.**

Telephone number: **332-6106**

Speed: **2,400**   Data bits: **7**   Parity: **Even**   Stop bits: **1**

Local echo: **ON**   Terminal type: **VT102**

Login prompt: **"Username: "**   Login name: **"frog"**

Password prompt: **"Password: "**   Password: **"crunchy"**

FIGURE 6.8: Sample dialing-directory entry

Automatic Log-in. In addition to dialing up a host, a program may be able to log you in. Sometimes a single keystroke will get you connected and logged into the system of your choice. Although very convenient, programs that store user name(s) and password(s) may present a security problem.

Canned Directories. Some software packages include directory entries already set up for popular systems, such as MCI Mail, Dow Jones, and CompuServe. All the user need add is the local telephone number. Also useful are "template" directory entries for different types of host systems.

File Capture and Insertion. File capture is the ability to transcribe part of a terminal session to a disk file. File insertion is the complementary process of copying a disk file into the input stream to the host. This may be a valuable method of effecting a file transfer when no other means is available.

Multiple Sessions. Some products, such as CROSSTALK® Mk.4 and Smartcom III™, allow two or more concurrent terminal sessions.

What's Half a Duplex?

Many terminal emulators for PCs allow you to request either "full-duplex" or "half-duplex" operation. What does this mean? It turns out that the terminology is being misused here. Almost all communication paths used by PCs emulating terminals are full-duplex in the original, correct sense of the term. The misuse of the terms relates to the device that performs echoing of the user's keyboard input. Here, "half-duplex" means that the terminal emulator will copy to the screen each character typed by the user. "Full-duplex" means that the terminal emulator will not echo input; this is normally selected when the host does the echoing—that is, when echoplex is in effect.

The rationale behind all this is that echoplex cannot be performed on a true half-duplex communication link; it is not practical to reverse the direction of data transmission to let the host echo each character. This leaves it up to the terminal to do the job instead (as was shown in Figure 6.7c). On a true full-duplex link, it is assumed that the host will echo, so the terminal need not do so. In the terminal-emulation realm, however, the usage of these terms has degenerated to the point where they indicate only whether echoing is local, and tell us nothing about the nature of the link itself.

Half-duplex and *full-duplex*, then, are terms to be wary of. They are often used correctly, as defined in Chapter 1, but their misuses are sometimes even more confusing than they are here.

Using a Terminal Emulator

A terminal emulator must provide two modes of operation, which we'll call *command mode* and *on-line mode*. (Some products have different names for these modes, or don't name them at all.) Let's consider how a terminal emulator is used. In command mode, you are interacting with the emulator program itself. Any emulator product will start up in this mode, allowing you to use its command or menu system to establish a connection to the desired host. Once that connection is established, you want to interact with the host, not the emulator, so you switch to on-line mode. Generally, the program switches modes automatically once the connection is made, but in a few cases a user command is necessary.

To appreciate the vital importance of this distinction between modes, imagine the havoc that might result from the lack of a clear distinction. Consider an activity analogous to using a terminal emulator: giving dictation. Again, you are speaking to the desired party (the "host") through the agency of a third party, a secretary (the emulator). "Dear Mr. Parrott. . .What on earth is that man doing? No, no, don't write that down. I'm sorry, I was just looking out the window. Let's start again. Dear Mr. Parrott. . .I. . .oh, you've got that already? Okay. I am pleased to inform you that the Management Committee has approved your promotion. No, not *you*—Mr. Parrott. Okay, look. When I'm holding my left hand up in the air that means I'm talking to you; when my left hand is in my jacket pocket, like this, I'm dictating. Ready? Oh, *here's* my Swiss Army knife. . . . No, no, I wasn't dictating just then. . . ."

Certainly, anything entered in command mode should not be, and is not, sent to the host. In on-line mode, on the other hand, the emulator program is "transparent" to most, if not all, ASCII characters; instead of interpreting the typed characters, it forwards them directly to the host, as any good terminal would. (Non-ASCII keys pressed while in on-line mode will have no effect unless they have a defined meaning to the emulator.) Some escape route must be provided, however, so that the emulator program can be forced back into command mode. This switching operation may be invoked automatically if the host connection is lost, but it's essential that the user have a means of bringing it about deliberately. The emulator reserves one key on the PC keyboard as an *escape key* for this purpose. By pressing this key, the user can escape back to the PC and enter commands to the emulator; the host connection is customarily left open, awaiting further use if the on-line mode is selected again.

Do not confuse the *mode* escape key discussed here with the key labeled Esc, which generates the ASCII Escape character. The Esc key is sometimes used as the mode escape key, but this is not its intended function. Rather, Esc is meant to provide escape from the normal interpretation of the data stream, as required in X3.64.

The foregoing discussion may remind you of smart modems (Chapter 3), which have equivalent requirements for switching between command and on-line states.

Again, when you're on-line, pressing any key that generates an ASCII code should cause the emulator to send the associated character to the host. The sole exception crops up when an ASCII key is chosen as the escape key. A non-ASCII key, such as a function key, is obviously a better choice for mode escape, since it will not interfere with the sending of any ASCII character to the host. An emulator that does use an ASCII key for mode escape must allow that choice to be altered, in case the user needs to transmit the corresponding character.

Any competent terminal emulator will maintain a constant reminder of the escape key on the screen. Since the emulation of most terminals requires a display of only 24 lines, emulators typically take over the bottom (25th) line of the PC screen for status information of this kind.

Even if you're thoroughly confused, this would be a good time to go and try out your terminal emulator. With a little practice, the necessary mechanisms should quickly become obvious. If you're not confused, then imagine using your PC terminal emulator to connect to a host, where you run another terminal emulator program to connect to a second host, where you run a third terminal emulator to connect to a third host, and so on. Believe it or not, there are perfectly valid reasons for doing such things. You may have to make note of all the escapes involved, however, to avoid losing track of which host you're communicating with at any moment.

How to Generate Rubouts, Nulls, and Pleas for Clemency

If you spend enough time using a PC as a terminal, sooner or later you'll be faced with a situation like this: You do something that prompts a host to send screenful after screenful of data you have no interest in seeing. The host graciously pauses after each screenful and asks you to hit a *Rubout* if you wish to terminate the output; any other character causes it to proceed with the next screen. You need the output like you need a copy of this book written in Middle English; enduring the avalanche of text is frustrating and expensive; and *there is no Rubout key on the PC keyboard*. You try every key you can think of, then pound out combinations with Ctrl, Alt, and Shift all at the same time while Scroll Lock is on and the keyboard is upside down; the output keeps right on coming. You have one leg out the window when you realize that all you have to do is disconnect.

After you've calmed down, you decide to research Rubouts so you'll be better prepared the next time around. Most ASCII tables, and even the original ANSI document, make no mention of Rubout. You notice, however, that ASCII does have a character called Delete, which sounds suspiciously similar. The next time you are faced with an urgent need for a Rubout, you optimistically strike the PC's Del key. And nothing happens. You strike it a few more times. Still nothing. Believe it or not, Rubout and Delete *are* the same; your mistake was in assuming that the Del key generates a Delete. It doesn't. The Del key does not generate an ASCII code at all. To get a Rubout/Delete you must use the key combination Ctrl-Backspace.

How, in general, do you find out about this sort of thing? Now that you have this book, you can look at the ASCII table (Appendix E), which lists the PC keystrokes for all ASCII codes. Very few terminal emulators are any help, although Hayes' Smartcom II™ is an exception worthy of some praise. Appendix G of the Smartcom II manual includes a fold-out ASCII chart complete with the keystrokes recognized by the program.

Another feature of the PC keyboard worth remembering is that any ASCII character, except for the Null, can be generated by holding down the Alt key and then entering the appropriate decimal code from the ASCII table on the numeric keypad. A Rubout could thus be created by depressing Alt and typing 127; the keyboard handler completes the code and sends it to the program when the Alt key is released. Similarly, if you wanted to generate an ASCII Bell and didn't know that it corresponds to Control-G, you could hold down Alt and press 7 on the numeric pad. This method can be used to generate not only true ASCII codes, 1 to 127 decimal, but also extended codes, 128 to 255. This is, in fact, the only way to generate extended codes from the keyboard. It's a good idea to keep an ASCII chart within easy reach—preferably the one in this book—so you'll always be safe. Or will you?

Generating the appropriate ASCII code is only half the battle. The next question is: Will your terminal emulator deign to transmit the character, or will it instead treat it as some weird glitch unworthy of attention? Most terminal emulators will cooperate with you for Rubout, at any rate, but you may not be so lucky with Null, ASCII code 0. You can generate a Null with the key combination Ctrl-2, but most programs of any kind, to say nothing of terminal emulators, will joyfully throw it away (that's what Nulls are for, after all). Of course, they do this without telling you. (Smartcom II, incidentally, will transmit Nulls, while CROSSTALK XVI will not.) Fortunately, it's very unlikely that you'd ever have to send a Null to a host. Nulls are used mainly by hosts as "padding" for mechanical terminals. After sending a carriage return, say, to a printing terminal, the host may need to pause before sending another character, allowing time for the print head to move back to the left margin. It's almost always easier to time such a delay by sending a certain number of Nulls than by using a clock and leaving the line idle.

Most other control characters present no problem, being generated by a Ctrl-letter combination and handled by terminal emulators just like any regular character.

The last question here concerns BREAK. The PC keyboard has a key labeled Break, but it does not necessarily generate a BREAK signal. Every terminal emulator should be capable of sending a BREAK and should associate some key with this function. There is little consistency, however, as to which key is assigned for this purpose; certainly, very few emulators use the Break key itself.

Products

Emulation and file transfer are the two most popular PC communication applications, and most terminal emulation products for PCs also offer file transfer capabilities. Such products, usually called *communications packages*, will be examined more closely in Chapter 10.

Besides programs that emulate specific terminals, a few emulate only a generic terminal, something akin to a glass teletype. Included in this category are PC-TALK™ III and IBM's Personal Communications Manager.

In many products, emulation of certain terminals is intentionally incomplete. For example, many VT100 emulators do not support the 132-column mode of the DEC product, simply because no more than 80 columns can be displayed on a PC lacking a graphics adapter. Several other such limitations are inherent in the PC architecture. Another problem with VT100 emulation is that a PC cannot display double-size characters, except in graphics mode, or use different speeds for transmission and reception. Fortunately, these restrictions are unimportant to most people.

If you need high fidelity in a terminal emulator, you might want to consider products that specialize in terminal emulation in preference to general communications packages that claim to emulate the terminal(s) you need. Notable among the specialized products is the SmarTerm® series from Persoft®, which includes precise emulators for most DEC terminals, various models of the Data General™ Dasher™, and the Hewlett-Packard 2392. Another outstanding product, designed for DEC VT220™ emulation, is available from AST Research.

GRAPHICS TERMINALS

Graphics terminals are those capable of displaying graphics images and/or text. They are widely used by engineers for computer-aided design (CAD), by scientists for technical data analysis (making sense of masses of data by forming images from them), by business people for presentation graphics, and in many other application areas.

There are two main types of graphics terminals: *raster* and *vector*.

Raster terminals form images using scan lines; all PC monitors work in this manner. Typically, a monochrome cathode-ray tube (CRT), whether in a black-and-white television set or a PC monitor, sweeps an electron beam back and forth across its screen while making incremental shifts in the beam's vertical position. This process creates a succession of several hundred horizontal lines (collectively, the raster) covering the screen from top to bottom. The beam excites the atoms of a phosphor coating on the inside of the screen, causing them to emit light. In a television, the beam strength is rapidly varied as it traces the raster to produce the required image. In a PC monitor, the beam is rapidly switched on and off. Each screen character is composed of an array of dots, but two or more horizontally adjacent dots merge into a line. The lines that form a single character then blend, in the eye of the beholder, to form a single recognizable pattern. The principle is similar to that of a dot-matrix printer. A raster display of an asterisk is shown in Figure 6.9a.

A color CRT uses three electron beams, one for each primary color (red, green, and blue). Each beam is focused through a set of holes in a mask so that it hits phosphor dots of the appropriate color. A bundle of three such dots is placed at each picture location, called a *pixel*, or *pel*. Each beam traces a raster and is modulated in keeping with the intensity of its associated color, contributing to the composite color of the beams at each pixel. An asterisk drawn by this method is shown in Figure 6.9b. This type of display is still a raster, since each of the electron beams traces out the same formation as in the monochrome case. Other display technologies, such as the liquid-crystal display (LCD) and plasma screens popular on laptop computers, also use a pixel-based system.

Vector terminals, also called *storage terminals*, use an electron beam to excite phosphor dots in the same manner, but instead of tracing a raster, the beam directly draws each line, or *vector*, required to produce the image. Figure 6.9c illustrates the vector tracing of an asterisk. Vector screens are widely used in arcade video games. Although two of the best-known graphics terminals, the Tektronix 4010 and 4014, are of the vector type, we will not consider vector terminals here; raster types are now preferred, and PCs can emulate terminals only in raster mode. Moreover, the 4010 and 4014, both long discontinued, were

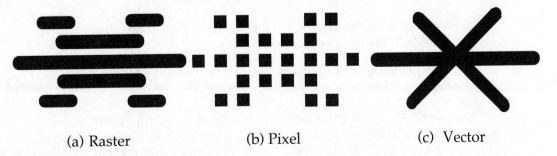

(a) Raster   (b) Pixel   (c) Vector

FIGURE 6.9: Graphics display types

monochrome units; most people now prefer color, which is more readily reproduced by raster technology.

If you peer closely at a graphics image on a raster screen, you'll observe that the image is composed of myriad dots—the pixels discussed above. Raster screen resolution is measured in terms of these pixels. A screen with "620 by 200" resolution displays an array of 620 pixels in its longer dimension by 200 pixels in its shorter dimension, for a total of 620 times 200, or 124,000, pixels.

It's worth commenting on the difference between a PC video adapter designed for text display and one designed for graphics display. Both are hardware items. A *text-display adapter* accepts character codes, which it translates into dot matrices for display. It can display only those characters with "known" dot patterns, normally the 256 of the standard PC character set. Furthermore, each character must fit into a predefined "box," or character position, on the screen. These boxes correspond to the intersections of the 25 rows and 80 columns on a regular monitor. A *graphics adapter*, on the other hand, can be fed images pixel by pixel. Since each dot on the screen can be independently lit and (on a color screen) colored, such devices are sometimes described as *all points addressable (APA)* adapters. To simplify the display of text, graphics adapters can also be instructed to behave like text adapters, accepting data in the form of character codes.

A list of popular graphics terminals is given in Appendix F. Models differ in such attributes as resolution, number of displayable colors, size of screen, and support for peripherals, including digitizers and secondary "slave" monitors. Most color terminals can display simultaneously some modest number of colors chosen from a "palette" which may contain a much larger number. A large stock of available colors enables the user to create more realistic and artistic pictures, but since each pixel must be colored independently, the amount of memory required to hold the image is proportional to the number of colors on the screen. Therefore, to keep RAM requirements within reasonable bounds, the number of simultaneously displayable colors is necessarily limited.

Host application programs generate graphical output in the form of function sequences similar to those for text only in ANSI X3.64. These function sequences are used to draw on the screen "primitives" such as simple lines, curves, and circles. A succession of primitives constitutes a picture.

A set of graphics-oriented function sequences forms a *graphics-output language*. Among several such languages that have been developed, one of the most important is PLOT-10™, originated by Tektronix and adopted internationally by many other companies. Each PLOT-10 command consists of an escape character followed by two capital letters and, when necessary, numeric arguments. Here are two examples:

<Esc>ML*n* sets the line index to the integer *n*. The line index
  determines the color used to draw lines; $n = 2$, for
  example, denotes red.
<Esc>LF*xy* repositions the cursor to the coordinates given by
  integers *x* and *y*.

The primary task of a graphics terminal emulator is the interpretation of the appropriate graphical output language, and the mapping of its primitives, onto whatever screen hardware is in use. Some emulator products include special display adapter hardware that performs double duty as a regular PC graphics board, emulating an IBM CGA, EGA, or

VGA, and as a video driver for the terminal emulator. Other products attempt the job in software only, making the best of whatever ordinary graphics adapter is installed in the PC. If the resolution of the PC screen does not match that of the terminal being emulated, there is no big problem. The PLOT-10 language, for example, addresses a *virtual screen* of 4,096 by 4,096 pixels; an emulator, or a real terminal, maps the virtual screen onto the screen actually used. The large virtual screen makes *true zoom* possible: since the amount of information exceeds screen resolution, a small part of the picture can be blown up to show more detail than was visible prior to the zoom.

Graphics terminals, and graphics technology in general, are forever improving, driven by the maturing of computer-aided design and manufacturing (CAD/CAM). Design engineers nowadays rarely need to build physical models of new products for testing; instead, they build computer models and programs to simulate test conditions. Even wind tunnels for testing airplane and automobile models are becoming, if not obsolete, at least less important to the early stages of product planning, as computers do the job at ever-lower cost. And airline representatives, instead of viewing reduced-scale mock-ups, can gaze at pictures of their planned purchases already emblazoned with the company's name and colors.

FILE TRANSFER PROTOCOLS

A *protocol*, in general terms, is a set of formal rules governing behavior in an interaction among two or more parties. For example, protocol leads us to say "Hello," or to offer some other customary salutation, when we answer the phone. In the realm of data communications, a protocol is much the same: a set of rules governing the behavior of the interacting entities that follow it.

We'll first consider the need for communication protocols in general, and then concentrate on the particular class used to effect file transfer between pairs of computers. Somewhat different types of protocols, discussed in the next chapter, are used in other areas of computer communication, especially networks.

WHY PROTOCOLS ARE NEEDED

To illustrate the need for protocols, consider the prospect of data transfer *without* one. We'll analyze the simple case of a serial link connecting two PCs. Ignore the link's speed and length, and assume that raw data are being piped across it. "Raw" here means that nothing has been added for control purposes; for example, data straight from a disk file could be called raw. Briefly, the major issues are as follows:

- The danger of data in transit being corrupted by transmission errors.

- The possibility of the transmitter sending data more rapidly than the receiver can cope with them—in other words, flow-control problems.

- The lack of a means to mark the end of a file. When the receiver stops getting data, is the file complete? Or has the sender died? Or is the link broken? Or does it just mean that there's been a delay?

- The inability to provide information that explains (and, in other settings, accompanies) each file, such as its name, length, and creation date.

- The inability to transmit eight-bit data over a connection that demands the use of parity, and allows the passage of only seven data bits per character.

A file-transfer protocol will overcome many of these obstacles. The best protocols will nullify all of them.

Protocols must sometimes bear a few additional responsibilities. One important example is *addressing*. On the simplest point-to-point link, the data's destination is never in question; they flow from the station at one end to the station at the other, and that's that. On a communications link that interconnects several stations, however, we need some method

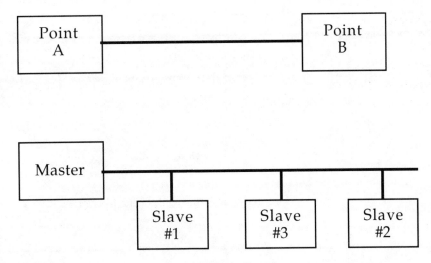

FIGURE 7.1: Point-to-point and multipoint communications

of tagging chunks of data with their intended destination. For this purpose, stations are assigned distinct addresses, and a protocol accomplishes the labeling of data before they leave the transmitting station. Point-to-point and multipoint arrangements are shown in Figure 7.1.

Such addressing, while essential in a multistation network, may also be required on a two-station hookup if the two stations happen to be multitasking computers. After all, you send data not to a computer but to a program running on a computer. Therefore, whenever any doubt can arise as to the ultimate destination of some particular data, each active program must be uniquely identified, and data must be tagged with the appropriate identifier. Each program then becomes a "logical station" on a channel that may be shared by several other such logical stations.

Protocol Basics

In a raw data stream, the unit of transmission is the byte; all bytes are considered to be data except in cases where a few values, such as Control-S and Control-Q, are singled out for control purposes. In a protocol data stream, the unit of transmission is the *message*. Fortunately, all the demands made on a protocol are met by the single, simple technique of ordering communication in terms of messages. A *protocol message* is a transmission sequence with a well-defined structure. It may or may not contain data, but always contains *control information*, used by the protocol for its own purposes—primarily, identifying and addressing the message, and describing and delimiting any data contained in the message. In this sense, a message is analogous to an envelope, as shown in Figure 7.2, that may contain a portion of the data being transferred, and will always be marked on the outside with control information indicating how and where it is to be delivered.

In order for two stations to communicate by means of a protocol, both must be equipped with a suitable program to operate the protocol. The transmitting station takes successive fragments of the data to be transferred, packages each fragment in a message envelope, and sends it off. As each message arrives, the receiving station checks its control information,

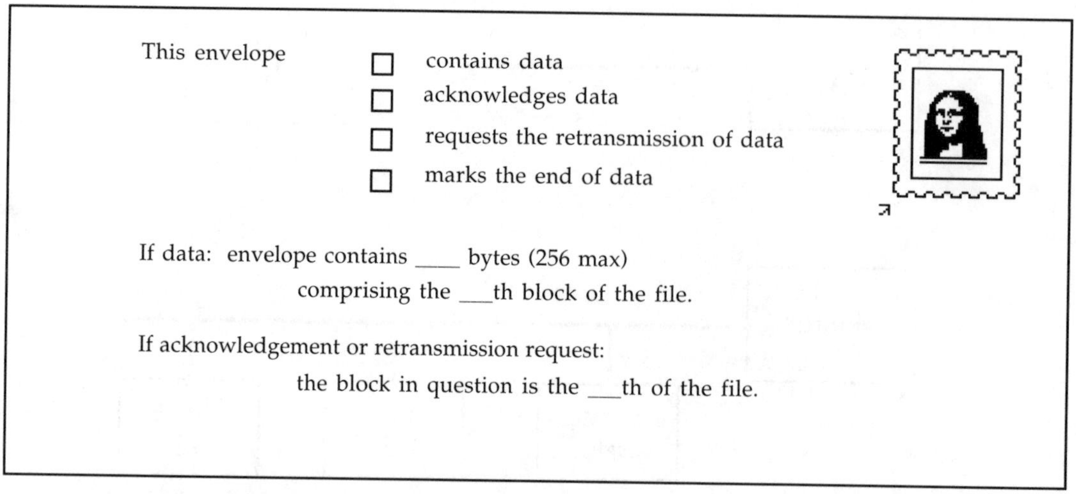

This envelope
- ☐ contains data
- ☐ acknowledges data
- ☐ requests the retransmission of data
- ☐ marks the end of data

If data: envelope contains ____ bytes (256 max)
comprising the ___th block of the file.

If acknowledgement or retransmission request:
the block in question is the ___th of the file.

FIGURE 7.2: Protocol envelope

extracts the data, and discards the envelope. From time to time, the receiver responds with empty envelopes serving to acknowledge receipt of the data.

Data-bearing messages are identified as *data messages,* while those sent purely for control purposes (the empty envelopes) are called *control messages.* Some protocols give other names to the unit we've called a message; *block, packet,* and *frame* are the most common. Any protocol will establish an upper limit on the amount of data that can be sent in a single message, typically between 80 and 1,024 bytes. Figure 7.3 illustrates how a file is split into a succession of messages for transmission.

Stations manage flow control by pacing the transfer of data messages. In particular, a receiving station has some way of indicating to the sender how much data it can accommodate. Depending on the particular protocol design, this may be achieved by sending control messages encoding such indications as "Okay to send me the next six messages," or "I can handle 5,000 more data bytes," or "Whoa! My buffers are full."

TECHNIQUES OF ERROR CONTROL

We will now examine how protocols provide *error control*, a process involving two distinct steps. The first is *error detection;* the second, carried out only after errors are found, is *error*

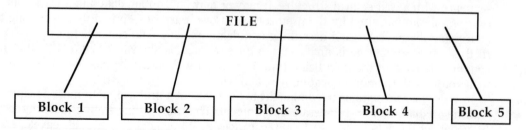

FIGURE 7.3: Division of file into blocks for transmission

correction. We have already investigated two common methods of error detection: parity and echoplex. Error correction entails retransmitting any data message in which an error has been detected—essentially the method people use in conversation when some of the data are garbled.

Error-Detection Methods

Suppose you have an urgent need to send a file from your PC to another over a telephone/-modem link, and no protocol is available. The file is the executable version of a program, and it is imperative that the receiver obtain an intact copy. Assuming that you have a means of transferring the raw data, how can you verify correct reception? Take a moment to ponder the problem.

One solution is to send two complete copies of the file, so the receiver can check one copy against the other. If the two prove to be identical, both are probably correct, since it's unlikely that exactly the same error(s) would occur on two successive transmissions of the file. If the two copies differ, one or both must be damaged; to "recover" from the error(s), a further copy must be sent and checked against the first two, and so on.

Although it might be worth trying in extremely pressing circumstances, the above technique is only barely practical. If the file is long and the telephone line noisy, the chances of transferring an entire copy without an error may be formidably low. In addition, the cost in money and/or time for transferring duplicate copies may be prohibitive.

A second, equivalent solution is to send the file to its destination and then have the recipient send a copy back to be compared with the original—a ploy much like echoplex. All the arguments leveled against the first solution apply equally to this one.

The point of the preceding exercise, besides giving you a chance to think through the problem, is to introduce the important concept of *redundant information*. Redundant information, like the second copy of the file in the cases above, is transferred only for the purpose of detecting errors, and is otherwise superfluous.

To enable the receiver to detect errors, the sender transmits some redundant data whose consistency with the "real" data can be checked by the receiver. Normally, the redundancy adds only about 1 or 2 percent to the total quantity of "real" data transmitted, as opposed to the 100-percent redundancy in the first example above. Taking advantage of the data's binary form, the sender generates redundant information by performing some arithmetic or logical operation on the data and transmitting the result as part of the control information. The receiver performs the same calculation on the data it receives, and checks its result against that obtained by the sender.

Now suppose that you're out in the jungle benefiting mankind by researching a rare population of the butterfly species *Morpho Genesis*. You are required to summarize the number of individual specimens sighted during each daylight hour. Every day, your written report is carried back to base camp by your trusty chimp, Darwin. Unfortunately, the frequency of tropical rainstorms in the area is such that many reports are smeared in transit, resulting in an uncertain interpretation of the figures by your diligent support staff. The strategy of totaling each day's counts and appending the sum to the report would provide a primitive, but worthwhile, check for colleagues back at headquarters on whether they are reading the numbers correctly. If the numbers, as they read them, add up to the same total as yours, the chances are that all is well. If there's a discrepancy, they can send back a message with Darwin requesting you to repeat the data along with the following day's report.

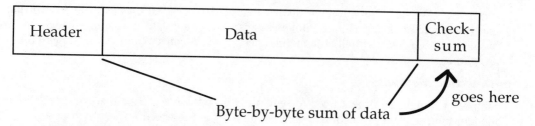

FIGURE 7.4: Checksum

The simplest error-detection scheme, called a *checksum*, makes use of just such a form of redundant information. A checksum is simply the arithmetic sum of all the bytes in a message. The sender calculates this sum for each message and tacks it onto the end, as illustrated in Figure 7.4. The receiver computes the sum of the bytes as they arrive and compares it with the checksum received. Any discrepancy is evidence that the data are damaged. A checksum error may also occur because the checksum itself is damaged in transmission, while the data remain uncorrupted. It is, of course, impossible for the receiver to tell whether the data proper, the checksum, or both were damaged in any instance of a checksum discrepancy.

No matter what the data represent (characters, instructions, pictures, or whatever), they can always be treated as a sequence of eight-bit bytes, and the simplest computer can add these bytes together. The sum of a few dozen or a few hundred bytes, though, may be a number too big to be represented in eight bits. If the bytes are summed as unsigned, and therefore positive, integers, the number of significant figures is bound to increase. This is like saying that you can't add up 843, 598, and 610 and write the total as another three-digit number. In order to keep things in manageable byte-size pieces, a protocol uses a specified group of 8 or 16 bits of the sum, discarding any excess.

As you may already have deduced, no error detection method is perfect. No matter how clever the method may be, there will always be some errors it will fail to detect. Consider, for example, the weakness of a checksum scheme. Suppose that exactly two data bytes in a given message are damaged, and damaged in such a way that the value of the first byte is increased by one, while that of the second is decreased by one. The sum, clearly, will remain the same, and the error will be missed. Even if we were to transmit a redundant copy of the entire data file, it's always possible that both copies could be damaged in an identical way. This problem persists no matter how many extra copies we send. While the probability of every copy being damaged identically may become ridiculously small in practical terms, it will never truly reach zero until the number of copies reaches infinity, at which point the telephone bill would also be infinitely large.

Since the efficacy of error-detection schemes varies, we need a way of measuring their power. The measure employed is called the *undetected error rate*, which expresses the proportion of all errors the technique will fail to detect. For an 8-bit checksum, the undetected error rate is approximately 1 in 250; for a 16-bit checksum, the rate is roughly 1 in 1,000—"roughly" because the exact rate depends on both the message size and the nature of the errors on the link. It should be evident that the more redundant data is transmitted relative to the "real" data, the better the protection; a one-byte checksum represents a much larger proportion of redundant information to a 10-character message than to a 100-character message. In any event, an undetected error rate of 1 in 1,000 means that, on average, of every 1,000 flawed messages, 999 will be caught and 1 will slip through undetected. Now, imagine a practical situation where this undetected error rate applies: if only 1 message in every 100 transmitted is actually damaged, then only 1 message in 100,000 will get through with an undetected error.

Do these rates, 1 in 250 and 1 in 1,000, sound satisfactory? The practical implications of an undetected error rate may become clearer if you calculate the *mean time between undetected errors,* which is primarily a function of the undetected error rate of the protocol and the actual error rate on the line. For example, if we used an eight-bit checksum to protect data on a channel that suffers an average of one glitch per minute, the mean time between undetected errors would be around four and a half hours of continuous operation. (This calculation involves a host of minor assumptions; including all possible variables would be pointlessly complex.) The error-detection power of checksums, while decidedly better than nothing, is none too impressive in practice. Unfortunately, checksums are frequently employed in PC protocols. Much better techniques are available, most notably the *Cyclic Redundancy Check (CRC),* which is becoming increasingly common in PC protocols. Sometimes, all error checks, even CRCs, are referred to generically as checksums.

Conceptually, a CRC is almost as simple as a checksum. Instead of treating the data in a message as a sequence of bytes to be added together, however, it is taken as one huge binary number, perhaps hundreds or thousands of bits wide. We divide that huge number by a constant divisor, and use the remainder as the error-control reference. A 16-bit CRC, the most common size, detects all errors affecting 16 or fewer adjacent bits, 99.997 percent of 17-bit errors, and 99.998 percent of errors affecting 18 or more contiguous bits. (These figures were published in Andrew S. Tanenbaum's *Computer Networks*, Prentice-Hall, 1981.) With a typical error distribution, a 16-bit CRC has an undetected error rate of about 1 in 10^{10}, sufficient for many needs. 32-bit CRCs, found, for example, in Ethernet LANs, are the "ultimate" error-detection method in common use.

While checksums are universally calculated by software, CRCs are best generated by special hardware. Many computers, such as the DEC VAX® and Apple Macintosh, have CRC capability built in as part of their I/O hardware. The PC, however, is not so equipped, so one must either add appropriate hardware (an expensive undertaking), or set up software to perform the calculation, which can be unpleasantly slow. In practice, for asynchronous protocols, CRC calculation is usually done in software; for synchronous protocols, since hardware has to be added anyway, it is generally done in hardware.

Despite all the seemingly horrendous long division, CRC programs can be short and simple, but traditional algorithms for them eat up a lot of processor time due to the huge amount of *shifting* required—a task at which the PC is not exactly a hot-rod. (Shifting, a basic operation of all computers, is the displacement of a data item some number of bit positions to the left or right.) Faster algorithms, now coming into widespread use, trade off memory for speed. By maintaining tables of precalculated partial results, they speed up the calculation substantially. Several standard CRCs are defined, each specifying the particular divisor to be used. Important examples are named CRC-16 and CRC-CCITT.

The above statement that PCs are not normally equipped with CRC hardware is not strictly correct. PCs do not come with stock CRC hardware that's accessible by communications software, but they do have CRC circuits buried in their disk controllers. Data stored on disks are recorded in the form of flux variations induced in a magnetic material. The material, and hence the stored information, is susceptible to damage from various sources, including dirt, external magnetic fields, and wear caused by heads landing on the disk surface when the drive is shut down. (Take heed: Don't "store" floppy disks by fastening them with refrigerator magnets to the side of a metal cabinet.) Just as the program stored on an audio or video cassette deteriorates with time and use, so does the information stored on a disk. Therefore, *disk controllers*, the electronic servants that handle the low-level details of disk I/O, are designed to store each block of data with a CRC. The CRC is checked whenever the disk is read, and it is a testament to the quality of today's disk components that CRC errors are very rare.

Error-Correction Methods

All common protocols correct errors by means of retransmission. When a receiving station detects damage in a data message, it returns a control message requesting that the sender retransmit the data. A data message may be retransmitted several times before arriving intact.

Protocols can employ various methods to effect retransmissions. In the simplest, the sending station transmits one data message at a time and then waits, before sending another, for a notice from the receiving station indicating whether or not the message was received correctly. Control messages returned by the receiver are called, appropriately, *acknowledgments.* These come in two flavors: positive and negative. A positive acknowledgment, abbreviated ACK, indicates that the data message was received correctly, as far as the error-detection scheme can judge, and invites the sender to proceed with the next data message. A negative acknowledgment (NAK) indicates faulty reception, mandating retransmission of the last data message.

The system of alternating data messages and acknowledgments is referred to as *Stop-and-Wait ARQ*. ARQ stands for Automatic Retransmission reQuest; Stop-and-Wait is self-explanatory. This scheme is used in most protocols, including XMODEM, Kermit, and Bisync, all of which will be discussed later. Stop-and-Wait ARQ is appealingly simple, and is straightforward both to understand and to implement, but it does not offer the greatest possible efficiency.

Two steps can be taken to accelerate transfer and, consequently, error correction. First, the sender can transmit several data messages before stopping to wait for a response. A limit is set on the number sent in such a group because, when a damaged message is detected, the receiver must wait until that message is correctly received before it can deliver any subsequent data to their final destination. Suppose the receiving station is directly printing the received file. To ensure that the file is printed in sequence and without gaps, one of two courses must be taken. Either the receiver keeps in memory all data correctly received after the corrupted message, or the sending station retransmits not only the damaged message but all subsequent data messages as well. In practice, both methods are used, some protocols adopting one, some the other. The first alternative, called *Selective-Reject ARQ*, is more efficient; the second, *Continuous ARQ*, is easier to implement.

Note that continuous ARQ is somewhat more efficient than stop-and-wait ARQ with a single, relatively long data message. The longer the message, or batch, the greater the time required for its retransmission, but continuous ARQ at least does not require retransmission of messages previous to the damaged member of a batch.

The above schemes for trading data messages and acknowledgments involve transmission in only one direction at a time. This is fine for a half-duplex link, but it wastes the resources of a full-duplex channel. To make the best use of full-duplex, data messages and acknowledgments can be made to flow simultaneously, as shown in Figure 7.5. This wastes no time at all on the sender-to-receiver path. Much better use can be made of a full-

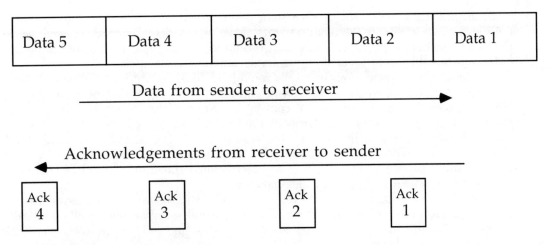

FIGURE 7.5 A full-duplex protocol

duplex link by permitting bidirectional data transfer. Although we will not study these more elaborate schemes in detail, we will touch on a few instances of their use with particular protocols.

Forward Error Correction

No matter how it's organized, any retransmission of data to correct errors introduces significant inefficiency. A technique called forward error correction reduces the need for retransmission by slightly increasing the amount of redundant information sent and organizing the extra information so that it can be used by the *receiver* to correct certain errors. A typical basic technique of forward error correction can correct any single-bit error in a message and detect the vast majority of multiple-bit errors.

We won't study methods of forward error correction in detail; the simplest types are not very complex, but explaining them is laborious. More to the point, they're seldom used with PC protocols. Why mention them, then? Because they are used in current high-speed modems that must contend with frequent errors. Forward error correction, generally used only where high error rates are anticipated, allows such modems to overcome a significant percentage of errors without resorting to retransmission.

DIFFICULTIES WITH PROTOCOLS

Some serious practical problems can arise with the implementation of protocols on different kinds of computer systems, or when protocols are used for transferring data between unlike application programs. Before discussing these problems, we repeat an obvious but essential fact: a computer can't communicate using a given protocol unless it is supplied with a program that understands that protocol. The protocol-handling portion of such a program is sometimes called a *driver* for the protocol.

Synchronous vs. Asynchronous Protocols

As indicated previously, whenever two computers are connected for file transfer, a choice must be made between synchronous communications with a synchronous protocol and asynchronous communications with an asynchronous protocol. For PC connections, async is usually preferable, unless the user has some particular motivation to choose sync. This is not the moment to discuss the relative merits of the two modes of connection (we'll get to that in the next chapter). Here, we contrast certain aspects of the two kinds of protocol in order to expose the obstacles confronting async communications users.

In principle, all asynchronous protocols could be used on synchronous links, and many synchronous protocols could be used on async links. The segregation of protocols into the two groups is largely a matter of convention. Nevertheless, as we shall see, design considerations arise with async protocols that are not an issue for sync protocols. Only two popular protocols are actually used in both realms: DEC's Digital Data Communications Message Protocol (DDCMP™) and X.25. DDCMP is a rather well designed protocol, but it is of little relevance to PCs. X.25 is an international standard protocol of enormous importance, and we'll study it in the next chapter.

In practice, the primary functional distinction between synchronous and asynchronous protocols stems from the fact that the former are generally used on links built specifically to accommodate them, while the latter are often pushed and prodded to work over links intended for terminal traffic.

Before personal computers appeared on the scene, asynchronous protocols were rare. Raw async communication was used for terminals, and synchronous protocols predominated for other applications. The needs of microcomputer users spurred the development of async protocols for file transfer, in the process presenting protocol designers with many new challenges.

Trouble on the Road

What constitutes an ideal data link for file transfer? Setting aside concern with transmission errors, we can say that such a link would provide a channel that carried eight-bit bytes between two intercommunicating programs, with no delays and no impediments. Generally speaking, synchronous protocols are blessed, in that they get to operate over synchronous links closely approximating the ideal. Typical async connections, however, fall far short of the ideal. Thus, asynchronous protocols are somewhat damned, in that they must contend with four specific kinds of problems. These hazards, except as otherwise noted, are relevant only to async protocols:

Data may be delayed during their journey across the link.

The link may not be able to support the flow of data at its full rated capacity.

Certain characters may "disappear" in transit.

Some links will pass only seven-bit bytes.

Here, we examine the likely sources and implications of each problem.

Data Delays

Data may be delayed in transit because of a very long propagation path or because they are briefly stored by devices in the link before being passed on. In practice, satellite links are the only data paths long enough to cause noticeable delays by virtue of length alone. When data are bounced across a continent or an ocean by a communications satellite, propagation time becomes significant. Such satellites orbit at an altitude of approximately 22,380 miles; even at the speed of light, it takes a little while, typically close to a third of a second, for a radio signal to get up there and back. In contrast, propagation time across a 3,000-mile terrestrial (i.e., Earth-bound) cable is only about one-tenth as long. When a computer must send a message over a satellite link and then await a response, the delay is nearly two-thirds of a second. Since any cross-country dialed telephone call nowadays may be routed via a satellite link, it might be advisable to ask an operator for a terrestrial link for your data call.

Even when distances are short, considerable delays can creep in if a connection is routed through one or more *store-and-forward devices*. These devices read an entire message into memory and then transmit it onward. The classic example of data's encounter with such devices is the packet switching network (PSN). In traversing a PSN, each message is stored and then forwarded by every network node along its path; this could involve four or five stops for a coast-to-coast connection. Actually, despite this multiple relaying of messages, most PSNs are impressively fast, but traffic jams are always possible, especially at the busiest times of day. To complicate matters further, long messages may be fragmented during their passage through PSNs, occasionally resulting in gaps between the arrivals of successive fragments at their destination. Many protocol drivers are designed with the expectation that an input message will flow in an unbroken stream once it appears; such drivers may have difficulty with PSNs.

Time delays in the two cases discussed are rather different in nature. With satellites, delays are large but constant and predictable, so protocol drivers can easily adjust to them, at least in principle. PSN-induced delays are likely to be shorter but variable and unpredictable. Delays of these kinds, especially those introduced by satellite links, affect both synchronous and asynchronous protocols.

Rated Speed vs. Practical Capacity

The designers of many big computer systems assumed that, for asynchronous communication, their equipment would never deal with anything but terminals. This creates several problems for the asynchronous protocols used by PCs.

One problem relates to the input load a host port can cope with. Many systems conform to the notion that an async port will never receive data from any source but a human typist. Since human operators don't type very fast, the substitution of a PC, spitting out characters at top speed, can cause a serious mismatch. Even if a speed of 9,600 bps can be selected for the host port, the software driving it might not be capable of keeping up with a sustained data rate of even 150 characters per second. The result of this mismatch is that incoming characters are occasionally lost. This problem has been known to crop up even in DEC systems, which, in other respects, are models of good behavior. Although an error-correcting protocol detects most such losses, frequent message retransmission can drastically reduce efficiency. Moreover, if the losses are substantial, it may be impossible to get a complete message through intact; even elaborate error control may not suffice to restore the original data. Communications software cannot be made to circumvent sluggish input handling unless the program places artificial limits on the rate at which characters are transmitted to the host. Such limits may be enforced by either reducing the transmission rate or prescribing intercharacter delays. The latter method is discussed in Chapter 10.

Characters Missing in Action

Some devices on a communications link may intercept certain characters, possibly removing them from the data stream. The device may only be trying to help: for example, it may interpret Control-S and Control-Q as flow-control signals when they weren't meant to be. Less common is the opposite problem of characters being added to the data stream by zealous devices, primarily those generating Control-Ss and Control-Qs.

Port selectors are frequently troublesome in this regard. A port selector is a device that switches async terminals among a number of hosts. When a computer center has several host systems that support terminals, it may be cumbersome or wasteful to provide a separate set of dial-in lines for each host. Instead, the installers may opt for a single set of lines and a port selector. On initial connection, the port selector provides the terminal user with a menu of systems available to him or her. Most port selectors allow a user to "break back" from a host to the port selector and then switch to another host. Many such devices respond to software flow control, and some may interpret certain character sequences as invitations for them to break into the session. Thus, they may cause two kinds of problems, removing what appear to them to be control characters and/or inserting characters (prompts to the user) when they think it's time to break in.

While some port selectors rely on a character sequence to provide an escape mechanism for terminals, many adopt the BREAK signal for this purpose. BREAK is a superior choice in guaranteeing noninterference with protocols.

Often, the worst impediments to the flow of characters are timesharing systems. The driver of an asynchronous protocol for a host usually takes the form of an application program running under the timesharing system. This is often the best method, despite the fact that the driver must then work within the constraints imposed by the timesharing system.

What sorts of restrictions do these systems impose? To begin with, they may appropriate some input control characters, almost certainly including carriage return, backspace, and Control-C, for their own purposes, and discard any incoming control characters that do not have functions prescribed by the system. They may demand input framed as lines of text, discarding any characters that stray beyond the 72nd or 80th position in a line until a carriage return is entered. After accepting a line of input, they may insist that we wait for a prompt such as "Command?" before presuming to enter another line. Mercifully, timesharing systems are usually much less restrictive when it comes to output.

The Seven-Bit Syndrome

A major obstacle to the use of an asynchronous protocol by many large systems is their insistence on using parity. This parity loyalty stems from the designers' preoccupation with terminals, as mentioned earlier. Parity commandeers one bit in each eight-bit character for its own purposes, leaving only seven for data. (Transmission with eight data bits and a *ninth* bit for parity is possible, but very uncommon.) This means that only pure ASCII text can be accommodated; the transfer of files containing anything else becomes very complicated.

Being limited to pure ASCII is not always a severe handicap, because the ability to move binary data between dissimilar machines is seldom important. After all, a typical binary file, such as the executable form of a program, is intelligible only to the type of computer that created it. Occasions do arise, however, when you may find it convenient to be able to send a binary file from a PC to a host system. Such acceptance would let several PCs use a common host as a forum for sharing files; likewise, individual PCs could use a host as a repository for both text and binary PC file back-ups.

If the host does not directly accept binary data, a file can be converted to an ASCII format for transfer. There are plenty of utility programs available on the market and in the public domain to handle this task. The simplest approach is to convert each binary byte to two ASCII-coded hex characters, dividing the resultant data file into lines of uniform size. Thus, for example, the binary value 10100100 (hex A4) would be expanded to the ASCII codes for "A" and "4"; this process continues for each binary value, with the conversion utility inserting a carriage return/line feed after, say, every 40 characters.

Hosts are not alone in restricting data to seven-bit data paths. Although PSNs are universally capable of supporting eight-bit paths, the default parameters of many such networks restrict async-terminal connections to seven bits.

Implications for Asynchronous Protocols

The constraints described above suggest that protocols may have to confine themselves to the use of ASCII codes, cooperate with flow control mechanisms, disguise messages as lines of text, keeping those messages within strict size limits, and shun control characters. The dismal fact is that few protocol designers have bothered to confront such difficulties. One sterling exception is the research group at Columbia University who developed Kermit, a gem of a protocol we'll meet a little later on. Another protocol that manages to cope with several such environments is BLAST®, also covered in this chapter.

The four areas of difficulty outlined above are common enough to present serious hurdles to the designers and implementers of protocols. Although we've cited host computers as the sources of these impediments, some big systems present no such problems at all. Many timesharing systems, for example, permit a program to set a port in a *binary* or *transparent* mode. Such modes, which originally enabled appropriately equipped terminals to read and write punched paper tape, allow the unrestricted flow of data in both directions.

Data Translation and Formatting Problems

When you transfer a file from one computer system to another of identical kind, there should be no problems of interpretation when the data reach their destination. If, on the other hand, the computers are not of the same kind (or, for that matter, are simply running two different operating systems), you may run into trouble even when transmitting text.

For our purposes, we can divide files into two categories: "text" and "other." We will refer to the "other" files as "binary." As noted above, binary data can always be transformed into pure ASCII for transfer and, if appropriate, converted back to binary afterwards. Therefore, we'll set aside consideration of binary files and concentrate on text files, which we often wish to copy between heterogeneous systems.

Unfortunately, even with plain text files, different systems behave in different ways. To begin with, there are two distinct character sets in common use. All personal computers use ASCII, but many bigger machines grew up on EBCDIC. Translation between these two codes is fraught with potential pitfalls. No standard exists for mapping one set into the other, and, since EBCDIC has more characters than ASCII, there can be no one-to-one correspondence. The translation of letters, numbers, and standard punctuation marks is straightforward, but when it comes to special symbols and control characters, any two translation schemes are likely to be different. If you start with an EBCDIC-coded file, translate it to ASCII, and then back to EBCDIC, the result may not be the same as the original. The problem is that, in some cases, two EBCDIC characters must be translated into the same ASCII character, but the ASCII character can be retranslated into only one EBCDIC code. This may happen, for example, with the cent sign (¢), which exists in EBCDIC but not in ASCII. Fortunately, translation from ASCII to EBCDIC and then back to ASCII, the more likely sequence for PC users, should produce a result identical to the original file.

Even among personal computers, there are different ways of formatting ASCII files. A good example is the varying representation of "end-of-line": some micros use a carriage return followed by a line feed, while others use a line feed alone. And in the transfer of document files maintained by word processors (as opposed to, say, program source-code files), incompatibility reigns.

The ideal solution to these and other formatting problems is a *virtual file format*, which prescribes a uniform way to represent every possible element of a text file. During transmission, the file transfer program converts a text file's contents from the local format into the virtual format. The receiving program inverts the process, translating from the virtual format into whatever local format prevails. This ensures the text's transferability whether the systems are the same or different.

Several virtual file formats have been proposed as standards, but none has been widely adopted. The only format that seems at all likely to attain such status is IBM's Document Content Architecture (DCA), discussed further in Chapter 12. DCA is a complex blueprint for highly formatted documents and is very important in IBM's larger systems. It is now seen in many PC products, including Microsoft Word®and other leading document processors. Some of the communications packages sold for a number of different systems have their own virtual format schemes; a good example is the Communication Research Group product BLAST, covered later in this chapter.

XMODEM AND VARIANTS

XMODEM is an important protocol historically—indeed, it was at one time the predominant protocol for microcomputer use. Nevertheless, for reasons that will be made clear, XMODEM hardly merits serious consideration for professional use today. In spite of this negative prognosis, we have chosen to accord XMODEM substantial attention, principally because, being of very simple design, it constitutes a convenient tutorial on the inner workings of protocols, and it is also a case study of how a poorly constructed protocol can prove inadequate. The XMODEM variants XMODEM CRC, XMODEM-1k, and YMODEM™ will also be discussed briefly.

The Origins and History of XMODEM

XMODEM dates from the early days of personal computing, when most micros were in the hands of hobbyists. Little commercial software was available, but enthusiasm for sharing user-written software abounded. Programs were distributed among friends and through user groups, and later were disseminated via electronic bulletin boards. Since most programs were written in BASIC, it was easy enough, in principle, to move them even between differing brands of microcomputer. However, another aspect of computing in those days made such sharing difficult: the many incompatible media formats adopted by different manufacturers. While most companies used eight-inch diskettes or (heaven help us) audio cassettes for data storage, each maker developed its own format, carefully designed to be unreadable by the competition. Admittedly, this somewhat overstates the conflict, but even today, when both the Apple Macintosh and newer IBM PCs use 3 1/2-inch diskettes, it remains impossible for one system to read a diskette written on the other, except for those machines that handle the latest 1.44-MB HD (high-density) floppy disks.

In 1977, a bright fellow named Ward Christensen, who happened to work for IBM in Chicago, was frustrated by this state of affairs and, on his own time, came up with a workable solution. He recognized that many computer users also owned modems, all perfectly compatible Bell 103-type, 300-bps units, and he reasoned that these modems could be used to transfer program source codes from one machine to another. He designed a protocol for this purpose and implemented it in a program he called MODEM, which was placed in the public domain. MODEM was distributed through CP/M user groups and became a worldwide hit.

Several versions of the MODEM program evolved over the years, and the protocol itself came to be known by that name. The version most widely used today, formalized in 1982, is called XMODEM, and it is about as simple as a protocol can get and still *be* a protocol. XMODEM is also sometimes called the "Christensen protocol."

How XMODEM Works

Let's examine the structure of XMODEM messages, and watch two XMODEM drivers conduct a file-transfer session. This study will serve to introduce many vital concepts of protocol operation. The only other protocol we'll cover in depth is the more advanced X.25, discussed in Chapter 8.

References here to a *sender* and a *receiver* apply only to the stations' roles in moving a particular file from one to the other. In the course of transferring a given file, each station will actually transmit and receive messages. Of course, the stations may transfer a file in one direction, then switch roles to conduct a transfer in the reverse direction. Indeed, within a "file transfer session," the period during which two XMODEM programs are connected to each other, many files may be sent back and forth, but only one at a time.

Here's a catalog of XMODEM message types. The formats are shown in Figure 7.6. Messages transmitted from sender to receiver:

> *data* carries a portion of the file data.
>
> *EOT* marks the end of the current file.

Messages transmitted from receiver to sender:

> *ACK* announces the safe arrival of a data message.
>
> *NAK* indicates the receipt of a damaged data message, implying the need for retransmission of that message.

Every message starts with a control byte, whose value identifies the *message type*. The type is the first thing the station receiving the message needs to know; it indicates not only what action the station should take, but also identifies the message length. In the case of XMODEM's control messages, ACK, NAK, and EOT, the type is all there is to the message—there's nothing more to say.

A data message, called a *block*, carries a fixed complement of data, 128 bytes in length. As shown in Figure 7.6, the data portion of the block is prefaced by a block header comprising the following control fields:

> *SOH* is an ASCII control character with a value of 1, identifying a data block.
>
> *N* carries the block sequence number.
>
> *N'* contains a repetition of the sequence number in complemented form.

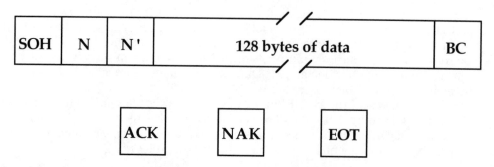

FIGURE 7.6: XMODEM message formats

Following the data is a one-byte checksum called the *block check character (BCC)*. The sender adds up the data bytes in the block to form a 16-bit sum whose low eight bits become the BCC. (The high 8 bits are discarded.) The bytes in the block header are not included in the checksum. Including the initial SOH in the block check would be superfluous because, if the SOH were damaged, the receiver would not even recognize the message as a data block, and therefore would not verify its BCC. The sequence number is excluded from the checksum because it is sent with full redundancy anyway, as discussed below.

The block sequence number is set at 1 for the first block of a file, is incremented for each subsequent block, and, upon reaching 255 (the highest number that will fit in a byte) cycles back to 0. Hence, for a long file, sequence numbers follow the repeating pattern: 1, 2, 3, ..., 254, 255, 0, 1, 2, ..., and so on.

Repetition of the sequence number in the block header represents an interesting design choice; it gives this crucial piece of information extra protection from corruption by transmission errors. But why is the second statement of the sequence number *complemented*, with each 1-bit in the original represented by a 0-bit in the copy, and vice versa? This reflects the one stroke of genius in XMODEM's design. Suppose the copy of the sequence number were not complemented. Then, if an *error burst* (a sustained transmission error that forces a succession of signals to take on the same value) just happened to change all the bits in both sequence-number fields to zeroes (or to ones—the argument is the same in either case), the sequence numbers would still appear valid by virtue of being identical. Making the two copies complementary significantly reduces the likelihood of the sequence-number values masquerading as legitimate when, in fact, they have been damaged. This is an important issue because the kind of error hypothesized was especially likely to occur with the 300-bps modems commonly used in XMODEM's heyday.

Figure 7.7 illustrates an XMODEM exchange involving no transmission errors. A transfer is always initiated by the receiver, which sends a NAK to indicate its readiness to accept data. If this initial NAK elicits no response from the sender, the receiver will repeat it at 10-second intervals. The sender, upon receiving a starting NAK, transmits the first data block and then, because XMODEM adopts the stop-and-wait ARQ scheme, pauses for an acknowledgment, as it will do after each block transmission. After the last block of the file has been successfully transferred, the sender transmits an EOT. The receiver acknowledges this EOT in the same manner as it does a data block. Once the sender has received an ACK for the EOT, the transfer is complete.

Figure 7.8 shows a portion of a transfer illustrating XMODEM's behavior when a block is damaged. Here, block number 1 is hit by errors twice in a row; the receiver returns a

NAK each time, prompting the sender to repeat the block. On the third attempt, the block gets through undamaged, eliciting an ACK from the receiver; transmission then continues with block 2.

If a block is NAKed 10 times, the sending program should ask its user whether it should continue trying or else give up. Many implementations ignore this requirement and, after experiencing 10 consecutive NAKs, just give up, deeming the line to be too noisy to be usable.

Figure 7.9 shows how the sender handles the absence of a response to a block it had transmitted. Perhaps the SOH of block 1 was damaged, with the result that the receiver never even recognized it as a block; alternatively, the receiver's ACK or NAK may have been wiped out by a transmission error. After transmitting each block, the sender waits 10 seconds for the receiver's response. If no acknowledgment arrives within this period, the sender transmits the block again. The 10-second wait, called a *time-out*, is essential to protocol operation in ensuring that a station does not wait forever for a message that is never going to materialize. It's like having an arrangement to meet someone who doesn't show up: you'll wait perhaps a few minutes, or even an hour or two, then storm off. Computers must be told when to give up or they will wait indefinitely. There is one highly publicized case of a robot waiting in a restaurant parking lot for well over five hundred thousand million years.

The 10-second time-out used by XMODEM may seem surprisingly long, but there are excellent historical reasons for this choice. As we suggested earlier, although the system of acknowledgments is primarily a means of error control, it may also be used for flow control.

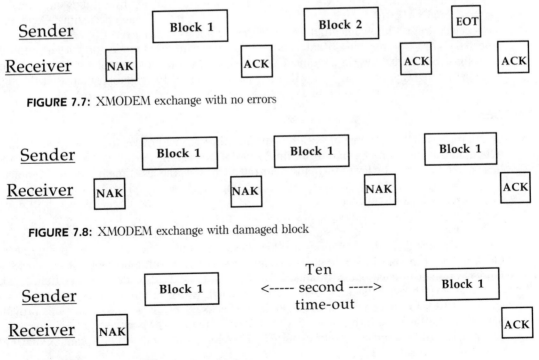

FIGURE 7.7: XMODEM exchange with no errors

FIGURE 7.8: XMODEM exchange with damaged block

FIGURE 7.9: XMODEM exchange with lost response

When a station receives a block, it must dispose of the data contained therein, normally by writing them to a disk file. If the station has only one buffer for receiving data, it should delay sending an acknowledgment until the disk write is complete, to foreclose the possibility of new data arriving and overwriting the old before they've been saved. The choice of 10 seconds relates to the fact that early implementations of XMODEM typically used a single receive buffer and could take quite a while to relay received data to their final destination, which might well have been an audio cassette. In other protocols, acknowledgment time-outs are often one second or less.

The possible loss of acknowledgments underscores the need for sequence-numbering of blocks. If the receiver depicted in Figure 7.9 did indeed send an ACK, the second copy of block 1 would be a duplicate and would be discarded by the receiver. The receiver keeps track of the sequence number of the last block it received correctly, thus enabling it to detect duplicates. But what if, rather than a duplicate, the receiver got a block with an out-of-sequence number—for example, block 3 immediately after block 1? Only a malfunctioning sender, or some freakish line error, could explain that. A receiver should be able to detect, but has no way of recovering from, such an occurrence; it will most likely report a fatal error to the user and abort the transfer.

We will now consider two extensions to XMODEM.

XMODEM-CRC

The original XMODEM's greatest weakness, the 8-bit checksum, was substantially over-come with the addition of a CRC option, which replaces the checksum with a 16-bit cyclic redundancy check (CRC-16). The design of XMODEM-CRC ensures compatibility with regular XMODEM. An XMODEM-CRC receiver initiates a transfer by sending an ASCII C rather than a NAK; the C invites the sender to use CRCs rather than checksums. Generally, the receiver doesn't know ahead of time whether or not its partner has CRC capability, so if repeated Cs draw no response, it falls back to the checksumming mode and tries a couple of NAKs instead. Under certain circumstances, XMODEM transfers can take half a minute or so to get under way, as is the case when a sender without CRC capability must sit through a few Cs, arriving at 10-second intervals, before the receiver drops back to NAK.

XMODEM-1k

Standard XMODEM's habit of breathlessly awaiting an acknowledgment after each 128-byte data transmission is a significant limitation; if it could be curtailed, file transfer would be faster. Of course, the fewer the pauses during a transfer, the less time it takes to complete. The XMODEM-1k extension, while still operating under stop-and-wait ARQ, allows data to be sent in 1,024-byte blocks as well as 128-byte blocks. The larger blocks are known as 1k-byte (or simply 1k) blocks. A sender transmits the larger blocks as long as there are sufficient data to justify doing so but, when appropriate, sends the tail end of a file using the smaller blocks. A file containing 1,025 bytes, for example, would be sent using one 1k block followed by one 128-byte block. To alert the receiver to the presence of 1k blocks, a sender commences each one with an ASCII STX (Start Of Text, code 2) rather than SOH.

XMODEM-1k is really an extension of XMODEM-CRC in the sense that it always employs CRCs for error control. A single-byte checksum on a 1k message would provide pathetically little error protection. XMODEM-1k's main drawback is that, when errors occur, large blocks must be retransmitted. Therefore, on a noisy line, plain XMODEM would be a better choice.

XMODEM Availability

XMODEM is now available not only in several public-domain programs but also in a good deal of commercial software, on many public systems such as CompuServe, and on most bulletin boards. It has been implemented on almost all personal computers and on many larger systems. There are, for example, several versions for UNIX. Many newer products include both the CRC option and the 1k extension.

XMODEM's wide acceptance stemmed partly from its simplicity, which made it easy to program, and partly from its origin (in the early years, it had little or no competition). Its popularity, in turn, led to its being considered a standard. But, while almost any standard is better than none, XMODEM is not good enough to warrant such status, even with the CRC and 1k options. There remain five other significant weaknesses:

Fixed Block Size

The protocol's fixed block size gives rise to an annoying problem. If the length of a file is not a multiple of 128 bytes, then the last transmission block must be padded, that is, filled out with extra characters to fit. (The fill character used to pad blocks is Control-Z, a vestige of CP/M, whose operating system used Control-Z as an end-of-file indicator.) This virtually guarantees that the received copy of a file will not be identical to the original—hardly a satisfactory situation. As we shall see, nearly all other protocols accommodate data blocks of variable size.

Vulnerable Control Messages

While XMODEM data blocks may be adequately protected from transmission-error damage when the CRC option is employed, control messages are afforded no such protection. Imagine the consequences if a line hit happened to convert a NAK into an ACK, or the SOH of a data block into an EOT. Again, we'll see that most other protocols do not take such risks.

Lack of Sophistication

XMODEM lends itself neither to automation nor to a sophisticated user interface. It's convenient to be able to send filenames as part of a protocol, as, for example, when sending multiple files or communicating with unattended systems. Extending XMODEM to defeat this limitation is not overly difficult; in fact, it has been done, in a variant called YMODEM (see below). "Standard" XMODEM, however, still lacks an accepted way to facilitate such automation.

Eight-Bit Requirement

XMODEM requires a fully transparent eight-bit data path, and therefore is not adaptable to hosts and networks that constrain async connections to seven-bit data. Admittedly, few protocols manage to cope with seven-bit hosts, and protocol designers should not be condemned for failing to address the problem. Therefore, XMODEM's dependence on an eight-bit path need not be considered a serious failing. Nevertheless, it has severely limited the protocol's spread outside the world of personal computers.

Possible Inefficiency

As noted in the discussion of XMODEM-1k, XMODEM has a nasty habit of waiting for an acknowledgment after each data block. On connections with large propagation delays, such as PSN circuits (where the lag can be as long as a second), this stopping and waiting can depress efficiency to an intolerably low level.

Christensen himself is not to be faulted for the deficiencies of XMODEM. He designed the protocol as a quick-and-dirty means of sharing files with a few friends; not in his wildest dreams did he imagine it would become a popular standard. He once told a colleague, "Why, if I'd known that everybody in the world was going to use XMODEM, I'd have put an extra evening's work into it."

In an effort to overcome some of its limitations, several designers have developed extensions to, and new versions of, XMODEM. Variants of the protocol include MODEM7, Telink, and WXMODEM. We'll examine only the most prevalent: YMODEM.

YMODEM

YMODEM was designed by Chuck Forsberg, author of the splendid Pro-YAM communications package. YMODEM incorporates both XMODEM-CRC and XMODEM-1k, and addresses many other deficiencies of the original.

YMODEM prefaces the transmission of each file with a *header block*, always numbered zero, which contains the name of the file, its length, and, optionally, the time and date of its creation. An example is shown in Figure 7.10. Although each transmission block must still be of a fixed size, the *file length indicator* permits the receiver to discard any fill characters in the last block.

This header, the "zeroth" block of each file, amounts to a directory entry for the file; it is the seat of YMODEM's flexibility. Thanks to it, the user can transfer multiple files with a single command and will need to supply the names of files to be transferred only to the sender, rather than to both sender and receiver. This might be effected, for example, by a command such as SEND YMODEM *.*. The sender signals the completion of a session (i.e. a batch of transfers) with a header block containing a null filename.

A YMODEM variant called YMODEM-g facilitates file transfers over error-free links in a manner that does not require an acknowledgment for every block. (An "error-free link"

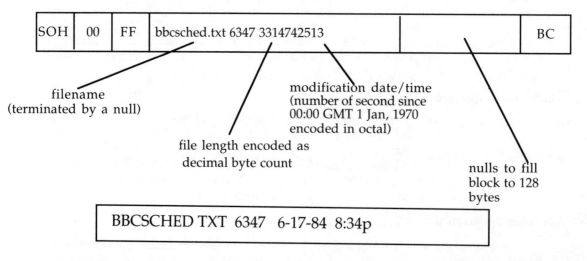

FIGURE 7.10: YMODEM file header block, with listing of corresponding directory entry

is one that can generally be assumed to deliver data reliably. Examples are short direct-connect links and links managed by error-correcting modems.) Under YMODEM-g, a file is transported in the same blocked format used by regular YMODEM, but the sender transmits continuously. The receiver acknowledges only its receipt of an EOT. This synchronization at end-of-file gives the receiver some time to open and close files. The receiver can pace the sender with simple XON/XOFF flow control. Although data blocks are not acknowledged, a YMODEM-g receiver does verify the block check just in case. If an error is detected, the receiver sends some CANs to abort the transfer. (CAN, for Cancel, is an ASCII control character, decimal 24. It's commonly associated with Control-X.)

YMODEM also defines a method of aborting a data transfer. Either station may transmit two consecutive CANS—OUTSIDE of a data block—to interrupt and cancel the transfer. The use of two characters for this function eliminates the possibility of a transfer being terminated by an ACK or a NAK that happens to be changed into a CAN by a transmission error. Some implementations of plain XMODEM also recognize the CAN-CAN as an abort sequence.

While YMODEM is a worthy improvement over XMODEM, the attempt at enhancement seems a bit like trying to make a silk purse out of a sow's ear. There are plenty of fundamentally better protocols from which to choose. XMODEM, and all its derivatives, are weak, obsolete protocols that should be avoided for serious applications. ZMODEM, a distant cousin, deserves considerable attention—and gets it, later in this chapter.

KERMIT

Kermit is unique in many ways. It is the only asynchronous protocol to which an entire book has been devoted (see Page 179); it is almost certainly implemented on more different systems than any other design; and it is the only protocol whose namesake is a frog. (*Kermit* is not an acronym; the protocol is named after Jim Henson's amphibious Muppet, with Henson's approval.) Kermit also moves files unscathed through data links where other protocols would fear to tread.

We have Columbia University in New York City to thank, heartily, for Kermit. The protocol was originally developed there in 1981 by Bill Catchings and Frank da Cruz, with help from many other people. There are now Kermit versions for over 200 systems, some written at Columbia and others by enthusiastic users worldwide.

Implementations and Availability

Certain programs implementing the Kermit protocol, modeled on the original versions designed at Columbia, are themselves, somewhat confusingly, referred to as "Kermits." Kermits abound for computer systems of all sizes, both common and esoteric. While many such programs are free, they are not necessarily in the public domain; some are copyrighted. (In such cases, though, the copyright owners have granted blanket permission for others to use the programs freely as long as copyright notices and credits remain affixed, and provided that they are not used for commercial purposes.) Kermits written for personal computers also provide terminal emulation, as do versions for many larger systems capable of originating dial-up connections. Source code is available for all Kermits, so anyone may add features, fix bugs, etc. Users who make such modifications are asked to send the results to Columbia so that everyone else can benefit.

Each such Kermit provides everything necessary for a user to connect to another Kermit and exchange files. In general, Kermit user commands loosely follow the Columbia standard, so an experienced user may move easily from one Kermit to another. Later, we'll discuss the PC version, known as "MS Kermit."

The protocol is also provided by a number of commercial communications packages for PCs, including CROSSTALK. In such cases, Kermit is usually one of several protocols supported, and the user interface is the communications package's own.

Columbia maintains its copyright over the Kermit protocol design. Companies incorporating the protocol into commercial products must meet certain conditions imposed by Columbia, a list of which is available from the address given on Page 179. In effect, commercial vendors are prohibited from increasing their profit on a product by adding Kermit to it.

Strengths and Features

Here is a synopsis of Kermit's features:

Flexibility

Kermit's flexibility is its greatest strength. It was designed to overcome the problems cited in Chapter 3, such as difficulty in transferring files to minis and mainframes, especially when working within the confines of timesharing systems. In this regard, Kermit is superior to any other protocol. It forms its messages to make them appear as lines of text, eschews control characters, and, when necessary, transforms data to fit a seven-bit connection.

Availability for Many Computer Systems

Kermit implementations can be found for machines ranging in size from the Sinclair handheld computer to the Cray-2 supercomputer. In fact, the only well known computers for which no Kermit exists are the IBM System/3Xs, excluded due to their lack of asynchronous communication capability.

Portability

A concern for portability underlies the wide dissemination of Kermit programs. *Porting* a piece of software means moving it from one computer system to another—rarely a trivial exercise. The *portability* of a program is the ease with which it can be ported.

Kermit is easily implemented because, with the exception of the advanced options to be discussed later, all its numerous features are designed for ease of programming. Source versions of Kermit in C, Pascal, and other languages are available to developers wishing to port them farther afield. The C version, at least, is extremely well written.

Compatibility

Kermits are mutually compatible, despite the great variation in features found in different implementations. There are some things all Kermits must do, such as disguising control characters, error-protecting messages with checksums, and so on. There are also several other things they *may* do, such as using CRCs instead of checksums. Many of the optional features were not part of Kermit's original design, but have been added over the years.

When two Kermits start communicating, each tells the other a good deal about itself, negotiating, so to speak, the terms of their conversation. Each transmits a list of its requirements

("Here's what I need you to do for me") and capabilities ("These are the options I can handle; let's use any that you, too, can handle"). This approach allows two full-featured Kermits to work together using all the latest whizbang improvements, while assuring that the latest program can still operate with even a bare-bones Kermit implementation from the early days.

Reliability

Reliability is not Kermit's most consistent virtue, but at its optionally equipped best the protocol is quite trustworthy. Any Kermit can generate a single-byte checksum; the use of a two-byte checksum or a CRC (CRC-CCITT) is optional. Certainly, if you have a pair of CRC-capable Kermits, you are in fine shape. Even with a one-byte checksum, Kermit is more reliable than XMODEM, because every message, including acknowledgments, is checksum-protected. XMODEM error-protects only its data messages.

Virtual File Format

All Kermits use a virtual file format, albeit a simple one, for transferring text files. This suffices to ensure delivery in a form readily usable by all systems that do not impose bizarre requirements in that regard.

Operation as Servers

A *server*, as used here, is an automated file repository located in a remote computer to which users may connect for the purpose of uploading and downloading files. Some Kermits can operate as servers. A server depends on a protocol that is, like Kermit, sophisticated enough to let the user direct transfer operations from her own (local) end of the link, entirely from within that user's Kermit. The local Kermit sends commands to the remote server and receives replies via the protocol itself. The user may command the server to issue directory listings and other information.

That's it. You may have noticed that we omitted *efficiency*. Efficiency was not an over-riding concern in the original design of Kermit, and indeed was sacrificed for the sake of simplicity and flexibility. As it happens, Kermit relies on the same slow stop-and-wait acknowledgment strategy employed by XMODEM. This is not to say that Kermit is horribly inefficient, but it does suggest that some other protocol may be a better choice where speed is a prime criterion. In practice, Kermit *is* sometimes very inefficient, and sometimes phenomenally fast. It is inefficient only under conditions of extreme duress, as exist with some half-duplex timesharing systems—an environment in which, typically, Kermit has no competition. High speed, on the other hand, is the likely outcome of communication between Kermits incorporating the latest and greatest extensions to the protocol.

If you wish to know how Kermit manages its clever tricks, read on. If such technical information doesn't interest you, skip to the subsection titled *MS Kermit*.

Where Kermit Dares to Tread

As noted above, Kermit can move any file, text or binary, over almost any seven- or eight-bit connection. Not all Kermit implementations support seven-bit paths, but since that option is both very common and closely tied to the protocol's prestige, it warrants our attention.

Kermit carefully disguises its messages, called *packets*, to resemble lines of text. Let's look at the steps it takes to accomplish this:

1. Kermit encodes its control bytes so that only *printable* ASCII characters, those assigned graphic representations, are ever used. Control characters, those without graphic representations, correspond to ASCII codes 0 through 31, plus 127. This means that Kermit has to count in a rather strange way, "32, 33, 34 . . . ," instead of counting "1, 2, 3 . . ." as people do, or even "0, 1, 2 . . ." as computers are inclined to do. Your faithful ASCII table shows the reason. The decimal codes for the printable ASCII characters form a sequence from 32 to 126. Since "32" really means "0," it follows that "33" stands for "1," and so on; "126," then, means "94," which is as high as Kermit can go. So when a Kermit wants to indicate that there are, say, 10 bytes in a message, it declares that there are 42 of them; any other Kermit will know to subtract 32 from the value given. This system of enumeration ensures that any count sent by one Kermit to another is safely represented by a normal, printable character, which even the most persnickety system is likely to accept.

Figure 7.11 shows the layout of a Kermit packet. The LEN field records, in the notation just described, the number of bytes in the balance of the packet—that is, from SEQ through CHECK, inclusive. The maximum length is, of course, 94. The SEQ field holds the sequence number of the data, using the same modulus-95 counting method.

To avoid an elaborate discussion of modular arithmetic, we'll simply say that a modulus-n counting scheme has n integral elements, ordinarily running from zero to $n - 1$. When items are counted in this way, the count starts at zero, rises to $n - 1$, and then "cycles" back to zero, continuing until no items are left. For example, "98 mod 95," or 98 in modulus-95 notation, is 3. Here, $n = 95$. Generally, for nonnegative integers m and n, m mod n is the remainder when m is divided by n.

The TYPE field contains a capital letter that identifies the packet: D for a data packet, Y for a positive acknowledgment, N for a negative acknowledgment, and others, a couple of which we'll meet later. A data packet is said to be "of type D," and so on.

We stated above that Kermit uses only printable characters. But what about the MARK field? Well, we lied to you. The MARK field normally contains an ASCII SOH character, that is, a 1, which happens to be one of the few control characters most systems will let through. If a Kermit receiver gets out of sync and loses track of where packets begin and end, it can recover by looking for an SOH.

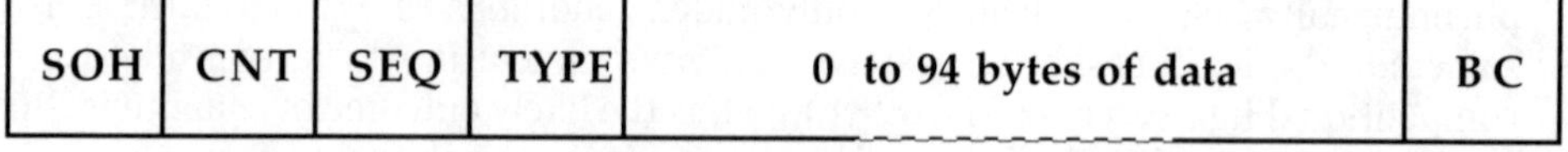

SOH	CNT	SEQ	TYPE	0 to 94 bytes of data	B C

SOH is an ASCII Start Of Header (code 1)
CNT is the encoded count of data bytes
SEQ is the encoded sequence number of the block
TYPE is the type of block (data, ack, etc.)
BC is the Block Check.

FIGURE 7.11: Kermit packet layout

2. Kermit takes absolutely no chances with control characters. It eliminates them from data as a matter of course. In fact, the only place Kermit ever sends a control character is in the MARK field.

Kermit translates data as it prepares each packet for transmission. Any control characters encountered are converted to two-byte sequences by a process called *prefixing*. A Control-A, for example, becomes a # followed by an A. A Carriage Return/Line Feed sequence is converted to #M#J (remember that CR is really Control-M, and LF really Control-J). A receiving Kermit, of course, performs the inverse translation. The # character itself is sent by doubling it: a # symbol in the data is transferred as ##.

This algorithm for squeezing out control characters means that in the worst possible case, that of transferring a file composed of nothing but controls, Kermit would double the amount of data during transmission. When we balance the rarity of such a file against the simplicity of Kermit's method, however, the algorithm seems quite acceptable.

3. The CHECK field at the end of the packet contains an error-check, also constrained to consist wholly of printable characters.

4. Every packet is terminated by a carriage return. This is a necessary crutch for Kermits that can read input only in units of lines. It also benefits many other Kermits that, while capable of performing character-at-a-time input, operate more efficiently on a line-at-a-time basis.

5. If Kermit has an eight-bit-wide path to work with (that is, if parity is not in use), it takes no steps beyond those listed above to protect the data in transit. In such a case, any character whose high (eighth) bit is set to binary 1 (i.e., whose value is in the 128–255 range) is transmitted without alteration of the eighth bit. Even with characters of this kind, however, if the low seven bits alone would otherwise represent a control character, then the byte will still be prefixed as above. This step is taken in order to outsmart any devices that might ignore high bits and eat control characters.

For a seven-bit path (that is, when the eighth bit is used for parity), Kermit expands all extended characters (those above 127) to two-character sequences, again by prefixing. A byte of value $128 + N$ is converted to the sequence &N. If the resultant N is a control character, it is prefixed in turn by the method previously described. Thus, 176 gets translated to &0, and 129 becomes &#!. Any & in the data is sent as #&.

Taken together, these two prefixing techniques increase the size of an average binary file by 76 percent. Techniques that produce more compact encoding are available but, again, there's much to be said for the simplicity of Kermit's method.

The combination of steps (1) through (4), with (5) included as necessary, is sufficient to get data through the roughest territory encountered in common practice. Kermit's avoidance of control characters not only precludes trouble in settings where such characters may trigger undesirable effects, but also grants Kermit the considerable benefit of compatibility with links using Control-S/Control-Q flow control.

Text Files, Binary Files, and Compression

Kermit's philosophy in moving files is to keep text files as useful as possible, and to keep binary files identical. Text files are transferred in a simple but effective virtual file format called *Kermit canonic form*, which uses ASCII codes with CRLF ends-of-line (EOLs). As an example, suppose a Kermit on a UNIX system is sending a text file to a Kermit on an IBM mainframe. The original file would already be in ASCII, but the sending Kermit would have to convert the LF-only EOLs, which are standard in UNIX, to CRLFs. The receiving Kermit would translate all characters from ASCII into the local character code, EBCDIC. Life is easy for Kermits running on PCs, because the canonic form is identical to the form in which DOS and OS/2 maintain text files.

Kermit must be told whether the files being transferred are to be treated as text or binary. On some occasions, it may be wise to transfer text files as though they were binary. For example, if you're moving text files between two systems that represent such files identically, transferring them as binary will save the Kermits the processing time associated with conversion to and from canonic form.

One of Kermit's unfortunate deficiencies, except when a rarely-implemented advanced feature is available, is the failure of the protocol itself to distinguish between text and binary files. The user must apprise *both* the sending and receiving Kermits of the nature of the file being transferred. To make matters worse, conventional Kermit programs provide rather awkward means of inputting this information. If the user becomes careless, a not-uncommon outcome is that one Kermit will deal with text files while the other treats the same files as binary.

Many files contain sequences of repeated characters that can be compacted during transfer. Highly formatted text files, for example, often contain long runs of spaces, and executable files typically include blocks of binary zeroes. Some Kermits have the ability to compress such files, reducing the number of bytes to be transmitted and, consequently, the transfer time required. Thus, instead of sending "000000000000000," a Kermit might send a message saying, in effect, "15 zeroes," just as a human speaker would. To be precise, a run of four or more identical characters can be represented as a three-character sequence: [Flag][Length][Repeated character]. The *Flag* is another prefix character of the kind we met above, in this case a tilde (˜). The *Length* is the number of repeated characters compressed, expressed in Kermit's standard biased-by-32 form. The last element of the sequence is the repeated character itself. Thus, the run of 15 zeroes would be encoded as ˜/0. Readers following this chapter closely will realize that this method can compress up to 94 repetitions of one character at a time. A run of 95 question marks would be represented as ˜??, while 99 of them would come out as ˜?%?.

The analysis of a large number of typical files shows that this simple technique, called *run-length encoding*, suffices to compensate for most of the expansion of data that Kermit performs for other reasons. We'll have more to say about this technique, and other methods of data compression, in Chapter 9.

Negotiation

Kermit gives us an opportunity to study a well-designed system of parameter negotiation. At the start of a file-transfer session, two Kermits exchange *Send Initiation* packets (type S) stating their respective requirements and capabilities. Requirements are statements such as "You must not send me packets longer than 72 bytes." Kermits will always honor such requests. Statements of capability are those such as "I can do run-length encoding." In practice, each requirement, and each capability, is expressed as a single character code. Two Kermits settle on what might loosely be termed "the least common denominator" of each of their respective capabilities. If both can handle compression, for example, then they'll use it; if only one admits to having that talent, then the Kermit so endowed recognizes that, for this session, it must not use it.

Here is a summary of what each Kermit tells its partner at the start of a session:

- The maximum packet length the partner may send. Since each Kermit adapts to its partner's wishes, the maximum packet size may differ for the two directions of transfer.

- The amount of time the partner should wait when it expects a packet. After this time-out, recovery action should be taken, such as retransmitting the previous packet.

- The character the partner should use to terminate the packets it sends. We suggested earlier that a packet is always terminated by a carriage return; this is usual, but, if some other character will work better, it can be specified here.

- The *control prefix character*. This is the prefix the Kermit will use to "quote" control characters. By default this is #, but an alternate character may be chosen. In practice, the control prefix character is almost never changed from the default.

The foregoing are mandatory parameters that all Kermits specify. Optional parameters may be added to indicate readiness to perform eighth-bit prefixing, run-length encoding, and some advanced, optional operations outlined below.

Compatibility between Kermits that cannot both handle extended features is ensured by the design of the Send Initiation packet. If a Kermit does not supply parameters for a given feature, its partner, concluding that the first Kermit does not support that feature, makes no attempt to use it. Conversely, a Kermit ignores parameters supplied for a feature it does not itself support.

Kermit comes as close as we have seen to a self-configuring protocol. Conceivably, the precise details of communication (parity, maximum packet length, choice of prefix characters, etc.) established between any given pair of Kermits might be unlike that between any other pair, and each unique pair could probably communicate with a minimum of intervention by the operator.

Advanced Features

No one can say that Kermit doesn't move with the times. Thanks to its design, it has managed to absorb numerous incremental improvements. Its advanced options enable it to convey file attribute information, accommodate long packets, and overcome the limitations of the protocol's stop-and-wait transfer tactics.

It's important to distinguish "classic Kermit," without advanced features, from "advanced Kermit," also dubbed "SuperKermit," which incorporates some or all of the latest options. Again, since the use of any option, advanced or otherwise, is negotiated by means of the standard Send Initiation exchange, classic and SuperKermits remain compatible. There are two significant differences between the recent, advanced options and the "regular" options. First, while all the regular options are designed for easy programming, the advanced options are tough to implement, with the result that they're not being adopted very quickly. Second, the new long-packets option and selective-reject ARQ scheme (see below) can, under the right circumstances, tremendously improve the protocol's efficiency compared to anything attainable with regular options.

The *file attributes* option allows a Kermit to transmit "type A" information packets prior to a file. In addition to such obvious file attributes as date and time of creation, access-permission data, and system of origin, these packets may contain various esoteric tidbits of information. More importantly, instructions may be transferred that detail the proper disposition of the file. This last feature is very powerful, enabling the receiver to deliver files as mail messages, submit them as batch jobs, or load them into memory for execution.

The *long packets* option permits packets to hold up to 9,024 bytes. The fact that this maximum size is equivalent to $95^2 - 1$ might tell you that the option is implemented by using two extra characters in each packet header to encode the length information. With the *extra long packets* option, using three extra header bytes, packets may expand to 857,374 ($95^3 - 1$) bytes in length. That ought to be a long enough packet for just about anybody.

The *sliding window protocol extension* allows the sender to transmit multiple packets before receiving an acknowledgment, changing Kermit from a stop-and-wait ARQ into a *selective-reject* ARQ protocol. Under this scheme, the sender may transmit packets continuously as long as acknowledgments arrive promptly enough to allow constant recycling of the sender's buffer space. After transmitting a packet, the sender must retain a copy until the packet is ACKed, against the possibility that a retransmission may be needed. The buffer space occupied by the copy is freed to accommodate new packets by the arrival of ACKs. Should the buffer become filled with unacknowledged packets, the sender will pause, awaiting an ACK before resuming transmission.

When a packet is NAKed, that packet alone is retransmitted. Since a retransmitted packet may turn up out of order, the receiver must maintain sufficient buffer space of its own to plug retransmitted packets into their proper positions before dispatching data to their final destination. This is illustrated in Figure 7.12.

The term *sliding window* thus refers to a "frame" encompassing unacknowledged packets stored in the sender's buffer. The rear edge of the window slides forward as acknowl-

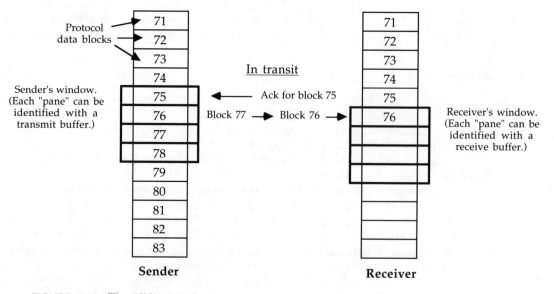

FIGURE 7.12: The "sliding window"

edgments are received and the associated packet copies overwritten; the front edge slides forward as new data packets are sent and copies placed in storage.

The two long packet options on the one hand, and the sliding window extension on the other, are intended to increase efficiency under different sets of circumstances; they are not normally used together. Long packets are valuable on half-duplex links where errors are infrequent. It should be easy to see why. Long packets have also proven ideal for use with high-speed error-correcting modems. The sliding-window extension is designed for connections with high propagation delays, such as satellite links and paths through PSNs; it also serves for any full-duplex channel with a high error rate. Since the ability to send acknowledgments concurrently with data packets is essential to selective-reject ARQ, the sliding window extension can be used only on full-duplex links.

MS Kermit

MS Kermit is the Kermit program designed for PCs running MS-DOS or PC-DOS. It is the result of a collaboration between the Columbia University Center for Computing Activities, where it originated, and Professor Joe R. Doupnik of Utah State University, who has produced several versions, for example, 2.3. Written in assembly language, it rates as one of the finest pieces of free software available for the PC. MS Kermit is easy to use, offers VT102 terminal emulation, and includes a modest script language (see Chapter 10). Newer releases support key redefinition, the long packets option, screen rollback (which provides for "scrolling backwards" to view bygone portions of a telecommunications session), special facilities for disabled users, and the ability to operate on NETBIOS-compatible LANs. (The NETBIOS, described in Chapter 14, is an IBM software-interface standard for local area networks.) A user with no specific requirement for other protocols might very well find that MS Kermit meets all of his or her communication needs.

MS Kermit also has server capability, meaning that it can be used to host a PC-based file distribution point—a restricted-function bulletin board system, as it were. We'll have more to say about servers in our discussion of LANs in Chapter 13.

Book of the Month

KERMIT: A File Transfer Protocol by Frank da Cruz (Bedford, MA: Digital Press, Division of Digital Equipment Corporation, 1987) will satisfy your appetite if you wish to learn more about this fascinating protocol. Laced with lighthearted analogies and drawings that are often as amusing as they are illustrative, the book is also well written and full of sound information. For those implementing the protocol, it includes a large section on writing a Kermit. The text is also highly recommended for anyone designing a file-transfer protocol.

Wrap-up

Kermits are available for nearly all popular systems, including PCs, Macintoshes, and most other personal and home computers, as well as DEC and other minis, UNIX systems, and IBM mainframes. A collection of freely distributed implementations (including sources) is available on industry-standard magnetic tape from Kermit Distribution, Columbia University Center for Computing Activities, 612 West 115th Street, New York, NY 10025. A handling fee is charged. Columbia also distributes MS Kermit and the Macintosh version on diskette. These same Kermits can also be obtained from bulletin board systems, PC user groups, and other sources, but Columbia provides a printed copy of the manual and a guarantee of receiving the latest revision. Columbia encourages users to copy and redistribute these Kermits, subject to the following conditions: Kermit must not be sold for profit; credit should be given where it is due; and new Kermit material should be sent to Columbia so the Trustees can maintain a definitive and comprehensive set of implementations for further distribution. Columbia also asks that Kermit be used only for peaceful and humane purposes.

As you may have gathered, Kermit found its early success in universities. It was greeted enthusiastically by the academic community for at least three reasons. First, universities tend to have many heterogeneous computers, and Kermit proved a boon for linking such systems together. Second, as PCs appeared on campuses, students began to use personal floppies for their files in preference to burdening mainframe disks with them. Kermit provided an ideal mechanism for transporting such files between mainframes and diskettes. Third, since universities never seem to have much money to spend on software (or anything else, for that matter), they eagerly snapped up the high-quality freebie that Kermit represented. The result was that volunteers, or perhaps manacled graduate students, were set to work porting Kermit to just about every known computer system.

Kermit is now rapidly achieving acceptance in the business world, after a considerable delay that undoubtedly stemmed from the protocol's initial lack of commercial support. Both commercial and academic Kermit users tend to be very happy with it.

When would you want to use Kermit? Kermit is often called for when you must negotiate file transfer over a seven-bit data path, or whenever you need a file transfer system that need not be fast but must be inexpensive. Generally, Kermit is likely to be a good choice for moving files between dissimilar systems, and may in some cases be the *only* choice. For PC-to-PC communication, where an eight-bit connection is generally in place, the relative inefficiency of basic Kermit may render it inferior to other CRC-protected protocols, except when its server capabilities are to be exploited. Advanced Kermit, however, makes an excellent PC-to-PC protocol.

In order to capitalize on the trend spawned by Kermit, the authors have designed a competitive protocol called Piggy, named after Kermit's lovely porcine companion. It is distinguished by acknowledgments in French, in keeping with Miss Piggy's penchant for the Gallic tongue. If this fails to establish our credentials, we will unleash Bill—named, without permission from Berke Breathed, for Bill the Cat, and consisting of nothing but ACKs.

ZMODEM

ZMODEM comes from the same source as XMODEM and YMODEM. It is accorded separate treatment here because it is on a much higher plane than, and only suffers from association with, its nominal forebears. In fact, ZMODEM is a superb protocol whose design has little in common with its X and Y namesakes.

ZMODEM was designed by Chuck Forsberg under a 1986 project for the development of a public-domain file-transfer protocol optimized for PSN use. The project was funded by Telenet with the intention of alleviating the network throughput problems cropping up with the then-predominant XMODEM and Kermit. As we have already pointed out, the timing strategies employed by XMODEM and Kermit render their use over PSNs somewhere between inefficient and impossible. (Kermits with the advanced sliding window option are more practical for PSN use.)

The designers briefly considered modifying YMODEM to provide the desired capabilities, but wisely decided to start with a clean slate. While borrowing ideas from Kermit,

Bisync, HDLC (described in the next chapter), and UUCP (UNIX-to-UNIX Communication Protocol), they also aimed to carry over one feature of XMODEM: its simplicity.

The design goals for ZMODEM were ease of use, high data transfer rate, robustness, and ease of implementation. Special attention was given to ensuring that the protocol would operate efficiently in the following situations:

- Over networks with significant propagation delays but low error rates, especially PSNs.

- Under the many timesharing systems and operating systems that place onerous restrictions on a program's ability to perform multiple simultaneous I/O operations.

- Over direct modem-to-modem links with modems that use adaptive duplex, that is, offer dynamic partitioning of the modems' bandwidth between the two directions of data flow.

- Over direct modem-to-modem links with high error rates.

The ZMODEM designers specifically chose not to address certain types of link. Seven-bit paths, for example, are not supported; ZMODEM requires a connection carrying a full eight bits per character. Also, while ZMODEM can operate on the rare path that exhibits both substantial propagation delays and high error rates, it does so rather inefficiently.

The protocol is easy to use: either of two communicating ZMODEMs may initiate a transfer, passing filenames and other necessary information between them. Batch transfers of multiple files, using wildcards (* and ?) in filenames, are possible. For robustness, data are protected by at least a 16-bit, and optionally a 32-bit, CRC.

For compatibility with links that restrict the flow of ASCII control characters, ZMODEM provides a means, similar to Kermit's, of disguising any control codes appearing in messages. This feature is activated only when required.

Here's a rundown of ZMODEM's strong points:

ZMODEM incorporates a range of ARQ schemes. The file receiver dictates which scheme is used, choosing the most efficient one it can handle. When both sender and receiver can manage it, the sender transmits data continuously in a process called *streaming*. A file, no matter how long, is sent as a single frame divided into data subpackets of up to 1,024 bytes each, as depicted in Figure 7.13. Each subpacket is CRC-protected, as are the frame header and most control messages. If the receiver detects an error, it interrupts the sender, requesting it to resume transmission beginning with the subpacket where the error occurred. The subpacket size is chosen to suit prevailing conditions. For example, 256-byte packets might be used when frequent errors are anticipated.

Streaming is intended for links capable of passing data full tilt without loss or for links that use XON/XOFF flow control. Streaming is *not* possible in the following settings, among others:

- On half-duplex circuits

- Where a sender is unable to read data arriving on the communication line without pausing in its transmission

- Where a receiver cannot simultaneously receive data from the line and write to disk.

ZMODEM adopts other ARQ tactics when such limitations prevail. One design factor partly responsible for this flexibility is the definition of three distinct types of data subpacket. The

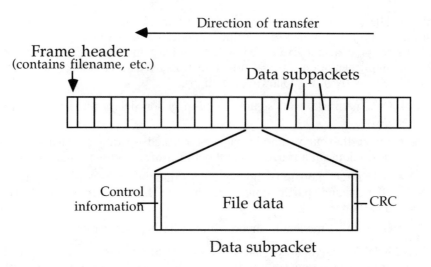

FIGURE 7.13: Format of a file in transit when sent by a protocol such as ZMODEM with streaming in effect

first type will not be acknowledged unless the receiver detects an error in it; the second always requires an acknowledgment, but the sender doesn't wait for it; the third requires an acknowledgment for which the sender immediately stops and waits.

When the ZMODEM program makes reference to a position in the data stream, it does so in terms of an *absolute byte ordinal* within the file being transferred. Thus, a receiver requests a retransmission not by telling the sender something like "back up to message 5 in the current cycle" but by requesting it to "restart transmission at the 24,654th character of the current file."

ZMODEM is unusual in that it permits the resumption of an interrupted file transfer at the point of suspension. A user who loses her connection, crashes the system, or runs out of disk space can easily restart the transfer where it left off. (Not only ZMODEM, but at least two other protocols, DART™ and BLAST, have a restart feature.) Although typically invoked when a transfer is stalled by a system failure, restart is also useful if a transfer involves a computer that becomes loaded down and sluggish; the user can deliberately halt the operation and resume it at a quieter time. Incidentally, ZMODEM's use of absolute byte ordinals greatly simplifies the business of resuming an interrupted transfer at the point at which it was broken off.

Where identical copies of certain files already exist at both ends of a link, a special ZMODEM option can automatically bring the two filebases into conformity without wasteful file-transfer operations. Before transferring a file, a ZMODEM sender calculates its CRC and transmits the information across the link; if the receiving ZMODEM has a file with the same name and CRC, both stations will assume the files are identical, and skip the transfer.

Another valuable ZMODEM option is data compression, using the very general and well-accepted Ziv-Lempel algorithm (see the IEEE publication *Computer*, volume 17, number 6, June 1984). "Very general" means that the algorithm is effective on almost any data susceptible to compression, in contrast to the many other compression methods oriented to some particular type of data, such as English-language text. The CRC-based selective-transfer feature and Ziv-Lempel compression are included in the ZMODEM specification but, as of late 1988, had not yet been implemented.

ZMODEM's designers learned a lot from the mistakes and shortcomings of other protocols. It is already a top-flight performer. But it is not set in stone, and future modifications, especially to handle seven-bit paths and bidirectional transfers, are likely.

PROPRIETARY PROTOCOLS

All the protocol designs discussed so far have been in the public domain. Several proprietary protocols are also to be found in PC communication packages. Among the best known are:

- BLAST, in the Communications Research Group's communication packages BLAST and BLAST II
- DART, in DCA®'s CROSSTALK Mk.4
- HyperProtocol™, featured in Hilgraeve's HyperAccess®
- RELAY™, in RELAY Silver™ and RELAY Gold®, both by VM Personal Computing
- CCDOS, in Carbon Copy PLUS™ from Meridian Technology

Little information can be given here about these protocols, because little is publicly available. Some copyright holders license proprietary protocols for use by others, but in all such cases the message formats and other details of protocol operation are kept more or less secret. It is tempting to assume that protocols designed by reputable companies must be of high quality. Protocols in this category are indeed of at least moderate quality, but it may be dangerous to assume more. In any case, the proof of the pudding must be in the eating.

The following is as much information as could be rooted out about some of these proprietary protocols.

BLAST

BLAST (BLocked ASynchronous Transmission) is the name of both a proprietary protocol and a communications package. Although the protocol's precise specifications are secret, general design details are known.

The BLAST protocol scores high marks for efficiency, but its outstanding selling point is the off-the-shelf availability of different versions for an impressive array of computer systems. BLAST is not particularly identified with PCs, and is equally at home on other micros, minis, and mainframes. It is sold for most popular personal computers and minis, many UNIX systems, and some mainframes, including IBM's. No other asynchronous protocol can claim commercial support by a single vendor across as wide a range of systems.

Like ZMODEM, BLAST achieves its efficiency by means of a sophisticated ARQ scheme that, under suitable conditions, allows data to be sent in a more-or-less continuous stream. Two other strong points are the protocol's ability to transfer files in both directions across a link at the same time and to resume an interrupted transfer.

BLAST employs 16-bit CRCs for error control, has a sliding window acknowledgment scheme, handles seven-bit connections, eliminates ASCII control characters from the protocol data stream, and offers data compression to boost transfer speed. It is tailored to connections with large propagation delays. At 1,200 bps, for example, BLAST can cope with a round-trip delay of 12 seconds (6 going, 6 returning) without loss of efficiency. Packet size is set by the user. The default size is 84 bytes, while the maximum is system-dependent (2,048 bytes for the PC). Two BLASTs with different maximum packet sizes will settle on the smaller one.

BLAST products use a copy-protection ploy also found in a few other communication products, including HyperAccess. Each BLAST package has a serial number built into the software. When two BLASTs start a communication session, they exchange serial numbers; if they both have the same number, they refuse to go any further. Unlike many other methods of copy protection, this scheme does nothing to inconvenience the legitimate customer.

BLAST products are not inexpensive, and for PC-to-PC communication in particular, BLAST II has plenty of competition. For heavy duty file transfer between PCs and other computer systems, though, or between dissimilar systems generally, BLAST may be hard to beat. Indeed, in the right setting, BLAST is dynamite.

DART

DCA is very tight-lipped about DART, one of two proprietary protocols in CROSSTALK Mk.4. (The other is the CROSSTALK® protocol, provided for compatibility with the older CROSSTALK XVI and Transporter™ products.) It seems that DCA is almost ridiculously reluctant to reveal information about DART. For example, DART appears to include a measure of data compression capability, which the CROSSTALK Mk.4 manual does not even mention. While it is entirely appropriate for DCA to keep the details of DART's data compression *techniques* confidential, it seems counterproductive to conceal the *existence* of data compression, a significant virtue of the protocol. Regrettably, this is not the only respect in which the Mk.4 manual is inadequate.

What we do know about DART is that it is a sliding window protocol that allows as many as 16 packets to be outstanding at any time. Perhaps DART's best feature is its adaptive packet size: the software dynamically adjusts the number of data bytes sent in a packet in response to error conditions present on the line. As errors increase in number, packet size is reduced; conversely, as line conditions improve, packet size is enlarged. The documentation suggests, however, that the minimum packet size is 512 bytes. This could be too large for efficient performance under an onslaught of line hits.

HyperProtocol

HyperProtocol is another speedy design that operates by streaming and takes advantage of data compression. In a survey of PC protocols published in the October 1987 edition of *Software Digest*®, HyperProtocol achieved distinction in accomplishing the fastest PC-to-PC file transfers.

The form of streaming used in HyperProtocol keeps data packets flowing continuously, under suitable line conditions, not only during a single file transfer, but also across file boundaries during a batch transfer. In the absence of transmission errors, the receiver sends an acknowledgment only at the end of each file batch, plus one "deadman" acknowledgment per minute during a transfer just to let the sender know that the receiver is still alive. When the receiver returns a negative acknowledgment, the sender retransmits the damaged data packet and all subsequent data packets. For error detection, the user can choose between checksums and 16-bit CRCs. The protocol automatically reduces its packet size in the presence of line errors.

HyperAccess offers a powerful compression facility capable of compacting almost any kind of data. When one HyperAccess communicates with another, it ordinarily compresses all file-transfer data no matter which of the available file-transfer protocols is used. (XMODEM and Kermit are also implemented in HyperAccess, but with a HyperAccess at each end, it seems foolish not to use HyperProtocol—except over a seven-bit connection, which favors Kermit.) HyperAccess checks whether its compression is improving efficiency, and disables the feature if it isn't doing much good. This means that the program wastes no time trying to compress random data and that, when running on slower PCs, its compressor will give up if it cannot keep pace with a high-speed (19,200 bps or above) connection. That's significant because, if a compressor cannot deliver compacted data fast enough to keep the line occupied, the transfer is likely to take less time without compression.

HyperProtocol was originally implemented only in HyperAccess, which is available only for PCs. HyperProtocol implementations for UNIX and other environments have recently appeared. HyperAccess incorporates a respectable script language, and may be a fine choice for PC-to-PC transfers when efficiency is a major concern.

RELAY

The RELAY protocol may be used between two PCs equipped with RELAY Silver or RELAY Gold, or between a PC running RELAY Gold and an IBM mainframe running RELAY/VM or RELAY/TSO. RELAY is "unsophisticated," in the sense that each end of a link must be separately primed for a transfer—that is, each station must be told to send or receive a file and must be provided with the filename. Batch transfers of multiple files are not supported. Nevertheless, RELAY remains an attractive option for PC-to-mainframe async transfers.

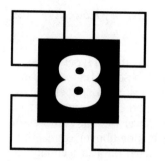

8

ADVANCED PROTOCOLS

The previous chapter dealt with protocols for asynchronous file transfer. Here we consider protocols a bit more generally, concentrating, as always, on those of importance to PCs. We'll start with a look at the synchronous kind, and then turn to networking protocols.

SYNCHRONOUS PROTOCOLS

In Chapter 1, we explored the basic concepts of sync versus async communications and learned that, technically, the difference between them is one of clocking. Synchronous devices share a common clock, while async devices each have individual clocks brought into temporary synchronization by triggers within the data stream. The more practical distinction is that async is ideal for traffic consisting of intermittent characters while, all other factors being equal, sync is more efficient for traffic consisting largely of data blocks of substantial size. Another practical difference between sync and async communications is that a protocol is almost always used in the synchronous case.

In synchronous communication, bit synchronization between stations is a given; start and stop bits are not required. Bit synchronization, however, is not the only kind needed. The receiver may have no trouble telling where bits are positioned in the data stream, but what about bytes? In a synchronous data stream, extra information is needed to enable the receiver to assemble bits into the correct groups of eight, and thus reconstitute the original message.

A few interfaces, including that defined by the CCITT recommendation X.20, provide a special circuit for the transmission of byte timing pulses. The most widely used method of byte synchronization calls for the transmitter to preface each protocol message with one or two fixed bytes called *sync characters*. Whenever a receiver is idling, it remains constantly on the lookout for such a sync character. As each bit arrives, the receiver puts it together with the previous seven bits and checks to see whether the result matches the sync character, as illustrated in Figure 8.1. The recognition of a sync character establishes byte synchronization for the message that follows. Both ASCII and EBCDIC define a character, called a SYN, specifically for this purpose. ASCII assigns its SYN the hexadecimal code 16, while EBCDIC uses hex 32. It would be correct to say that this byte synchronization is established *asynchronously*.

When synchronous protocols are employed on half-duplex links, byte synchronization is lost each time the direction of transmission is changed, so each message must be prefaced by SYNs. Although at least one SYN is required, two or three are most often used for greater safety. The receiver thus has an opportunity to regain byte synchronization with the first

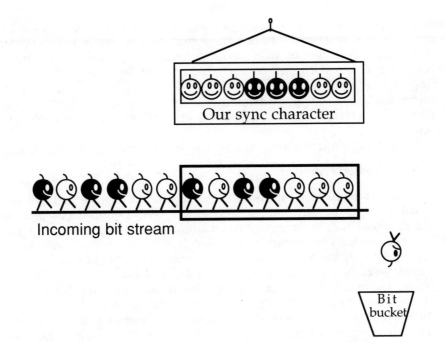

Our sync character

Incoming bit stream

Bit bucket

FIGURE 8.1: "Hunting the sync"

SYN and to confirm it with the extra SYNs. On a full-duplex link, sync characters are used for "idling" between messages; thus, except in the event of a substantial transmission error, byte synchronization is never lost.

The efficiencies of sync and async transmission can be compared in terms of overhead requirements, for sync characters in the former and for start and stop bits in the latter. The overhead for async transmission, assumed to be one start bit and one stop bit per eight-bit data byte, remains constant at 25 percent, regardless of traffic patterns. For a file transfer involving 512-byte blocks of data, the overhead for synchronous transmission, assuming two SYNs per block, is only 0.39 percent. (This comparison was illustrated, in a cruder manner, in Figure 1.18.) With half-duplex operation, the overhead for synchronous transmission is slightly higher, because a pad character is required at the end of each message.

Many people ask: Which is better, synchronous or asynchronous communication? This is a decidedly tricky question to answer. Don't let the figures given above fool you into thinking that, for file transfer, synchronous communication must inevitably be better. It's a simple matter of arithmetic that, if data traffic falls into suitable patterns, then at a given speed synchronous communication will be more efficient than async. Nevertheless, if the fastest async modem you can buy, or afford, runs faster than the fastest synchronous modem, then async may prove to be the better choice. Then again, async modems are not necessarily faster. The issue is also confused by the fact that, internally, many so-called asynchronous modems operate synchronously.

The safest and, indeed, most pertinent response is to point out that the question is misleading and irrelevant. It is misleading because it is too general: the answer may be clear for a specific instance, once many other factors are nailed down, but the general case is simply too nebulous. It is irrelevant because a bare choice between the two communication modes almost never arises. For the vast majority of connections between two machines capable of supporting either sync or async communications, other factors dictate the choice.

The block orientation of synchronous communication makes it inviting for batch or Remote Job Entry (RJE) and certain other types of terminals. RJE, or Remote Batch, terminals serve as remote submission points for batch jobs to a computer. Traditionally, such terminals were equipped with punched-card readers for job input and line printers for output. Synchronous communication is heavily used on both half-duplex and full-duplex links.

The most important protocols used for synchronous work are Bisync, SDLC, and HDLC.

Bit- and Byte-Oriented Protocols

Synchronous protocols fall into two distinct classes: bit-oriented and byte-oriented. Byte-oriented protocols transfer data in units of bytes. All asynchronous protocols are byte-oriented; indeed, with asynchronous communication you couldn't have it any other way. In the case of synchronous byte-oriented protocols, data are always transmitted in full eight-bit bytes, never as the seven-bit characters sometimes transmitted on async links. Bisync, for many years the most important and still the most common byte-oriented synchronous protocol, is the only one adopted by a large number of computer vendors. The other protocols discussed in this chapter, SDLC and HDLC, are bit-oriented.

Bit-oriented protocols, which do not, in principle, require that any aspect of communication be conducted in terms of bytes, can transfer blocks of data consisting of 1, 29, or 555 bits. A typical data stream for a bit-oriented protocol is shown in Figure 8.2. When the line is idle, patterns of bits called *flags* are constantly transmitted. They serve much the same purpose as the sync characters described above. The usual binary pattern for a flag is the eight-bit sequence 01111110. A receiver idles as long as it sees flags arriving, starts accumulating data as soon as it sees something else, and continues until it sees the next flag. If enough data are assembled to constitute a message, they are processed as such; otherwise, they are discarded. As you might imagine, line noise or interference may occasionally transform a data sequence into a flag. The false flag will be thrown out, causing the rest of the associated message to fail its CRC, and the message will ultimately need to be retransmitted.

Although messages must be able to carry arbitrary data, they must also be constrained not to contain flags. These requirements are reconciled by a simple encoding process: in transmitted data, an extra 0-bit is inserted after any sequence of five 1-bits. This alteration forecloses the possibility that a message will contain the six or more consecutive 1-bits needed to form a flag. The receiver, of course, performs the reverse transformation, discarding any 0-bit that follows five 1-bits. This encoding process, illustrated in Figure 8.3, is called *bit-stuffing* or *zero-insertion*. Readers with programming experience will quickly recognize that bit-stuffing implemented in software would be awkward and slow on most computers; the job is universally performed in hardware, which makes it a fairly trivial operation. The necessary hardware is built into the serial port.

Flag	Flag	Flag	Frame	Flag	Frame	Flag	Flag

FIGURE 8.2: Sample data stream for a bit-oriented protocol

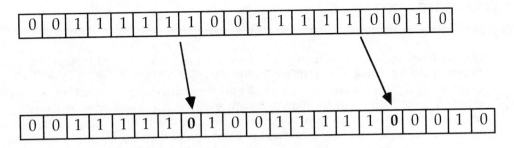

FIGURE 8.3: Bit stuffing/zero insertion

Despite the latitude bit-oriented protocols offer in principle, most actual examples handle data only in units of integral bytes. Thanks to the low overhead for data transparency afforded by zero-insertion, bit-oriented protocols tends to be more efficient than byte-oriented protocols.

Synchronous Ports for PCs

IBM sells a Synchronous Communications Adapter for PCs that includes an RS-232 port capable of synchronous operation. To go with the adapter, they offer a bewildering number of software packages, seven at last count. It is possible to buy a plain synchronous port from other vendors, but such ports are most often bundled with the software required to make them do something useful. Since most people will use a synchronous port for a single purpose only, typically that of emulating a synchronous terminal, this approach makes a lot of sense.

Synchronous Modems

A synchronous port is normally used with a synchronous modem, although synchronous modem eliminators are available for direct connect. (Modem eliminators were described in the first section of Chapter 5.) Synchronous modems, like asynchronous types, are available in both PC-internal and external models, although the external variety are much more common. There is no such thing as an acoustically coupled synchronous modem.

A synchronous modem will handle bit- and byte-oriented protocols equally well; in either case, the modem just sees streams of bits.

As we observed in Chapter 3, the clocks that synchronize synchronous connections are usually located in the modems; the transmitter section of each modem provides timing for the associated data stream.

The connection between a PC and an external synchronous modem is akin to that between a PC and an async modem, except that the cable must be set up to carry RS-232's timing signals on Pins 15 and 17. (RS-232 connections are diagrammed in Appendix A.) The modem sends a pulse on Pin 15, Transmitter Signal Element Timing, each time it is ready to have the DTE present the next bit for transmission on the Transmitted Data (TD) circuit. The modem pulses on Pin 17, Receiver Signal Element Timing, whenever it has a newly received bit ready for the DTE on Received Data (RD). Under RS-232, Pin 24 is also reserved for timing, providing Transmitter Signal Element Timing in cases where the transmitting DTE supplies the clock—a less common method of transmission timing.

BISYNC, SDLC, AND HDLC

Bisync

Bisync, developed in 1966, is an old warhorse that, like many things in the world of computers, has become so entrenched that many organizations still use it extensively; a few stragglers will probably continue to do so into the next century. It's not a bad protocol—it does a decent job—but its internal design is ugly and old-fashioned. Although its very name and the use of the protocol are strongly associated with its inventor, IBM, Bisync has become an industry-wide standard, and remains one of the very few protocols to facilitate communication among certain computers of different manufacturers.

Bisync is also known by the alternate abbreviation BSC, for Binary Synchronous Communications, its official name. The word *binary* here does not derive from the protocol's use in transmitting binary information, but from the *two* sync characters transmitted prior to each message.

Bisync is strictly a stop-and-wait ARQ protocol; any single exchange of messages is a "Ping-Pong" procedure, with each station transmitting in alternation. In the absence of errors, this normally entails a sequence of data block/acknowledgment, data block/acknowledgment, etc. Note that this does not prevent Bisync's use on full-duplex lines; in fact, it is often put to such use. By eliminating the delays required to reverse direction on a half-duplex line, full-duplex capability slightly improves Bisync's efficiency.

Several versions and variants of Bisync exist for use with different types of equipment. For example, 2780/3780 Bisync is used with the IBM RJE terminals of those numerical designations, while 3270 Bisync serves 3270-style interactive terminals. The protocol can also be used with several character sets. For EBCDIC, the most common case, 16-bit CRCs are used for error control; for ASCII, parity is applied to each character, and the entire message is checked by a similar method, called Longitudinal Redundancy Check (LRC). (This was shown in Figure 6.6, where LRC corresponds to the "horizontal" parity check.) When used in protocols, character parity is also referred to as a Vertical Redundancy Check (VRC), in part to help distinguish it from the LRC. Most Bisync equipment made by IBM is designed for EBCDIC use only.

Bisync is versatile enough to permit operation on both point-to-point and multipoint lines. The distinction was illustrated in Figure 7.1. Multipoint, also called *multidrop*, is a setup in which more than two stations are connected on the same line, calling for specially designed modems. The use of Bisync on such a line requires that one station, normally a mainframe, act as the master and that the other stations, normally terminals, act as slaves. Only one slave may be in active communication with the master at any given time, while the other slaves remain quiet. When the master has data for a slave, it transmits a short message, called a *selection*, addressed to that slave; the slave's response indicates whether or not it is capable of receiving data. (If the slave were a printing terminal, for example, it might be unable to receive data because it was out of paper.) When the master is not busy with output, it constantly cycles through its list of slaves, sending each one a "poll" asking whether that slave has any data for the master. The response is effectively "yes" or "no." When a slave answers "yes," the master invites it to start sending data. This organization precludes any direct communication between slaves.

Bisync has one wrinkle not found in the other protocols we've studied so far: a special control message called a WACK, or *Wait Acknowledgment*. A receiver sends a WACK when it has received a data message intact but wants to defer formal acknowledgment because it is temporarily unable to receive any more data. The WACK essentially means "I got that last message okay, and I'll ACK it when I'm good and ready." A WACK must be followed, within a certain period of time, by a proper ACK. This provides an effective yet simple means of flow control.

Bisync's greatest shortcoming is that it provides no error detection for control messages. As with XMODEM, Bisync data messages are error-protected, but ACKs, NAKs, EOTs, and the like are not. Although this does not diminish Bisync's importance, it does compromise its reliability, because a transmission error may generate a spurious control message.

SDLC

Synchronous Data Link Control (SDLC) was designed by an IBM technician, working overtime, who was frustrated with Bisync. One can only hope that this achievement was rewarded, as it deserved to be, with a huge pay raise, a promotion, and every other form of encouragement IBM could muster.

Data link control is basically another term for *protocol*. SDLC stands as the original member of a class of bit-oriented protocols that share the zero-stuffed transmission scheme described in the previous section and the frame format shown in Figure 8.4. Technically, an SDLC frame includes the flags that bracket it. When one frame immediately follows another, the single flag separating them serves as both the closing flag of the first and the opening flag of the second.

SDLC operates on a point-to-point link, a multipoint link, or a loop. An *SDLC loop* consists of a ring of stations, each of which forwards frames in one direction around the ring's periphery. In a loop or multipoint arrangement, as in Bisync, one station must be the master (called the *primary station*); the rest are slaves (called *secondary stations*). And, as with Bisync's "polled" mode, all communication involves the primary station; secondary stations cannot talk to each other directly. The address field of each frame contains the number of the addressed secondary station. The control field indicates the type of message, the information field carries any data (always in multiples of eight bits), and the Frame Check Sequence (FCS) contains a 16-bit CRC. We won't go into the details of the various frame types except to say that, in principle, they include acknowledgments, various frames used to initiate and terminate communication on a link (to say "hello" and "goodbye," as it were), information frames for transporting data, and a special frame transmitted by a secondary station when it receives an invalid frame.

SDLC is a continuous ARQ protocol. It does not pause after every frame, but sends several frames at a shot. Every communication transaction is initiated by the primary station, which sends a batch of frames to a secondary station and then awaits a response. A flag called the *poll bit* is set in the last frame of the batch to indicate that it's time for the secondary station to reply. (A bit is said to be simply *set* when it is set high, that is, to 1, and *cleared* when it is set low.) On receiving a poll, the secondary station sends whatever frames it has for the primary station, and marks the last frame of its sequence by setting the flag just mentioned—known, for this purpose, as the *final bit*. The secondary stations get regular

Flag	A	C	Information	FCS	Flag

FIGURE 8.4: SDLC frame format

opportunities to send data to the primary, despite their inability to initiate communication, because the primary, when it has nothing else to do, periodically polls them, as described above for Bisync.

Each frame batch may include up to seven frames containing data. Called "information frames," these are numbered in modulus-8 sequence (i.e., by a count cycling between 0 and 7). It is primarily this ability to send several data frames at once that makes SDLC significantly more efficient than Bisync. Greater efficiency, coupled with the higher reliability afforded by SDLC's use of error detection on all frames, makes it a much better choice than Bisync. Both protocols are used in IBM mainframe environments, notably in 3270-terminal networks, but SDLC is the choice of an ever-increasing majority of 3270 users.

HDLC and Others

High-level Data Link Control (HDLC) is an ISO standard protocol based on SDLC. Several other versions of SDLC/HDLC have been adopted by various organizations. For example, Advanced Data-Communications Control Procedure (ADCCP) is ANSI's standard bit-oriented protocol.

NETWORK ARCHITECTURES AND PROTOCOLS

Suppose that two application programs, A and B, are running on separate computers connected to a complex network. Suppose further that some useful purpose would be served by having these programs engage each other in a dialogue. Setting up a communication session for them is no easy task, especially if they are separated by a string of a dozen heterogeneous computers all connected to each other in different ways. Clearly, it would be dandy if A and B could communicate without concern for the network's underlying details or the intricacies of effecting the communication, as easily as picking up the phone and dialing a friend's number. Unfortunately, networking is not that simple. It is equivalent to giving the phone system step-by-step instructions on how to route the call, telling it what bandwidth is required for the conversation, specifying how it should bill charges, and so on. Thus, it is immensely important that networks be built, to the greatest extent possible, in ways that are both precisely organized and strongly standardized.

Faced in the 1970s with many complex and incompatible proprietary networking systems, notably IBM's Systems Network Architecture and DEC's DECnet™, the CCITT undertook to develop a new networking scheme free from the entanglements of specific vendors. The first fruit of this admirable endeavor was the network architecture known as "Open Systems Interconnection (OSI)/Basic Reference Model" (International Standard ISO 7498). Since it defined a hierarchy of seven functional layers, OSI came to be called "the seven-layer model." Each layer performs a well-delineated part of the work required to create, maintain, and terminate a dialogue between A and B. Further development, still in progress, has served to define implementations for each of the seven layers.

The layered architecture may be viewed in three ways. First, we can describe the model in terms of the *services* each layer provides. Second, we can discuss network operation in terms of layered *protocols*. Third, we can dig a little deeper and examine the *modules* that implement each layer. We will do each in turn.

Network Services

Conceptually, it's convenient to discuss the network layering in terms of services. Each layer performs a certain set of services for the benefit of the layer above it. In effect, each layer's

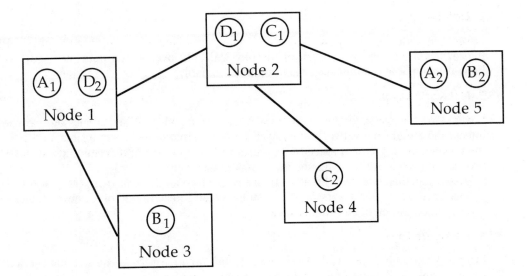

FIGURE 8.5: Nodes in a network

services consist of adding value to the services provided to it by the next lower layer. The bottom layers provide low-level services such as transporting and routing data. The top layers provide high-level services such as establishing network sessions and transforming communicated data according to a user's needs.

We speak of the member stations of a network as *nodes*, and of programs that use the network as *user programs*, a term that distinguishes them from programs that play roles within the network. (A user program in this sense can generally be considered an "application program," which is itself a regrettably vague term.) The user programs involved in a dialogue reside on the two *end nodes*; other network nodes, which may be responsible for relaying messages between the end nodes, are called *intermediate nodes*. Any node may function as an end node for one set of dialogues and as an intermediate node for other dialogues, as shown in Figure 8.5.

We'll summarize the services each layer provides, taking the layers in ascending order.

1. Physical Layer

The Physical Layer provides the services associated with a physical link, those of electrically encoding and physically transferring messages between nodes. The physical connection may be embodied in a dialed telephone connection, a leased line, a private cable, or any other communications link. Layer 1 is responsible for:

- Establishing the connection when necessary (e.g., dialing a call)
- Configuring the link (i.e., setting line speed, transmission formats, sync or async operation, etc.)
- Moving bits across the link
- Disconnecting the physical link, when necessary

In a nutshell, Layer 1 provides Layer 2 with a method (typically error-prone) of moving bits between two machines.

2. Link Layer

Layer 2 provides reliable flow- and error-controlled communication over the physical link. It provides a logical link, on top of the physical link, over which data messages, usually limited to some maximum size, may be moved reliably.

3. Network Layer

Layer 3 routes messages for data transfer between nodes. When a message reaches an intermediate node in a network, the Layer 3 entity at that node is responsible for forwarding the message onto the next stage of its journey. This may entail determining which link, of several connected to the node, should carry the message.

Taken together, the first three layers are referred to as the *subnet layers*. To provide full connectivity, all subnet layers must be implemented in each node of a network. Figure 8.5 shows the operation of the subnet layers.

4. Transport Layer

Layers 4 through 7 are collectively called *end-to-end layers* because their services are required only in the end nodes, not in intermediate nodes.

Layer 4 manages end-node-to-end-node communication, delivering units of data, of whatever size the user wishes, from end to end across the net. While the Link Layer ensures that a message will be delivered without damage *if it's delivered at all*, the subnet may not guarantee that all messages will, in fact, be delivered, or that they will be delivered in the order in which they were dispatched. Thus, the Transport Layer may be called upon to handle flow control, retransmission, and message sequencing.

5. Session Layer

Layer 5 is responsible for establishing, managing, synchronizing, and terminating network sessions (dialogues) between users.

6. Presentation Layer

Layer 6 takes care of translating data to and from standardized formats, as may be negotiated by the users. This job may include character set translation or any of several other forms of data conversion as, for example, between two different representations of floating point numbers. While Layer 6 transformations often serve to present data to the receiving application in a convenient form, they are also carried out for purposes directly related to the communication: data encryption to protect data on their way through the network, compression to hasten the data's passage, and so on.

7. Application Layer

Layer 7 constitutes an interface for a user program. This layer is often understood to encompass an application program that performs a network-specific user service, such as file transfer.

Another way of looking at this model is to regard the layers as providing logical channels of progressively greater value. Thus, Layer 1 supplies a link connection that carries raw bits; Layer 4 furnishes a network connection that reliably transports user messages; Layer 6 provides a network connection that will, when required, convert the data flowing through it according to the user's needs; and so on.

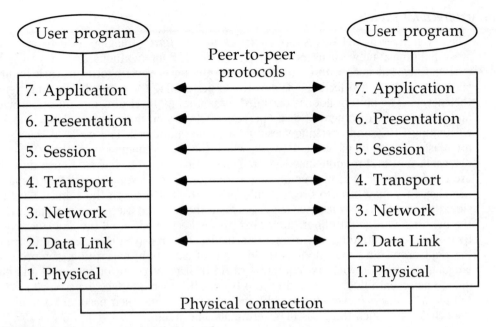

FIGURE 8.6: Peer-to-peer network protocols

Layered Protocols

To the user, a layered network embodies several levels of services. An operational view would focus on protocols. The Physical Layer is normally implemented by a physical interface such as RS-232, while the other layers, 2 through 7, are each implemented by a peer-to-peer protocol. *Peer-to-peer* means that each such protocol serves communication between two network entities found at the same level in different nodes, as shown in Figure 8.6. At the top of the hierarchy of layers sit the user programs themselves.

The intent of the seven-layer division is that each layer be implemented on each computer in a given network. Within a node, a layer communicates only with its immediately adjacent layers. Between nodes, a layer communicates with a partner layer at the same level via the appropriate peer-to-peer protocol.

The ISO standard protocols are: X.25 for Layers 1, 2 and 3, ISO Transport (X.224) for Layer 4, and ISO Session (X.225) for Layer 5. (While not part of the ISO standard, a protocol known as ASN.1 [Abstract Syntax Notation] is commonly used in Level 6.) For Layer 7, different types of network use call for different protocols, such as File Transfer and Access Management (FTAM), Virtual Terminal Protocol (VTP) for remote login, and X.400 for electronic mail.

Modules

The third view of the model focuses on software modules that implement each layer in a given node. Ideally, each module is a discrete software component that provides "clean," well-defined interfaces to the modules immediately above and below it. If changes are required at one level—such as bug fixes, implementation of standard revisions, or the wholesale replacement of one protocol by another—it should be possible to replace the relevant module with minimal impact on the rest of the network.

An Architectural Sketch

The seven-layer model serves as a *network architecture*. Imagine a "network" of eight-story buildings: network users, who live in eighth-floor penthouses, spend their lives in ever-shifting dialogues with each other, while the lower seven stories in each building are staffed by well-trained technicians devoted to performing the network functions defined for their levels. The bottom floor is occupied by pounding physical communication machinery and its cheerful but somewhat deaf operators. The second floor houses clerks who are busy calculating CRCs and checking message sequence numbers. The walls of the third floor are plastered with maps of the network, which the middle managers on this level consult to determine how best to route messages to their destinations. The harried fourth-floor dwellers are responsible for getting user messages from origin to destination. Before dispatching a message, they may have to break it into pieces to fit it through the subnet. On the input side, they must reconstruct user messages from the bits and pieces of data that arrive from the network. On the fifth floor, junior executives keep track of all the dialogues conducted by users in their building, ensuring, in particular, that received messages are distributed to the right users. The sixth floor is the domain of experts in encryption, compression, and language translation who, on request, perform their conversions on incoming and outgoing data. The seventh floor is staffed by top brass—the user interface experts who know how to talk to the users (never an easy job) and who understand their peculiar vocabulary when they chat about such things as files, terminals, and mail.

The staff on each floor communicates directly only with the staff on the two adjacent floors. They pass data messages back and forth, together with pertinent instructions, parameters, and status information. For outbound traffic, each group accepts a message from the floor above, performs whatever transformations are required, adds information to the head or tail for the benefit of their peers at the receiving end, and then passes it down to the layer below. Similarly, an inbound message is passed up layer by layer; each group examines and then strips off information added for its use, converts the rest of the data as required, and finally hands it to the next layer up. A group may also discard a received message, as is the case when a bad CRC is found.

Summary

The OSI Reference Model has been very influential, and many networks today are designed in accordance with its guidelines. Even many companies that do not choose ISO protocols to implement their nets still conform architecturally to the model. The seven-layer model is well known and frequently cited in articles, books, and reviews. Familiarity with the model will help you to understand the rest of this book and to cope with the world of networking.

It must also be acknowledged that the OSI model has come in for a fair amount of criticism. Some writers have argued compellingly that it imposes too narrow a view on network structure, failing, for example, to adequately address questions of internetworking (networking networks together). One reply to such complaints is that a fairly decent standard is better than none at all, but there is also merit to the claim that a flawed standard that neglects substantial practical achievements is sadly constricting. For a masterly commentary on these issues, see *The Elements of Networking Style* by Michael A. Padlipski (Prentice-Hall, 1985).

The protocols we've examined so far do not fit the OSI model. Since they are intended for use on direct point-to-point links rather than within networks, there is no reason why they should conform to it. The functions addressed by these protocols straddle several OSI layers, typically incorporating elements of at least Layers 2, 6, and 7. We will proceed in this chapter to examine three protocols, MNP, X.25, and X.PC™, that were designed to fit the model. X.25 and MNP are really "protocol suites" rather than single protocols, each constituting a set of protocols covering several layers. We will pay most attention to the Link Layer of the model, whose functions are addressed by most of the protocols to be discussed. A Link Layer protocol, remember, is one that attends to the reliable (error-controlled and flow-controlled) transportation of a data stream across a point-to-point link.

MNP

MNP, for Microcom Networking Procotol™, is the de facto standard protocol in two settings: in error-correcting modems (the subjects of a later section in this chapter) and for error-protected asynchronous access to packet switching networks (PSNs). These two uses frequently go together; people use MNP-based modems to gain reliable dial-up access to public networks. For modems, MNP stands a good chance of becoming a formal standard as part of CCITT recommendation V.42, published but not yet adopted at this writing.

Microcom, a leading manufacturer of error-correcting modems, originally designed MNP for use in electronic mail systems. The MNP specification actually includes three protocols, called the *link*, the *session*, and the *file transfer* protocols. The link and session protocols implement their namesake layers in the OSI model; the file transfer protocol performs functions of OSI's Presentation and Application Layers. The higher-level, session and file transfer portions of MNP, proprietary to Microcom, are little used and of negligible importance. The link protocol, on the other hand, has been so successful that most references to MNP are made as though the link layer were all there was to it. The balance of this discussion, then, applies solely to the link protocol.

Microcom developed its link protocol for incorporation into protocol modems, and later put much of that design into the public domain.

There are six distinct classes of MNP operation, identified as Class 1, Class 2, and so on. Class 1 has the least capability, and each successively higher class represents an incremental increase in the protocol's capability and performance. Here is a summary of the classes:

- Class 1 provides asynchronous byte-oriented data exchange in two-way alternate (half-duplex) mode.

- Class 2 provides asynchronous byte-oriented data exchange in two-way simultaneous (full-duplex) mode.

- Class 3 provides synchronous bit-oriented simultaneous two-way data exchange.

- Class 4 adds Adaptive Packet Assembly™and Data Phase Optimization™. The first provides procedures for adjusting packet sizes according to prevailing error conditions. As in DART and similar cases already described, packet size is increased when errors are relatively few, and decreased when line noise is necessitating frequent retransmissions. The second addition reduces the amount of redundant administrative information in each packet to further trim protocol overhead.

- Class 5 adds a data compression algorithm to increase data throughput. The algorithm continuously analyzes user data and adjusts the compression parameters to maximize performance. Since the compression is carried out as part of the transmission process, both interactive-terminal data and file transfer data can be compacted effectively.

- Class 6 adds two more features. Universal Link Negotiation™ allows two MNP modems equipped for operation at several speeds to initiate communication at a low speed and then to negotiate the use of a higher speed. Statistical Duplexing™ offers an algorithm that monitors data traffic patterns and dynamically allocates half-duplex modulation to simulate full-duplex service.

Classes 1 through 4 are in the public domain; Classes 5 and 6 remain proprietary to Microcom and may be licensed for a substantial fee. The progression of MNP performance levels allows a product designer to choose the level suited to the processing functions of a particular device, and to optimize the price-performance mix for the product's area of application.

MNP is one of few protocols designed to operate either synchronously or asynchronously. Two MNP modems begin communicating with each other asynchronously, then switch to synchronous mode if they determine that both are capable of doing so. The protocol employs continuous ARQ with 16-bit CRC (CRC-16) error detection.

MNP has won great favor in Europe and has been adopted by the major United States PSN vendors, Telenet and TYMNET. Among other networks supporting MNP are Transpac in France and Britain's ICL/Mercury network.

The document describing the public domain portions of MNP may be purchased from Microcom for $100. If the protocol is ultimately adopted as a CCITT standard, its specs will also be published as part of a CCITT document.

X.25

CCITT Recommendation X.25 defines a fixed-connection interface between a PSN and a computer or terminal. This very popular standard is now found on almost all commercial PSNs. X.25 has also been extended, expanded, and contorted to fit many other applications, so that variants and subsets of X.25 are currently used in ISDNs, teletex (a successor to telex), Hayes V-series modems, and for many other purposes. Since X.25 may well come to stand as the most important protocol in data communications, we will describe it at some length.

XMODEM was presented in Chapter 7 as an example of a simple and easily understood, although far from perfect, protocol. Readers who want to learn about a much better but more complex protocol, the foremost representative of its class, will do well to read about X.25. This section is an introduction; a technical synopsis is given in Chapter 16. These materials are not intended to be a definitive text on X.25, but will help those studying the protocol to deal with the typically terse tracts, such as the standard document itself, that do provide a complete description.

X.25 addresses the lowest three layers of the OSI model, which collectively define an interface between a DTE (piece of Data Terminal Equipment) and a DCE (piece of Data Communications Equipment). The DTE is the network user (a computer or terminal) and the DCE is, at least conceptually, the network to which the DTE is connected. Let's examine X.25's layers.

The Physical Interface

The X.25 physical interface between the DCE and DTE may follow the conventions of either X.21 (another CCITT standard) or X.21 *bis*, an alias for RS-232. In North America, RS-232 is normally used for X.25 connections, while in other parts of the world the X.25 physical interface more often adheres to X.21.

The Frame Level

Layer 2 of X.25 is called the *frame level* because its protocol message unit is a frame of the kind described in our discussion of SDLC and HDLC. This protocol is intended for use on permanent full-duplex connections, as opposed to the sort of transitory connections created by dial-up telephone links.

The job of the frame level is to carry data in a timely and reliable manner over the DTE-DCE link, as shown in Figure 8.7. Layer 3 supplies Layer 2 with data in units called *packets*; Layer 2 encapsulates packets into frames for transport across the link. Frames received by Layer 2 are unpacked, and the packets are delivered to Layer 3. Frame and packet traffic flow independently in both directions across the link. Each PSN dictates a maximum size for the frames.

Layer 2 messages are transmitted using the HDLC framing technique described earlier in this chapter. To recap: Each message is bracketed by *flags*, bit patterns of the form 01111110. This bit pattern is prevented from appearing within messages by means of the zero-insertion algorithm, which mandates the insertion of a 0-bit in the transmitted data stream after any five consecutive 1-bits. Successive messages must be separated by at least one flag; flags are also used to fill idle time on lines. A station recognizes as a message any received sequence not consisting of flags.

There are two versions of the frame-level protocol: *Link Access Protocol (LAP)*, an antique rarely found in practice and not discussed further here, and *Link Access Protocol Balanced (LAPB)*, the version in standard use with PSNs today. The frame level of X.25 is almost always referred to as LAPB when used in a context that does not involve Layer 3.

In X.25 parlance, a byte is called an *octet*, stressing the fact that data appear exclusively in eight-bit units. As previously noted, a byte in the world of microcomputers is universally understood to be an octet. In general, however, *byte* may identify any small unit of data. In this discussion, we follow X.25's nomenclature.

LAPB's frame format is shown in Figure 8.8. Each frame commences with a single-octet address field (A), followed by a control field (C) of the same size, and then a variable-length

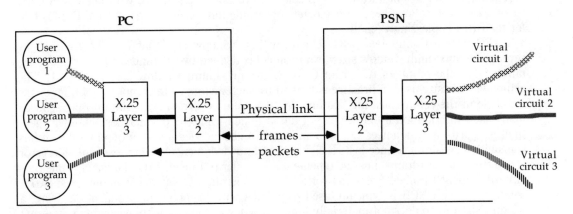

FIGURE 8.7: X.25 link between a PC user and a packet switch network

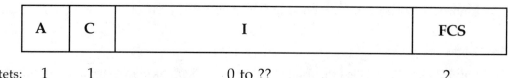

Octets: 1   1   0 to ??   2

> A is an address
> C is the control field
> I is the information (i.e., data) field
> FCS is the frame check sequence (16-bit CRC)

FIGURE 8.8: X.25 frame format

information field (I). The frame is terminated by a two-octet frame check sequence (FCS), which carries a CRC.

The frame level carries a single stream of data between two machines. There being no requirement for addressing, the A-field is used for another purpose, establishing a certain coordination between the two stations. This coordination technique is not easily explained; interested readers can find more on the subject in Chapter 16.

The control field contains the frame type identifier and, where necessary, sequence numbers. Frame types include the data-carrying information frame (I-frame), various acknowledgments, and some control frames used to initiate and terminate the logical connection. A logical connection, or *session,* must be established before data can be transferred. The process of establishing a logical connection enables each station to verify at the outset that the other is alive and operational. Similarly, reinitialization resets the link and allows the stations to "start clean" after a serious error, such as a station crash or an apparent breach of protocol.

The I-field of an I-frame contains data (i.e., packets) carried on behalf of Layer 3. The frame level itself has absolutely no concern for the nature of the data it carries. Generally, frames other than I-frames must have empty I-fields.

The maximum size of a frame is typically 128 or 256 bytes. Thus, with fairly well filled I-fields, the protocol overhead of five octets per frame (one each for flag, A, and C, plus two for the CRC) is pleasingly small.

LAPB uses a Continuous-ARQ scheme with a window size that may be as large as seven. The maximum window size for a protocol is defined by the range of packet sequence numbers; if the numbers run from 0 to R, the maximum window size is $R - 1$. The actual window size used in practice is limited by such factors as the amount of buffer space available in the communicating stations. With a window size of N, a station may send as many as N information frames ahead of the last such frame its partner has acknowledged. In other words, a station need not stop and await an acknowledgment until and unless it has transmitted N I-frames since last receiving an acknowledgment. When a transmission error is detected and an I-frame must be repeated, the sender retransmits the damaged frame plus any subsequent I-frames. Some networks restrict operation to smaller window sizes; two is common. Since LAPB is typically used over links with insignificant propagation delay, a window size of two does not materially limit efficiency as long as acknowledgments are sent promptly.

As we stated earlier, X.25 was intended for use over fixed links. It may prove unsuitable for transient links because LAPB does not provide means for a station to determine its partner's identity; on a dial-up link, where "anyone" can call in, this presents a potential security problem. It may also present another kind of problem: the network does not know whom to bill. However, such limitations have not totally prevented LAPB from being used on dialed connections.

The Packet Level

X.25's Layer-3 protocol is called the *packet level*. It acts as an interface between a network user and the communication services provided by the network. While conceptually the packet level is an interface to a network as a whole, the protocol essentially mediates between the user's machine and the network node to which it's attached, much as the Layer 2 protocol does.

As noted above, packets are carried across the DTE-DCE link by the frame level; each Layer 2 I-frame carries exactly one Layer 3 packet in its I-field.

The network services accessible at the packet level are classified as two kinds of *virtual circuit*. Services in one category are known as *switched virtual circuits (SVCs)*, often called simply *virtual calls*; less common are *permanent virtual circuits (PVCs)*. These terms were previously described in the section on PSNs. (Older versions of the standard mention *datagram services*, but these have been dropped.) Virtual calls will be the main focus of this discussion.

A connection over a packet network is termed "virtual" because it is normally allocated no physical resources within the net. This contrasts with a telephone call in which an exclusive channel is usually switched into place, connecting the two parties for the duration of the call. In other respects, a virtual call *is* similar to a dialed telephone call: a user requests a connection to a given host, and the network attempts to set up a relationship between the two parties. A single fixed path may not exist, however; each packet may be routed independently. Relatively speaking, a PVC is more like a leased telephone line— permanently available, but still "virtual."

At Layer 2, the user-network link appears as a single logical channel; again, the Data Link Layer may be carrying packets for many users simultaneously, but this is of no concern to frame-level software. At Layer 3, explicit support of multiple simultaneous users is required, since each user occupies a separate virtual circuit over the network. For this purpose, each virtual call or PVC is assigned a unique *logical channel*, identified by a 12-bit number. A logical channel may be thought of as a "connection index." In principle, each DTE has access to 4,095 such channels numbered upward from 1. In practice, some subrange of logical channel numbers is assigned for a host's use upon subscription to a particular network. The packet-level software allocates a logical channel for a virtual call upon initiating that call. A PVC will have a single logical channel assigned by the network administration. The basic format for a packet is shown in Figure 8.9.

The GFI and Type fields together identify the type of the packet. Packet types exist for the following purposes:

- Initializing (and reinitializing) the packet-level interface

- Establishing and terminating virtual calls

- Moving data

- Controlling the flow, and acknowledging receipt, of data

GFI	Logical Channel Identifier	Type	etcetera

Bits: 4   12   8   0 to ??

GFI is the general format identifier.
Type is the packet type identifier.
etcetera are anything else (packet-type dependent).

FIGURE 8.9: X.25 packet format

The packet level moves data for the layer above it, which may be Layer 4 or, since certain layers may be null in any given implementation, a higher layer, even the application program itself.

When establishing a virtual call, a user may request one or more network *facilities*. A facility, in this sense, is an optional service feature. Popular among the X.25 facilities are nonstandard default packet and window sizes, *reverse charging*, and *fast select*. Reverse charging, like a collect telephone call, bills network costs to the called station. The fast select option allows call setup packets to contain data, which they normally could not. A facility is requested by the calling DTE and accepted or rejected by the called DTE. Generally, a DTE is free to refuse any such option unless otherwise constrained by a particular network.

X.25 PADs

Packet assemblers/disassemblers (PADs) were briefly described in Chapter 2 in the discussion of PSNs. The PAD, a hardware/software combination, converts between an ASCII-terminal data stream and X.25 packets in various settings. With a dumb character-mode terminal on one side, and a sophisticated block-oriented network on the other, a PAD must do a fair amount of work to facilitate communication. (The PAD's responsibilities are less onerous if the terminal is operating in block mode.) PSN access nodes serve as PADs for terminals that dial into them. PADs can also be installed at user sites, where they typically support several terminals, communicating with the network via X.25 or X.32 over telephone lines. X.32, a dial-up version of X.25, enables the calling DTE to identify itself to the network.

PAD operation is governed by three more CCITT recommendations: X.3, X.28, and X.29. The most important, X.3, defines the services to be provided by a PAD. For a start, the PAD must offer a user interface to enable the terminal user to establish network connections; the usual approach is to prompt the user for a network address. X.3 also addresses such issues as:

- How characters arriving from the terminal are to be packaged for network transmission
- How BREAK signals from the terminal are to be dealt with
- Whether or not the PAD is to provide input echoing
- Whether or not the PAD should provide XON/XOFF flow control to the terminal

The first issue listed is particularly thorny: when should a packet containing terminal input be dispatched? Of course, packets are dispatched when filled, but with a typical character-mode terminal, there's no sure way of determining when a user has completed an input message. Although a unit of input is most commonly terminated by a carriage return, this is hardly universal. PADs deal with the problem by means of short time-outs: after a brief period has elapsed without the appearance of input, the PAD sends off a packet. The PAD also recognizes and acts upon typical input terminators including, but not limited to, carriage returns. However, these techniques are not adopted for block-mode terminals, which send one or more packets each time the user hits the Enter key or its equivalent.

X.3 defines a total of 18 numeric parameters that control PAD operation, including the time-out period for dispatching messages, the bit rate of the terminal, and a character-echo switch. The PAD parameters, somewhat similar to those set by the user of a PC communications package, must initially be set by the PAD itself for a given terminal session, and may later be adjusted by the terminal user or the host. Appendix G summarizes the complete parameter set and indicates how users of certain networks may change the settings.

X.29 prescribes methods by which the host can determine and change the PAD parameters for a terminal session. X.28 sets forth ways for the terminal user to alter PAD parameters.

Many vendors, including PSN companies, sell PADs for use with real terminals. PADs designed for PC use are available from Hayes, in the form of their X-series modems, and from other vendors, including Emucom. PC products often combine the PAD with a synchronous modem for making the connection to the PSN; the PAD and modem may be packaged together on a PC board or in a cabinet for external hook-up. Emucom also sells a stand-alone PAD that can be used with an existing PC modem capable of synchronous operation.

A PSN company will usually require that a product, such as a PAD, be "certified" before it may be attached to their network. In this process, the vendor subjects its product to a battery of tests prescribed by the PSN company and designed to lay bare any weaknesses.

Summary

The packet level of X.25, being a comparatively special-purpose protocol, has been adopted less widely than the frame level for non-PSN uses. The subset of Layer 3 that supports the data-transfer phase of virtual circuits, however, has been adopted for ISDN use. ISDNs handle call setup and call clearing differently than X.25 does. Among other things, such exchanges are conducted over a signaling channel (described in Chapter 2) separate from the one used for ISDN data.

The frame level of X.25 does an impeccable job of moving data across any fixed link capable of synchronous operation. It's not surprising, then, that LAPB has been adopted intact for many uses unrelated to PSNs. For example, it forms the basis of links used to download information from computers to other intelligent devices. In addition, many variants of LAPB have been developed for other specific applications: LAPD for ISDNs, LAPX for Teletex, and LAPM for error-correcting modems.

X.PC

X.PC was developed by TYMNET, the company behind the TYMNET PSN, which happens to be the second largest such network in the United States. TYMNET's goal was a protocol by means of which PCs could gain reliable dial-up access to packet networks. As its

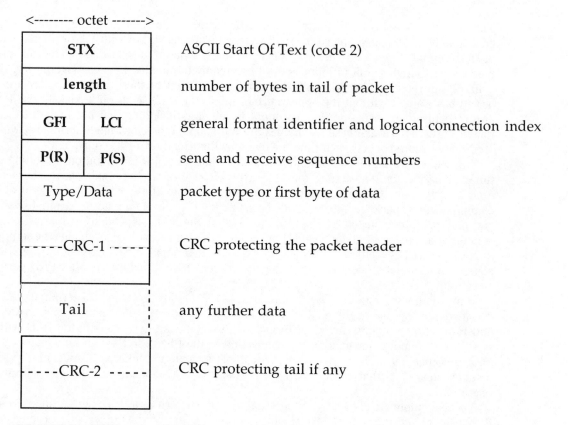

<----- octet ----->

STX	ASCII Start Of Text (code 2)
length	number of bytes in tail of packet
GFI	**LCI**	general format identifier and logical connection index
P(R)	**P(S)**	send and receive sequence numbers
Type/Data	packet type or first byte of data
-----CRC-1 -----	CRC protecting the packet header
Tail	any further data
-----CRC-2 -----	CRC protecting tail if any

FIGURE 8.10: X.PC message format

name might suggest, X.PC is modeled on X.25, incorporating X.25 features into a protocol designed for asynchronous links.

X.PC has the look and feel of X.25, and duplicates the latter's essential features, but it achieves this by means of a streamlined design which, in its detail, departs substantially from X.25.

X.PC Message Format

Although its specification addresses the packet and frame levels separately, X.PC in practice is best viewed as a single protocol that incorporates the functions of both layers.

The X.PC message format is shown in Figure 8.10. Each message commences with an ASCII STX (code 2), followed by an octet indicating the length of the message. A message can carry up to 256 octets of data and, with all the control fields included, can occupy a total of up to 264 octets.

Both the third and fourth octets are split into four-bit *nibbles* for a total of four such nibbles. The first nibble is the *general format identifier (GFI)*, which distinguishes data packets from all other types. The low four bits of the same octet hold the *logical channel identifier (LCI)*. The fourth octet contains sequence numbers for identifying (P[S]) and acknowledging (P[R]) data packets. The fifth octet, called the *packet type identifier*, encodes the type for all packets other than data packets. In data packets, the fifth octet contains the first data byte; a data packet must contain at least this one byte of data.

The message header is protected by a 16-bit CRC, which occupies the next two octets. Any further data octets follow; these are protected by a CRC of their own, which completes the message. The *length field* contains the count of data octets in this "tail" portion of the message. If there are no data in the tail, there's no second CRC, either.

How X.PC Differs from X.25

Examination of the X.PC message format reveals two major differences from X.25. First, X.PC supports a much smaller number of logical channels (15, as opposed to X.25's 4,095). Evidently, the designers believed that a PC would never have need for more than 15 simultaneous sessions. Second, X.PC, by virtue of its four-bit sequence numbers, allows a window size of 15 messages.

Unlike X.25, X.PC can be used directly between two DTEs without an intervening network. With this end in view, the packets are designed so that the protocol is symmetrical.

Facilities in X.25, remember, are user options selected when a call is established. X.PC permits the use of standard X.25 facilities, but dictates adjustments to the two negotiated flow-control parameters, packet size and window size. This is necessary because X.PC's maximum packet size is 256 octets (compared with X.25's 1,024) and its maximum window size is 15. Furthermore, X.PC adds a facility not found in X.25: a *reconnect option* that allows virtual calls to be maintained if the physical connection is temporarily broken.

Strengths of X.PC

X.PC is one of very few asynchronous protocols that support the multiplexing of logical connections. This virtue alone makes it an excellent candidate for connecting PCs to PSNs. The same virtue, combined with its symmetrical design, makes it an ideal choice for either a direct PC-to-PC link or a multisession PC-to-host link. For example, by using a communications package supporting X.PC to connect to a host that also supports the protocol, you can establish multiple concurrent terminal sessions.

X.PC's multiplexing capability makes it very attractive for use with the multiapplication operating systems becoming more and more important to microcomputer users. With X.PC and suitable higher-layer protocols on a PC, you could start up three concurrent file transfers, open a couple of time sharing sessions, check your electronic mailbox, plug into a newswire, get the weather in Pasadena . . . and lose track of everything you're doing, all at the same time. It was once rumored that X.PC would be built into the operating system we now know as OS/2. It is fair to say that, to facilitate networking, a multiapplication operating system should have a multiplexing protocol implemented within or very close to the operating system, so that it can easily be shared by all programs. OS/2 has appeared, however, with neither X.PC nor a substitute.

ERROR-CORRECTING MODEMS

Error-correcting modems, also known as *protocol modems,* are capable of transferring data using a Link Layer protocol. Most high-speed (9,600 bps and above) PC modems are of the error-correcting type, and low-speed versions can also be found. The modems decribed in this section, designed to provide error control between two devices, should not be confused with modems that incorporate protocols for other purposes, such as the X.25 PAD products mentioned earlier.

Two factors make the use of protocols in high-speed modems particularly attractive. First, error correction is almost invariably necessitated by the error rates encountered at such speeds. Second, on slower PCs, an error-correcting protocol implemented in software may find it difficult to keep up with the high-speed data stream.

The Link Layer protocol incorporated within an error-correcting modem is most often MNP, some variant of LAPB, or both. MNP, remember, was developed specifically for modem use.

The use of protocol modems raises two important issues:

First, for flexibility, a protocol modem should be capable of operating with other modems that share the same signaling standard(s), but not the protocol. Further, such a modem should automatically recognize one of its kin upon establishing a connection with it. In other words, a properly designed protocol modem will attempt to use its protocol only when appropriate, and will be able to resolve for itself the question of whether such use is possible. When a protocol is to be implemented in modems, its designers define a special detection scheme that calls for one modem to transmit a given sequence of characters upon initial connection and then to await an appropriate response from the other modem. If the response is forthcoming, both modems use the protocol; otherwise, they resort to plain old async. The characters used for detection are chosen to be minimally intrusive because, if detection fails, they may turn up on a terminal screen or in the input buffer of a host.

Just this sort of "transparent" detection scheme enables Telenet to support regular asynchronous dial-up and MNP access on the same telephone lines. Telenet has Microcom modems installed in many cities. When users without MNP capability dial in, they see nothing different from regular network behavior, but callers with MNP modems are automatically dealt a protocol-protected connection.

The second issue concerns the temporary drop in data throughput rate that occurs when retransmissions are required to correct transmission errors. A modem rated at 9,600 bps, for example, may effectively move data at only 7,000 bps when errors show up. What would happen, then, if the PC continued to pour data into the modem at 9,600 bps? At some point, an overflow would occur. For this reason, it is imperative that error-correcting modems be able to exert flow control over their own source of transmitted data. This is not as simple as it might seem. Software flow control, XON/XOFF, works fine as long as the data being passed are limited to printable ASCII characters, but is useless for binary data streams because the PC can't distinguish flow control characters from received data. Hardware flow control is therefore more promising. But which RS-232 circuit should be used? Although none is defined for this purpose, Clear To Send (CTS) seems an obvious choice. Unfortunately, because this need for flow control is rather new, many communications software packages pay no attention to CTS.

It has happened that companies have invested large sums in error-correcting modems, only to lose more data than they had with ordinary modems—not to transmission errors, of course, but to lack of flow control.

If you spend much time thinking about error-correcting modem operation, you may develop a few worry lines mulling over how a transmitting modem decides to package the data it sends. When does it initiate a packet? And when does it terminate and dispatch one? The simple answer, valid for LAPB and MNP units, is that such modems employ a form of *streaming*, whereby the process of assembling a packet for transmission is practically indistinguishable from the act of sending it. In other words, the packet is not buffered in the modem, but is fired off as it is assembled. When a modem receives a byte from the PC, it queues the byte for transmission and then checks to see whether a packet is currently being sent. If there is no active packet, the modem starts one. Data bytes are loaded into the packet until either it reaches its permitted maximum size or the data queue is empty, whereupon the packet is terminated. As you might imagine, this simple procedure serves well for both interactive and file transfer communications.

When two modems communicate with each other by means of a protocol, the opportunity arises for them to optimize that communication by transmitting data synchronously, that is, by dispensing with start and stop bits. Most protocol modems take advantage of this opportunity. The initial interaction between two such modems is carried out asynchronously; then, after each unit has established that the other is capable of synchronous operation, they switch to it. The efficiency gain realized by "switching to sync" more than compensates for the normal protocol overhead. For example, a 2,400 bps modem operating with MNP can move data noticeably faster than a plain 2,400 bps unit.

A common question: Must the protocol be used strictly between two modems, or may it be operated by a modem at one end, and by software running in a PC (or other computer) at the other end? In most cases, one may indeed mix protocol operators, although suitable software implementations of the requisite protocols are not common. "Suitable" here primarily implies compatibility with the detection schemes by means of which protocol modems recognize each other, as discussed above. But isn't this claimed interoperability between error-correcting modems and software protocol drivers at odds with the "switch to synchronous operation" just described? In fact, most modems "negotiate" the use of a protocol and the switch to sync separately, so no problem results. In MNP, for example, the ability to switch to sync is inherent in Class 3; two MNP drivers will conduct their communications in accordance with the highest class for which they are both equipped.

Deciding on a Protocol

In many cases, your choice of protocol for error-correcting modems will be circumscribed by compatibility requirements. Can the modem you're considering get along with units already installed, or with the protocol supported by the network or host to which you wish to connect? If you have a freer choice, you may wish to concentrate on the standards, if any, that prevail at the moment.

As of early 1989, well over 400,000 MNP-based modems from many vendors have been sold. A battle is being waged between MNP and LAP-based protocols for supremacy in this application, especially in regard to possible adoption as a formal standard by the CCITT. Despite many claims and counterclaims, the two protocols are, in practice, about equally well suited to the job. The question of which deserves to be chosen as a standard is not easy to answer: MNP dominates the market, but LAP-based protocols are based on formal standards that are well accepted for other applications. If the CCITT does settle on a standard recommending protocols for modem use, as many people expect will happen by 1990, that standard may well incorporate both contenders, leading to a situation in which most error-correcting modems will be equipped to use either protocol.

Although modems implementing X.PC are available, this protocol appears to be a poor choice for modem operation because it presents an obstacle to adoption of the streaming technique described above. Streaming is possible with LAPB and MNP because each packet is terminated by a fixed data pattern (a flag, in the case of LAPB). Since X.PC denotes packet length by a byte-count field in the header, the modem must know the length of each packet as it begins to transmit it.

A modem implementing XMODEM was once advertised, but this product was apparently unsuccessful and is, we suspect, no longer on the market.

Manufacturers of LAPB-based modems include Anderson Jacobson, Cermetek, Concord Data Systems, Eicon, and Hayes. Unfortunately, such modems from different makers are not universally compatible with each other. Among other things, incompatibility may arise from the use of varying protocol-detection schemes. MNP-based modems are offered by Concord Data Systems, Microcom, and many other manufacturers. Two MNP units from different vendors can be relied upon to be compatible, assuming, of course, that they share a modem signaling standard.

A recent development has intriguing implications for the area of modem compatibility. Design features of the NeXT™ microcomputer, demonstrated late in 1988, will allow the computer itself to act as a modem, obviating the external units or internal cards required by other machines. The NeXT-1's built-in Digital Signal Processor (DSP) and special processing hardware allow the user to write an application program that, in effect, creates this integral modem. The user adds a simple telephone-interconnect box that isolates and adapts the machine's Audio In and Audio Out ports for connection to the modular phone jack. Since the modem is an integral part of the computer, most of the various conversion steps normally associated with modem operation are either carried out within the machine or eliminated altogether. For example, the computer can create and interpret the analog waveform directly; there's no need to perform serial-parallel conversion on the data; and even a command set, as such, is no longer called for.

APPLICATION-LAYER PROTOCOLS

Application-Layer protocols address the highest level of the OSI model and are oriented to particular network applications. The most frequently encountered are designed for file transfer, virtual terminal, and electronic mail applications.

Virtual-terminal protocols support *remote login*; that is, they allow users to conduct terminal sessions with hosts over network connections. The term *virtual* forms part of the name because such protocols define a virtual terminal that is universal in scope. At the terminal end of the connection, data are converted between the formats used by the physical terminal and those defined for the virtual terminal. At the host end, the data stream is translated between the virtual format and the format used by the type of terminal preferred by the host. Similar in principle to the virtual file formats discussed in Chapter 7, a virtual-terminal protocol allows any kind of ASCII terminal to establish a connection to any async host.

The ISO standard protocols for the three applications named above—FTAM, VTP, and X.400, respectively—were listed earlier in the discussion of the OSI model. FTAM supports much more than simply file transfer, also allowing users to remotely access files and perform many operations on them: reading, writing, deleting, renaming, and so on. Among other application protocols are TELNET (a virtual-terminal protocol not to be confused with the PSN, Telenet), FTP (File Transfer Protocol), and SMTP (Simple Mail Transfer Protocol), all of which are part of the Defense Data Network (DDN) Protocol Set.

Several file transfer protocols are suitable for use by PCs where error control and other "low-level" functions are already taken care of, as when two PCs are connected via internal error-correcting modems, or when a PC is connected to a PSN host, with the PC-to-PSN link operating under X.PC. When only Application-Layer functions are required for file transfer, it may well be possible to use any standard PC file transfer protocol, such as Kermit or XMODEM. The lower-layer functions incorporated into such protocols may be "wasted," but this needn't hurt. The only potentially ruinous factor would be propagation delays, which could interfere with protocol time-outs. Even if delays aren't a problem, under such circumstances, when reliable data transport is assured, the comparatively low efficiency of these protocols is likely to render them unattractive. The file transfer need is better served by an Application-Layer protocol that concentrates on moving files and does not duplicate effort by performing tasks such as error detection. There are, however, few such protocols, and implementations of them are also scarce. Here are some candidates:

- Fast, another Hayes invention. *Fast* was not intended to stand for anything, but might well denote "Fast And Simple Transfers."
- YMODEM-g, a stripped-down version of YMODEM.
- IMODEM, a derivative of XMODEM.
- The little-used file transfer layer of MNP.

Certain other protocols, including Kermit (with its long-packets option), ZMODEM, BLAST, and HyperProtocol, also fit the bill, despite not being strictly Layer 7 designs. These are also ideal choices for links that can be considered "almost error-free," such as those constructed using external error-correcting modems. We use the "almost" qualification because errors could conceivably be introduced during the data's passage over the cable connecting the PC and modem.

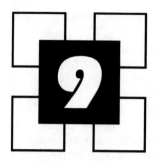

MOVING FILES

USING PROTOCOLS TO MOVE FILES

Now that we know how protocols operate, we have to learn how to use them. Putting protocols to work transferring files can be tricky; even experienced professionals sometimes have to try several times before getting things moving. We'll present this section as a question-and-answer session.

What Do Download and Upload Mean?

Download originally meant "to move a file from a big machine to a little machine." Typically, the term was applied to the process of sending a program from a host, where it was generated and stored, to a little computer, where it was run. When such a program crashed, the memory contents of the little computer would be *uploaded* to the host for postmortem analysis.

Since the advent of personal computers, these terms have taken on new meanings. In this context, download means "transfer a file *to* a PC," no matter where it's coming from. Similarly, upload means "send a file *from* a PC" to almost anywhere else.

What is a Server?

A server is a program that acts as a host for file transfers. A server sits and waits for a user to connect and transfer some files. Users and servers are essential counterparts in this process. Many Kermits and some ZMODEM programs have server capabilities.

Which Protocol Should I Use?

This question is addressed in the next section, which compares file transfer protocols using several criteria.

Do I Need the Same Program at Both Ends?

Generally, no. The protocol is important; the program isn't. An implementation of a given protocol in one worthwhile software product should be compatible with an implementation in any other such product. Nevertheless, exceptions do occur, especially with more complex protocols, like Kermit. YMODEM represents a special situation: Certain purported YMODEM drivers lack critical elements of the protocol, apparently due to confusion created by the profusion of XMODEM variants. This failing has led to grave incompatibility problems.

Although programs at both ends of a link need not be the same, identical software, if practicable, may be more readily cajoled into working as advertised. When files are to be transferred between different kinds of computer systems, the programs may have to be different.

What Steps Must be Taken to Start a Transfer?

1. The two systems must be connected via a link that provides the right kind of data path for the protocol to be used. This bears on the number of data bits per character, parity option, flow control settings, and so on. Any protocol can work on a link that passes full eight-bit characters, enforces no flow control, and does not subject its traffic to delay. On the other hand, very few protocols will work on a link that uses the eighth bit for parity, demands obedience to Control-S/Control-Q, throws away NULLs, and out of pure perversity inserts a two-second delay after every 516th character.

2. Appropriate software must be started on each computer and configured for the link described above.

3. The software must be told which protocol is to be used, if there is a choice.

4. The software must be told which files to transfer.

Okay, How Do I Tell the Software Which Files to Transfer?

This is where matters can get complicated. Steps to initiate the transfer must sometimes be taken at both ends of the link; in other cases, one end can exercise complete control over the process. The protocol itself is the primary determinant of transfer technique, although it may vary by implementation.

XMODEM is an example of the first case. Because XMODEM does not carry filenames across the link, both sender and receiver must be explicitly told the name of each file to be moved. A common beginner's mistake is to give a transfer command at only one end and then wonder why so little happens.

ZMODEM is an example of the second case. With ZMODEM you can, for example, say "send *.ARC" at the sending end or "receive *.ARC" at the receiving end. Either way, the program will start sending all files with names matching the pattern.

Obviously, the second method, which essentially involves a server-user relationship, is preferable, especially when you have several files to transfer. Fortunately, most protocols used today permit this simpler procedure. The precise commands vary, of course, with the program; they are not determined by the protocol.

Does it Matter Which End is Started First?

It may, or it may not. When a protocol driver is fired up, it will usually get busy trying to set the transfer in motion. This may entail sending a message and waiting for a reply, or just sitting and waiting for a message from the other end. In either case, it means waiting—and normally a program will wait only so long. If it sees no action after a certain period, perhaps after sending its initial message a few times, it will assume something is wrong, alert you to that fact, and give up. Thus, if you wish to transfer a file between two PCs a mile apart, you may not be able to start the receiver and jog to the other PC in time to start the sender. The good news is that as long as you start both ends within a reasonably short time (say, 30 seconds) it usually will not matter which you start first.

When transferring a file between a PC and a timesharing system, it's almost always essential to do everything necessary to get the transfer going on the host *before* starting the operation on the PC end. This is because the PC communications package, once instructed to do a file transfer, will prevent the terminal user from talking to the host again until the transfer is finished. That's as it should be. After all, anything you typed while a transfer was in progress would almost surely mess up the transfer.

What if I Transfer a File that's Already There?

So you've just started downloading file THINGME.WUG to your PC when you suddenly realize you already have a file called THINGME.WUG containing data that are very interesting, vital to national security, and totally different from those you are now receiving. Does this mean you've lost a precious file? Probably, if you didn't back it up. A more pertinent question is: should a file-transfer program overwrite an existing file when told to receive one with the same name? Some protocol recommendations address this question, but it's usually left to the software designer. Here are some approaches.

- Kermits generally have a user-selectable parameter determining whether or not existing files will be overwritten.

- Some programs, when told to receive to a filename that already exists, will instead invent a new and unique filename, store the file under the new name, and give you a message telling you so.

- Some programs will query you as to your preference, if and when the problem arises. This is considerate, but may not be desirable if a duplicate filename turns up only after you've started the transfer of a batch of 100 large files and gone off to lunch. Some clever programs give you a minute or so to respond before taking some other course of action.

Why Can't I Send a File Called \\[]/,... to my PC?

Different operating systems allow different characters in filenames. Be careful when transferring files between unlike systems. Macintosh filenames, for example, may contain slashes; PC filenames may not. What's a transfer program to do? Some simply refuse to transfer an unacceptable filename and, in a few cases, won't even tell you why (Grrrr). Others will translate a foreign filename into something acceptable that's as close as possible to the original. Many programs allow the user to specify two filenames, both the one at the sender and the one at the receiver.

Special care must be taken with UNIX systems, which, unlike most, are case-sensitive. To UNIX, the filename Blah is not the same as the filename BLAH. Nor are either of these filenames the same as bLah, BlAH, BlaH, or, for that matter, bLAh.

What if the Communication Parameters are Wrong?

As should be clear by now, you need an eight-bit connection to be able to use a protocol like XMODEM or MNP. What if you open a connection with, say, seven data bits and even parity, and command your communications package to perform an XMODEM transfer? Some CPs will switch to eight-bit mode. This is correct behavior on packet networks that establish default terminal connections with seven data bits and parity. The host can instruct the network to switch to eight data bits and no parity, and will indeed do so on commencing a protocol transfer. If the communication package also switches, all will be well. Some PC communication programs, however, are known to attempt XMODEM transfers over seven-bit connections, and don't notice that the connection setup ensures that the protocol can't possibly work.

What Else Should I Know about Transfers over PSNs?

As noted in Chapter 2, the use of file transfer protocols over PSNs can be problematic, primarily due to transmission delays. You can, of course, try to use any protocol and see how it goes: some will simply fail, while others will work, but at a snail's pace. If possible, use a protocol, such as SuperKermit or ZMODEM, designed specifically to cope with packet networks.

How Should I Set Protocol Parameters?

Many of the more sophisticated file transfer protocols have configuration parameters of their own, which the user may alter. For example, several protocols allow the user to specify a maximum message size. Kermit has a great number of user-settable parameters, a necessity in allowing it to operate in many hostile environments. Some of Kermit's parameters were described earlier; a full description is given in Kermit manuals. When using Kermit, be careful about the file type parameter, which must be set to either *text* or *binary*.

Rarely must a protocol's configuration be changed to make it work at all, but adjusting parameters sometimes enables it to work more efficiently. If the data message size can be changed, choose a large size for a relatively error-free channel, because longer messages mean less time will be lost in waiting for acknowledgments; conversely, select a small size when line errors abound. Small messages reduce the chance of a given message being struck by an error and require fewer data to be retransmitted when a message is damaged. The proprietary CROSSTALK protocol available in CROSSTALK Mk.4, for example, can be instructed to use a block (data message) size ranging from 256 to 65,280 bytes, variable in increments of 256. Kermit, equipped with the extra-long-packets option, can send anything from 20 to 857,374 bytes at a time.

Other common parameters relate to time-outs and the conditions under which a transfer should be aborted. As explained in the discussion of XMODEM, time-outs enable protocols to recover from lost messages. With some protocols, the file receiver is responsible for timing out; if the receiver fails to get an expected data message within a reasonable time, it reacts by sending a probe to the sender to stimulate a retransmission. With other protocols, the file sender handles timing; if the acknowledgment expected for a transmitted data message does not arrive within a certain period, then the sender retransmits the message. Time-outs that are too short may result in inefficiency due to unnecessary retransmissions. Excessively long time-outs may also reduce efficiency because, when a message is lost, a program will wait long past the point when all hope should be abandoned.

The selection of a suitable time-out period usually depends on the propagation delays inherent in the communications channel, and possibly on how busy the communicating systems are. For links involving satellites, a long time-out (of several seconds) is needed; PSN connections require a moderate time-out; for most other situations, a short time-out (say, a few dozen milliseconds) should work well. Beyond these general guidelines, only experimentation will indicate the best choice.

The setting of message size and time-out parameters amounts to a way of tuning the protocol to a particular link. A really intelligent protocol should be capable of dynamically adjusting these parameters for itself, according to the transitory conditions on the line.

Now, let's consider parameters set to indicate when a transfer should be abandoned. If a protocol message is repeatedly damaged in transmission, you normally don't want to keep trying relentlessly to get it through. The most common option is to specify the number of consecutive errors that should be tolerated before the link is declared impassable and the protocol gives up. Typical choices are in the teens. If you are very stubborn (or simply must get a file through, no matter what, and have no alternative means of doing so), you may elect to set the parameter to the highest allowable value.

Certain protocol drivers allow selection of a preferred error-checking method. This is typical of Kermits and a few others, such as HyperProtocol. Normally it is best to choose the most powerful error check available, such as a CRC rather than a checksum. Be careful, because the default error-detection method is often *not* the strongest. If you select CRC error-checking and then initiate a transfer with a system that can do only checksumming, then (for XMODEM variants and Kermit, at least) all will be well; the two programs will negotiate to use their lower common denominator.

Why would someone choose any but the best available error-detection method? Because a file transfer is likely to proceed more quickly with a simpler error check that can be calculated more rapidly.

I Have Error-correcting Modems. Do I Still Need a Protocol?

Goodness, yes, you certainly do. Remember that protocols do much more than just control errors. A more pertinent question is: Do I still need a separate *error-detecting* protocol? Some people insist that a regular error-detecting protocol is still essential to deal with errors creeping in on the links between modems and computers. They may be putting it a bit too strongly; in typical cases, the chances of errors impinging on modem cables are awfully small. But, to be safe rather than sorry, we do recommend full end-to-end, rather than mere modem-to-modem, error control. An exception can, of course, be made where internal modems are installed at both ends of the link.

Another incidental factor favoring the use of an error detecting protocol is that very few protocols for PC file transfer do *not* incorporate error control. Most of them were listed in the previous chapter's section on Application-Layer protocols. Probably the most common example is YMODEM-g. Bear in mind, too, that protocol modems normally activate their protocols only when communicating with modems of the same kind.

Should I Ever Consider Transferring Files without a Protocol?

Only if you have no choice, as is the case when you're exchanging files with a system that offers no protocol option. Some communication packages list ASCII among their protocols. This, of course, is not a protocol at all, but refers to a way of sending or receiving files as raw data streams. If, in a desperate situation, you ever resort to performing ASCII transfers, consider whether or not you can press XON/XOFF flow control into service to help a little.

What Should I Do if a Transfer Seizes up in the Middle?

Unfortunately, there is no good answer to this question. With today's protocols, seizures should be rare, but they're by no means unheard of. Furiously striking keys in hope of provoking the program into further action is usually useless. Most often you'll have to give up and start again.

ACCELERATING FILE TRANSFERS

If you do a lot of bulky file transfers, especially over long distances, you're likely to seek ways to speed them up. Increasing transfer speed may reduce phone bills and improve business efficiency by getting the information to its destination faster.

The most obvious way to increase speed is to buy faster modems, but twice the bps costs roughly twice the bucks. Also, the speed ceiling on dial-up modems is around 14,000 bps, possibly less if line quality is not the best, as is often the case in rural areas.

Moving to a faster protocol will help, too. You might consider upgrading XMODEM to ZMODEM, Kermit to SuperKermit, or YMODEM to HyperProtocol. But the best is only about 50 percent faster than the worst.

A third method is simply to send less data. We've mentioned *data compression* before; now let's look more closely at what it can do for us.

There are many algorithms for compressing data without losing information. Text, pictures, and spreadsheet files are particularly suitable candidates. If a data file is compressed for transmission, it must be expanded back to its original form at the destination.

The amount by which data can be compacted ranges widely. Some files can't be compressed at all, while others can be reduced to one-eighth of their original size. Forty to sixty percent compression is fairly typical, especially for text files, the least cumbersome of all to compress. We'll focus on some techniques for compressing text.

Text Compression

You may have seen an advertisement on a bus or subway promising "if u k rd th msj u k bkm a sec & gt a gd jb." This graphic demonstration of text compression is brought to you by a school that teaches Speed Writing, a compromise between longhand and shorthand (mediumhand?). In the ad, a 59-letter sentence is compressed into a 28-character message that can be unambiguously understood by any competent reader of English. The 28 symbols form a skeleton that provides the gist of the message; the context supplies the rest. Undoubtedly, gt here means get, but out of context the same abbreviation might be interpreted as got, gate, great, gait, and so on.

Written English is, in fact, about 50 percent redundant: we use twice the number of symbols (letters) theoretically required to convey our meaning. This is not to say that you can throw away half of this book without losing any content. Rather, it suggests that we could, if we chose, replace the word *antidisestablishmentarianism* with the neologism *smerg* or with any other small group of characters that sounded or looked like a plausible English word and didn't already mean something else. It might make our beloved language hideous, but think what it would do for the world paper shortage. Actually, computer users have been doing this for years to reduce their typing burden. For example, the word *character* is often abbreviated as *char*, and we are so used to it that we hardly think of it as text compression.

Fifty percent redundancy happens to be aesthetically pleasing in a language, allowing virtually infinite variety in expression. If the rate were lower, poetry and prose in English would be pitiful, crosswords would be dull, and few of us would be able to sustain interest in a game of Scrabble®. For the purpose of compressing English text for transmission, the degree of redundancy suggests that optimally encoded text would have about half as many symbols as the original.

Creative text compression is displayed on the vanity license plates of cars in the United States. For example, a friend of ours gently taunts RU-NVS on her sleek Porsche; a New York dentist has 2TH DR; and probably every state has one vehicle sporting the classic 10S-NE1. While not strictly containing a compressed message, the plate reading RS232C crisply conveys the computer interest of the lady who owns the car. Sometimes, a popular plate's unavailability inspires drivers to use roundabout codes requiring more symbols than the written English equivalent: Bill Howard, writing in the BMW Car Club of America publication *Roundel*, cited the Nissan 280-Z owner whose plate reads ALT-90 (if you're lost, look up 90 in the ASCII table).

Computerized text compression often takes advantage of the wide variation in frequency of letters' occurrence in written English. The letter E appears most often, X or Z most rarely. If we examine the occurrence of letters in pairs, the range is even greater. Letter pairs are called *digrams* or *digraphs*. The most common digrams, such as TH, ES, and RE, appear more often than the rarest individual letters. QI and HH, on the other hand, are very seldom encountered, and some, like XQ and QH, never appear at all. Going a step further, we can exploit the tendency of one letter to be followed by another. The most obvious case is Q, which is nearly always followed by U.

Text encoded in ASCII always involves seven or eight bits for each letter, regardless of its frequency. We can save space, overall, by using variable-length codes, representing E by perhaps 1 or 2 bits while Z might require 12 or 16. By extending this method to digrams or even trigrams, we can easily achieve a compression rate approaching 50 percent. Throw in some other techniques, such as compacting frequently repeated words, and compression rates of 66 percent are possible. While the value of compressing data by 50 percent approximates that of doubling line speed, the cost should be much lower because the process can be carried out in software. In practice, halving the size of a transmitted file reduces transmission time by slightly less than 50 percent, due to protocol overhead.

The use of variable-length codes for letters is called *Huffman coding*. A simplified example for single letters is:

Character	Frequency	Huffman Code
space	16.0%	0
E	8.6%	10
T	6.4%	110
A	6.3%	1110
O	5.9%	11110
. . .	. . .	. . .
X	0.08%	111111111111111111111111110

In this version of Huffman coding, the 26 letters of the English alphabet (plus the space) are arranged in order of frequency. The most frequently written letter, E, is assigned a 2-bit code; the second most frequent, T, a 3-bit code, and so on down to X, which ends up with a 27-bit code. In variable-length coding, each code must be uniquely distinguishable by its content. In other words, codes must be so structured that the boundaries between them can be detected without reference to a standard pattern; such codes can't be separated by counting bits. Thus, in the above example, each code ends with a binary 0, which never appears except in the last bit position. This makes decoding easy: just count binary 1s until you hit a binary 0, and then use the count to index the table.

In practice, codes are more sophisticated. For example, some algorithms for Huffman codes don't require every code to have a different length. So-called arithmetic codes, which do not depend on an integral number of bits per code, offer the best compression of all.

The authors have found compression techniques to be a fascinating subject. Readers interested in pursuing it are urged to investigate the book by Gil Held listed in the bibliography.

Products for Text Compression

Text compression products fall into three categories: hardware, communications packages, and add-on software. Whatever you choose, it's essential to equip both ends of the link with the same product.

Data compression by PC software may be carried out either as a step preparatory to the transmission session or as an integral part of the communication process.

The first method entails some work for the user. Each file to be transferred must be compressed on disk before the communications program is run. After transfer, each received file must be run through the matching expander program to recreate the original. In spite of the extra work, products in this category have a major advantage for some users: it may be possible to select a product oriented to the kind of data being transmitted. A prime example is SQZ!™ from Turner Hall, which squeezes files created by Lotus 1-2-3® and Symphony®. The compression can be spectacular, and anyone transferring much data of this kind should certainly consider using it.

SQUEEZE and UNSQUEEZE are slow-working stand-alone programs for compression and expansion, respectively, that typically provide about 42 percent compression. They are in the public domain, and can be obtained from many bulletin board systems (BBSs) and other sources. ARC and its successor, Zip, are shareware compression programs from System Enhancement Associates. Well known to BBS addicts, these programs are widely used for *packing* public domain and shareware products. Packing involves merging several files, typically the executable, documentation, and accessory files for a product, into one file, with some compression thrown in. This makes downloading from bulletin boards very easy because you transfer only a single file per item, you are sure of getting everything you need for a given program, and the compression reduces transmission time. After completing the download, you unARC or unZip the received file to recreate the original set of files. Commercial stand-alone compression programs are also available from a number of vendors.

The second method of compression by software requires a communications package that incorporates code to compress data as they are transmitted. Surprisingly few products for PCs offer such capability. Most common is the compression scheme specified for the Kermit protocol; as noted in the section on Kermit, this can compact files to a significant degree despite its simplicity. More sophisticated data compression is provided by BLAST II and HyperAccess.

Since data compression takes a lot of processing time, PC software performing compression on the fly may be able to do a useful job only when line speeds are relatively low. Practical data-rate limits depend on the software used and, most of all, on the speed of the PC involved. The software approach, then, is usually attractively inexpensive, but hardware may be needed for real-time compression at high communication rates.

Hardware products include modems with integrated compression capability and devices installed between a computer and a modem to compress or expand the data as they go by. The Hayes V-series modems compress whenever they're talking to each other, and many other high-speed modems, such as models from Microcom, also provide compression. Unfortunately, modems from different manufacturers tend to use proprietary and incompatible compression schemes. Despite the lack of standardization, data compression is likely to become very common for long-distance communications, and the work may well be done predominantly by modems.

Stand-alone hardware compressors that fit on an RS-232 link have the advantage of being usable on links that do not involve modems, but they are rather expensive. A company called Datran makes PC-specific hardware add-ons for compression, some of which can handle data encryption as well. Hardware compression products are also available from Chung Technologies, Racal-Vadic, RAD Computers, Symplex Communications, and Kinex.

COMPARING PROTOCOLS

The availability of so many protocols for PC asynchronous file transfer makes comparison a difficult matter. In the public domain, there are CompuServe A, CompuServe B, Kermit, SuperKermit, MEGAlink, MODEM7, PDIP™, SEAlink, Telink, WXMODEM, XMODEM, XMODEM-1k, XMODEM-CRC, YMODEM, YMODEM-g, and ZMODEM. Among proprietary protocols are ASCOMIV, BLAST, CROSSTALK, DART, HyperProtocol, RELAY, and Softrans™. Having conducted personal evaluations of most of these protocols, the authors are prepared to challenge the exalted status of some of them and state flatly that, should you have any choice, only a handful are worth using. It is prudent to consider candidates from the two groups separately.

Among the public domain protocols, only Kermit (preferably SuperKermit) and ZMODEM merit serious consideration. We include ZMODEM somewhat tentatively, because it is fairly new and not yet in widespread use.

Proprietary protocols must be evaluated a little differently from the public domain variety for a couple of reasons. First, proprietary designs cannot be considered apart from their implementations. Second, since the detailed workings of proprietary protocols are hidden, they must be judged primarily from observations of their behavior, rather than a study of their design. In the proprietary group, BLAST, HyperProtocol, and RELAY appear to be the most worthy of attention.

Naturally, such pronouncements cannot be made without some disclaimers. First, remember that we are considering only protocols for file transfer here; thus, X.25 and other protocols that are not file-transfer-oriented are excluded. Second, we don't mean to suggest that other protocols are without merit, or that they should necessarily be avoided. If your company has standardized on CROSSTALK Mk.4, uses the DART protocol, is happy with it, and needs nothing else, then that should be fine. (However, one might well hesitate to use any protocol whose error control scheme has not been published; in DART's case, not even an indication of undetected error rate is provided.) Third, while each of the protocols given preference here has important strengths, none comes close to being ideal. Each has deficiencies. None is a standard in the formal sense, and none is likely to become one. Fourth and last, even more new protocols, heaven help us, may appear after this writing, and some may also claim a place in the highest ranks.

We've put the bottom line at the top. Now let's consider the following criteria for comparing file transfer protocols:

- Availability
- Efficiency
- Features
- Reliability
- Support
- User Interface

Notice that this list is in alphabetical order. We leave priority-setting to the individual reader.

Availability

For transferring files only among PCs, there are plenty of protocols from which to choose. Your choice may be very limited, though, if you need to perform transfers between PCs and other types of computers. Some of the protocols listed above can be found in products for other microcomputers, but when it comes to larger systems, very few may be available. Due to restrictions of the kind noted in Chapter 7, such as forced use of parity, many async file transfer protocols simply cannot be implemented on most minicomputers and mainframes. UNIX users can certainly take advantage of BLAST, Kermit, XMODEM, and ZMODEM. IBM mainframers, depending on their operating system configuration, may be able to find implementations of BLAST, Kermit, and RELAY. BLAST and Kermit are both available for a wide array of other systems, but further options are scarce.

Efficiency

Efficiency is important to most users and is the simplest objective basis on which to measure and compare products. Efficiency in practice results from a combination of the inherent efficiency of a protocol and the quality of a particular implementation.

We can derive an efficiency rating for a given implementation of a protocol by measuring its effective throughput and comparing that against the raw data rate of the connection. Say we connect two PCs at 1,200 bps, run the same software in both machines, and transfer a 51,200-byte file from one to the other. Suppose the transfer takes exactly eight minutes (or 480 seconds). The effective throughput is then 51,200 divided by 480, or 106.67 characters per second. Assuming the communication link runs with eight data bits per character, no parity, and one stop bit, the raw data rate is 1,200 divided by 10, or 120 cps. The efficiency derived from the ratio of 106.67 to 120, is 88.89 percent. This figure suggests that 11.11 percent of the capacity of the link is either taken up by protocol overhead or lost to idleness.

To minimize the number of uncontrollable variables in the above process, the two machines should be directly connected in an environment free of transmission errors. Furthermore, care must be taken to eliminate the effects of delays typically involved in reading and writing disks. This can be achieved, for example, by sending the file from a RAM disk to the NUL device supported by DOS (data written to NUL are immediately discarded).

Also note that the above calculation gives a very static indication of performance. Dynamic ratings of efficiency might be generated by measuring protocol behavior under conditions where transmission errors occur in a known pattern, and where propagation delays are significant. Remember that, as discussed in Chapter 7, the relative efficiencies of protocols can vary greatly under different error and propagation-delay conditions.

Let's return to considering what contributes to protocol efficiency. Factors inherent in the protocol design include:

The Quantity of Data Carried in Each Message. Some designs rely on the user to set the data message size, but a better method has the software adjust the size automatically according to the existing error rate. Software incorporating the dynamic adjustment method is not hard to write but, sadly, few products have this feature.

The ARQ Method. This bears directly on the amount of transmission time potentially wasted while the sender waits for acknowledgments. The ARQ scheme, in combination with message size, also dictates the amount of data that must be retransmitted when a message is damaged.

The Amount of Control Information Used by the Protocol.   Some people are surprised to learn that, despite its poor ARQ scheme, XMODEM can be extremely efficient over a low-propagation-delay link. The reason lies in its great simplicity; very few control bytes are needed to shepherd the data from PC to PC.

Other efficiency factors are tied to the protocol implementation. They include:

The Care Taken to Overlap Disk Accesses with Message Transmission and Reception.   The speediness of a fancy ARQ method can be completely wasted if, after transmitting each data message, the sender takes a second or two to extract the next chunk of data from the file.

The Promptness of Actions Taken in Response to Acknowledgments and Other Control Messages.

The Slickness with which the Software Generates the Error-checking Information (i.e., Check-sum or CRC).   A receiver, for example, usually does better to calculate this figure on the fly, as each character is received. Otherwise, once the entire message has been read, the program must take the time to go through it all again to perform the necessary calculation. The second method may be chosen because, at high data rates, there isn't sufficient time between arriving characters to do it the first way.

Another factor that contributes to efficiency is data compression. Indeed, given sufficiently compressible data, this factor is likely to outweigh any of the others mentioned above. It may be misleading, however, to evaluate protocols in terms of compression facilities, because data may often be compressed independently of the protocol in use. As stated above, compression may be available in any of four ways: specified as an optional feature of a protocol, integrated into a particular protocol implementation as a bonus feature, provided by the communicating modems, or carried out by the user as separate processing steps before transmission and after reception.

Features

What features do you need in a protocol? Above all, you need the combination of features that renders the protocol suitable for the communication link(s) you'll be using. It's also worth considering the protocol's ability to do each of the following:

- Resume an interrupted transfer at the point of failure. Suppose you've nearly completed the cross-country transfer of a one-megabyte file when your dog knocks over an extension telephone on the same line as your modem. You'd give anything to avoid having to start again from the beginning. A few protocols, including ZMODEM, BLAST, and DART, will let you continue from the point where you broke off, once the communication link has been reestablished.

- Deliver text files in a useful form (for transfers between unlike systems) and transfer file attributes, such as creation date and time, along with the contents. The first issue was discussed in Chapter 7, where such helpful features as virtual file formats were mentioned.

- Handle simultaneous file transfers in both directions. Imagine a company that must transfer sales figures every night from a branch location to headquarters and send price quotes for the next day's business from headquarters to the branch. If full-duplex modems are employed, it would be faster, and therefore usually cheaper, to conduct the two transfers simultaneously. With half-duplex modems, or the adaptive-duplex type mentioned in Chapter 7, it would be more efficient to do one at a time, since that should minimize the required number of line turnarounds. Few communication products support bidirectional transfers; BLAST is one that does.

Reliability

Several factors contribute to a protocol's reliability. As with efficiency, some inherent in the protocol, others in the implementation. The most important are *integrity* and *robustness*. Integrity refers to the protocol's ability to deliver data without error; properly speaking, it's a measure of the avoidance of undetected errors. High integrity results not only from the use of a strong error-checking method but from its application to *all* messages. (Some protocols, remember, error-protect data but not control messages.) Ideally, a high-integrity system also keeps the quantity of information protected by each check reasonably small. Robustness can be thought of as a measure of a protocol's ability to continue working under the most adverse conditions created by transmission impairments. In practice, both design and implementation must be robust for a protocol to have that quality.

Protocol implementers adopt various strategies to ensure the robustness of their software. Special "torture devices" that simulate noisy transmission lines are often used for software testing; a fiendish assortment of controls allows the implementer to select both the amount and nature of the noise and interference inflicted on the line. Also, test sequences that run on special Data Line Monitors (DLMs) are available for certain protocols. These sequences, called *test suites*, reveal a program's behavior under unfavorable conditions such as the receipt of inappropriate, malformed, or invalid messages from a protocol partner. DLMs are special-purpose microcomputers that can be hooked into a transmission line to monitor and graphically display link traffic, or placed at a link termination and programmed to emulate some other device.

Some critics condemn all public domain protocols because their implementations so often lack robustness. This is not quite fair. It makes more sense to condemn all proprietary protocols because their integrity cannot be objectively analyzed. If a protocol, like XMODEM, is inherently unrobust, clever implementation tricks incorporated into some public domain programs can actually improve it. But who cares? Implementations of intrinsically robust protocols in name-brand products are usually, but not always, robust themselves.

Support

Don't overlook support. When a file transfer link starts to go haywire, diagnosis can be very elusive. So many components are usually involved that even identifying the culprit can be a monumental task. One of your modem cable wires may be loose; your communications software may be incompatible with the new version of DOS to which your PC was just upgraded; some helpful soul may have changed a parameter in your communications package without telling you; your time-outs may be set wrong; a PAD parameter may need changing when you connect to the PSN; or any of several hundred other problems may have arisen. It can be a nightmare. There's no substitute for an on-the-spot expert, but solid customer assistance at the end of a phone line comes close. Remember: a product that's cheap to buy may not be cheap to use if a large number of mistakes and mishaps are sold, so to speak, along with it. Many people, including plenty of business users, love Kermit, appreciate its value for money, and want for nothing more. Others write off Kermit in favor of products like BLAST and RELAY that are backed by strong single-source support.

User Interface

The user interface to a protocol is influenced by user-settable parameters and similar features, but it is attributable more to the design of the implementation than that of the protocol itself. The user interfaces of public domain Kermits are fairly consistent, but such conformity is the exception rather than the rule.

A simple menu-based user interface often helps to accommodate people who are not comfortable using computers. A customizable interface can be tailored to individual preferences. A programmable interface may be needed to facilitate unattended transfers in off-hours. Various styles of user interface will be examined in the next chapter.

ALTERNATIVES FOR LONG-DISTANCE FILE TRANSFER

Most people would consider dialing a connection from a PC to another computer using a communications package, and exchanging files by means of a protocol, to be the conventional means of file transfer. This section is about unconventional means: alternative products, services, and gambits for getting files from one place to another.

Long-distance file transfer affords the PC communicator a great deal of creative latitude. Plenty of obvious methods are available, and others can be dreamed up; homing pigeons were most successful in one case. It can even be fun to figure out what will work best for a particular purpose. The factors directly affecting the choice of method will almost certainly include cost (both initial and long-term), reliability, security, and speed of delivery.

Here are a number of attractive possibilities for getting files from here to there in a hurry:

- Federal Express and similar package network services
- Electronic mail
- Electronic bulk data delivery
- Facsimile transmission

Now we'll describe some of the products and services that have been successful in the past, citing specific cases where possible.

Some Solutions for Short Distances

Large corporations whose offices are dispersed among buildings in lower Manhattan have adopted some innovative data transfer methods. These companies always want high bandwidth, which rules out regular leased lines.

Light Links

If the buildings are in line of sight, then light links, which typically use modulated laser beams to carry information, are feasible. Light link bandwidth is wide and installation fairly simple. But a bit of fog, a heavy rainstorm, or a flock of birds is enough to compromise the method's reliability, so some form of back-up is needed.

Microwave Transmission

Microwave transmission is another line-of-sight option. Although less affected by bad weather than light-based links, it is still very sensitive to the effects of rain. Further, microwave, like all radio-based transmission media, is regulated, so U.S. users must obtain an FCC license for anything except low-power gear.

Vacuum

One New York bank has had great success with a vacuum system. Old-fashioned sucker tubes, carrying capsules full of floppy disks, run from upstairs offices, down through the basements, and between two buildings about a block apart. Since the capsules are packed very full, and the vacuum pulls them very fast, this system is said to constitute the most rapid method of data transfer, per megabyte, in the world today—but only for about two seconds at a time. (The same has been said of a CD-ROM in a Federal Express pouch, whose journey lasts a bit longer.)

Optical Fiber

Optical fiber is the single best solution for close quarters, if it can be installed affordably. This method often turns out to be substantially less expensive than line-of-sight techniques over short distances. A minimum capacity of 45 Mbps is available for fiber links, and the maximum (several hundred Mbps at this writing) is getting higher all the time.

Programmable Modems

The programmable, or stand-alone, modem introduced in Chapter 3 has a built-in RAM, a clock, a printer port, and a script-language processor for communication and data transfer functions. The RAM is used in the manner of a RAM disk; it holds script programs, files to be uploaded, and files that have been downloaded. These little-known but remarkable units are invaluable for a few special applications, and you'll pay only a moderate premium over the cost of other high-quality modems.

A stand-alone modem may be useful for the lone PC user who wants to check each of his two dozen electronic mailboxes every hour, but most such units are put to work broadcasting data. A programmable modem may serve handily at either end of a broadcast link, as in the following two case studies. Facsimile transmission, described in Chapter 11, might also work in the same circumstances.

1. A network for tracing uncommon car parts in wreckers' yards uses three programmable modems at its central office. During each business day, requests for hard-to-find parts are collated on a PC at this central location. During the night, the three modems dial up each member yard and download a copy of the day's request list. Each modem, covering a different area of the country, permanently holds a list of telephone numbers for its assigned area. If a modem gets a busy signal, it skips that number and tries it again after completing the remainder of its calls. Messages from the yards, such as responses to the previous day's requests, can be uploaded as part of the same process. A clever wrinkle in this scheme is that the master list to be distributed each day is loaded into the three modems in tandem; their Transmit Data lines are tied together, enabling them to be programmed simultaneously. In the morning, any uploaded files are, of course, extracted from each modem separately. If the network expands and the work becomes too much for three modems, more can be added with very little effort.

If the workload can be handled by a single modem, it probably makes more sense to use a regular modem and a PC communications package capable of unattended operation.

Once the operation outgrows a single modem and expansion is warranted, however, programmable modems come into their own. Clearly, it will cost much less to buy only additional programmable modems than additional standard modems and a PC for each.

2.   In our second case, system designers exploit the fact that a modem script file can be downloaded to a remote modem just like any other file, making such modems *remotely* programmable. A chain of grocery stores has equipped each of its branches with a stand-alone modem and printer to assist in the broadcasting of pricing information. As each modem is installed, a PC at headquarters calls it up and downloads the single script file it will need for future use. Thereafter, at an appointed weekly time, each store manager presses a button on the local modem to stir it into action. It dials up an electronic mail service, pulls down a long message containing that week's prices, and sends the message to the printer, all in accordance with the script. Apart from the microprocessors in the modems, no computers are required in the stores. This excellent arrangement supplanted the use of an overnight courier service, saving a lot of money and expediting data dissemination into the bargain.

Incidentally, the printer ports on these modems are generally serial rather than parallel, facilitating the connection of plotters or other serial devices as readily as ordinary printers.

Electronic Mail

Public electronic mail services, surveyed in Chapter 11, are oriented to delivering small structured text messages. Generally, they can also be used to move arbitrary data files, but with a couple of complications. First, many will accept only files that appear to be text messages (i.e., those composed of printable ASCII characters organized into lines). A few telex-oriented mail services restrict characters even further, allowing, for example, only uppercase letters. Any file can be converted into a format suitable for transmission through an e-mail (electronic mail) system, but such conversion involves extra steps in the transfer procedure and, on average, greatly increases the volume of data to be moved. Plenty of products are available to enable PCs to perform such conversions, notably Lotus Express®, which also provides an interface to MCI Mail[SM]. The second potential problem in using e-mail for file transfer is that the pricing structures of most mail systems are skewed in favor of small messages; the cost of sending large data files may prove prohibitive. A third possible problem is that, while many electronic mail services have been moving to accommodate protocols for uploading and downloading messages, the practice is not universal.

Although, as we've pointed out, electronic mail may not be ideal for file transfer, many companies have found it quite satisfactory for the purpose and use it regularly. One major advantage of e-mail over direct computer-to-computer transfers is that distribution of a file to multiple receivers becomes child's play.

Delivery of an e-mail message addressed to many recipients may be accomplished in two ways. Public mail systems usually hold a single copy of the message, reading it out to each addressee as he or she logs in. The message is discarded after all addressees have read it or, perhaps, after a time limit (even if some addressees have not seen it). Note that this is different from the organization of most private and network e-mail systems, which make a copy of a message for each addressee and deliver it to the appropriate electronic mailbox.

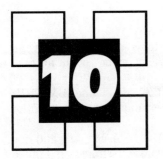

10 PC COMMUNICATION PACKAGES

Software products for terminal emulation and file transfer are generically called *communication packages*. Some well-known examples are CROSSTALK XVI and CROSSTALK Mk.4, Smartcom III, PC-TALK™, HyperAccess, and RELAY Silver and Gold. We will discuss what to expect from such products, how to evaluate them, and what the popular ones can do for you.

OVERVIEW

A communication package, which we'll sometimes call simply "package" here, allows a PC user to communicate with other computers over asynchronous and, in some cases, synchronous links. "Other computers" includes not only other microcomputers but, in addition, that miscellany of mainframes, minis, and super-micros often lumped together as "hosts." A competent package will permit you to conduct a terminal session with a minicomputer, connect to electronic mail services to send and receive messages, and execute protocol file transfers to and from remote PCs. A sophisticated product, on a PC equipped with sufficient communications hardware, will perform all these tasks at the same time.

A good package will allow the PC to function as either terminal or host. In *terminal mode*, the PC establishes a connection to a computer system operating as host, so the user can conduct an interactive session with it. A package running in *host mode* can answer a telephone call, communicate with another computer running a package in terminal mode (or even with a real terminal), and perform services for the remote user. At first it may seem remarkable that the same program should do both jobs, since they are conceptually very different. But the two functions have much in common when it comes to accessing files for transfer, driving COM ports, and interfacing with modems.

Communication Package Features

The rest of this section is a summary of the important features found in packages. Some of these were introduced in Chapter 6 as items common to ASCII terminal-emulator products for PCs. To recap, we described:

- Dialing directory
- Automatic login
- Canned dialing-directories entries
- File capture and insertion
- Multiple sessions

Here, we'll provide additional information about a few of these items, and describe several other fairly standard communication package features of significant value to the average user.

A *choice of emulated terminals* is likely to include the popular DEC VT100 and IBM 3101, plus some others. The dialing directory should store the type of terminal to be emulated for each host.

A good *selection of file transfer protocols* ought to include XMODEM, Kermit, and one or two others. Some packages also offer proprietary protocols, whose usefulness is limited to connections between two packages of the same kind.

Macros are user-defined mappings between text strings and non-ASCII keys, such as function and Alt-shifted keys. For strings of characters that you must type frequently (your name, for instance), or those that are an occasional nuisance (such as long commands), macros may save time and energy. One of the authors might, for example, define a macro such that when he hits Alt-N, the program will send the string "login kenton" to the host. While some people use macros religiously, there are plenty of others who rarely bother with them, having found it more troublesome to remember which key invokes a given macro than it is to type the string itself.

File capture and file insertion capabilities were introduced in Chapter 6. *File capture* allows the user to transcribe a terminal session onto a PC disk file. The complementary facility, *file insertion*, injects the contents of a disk file into the host-bound input stream. The facility names given here are not universal; terms vary from one package to another. Although capture and insertion may be used to transfer files, they should not be confused with "file transfer" as it's normally understood—that is, implying that a protocol is involved. Still, file capture and insertion are valuable for moving files to and from hosts offering no PC protocols. File capture also serves a very important function in storing host-generated data that don't reside on a host file as such.

For file insertion, *line* or *character pacing* may be provided to prevent the host's being ground into the dust by a stampede of data from the PC. Line pacing directs the transmitting PC to wait for some event between lines of text. The event may be the passage of a fixed time interval, receipt of a prompt from the host, or, when echoplex is in effect, the host's echoing of the carriage return at the end of each line.

Many hosts process received data one line at a time, and therefore need the delay between lines provided by line pacing. Within a line, some of these hosts are able to "absorb" data as fast as the PC can send them. Others, however, programmed to accept relatively leisurely input from typists at terminals, cannot keep up with the breakneck pace at which individual characters are normally emitted by PCs. Such slow-witted hosts need character pacing, which introduces a delay after every character transmitted. The delay may again be a fixed interval, or may reflect the time required for the host to echo the character. When necessary, both line and character pacing techniques can usually be employed without interfering with each other.

Background operation is great for doing file transfers without tying up the PC. Once a file transfer has been set in motion, the communication package has no essential need of the screen and keyboard; with background file transfer, the user may reclaim them for word processing or other tasks while the transfer is under way. The package sits in memory, becoming briefly active when necessary to send or receive data, but allowing another application program to run. Background operation is automatically available on computers running OS/2 or, with some packages, such DOS extensions as DESQview™ and Microsoft Windows/386™, but relatively few packages support it under basic DOS.

Packages that do offer DOS background operation are discussed in a later section of this chapter.

Context-sensitive help is an especially desirable feature. When both the host and the phone company are eating up your money at a brisk clip, and you forget, say, how to abort the insertion of a file, you want timely and accurate help. Flipping through the manual to retrieve the name of some obscure command can be time-consuming and frustrating. If the help facility is context-sensitive, you can hit a single key and immediately get the command information you need.

Script languages allow the user to automate communication functions by programming the relevant software. The normal use of a communication package, with what might be called the "standard user interface," involves the PC keyboard (to type commands to the program) and the monitor (to display output). Of course, the style and quality of this interface vary greatly from product to product. With a script language interface, the user can create a file of commands that will later be fed as input to the program. (The command file is usually created off-line, when the package is idle.) For example, a set of commands might direct the program to dial a host computer, log in, upload a file, log out, and hang up. Once the completed file of commands has been tested, the package can perform the sequence of actions by itself, without any user attention.

A script language interface has two advantages. First, scripts written to automate repeatedly performed actions, such as logging in or checking for electronic mail, save a lot of wearisome typing, eliminate typographical errors, and leave you free to do more productive or more enjoyable work.

Second, scripts facilitate *unattended operation* of the program. If you want to take advantage of the cheapest phone and network rates by executing file transfers in the dead of night, you can compose the appropriate command sequence and sleep through the whole thing.

Customization capability, offered with a couple of the leading packages, could apply to numerous areas of operation, but is primarily used to allow users to create new menus and extend existing ones. In many cases, menu customization is implemented via script language commands; this is carried out especially well in RELAY Gold and CROSSTALK Mk.4. The CROSSTALK script language is sufficiently powerful that it can even be used to add extra protocol drivers.

Multiple-session capability, offered by a few of the more sophisticated packages, such as CROSSTALK Mk.4 and Smartcom III, allows the user to conduct a number of communication sessions simultaneously. Such products will appeal to insatiable communicators with two or more COM ports and modems, and to users who have direct connections to local hosts and want to stay logged into them while dialing up remote systems. Concurrent sessions normally involve the use of multiple ports, but multiplexing protocols such as X.PC may allow multiple sessions over one physical connection.

Multiple-session capability is obviously a bigger bonus under DOS than under OS/2, where several packages could be run concurrently. Nevertheless, even in the latter case, use of a single package is likely to provide a more seamless transition between sessions.

CONFIGURING COMMUNICATION PACKAGES

Communication packages nowadays bristle with options and parameters, most of which must be set by the user. For the novice, the screenfuls of unfamiliar names and numbers may be quite daunting. Every option has its value, however, and there may come a day when you are thankful for it. Here, we look into the parameter-setting procedures that make these options available.

It's helpful to categorize the kinds of information that communication packages need from the user. The first step is to distinguish between what we might call *global* and *host parameters*. Global parameters relate to configuration of the PC itself, describing, for example, which COM port(s) are involved, the model of modem, where to find the printer, the kind of monitor, and the name of the file containing the user's favorite word processor. Host parameters comprise the settings that go into the dialing directory, that is, data that the communication package uses to manage communication with each host.

Host parameters can be further divided into what we will call *required* and *general groups*. Required parameters are those the user must supply specifically for each host. Fortunately, there are not many of these. They include the telephone number, data rate, number of data bits, parity setting, and maybe an echo switch. General parameters are not relevant to the initial establishment of a host connection, and can usually be left at their respective default settings until experience shows that another setting will serve better. Examples of general parameters are a host's preferred file transfer protocol, the type of terminal the package should emulate, and details of end-of-line handling (discussed briefly later in this chapter). The composition of the end-of-line group varies from one package to another, as does the way the user can modify its elements.

When connecting to a given host for the first time, you can expect the host's administration to supply the required parameters, along with details of the account you will use. Once you enter these, you should be in business, or at least in communication. You shouldn't need to bother with general parameters at first, unless the host has some eccentric communication habits. It may later become advisable or necessary to change one or more general parameters to accommodate the host's characteristics or work with it in more sophisticated ways.

One measure of a good package is convenience in setting required parameters while the rest are kept more or less out of sight until the need to change them arises. Another attractive, but not universal, feature is sensible default settings for the general parameters.

Modem Particulars

Assuming that we're dealing with dial-up hosts, rather than directly connected systems, a communication package almost invariably uses a COM port and modem to establish connections. Hence, the package needs to know precisely what kind of modem is available and which port it's connected to. A common mistake is to configure a package for the wrong COM port so that it ends up trying to dial up MCI Mail using the serial printer. Most packages assume they should work with COM1 unless told otherwise. Putting the serial printer on COM2 and the modem on COM1 can save a lot of configuration work for those who deal with a number of different packages.

If you're lucky, you won't have to configure a package for your modem. This should certainly be true if both software and modem were sold together. Otherwise, the issue is likely to depend on how compatible your modem is with the Hayes Standard AT Command Set. Most packages are set by default for Hayes-compatible modems; a few tolerate nothing else. Some packages have a menu list of supported modems, from which you may select the one you're using, but this limits the software's ability to work with new modem models as they appear. Most commonly, configuration requires the user to supply suitable command strings for a small set of modem functions, such as those used to preface a telephone number to be dialed, and to hang up after a data call. If a modem imposes special requirements for such tasks, its manual will almost certainly supply examples of commands that can be abstracted for the communication package.

One configuration issue confronting many users involves the choice between pulse and Touch-Tone dialing. Nearly all modems support both modes, with pulse as the default selection and a command to switch to Touch-Tone. In most communication packages, on the other hand, tone dialing is the default setting; unless told otherwise, the software will override the modem's default and command it to use Touch-Tone. In the Hayes language, Touch-Tone is set by incorporating "DT" into the string of commands used to initialize the modem or by prefacing each dial command with "DT." Used in the same way, "DP" indicates pulse dialing. Here are some typical Hayes command lines:

ATDP5551212	dials the given number in pulse mode
ATDT5551212	dials the number in Touch-Tone mode
ATD5551212	dials the number in whichever mode was last set

Required Host Parameters

To establish a connection to a host, a communication package needs, at the minimum, the host's telephone number and the parameters that define the make-up of the data stream: the preferred line speed, number of data bits per character, number of stop bits per character, and the choice of parity. It may be annoying to have to spoon-feed such details to the software for every host, but there's no getting around it. Very few packages have even the modicum of artificial intelligence that would be needed to perform this chore. The only relief is provided by those popular systems for which canned communication-package directory entries incorporate the appropriate settings.

In any event, the user's task is normally straightforward, because there should never be any secret about the parameters required for a given system. (If you dial into systems at random, of course, you're on your own.) A "regular" host, whether mainframe or BBS, should publish the parameters it requires. For PC-to-PC links, there would seem to be little reason to deviate from eight data bits, one stop bit, and no parity.

Most packages provide five options for parity: none, odd, even, space, and mark. *None* means that all bits in each character are handled as data. *Odd* and *even* select the normal uses of parity. *Space* means that each transmitted character's parity bit is set to zero; *mark* means that each parity bit is set to one. The space and mark options are seldom appropriate for modern hosts.

The number of data bits stipulates the size of characters, excluding the parity bit, to be handled by the port. While PC serial ports are capable of transmitting characters of five to eight bits, only seven- and eight-bit characters are supported by communications software. (The ability to send and receive five-bit characters would allow communication with a teletypewriter using Baudot code, probably requiring operation of the serial port in current-loop, rather than RS-232, mode.)

The number of stop bits may be one, one and a half, or two, with one being the most common setting. Selecting two stop bits is one of several ways to artificially slow down host input, should that prove necessary for file transfer.

In principle, any combination of character size, parity option, and number of stop bits is possible, but only a few are often used in practice. The three most common combinations, shown in Figure 10.1, are often abbreviated as 8N1, 7E1, and 7N1, meaning, respectively, eight data bits/no parity/one stop bit, seven data bits/even parity/one stop bit, and seven data bits/no parity/one stop bit.

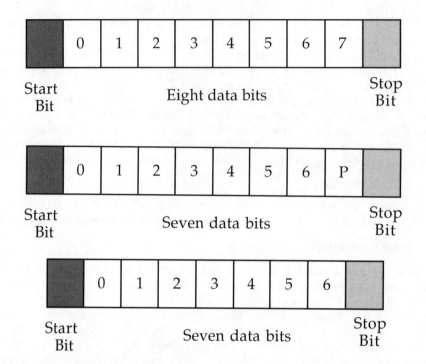

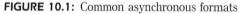

FIGURE 10.1: Common asynchronous formats

If you supply these communication parameters incorrectly, all is not necessarily lost. In many cases, you can still provoke the host into sending some output; it may look like garbage on the screen, but with a little ingenuity, it can still help you to adjust the parameters properly.

Another, less essential parameter, often set with those just described, involves the choice of local or remote *echoing*, discussed in Chapter 6. To recap, for normal terminal operation, characters typed on the keyboard must somehow be echoed onto the screen. Echoing may, in principle, be effected by the host, the user's modem, or the communications software. Host echoing ("echoplex") is usually the best method, since it can reveal some transmission errors.

A typical communication package defaults to host echoing, so it must be told if local echoing is desired. When set for local echo, most packages will perform the task themselves, although some rely on the modem for this. As we've mentioned, some packages may rather imprecisely list local and remote echoing options as "half-duplex" and "full-duplex," respectively. If you are unsure of the correct setting, you should start with the one that turns on local echoing. Then, if "ttwwoo ccooppiieess" of each typed character appear on the screen, reverse the setting. If you get no echoing at all, either the host or the package must be told to start echoing.

General Host Parameters

Host parameters in the next group will not altogether obstruct communication if improperly set, but they must be set correctly for best results.

Selecting the *terminal type* to be emulated is usually straightforward. When the host supports only a generic teletype-style device rather than a specific model of terminal, it's generally safe to select emulation of a VT100 or similar terminal, assuming the communication package offers nothing more suitable. If strange character sequences containing lots of square brackets appear on the screen along with readable text, the choice of terminal was probably inappropriate. (The strange characters are function sequences such as those defined by ANSI X3.64.)

For some hosts, attention must be paid to the package's handling of *end-of-line*. This may be an issue for *host input, host output*, or both. Most host systems that handle terminal input in units of lines require only a carriage return (CR) as a terminator for each line. A few, however, also demand that the terminal send a line feed (LF), which any package should be capable of supplying automatically every time the Enter key is pressed to send a CR. On the output side, most host systems terminate each line sent to terminals with a CR/LF combination, but some supply only the CR and expect the terminal to provide the LF. Again, a package should be capable of behaving appropriately. The appearance of output from the host on a single, repeatedly overwritten line is a signal that the user should turn on automatic line feeding. Conversely, if host output appears consistently double-spaced, then presumably auto-LF mode was set when not required.

A *flow-control parameter* tells the package whether or not to pay attention to XONs and XOFFs sent by the host. (Normally, flow control is separately selectable for both directions of data transfer, i.e., to and from the host.) With flow control selected, the package, upon receiving an XOFF from the host, will send no further input until an XON arrives. Direct keyboard input, whose data rate is quite slow, would hardly ever be suspended by this technique. Flow control is important, however, when input is being sent from a file during a file insertion or similar operation; it may also be employed during protocol transfers if the protocol is compatible with it. This type of flow control is crucial on PSNs, since a PSN node packetizes data for forwarding through the net. When flow control is enabled in the node, the node accepts one packet-load of data, typically 128 or 256 bytes, then sends an XOFF to inhibit further input until it has sent that packet on its way, at which time it will be ready to fill another one. Protocols operating over PSNs must handle such flow control (or use small messages to circumvent it), or suffer possible loss of data as a result of swamping the PAD.

When Parameters are Too General

One apparent shortcoming of a fair number of communication packages is that they maintain, as global parameters, settings that ought to be kept independently for each host. For example, in the handling of received flow control, one package allows only a single setting for XON/XOFF, which then applies to every host unless specifically changed at the time of connection. This is a nuisance if some of the user's hosts employ flow control while others send Control-Ss and Control-Qs for other purposes. In an even more irksome instance, although one likely to affect fewer people, many packages assume that the user has but a single modem. Thus, if you have two modems attached to separate ports, and use each one to connect to different hosts, you are forced to spend time "adjusting" parameters that really haven't changed.

The ideal solution, of course, is for package designers to get it right in the first place. Separate storage of every significant parameter for each host would impose little additional burden on the user, who can simply establish a default set. A generally practical solution is to arrange your disk so that the dialing directory entry for each host is stored in its own separate disk directory. Clearly, keeping a copy of the communications software in every directory would be a terrible waste of space, but this can be prevented through judicious use of the operating system's PATH command. Just arrange for the package to set up a "global" parameter file in each directory. Experienced communicators often use multiple directories, even in the absence of the problems outlined above, to keep separate the many other files associated with each host.

A similar issue arises with file transfer protocols. Since, in most cases, you'll use only one protocol with a given host, it is beneficial if the package can "remember" your preferred protocols. Many packages, unfortunately, insist that you respecify the protocol to be used at every file transfer.

TIPS AND TRICKS

Script Languages

Script languages are the rule rather than the exception in communication packages today. Early script languages provided means to automate straightforward dialogues with a host where every detail of the exchange could be anticipated, largely because details were so few. A generic example to connect to a host and login is

> CALL mine_host
>
> WAITFOR "Username:"
>
> SEND "frog"
>
> WAITFOR "Password:"
>
> SEND "crunchy"

Figure 10.2 shows a transcript of a login sequence for which this script would serve. Note that the SEND command must append a carriage return to the input string that it sends to the host. Following common practice, the host does not echo the password.

These early languages served adequately to automate login sequences, but were limited from more powerful applications primarily by their paucity of control commands, that is, their inability to test items, branch within the program, call subroutines, loop, or process error conditions.

Today, the leading script languages, such as SCOPE™in Smartcom III and CASL®in CROSSTALK Mk.4, are as complex as some programming languages. In fact, one could justly call them programming languages. It would be ridiculous, but one could probably write a spreadsheet program in CASL. Script languages take some getting used to, but are substantially easier to learn to use than "regular" programming languages for three reasons: (1) they are functionally oriented, that is, they include powerful commands to perform communication-related functions; (2) they make testing and debugging programs relatively easy because their performance is very graphic; and (3) the best are designed with simple syntax structures, good help systems, and excellent diagnostics to make life easy for users who aren't "real" programmers.

Script languages can be used to develop programs for the following classes of function:

- Assistance in the performance of routine functions in regular hands-on sessions, of which the login example above is a trivial illustration.

Welcome to the Whizzo Chocolate Company mainframe.

Username: **frog**
Password:

Logged in at 15:00, Friday 26th February, 1988.

Command:
 —

FIGURE 10.2: Login sequence corresponding to script file in the text

- Conducting entire communication sessions to facilitate unattended operation of the package: checking for, downloading, and uploading electronic mail; performing long file transfers during off-hours; and performing routine database queries.
- Customization of the package user interface.
- Servicing callers who connect to the package in host mode.
- Distributed processing to provide, for example, a customized user interface to a mainframe application program.

Running Other Programs from a Communication Package

Many communication packages for DOS permit the user to run another application program from within the package. A "RUN" command, for example, is very common. Typically, this suspends the communication session, rendering the package temporarily dormant, while another program is loaded above it in memory and executed. Once that other program terminates, the package regains control. Such a feature is tremendously useful: you can perform tasks unrelated to the communication session and still be sure of keeping your connection. Considering that this facility is not hard to implement, it belongs in every package.

The most common opportunity to take advantage of this feature is in the use of a word processor to compose, say, a reply to an electronic mail message. Many packages, in fact, have two types of run command: one to start up your favorite word processor (whose name they'll remember), and one to run an arbitrary program whose name is entered at the time you wish to run it.

The choice of programs to be run from within packages is limited primarily by the amount of memory available. Since communication packages tend not to be memory hogs, the user usually has a fair amount of latitude. In particular, it should be possible to run COMMAND.COM, the DOS command interpreter. This provides access to all the usual DOS utilities, including COPY, FORMAT, etc. (To terminate the command interpreter and get back to the package, one invokes the DOS EXIT command.) It won't usually be necessary to exploit COMMAND.COM for such purposes as getting directory listings and deleting files, because many packages have built-in commands for these tasks.

One kind of program that generally cannot be run from within a communication package is another communication package. Obviously, it would be silly to attempt such a maneuver on the same COM port, but it may well cause trouble even on a different port due to interrupt-line conflicts (see Chapter 4).

There are exceptions to the general rule that running another program within a package renders the package itself dormant. A few products, such as RELAY Gold, will allow you to start a file transfer, then run another program; the transfer will continue merrily on its way, and you can break back to the package once the transfer is complete.

With many communication packages, it's actually possible to go one step beyond the feature just described. You can exit the package as if you were finished with it, run other programs, and then restart the package to resume your session, all without losing your connection. This depends on the package's not resetting the modem on either entry or exit. A few, like Smartcom, do reset the modem, but many others don't.

What's the advantage of this method over a RUN command? Well, it's certainly useful if your package lacks a RUN. It would also allow you to run a huge program for which you might not have room with the package resident. This method of leaving the first package dangling can be quite handy for switching among packages. Of course, not everyone plays with many such programs, as the authors do. But if, for example, you have a connection somewhere and need a certain protocol not supported by the active package, you can switch to another package that does have it. Incidentally, booting a PC does not affect COM ports, so if a package crashes, you can press Ctrl-Alt-Del (or the reset button), get DOS back up, rerun the package, and continue where you left off.

Moving Dialing Directories Among Communication Packages

When a large organization has standardized on a particular package, the need to share dialing directory entries inevitably arises. One person might determine which parameters work best for a particular host, and then distribute them to other users who will access the same system. Often, the other users have no knowledge of communications and no understanding of the parameters involved. How is this distribution best accomplished? The issue here is not that of physically moving the data, but of getting them into a form in which they *can* be conveniently transferred. First, how do you get the single desired dialing directory entry out of the package that created it and into a file that can be transferred to another PC? And, second, how do you feed that file into another copy of the same package? There are several possible approaches. The correct one depends on how the creator communication package maintains its dialing directories.

Many packages, especially those that store a lot of information about each host, maintain each dialing directory entry on a separate file named for the host. CROSSTALK XVI, for example, would keep all the necessaries for a host called CHARIOT on a file called CHARIOT.XTK. When these distinct files are used, moving them among PCs is utterly straightforward: just copying a file into the directory belonging to the recipient package ensures that the recipient will automatically find it. This implies that such a package keeps no explicit record of its dialing directory entries. Instead, at each start-up, it checks the current disk directory for all files that fit the pattern of a dialing directory entry—for example, *.XTK in the case above.

A more difficult situation arises when a package keeps its entire dialing directory on a single file. A few packages not only take this approach, but offer no help to the user who wants to extract a few entries for use by somebody else. Moving the whole lot, with the intention of subsequently deleting unwanted portions, will not really solve the problem if the recipient has already set up her own dialing directory, since there will normally be no way to merge the two. The simplest solution is to make sure that this problem will not occur *before* standardizing on a package product.

EVALUATING PC COMMUNICATION PACKAGES

Someone once claimed that communication packages were like religions. Some people take to a particular package and stick with it fiercely; others use two or three and never settle on a clear favorite. The total number of PC communication packages on the North American market must be over 200, and quite a few are worthwhile products. In this section, we present some ideas for evaluating and choosing a package. First, consider three objective issues:

> The modems supported
> The terminals emulated
> The protocols provided

Here are some things to look for:

Modem Support

Communication packages may be finicky about whose modems they will talk to. This is due primarily to the different command languages used, but may also be affected by such aspects of modem design as how RS-232's modem control circuits are employed. Most packages will at least talk to Hayes modems and compatibles—hardly a surprise, since they constitute the great majority. Many products come set up for Hayes-type modems, but can easily be adapted for any other.

Terminal Emulation

Consider what types of terminal you might need to emulate. If two or more of them are obscure types, you may not be able to find a single product that emulates the entire set.

Protocols

Consider what protocols you might require. This is most likely to depend upon the protocols offered by hosts with which you plan to work.

Other Tips for Picking Communication Packages

When choosing a package to be used by many people in an organization, it's wise to note that users will want to share dialing directory entries and script files. Sharing script files should be straightforward with any package: a script, after all, is just an ASCII file created with a word processor. As indicated in the previous section, however, sharing dialing directory entries is not necessarily so easy.

Anyone who uses a package frequently is likely to appreciate one accommodating a command line parameter that directs it to connect and log in to a particular host. This was a rare feature in the early days of communication packages, but most of the leading products now have it. One of its virtues is that the package can be invoked from a batch file. A user might set up a batch file, for example, to invoke CROSSTALK XVI to connect her to CompuServe; this file, called CS.BAT, would contain:

```
C:
CD \XTALK
XTALK CSERV
```

The user simply enters CS at any DOS prompt, and can then sit back and relax while CROSSTALK does all the work, taking over again only after being logged in. Here, the CSERV parameter in the line that starts up CROSSTALK identifies a command file containing a dialing directory entry for CompuServe and a login script. The program dials up CompuServe, and automatically invokes the login script upon completing the connection.

While the leading commercial packages, such as CROSSTALK Mk.4, HyperAccess, RELAY Gold, and Smartcom III, are all excellent products, they may be too much of a good thing for some users. If you don't need the power of their numerous automatic features and the versatility of their script languages, you might prefer a simpler and less expensive package, such as one of the several fine shareware programs for this purpose. Typically, shareware programs are distributed through various public networks; their authors permit copies to be made and shared under certain conditions so that potential users can freely evaluate them. After a trial period, users are expected to pay a fee that is generally below the cost of regular commercial software. Perhaps because those who are apt to write shareware are also keen on telecommunication, their packages stand out as some of the best shareware offerings. In the early years of PCs, PC-TALK III, written by the late Andrew Fluegelman, enjoyed wide popularity among both business and hobbyist users. The shareware program in vogue at the time of writing is a little gem called ProComm; its successor, ProComm Plus®, is a mainstream commercial product distributed by Datastorm Technologies.

A few communication packages, particularly older ones, are designed primarily for use over modem links, with little attention given to local, direct-cabled connections. Their major shortcoming in this regard is a ceiling on transmission speed. As we have seen, RS-232 interfaces on PCs can run at speeds up to 115,200 bps, but many software packages impose a maximum of 9,600 bps. This may be sensible in some cases, because the software might not be able to keep pace with data at higher rates, but generally the limitation is artificial and unnecessary. For terminal emulation, 9,600 bps is almost always adequate because few hosts support greater speeds no matter how the PC is connected. File transfer between local PCs, however, is another matter. Why not let it rip at 56,000 or 115,200 bps? A couple of vendors have spotted this niche and sell PC-to-PC, file-transfer-only products oriented to these higher speeds.

Product reviews and evaluations are a source of information and guidance on the availability of context-sensitive help, the extent of user control and flexibility, and the ease of learning and use. A more personal determination must be based on your individual preferences for menu or command operation and on whether you want access to, or protection from, the low-level technical details of communication.

OTHER PC COMMUNICATIONS SOFTWARE

Remote Control

A class of products called *remote access, remote control,* or simply *remote* packages offers the ability to link two PCs together so that they act, more or less, as one. This amounts to turning one PC into a single-user host, which we'll call the "host PC," controlled via the screen and keyboard of the other PC, which we'll call the "remote PC." The two machines may be connected by any type of RS-232-based link, usually a dial-up modem connection, as illustrated in Figure 10.3.

A remote control package supplies two programs, one for the host and one for the remote PC. These programs conspire to duplicate the screen display of the host PC on the monitor of the remote PC, and to permit the host to receive input from either keyboard interchangeably. The host software runs in the background, communicating with the software in the remote PC and making possible the "mirroring" provided by the remote. The net effect is the illusion that any program running in the host is also running in the remote. Direct and remote operation of the host PC are essentially indistinguishable, except for three aspects of remote operation:

- First, the appearance of output on the screen and the response to keyboard input are slowed by the speed limitations of the communication link.
- Second, the host PC cannot be rebooted from the remote.
- Third, the remote user (obviously) cannot perform physical actions at the host, such as inserting diskettes into drives or loading paper into a printer.

Remote access is useful under various circumstances, as in the following examples:

Remote Access to PC Resources.   A user wants to access an office PC, which is loaded with lots of memory, a hard disk, and add-in boards, from a lightly configured PC at home.

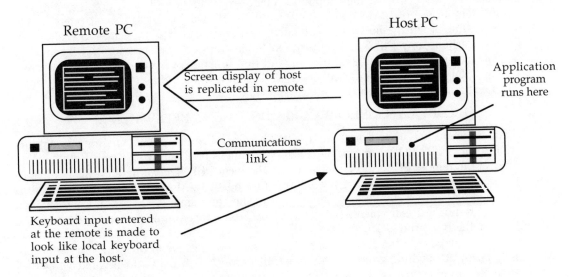

FIGURE 10.3: Remote-control software

Remote Access to PC LANs. A remote access product can provide a very effective means of dialing into a PC LAN. (We'll say more about this in Chapters 13–15 on LANs.)

Remote Diagnosis. A software developer wants a firsthand look at a problem reported by a user. Remote access in this context is especially helpful when a software bug cannot be reproduced except on one particular user's PC, located far from the program's author.

Training. Instruction in the use of a software product may be facilitated by supplying a pair of PCs, one for the trainer and one for the trainee, linked by a remote control package. In this case, unlike most others, the two PCs are typically directly cabled together and placed right next to each other.

Software Demos. A software vendor can give a prospective buyer practical experience with a product without supplying a copy of the program and risking its loss or piracy.

Two-Way Conferencing. Two business people, working at their own PCs, can view the same spreadsheet, document, or other material, discuss it, and key in changes that will be displayed on both screens. For people working in separate locations, this technique will require two telephone connections, one for the computers and one for human conversation.

Note that DOS affords a degree of remote control capability with its CTTY (Change Console) command, which redirects keyboard input and screen output to a given COM port. But so few application programs make use of DOS services for their keyboard and screen I/O that CTTY is useful for little beyond remote entry of DOS commands. A competent remote control package, by contrast, can redirect keyboard input at the BIOS level and copy screen output directly from the video buffer, thus rendering it compatible with almost any user program. A specialized product, moreover, provides such extra features as access control (with passwords, etc.), greetings messages, and file transfer.

Carbon Copy PLUS from Meridian Technology is one of several excellent remote control products for PCs. This package supports remote reproduction of both graphics and text output, remote use of IRMA® cards, and compatibility with many LANs. It offers a chat mode so that, when the host PC is attended, two users can type messages to each other. Finally, Carbon Copy PLUS not only supports file transfers, but provides an ingeniously sensible means of initiating them: a command that functions very much like the operating system's COPY utility. A user at either of two PCs linked by Carbon Copy PLUS may enter a command such as:

(4) COPY LA:\CC\BEESWAX RD:\DOCUMENT\BEESWAX.DOC

An argument to Carbon Copy Plus's COPY command can be almost anything acceptable to DOS's or OS/2's COPY, except that each pathname is prefixed by either an *R* (to indicate a file on the remote PC) or an *L* (for a file on the local PC). *Remote* here means relative to the user who starts the transfer, not relative to a host PC. Most PC users, accustomed to COPYing files, will easily take to this variant of the command. And Carbon Copy PLUS's COPYs are not just convenient, they're fast; the proprietary protocol used for the purpose is one of the best around.

The marketplace offers remote control products with a range of talents. Some are especially adept at handling graphics; some permit more than two PCs to be linked together (great for large demos); and a few support remote access from an ASCII terminal as well as from a PC. Another acclaimed product is PC Anywhere™ from Dynamic Microprocessor Associates.

An interesting subclass of remote control products operates in a slightly different fashion that might be called *tandem control*. Unlike the software described above, tandem control operates symmetrically. Two connected PCs act as peers, and mirroring software duplicates any keyboard input typed at one PC in the other. This facility is normally used on two similarly configured PCs running the same application program; the control software, running in the background, ensures that both copies of the application program receive the same input. A product of this type does not fill such needs as remote LAN access or off-site diagnosis, but might be preferable to a regular remote package for training and demonstration, since it allows two PCs to run in a mirrored fashion without the burden of carrying screen data between them.

Background Communications Packages

If your operating system is DOS *ordinaire*, as opposed to DESQview, Microsoft Windows/386, OS/2, or some other multiapplication environment, you can run only one regular application program at a time. True, you can also install a few special memory-resident programs, but the restriction to a single application program can make life frustrating when you initiate a lengthy file transfer. While the PC is tied up, the communications program denies you the use of the keyboard, displays inessential information (if any) on the screen, and makes only limited use of the processor, especially irksome if it's a powerful one. How much nicer it would be if you could start the data transfer and go on to some other work, letting the transfer chug along in the background. Well, of course, you can do so with the aid of a background communications package. Such programs are memory-resident, ready for use at the drop of a hotkey.

The most obvious motivations for using a background communications package are negative ones: avoiding being bored to death, or going bankrupt due to lack of productivity, while your PC is busy with file transfers. But other common motivations are sunny and positive. Suppose, for example, you use your PC as a terminal and like to remain logged into a certain host all the time, whether you are actively using your session or not. This may be because you wish to avoid the hassle and delays involved in frequent logins and logouts, or perhaps you want to be available for other users on the host to send you messages. Whatever your reasons, a background package is the most cost-effective way to free such a PC for other tasks.

Since demand is modest, only a few background communication packages are to be found on the market and, in view of the rise of multiapplication capabilities for PCs, it seems unlikely that many new ones will emerge. SideTalk™ from Lattice, a company better known for its splendid C compilers, has shown the greatest longevity.

A common, and perhaps inevitable, shortcoming of background communication packages is that they occupy a good deal of memory, much more than the average memory-resident program. If you like to work with monster spreadsheets or large database programs, you may find yourself a little cramped.

Among the features to look for in a background package is the ability to unload the program when you're finished with it, which allows you to reclaim the memory hogged by the product. You can, of course, unload any such program by rebooting your machine, but that is time-consuming and may be unacceptably disruptive to your work. *Batch-transfer* protocols are another especially valuable feature of a resident communications package. Protocols such as YMODEM and Kermit, which permit the transfer of multiple files with a single command, are ideal: if you're going to be transferring files in the background, you probably want to streamline the process as much as possible.

Building Communications Capabilities Into Application Programs

A number of companies sell libraries of program functions for accessing serial ports, mostly for programs written in C, but a few for Pascal. Some are targeted for particular compilers. Usually, such packages include source codes, and the vendor asks no royalties for functions incorporated into the purchaser's commercial or in-house programs.

A library typically includes functions for configuring a COM port, with data rate, parity option, etc.; managing queues, for example, of input data awaiting processing, or output data awaiting transmission; receiving and transmitting characters, using either polling or interrupts; running XMODEM; and controlling Hayes modems.

A library of this kind would make writing your own communications package much easier than starting from scratch, but you are likelier to use it to add communication capability to some other kind of application program or to create a program to talk to a strange RS-232 device.

Products in this category are available from Blaise, Greenleaf, and Software Horizons, among others. Library products for various application areas, including serial communications, are frequently advertised in trade publications.

ELECTRONIC MESSAGING AND ON-LINE SERVICES

ELECTRONIC MAIL SYSTEMS

Some readers may be familiar with electronic mail systems available on hosts or networks within organizations. Others may have used e-mail services that are run more like public utilities, to which individuals or corporations can subscribe, and which fill a role similar to that of the post office. We will first consider the latter category.

The leaders in public e-mail are MCI Mail, Western Union's EasyLink, British Telecom's Dialcom, McDonnell Douglas' OnTyme™, and, in Canada, Envoy™. Other popular services include Telenet's Telemail®, GE Quick-Comm®, CCI Multilink™, and AT&T Mail®. To add to the confusion, many information utilities, including CompuServe, offer electronic mail. Unfortunately, there are few gateways (special-purpose connective paths) between different services. MCI Mail and CompuServe subscribers can send mail to one another, and some other links are in the works, but we are a long way from a universal electronic mail system. A new international standard protocol for electronic mail, X.400, may prove to be the keystone of a bridge linking all of today's disparate systems by the mid-1990s.

Electronic mail is an umbrella term for a variety of services. The common feature is electronic messages created either on a personal computer (with the aid of a word processor) or with an editor provided by the mail service itself. The message may then be delivered in four ways:

To an Electronic Mailbox.   This is simply a file to which messages are appended. The owner of the mailbox must usually poll the system (i.e., log in to it once in a while) to learn whether newly delivered mail is waiting.

To a PC.   Some services can dial out to a recipient's PC and deliver mail directly to it. The PC, of course, must be set up with a modem ready to answer such a call.

To Paper.   The message is transmitted electronically to a location close to its point of delivery and then printed. The printed copy is then either injected into the regular mail system or delivered by courier.

To Another Network.   Although, as noted above, gateways among e-mail networks are uncommon, some mail services have gateways to telex and similar networks. The message may be delivered to a telex or TWX machine, or as a telegram or cable, giving someone without a telex machine access to the world's 1.8 million telex subscribers. Some services also deliver messages to fax machines.

Ordinarily, electronic mail services can be accessed by any ASCII terminal, or a PC emulating one, with no special software. However, some PC software products are designed to make the use of these services even easier and more automatic.

MCI Mail

MCI Mail can be accessed through its own network reaching over 50 U.S. cities, through TYMNET in over 500 domestic locations, via a toll-free telephone number, or from 50 other countries. If you connect via MCI's own network, access is free; you pay only for mail you send. Checking a box for mail costs nothing.

MCI can deliver mail as "instant letters" to another MCI mailbox, "overnight letters" for delivery with regular mail, or "telex dispatch" to any telex terminal. In addition, every subscriber is given a telex number to facilitate receipt of messages from telex users. Optional services include registration of a letterhead to be used for printed mail, telephone notification that electronic mail is waiting, and mail forwarding.

Registration with MCI Mail also automatically gives the user access to the Dow Jones News/Retrieval™ service, for which substantial usage-based charges are assessed.

Many MCI users find the service almost addictively versatile. One communications consultant reports that he has subscribed to MCI Mail for several years and finds it a convenience he would hate to give up. Among many other things, he has used it to exchange telexes with clients overseas, as a demonstration tool in seminars, and to correspond with business associates all over the United States.

EasyLink

EasyLink, a service of Western Union, delivers electronic messages to mailboxes, telex machines, or PCs, or in the form of mailgrams, telegrams, or cablegrams. It may be accessed through its own network or via inbound WATS lines. Billing is based on time used to input messages, rather than total connect time, with surcharges for specific services. There is a minimum monthly charge.

Mailbox messages not read within 10 days are forwarded as mailgrams. Optional services include mail forwarding, delivery alert, and detailed customer reports. Subscribers to EasyLink also have access to over 600 popular databases in a system called Infact.

While MCI Mail and EasyLink offer a similar array of services, MCI Mail is a little more user-friendly. EasyLink's user interface, oriented more to terminals than PCs, is somewhat old-fashioned.

Using Electronic Mail Systems for File Transfer

A service like MCI Mail allows a PC user to prepare an electronic message and dump it into the mail system, from which other subscribers can extract it by downloading to their PCs, usually with no delay. As may be pretty obvious, such a service is too valuable to use solely for electronic mail. Since an e-mail message is essentially a file, it should be possible to use the service as a transfer mechanism for arbitrary data files. This generally proves true, but, as we discussed in Chapter 9, there are a few potential problems. We'll briefly review the main ones here. First, e-mail services often impose restrictions on the structure of messages, possibly requiring conversion on both ends of a transfer. Second, the pricing schemes of some e-mail systems may make their use for file transfer less attractive. Finally, not all systems support protocols.

Associated Products

Digisoft Computers' Mail-Com™, available from Digisoft or MCI Mail, is designed to streamline the use of MCI Mail on PCs. It provides an environment for creating, retrieving, and managing electronic mail right in the PC. The user never even has to connect to MCI, let alone learn how to use it; he works only with Mail-Com, which automatically dials MCI Mail and handles all interaction with it. This powerful front end provides a way of using MCI Mail that, for some users, may be more appealing than direct contact with MCI itself. In addition to handling letters and memos, the program can encode any binary file for transmission in e-mail form to recipients who also have Mail-Com.

Software is available to assist PC users in the automatic checking of electronic mailboxes. Such programs dial into a mail service at any programmed interval and report back if mail is waiting. It's important that these operations are performed in the background, so the user is not disturbed unless a message is found. While some products will also download mail to the PC, others just indicate the presence of waiting mail. (Automatic downloading of mail may sometimes cause annoyance and unwanted data transfer expense, as is bound to be true for people who get a lot of "junk e-mail." At worst, it could be dangerous: since some networks automatically delete mail after it is read, a crash or power failure at the PC end may result in the loss of messages.) These programs seem ideal for users who get lots of e-mail, especially if their productivity is so tied to such messages that they wish to be alerted automatically when each load arrives. Automatic mailbox checking may also be handy for people who get so little mail that they rarely bother to look.

TeleVision, from LCS/Telegraphics, converts graphics files for transmittal by electronic mail. The process involves not only conversion to ASCII codes, but also data compression that allows a full-screen Color Graphics Adapter (CGA) image to be sent in less than a minute at 1,200 bps.

PC Mail Systems

A few years ago, a British communications expert known to the authors decided that the world needed a PC-based mail system that could perform the following feats:

- Deliver mail messages via any standard communication link (telephone, PSN, LAN, and perhaps even telex).
- Interface to the major public e-mail systems (MCI Mail, EasyLink, Telemail, etc.).
- Transport arbitrary files as attachments to mail messages.
- Efficiently exchange mail among geographically separated communities.
- Broadcast mail to named user groups, forward mail, and provide delivery receipts.

Much of the power of the system he envisioned would result from the establishment of mail "posts" or "hubs," PCs dedicated to the job of handling mail, whose services would be optional for small communities of users and particularly advantageous for large groups. He even toyed with the idea of building such a system himself. Fortunately for the communications industry, someone else beat him to it. Several such products soon appeared, including The Coordinator™ from Action Technologies and Higgins™ from Conetic Systems.

These products represent a new class of application programs designed to support work-group productivity, addressing such needs as project planning and management, scheduling of meetings and other activities, and, of course, interpersonal communication. Such programs differ from traditional PC application programs in that their use by a single person in isolation is meaningless; they are relevant only to a band of communicants and require some communications infrastructure, usually a LAN. We'll use the example of The Coordinator to show how they work.

The Coordinator

The Coordinator's job is divided between *connectivity management*, which creates a sophisticated electronic mail system with many of the features outlined above, and *conversation management,* which requires further explanation.

Ordinary e-mail systems deal with messages largely in isolation. Even when one message is a reply to another, the association between the two is maintained weakly, if at all. Any meaning and structure that exist in a thread of messages are apparent only to the communicants. The Coordinator, on the other hand, treats every message as part of a conversation and takes an active role in directing each conversation, recording it, and interpreting its meaningful parts. The Coordinator manages two general kinds of conversation: those for furthering action and those for brainstorming. Brainstorming conversations are forums for sharing ideas, propositions, and speculations.

The Coordinator's way of directing conversations tends to enforce a certain management style that may not be everybody's cup of tea. It is not coercive, but does encourage communication according to preset forms, such as an automatically generated "yes-indeed-I-will-do-that-by-such-and-such-a-time" response to a request for action. In its distributed database of conversations, The Coordinator records the participants, the dates, the kind (action or ideas), the status, commitments made, and times of pending actions. When they want to retrieve messages, users may "key into" such conversational attributes, including, most significantly, types of agreement made, actions due, and similar elements of meaning.

In addition to all the above, The Coordinator incorporates a multiwindow word processor, tools for time and project management, and features for ensuring the security and confidentiality of data. It promises to increase productivity, reduce "telephone tag," cut down on meetings and travel, and, of course, save money.

It has been claimed that all problems in interpersonal relationships are problems of communication. Products that facilitate easier and clearer communication have a bright future. In business, the emphasis on clarity is addressed to defining responsibilities, nailing down commitments to oneself and others, and avoiding fuzzy information. Another factor contributing to the success of these products is that, given a decent user interface, people love to use electronic mail.

CONFERENCING SYSTEMS

A computer conferencing system enables people to join in a group discussion via PCs or terminals. It gets them together for discussion, planning, argument, brainstorming, or problem solving, while eliminating many of the obstacles involved in face-to-face meetings: scheduling, travel, pontification, boredom, and difficulty in documenting the proceedings.

A conference is managed by software running on some host computer, and is made available to PC users by standard communication methods, typically terminal emulation via async dial-up or a PSN. Two basic types of conferencing are found.

One type enables scattered participants to conduct an on-line meeting, with all the users involved hooking up to the host computer at the same time. Both public messages, seen by everyone, and private messages, directed to a particular user, are entered and immediately distributed. We'll refer to this as a *real-time* conference system.

The other kind of system, which we'll call the *stored* type, supports nonsimultaneous use, managing a database that holds messages entered by users at various times. A user can check into the conference at any time, view all the messages posted since the previous visit, and add new messages in response. Older messages, if still present in the database, can also be reviewed. A conference may contain many "departments" for discussion of different matters, variously called *topics, subjects, subconferences*, or *threads.*

Some conferencing systems offer both real-time and stored access. Although the added option of on-line chatting can be convenient, users greatly prefer stored conferences for most applications, so we'll focus on the stored type.

Stored conferences are the principal fare on such services as BIX, CompuServe, and GEnie™. (These "electronic meeting places," open to public subscription, are described further later in this chapter.) The conferences hosted by such services are variously called *forums, SIGs* (special interest groups), or simply *conferences*. On CompuServe, for example, you can find conferences devoted to PC Communications, CROSSTALK products, and Telecommunications generally, among many others.

A stored conference requires a leader, called the *host* or *sysop* (system operator), who manages and mediates the proceedings. The leader may stimulate use of the conference, keep discussion "on track," ensure that proceedings are conducted in a proper manner, and prune old messages at suitable times to keep the message base to a reasonable size.

Here is a checklist of some features often found in computer conferencing systems:

Selective Search. Users can search the database for all messages conforming to given criteria. Typical examples are the presence of a particular word, authorship by a certain person, or entry after a given date.

Security. Not only may access to the conferencing system itself be controlled by means of usernames and passwords, but access to a subconference may also be limited to certain users, granted in some cases on a read-only basis that does not permit them to add messages.

Accounting on a User-By-User Basis.

Vote Tabulation. This is not a common feature, but some systems can conduct "opinion polls" among users and publish the results.

A Text Editor. This allows a user to compose a message and then revise it before posting it to the conference. A file-transfer protocol may also be provided to facilitate the uploading of messages written on PCs.

An organization wishing to establish a computer-based conference can choose to set it up on an in-house computer system or "rent" a private conference from a commercial provider. The in-house method is likely to cost less as long as system users are located within a small geographical area. "Rented" conferences usually include system access via a public data network, and hence may be a better choice for widely dispersed user communities.

A minicomputer implementation may be best for an in-house conferencing system, because conferencing products for PCs are few in number, low in user capacity, and limited in features. As PCs grow ever more powerful, this situation will undoubtedly change.

Many companies sell electronic conferencing facilities by the hour, but prices can be high. Vendors include certain electronic mail outfits, such as Dialcom with its Caucus service, some of the information utilities, such as CompuServe's Participate (formerly offered by The Source®), and other miscellaneous companies. Advertel Communications, for example, markets a mainframe-based system known as Confer II™, accessible via Telenet, TYMNET, and other paths.

When considering either an in-house or rented conference, take care to evaluate the user interfaces, especially if the group of users is likely to include some non-computer-literate types, as is often the case. The user interface quality of conferencing products is, on the whole, uninspiring. A conference that is awkward to use may lead to costly mistakes and, worse, make itself unpopular.

FACSIMILE TRANSMISSION

Fax Facts

Facsimile, or fax, machines are used to transmit documents among offices. At the originating office, a fax machine scans a document to create a digitized image and then sends the image over a dialed telephone connection to a similar machine, which prints it. Approximately 10 million fax machines are installed around the world. If that number seems surprisingly large, it may be because, although fax technology is very important to North America, the Japanese account for a disproportionately large share of fax usage. The Japanese favor fax over telex and other alternatives because of *kanji*, the set of characters used in writing their language. Since there are perhaps 10,000 *kanjis* altogether, and about 2,800 in common use, a Japanese typewriter is to an American one as a church organ is to a toy piano. *Kanji* input for computers has only recently become standardized or widely accepted. Clearly, since most documents in Japan are hand-scribed, fax has little competition there.

Elsewhere in the world, fax is also heavily used for transmitting text, although it's far less efficient for this purpose than ASCII encoding. For graphics transmission, on the other hand, fax is hard to beat, as long as its resolution and lack of color are acceptable for the application. No other standardized system of communication can transmit any image printed, written, or drawn on an 8.5 × 11 inch piece of paper.

Fax machines widely conform to CCITT international standards. The dominant fax standard, called Group 3, specifies a resolution of 200 dots per inch (dpi) horizontally and 100 dpi vertically. An optional "fine" mode uses 200 dpi in both dimensions. There is no contrast adjustment or grey scale; each dot is mapped into one bit to produce the digitized image. Thanks to the fairly high resolution, however, the effect of a grey scale can be achieved by varying the density of dots. The quoted resolution suggests that a raw fax image of an 8.5 × 11 inch page would occupy 234 kbytes, but Group 3 includes a data compression scheme that can reduce this number by as much as a factor of 8. Fax machines communicate via specially made, half-duplex, 9,600-bps synchronous modems.

A facsimile machine is a large, complex, and (for the best units) expensive item consisting of a document scanner, a printer, a modem, and logic circuitry to drive it.

The use of facsimile transmission as a form of electronic mail has many attractions. Fax machines are easy to use: they're operated much like photocopiers and are thus less intimidating than computers. (Two communicating fax machines could even be thought of as a single photocopier whose input and output sections are separated by a telephone line, although the technology is totally different.) Fax operating costs are very reasonable because the combination of a 9,600-bps data rate and substantial compression means that documents can be fired off at one to four pages per minute. This makes fax practical even for international transmission. Adherence to the standard is very strong, so incompatibility problems rarely arise. The system is so foolproof that the only thing a user might do wrong is feed a document into the scanner upside down.

Of course, fax is not without limitations. First, there is no transmission error control, so if data are damaged on the phone line, the received image will be botched up. For most applications, this is not a serious flaw: the occasional error may slightly disfigure an image, but will rarely render it unreadable. Second, the resolution provided by the Group 3 standard is not high enough to suit some users. Engineering drawings, for example, constitute a large proportion of the graphics documents being distributed among offices. Fax suffices for rough drafts, but an overnight-delivery or courier service is still needed for final versions. Third, since fax is strictly a high-contrast monochrome system, it cannot reproduce color images and can only mimic a grey scale. Fourth, fax does not facilitate document broadcasting the way some other electronic mail systems do. To send an image to several locations you must normally dial, scan, and transmit individually for each recipient. Finally, although an alternative to this tedium, in the form of automated multiple-recipient fax transmission, is now feasible (see below), such "improvements" have already begun to menace users with the prospect of "junk fax," unwanted commercial solicitations that tie up the machine. Several state legislatures have recently passed laws restricting junk fax transmission.

Group 4, a successor to the Group 3 standard, is a step up in resolution (to 400 dpi), but has not caught on widely yet. It's not intended for use over dial-up connections, but rather over networks (PSNs and ISDNs) or leased lines.

Mixing PCs and Fax

Because both PCs and fax machines deal with digital data, it seems inviting to try combining the two, for several reasons. First, the combination would constitute a fax machine with intelligence, providing, as the most obvious examples, the ability to arrange for transfers to be executed automatically during the night, and to broadcast a single fax image to several recipients. Second, the PC can synthesize fax images: appropriate software can convert a file into a better image than one obtained by printing or plotting the file and then digitizing it with a scanner. Third, PCs and fax machines share several hardware components, notably dot-matrix printers and, in the case of fancier faxes, fixed disks. Adding fax capability to a PC, it has been said, gives it access to millions of remote printers in all parts of the globe.

Obstacles to the integration of PC and fax hardware arise mainly from resolution requirements. To begin with, fax resolution exceeds that of many PC devices. A PC monitor driven by a Hercules monochrome graphics card, for example, could show only about a 2 × 3 inch section of a fax document at full resolution. A typical PC dot-matrix printer has sufficient resolution to print a fax image, but lacks the sharpness of the kind of printer built into fax machines. Even PC devices that do have high resolution often suffer from incompatibilities with fax requirements. PC laser printers are a case in point: they have the necessary print quality, but most of them have 300-dpi output. This is too high for Group 3 operation (resulting in some distortion of output), but not high enough for best results under the Group 4 standard.

A PC can be equipped for fax in stages. A sensible first step is to install a Group 3 modem plus software to handle facsimile transmission and reception, to synthesize fax images, and to print them. You may not need a scanner at all, but if you opt for one, you may be able to gain the added benefit of *optical character recognition (OCR)*. Here, as usual, the scanner generates a bit-mapped image of a document; OCR's trick is that, if the document consists of clearly printed text in a common font, appropriate software can convert the scanned image into ASCII. Such conversion may sometimes be less than 100 percent successful, but a brief editing job will quickly fix it up.

While PC scanners may also earn their keep as OCR devices, they must do so by operating at a higher resolution than the 200 dpi called for by the Group 3 standard. Unfortunately,

200 dpi is insufficient for dependable conversion of even typewritten text, so a document that a PC receives by fax generally cannot be coerced into ASCII form. (Group 4 resolution, however, would make such conversion feasible.) Thus, fax transmission from a fax-equipped PC to stand-alone fax machines looks very promising, especially in a broadcasting mode, such as sending documents from a head office to multiple branch offices; transmission from a dedicated fax machine to a fax-equipped PC has some limitations; and image transmission among PCs, whether fax-equipped or not, is almost always better done another way.

A PC taking the place of a fax machine is likely to be on the job full-time, as a true fax machine would be, standing by to accept an incoming fax call at any moment. This requirement created a problem with the first add-on fax products made for PCs, which tied up the whole PC so that it had to be dedicated to its post even if operating only sporadically. To add insult to injury, the expense of equipping a PC to waste most of its time this way could be substantial. This snag could be circumvented by setting appointments or restricted hours for facsimile reception, but many organizations found this unacceptable.

A compromise seized upon by a few manufacturers was to give fax machines internal storage and RS-232 ports so that they could be used much like buffered modems; images were moved between the PC and fax machine at convenient times, with the latter managing the transmission and reception independently. The latest products, however, provide the best of both worlds by incorporating special boards to be plugged into the PC. They use the PC's disk for storage, are programmed and controlled by PC software, and yet do their basic jobs independently so that the PC can still be used to run application programs with minimal performance degradation.

No doubt the ever-decreasing price of PC clones will eventually lead to the widespread use of PC-based fax machines, spurred on, perhaps, by "desktop communications." A struggle may therefore arise between users who want to stick with the dependability of the universal Group 3 standard and those pushing for color, higher resolution, and a broad range of features to make fax practical for many more applications.

Extra Features in PC Fax Products

Manufacturers of PC fax products offer a plethora of extra features, such as broadcasting capabilities, encryption options for the secure transmission of documents, LAN interfaces that allow all the PCs on a network to share the fax capability, use of PC modems as an alternative to fax-standard units, use of fax modems for PC-to-PC file transfer, background operation, unattended operation, logging of faxes sent and received, a directory to store the telephone numbers of fax systems commonly dialed, conversion of graphics files to fax, graphical editing of fax files, and diagnostic software. Also, specialized software facilitates fax use in certain business settings, such as law offices.

Fax and Desktop Publishing

Think of high-resolution, monochromatic PC graphics today and you're bound to think of desktop publishing. Imagine a PC equipped with a document scanner, a laser printer, a fax board, and desktop publishing software that includes a pixel-based graphics editor, and you have a tremendously powerful workstation for writers, journalists, publishers, students, and a host of others. Add optical storage (e.g., gigabytes of space on a laser disc) and some OCR equipment, and you'll have a lot of people wide-eyed and drooling. The trouble with this "dream system" is that fax is the weakest link in it.

GMS offers particularly impressive fax products for use with PCs. Other vendors include Datacopy, Gammalink, and Panasonic Industrial.

INFORMATION UTILITIES

We are said to be moving into an "information age." The rapid growth of businesses selling information services to terminal and PC users certainly supports this notion.

The typical information utility has one or more databases containing information of value to professional people, made accessible over a packet switching network (PSN). Prime examples are lists of the latest stock market quotes together with historical highs and lows, scientific and financial news, opinions in legal cases, and the electronic edition of the Official Airline Guide (OAG$^®$). Users connect to the utility, access a database, and pick off whatever records are of interest to them.

There are several compelling reasons for marketing information in this way. First, the information comes in a form that can easily be computer-processed; stock quotes, for example, can be fed into spreadsheet programs without retyping. Second, the data may be too ephemeral, too cumbersome, or too valuable to be published in any other way. Third, PSNs and public databases have grown up symbiotically; a PSN makes a database instantly available to potential users almost anywhere in the world at reasonable communication cost. Finally, in searching huge databases, the PC may be able to process instructions embodying search criteria before connecting to the utility, thus reducing the time and cost of on-line usage.

Some information utilities charge on a connect-time basis, some according to the amount of data retrieved, and some for a combination of the two. Access to the highest-priced databases typically runs around $100 per hour; a few very specialized ones are costlier.

PCs gain access to most databases simply by running a terminal emulator. A few utilities, however, have their own proprietary PC software. Some special-purpose systems, notably LEXIS$^®$ and WESTLAW$^®$, were once accessed predominantly through dedicated terminals, but are now increasingly available via PCs, with or without the aid of proprietary software.

Several books are available cataloging information utilities. *Online Database Directory*, for example, is published by Omni magazine and updated sporadically.

Here's a sampling of choice services:

NewsNet offers a wealth of databases relevant to general business needs, plus a few specialized ones. It stresses business newsletters, offering more than 275 publications, but has much else, including on-line stock quotes, wire services, and airfares. A monthly or yearly subscription fee is levied, plus connect charges.

DIALOG$^®$, set up by Lockheed, offers the largest number of databases, covering engineering, publishing, agriculture, social sciences, and national resources.

Chase Econometrics/Interactive Data specializes in economic data, with well over 100 databases.

Dow Jones News/Retrieval offers financial and economic services, stock quotes, general news, weather and sports reports, movie reviews, and electronic shopping.

Mead Data Central features the popular LEXIS, NEXIS, and MEDIS databases. LEXIS, a legal database of more than 6 billion words, has become a standard tool for attorneys and law students. NEXIS contains the full texts of articles from many major newspapers, magazines, and newsletters, plus the *Federal Register* and *Encyclopaedia Britannica*. Publications represented include *The New York Times, The Washington Post, The Guardian Weekly, ComputerWorld, Byte, Data Communications*, the *Economist*, and the BBC Monitoring Service's *Country Notes*, daily transcriptions of all radio broadcasts in most countries of the world. NEXIS is astounding! MEDIS, an international medical database, is not bad either.

WESTLAW, a service of West Publishing, is another huge legal database, a complement to and competitor of LEXIS. Since it is more library-oriented than LEXIS and uses a different billing scheme, WESTLAW is thought to be especially valuable to smaller law firms.

Instant Yellow Page Service combines information from some 4,800 U.S. yellow page directories, with listings for several million businesses. It serves as a source for generating sales leads and mailing lists, an aid to market research, and a handy guide to suppliers and services. (Want to know how many doughnut shops there are in Oshkosh, Wisconsin?) In addition to on-line access, the company provides tapes, diskettes, mailing labels, and other services.

ELECTRONIC COMMUNITIES

Here we turn our attention to on-line systems, open to public subscription, that serve as virtual meeting places for electronic communicators. BIX (BYTE Information eXchange), CompuServe, Delphi™, and GEnie are the best known examples, offering information utilities, conferencing systems, e-mail services, and much more. There's no generally accepted name for such systems; variously described as "virtual communities" and "electronic cocktail parties," they are perhaps the electronic age's equivalent of the corner pub.

CompuServe, Delphi, and GEnie

CompuServe is a database service, mail and conferencing system, bulletin board, time-sharing system, and much more, all under one electronic roof. It offers an Executive Information Service (EIS) and a Consumer Information Service (CIS). One of the authors uses CIS for electronic mail, checking airline schedules and fares, booking flights, and enjoying a conference on travel. CIS also offers games, electronic shopping, and so many other services that no summary could be comprehensive.

EIS offers access to everything in CIS, plus business data: professional forums on legal, medical, and other matters, newswires, and a wealth of investment information.

CompuServe is accessible through its own national network or via TYMNET, Telenet, or Datapac. EIS imposes a minimum billing, while CIS has no minimum. Surcharges are added for some services, including access to the OAG.

In June 1989, CompuServe acquired The Source, which had been CompuServe's main competitor, offering a similar array of services at roughly comparable prices. Several of the former Source services will remain available to CompuServe customers.

Although The Source is out of the picture as an independent entity, GEnie (the General Electric Network for Information Exchange) and Delphi are still among the top contenders in this market.

The WELL

The WELL ("Whole Earth 'Lectronic Link"), located in the San Francisco Bay Area, is one of several regional systems that have succeeded by creating a much greater sense of community for their users than is possible on their larger competitors. (Another such system, called Chariot, is headquartered in Colorado Springs.) Among the WELL's users are many outstanding writers, artists, and software authors. The level of intelligent discourse on the system attracts such thinkers and writers; the WELL is also a great networking tool for independent business people who find it a source of valuable contacts and a sounding board for ideas. WELLites also get together in the flesh to enjoy recreational activities.

On the WELL, you'll find public conferences on subjects as varied as adoption, word processing, telecommunications, one-person businesses, and the stock market. It also hosts private conferences for outside organizations. Last but not least, public e-mail and news access is available to USENET (see below).

DISTRIBUTED COMMUNITIES

The electronic communities we've just discussed are typically gathered around a single host computer that serves as a clearinghouse for many users, scattered either regionally or nationally. A special case is the *distributed community*, created by interconnecting many machines called *local computers, hosts*, or, somewhat confusingly, *local hosts*. Some local hosts of distributed communities also happen to constitute electronic communities of the single-host kind. The WELL, for example, is a USENET node, as are quite a few universities and research facilities. Others may simply be minicomputers used by software developers or other small companies. By establishing an appropriate electronic link between the local host and other computers in an existing distributed community, the users of each host become community *members;* all users of all local hosts can then exchange e-mail, post news articles, or subscribe to a "newsletter" mailing list. The participation of individual members of a distributed community is limited only by the hardware and software involved. Some examples of such communities are USENET, FIDONET, and the DARPA Internet.

USENET is a network made up of UNIX computers from all over the world. The heart of this community is the "netnews" system, an application that transfers news items submitted by members to all the hosts on the network. With over 2,500 local hosts and perhaps several hundred thousand members, the USENET system usually contains plenty of news. The system is subdivided into many different news groups appealing to various interests, such as *ba.food* (good restaurants in the Bay Area), *comp.unix.aux* (Apple's UNIX-like product), *rec.music.gdead* (The Grateful Dead), and so on. USENET also supports electronic mail between users.

The local hosts making up USENET, when connected to each other, perform an operation known as *uucp* (UNIX-to-UNIX copy) to move files from host to host. (Don't confuse this operation with UUCP, the UNIX-to-UNIX Communication Protocol mentioned in Chapter 7.) The connections themselves may be of many types—dial-up, PSN links, leased lines (favored by large corporations with widely dispersed machines), LAN connections, and so on. Each host is usually connected to several others, and some pairs of hosts are linked in more than one way. An important advantage of this approach is that it makes the network difficult to disrupt. A potential disadvantage is that, since data are sent in "daisy-chain" fashion, mail and news could take a long time to trickle through the net. To overcome this problem, a number of corporations have allowed their computers to become hubs (in the airline sense) for USENET connections. Because this set of machines, known as "the backbone," now handles most of USENET's U.S. and international traffic, its corporate owners are faced with large telecommunications costs, requiring the promulgation of "community laws" to limit superfluous postings. For example, gleefully correcting other members' grammar or spelling is frowned upon.

FIDONET is a network of local BBS systems (see below) joined by a mechanism similar to USENET's. However, as corporations do not foot the bill for FIDONET data calls, transmission of mail to members outside one's local BBS system is normally restricted to what are euphemistically called "trusted" users (i.e., those who pay for the transfers). Most local BBS systems in the United States are now FIDONET nodes, substantially extending the local electronic communities provided by the BBSs. Also, FIDONET is connected to USENET at a few points, allowing mail to be passed between users of the networks.

The DARPA Internet, introduced in Chapter 2, was the original distributed community and serves as a "model" for others. In addition to exchanging mail and transferring files from computer to computer, its users can log in to other host computers, any of which may be running different operating systems or, even more remarkably, come from different manufacturers. (Contrast this with the relative simplicity of constructing homogeneous IBM PC, PS/2, or UNIX-based networks.) Moreover, since DARPA community members are "peers," they are accorded equal treatment, without regard to operating system, memory capacity, or disk size. Of course, this description is somewhat idealized. For example, you cannot currently log into an MS-DOS machine and play Flight Simulator™ across The Internet because DOS, unlike OS/2, doesn't deal very well with remote login sessions; and without the special protocols available for larger machines, the graphics won't travel very well, either. To other hosts in The Internet, however, your machine, even if a lowly PC, still looks like any other host.

The Internet has served as a sort of "glue" for numerous electronic communities. Many research facilities operated by corporations (such as Ford Aerospace) and universities (including the University of California at Berkeley) chose to use The Internet protocols to link together their own local computing systems. These local networks were then connected to the Internet via gateways. As discussed in later chapters, a *gateway* is a computer connected to, and equipped to interpret the protocols of, two or more dissimilar networks. It serves as a message switch, a kind of traffic cop, that sorts out messages dispatched from one network to another, reformats them as necessary, and shoots them on their way. In the research facility/Internet setting, the gateways give local users access to the resources of the larger network and also allow Internet users to access desirable local-host resources, such as supercomputers.

Joining many of the larger networks, and even some of the larger electronic communities such as BIX, are special gateways that pass mail from one system to another. In most cases, such mail can pass through several networks, although it often must be explicitly addressed to traverse the various nets. For example, a user on AppleLink® (operated by Apple for its internal staff, external software developers, and retail dealers) could send mail to a user on USENET with the address

shibumi@speedo@DASNET#

where the # symbol forms part of the DASNET address. AppleLink will send the mail to the DASNET gateway, with instructions to route the message to the USENET host "speedo." DASNET, a commercial network accessible to AppleLink, will then send the message to the USENET gateway, a computer connected to USENET. Finally, this gateway will use the USENET mail routing system to send the message to the user "shibumi" on "speedo."

BULLETIN BOARD SYSTEMS

Traditionally, the bulletin board system, or BBS, has been associated with computer hobbyists and hackers (in the best sense). It was a vital meeting point for early microcomputer users, providing a forum for sharing software and experiences. BBSs thrive in this community today. There are at least 1,500 nationwide, more than 40 in the San Francisco Bay Area alone. Access to many is free; some charge a modest fee. Although a widely available and cheap resource, even the best public BBSs are likely to be of little value to business PC users as such. They are often oriented toward entertainment, fun, and other ostensibly "nonbusiness activities."

Despite these pro-social tendencies, the BBS concept has begun to attract the attention of the business world, which is adopting such systems as communication posts. A computer BBS is far more versatile than a cork board, and can be accessed just as easily. It can be used for mail, conferencing, announcements, calendars, and whatever else the MBAs can dream up.

Many software vendors use BBSs for customer support. Licensed users of a software package can download updates from the board, post questions to be answered, and conduct conferences among themselves. Among the companies offering such BBSs are Borland International, Lattice, SoftLogic Solutions, and TOPS®. Many companies also offer support on some of the more traditional electronic community systems, including Delphi and CIS.

Some BBS products for the PC support only one user at a time, but the better commercial offerings support several concurrent callers. One popular product with multiuser support is Chairman™ from Dynamic Microprocessor Associates. For large numbers of simultaneous users, a UNIX-based BBS might be preferable to a PC-based system.

12 COMMUNICATING WITH IBM MAINFRAMES AND MINIS

The world of IBM hosts is a vast tangle of hardware and software options. In addition to the assorted mainframes and minis that can act as host, there are four important operating systems (including a version of UNIX called AIX™, formerly IX/370), numerous subsystems, a quagmire of acronyms and nearly meaningless names, and complex product interdependencies ("If you want to perform task X, then you must have software Y; to accommodate software Y, you must have hardware A, B, and C; to use hardware B, you must have license Z and software Q..." and so on). Even a modest installation requires a small army of support personnel, with heavy emphasis on systems programmers. Although such aspects of IBM systems may be daunting, the power of these machines, their importance to the market, and their communications flexibility justify their extended treatment here.

In this chapter, we'll examine the ways in which large IBM systems communicate (a body of law unto itself) and discuss methods of connecting PCs to them.

IBM MAINFRAMES: OPTIONS AND PROBLEMS

Many IBM products are identified by four-digit numbers such as 3278, 4341, and 7171; to help readers cope with the confusion, a list of the most popular designations is provided in Appendix H.

A PC can communicate with an IBM mainframe system by four principal routes:

Asynchronously, via a standard ASCII terminal

By emulating an IBM remote job entry (RJE) terminal, such as a 2780 or 3780

By playing the role of an IBM 3270 terminal

By means of IBM's Advanced Program-to-Program Communication (APPC) system

The choice of route depends on whether the IBM host will support a given method, the location of the PC relative to the host, and the user's purpose in accessing the host system. For most people, the best and sometimes the only viable choice is 3270 terminal emulation; traditionally, about 85 percent of IBM mainframe access has been provided by 3270 networks. Before dealing with 3270, we will briefly discuss the first two options listed above; the still-young APPC option is treated in Chapter 16.

The Asynchronous Route

While IBM mainframes are strongly associated with synchronous communications and proprietary devices, asynchronous terminal access should not be dismissed out of hand. It is entirely possible to connect a regular asynchronous ASCII terminal to an IBM host, as long as the host is suitably configured. In a few IBM environments, such as certain university computer centers, asynchronous access is the rule.

A salient disadvantage to such hookups is the sometimes severely limited resources available to the asynchronous user. IBM's two main time-sharing systems, TSO™(Time Sharing Option) and CMS™(Conversational Monitor System), support async terminals, but many other popular interactive environments, such as IMS (a database system) and CICS (a transaction processing system), do not. On the other hand, AIX, like other UNIX systems, supports only ASCII terminals, but AIX is not very popular because IBM mainframes are not well suited to UNIX.

IBM's support for async terminals, unlike almost everyone else's, is confined to half-duplex operation. This is not to say that a half-duplex modem is required—IBM manufactures and supports regular full-duplex modems—but rather that the system does not support echoplex or *type-ahead*. (Type-ahead allows users to key in characters in anticipation of their acceptance before the system is ready for them. DOS supports type-ahead with a 15-character buffer in its command processor.) Furthermore, IBM systems restrict synchronous data traffic to seven bits per character.

For the PC user, asynchronous access is effected with the same modems and communication packages as are used for any other asynchronous host. Any ordinary type of asynchronous terminal, including IBM's own 3101 or 3161, will also do.

What about asynchronous file transfer? For many reasons, including those outlined in Chapter 7, implementing a protocol on an IBM mainframe is a nightmarish proposition. IBM itself offers no asynchronous protocols, and the seven-bit data limitation rules out even XMODEM. Only two options appear to be available—fortunately, both good ones. They are Kermit and BLAST, covered in previous chapters. Even these protocols, however, do not operate at their best with IBM systems. Due to the half-duplex restriction, for example, Kermit's advanced sliding windows option cannot be implemented. If mainframe access is needed only for the occasional transfer of files of modest length, Kermit or BLAST may be satisfactory.

Emulating A 2780/3780 RJE Terminal

In the 1960s, the early days of mainframe computers, users worked primarily by submitting batch "jobs" on decks of punch cards, awaiting output in the form of printed listings. At sites local (very close) to the mainframe, huge card readers and fast line printers were employed. Remote access stations were equipped with RJE terminals, also called "batch terminals," which consisted of a small card reader, a modest printer, and a box of electronics to operate a synchronous protocol over a telephone link, typically running at 1,200 or 2,400 bps. Some of these stations also included a console (screen and keyboard) for directing operations and querying the status of submitted jobs.

IBM's widely used RJE terminals were the 2780 and 3780, which employed the Bisync protocol. Other computer manufacturers created their own batch terminals using proprietary protocols, although some also supported 2780/3780 access to their mainframes.

Most 2780s and 3780s have now been laid to rust, but a few installations remain, and a small number of manufacturers, notably AST Research, has marketed PC-based emulators for them. Obviously, a PC doesn't need a punch-card reader; instead, the emulator reads disk files to generate host input.

Consider 2780/3780 emulation for a PC only to hook up to a mainframe for which RJE access is the preferred mode. Otherwise, this route has nothing to recommend it; 3270-style access is much superior.

THE 3270 FAMILY OF EQUIPMENT

The mainstay of IBM network hardware is the 3270 series of equipment, known in IBM parlance as an "Information Display System." The 3270 family, the first members of which were introduced in 1971, includes video display terminals, printers, terminal controllers, and a few ancillary items such as multiplexers, which serve as the primary means of interactive access to IBM mainframe systems. Here we will meet the important family members and see how they work together to form networks. We'll ignore PCs for now, and return to them later to discuss various means of hooking them into 3270 networks.

In reading this section, bear in mind that the range of 3270 equipment is broad and its complexity fearsome. No simplifications are made here, but many unimportant details are omitted.

3270 Terminals

IBM offers about 10 different terminal types in the 3270 family, with designations like 3179, 3180, 3278, and 3290. Despite the variety of names, all may be generically called "3270 terminals." The types vary considerably in size, physical appearance, cost, and features. Most are stylish and designed with considerable attention to ergonomics. (Ergonomics is the science of designing desk chairs, keyboards, automobile controls, and other objects to be comfortably and efficiently used by human beings.) The 3270 terminal family includes monochrome and color units, text and graphics models, plus a wide selection of screen sizes and keyboard layouts. While terminals may differ greatly from the user's point of view, all interact with a host in the same manner, using the *3270 data stream.*

IBM literature describes 3270 terminals as both *workstations* and *display stations.* They are semi-intelligent, capable of communicating with a distant host by means of a synchronous protocol, and screen-oriented, with local editing facilities. When a 3270 terminal is connected to an application program running in a host, the program presents output to the user, then waits for the user's input, and so on repeatedly. This strict alternation is enforced by the half-duplex behavior of the terminal. In fact, the keyboard is physically *locked* except when the application program is soliciting input. (This doesn't mean that keys literally can't be pressed, but indicates that keystrokes are ignored.) Data are passed between terminal and host, not one character at a time, but in large packets. Indeed, an application program may deliver several screenfuls of output at a shot. Keyboard input is held locally and may be edited before being dispatched, by use of Enter or some other special key, to the host.

For a text-mode terminal, the 3270 data stream contains characters represented in the EBCDIC code, and may also contain control bytes describing screen and field attributes. Many 3270 devices can be used with ASCII instead of EBCDIC, but this is rarely done. The control information is, in principle, much like the ANSI X3.64 function sequences used with ASCII terminals. Among other things, it can be used selectively to erase parts of the screen and to display blinking, reverse-video, and color fields. An application program may interact with a terminal user by means of either *formatted* or *unformatted screens.* A formatted screen's text is divided into fields, with each field described by an *attribute byte.* An unformatted screen consists of homogeneous text.

Various keyboard styles are available for 3270 terminals to suit different needs, such as data entry, word processing, and programming. Some terminals even offer a user-modifiable keyboard, which allows users to define their own graphics characters and engrave custom keycaps to match. This option is obviously appealing for foreign language applications and in industries that make regular use of nonstandard characters. IBM has used this capability to ensure market penetration internationally and in many industries. As of April 1987, IBM offered 118 different keyboards for 3278 and 3279 terminals, with national keyboards for 22 foreign regions, including Iceland.

Transaction Processing

3270 terminals were designed to be ideal for transaction processing, a class of computer applications that involve repetitive, on-line procedures such as taking product orders, making hotel and airline reservations, and processing payments. In everyday usage, "transactions" are relations between customers and merchants, but here they are typically conducted between a terminal operator and a database application in a host. In the case of order processing, for example, an operator answers a customer's call, requests pertinent information, and enters it at a terminal. One call may involve a sequence of related transactions between the operator and the database—perhaps one to identify the customer, a second to enter details of the order, and a third to check inventory for the required items.

Transaction processing systems generally send "forms" to a 3270 terminal, or rather screen images of forms, to be filled in by the operator. A form has two kinds of data field: *prompts* and *input fields*. Prompts (such as "Customer name:" or "Purchase Order number:") are defined as *protected fields*, meaning that the operator is prevented from overwriting them. Input fields are, of course, *unprotected*. Where appropriate, an input field can be further defined as *numeric*, meaning that the operator can enter only numbers. Dashes or spaces, in the appropriate slot(s), may be prepositioned in such a field.

The operator may fill in the fields in any order, skipping among them by means of a tab key, and make corrections as necessary until the form is complete—all without any host involvement. If the operator attempts to enter a character that is invalid for a particular field, the terminal will protest, locking its keyboard until the operator presses a special reset key. A form may also be configured so that certain fields must be completed before the terminal will permit the form's return to the host.

For applications requiring the operator to fill in one form repeatedly, the host, instead of sending the form to the terminal for each transaction, transmits it only once at the start of a session. Subsequently, after each input, the host commands the terminal to "erase unprotected data," clearing the form for reuse. More will be said about terminal-to-host data traffic later in this section.

While this arrangement makes 3270 terminals especially valuable for transaction processing, they are also commonly used for general purposes, including word processing, programming, handling electronic mail, and other applications that may take little or no advantage of the terminals' fancier capabilities.

3270 Terminal Configurations

The primary characteristics in which terminal models differ are size and type of screen and type of display (e.g., monochrome text, color text, or color graphics). The best known terminal types are the 3278 and 3279, which, like most other types, are really subfamilies, each covering several distinct models. Members of the 3278 group all have text-only monochrome displays and vary in screen size. The 3279 models offer colors and graphics capabilities. Other terminal units in the 3270 line include the 3178 and 3179, lower cost versions of the 3278 and 3279, respectively, and the 3290, equipped with a snazzy plasma display instead of the usual cathode ray tube (CRT).

The most common 3270 screen size is 24 lines by 80 columns, but some models have larger formats. The screen size quoted for a 3270 terminal indicates the number of rows (lines) and columns used to display data; there is always one additional line for displaying terminal status information. One 3270 product, the 3180 terminal, has keyboard-selectable 24 × 80, 43 × 80, and 27 × 132 display formats.

In addition to the wide range of basic models, IBM offers options such as light pens, mice, security locks, and support for the APL character set. APL is a powerful programming language distinguished by a terse syntax. It employs many special symbols instead of the keywords used by most other languages.

The 3270 Control Unit

A 3270 terminal is not autonomous, but must work in conjunction with a so-called control unit, commonly known outside of IBM as a *cluster controller*. IBM's 3274 and the newer 3174 are prime examples. A control unit serves as manager for a community of up to 8, 16, or 32 terminals, depending on the model. As you might guess, control units are really just special-purpose computers. They come equipped with diskette drives for loading the software that controls them, and share their centralized processing power among a number of terminals. This is cheaper than replicating a processor in each terminal and, because it permits several terminals to share a single communications path to a host, provides multiplexing into the bargain. As we shall see, though, some 3270 terminals have their own processing power.

Each terminal is normally connected to its control unit by a separate RG-62 A/U coaxial cable, using a proprietary electrical interface. IBM and other companies offer alternative cabling methods, but all require some form of direct wiring; telephone connection is not possible. While standard practice limits cable length to 4,900 feet, several products on the market can extend this range. Transmission speed between terminal and controller is a hefty 2.3587 Mbps.

Newer control units, including some models of the 3174 series, can be fitted with either an RS-232 or Token-Ring interface, in addition to the standard coax port. A PC may connect by any one of the three, as long as both the cluster controller and the PC are suitably equipped. The RS-232 option, comprising not only the requisite ports but also software (called *microcode*) to support ASCII devices, provides two complementary enhancements. First, an ASCII terminal can connect to the control unit and access IBM hosts as if it were a 3270 terminal. Second, a 3270 terminal attached to the controller can access ASCII hosts as if it were an IBM 3101 or DEC VT100 asynchronous terminal. Similarly, attached 3270 printers can operate with an ASCII host.

A terminal can interact with its control unit in either of two modes, designated by IBM as *Control Unit Terminal (CUT)* and *Distributed Function Terminal (DFT)*. In CUT mode, used by the older and simpler terminals, the controller itself interprets the 3270 data stream, and interacts with the terminal by sending characters directly to the screen. A CUT terminal, such as a 3278, consists of precious little apart from a power supply, a CRT, and a keyboard; the brains of this outfit reside in the control unit. CUT is supported by all control units in the sense that any CUT-mode terminal can be connected to any 3270 controller.

DFT mode is used by more sophisticated terminal types, such as the 3290. DFT allows terminals to conduct multiple concurrent host sessions. The control unit passes the full 3270 data stream through to the terminal, which then does the work of interpreting it. Although a DFT terminal must have significant internal processing capability, the control unit is not deprived of useful work, since it still performs all the communications and multiplexing chores. Only certain control unit models support DFT.

The Display Buffer

We must consider here a technical aspect of 3270 terminals that has profound implications for PCs operating in a 3270-emulation mode. Central to the operation of each 3270 terminal is a display buffer consisting of a block of RAM. This buffer contains the data that form the display on the terminal's screen, including all the "behind-the-scenes" information needed to define the attributes of each field. As new data arrive from the host or are typed on the terminal keyboard, they enter the display buffer, and the screen is updated accordingly.

The 3270 terminal keyboard has three types of keys: text keys for entering characters; local control keys for manipulating the cursor position, erasing the contents of fields, etc.; and control keys for initiating transmission to the host. (Unlike their ASCII cousins, 3270 terminals have no Control key and cannot generate control characters.) Among the transmission-initiating keys are an Enter key and up to 24 Program Function (PF) keys. When a text key is pressed, the appropriate character is stored into the display buffer at the byte corresponding to the current cursor location. If the character is acceptable in the current field, it is then echoed back to the screen. Only when the Enter key or one of the function keys is pressed is anything actually sent to the host. When it comes time to transmit a completed transaction record, the control unit will normally send only the data in the fields modified by the user; it is pointless and wasteful to return the form itself to the host.

A crucial element of this scheme is that both input and output pass through the same display buffer. The common-buffer method implies, among other things, that the software component of a 3270 emulator operates by intercepting keystrokes, writing text characters into the display buffer, and simulating the function of a control key. For traffic in the other direction, the emulator program receives host output, writes it into the display buffer, and sends it to the screen. (Some fortuitous side effects of 3270 display buffer operation will be pointed out below.) The bidirectional use of the display buffer makes 3270 terminal operation critically different from other forms of terminal communication, in which input and output constitute discrete data streams. With a typical ASCII terminal, for example, the only association between input and output is in the operator's mind.

Types of Control Unit

Cluster controllers are of two basic types, one attached locally to a host, and the other intended for use at a remote location, as illustrated in Figure 12.1. The local type normally supports terminals on the same site as the mainframe, while the remote type normally supports off-site terminal users. The 3174 and 3274 series include several models of both types.

A local control unit, also called a *channel-attached controller*, plugs directly into a mainframe *channel*, a high-speed conduit through which the mainframe performs I/O. Typically, IBM mainframe channels carry data between system memory and the controllers that manage various peripheral devices, and they operate at 3 Mbps. A channel-attached controller must normally be situated within 200 feet of its host but, as usual, the market offers means of extending this distance. One source is IBM itself, which offers a fiber-optic channel extender.

Local 3270 terminals can be connected to any IBM mainframe via control units, and this is the standard arrangement for larger systems. IBM's newer, smaller mainframes can also be equipped with internal adapters that perform the same function as local control units. For the 9370 line, for example, a Workstation Subsystem Controller card is a simpler and less expensive option for supporting small numbers of 3270 stations.

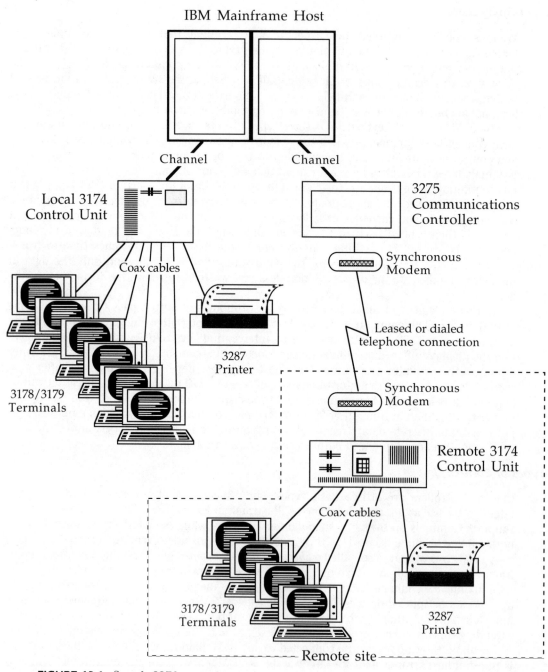

FIGURE 12.1: Sample 3270 network

A remote control unit normally communicates with its host over a synchronous modem link to a front-end processor (*FEP*). The controller is then also referred to as *telecommunications-attached*. The FEP, a minicomputer specially designed for communication purposes and available from most makers of large computer systems, relieves the mainframe of the burdens of port driving and protocol management. IBM has offered two generations of FEPs, which it calls *Communications Controllers*, for its mainframes: the older 3704 and 3705 series, and the contemporary 3720s and 3725s. As usual, both the 3720 and 3725 come in a variety of sizes and offer myriad options. A few mainframe models, including the 4321, 4331, and 9370 line, can be ordered with built-in communications adapters to which remote control units connect, obviating the FEP. (This alternative to the traditional front-end is essential since, although even a 9370 can be configured with a 3725 if desired, a 3725 can easily cost more than a 9370.) For the rest of this discussion, we'll refer to FEPs as if all IBM mainframes were equipped with them for remote communications, but the reader should bear in mind that the function of the FEP is sometimes more likely to be performed by an internal controller, as described above.

Both dial-up and leased lines commonly complete the link between the remote control unit and the FEP. A leased line allows the user to establish a multipoint connection, with several controllers sharing the link to an FEP. Dialed-line speeds range from 2,400 to 4,800 bps; the range is 4,800 to 9,600 bps for most leased lines, but may be as high as 64 kbps. A remote controller may also be cabled directly into an FEP via a synchronous modem eliminator.

No matter how it's connected, a remote control unit communicates with the FEP by means of a protocol, which may be Synchronous Data Link Control (SDLC), BiSync (BSC), or X.25. SDLC is generally preferred, being an integral part of SNA and offering slightly superior performance to BSC. IBM BiSync units are more limited in transmission speed, the fastest being capable of 9,600 bps. X.25 is normally employed only for links made via PSNs. Not all controllers can support all three protocols, and within any network, protocols may be mixed as needs dictate.

While remote control units differ greatly from local models with respect to their connection to the host, both types accommodate the same terminals. Not surprisingly, though, there are often considerable differences in efficiency between locally and remotely connected terminals. Remote controllers can be made to drive terminals at respectable speeds, but they cannot avoid the bottleneck presented by the telephone connection. Local controllers, which communicate directly with their mainframes at multimegabit/second channel speeds, can often provide truly dazzling terminal response.

The data path between a control unit and a host-based application program is essentially error-free—thanks, in the case of remote controllers, to the synchronous line protocol. Similarly, the coax link between a terminal and its control unit involves a proprietary protocol of its own.

Suppose you have a control unit in one room and want to connect it to a slew of terminals in another room, perhaps six floors away. Can you avoid laying a separate coax cable for each terminal? A 3299 multiplexer can help you. It will multiplex up to eight terminals' worth of 3274 traffic over a single coax link. Unlike other multiplexers, 3299s are not used in pairs. A single 3299 does the multiplexing and demultiplexing at the terminal end, and the 3274 itself performs these functions at the controller end. Such an arrangement is shown in Figure 12.2. Multiplexers of this type are usually called *concentrators*.

Control units with Token-Ring attachment capability may also use such a network to connect to each other, thus providing another multiplexing option.

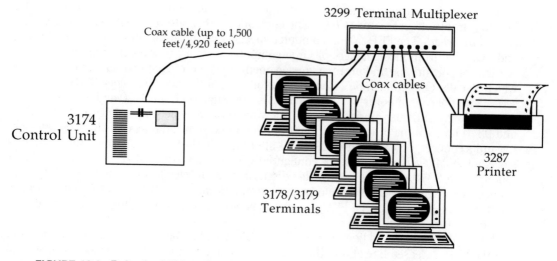

FIGURE 12.2: Role of a 3299 multiplexer

3270 Printers

Printers are normally connected to a 3270 network via coaxial interfaces to control units, just as terminals are. The user must configure the controller with the current use of each port, but any mix of terminals and printers is allowed. IBM offers a fair range of 3270 products in this category, including fast line printers, color dot-matrix character printers, and letter-quality printers. The best-known model of 3270-compatible printers is the 3287, so, following common practice, we will use the term *3287* generically to refer to any printer connected to a 3270 network.

A user may print on a 3287 either locally or from a host. When connected to the appropriate model of control unit, any terminal may execute a "print screen" function directed to a printer also attached to the control unit. As with a PC, this causes the printer to spit out a copy of the current screen image. Printers are more commonly used by directing a file on the mainframe to be dispatched to a 3287; any 3287 in a 3270 network can be so addressed.

The Big Picture

Figure 12.1 ties together all the elements described in this section in a small installation with a host, one local control unit, and one remote. An actual 3270 network would usually be much bigger, with several terminal clusters. Such networks can get more complicated than the one shown in any number of ways. For example, multiple hosts can be supported. (To many people, "network" implies a web of computers, and a network involving a single host may seem puzzling. While 3270 networks may now involve multiple hosts, they originally did nothing of the kind; they were supposed to be networks of *terminals*, not of computers.)

A large 3270 network can encompass several dozen computers, support thousands of terminals, and span a continent.

IBM ARCHITECTURES

IBM is very fond of architectures, which they have developed for computers, networks, documents, and application interfaces. Architectures are best viewed as IBM's internal standards, which may or may not become accepted industrywide. By IBM's own definition, architecture "refers to a set of design principles that define the relationships of and interactions between various parts of a system or network of systems."

We will consider three: Systems Network Architecture (SNA), Document Content Architecture (DCA), and Document Interchange Architecture (DIA). As a point of interest, there are also two others: VM/XA™(the System/370 Extended Architecture) is IBM's current mainframe computer architecture, and Systems Application Architecture™(SAA) is their application program interface architecture, an attempt to standardize the user interface for application programs across the entire range of IBM computers.

SAA may soon become very important to some PC users. In May 1989, IBM announced a sweeping new software line called the OfficeVision™Family, designed to provide a uniform user interface for office applications. PS/2 components of OfficeVision will run under OS/2 Extended Edition Version 1.2, and will be the first software to take full advantage of Micro Channel Architecture. (Micro Channel, mentioned in Chapter 3 as a standard bus in PS/2s, has been touted as a major feature of the PS/2 line since its introduction, but has more or less lain dormant until now.) While details are lacking as this book goes to press, the OfficeVision system will facilitate enhanced networking and cooperative processing among disparate IBM machines, including PS/2s, minis, and mainframes. Equally significant, users of OfficeVision application software (communications, word processing, database management, and so on) will be presented with a consistent and integrated icon-based user interface irrespective of the machine they happen to be using. As you might have guessed, this is where SAA comes in. The new software line, to be marketed by both IBM and third-party developers, is to include modified versions of established applications that will "snap in" to the OfficeVision system by adhering to SAA standards. Of course, there's a catch: OfficeVision reportedly requires huge amounts of RAM.

Many of the architectures listed above, including SNA, are *open* in the sense that IBM publishes their full technical specifications. An open architecture paves the way for other companies to manufacture and sell compatible products, although the range of such products may sometimes be limited by IBM patents.

SNA

IBM announced its SNA in December 1973 as a unification of, and replacement for, several already established methods of terminal-to-mainframe communications. It has grown to be a huge networking scheme capable of interconnecting almost all data-processing devices made by IBM, including mainframes, minicomputers, PCs, and terminals. Since its basic constituent parts are close to 20 years old, SNA is showing its age. Nevertheless, it still provides staunch service, is growing with the times, and will be with us for a good while yet.

A complete appraisal of SNA would fill a book—has, indeed, already filled several fat volumes. Only the briefest overview will be presented here.

SNA was originally designed as a framework for building terminal networks around single mainframe hosts, with remote connections made over switched or leased telephone lines. It has evolved to support multiple hosts, minicomputers and PCs, and modern transmission facilities such as PSNs and satellite links. SNA is intended for both local- and wide-area intraorganization networks.

Most large networks are built according to architectural models, such as the OSI seven-layer reference model described in Chapter 8. Since their structures are dauntingly complex, our understanding of their design is enhanced by division of the system into neat, compact, modular areas. SNA is also a seven-layer architecture, as shown in Figure 12.3, but differs

	OSI Layer	SNA Layer	Major SNA Functions
7	Application	NAU Services Manager	Application services
6	Presentation	Presentation Services	Data translation/compression
5	Session	Data Flow Control	Dialogue synchronization
4	Transport	Transmission Control	End-to-end flow control
3	Network	Path Control	Routing & traffic control
2	Data Link	Data Link Control	Point-to-point data transfer
1	Physical	Physical	Physical/electrical interface

FIGURE 12.3: SNA Layers-with OSI layers for comparison

considerably from the OSI model. Thus, although networks of the two types can still communicate with each other, their interaction is not straightforward. IBM, of course, is fundamentally committed to SNA, but offers some support for OSI, primarily in Europe, where OSI is more prevalent.

A comparison of the SNA layers in Figure 12.3 with the OSI layers (Figure 8.5) reveals strong superficial similarities. When it comes to detail and implementation, differences are more pronounced.

We can regard SNA in three ways:

1. As an abstract model that describes the design and operation of a network.

2. As a set of specific protocols used to create a network.

3. As the realization of (1) and (2) in the equipment sold by IBM (and others) to construct actual networks.

We will examine SNA from each of these points of view.

SNA as a Model of Network Design

SNA serves as an architectural model for IBM's networks by defining various component entities, their functions, and their interrelationships. Its primary building blocks are *physical units (PUs)* and *logical units (LUs)*. A PU manages network resources; prime examples are host CPUs (which manage application programs), FEPs (which manage network connections), and cluster controllers (which manage terminals). An LU, by contrast, is a user's port into the network. LUs include terminals, printers, and application software products.

SNA defines several PU types. The scheme of type definitions is somewhat arbitrary, but on the whole useful, as it codifies a bewildering and ever-expanding array of devices. For example, 3270 cluster controllers are PUs of type 2, usually specified as "PU 2." The Network Control Program (NCP), IBM's SNA software that runs in a 3705 or 3725 front-end processor, is a PU 4. Host computers are PU 5s. An LU can be said to define a generic network interface for a specific class of devices. It is the logical entity that communicates on behalf of a network user. One LU class comprises all 3270 terminals which, as we saw in the previous section, vary considerably in physical characteristics yet interact with the network in a uniform way.

PUs, LUs, and other network components interact through *sessions*. Sessions are temporary logical connections between pairs of network entities that enable them to conduct a dialogue. SNA defines several classes of session for various network needs, the chief class being the "LU-to-LU session." This is the kind normally engaged in by a network user, and commonly known as a "host session" or "terminal session." (Note that these expressions are two sides of a coin; they both refer to the same thing.) In the early days, LU-LU sessions were always established between a mainframe subsystem and a terminal or printer, but nowadays program-to-program sessions are also important.

SNA assigns numerical type designations to various LU-LU sessions. For example, a session between a 3270 terminal and a host subsystem is of type 2; one between two programs is of type 6. (The assignment of designations was more chronological than logical.) The session type specification lays out the kind of data that may be transferred, how those data should be formatted, and other elements of the interaction. A special kind of session, designated type 0, is intended as a sort of do-it-yourself LU-LU interaction kit with no predefined parameters. Type 0 sessions are used, for example, with Automated Teller Machines (ATMs).

Terminals and printers are themselves frequently identified by LU type; a 3278 terminal, for example, may be referred to as an "LU 2." SNA gurus hold that naming a network device after the type of LU-LU session it engages in is technically incorrect. Although unambiguous for most hardware LUs, which support only one session type, such nomenclature is problematic for software LUs, which often support several types so that they can communicate with different devices. Since even IBM often uses session type names to refer to hardware LUs, however, we must deem it acceptable.

Figure 12.4 illustrates a network abstracted to show users, LUs, some sessions between users, and what is called the *Common Transmission Network*. The Common Transmission Network is the conglomeration of the three lowest layers of the network, collectively responsible for the delivery of messages between LUs. LUs can treat the Common Transmission Network, called the *subnet* in other types of network, as a "black box" that, given the right instructions, will route a message to its correct destination and deliver it reliably.

A special network entity, the *System Services Control Point (SSCP)*, is given overall responsibility for network management. The SSCP is part of the networking software running in a mainframe. A multihost network will have several SSCPs, each controlling the portion of the net that falls within the domain of its host. It is the SSCP that brings the network up and down, deals with network outages, executes commands entered by a system operator, and maintains information about the status of the network. In addition, the SSCP is pivotal in establishing user sessions. When a network terminal comes online, for example, it begins by opening a session with the SSCP, which is likely to present the user with a menu of subsystems available for connection. When the user selects a subsystem, the SSCP coordinates the establishment of the required LU-LU session. (Note that the SSCP itself is not an LU.)

SNA Protocols

A network consists of a well-defined organization of software and hardware components, each of which performs specialized functions essential to network operation. Pairs of components located at different points in the network establish working relationships, or sessions, that permit them to interact in defined ways. The final products of these interactions are services rendered to network users, most commonly terminal sessions.

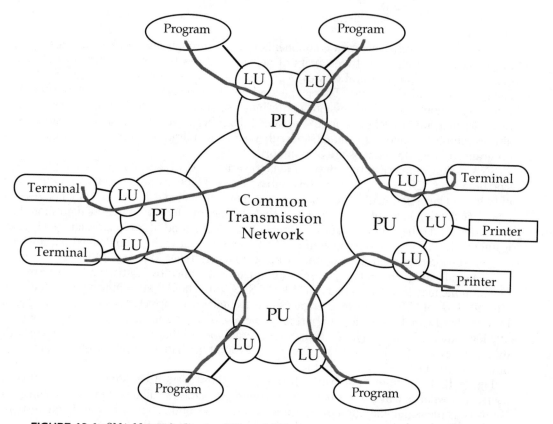

FIGURE 12.4: SNA Network showing LUs and PUs

The actual communication that supports the above organization is provided by several protocols, usually one protocol per network layer. These are called *peer-to-peer protocols* because they are used for communication between components that provide the same level of network function. The modular network design mentioned at the outset demands that communication between network nodes be conducted strictly between peers.

Each protocol is designed to handle the functions of the layer it serves. A protocol for the lowest layer, for example, is primarily concerned with error control. A layer or two up, a protocol attends to message addressing and routing.

SNA employs a set of proprietary protocols, of which just one, *Synchronous Data Link Control (SDLC)*, is worth mentioning here. Described further in Chapter 8, SDLC is the protocol used at the second layer (data link control) to ensure reliable data transfer over a single network link—notably the link between a remote cluster controller and an FEP. SNA also supports X.25 and 3270 Bisync as alternate data-link protocols. The SNA layer below SDLC, called *physical control*, is implemented by a physical network interface such as RS-232.

SNA Equipment

The primary equipment used to build SNA networks consists of 3705/3725 FEPs, the 3270 series of devices described in the previous section, and IBM's Token-Ring LAN products, outlined in Chapter 14. (A Token-Ring network may either be integrated into an SNA environment or used independently.) While 3270 terminals are standard in office environments, IBM also offers several special-purpose terminals with SNA capability, including point-of-sale terminals for use in stores, a line of document scanners, and a Japanese-language workstation. In addition, there are devices for directly linking pairs of mainframes, devices for interconnecting mainframes with System/36™ and System/38™ minicomputers, encryption boxes, and other equipment that need not concern us.

Network architectures must necessarily leave certain factors undefined, lest all flexibility be "specified" right out of the system. Accordingly, SNA does not define every single aspect of network operation. For example, it says nothing about what kinds of modems should be used in networks, except that they must be synchronous. In practice, the choice of modems is left to the user, who selects a unit complying with the standards followed in the country concerned. IBM offers a line of modems that incorporate especially powerful diagnostic and network management features.

Integrating PCs into SNA

A PC can operate in an SNA environment in two ways: by pretending to be a terminal, or by using session type 6.2, generally referred to as "LU 6.2" or *Advanced Program-to-Program Communication (APPC)*. The ".2" increment in the session type designation corresponds to the "Advanced" qualifier. APPC makes use of a recent and powerful addition to SNA to be discussed in Chapter 16. Here, we'll explore the more traditional method of having a PC play the role of a 3270 terminal.

There are two general approaches to enabling PCs to mimic 3270 terminals: emulation and protocol conversion. Emulation is effected by equipping the PC with the hardware and software necessary for direct connection to an SNA network; the PC plays the role of some standard component, such as a 3278 terminal. Protocol conversion involves having the PC emulate some *other* kind of terminal, typically a VT100 or IBM 3101, and then connecting the PC to the SNA network via a protocol converter. The converter makes the PC appear to the host as a 3270 terminal.

True 3270 emulation inherently equips a PC for greater functionality and higher efficiency in the SNA world, but protocol conversion is likely to be cheaper and more flexible. Because emulation is both the preferred and the more powerful method, we will consider it first (after discussing other architectures), and deal with protocol converters in a later section of this chapter.

SNA Summary

SNA is a mature networking scheme predominant in large IBM mainframe installations. With SNA, IBM largely realized its goal of overcoming the limitations inherent in async and BiSync communications, creating in the process a reliable and efficient networking system able to exploit the best communication facilities of its day. SNA is defined in the precise, modular fashion appropriate to a standard. It is also well documented. In fact, the quantity of documentation can best be described as staggering. An IBM engineer recently estimated that this printed material would fill two large rooms from wall to wall and from floor to ceiling. Think of that the next time you feel put off by the length of a magazine article or a chapter in this book.

On the other hand, SNA is harrowingly complex and very expensive to buy, install, and, most significantly, maintain. Its complexity is to some extent inevitable, as it was designed both for high performance and to be highly functional for all of IBM's diverse customer base.

Its evolution has been hampered by its stubbornly hierarchical design, in which mainframes have played the lords and masters, and terminals the poor dumb slaves. SNA is no lumbering giant, though; it is shedding its old image as IBM continues to develop it. In the late 1980s, SNA is growing in four main new directions. First, it is being extended to support smaller, less expensive, non-mainframe-based networks with *Low Entry Networking (LEN)*, announced in 1987. IBM also recognizes a need to reduce costs of SNA networks for all users to more closely match competitive networks. Second, with APPC, a significant measure of peer-to-peer communications capability is being grafted onto SNA, making it a quite viable networking base for distributed processing and for PCs. Third, software is being developed to simplify network design and operation, and to automate network management with such products as NetView™, an attractive network management tool. Fourth, moving (slowly) as ever to support newly emerging transmission facilities, IBM is adopting SNA support for LANs.

Office Information Architectures

IBM is developing standards to assist in office automation. We will look at two that define methods for formatting and distributing documents.

Document Content Architecture (DCA)

DCA, mentioned in Chapter 6, is IBM's standard for formatting documents. (This DCA is not to be confused with the company called Digital Communications Associates.) Different computer systems, even when produced by the same manufacturer, may employ very different means of representing and storing documents, especially documents with embedded format controls. (Embedded format controls are essentially shorthand format commands embedded in text, used to indicate such requirements as "Use a left margin of 9 when printing this," or "Print this word in boldface.") In fact, different document processors for a single computer system may involve wildly incompatible formats, as is evidenced by the variety of word processors designed for PCs. DCA is an attempt to specify standard formats for small documents in word processing environments.

DCA defines two types of format: one for "revisable form" documents, which may be edited, and one for "final form" documents, intended for printing or display. The distinction between these two forms is illustrated in Figure 12.5. IBM supports DCA with software products, most notably the DisplayWrite™ series of word processing programs, for its mainframes, System/36/38 minis, and PCs. DCA appears poised to become an industry-wide standard; many other companies, including several major vendors of PC word processors, have adopted it in such compatible programs as Microsoft Word, Multimate®, WordPerfect™, and PC-Write™. While DCA is a worthy and much-needed standard, it is rather complex and perhaps insufficiently flexible to be suited to all documents. It addresses the needs only of documents containing pure text, although extensions may appear to incorporate graphics, and perhaps even voice, documents.

Document Interchange Architecture (DIA)

DIA is a scheme for document distribution. It defines addressing systems for network users (both individuals and groups), accommodates document archivers and other services, and facilitates message broadcasting. DIA can be thought of as a means of creating virtual envelopes for documents, and addressing them for distribution.

DCA and DIA, together with a facility called SNADS (SNA Distribution System), form the basis of a good electronic mail system. Such a mail system is available in two office automa-

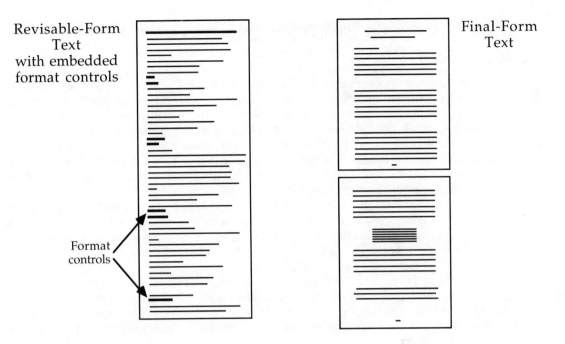

FIGURE 12.5: DCA's Revisable-Form Text and Final-Form Text

tion products made by IBM for its large systems: PROFS®(Professional Office System) and DISOSS (Distributed Office Support System). DIA and SNADS are both built using APPC.

3270 TERMINAL EMULATION

Emulating a 3278 or 3279

Equipping a PC with the hardware and software it needs to directly emulate a 3278 or 3279 terminal is the most straightforward method of facilitating its participation in a 3270 network. The hardware is an expansion card providing the required coaxial interface for connection to a cluster controller. The software is a program to make the PC behave appropriately. Since a plug-in board must be installed, it makes sense to incorporate as much logic circuitry into it as possible. The more work the card can do, the less the PC itself has to do, and so the better the overall performance. Thus, in practice, the hardware component of the emulator does a great deal more than just provide the coax port.

This type of emulation is sometimes referred to as "the coax connection," but it is perhaps more aptly characterized as "the IRMA method," after the product that has captured the lion's share of the market. IRMA, made by the long-established company Digital Communications Associates, was the first 3278 emulator marketed for PCs and one of very few early examples that worked well. Despite meritorious and plentiful competition in later years, IRMA has continued to evolve, maintaining both high standards and a strong position in the market.

The IRMA method of emulation is the obvious choice when cluster controllers are already in place, such as when real 3278s and 3279s are being replaced with emulator-equipped PCs.

Many corporations are making such substitutions these days; since a PC need not be much more expensive than a terminal, this is a very attractive option.

Emulating a 3274/3276

A second approach to emulation involves equipping the PC with a different hardware-software combination to emulate a 3274 or 3276 cluster controller as well as a 3270 terminal. In this case, the plug-in card usually comprises the entire controller emulator plus the synchronous port, while the software takes care of the terminal emulation proper. All current products in this category emulate the remote type of cluster controller, which is more in demand and, with the aid of a modem eliminator, can also be used locally. Another compelling argument in favor of this approach is that building the channel interface required for a local controller would be a difficult and costly task.

This type of emulation, and the associated category of products, is often referred to as the "modem connection." Most vendors sell emulators for SNA-style controllers, and a few also offer Bisync types but, unlike the case of IRMA, no single vendor has attained an outstanding position in the market. DCA offers IRMAcom®, and related products are available from AST®, IBM, and many others.

It is intriguing that a real 3274 cluster controller from IBM occupies a large floor-standing box and costs thousands of dollars, but you can buy a PC-based cluster controller emulator, consisting of a single printed circuit card, for a few hundred dollars. The comparison is unfair, of course, since "the real thing" is considerably more powerful, especially in its support of large numbers of terminals.

Cluster Options

As long as a PC product is emulating a cluster controller, it seems wasteful for it to support only one terminal. Why not design the product so that the emulated controller can support other terminals at the same time? Most manufacturers have, in fact, done so, but the manner in which extra terminals can be connected varies considerably among makers. Usually, the basic product emulates a controller and one terminal, while an add-on product, often called a "cluster option," supports additional terminals. In many cases, the add-on provides yet another plug-in board for the PC.

Let's call the extra terminals supported by cluster options "satellites," and the PC that houses the emulated controller the "hub." Some products support only PCs as satellites, while others support real terminals, generally asynchronous. Many users would like a PC-based controller emulator to which real 3278s and 3279s could be connected, but no such product has yet appeared.

We will examine a generic cluster option representative of many products. With the style of clustering illustrated in Figure 12.6, the satellites may be either ordinary async terminals (perhaps restricted to a few popular varieties such as the VT100 and IBM 3101) or PCs emulating such terminals. The satellites, typically a fairly small number (perhaps four), are connected via asynchronous RS-232 connections to a cluster board in the hub.

RS-232 connections between hub and satellites have two potentially valuable attributes: (i) they can be extended over telephone lines using regular PC modems, and (ii) the method is relatively inexpensive, since only software need be added to each satellite PC. A third benefit, generally less important, is that ASCII terminals can be substituted for PCs.

Controller emulation is often the method of choice when PCs require 3270 capability and are not within reach of an existing 3274/3276. Assuming that they can take advantage of a cluster option, a small single-location group of PCs, all requiring 3270 access to the same

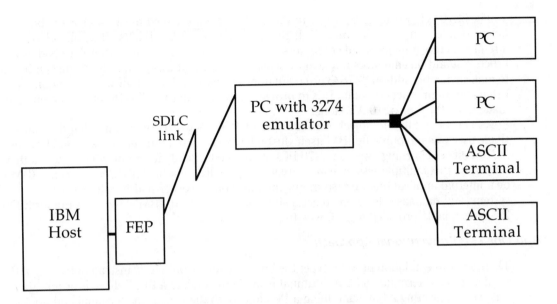

FIGURE 12.6: RS-232 Cluster Option with 3274 Emulator

SNA network, will benefit especially from this approach. The purchase of a real cluster controller purely to support a small community of PCs may be less cost-effective.

SNA and BSC Gateways for LANs

A third way of providing 3270 emulation for PCs is to install a LAN with an SNA or Bisync *gateway*. A gateway is a portal between one kind of network and another. Gateways have been developed to link Ethernets to SNA networks, token-ring networks to X.25 networks, and so on. A LAN gateway for 3270 emulation operates exactly like the second cluster option above: one PC on the net, acting as the gateway, hosts a cluster controller emulator, and other PCs emulate 3270 terminals communicating with the gateway by means of the normal LAN protocols. Emulation hardware is required only in the gateway PC.

The 3270 PC and 3270 AT

A fourth form of 3270 "emulation" must be mentioned even though it is already obsolete: the 3270 PC/3270 AT series, IBM PC models with integrated 3270 capability. To buy one was akin to getting a PC or AT, plus a 3278 or 3279, in a single box. In unmodified form, these machines, designed to be plugged into a 3274-type cluster controller, were quite powerful, and included a windowing control program, support for multiple sessions, an API (discussed below), and, in some models, graphics. The series was never successful; the original 3270 PC, in fact, was a bit of a disaster. Programs ran more slowly than on a regular PC; the 3270 control program occupied so much memory that it considerably restricted the user's choice of PC application programs; and the silly things weren't even 100 percent PC-compatible (they could not, for example, be hooked to certain LANs). Probably their greatest failing turned up on the invoice: it was much cheaper to buy an ordinary PC and equip it with a third-party 3270 emulator. The resulting setup was not as versatile as a 3270 PC, but was quite adequate for most users.

The 3270 AT was much superior to the 3270 PC and satisfied most purchasers, but also failed to catch on in a big way. With the introduction of the PS/2s, IBM abandoned its attempts to integrate personal computers with 3270 emulation. The marketplace had established that add-on emulators made more sense. (Throughout this period, IBM had continued to make available add-on 3278/3279 emulators as well.) And although several vendors marketed add-on products for plain PCs to provide emulation of the 3270 PC or AT, no one ever made a 3270 PC or 3270 AT clone.

As a postscript to the subject of 3270 PCs and ATs, it's worth mentioning that their largest single user was undoubtedly IBM itself. Just a few years ago, many employees could be seen in IBM offices churning away on 3270 PCs, zipping effortlessly from one window to another. Evidently, this multiple session capability was especially valuable for IBMers because IBM's own internal applications were so fragmented; a typical worker had to interact with several systems and databases in order to get a single job done. Also, IBM's own appetite for 3270 PCs presumably provided a good way to get rid of them.

And One Less Conventional Approach

There's a fifth emulation product type: the bolt-on conversion. Here, instead of making a PC emulate a 3270 terminal, a 3270 terminal is made to emulate a PC. Believe it or not, this is achieved by grafting a box containing a PC clone onto the side of the terminal and hooking it into the terminal's keyboard and screen. Maybe it beats junking a perfectly good terminal or cluttering a desk with keyboards and screens, but it certainly is an odd approach.

SELECTING AND USING A 3270 EMULATOR

The 3270 emulators offer a variety of optional features. We will describe the most popular and important of them and touch on many problematic issues specifically related to DOS. The use of 3270 emulators with OS/2 should be relatively smooth sailing.

Optional Features

The 3270 Keyboard

A real 3270 terminal keyboard has the usual alphabet, numerals, and symbols, up to 24 function keys, a small pad of keys for local editing functions and cursor control, plus a few unusual graphics keys. A 3278/3279 emulator should provide an equivalent set of keyboard functions. Although PC keyboard faces look like giant ears of corn compared to most, they still fall short of their 3270 cousins, so emulator makers must concoct key combinations (Ctrl-This, Alt-That, etc.) to match the real terminal. Because there is (wouldn't you know it?) no standard for this scramble, every vendor does it in a different way, making a template that maps 3270 key functions into the PC keyboard almost essential.

Manufacturers have developed two techniques to make 3270-style keying easier. The first allows the user to remap the key combinations according to personal taste. The second involves physically extending or replacing the stock PC keyboard. Someone accustomed to working on a real 3270 terminal might do well to buy one of the giant replacement keyboards that incorporate the keys normally found on both the PC and 3270. Keytronic and DCA are notable suppliers of such units. The question of replacement keyboard design, by the way, is not trivial, especially since IBM has gone through so many different styles for its various PC models. In general, each new keyboard has been given not only a different key layout but also a different interface to the PC. This means that a replacement-keyboard maker must come up with several models to provide plug-in compatibility with all PCs.

A less expensive, less elaborate product is the *keypatch*, or keyboard extension, which attaches to an existing PC keyboard and supplies the "missing" keys.

IBM's original PC keyboards had 10 function keys, while more recent models have 12 to facilitate emulation of the 3270's 24 function keys.

One of the more appealing features of the 3270 PC/AT series was a fully *3270-compatible keyboard*, that is, one equipped with all the same keys as appear on a 3278/3279. (A *PC-compatible keyboard* is one that will operate correctly when plugged into a PC.) IBM went overboard (so to speak) to provide every 3270 key plus every PC key, resulting in a versatile, if somewhat cumbersome, design.

Graphics and Color

As stated earlier, the 3279s are a series of color terminals, some with graphics capabilities. Many 3270 emulation products provide 3279 color support for text (this works fine as long as the PC is equipped with a color monitor), but graphics support is far from universal and usu-ally involves extra cost. Graphics options generally exploit standard PC graphics adapters, such as EGA and VGA modes. Light pen support is also an option with a few products.

Screen Sizes

Screens for 3270 terminals vary in size. In addition to the typical 24 lines by 80 columns, there are models with screens ranging from 12 $\times$40 to 27 $\times$132, and 43 $\times$80 is also common. Since some application programs may be oriented to the larger screens, it's fitting that PC emulators should cope with them. PCs with *Enhanced Graphics Adapters (EGAs)* can operate in a 43-row-by-80-column mode, which makes life easier for the emulators. The safest assumption for an emulator, however, is that a boring old 25-by-80 monitor is in use; larger screens are emulated by treating the PC screen as a window onto the larger virtual screen, with keyboard controls used to shift the window around.

Resident vs. Nonresident Operation with DOS

In Chapter 10, we mentioned that some asynchronous terminal emulators are capable of memory-resident operation under DOS, allowing the user to switch back and forth between a terminal session and a DOS application program. This feature is even more valuable under 3270 terminal emulation. Unlike asynchronous terminals, most often connected transitorily to hosts over switched lines, 3278/3279s tend to remain host-connected for long periods, so that simultaneous access to DOS application programs is really handy. Most leading products allow either resident or nonresident operation. The primary disadvantage of resident opera-tion is that access to some emulator features, such as screen capture (described below), may be restricted due to the limitations of DOS.

Screen Capture

The ability to capture the image on the terminal screen and direct it to a PC disk file or printer is a feature that seems too good to pass up. It can even be used to advantage as a primitive, impromptu means of file transfer. Weaknesses in DOS, however, make screen-capture-to-disk a risky operation for PC programs running in resident mode; it can be made to work, but some vendors, understandably, have not attempted to support it. Almost all emulators permit unrestricted capture in nonresident mode, however, and switching between resident and nonresident modes is seldom difficult. In general, because the host connection is maintained by the hardware portion of the emulator, the emulator software can be stopped and started at will without losing the session(s), making it easy to switch between resident and nonresident operation.

Multiple Sessions

IBM led the industry by supporting multiple concurrent host sessions in both the 3290 terminal and 3270 PCs. Emulator vendors quickly followed suit. There is much to be said for being logged in to several application programs simultaneously, since many mainframes are overburdened and respond sluggishly to input from terminals. By juggling multiple sessions, users can increase their productivity, working with one while waiting for another. Furthermore, emulators offering multiple-session capability usually make provision for moving data between sessions, as described below.

When a PC equipped for multiple 3270 sessions is hooked to a multihost SNA network, the user may log in to several hosts at once.

Multiple-session capability is normally implemented with multiple window displays on the PC screen. In the best implementations, such windows can be resized, moved around the screen, and hidden behind one another to suit the user's convenience, as in the Macintosh. In addition to several host sessions, the user will be provided with at least one DOS session. Some versions of IBM's own emulator products even permit multiple DOS sessions, albeit with a few awkward but unavoidable restrictions such as incompatibility with most memory-resident programs.

It's all very well to say let's make everyone super-productive by equipping all PC users with multiple 3270 sessions, but the cost must not be overlooked. A cluster controller is an expensive item and supports a limited number of sessions: 8, 16, or 32, depending on the model (one session per terminal). And then there's the cost of FEP ports, host memory, and CPU overhead. In spite of the convenience and potential productivity of multiple sessions, a user may ultimately be better off sticking with single-session emulators.

Moving Data Between Sessions

Most multisession emulators enable the user to move text between windows, and thus provide an expeditious way to move small quantities of data from one application program to another. One or more extra windows, called "notepads," may be provided to facilitate the reformatting often necessary when data are transferred. A block of text may be copied from one session into a notepad, where it can be edited to suit its new home, and then passed on to the other session.

Two underlying technical aspects of 3270 operation affect the copying of data between host sessions; one makes the transfer easy, the other may make it tricky. The display buffers (Page 259) that serve as a foundation for 3270 terminal operation act as a repository for both input and output characters. During multiple sessions, each session can be thought of as taking place in a separate virtual terminal, in the sense that each has its own private display buffer. In principle, then, data can be moved from one session to another simply by copying characters from one display buffer to another. That's the easy part. The hard part derives from the field orientation of 3270 terminals; you cannot arbitrarily grab the contents of one window and plunk them down into another. Instead, you must move data in units of individual fields.

The transfer of data from a DOS session to a host session is reasonably straightforward and is similar to inter-host-session copying. Getting data from a host session into a DOS session, however, is more difficult. DOS application programs expect their input to come from the keyboard or a disk file, not a memory buffer. A clever PC programmer could find some way to fake it, but other means are generally used. One method is to save data from the host window to a PC disk file, which the application program then reads. Another approach is offered by IBM's 3270 Workstation Program, which allows one DOS session to simulate keyboard input for another DOS session; thus, one program can read host data from a display buffer via an Application Program Interface (API) and then "type" those characters into a second application program, such as a spreadsheet.

Application Program Interface

The term "API" is used in various (and potentially confusing) ways. For now, we'll confine ourselves to discussion of APIs in the 3270 context. Such an API enables a PC-based application program to take control of an emulated terminal and thereby communicate directly with an application program in the host. The API comprises a library of functions available to the PC applications programmer. These functions simulate user operations such as entering keystrokes and examining host output.

An API for an emulated 3270 terminal serves as an interface between a PC program and the terminal's all-important display buffer. Two primary functions are required: one effects host input by simulating a keystroke, and the other obtains output by retrieving the contents of appropriate fields from the current display.

An API of this kind is a convenient, but hardly powerful, means of establishing program-to-program links. Its limitations are numerous and irksome: the awkwardness of terminal emulation, the rigidities of network hierarchies, and the bottleneck of terminal speeds. Still, it is the only way to build upon terminal emulation and, as we shall see, it has yielded some pretty impressive accomplishments.

No 3270 API has become a firm standard, but High Level Language API (HLLAPI), introduced by IBM for the original 3270 PC, is in the strongest position, having been cloned by several other manufacturers. It is offered in versions for several IBM language processors, including BASIC, Pascal, C, and COBOL. HLLAPI provides a total of 12 functions; in addition to the two described above, these include

- connecting the application program to a terminal session, and subsequently disconnecting it;

- detecting the status of the emulated terminal (transmitting data, receiving data, etc.) and awaiting status changes;

- copying the entire screen contents into the application program, searching the display buffer for a given text string, and determining the current cursor position; and

- setting and querying session parameters—functions effective for all sessions, not just the application program's own.

How do you use an API? Standard enhancement products for 3270 emulation, including file transfer packages and virtual device interfaces, are all built using APIs. As an example more likely to be developed by a user, consider a transaction processing system for order processing designed with distributed intelligence. In such a scheme, the order database resides on the mainframe, so that all operators may share access to it. Each PC used to enter orders, however, has a local copy of the customer file. Customers can be identified, their ID numbers picked out, credit ratings checked, account balances verified, and so on, all without bothering the mainframe. This arrangement both lightens the mainframe's workload and guarantees faster response to the customer.

A more general description of APIs is to be found in Chapter 16. Chapters 14 and 16 contain details of other special types of APIs.

Script Languages

Async communication packages commonly include a script language (see Chapter 10) but rarely an API. With 3270 emulators, the reverse is true. Nevertheless, some script languages (AutoKey/3270™ from CDI Systems, for example) are available as separate products to work with a number of emulator boards. Also, CASL, the script language incorporated into CROSSTALK Mk.4, operates in CROSSTALK's 3270-emulation mode with IRMA and compatible boards.

3287 Emulation

Many 3270 emulator products permit a printer connected to the PC to operate as a 3287, thus enabling it to accept printable output from the host. In principle, any printer that can be connected to a PC via a parallel or COM port can be made to work in this way.

In the case of a 3278/3279 emulator connected to a cluster controller, the provision of 3287 printer emulation—or, for that matter, of multiple host sessions—implies the use of multiple logical connections over a single coaxial interface. Such connections are possible with some, but not all, cluster controllers.

Workstation Control

Whether your emulator offers a meager single host session and single DOS session, or a cornucopia of multiple host and DOS sessions with windowing, notepads, and cut-and-paste functions, all in sixteen colors, you need a way to manage the whole show. In the early days, emulators provided a single "hot key" (Shift-Shift and Alt-Esc were popular combinations) to toggle between host and DOS sessions. Nowadays, you're likely to need controls for jumping between windows, resizing and moving windows, changing colors and other video attributes, and moving data between sessions. IBM calls this group of functions "workstation control." Unfortunately, but probably inevitably, such control becomes complicated, and you may have to manage obscure three-key combinations with your elbows even for simple functions. Make a mistake, and instead of skipping from one session to another, you may change the background color of some hidden window from red to blue. Keyboard templates or on-screen menus thus become indispensable.

File Transfer

Almost every vendor throws in at least some rudimentary file transfer ability with its basic emulator product. The furnished method may be slow and awkward, and possibly adapted only to moving text files. For faster and easier file transfer, consider buying an add-on product, which could include code for the host as well as for the PC. Note that for text transfer operations, the program will normally incorporate software for character set conversion between ASCII and EBCDIC.

Any file transfer option provided with an emulator will be set up for operation in a single mainframe environment. Software is most commonly offered for the two timesharing systems, TSO and CMS.

Advice on Selecting a 3270 Emulator

First, stick with recognized products. Emulating a 3270 is not simple, and some products do a spotty job. A competent programmer could throw together an asynchronous terminal emulator for a PC in less than a day; a full-blown 3278 emulator would take the better part of a year.

Second, be aware of possible upgrade paths. Even if you initially perceive your needs as modest, it's wise to choose products that offer scope for later enhancement. The time will probably come when you want multiple-session capability, graphics, or one of the other features discussed above, if not some wholly new gizmo not yet on the market.

Finally, proceed with caution if you have 3270-compatible equipment. PC-oriented people tend to regard any equipment that works with IBM's personal computers as "IBM-compatible," but there are clones of IBM mainframes, 3270 equipment, and even typewriters. The 3270-competitive products are often *function-compatible* but not *plug-compatible*. Plug-compatible equipment is (or should be) close enough to the original to be freely intermixed with IBM devices. Function-compatible equipment, on the other hand, does the same job as the real thing but is identical only where it absolutely needs to be (i.e., in the mainframe interface). A merely 3270-function-compatible cluster controller made by company X may well accept only terminals also made by X, and not those made by IBM. Be warned that a fair number of vendors of 3270-compatible equipment do indeed offer only functional compatibility—presumably to keep their customers captive.

A specific area of concern is the interface between cluster controllers and terminal emulators. Plug-compatible 3270 controllers should create no problems for 3278/3279 emulators in PCs. If you have function-compatible controllers, you must assume that most emulator products will not work for you, and you should consult the manufacturer of your network equipment. Some network vendors, ITT®for instance, offer their own terminal emulator products for PCs.

3270 PROTOCOL CONVERSION

A protocol converter transforms a data stream from one protocol to another. Its job is to receive data packaged in one manner, unwrap them, repackage them in a different form, and then send them on their way. A 3270 protocol converter allows a non-3270 terminal or terminal-emulating PC to appear to a host as a 3270 terminal. Most such products support asynchronous ASCII terminals. In such cases there is, strictly speaking, no protocol at all on the terminal side, but just a raw data stream; but the term *protocol converter* is usually applied anyway.

Many products are available for 3270 protocol conversion, distinguished primarily by the point at which they fit into the network. We will consider all the possibilities, beginning with those located farthest from the host.

Converters Installed Between the Terminal and Cluster Controller

Figure 12.7 shows a protocol converter sitting between a PC and a 3270 cluster controller. Such a converter consists of a box with a coax connection on one side and an asynchronous RS-232 port on the other. The box itself contains a microcomputer that does the converting. As you'd expect, the coax link belongs to the controller, while the RS-232 port can support either a real async terminal or a PC emulating one.

Such a device is unlikely to be cheaper than a PC 3278 emulator and, due to the relatively slow RS-232 link, is guaranteed to be less efficient, so it would be a poor choice for a local connection between a PC and a controller. However, because it gives a PC dial-up access to a cluster controller, it's a logical solution for those who need to support a few telephone

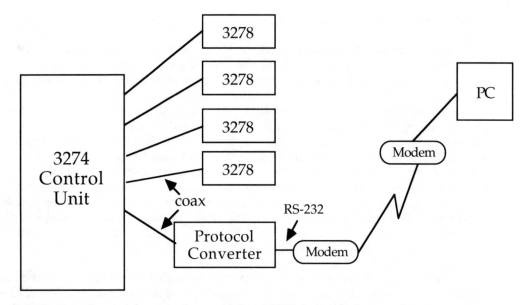

FIGURE 12.7: Protocol Converter between PC and 3270 Control Unit

ports to an existing controller. For a large number of dial-in ports, other options soon to be described may well be better.

Protocol converters of this first kind have not proven wildly successful in the marketplace. DCA, the IRMA company, is among the few vendors offering them.

Substitutes for Remote Cluster Controllers

The next device, shown in Figure 12.8, operates like a cluster controller, appearing to the host as a remote 3274 but supporting RS-232 connections for terminals. The illustrated device represents the most popular type of 3270 protocol conversion. This approach is particularly well established because it predates PCs, having been originally developed to support real ASCII terminals. Such converters fit neatly into the 3270 realm and can support a large number of PCs and/or terminals over both local and switched links.

In this category IBM offers both the 3174, described in the section on the 3270 family, and the 3708 Network Conversion Unit. The 3174 is a true 3270 control unit which, with one option in particular, supports ASCII devices. It's an obvious choice when both real 3270 terminals and either ASCII terminals or PCs are required in a remote location. The 3708 is a 10-port protocol converter that emulates a remote 3274. Two of its ports can connect to one or two SNA hosts (two connections can be made to the same host for more efficiency) by either direct cabling or leased line, but not a dial-up connection. Both the 3174 and 3708 support ASCII passthrough: RS-232 ports can be configured for connection to either a terminal/printer or an ASCII host. ASCII host connections are not, of course, multiplexed, as SNA host connections are; therefore, only one terminal at a time can use each ASCII host connection. (Incidentally, the cluster option of a PC-based 3270 control unit emulator essentially operates as this kind of protocol converter.) Other reputable manufacturers of such 3270 protocol conversion equipment are Local Data and Wall Data.

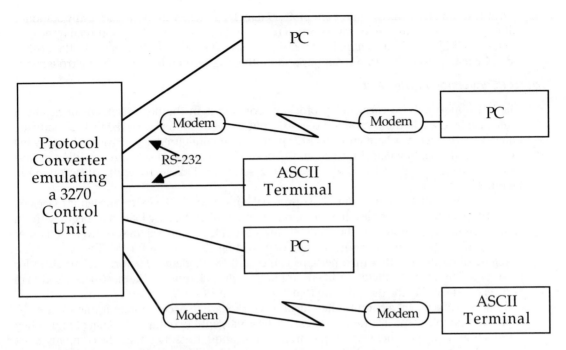

FIGURE 12.8: Protocol Converter replacing a 3270 Control Unit

Substitutes for Local Cluster Controllers

Dial-up connections from a PC to a protocol converter provide inferior performance compared to a real 3278/3279. Dialing right into the host site, of course, should work best, eliminating at any rate the second phone connection between the protocol converter and the host. Of the few products that permit such dialing, IBM's own 7171, which it calls an ASCII Device Attachment Control Unit, stands out.

The IBM 7171

The 7171 was reputedly built around the IBM Series/1™minicomputer, with protocol conversion software originally developed at Yale University. The biggest model supports a whopping 64-terminal complement.

Since the 7171 incorporates a general-purpose computer, it offers impressive versatility, supporting such useful features as software flow control (using Control-S/Control-Q), automatic line speed determination (autobaud), alternate screen sizes, file transfer, and even typeahead (potentially convenient, but decidedly foreign to "normal" 3270 operation). Built-in tables define the operating characteristics for several popular ASCII terminals, including the IBM 3101 and 3161, DEC VT100, Lear Siegler ADM3a, and Televideo 912/920/950™. A special additional table accommodates PCs, which are expected to operate in 3101-emulation mode. By attaching a PC as a console for the 7171, the user can add customized tables supporting additional terminal types, or redefine the built-in tables to change the way the standard terminals are driven.

ASCII terminals, printers, and even plotters may be attached to the 7171 by any standard full-duplex async means (line drivers, modems, or a modem eliminator), and then appear to the host as 3278 or 3279 terminals or 3286 printers. The 7171 itself appears to the host as a 3274 cluster controller or, if it supports more than 32 terminals, two such controllers.

Protocol Conversion in the Host

The last opportunity to carry out protocol conversion is in the host itself. (In principle, it could also be done in the front-end processor, but anyone familiar with IBM's FEP software knows why that'll never happen.) The FEP ports can be configured asynchronously, allowing PCs and terminals to connect directly to the host. The conversion software, residing in host memory, works closely with IBM's networking software. This approach is diagrammed in Figure 12.9.

A substantial disadvantage of in-host protocol conversion is the extra burden it places on memory space and CPU cycles, host resources that are often heavily loaded to begin with. In some circumstances, however, the relatively low cost of this approach may outweigh all other considerations. It remains the only method of providing 3270 access for PCs that involves no purchase of hardware other than perhaps cables and PC modems. The pricing structure for these products tends to dictate a fixed, although hefty, charge for the host-based software and very little outlay for the software that runs in each PC.

In-host protocol conversion is often ideal when PCs are to access a mainframe via a PSN. A classic example is the insurance company whose gargantuan databases of client and policy information reside on a network of mainframes at headquarters. Let's say the company must provide 3270-style access to both employees and widely dispersed independent insurance agents. These users already have PCs for other purposes, making PCs the logical choice for mainframe access. Since users access the system only sparingly and are not clustered, 3270

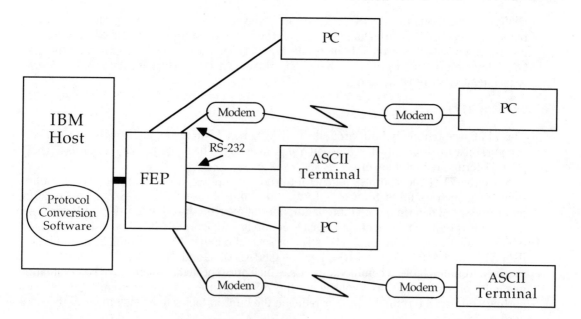

FIGURE 12.9: 3270 Protocol Conversion in a Host

emulation is not an attractive solution. The geographical spread strongly suggests the use of a public PSN. The large number (thousands) of users encourages centralizing the means of providing 3270 capability. Equally important, it may not be appropriate to demand that every insurance agent bear the substantial cost of a 3270 emulator for infrequent system access. All these factors clearly make host-based protocol conversion with access by PSN the best arrangement. A company that wants to ease gradually into providing 3270 support should also consider host-based conversion as an interim measure to hold down initial costs until real 3270 equipment is phased in. Products in this category include SIM, from Simware, and RELAY/3270™, from VM Personal Computing.

Conversion by PSN

Packet switch vendors are always falling over each other looking for value-added services to help sell their networks. Some offer 3270 protocol conversion within the network itself, providing a solution functionally similar to in-host conversion. Be aware, however, that PSN-based conversion may be limited in flexibility.

A General View of Protocol Converters

The Protocol Converter's Job

Now that we've seen how protocol converters fit into the scheme of things, let's pause to consider what such a product must do. It should be clear that at the heart of any protocol converter lies some kind of computer, whose responsibility includes the following for each terminal:

- Management of the display buffer, the operational core of every 3270 terminal. When data are received from the host, text must be converted from EBCDIC to ASCII. The converter interprets the 3270 field attributes so that the text is correctly positioned in the display buffer and, where necessary, generates X3.64 functions, or other screen-control codes used by the particular terminal, to create the appropriate image on the terminal screen. (The X3.64 functions would include field highlighting, clearing portions of the screen, and cursor positioning.) Finally, the terminal screen must be updated to match the display buffer.

- Processing input from the terminal keyboard. This entails recognizing certain character sequences used in place of Program Function keys, as well as other keycodes missing from ASCII keyboards. PF keys, for example, are often simulated by pressing the Escape key followed by 1 through 9 for PF1 through PF9; various other keys fill in for PF10 through PF24. Characters that represent local editing functions must be handled with appropriate adjustment of the display and cursor position, both in the display buffer and on the screen. Text characters must be checked for acceptability in the current field, correctly positioned in the display buffer, and finally echoed back to appear on the terminal screen. When the user enters a keyboard function that triggers the passing of input data to the host, the relevant data must be selected from the display buffer, translated to EBCDIC, and sent on their way.

- Special tasks where type-ahead is implemented. A real 3270 terminal is connected to its controller by a half-duplex link, and the controller keeps the terminal's keyboard physically locked except when an application program is soliciting input. The full-duplex communications employed by ASCII terminals, together with the system's inability to exclude terminal input, invite the amenity of anticipatory typing. Here, the protocol converter maintains a buffer for keyboard input, separate from the display buffer. This is needed for occasions when the user enters input prior to the appearance of the application-supplied screen to which the input is a response. Input characters can't go into the display buffer until the application program has delivered its output, because the fields and cursor position won't have been defined. The converter, then, won't know where to put such characters.

All of the foregoing are in addition to whatever the protocol converter does to communicate with the host, such as masquerading as a 3274.

Advantages of Protocol Conversion vs. Emulation

- Lower cost. Protocol conversion, appropriately implemented, is almost always less expensive than emulation.

- Much greater communication flexibility. This is especially evident in the easy incorporation of dial-up links with inexpensive async modems. To appreciate this, try sticking an IRMA card into your sleek laptop portable, checking a 3274 on a flight to Omaha, or hooking a synchronous modem into a public phone.

- In most cases, support of real async terminals in addition to PCs.

Limitations and Cautions

- The performance of protocol converters is unlikely to equal that of emulation, because they usually depend on RS-232 links to support PCs.

- The weakness of the async link means that the reliable data path guaranteed by true emulation is sacrificed. Still, extra steps can be taken to ensure reliability. Some vendors of protocol converters support asynchronous protocols for PCs; if these are not available, protocol modems can always be pressed into service. In fact, protocol converters present error-correcting-modem manufacturers with their biggest market.

- Keyboard mapping is complicated by the fact that the protocol converter does not have direct access to the PC keyboard.

- Options for the support of PC printers operating as 3287s, multiple host sessions, graphics, and file transfer, while not eliminated by protocol conversion, are much reduced in practice.

- Our assertion that protocol conversion is usually cheaper than emulation was qualified by "if appropriately implemented." One thing to watch for is how well FEPs are utilized. FEPs are expensive. With regular 3270 equipment, each FEP port normally supports a cluster of terminals. Host-based protocol conversion, in particular, implies that each FEP may be used by only one terminal at a time.

3270 Access via a System/36 or System/38

One means of protocol conversion has been saved for last. This technique is in a category by itself because it does not involve async operation. Moreover, the pros and cons of protocol conversion listed above do not apply.

PCs connected by means of 5250 emulators to an IBM System/36 or System/38, which is in turn connected to a larger network, can open 3270 sessions with any mainframe(s) on that network. The System/36 or /38, in this case, acts as a protocol converter. This is a boon to

PC users who work predominantly on the minicomputer, but who occasionally require access to the mainframe. It is unlikely to prove satisfactory for heavy 3270 use, however, because of the two levels of emulation involved: the PC is made to look like a 5250, and the System/36 or /38 makes the 5250 look like a 3278/3279.

COMMUNICATING WITH IBM SYSTEM/3XS

IBM's System/3X minicomputers, which the manufacturer describes as "departmental processors," include the System/34™, System/36, and System/38. They are well suited to small multiuser database applications, and their worldwide installed base is substantial. Like so many IBM systems, they use the EBCDIC character set rather than ASCII.

The System/34 is a small machine that is now obsolete; the 36 is a replacement for the 34. The larger 38 is not program-compatible with the other two models. Submodels of each designation offer different levels of power, amounts of memory, and so on, resulting in a wide system range. We'll study the communications capabilities of System/3Xs and examine how PCs may be tied to them.

Although the 36 and 38 are not compatible in other respects, they are alike in the way they communicate with the outside world. The 34 supports the same basic communication facilities as the other two machines but with comparatively limited options that we won't discuss in detail. The System/3Xs use SNA to communicate with one another and with IBM mainframes. IBM has a well-developed series of office automation products, such as PROFS and DISOSS, that take advantage of System/3X-to-mainframe links. On the terminal side, System/3Xs work with the IBM 5250 Information Display System. The 5250 system is to System/3Xs as the 3270 system is to IBM mainframes, and is organized in much the same way, with display terminals, printers, controllers, and auxiliary devices.

System/3X has no versatility in terminal communications; it can communicate only with 5250s or devices emulating 5250s. These computers are indeed unusual in offering no direct support for ASCII terminals or other async devices. 5250 equipment is itself very limited in application, being used exclusively with System/3X machines.

The 5250 Information Display System

The original, monochrome terminals in the 5250 family were the 5251s, later joined by the compatible but ergonomically improved 5291s. The 5292s offer seven-color display, Model 1 for text only, Model 2 with graphics capability.

The 5251s, 5291s, and 5292s are considered the standard 5250 terminals, and are the units most commonly encountered in System/3X installations. However, a few special models within terminal lines primarily associated with the 3270 family also belong to the 5250 group. These include the 3179 Model 2, the 3180 Model 2, and the 3196.

Here is a summary of the significant features of 5250 terminals:

- They are designed primarily for data-entry and inquiry applications. Programs may present terminal users with formatted screens much as they do for 3270 terminals.

- They are dumb. Terminal functions, such as ensuring that keyboard input is compatible with field attributes, are carried out by a controller. Input is collected by the controller and sent to the application program only when the user presses Enter or some other special key.

- All supported terminals have 24-by-80 screens except the 3180 Model 2, which has a 27-by-132 screen.

- Both data-entry and typewriter-style keyboards are available for many models.

- All 5250s offer the same video controls found on PCs: reverse video, highlighting, blinking, underscore, and combinations of these. In addition, column separators, in the form of thin lines between character positions, are available to enhance the display of tabular information.

- The 5251s support optional light pens and magnetic-stripe readers, facilitating input from credit cards, ID cards, etc.

There are several printers in the 5250 line (models 4210, 4214, 5219, 5224, 5225, 5256, and 5262), ranging from 40-cps printwheel units, through fast dot-matrix and color printers, to a 650-line-per-minute line printer.

Let's consider a typical configuration of terminals and printers connected to a System/3X machine. As is true for 3270s, stations may be connected either locally or remotely; again, the two connection schemes call for considerably different arrangements. Local stations connect via twinaxial cable at a speed of 1 Mbps, and up to seven stations in any combination of terminals and printers may be attached, in daisy chain formation, to a single cable run. ("Daisy-chained" devices are connected by cable segments in a linear string.) Since a cable run may extend up to 5,000 feet (1,525 meters), this arrangement is potentially far less expensive than systems requiring one cable per station. The controllers for local stations are built into the minicomputers themselves; the number of controllers, and hence the number of daisy chains supported, varies from one model to another.

Daisy-chaining is made possible by a feature called *Cable Thru,* which provides each station with two twinax ports not unlike the pair of side-by-side RJ-11 jacks found on many modems and telephone answering machines. Cable Thru is a standard feature on most 5250 terminal equipment and an option on the rest.

Remote stations are connected via a controller that communicates with the System/3X over a telecommunications link. Two forms of remote control units are available: the 5251 Model 12, an integrated terminal and controller, and the newer and more versatile 5294, a stand-alone controller. Either unit can be configured to support four or eight stations connected, much like local terminals, on either individual or daisy-chained twinaxial cables. For the 5251 Model 12, that means four or eight stations in addition to the 5251 itself.

The remote link normally uses SDLC over a synchronous-modem connection at rates up to 9,600 bps, but the 5294 can also run X.25 over a PSN connection at up to 56 Kbps. As with any RS-232-based link, local connection via a synchronous modem eliminator or synchronous line drivers is also possible. A System/3X computer does not require an FEP to handle remote control units; synchronous RS-232 ports are built right into the machine.

The 5251 also comes in a terminal-only Model 11 which, along with other terminals, serves equally well in local and remote configurations. The 5294 control unit supports remote connections for all terminals and printers; the 5251 Model 12 supports only certain older models.

Communication between host and remote controller is by SNA. The low-level protocols involved, such as SDLC, are identical to those used for 3270 gear and other SNA devices. The highest-level protocols, which relate to the functions of a specific class of terminal or printer, are unique to 5250 device groups; this is equivalent to saying that these device groups have unique LU types. 5250 printers are LU type 4, and 5250 terminals are LU type 7.

Getting PCs Involved

Although IBM sells a good selection of 5250 terminals, the company has declared PCs the preferred workstations for System/3X installations. Getting a PC to work with a System/3X, however, entails making it behave like a 5250 terminal. This can be done in several different ways, just as there are quite a few ways to make a PC play the role of a 3270 terminal. In fact, all the options available for PC emulation of 3270 terminals have their parallels here, except that protocol conversion in the host is not possible because the System/3Xs do not support direct asynchronous connections. Here is a summary of options:

- Emulation of a 5251 Model 11, 5291, or 5292 with attachment to either a local daisy chain or a remote control unit.
- Emulation of a remote control unit *and* a terminal in combination (for example, of a 5251 Model 12, or of a 5294 and a 5291 or 5292 terminal).
- Connection via a protocol converter that supports ASCII terminals.
- Connection via a LAN gateway.

5250 Emulators

The most popular way of connecting a PC to a System/3X is by equipping the PC with a 5250 emulator. This consists of a plug-in board that provides the proprietary twinax interface, usually with Cable Thru, and software to make the PC behave like a 5291 or 5292. (Since "behaving like a 5291" is roughly the same as "behaving like a 5251," the 5251 option is not expressly discussed here, although it may be in product literature.) The emulator board plugs into a twinaxial daisy chain, which may hook it either directly to a host or to a remote control unit. Vendors of such emulation products include AST Research, DCA, Emerald Technology Group, IBM, IDEAssociates, and Techland Systems.

For remote operation, a mixture of PCs and real 5250 stations is best supported by a 5294 control unit with individual 5250 emulators for each PC. A single PC should generally be equipped with a product, most often a 5251 Model 12 emulator, that emulates both a remote control unit and a terminal.

PC 5250 emulators offer many extra features, such as support for multiple (up to seven) sessions, keyboard remapping, file transfer, and support for PC printers as emulated 5250 printers. Multiple-session support is a simpler matter in 5250 emulation than in the 3270 case, because support for several stations per connection is inherent in 5250 architecture. Some remote controller emulators even include a synchronous modem with autodialer on the emulator card.

In preference to Cable Thru, some emulator products offer an RS-232 cluster option that permits the emulator to extend 5250 sessions to additional PCs connected by async RS-232 links, as shown in Figure 12.10. Since these satellite PCs require only software to gain 5250 capability, the method is considerably less expensive than providing an emulator board for each PC. Moreover, it allows PCs to gain async dial-up access to 3X systems and, in the better products, provides excellent performance. IDEAssociates is notable among manufacturers offering such cluster options.

Certain features of a real 5250 terminal cannot be realistically emulated by PCs. A prime example is the column separator that draws vertical lines between character positions on the terminal screen. Those who want "the real thing" can find special video adapters that duplicate all 5250 screen effects on a standard PC monochrome monitor. Similarly, 5250-style replacement keyboards are available from some vendors.

5250 Protocol Converters

5250 protocol converters support 5250 sessions for ASCII terminals and printers, as well as for PCs emulating ASCII terminals: they are available for both local and remote connec-

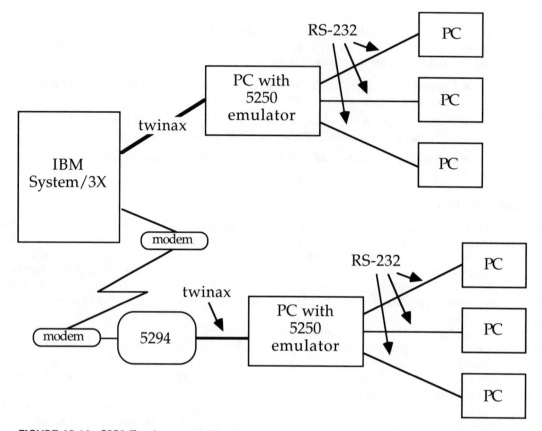

FIGURE 12.10: 5250 Emulators with Cluster Options

tion to a System/3X, as shown in Figure 12.11. Remote hookup is normally effected by the protocol converter's emulation of a 5294. Protocol conversion tends to be less effective than direct 5250 emulation for PCs because conversion schemes necessarily support fewer features. Nevertheless, protocol conversion is usually a cheaper approach than the use of emulator boards in PCs. It is a valuable option when both ASCII terminals and PCs must be provided with System/3X access, particularly if by async dial-in. Vendors of 5250 protocol converters include Local Data, PCI, Renex, and Wall Data. For small numbers of PCs, a 5250 emulator with an RS-232 cluster option, technically similar to a protocol converter anyway, is likely to prove a better choice.

5250 Gateways

A 5250 gateway consists of a PC connected to a System/3X and equipped with an emulator that allows it to provide 5250-terminal and 5250-printer sessions to other PCs via a LAN. A 5250 LAN gateway kills two or more birds with one stone. PCs can be networked for other purposes while being provided with 5250 access. Moreover, the 5250 sessions provided by the gateway can be shared, according to demand, among any of the PCs on the LAN. Potentially,

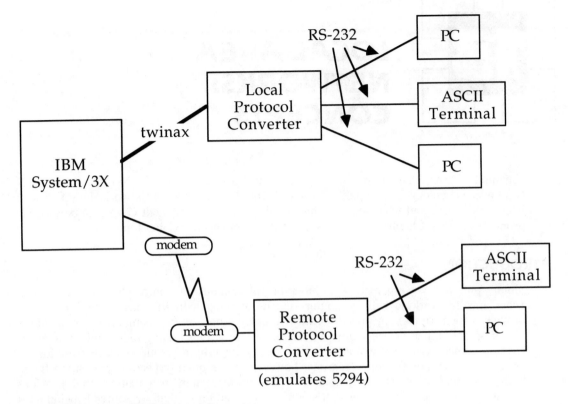

FIGURE 12.11: 5250 Protocol Converters

then, a gateway is far less costly than an arrangement requiring each PC to have an emulator that would probably see infrequent use. Gateway products are available for both local and remote host connection from Asher Technologies, AST Research, IBM, Wall Data, and others.

LOCAL AREA NETWORKS: CONCEPTS

This first of three chapters on the subject of local area networks (LANs) introduces LAN concepts, technology, and capabilities. Here, you'll learn how LANs work, how they can benefit PC users, and what some of their weak points are. The next chapter surveys LAN products for PCs. Chapter 15 finishes up with miscellaneous related topics.

INTRODUCTION

Simply put, a LAN organizes a number of autonomous PCs into a multi-user system. Schematically, working with computers means working with the various resources they provide, which we can categorize as *hard resources* (processors, memory, disks, printers, modems, and other devices) and *soft resources* (programs, data, files, and databases). Given a choice, each user would prefer to keep private hard resources exclusively for his or her own use. For economic reasons, however, it's frequently necessary to share them. Computers themselves can help manage such sharing, often in a manner that provides enough convenience for the user that she need not even know that a resource is being used by others at the same time. Some soft resources, such as personal files, are certainly best kept private; many others, such as corporate databases, were made to be shared and have value only, or at least predominantly, to the extent that they can be shared.

Since the mid-1970s, the focus of computing has swung from large, expensive multi-user hosts to small, inexpensive, stand-alone personal workstations. (To say "inexpensive" may be overstating the case, as we'll see shortly.) Not long ago, it was safe to say that everything except the keyboard and screen of a user's dumb terminal was shared by default. Users vied for processor cycles, memory, and access to peripheral devices; resources that had to be kept private were protected by permissions and passwords. There were substantial benefits to the host-computer regime: it centralized data processing and facilitated the sharing of essential soft resources such as programs and databases. The introduction of PCs, which gave users responsive computer power of their own, eliminated the often troublesome sharing of hard resources but made the desirable sharing of soft resources much more difficult. LANs fused many of the most worthwhile elements of the old and the new, giving PC users the best of both worlds; they keep their ever-increasing private processing power, favorite application programs, and customized workstations, and they gain the ability to share expensive devices and vital data. The transition would be painless were it not for the problem of cost. To begin with, although the price of LAN hardware has generally declined, vendors often load up their systems with snazzy and expensive extra features. More to the point, users have become enamored of increasingly sophisticated and powerful workstations, so that the networked PCs themselves (some of which are properly considered minicomputers) are driving up LAN costs.

Some people today maintain that mainframes are obsolete—that PC networks are just as powerful, much cheaper, and a lot more pleasant to deal with. This is not quite fair. Mainframes are still needed to handle huge databases, to support hundreds of simultaneous users, to perform heavy number-crunching, and to keep IBM in business. In 10 years' time, however, the picture might be very different.

PC LANs support the sharing of needed resources by providing a high-speed channel that is itself shared by a local community of PCs.

An Overview of LANs

LANs, widely used in computing, were developed before PCs and have many applications unrelated to PCs. All LANs exploit a local high-speed interconnection that provides a common path to tens, hundreds, or even thousands of devices for shared communication, and all depend on the same basic underlying technology. It typically involves a cable carrying data at a high rate, most often between 1 and 10 Mbps, but occasionally extending to over 270 Mbps; a method of hooking devices into the cable; a method of managing access so that only one device transmits on the cable at a time; and a protocol to ensure that data get to their destination intact.

Certain LANs, called *terminal* or *front-end networks*, are used to connect dumb terminals to hosts, and eliminate the individual cable runs otherwise needed between each terminal and its host port. Moreover, when several hosts are connected to the network, the terminal user can choose which host to connect to. The LANs then take the place of both multiplexers and port selectors.

Back-end networks connect mainframes to one another, as well as to tape drives, terminal controllers, and other high-speed devices. Such LANs allow a peripheral device to be located much farther from its host than is otherwise possible.

PC LANs interconnect PCs, and sometimes other machines, for the purpose of resource sharing. All our subsequent discussion of LANS concerns only the PC type.

Terminology

PCs and other devices on a LAN are commonly called *stations*. Stations may be described as *users* or *servers*, distinguishing the two basic roles in network operation. Servers manage network resources, such as shared disks, and give user stations access to these resources. User stations, sometimes called *clients* or *workstations*, are where people, the real users of the network, do their work. Some LANs enforce a deep separation between users and servers, requiring that each station be fixed as one or the other. Other networks, while maintaining the functional differentiation, allow stations to perform both roles simultaneously.

Features of PC LANs

PC LAN products may provide or support the following features:

- Disk sharing
- File sharing
- Printer sharing
- Modem sharing
- Sharing of other devices, such as tape drives (for disk back-ups)
- Distributed applications

- Electronic mail
- Fast file transfer between PCs
- Gateways to other types of network
- Bridges to other networks of the same type

The next section focuses on the broad subject of file servers. Other listed items are collectively dealt with in the subsequent section.

FILE SERVERS

PC LANs were first developed in the early 1980s primarily to permit the sharing of disk space. In those days, hard disks for PCs were very expensive (a 10-megabyte unit with controller sold for over $2,500), creating a powerful incentive to share them. Each user was allocated a certain portion of the disk's storage space, sometimes corresponding to a physical partition of the disk.

With a stand-alone PC, the space on a hard disk can be carved up into several volumes using the FDISK utility. Each volume then appears as a separate logical drive (C:, D:, etc.). (A hard disk whose capacity exceeds 32 megabytes [MB] may need to be apportioned in this manner, since a single DOS or OS/2 volume cannot exceed 32 MB.) A disk server takes the same approach, but makes each volume the private domain of a different user. Although each user's space is allocated on the same physical drive, files are immediately accessible only to their owners; at best, files can be copied from one user's area to another, but there's no provision for shared access to a single file. Hard disks have now become so cheap that sharing them like this is no longer of much importance.

In the mid-1980s, file sharing supplanted disk sharing as the primary application of LANs. With file sharing, designated files resident on a network disk could be simultaneously accessed by any number of users. A network station supporting such file sharing is called a *file server*. A given network might have several file servers, or only one. Users and application programs access files on file server disks in the same way that they access files on local disks.

Normally, file servers support the sharing only of files resident on fixed disks. LAN products have appeared that allow sharing of files on diskettes and even RAM disks, but they're exceptional. Attempting to share files on a removable-disk drive is rather dangerous: because a user cannot necessarily tell what volume is loaded at any moment, he may inadvertently write to the wrong disk.

You may be familiar with the DOS command SUBST, which allows you to substitute a drive specifier for a path. Thus, the command

SUBST E: C:\TOOLS\AID

sets up an association between the drive letter E and the \TOOLS\AID directory on drive C. Once this command is given, "E:" becomes a synonym for the given path. This may be nice just as a shorthand utility for your own use, but it's intended to smooth operations with old-style application programs that don't understand pathnames. In effect, this command defines E: as a virtual disk. (The importance of virtual devices, including virtual disks, is discussed in Chapter 16.)

Generally, the capability offered by networks is very similar to the above—mapping a local drive specifier into a shared directory—but the LAN operating system provides a different command for this purpose. Each shared disk on the LAN is given a symbolic name.

With IBM's network software, for example, a disk might be named "\\PETE\PETESC." The first component identifies the station, after its user, and the second names the device, Pete's C drive, on that station. The double backslash is an extension of IBM's pathname syntax. The command

NET USE D: \\PETE\PETESC\TOOLS\AID

gives a user access to the \TOOLS\AID directory on the cited disk, and establishes its new identifier simply as "D:." The first few drive specifiers, perhaps A to C, depending upon PC configuration, are reserved for physical drives directly attached to the PC. Subsequent letters—D, E, and (in principle) on to Z—refer to network volumes.

It's very convenient to be able to share files on a directory, rather than a volume, basis. It means, for example, that some directories on a file server may be made public while others can be kept private. Sharing a directory really means sharing the directory tree rooted in that directory; all subdirectories of that directory are included. Since a DOS or OS/2 volume is itself simply a directory tree, rooted in a directory called "\", there's little need for a distinction between volume and directory.

Efficient and reliable file sharing demands that attention be paid to five extra facilities in servers: *locking, security, caching, back-up*, and *power protection*.

Locking

Locking refers to the mechanism provided by a network, or other multiuser system, to ensure proper coordination among users competing for access to the same resources. To illustrate the need for locking, let's consider a scenario involving users of a primitive network that provides no means of regulating shared access to files.

Jane and John are business partners who like to maintain all their records, from company accounts to personal calendars, on their computers—specifically, on the file server of their fancy new PC network. One day John gets a phone call from his friend Mark, who invites him to lunch the next day. John fires up his trusty word processor and tells it to open his calendar file which, like everything else, resides on the file server. Inspecting his entry for the following day, John finds no previous engagement, agrees to meet Mark, and enters a notation in his calendar to that effect. John and Mark continue to chat while John idly browses through his schedule.

While this is going on, Jane answers a phone call from an important new customer, Barbara, who needs some matters straightened out. Jane decides that either she or John should get together with Barbara as soon as possible, and Barbara suggests a luncheon meeting on the following day. Jane runs her favorite word processor and starts editing her calendar. She finds that she is already booked up at the proposed time, so she opens John's calendar to see if he is free. The version of John's calendar that Jane consults is the same one that John looked at a minute before, because he has yet to save the results of his editing session. Thus, Jane wrongly concludes that John is free, and tells Barbara that she will arrange for John to meet her. Jane updates John's calendar, saves the result, and is immediately occupied by another phone call. A few minutes later she puts a message in John's electronic mailbox telling him about the scheduled meeting with Barbara. But in the meantime, John has checked his mailbox, as he does every afternoon, and found it empty. He has also saved his updated version of his calendar, overwriting the change made by Jane.

The next day John meets Mark for lunch, while Barbara is left sitting in another restaurant, rather disgruntled at having nothing but a dog-eared copy of *Widget Age* for company.

When Jane and John try to figure out what went wrong, Jane insists that she entered the engagement into John's calendar and left him a message to boot. John insists that there was no message, and no appointment in his calendar. When they look together at the calendar and mailbox. . .well, you know what they find. The partners quickly realize that they need some locking.

Locking allows one user to gain temporary exclusive control over a resource. Its most common use is to lock either a record within a database or a whole file when a user reads it with the intention of making a change. Other users who just want to read the data may be allowed in, but anyone who wishes to alter them will be forcibly kept away until the first user has completed his or her update. Of course, such a mechanism would not affect the empty mailbox, but it would solve the calendar problem. We'll look more deeply into the implementation of locking mechanisms in a later section.

Security

Whenever files are shared, the need to limit access in one way or another is likely to arise. It may be necessary to prevent some users from accessing particular files; for example, students are not generally allowed access to their instructors' files. Sometimes, certain network users must be able to read a file, yet be prevented from writing to it. Similarly, copy protection needs may dictate that users be able to execute a program in a certain file but be barred from making a private copy of it. All these constraints come under the heading of security.

The best security is managed through a set of *permissions* granted to each network user by a system administrator. User Andy might, for example, be given permission to access files in directory X in any manner (read, write, delete, etc.) but to "read only" in directory Y, while being prevented from accessing directory Z even to the extent of determining that it exists. Permissions may be organized in a hierarchical manner such that the overall network administrator allows selected users the privilege of setting permissions for certain groups of users who fall in their domain. Permission-based security depends upon each user logging in to the network with a username and password; often, however, users must log in separately to each file server they wish to access.

Some networks provide security directly by means of *passwords* rather than permissions. To be precise, the permissions method causes the system to check a list of permissions for the user on login, as described above. The password method requires an individual clearance step for each *directory* to be accessed during the session. To get at files in a directory, a user must supply the requisite password. A directory may have several passwords: one for read access, one for write access, one for delete access, etc. The amount of security provided by PC LAN products varies from "absolutely none" to "as much as you could want."

Disk Caching

Accessing data on a disk, even a fast fixed disk, is relatively slow compared to other computer operations. Many PC application programs spend the bulk of their time idly waiting for data to be read from and written to disk files. A *cache* is a high-speed memory buffer in which the most frequently used portions of a disk can be duplicated for fast access; disk caching is commonly used with PCs, networked or not. Caching programs use a portion of PC memory to store disk sectors so that, for example, a repeatedly read file may be kept in cache, from which it can be read more quickly. Caching can significantly speed up operation on a stand-alone PC, but the extent of improvement depends greatly on patterns of disk usage. On a server, with numerous users converging on the same data, caching can speed up operation so much that it becomes a virtual necessity.

Many file servers maintain a copy of the entire disk directory in memory at all times. This is not a cache, precisely, because even subdirectories that happen never to be referenced are kept in RAM. But the technique is the same, speeding up both file openings (when the directory tree must be searched for the file name) and the preparation of directory listings. In principle, disk caching proper can assist in three ways. First, frequently read files, such as popular application programs, can be kept in memory for almost instant availability. Second, data that are supposed to be written to a file (because of some operation undertaken by the user) can be temporarily parked in memory. The file server can write the data to disk at its leisure, without keeping the user waiting for a disk access operation to be completed. Third, if the file server has some idle moments, it can check to see whether any users are reading files sequentially, and preload data in anticipation of upcoming read requests.

Clearly, a file server needs a lot of memory, preferably a few megabytes, to provide substantial cache capability. This is one of several reasons why a newer PC, with an 80286 or 80386 chip, makes a better file server than an older 8088- or 8086-based machine would. The newer PCs can accommodate more memory, and access it more easily, than the older ones. Since file serving operations don't make intense computational demands on PCs, the newer machines' more powerful processors count for very little in making them better candidates for the job. Rather, it is their larger memory provision, faster buses, and larger disks that make the difference.

Back-up and Power Protection

The timely and orderly *back-up* of files is important for any computer user with a fixed disk. When multiple users share data on a networked disk, reliable back-up becomes critical. A single user may manage with back-up to diskettes, but back-up to magnetic tape is almost essential for a shared disk. Compatibility between tape back-up units and LAN software should be carefully studied when planning a network.

For the same reasons, *power protection* is more important for PCs incorporating shared disks than it is for user stations. An uninterruptable power supply (UPS) is worth considering for each file server. A UPS will not keep a file server alive indefinitely during a power outage, but that's not its purpose. All it must do is to keep the server going for at least a few seconds, enough time for an operator to initiate a manual shutdown. The server can thus flush its buffers gracefully and securely to disk, ensuring that no data will be lost when the power finally does disappear.

What Constitutes a File Server?

Most file servers on PC LANs are simply PCs of AT class or better, equipped with file serving software. A few, called *proprietary file servers*, are larger computers outfitted with disks and appropriate software. These were originally introduced because early PCs were too short on power to function as file servers for large groups of users. The special-purpose proprietary servers, which often used Motorola 68000 processors with large disks and fast buses, supported up to five times the load handled by a PC-based server. With more powerful 80286- and especially 80386-based PCs now available, proprietary servers no longer have such a competitive edge, but plenty are still sold. A third file-server possibility is a minicomputer. Only a few network vendors support such an option, but it's possible to use a DEC VAX, or one of a few other types of mini, as a file server on a PC LAN.

A key characteristic of a file server is whether or not it is *dedicated*. A dedicated server performs only file serving (and possibly other network tasks), but is not available as a user workstation. Some PC-based file servers are dedicated and others are not; it depends primarily on the vendor, and to some extent on the user. A nondedicated file server may be an attractive option for very small networks, where devoting a PC to the purpose seems inappropriately expensive. Some network vendors give you no choice; their file servers must be dedicated. Proprietary file servers are by their very nature dedicated. Minicomputer file servers need not be; they continue to support users while performing the service.

Centralized and Distributed Servers

With respect to file serving, some networks are *centralized* while others are *distributed*. A centralized network has a small number of servers usually, but not necessarily, dedicated. In a distributed network, every PC may be a file server, by implication not dedicated. A centralized design is best for a network oriented to heavy database use, in which case the file servers effectively become database machines. A distributed net may make more sense for LANs built to support general file sharing. Most LANs are better suited to one mode, centralized or distributed, than to the other.

When setting up a centralized network, it's usually wise to make the file server(s) dedicated even if the network software itself imposes no such requirement. Exceptions may be made on small networks, but running user application programs on a centralized server is generally a poor idea, both because it degrades the server's response to other users and because a crashing program may take the server with it, especially under DOS.

A dedicated server normally makes its entire disk storage available as a shared resource. With nondedicated servers, it's usually possible to share files on a directory-by-directory basis, so directories containing public files can be made available to other users while private directories are kept for local use only.

How File Servers Are Used

In practice, file servers not only manage databases and other files to which users require concurrent access, but offer other possible benefits.

With the aid of a file server, a community of PC users can reduce its total disk space requirement, eliminating the duplication of files necessary with private disks. For example, consider a university facility with 50 PCs, all of which are available for students to run a certain statistical analysis package. The software is complex, occupying 4 MB of disk space. If a copy were stored on each PC, the aggregate disk space required would be 200 MB. By maintaining only one copy, accessible to all users, on a file server, the university saves 196 MB of storage for other worthy purposes.

Although disk sharing, as described at the beginning of this section, is no longer attractive on purely economic grounds, it may be valuable in other ways. File security, for example, is certainly stronger on a file server than on a plain PC. A copyrighted program can be stored on a server in such a way that users can execute but not copy it. Likewise, diskless PCs can be attached to a LAN so that users work solely with server disks and cannot walk off with any data on floppies.

A few organizations, such as engineering design labs, have installed LANs and file servers primarily to facilitate the exchange of files among member PCs and to centralize back-up. In these environments, users don't need concurrent access to files, but do need to share them serially (consecutively), as is the case when several people must work on a document or blueprint in succession. By installing a central file server with tape back-up, and instituting a regimen that calls for each user regularly to copy critical files to the server, the organization can protect the integrity of the project by systematically backing up only that one disk. Both back-ups and serial exchange can thus be handled in a very efficient way.

Finally, a file server can also increase the speed of file access. Believe it or not, thanks mainly to caching, accessing data on a file server can be faster than on a local disk, as long as the server is lightly loaded. If you had ridiculous amounts of money to spend and wanted the ultimate PC-compatible system, you might do well to buy two PCs, connect them with a LAN, and put one to work as a file server for the other.

OTHER LAN SERVICES

Not all LANs provide the full complement of services described here, but you can expect to be able to get most of them.

Print Servers

Printer sharing arose as the function second most in demand by PC LAN users. Not surprisingly, a PC supporting shared printers is called a *print server*. A single printer might be shared on a small office network. Users on a large network might each have a private printer (perhaps of the less expensive dot-matrix variety) local to their respective PCs, and share letter-quality and/or laser printers over the net. Usually, files are sent to a shared printer by means of a DOS-level command such as "NET PRINT," in preference to mapping networked printers into standard DOS device names, because DOS supports only three names for printers—LPT1, LPT2, and LPT3. This restriction means that it may not be possible to print on network printers from within application programs.

Some networks integrate print serving with file serving, so all shared printers must be attached to file servers. Other networks allow independent print and file service, enabling any printer on the network to be shared. Supporting a shared printer is no big job, so placing one on a user PC causes almost no noticeable change in the responsiveness of the machine.

Most networks support spooling for shared printers. After giving a network print command, a user on such a system can go on to perform other tasks, instead of being held up until printing is complete. The spooling function is usually handled by a file server.

Distributed Applications

A distributed application has program components running on two or more computers at the same time. A multiuser application can take advantage of a network in two basic ways. One is by accessing shared files on a network disk, as described above. The other is by distributing its intelligence over a number of PCs, using the network facilities to support communication between its various parts. Distributed applications, which first appeared long before PC LANs, are now increasingly important. Although some run under DOS, multitasking operating systems such as OS/2 have largely facilitated the upsurge of distributed applications.

Modem Sharing

There is a fair amount of support for modem sharing on LANs. DCA, Hayes and VM Personal Computing, for example, sell network versions of their CROSSTALK, Smartcom, and RELAY communication packages. On suitable LANs, such a product permits attachment of a modem, or a pool of modems, to a networked PC, which then acts as a modem server. (A PC that manages shared modems is sometimes called a *communications server*.) A user at another PC can allocate herself a free modem from the pool and use it for dialing out. Since modems are not terribly expensive, few organizations opt to share them in this manner. Those that do are most often motivated, not by any scarcity of modems, but by a scarcity of telephone lines. When external lines suitable for data transfer are very expensive or difficult to obtain, modem sharing begins to look attractive, as might be the case, for example, when a company relies on a digital PBX for its internal phone system.

Clock Servers

If one PC on a LAN has a real-time clock, and others don't, it's usually possible for that PC to act as *clock server* for the others. This obviates the tiresome and error-prone manual entry of times and dates. It does not necessarily synchronize all PCs on a net (i.e., cause them all to maintain the time identically), because delays in transmitting the time from one station to another inevitably result in minor discrepancies. Nonetheless, it is likely to lead to a state closer to synchronization than any manual method. Since most newer PCs come with clocks built in, the value of this facility is rapidly waning.

Sharing Other Devices

The sharing of other devices on LANs is of comparatively little importance. Plotters, for example, can sometimes be shared, but most small plotters must be hand-fed with paper for each plot.

Electronic Mail

Electronic mail is popular on many networks. Mail facilities are included in some LAN products, and add-on facilities for others are usually available from either the network vendor or a third party.

Remote Booting

Normally, a PC loads its operating system from a local disk—the procedure called *booting*. When a PC is on a LAN, it may be possible to arrange for booting from a file server. The normal boot code is stored in read-only memory (ROM) in the PC. Remote booting is effected by code in ROM on a network card that overrides the standard, local ROM, causing the operating system files to be read from some suitable server. This facility is not supported by all networks, and is normally employed only for the benefit of diskless PCs.

File Transfer

Do not confuse file transfer (moving files as objects from station to station) with file sharing (concurrent on-line access). File transfer over LANs may be accomplished in several ways. Moving files between a user PC and a file server is as straightforward as a DOS COPY. Moving files between two user PCs may be trickier. Some networks provide a special command for the purpose, some leave the job to the mail system, and others fail to address the issue at all. The last case calls for a two-stage procedure: the originator of the transfer copies the file to a server, from which the recipient must then copy it.

Gateways

Gateways are portals between different networking environments. The commonest type links a PC LAN to an SNA network and provides 3270-terminal emulation to the PCs on the LAN; usually, such a gateway is itself a PC with a 3274 emulator on board. Gateways for X.25 networks allow, for example, PCs on a LAN to act as terminals on a PSN. There are even gateways to link different types of LAN together—for instance, to interconnect a Token-Ring and an Ethernet™. In many instances, 3270 and X.25 gateways could be dubbed protocol conversion servers, but the term *gateway* is standard.

Bridges

A bridge generally connects a pair of similar LANs. Local bridges interconnect two LANs in the same location; remote bridges connect a pair of LANs over a telecommunications link, which may be a dialed telephone circuit, a leased line, a virtual connection through a PSN, or just about any long-distance link. A *full-function bridge* will make two LANs appear logically as one: a user on one can transparently access resources on the other. Not all bridges provide full function.

We'll refine and expand these definitions of bridges and gateways in Chapter 15.

So, What's it Really Like to Use a LAN?

Let's compare the exciting experience of using a LAN to that of using a plain old stand-alone PC.

Sit down at a solo PC, and chances are you'll be faced with a prompt such as "C." Sit down at a *networked* PC . . . and chances are that you will still be faced with a prompt such as "C."

A LAN doesn't jump out and grab you; it doesn't alter the basic look and feel of using a PC (except for the few LANs, like Torus's, that provide an icon-based user interface). A LAN hovers in the background. It adds great power to the PC, but you have to know it's there to make much use of it.

Just what does a LAN do for you? Fundamentally, it does four things:

- It increases the number of disk volumes at your disposal—up to 26 if you use all of A: through Z:.
- It allows you to run multi-user applications.
- It provides access to other shared resources, such as modems, printers, and gateways.
- It provides some extra DOS-level commands for such utilities as determining the status of the network (who's on, what servers are active, how busy it is, etc.); sending files to network printers; and using such services as electronic mail.

THE DARK SIDE OF LANs

In the last section we regaled you with the wonders of LANs. Here, we'll note some of the problems and restrictions encountered with them.

How Local is Local?

LANs are not called *local* area networks for nothing; they are designed for use at close quarters. Many live in single offices, some cover large buildings, and a few extend over wide campuses or commercial installations. Generally, LANs are distance-limited by the user's right-of-way to run cable and by operational restrictions imposed by constituent products. The maximum spread of the various LAN products varies greatly, ranging from a few hundred feet to a few miles. Such distance limitations are alleviated to some extent by bridges.

Configuration Limits

Any LAN dictates a maximum spread, which may be expressed as a limit on the aggregate length of all the cable used or as the maximum cable distance between any two stations. In addition, each network imposes a ceiling on the number of stations that can be attached. The ceiling ranges from a handful to several thousand, but the most popular PC LANs have limits between 24 and 260 stations.

The specified maximum number of stations reflects either the number of possible physical connections or the number of defined station addresses. It does not have direct implications for performance "in the field": a LAN may, in principle, permit networking of 256 stations yet have a practical performance limit of a dozen stations. (We'll address performance again later.)

LAN Management

Generally, you don't just install a LAN and then leave it alone to do its work. It requires some attention. LAN management may call for anything from a small fraction of a person's work week to a full-time commitment with bonuses, overrides, and a gold watch upon retirement. The amount of time devoted to management depends primarily on the size of the installation and secondarily on such factors as:

- The demands of the particular LAN product
- The amount of security required
- The caliber of the people using the LAN. When appropriate, a LAN may be managed largely by its users.

The LAN manager's job may involve a wide range of tasks, including:

- Establishing and maintaining accounts and security
- Updating the network operating system and network application programs as new releases appear
- Producing documentation and conducting training on LAN use
- Dealing with hardware and software problems as they arise
- Adding new PCs to the network
- Setting up network commands in batch files to aid relatively naive users
- Ensuring that back-ups of shared disks are performed regularly and responsibly
- "Collecting garbage" from shared disks. Give enough people access to a disk, and it'll fill up with junk in no time.

Of course, not all of these duties will necessarily fall to a single manager. One person might take administrative charge of the network, tending to security and the like, while another looks after hardware and a third assumes responsibility for software.

PCs and Foreigners

What can you attach as stations to a PC LAN? You should have no trouble with PC- and AT-family machines but, in a few cases, support may be lacking for PS/2s. Generally, devices such as disks and printers are not attached directly to a LAN but are connected via a PC. Many products do allow the attachment of certain other computers: proprietary file servers, Apple Macintoshes, certain minicomputers, and, indirectly, mainframes. Exactly what can be hooked up, and to what advantage for the PCs, are highly LAN-product-specific questions.

LAN Costs

The prices of many LAN products, especially hardware components, have been declining in recent years, but LANs are still not exactly cheap. It could cost as much to put a single PC on a LAN as to buy the PC in the first place. In a later section, we'll survey some alternatives, some of which are less expensive. But, as we'll see, none of the other options offers the versatility and functionality of a true LAN.

Hardware Compatibility

The packing of many add-on boards into a PC, no matter what their function, can cause trouble because of competition for interrupts, address-mapping space, electrical power, and so on. LAN cards certainly have similar liabilities. IBM's 3270 PCs and 3270 ATs, for instance, are foreclosed by hardware conflicts from operating on many LANs. Also, memory-use conflicts render certain expanded memory boards and EGA adapters incompatible with IBM Token-Ring cards.

Software Compatibility

Once you've put your PC on a LAN, will you still be able to run the same programs as before? Ordinarily, yes: just because your PC is attached to a LAN doesn't mean that you have to use it. As long as you ignore the LAN and use only local resources, your connection to the net should have only two effects: first, a very slight, probably imperceptible slowdown in response time due to the software, which continually checks for any requests made to network resources; and second, possible trouble with memory-resident software under DOS. A large part of the network software is itself memory-resident, and may conflict with other such programs. It's not uncommon to find that keyboard enhancers, for example, will not work properly on networked PCs under DOS.

How about running single-user PC application programs (i.e., those not specifically designed for multi-user operation) with shared files? For example, can you safely use a word processor not designed for network operation to edit a file from a shared disk? In most cases, as long as you're the only person using the file at the time, there's no problem. A single-user program doesn't know or care where its files are. If someone else tries to access one of the files at the same time that you do, then nasty surprises are possible. In the same vein, some single-user programs work in ways that can cause unsuspected trouble on networks. For example, users of WordStar™ know that it creates automatic back-up files with the extension of ".BAK." Suppose that you use this program to edit a file called DOC.ONE in a shared directory. Another user tells WordStar to edit a file called DOC.TWO in the same directory. There is no conflict between the files being edited, but each WordStar will independently attempt to create a back-up file called DOC.BAK in the same directory. This spells trouble. Such snags may not be apparent until they crop up but, happily, they can usually be avoided. In the above case, you just have to make sure that WordStar uses local directories for its back-up copies.

Networking PCs with Other Types of Computer

Suppose you have PCs and Macintoshes in your office and want to network them together. Or PCs and Sun Workstations®; or PCs and Amigas®. What do you do? You are quite likely to find some LAN product that caters to the combination if you search far enough.

But your options may be very limited. You must also be prepared to find that, compared to the facilities enjoyed by users of pure PC networks, multisystem nets provide considerably restricted communication between dissimilar computers. Differing operating systems, file structures, and data formats tend to make file sharing between different types of computer quite a chore. But the same factors also conspire to limit the appeal and value of such file sharing. Most concurrent file sharing is performed via multi-user applications, few of which have as yet been offered for operation on more than one type of computer. A common motivation for linking PCs and Macs is to give the PCs access to Apple LaserWriter® printers. In such cases, sharing files is a convenience, but of secondary importance.

Some file servers have been designed to manage shared file bases for different operating systems (e.g., AppleProDOS® and DOS, or UNIX and DOS) on the same disk, but in such a manner that each base is maintained independently. It's usually possible to copy files from one shared file base to the other, but little or nothing else.

Different PC Configurations

We've noted that file servers allow a single copy of a widely used application program to be maintained for all PCs on a LAN, which saves on total disk space, ensures that all users in a group are running the same version, and simplifies updates. A complication arises, however, when the program is one that must be configured differently to suit different PC setups. The most common example is the application program especially configured for a PC's video adapter type: monochrome, CGA color, EGA color, etc. In order to suit all the PCs on the network, it may well be necessary to maintain several versions of the program on the server, each with a different configuration setup. Under such circumstances, the network manager can usually arrange for users to run the program uniformly by establishing for each user a batch file that executes the program indirectly. Some networks, notably the IBM PC LAN Program, provide assistance with the establishment of such batch files.

Despite this long list of bugaboos, LANs are still powerful agents, capable of greatly boosting the productivity, ease, and pleasure of PC use.

WHAT LANS ARE MADE OF

We will investigate PC LAN composition in several stages. The first and simplest step is to divide the system into *LAN hardware* and the *network operating system*. The hardware part moves the bits among the stations. The network operating system functions as an extension of the PC operating system. As you know, the PC operating system, such as DOS or OS/2, manages local PC resources and handles requests made by application programs to access these resources. In much the same way, the network operating system manages *shared* resources, and extends the PC operating system to give application programs convenient access to these shared resources.

You may well buy these two major LAN components—network operating system and LAN hardware—separately. Some measure of "mixing and matching" is feasible, but you must determine in advance whether the separate products will work together. Of course, if everything comes from a single vendor, you can count on getting a compatible combination. At least, one would certainly hope so.

The LAN Hardware

The hardware part of a LAN consists of a cabling system and a set of *Network Interface Boards* or *Network Interface Cards (NICs)*. One NIC is installed in each PC, and then hooked into the cabling system. The NICs are normally identical for all stations except, of course, for differences required by PC-family and PS/2 architectures. A few products, including IBM's Token-Ring, offer a sort of turbocharged version of the NIC for use in stations, such as file servers, that must cope with particularly heavy traffic. This makes a lot of sense: in a network that supports mostly file serving, the amount of traffic handled by each file server is the same as the total traffic handled by all of its users put together.

Media

LANs use many different cable types: coaxial, twisted pair, and fiber optic in various grades. A few LAN products even use radio transmission, rather than cable runs. A given product will mandate the use of one, two, or three (rarely more) specific media. Electrical cables have traditionally been used with LANs, but the fiber optic type is rapidly gaining ground. For networks whose wiring schemes involve point-to-point cable links, optical fiber may soon be the cable of choice.

Coaxial cable is the ideal electrical conduit for LANs. Its bandwidth, immunity to noise, and low loss enable it to perform effortlessly over many thousands of feet at the multi-megabit/second rates used by LANs. In the last few years, vendors have been vying to provide more PC LAN products capable of operation over twisted pair cable, which is much cheaper than coax to buy and to install, and in some cases will already be present in a building. A separate but related recent development has been the appearance of twisted-pair products with many of the same electrical attributes as their coaxial counterparts. Most of these offerings, from SynOptics, Cabletron, and other companies, are intended as twisted-pair replacements for coaxial cable in Ethernet, following a standard called 10BASE–T.

Although coax may cost up to 10 times as much as twisted pair, it's still affordable for many smaller installations; the extra expense becomes substantial only in widely spread networks. Unfortunately, the wider the cabling spread of a LAN, the greater the need to use coax to achieve adequate performance. Hence, networks that permit station-to-station cable runs in the range of miles specify coax or optical fiber, while twisted-pair nets are typically limited to a few hundred feet or, at most, about half a mile.

In large LAN installations, for which cable must be laid by contractors, cabling cost can be by far the greatest single expense. Companies situated in very old, thick-walled, multistory buildings have reportedly paid hundreds of dollars per foot for cable installation. Of course, not much can be done about our ancestors' lack of foresight, but it's prudent to incorporate cabling needs into the design right from the start when constructing a new building.

The Network Interface Card

The NIC's most obvious job requirement is the ability to provide a high-speed interface to the network. Remember, we're dealing in megabits per second here; RS-232 doesn't even come close. But a NIC normally provides much more than just a hardware port to the LAN. Most of them incorporate a microprocessor and a fair amount of memory, both RAM for buffering messages and ROM for holding the software that drives the NIC. Operating a PC on a LAN involves a great deal of work, and it's best to have the NIC do as much of it as possible. Otherwise, it has to be done by the PC processor, which, of course, leads to a degradation in response time to the user. The NIC can't do everything, though; many functions must be performed by the PC itself, and these are the tasks of the network operating system.

The bulk of the NIC's job is operating the protocols used on the LAN. Data that a station sends across the network are divided into packets transmitted as individual protocol units protected by CRCs. In fact, the protocols used on LANs are not significantly different from those we've already studied, such as HDLC. Addressing is a little more complex on a LAN, since each message typically contains the addresses of both sender and receiver. In addition, most LANs permit the broadcasting of messages from one station to all others. Broadcast messages may be used to relay information about the state of the network for the benefit of the network software (when a new station becomes active, for example) or to send informative messages to all users, such as "Server X going down in five minutes for back-up."

Baseband and Broadband

Although there are several other categorizations, LAN hardware is fundamentally divided into *baseband* and *broadband* types. The distinction is rooted in the type of signaling used on the network cable. Baseband LANs depend on digital signaling; broadband LANs use analog signaling on a cable that is divided into several channels.

A broadband LAN has a great deal in common with cable television; in fact, they use much of the same technology. When cable TV service is installed in a home, a coaxial cable drop is brought in. A selector box then allows the customer to tune into any of perhaps 30, 40, or 50 stations. The cable company can squeeze all those stations onto one skinny cable because they've mastered the magic of *frequency division multiplexing (FDM)*. The bandwidth of the cable is divided up into channels, each 6 MHz wide, as shown in Figure 13.1. Each channel is assigned to a different station, whose signal is modulated onto a carrier frequency within that channel. (The actual bandwidth of a TV signal is about 4.5 MHz; the 6-MHz channels ensure good separation and thus reduce interference between adjacent channels.) The cable selector box demodulates a station's signal from its cable channel and remodulates it onto a frequency handled by the television set.

In most cases, a broadband LAN uses only two channels on the cable. The remaining channels are available for other purposes, such as high-speed point-to-point data links, closed-circuit TV, building security, and video conferencing. It's possible for several independent LANs to operate on the same cable, using different channel pairs, but product support for this is limited. Not all channels are suitable for LAN transmission.

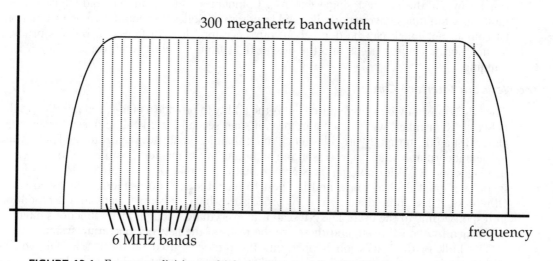

FIGURE 13.1: Frequency division multiplexing on a broadband cable

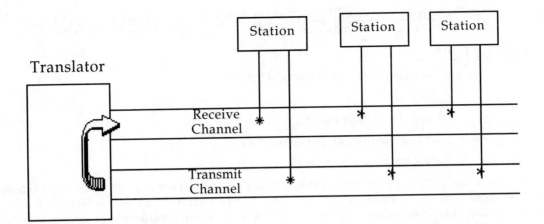

FIGURE 13.2: Broadband translator

Why do broadband LANs occupy two channels? Because each channel is unidirectional. All LAN stations transmit on one channel and receive on the other. A *translator*, a special device at one end of a broadband cable, moves all the traffic from the transmit channel to the receive channel, as shown in Figure 13.2.

Broadband LANs are a bit more expensive than the baseband type because they require extra components, a translator for the network and a modem for each NIC, not needed by a baseband LAN. (Granted, these modems are less complex than the telephone line kind.) Also, the cost of buying and installing broadband cable, which tends to be heavier than baseband, is likely to be higher. In spite of these differences, broadband LANs are remarkably competitive in cost with baseband.

Broadband LAN speeds are theoretically more limited than baseband, because the data capacity of a 6-MHz broadband channel is only between 5 and 10 Mbps. As a practical matter, however, the disadvantage is slight: although baseband LANs can, in principle, operate at rates up to a few hundred Mbps, none made for PCs is designed to work any faster than 10 Mbps.

Which type of LAN hardware should you choose? Although strikingly different kinds of electrical activity occur on baseband and broadband cable, the two types are indistinguishable from the network user's viewpoint. Both LANs support the same network operating systems and offer the same network facilities. Unless you have a particular reason for preferring a broadband LAN (see below), you should consider only baseband. The vast majority of PC LAN products are baseband; all the "standard" products are of this type; and baseband is less expensive to buy and easier to install and maintain.

There are several possible rationales for choosing broadband anyway. These include:

- For other reasons, you prefer a particular LAN product that just happens to be a broadband implementation.

- You need a LAN to cover a range of 20 miles or so. Since broadband technology has a slight edge in covering such distances, you may have to consider using it.

- Your organization has a broadband cable already installed, and you are told that you had better make use of it.

There were more broadband LAN products in the PC marketplace in the early years than there are today. The time may come when broadband options for PCs all but disappear.

Installing a LAN

There are four major steps in installing a LAN:

1. Laying the cable.
2. Putting the NICs in the PCs.
3. Installing the network operating system.
4. Setting up the network administration.

In a small office, you may choose to install the cabling yourself, but be aware of building codes, fire codes, union restrictions, and common sense safety precautions. For a large installation, it would be foolhardy not to let professional contractors do the job, especially if you are using coax.

The tasks of installing NICs and loading network software in PCs are usually straightforward ones for a technically competent person. For small networks, in fact, LAN installation often proves to be surprisingly easy. Unfortunately, if you do run into a problem, it may be hard to solve without sophisticated equipment of a kind you're not likely to have on hand. A single loose cable connection that's hard to spot can jam up a whole net. You may feel more secure having a consultant install the network for you, but you may learn more by doing it yourself. Then again, you might learn faster by watching an expert do it. If it makes you feel better, you can always do it again yourself afterwards.

There's not much that can be said in general about installing network software. Here again, product differences overwhelm the common points. Setting up user PCs is often a breeze: you just copy a few files onto the boot volume and add a couple of lines to the AUTOEXEC.BAT file. The installation of server software is usually well automated, so all you need do is pop in a few diskettes and make some menu selections. Some products, however, exhibit a few perversely obscure menu options.

The administrative phase of network installation entails organizing the file servers, loading network applications, establishing user accounts for LANs that require them, and setting up permissions or passwords. When the users are not competent to handle such tasks themselves, the administrator must also set up disk mappings (mapping local drive names into network volumes) for each user, and create batch files to simplify network operations (e.g., printing on shared printers).

Note the absence of a configuration step in the installation process. PC LANs are all self-configuring, so there's no need to do anything like supplying the network software with a list of the PCs attached to the cable.

When you're installing a LAN, start small. Don't attempt to bring up a network of 50 PCs in one shot. Begin with a few and expand gradually. Building a network incrementally is very easy. In most cases, new stations can be plugged into the network and put into operation without disturbing existing users in any way. It's also possible to power PCs on and off without disrupting network operations, except that turning off a server will incommode any users accessing it at the time. If you're installing a very large LAN, it's also a good idea to build a second "test" LAN on which you can check out NICs before adding them to the real network. Such an off-line network will also allow you to practice other tasks, such as bringing servers up and down, without inconveniencing users.

14 LOCAL AREA NETWORKS: PRACTICE AND PRODUCTS

This chapter explores the practical details of PC LANs and discusses the leading products.

LAN CABLING SYSTEMS

In May of 1984, IBM introduced the *IBM Cabling System*. Although IBM and other manufacturers market its physical constituents, the Cabling System is not so much a line of equipment as a set of recommendations for IBM customers on installing cable in new and old buildings. IBM then announced that its future products would be designed to make use of these cables. The first product to do so was the IBM Token-Ring Network.

The Cabling System specifies types of cable for both data and voice transmission, and lists associated connectors, distribution panels, faceplates, test equipment, and accessories. It also includes a software program for PCs, called the *IBM Cable Data Management System*. The Cabling System is designed for all types of communication, not just LANs. It is introduced in this chapter because of its relevance to the Token-Ring.

IBM proposed its Cabling System as a solution to three perceived problems in the office environment:

- The general lack of connectivity between different types of office equipment.
- A lack of standards for cables. Different office equipment lines, even from the same vendor, often required incompatible cable types.
- The rising costs of cable installation.

Here's a summary of the cable types described by the Cabling System:

Type 1 Data Cable, intended, as the name implies, for data communications, consists of two shielded twisted pairs of 22-awg solid conductors. Versions of this cable are sold for use in plenum, for outdoor use, and for "regular" use (indoor, nonplenum). Cutaway samples are shown in Figure 14.1.

Type 2 Data & Telephone Cable is composed of two shielded 22-awg twisted pairs for data (like Type 1) plus four unshielded 22-awg twisted pairs for telephone use. Type 2 cables comes in plenum and nonplenum versions, as shown in Figure 14.2.

Type 5 Fiber Optics Cable consists of two 100/140-micron optical fibers and is suitable for installation almost anywhere. Optical fiber, discussed in Chapter 4, has three advantages over electrical wire: freedom from electrical interference, absence of electromagnetic emissions, and inability to cause electrical fires.

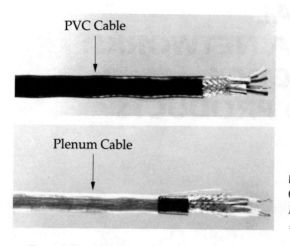

PVC Cable

Plenum Cable

FIGURE 14.1: IBM Type 1 data cables.
Q *Reprinted with permission of Black Box Corporation, Pittsburgh, PA. Copyright ©1987.*

Type 6 Data Cable comprises two shielded twisted pairs of 26-awg stranded conductors. Available for nonplenum use only, this very flexible cable is intended for making short patch leads.

Type 8 Undercarpet Cable consists of a single shielded twisted pair of 26-awg solid conductors. This low-profile data cable has beveled edges to minimize visual and tactile intrusiveness when laid under carpeting.

Three types of connectors are designed for use with the above cables. Two styles of telephone jack, similar in appearance to the familiar RJ type, are provided for use with the telephone cables. A self-mating (genderless) data connector, pictured in Figure 14.3, works with the data cables. All three connectors are affixed to their cables without wire stripping or soldering.

Oddly, the Cabling System includes no coaxial or twinaxial cables, the mainstays of cabling for the most common IBM terminal systems, the 3270s and 5250s. The System does provide gadgets for interconnecting coax and twinax cables with both Type 1 and Type 2 Data Cables, thus allowing 3270 and 5250 devices to make use of the Cabling System instead of their usual cables.

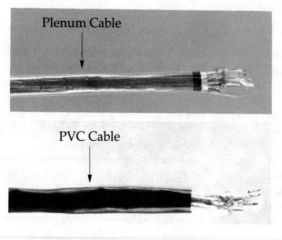

Plenum Cable

PVC Cable

FIGURE 14.2: IBM Type 2 data cables.
Reprinted with permission of Black Box Corporation, Pittsburgh, PA. Copyright ©1987.

FIGURE 14.3: IBM data connector.
*Reprinted with permission of Black Box Corporation,
Pittsburgh, PA. Copyright ©1987.*
All rights reserved.

The IBM Cable Data Management System is a utility program designed to assist in the planning, installation, and maintenance of the Cabling System. This software assists in laying out a building's cabling, calculating cable lengths and accessory requirements, estimating costs of hardware and installation, and preparing cable labels and location charts.

After IBM published its cabling system, AT&T, not to be outdone, came out with a similar scheme, the *AT&T Premises Distribution System*.

Topologies

Every LAN has a topology, or "network shape," which describes the physical pattern of its cabling. Figure 14.4 shows the four commonly encountered topologies: the *bus*, the *branching bus*, the *star*, and the *string of stars*. The simplest of these, the bus, consists of a single run of cable into which all stations are hooked. The branching bus, also called a *tree*, is a cable with multiple tributaries into which stations may hook at any point. The star has a master station at its center, with other stations individually connected by spokes. The string of stars is composed of a set of wiring centers, one at the center of each star, and stations on the periphery.

Most of the networks we'll examine in detail are organized in either branching bus (e.g., Ethernet) or string of stars (e.g., Token-Ring) form. The single star formation matches the wiring system used by a PBX; a few LANs, including the once-unassailable Novell®S-Net, have also been designed this way, but this is not a popular choice for LANs. Each of a single star network's stations has a private, rather than a shared, communication path, so such LANs are exceptions to the norm in many ways.

With the exception of single stars, the topology of a particular LAN has no direct bearing on network performance and no particular implications for the user beyond the layout and amount of cable required. Those who have notions of assembling a LAN using existing cable may find it essential to adopt one particular topology.

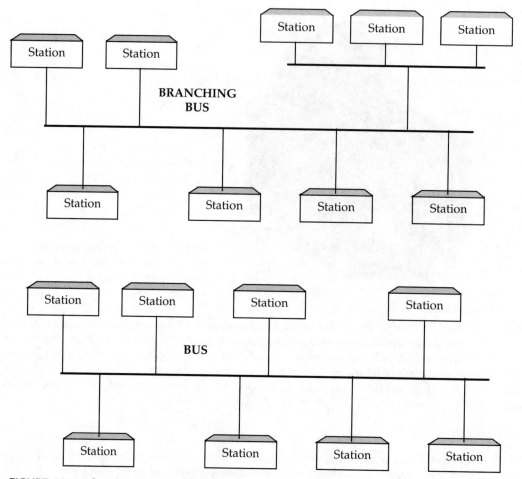

FIGURE 14.4a: Standard LAN Topologies

HOW LAN HARDWARE WORKS

Almost all LANs are engineered in keeping with two philosophical tenets:

First, no single station should be a single point of failure. Network design should not make any given station so critical to network operation that its failure will cause the whole network to go down. The concern here is with network hardware and the low-level communications infrastructure that the hardware creates. Of course, if a LAN's single centralized file server goes down, users may not be able to get much work done, but such failures are not relevant here. Even with the server out of action, the remaining stations should be able to continue communicating with each other (although this might not be very productive). This first criterion, then, implies that the responsibility for maintaining orderly communication must not be vested in any single station, but should be distributed equally among all stations. It also demands that network operation not be disrupted when stations are powered on and off.

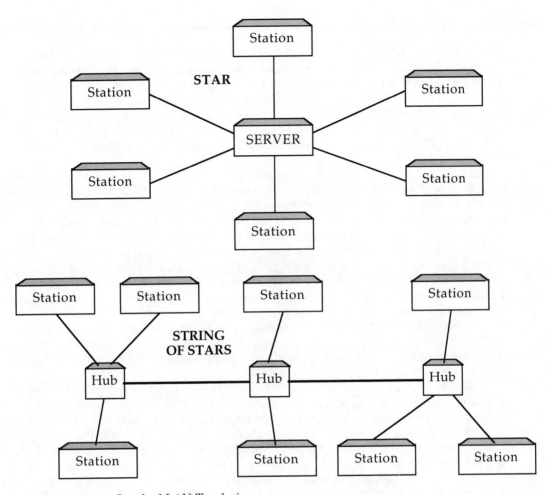

FIGURE 14.4b: Standard LAN Topologies

Second, stations should be equals. Networks should provide equal opportunity of network access to all stations; that is, no station should get to use the network more than another. This might not always be desirable in practice, since certain applications fit better into a prioritized network access scheme. When such prioritization is required, it is better to implement it at higher layers, specifically in network protocols. The Token-Ring, for example, while strictly peer-oriented at the hardware level, allows messages to be handled in priority order.

The lowest level of a LAN, a combination of Layers 1 and 2 in OSI terms, determines how stations transmit and receive on the network cable, and how access to the cable is managed. The second level, called *Medium Access Control (MAC)*, is the difficult one. The MAC must ensure that only one station transmits at a time, and that all stations have the same opportunity to transmit.

We will examine the two leading means of medium access control: *CSMA/CD* (Carrier Sense Multiple Access with Collision Detection) and *token passing*. Bear in mind that the flow of traffic on a LAN is affected by both its the topology (layout of cable connections) and its MAC, which dictates the movement of what might be considered control signals.

CSMA/CD

CSMA/CD is the MAC used by several LAN products, including Ethernet and IBM's PC Network. All CSMA/CD LANs are organized with a bus or branching bus topology. Since all stations are hooked into what is effectively a single cable, the LAN functions as a broadcast system at the transmission level: when one station transmits, its signal flows across the entire cable and is received by all other active stations. However, each message contains the address of the station it's destined for, so only the intended recipient will pay attention to it. The procedures prescribed by CSMA/CD ensure that only one station broadcasts its message at a time.

The CSMA/CD control technique consists of two steps. The first, the "carrier sense multiple access" part, is easy enough. It dictates that a station wishing to transmit must first check that no other station is transmitting. If the cable is quiet, the station starts transmitting; if there is already a signal on the cable, the station waits until the cable becomes quiet. CSMA is a straightforward procedure, but does not in itself suffice to prevent conflicts. If two stations attempt to transmit at the same instant and find the cable available, they will both begin transmitting; their signals will mess each other up, and communication will be ineffective. Such a conflict can occur even if the two stations don't pick exactly the same moment to attempt transmission. Suppose one station begins transmitting a few microseconds before another, physically distant from the first, decides to send a message. The second station finds the cable quiet because, due to propagation delays, the signal from the first has not yet reached it. Thus, there is a substantial "window" in which conflicts can occur. For any two stations, the time width of this window is proportional to the length of the cable connecting them.

CSMA/CD networks allow such conflicts, called *collisions*, to occur, but then resolve them very quickly by means of "collision detection," the second part of the procedure. The actual detection of collisions is easy: each station continues to listen to the cable while it is transmitting. In fact, every active station is always listening to the cable. If a transmitting station hears a signal for which it is not responsible, it recognizes that one or more other stations must also be transmitting and that a collision has occurred. Any other stations transmitting at that instant also detect the collision in the same way, and all stations "back off," that is, stop transmitting. Now comes the hard part: the colliding stations must "decide" among themselves which will get the turn to transmit. It would be easy enough to arbitrate among them by either a pre-established priority or the decision of some master station. Such options are ruled out, however, by the criteria set forth above: a master station would violate the requirement that there be no single point of network failure, and the priority method would prevent stations from being peers. Instead, the conflict is resolved by a method that resembles having the stations roll dice to choose their turns.

After backing off, each of the colliding stations picks a random number, using the pseudo-random-number generator built into its NIC, and then begins a waiting period of length proportional to its number. When a station's waiting period expires, it checks the cable again. If it hears any activity, it knows that it must wait until some other, luckier station completes its transmission. If the cable is quiet, the station knows it is the first one to time out, so it starts transmitting. Of course, two or more stations may occasionally generate the same (or nearly the same) random number, time out simultaneously, and collide again. That's fine: they simply repeat the procedure, generating new random numbers. When many stations collide, this procedure may be invoked several times until all stations but one are winnowed out. In practice, most collisions are resolved on the first attempt; there may sometimes be as many as eight or nine repeated collisions, but very rarely more.

Although CSMA/CD may seem a bit primitive, it's a well-established and very effective technology. Even the occasional eight-times-repeated collision is resolved within a few milliseconds, and network users are not aware of any problem. Of course, we could dream up a nightmare network on which every station was always ready to transmit. With CSMA/CD, such a LAN, even if only moderately large, would spend most of its time resolving collisions, and performance would be dreadful. Fortunately, the transmission patterns of real networks almost never get that bad.

Some details were purposely omitted from the above description of CSMA/CD. When a station detects a collision, it briefly transmits some garbage data, known as the *jamming signal*, before going quiet. This step ensures that every station involved in a collision will realize the fact. There's no danger that any station will treat such an aborted message as valid, because the jamming signal is designed to be shorter than the shortest acceptable message. Another refinement to the scheme is that, when repeated collisions occur, the colliding stations generate random numbers selected from increasingly large intervals, thus raising the chances that they will pick different numbers and avoid further collisions.

A frequently cited illustration of CSMA/CD is the cocktail party analogy. Picture a group of people, drinks in hand. At a sudden lull in conversation, several of the rather well lubricated guests jump in and start talking at once. Collision! After a few seconds (or more, depending on the lubrication level), all the speakers realize what has happened, back off, and look around trying to decide who will get his say. A couple of people pipe up again, causing a second, smaller collision. Eventually, someone—the most assertive, the best-oiled, or the one with good timing—gets the floor.

Token Passing

Token passing, the main competition to CSMA/CD, takes a much more orderly approach to medium access control. Here, a virtual entity called a *token* is passed around the LAN from station to station by means of a special protocol message. A station may transmit one data message only when it receives the token. After the transmission, or if it has no message to send, it must immediately pass the token to the next station.

In some ways, the token is like a baton in a relay race. Just as the baton is passed from runner to runner, the token is passed from station to station. And as a runner may use the track only while holding the baton, a station may use the cable only while holding the token. The token may thus be regarded as a symbol of temporary permission to use the network for data transmission.

There are two variants on token passing: the *token-passing bus*, as used by ARCNET®, and the *token-passing ring*, exemplified by IBM's Token-Ring. The evolution of token-passing schemes has been such that operational differences between the ring and bus types are now comparatively minor, but it's useful to explore their basic structures.

The Token-Passing Bus

The cabling system of a token-passing bus is topologically equivalent to that of Ethernet. Thus, it is fundamentally a broadcast network in the sense described above. Stations are given addresses consisting of numbers in a fairly narrow range, from 1 to 255 in the case of ARCNET. The token is systematically passed from station to station in address order. When a station receives the token, it may transmit one data message and wait for its

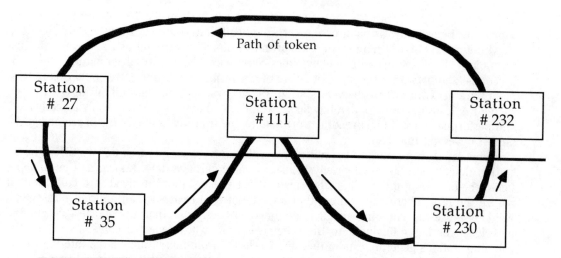

FIGURE 14.5: Token-Passing Bus

acknowledgment; it must then pass the token to the next numerically higher station. When a station with no outbound data message pending receives the token, it must pass it on immediately. The highest-numbered station passes the token back to the lowest-numbered. A station need not wait for the token before transmitting an acknowledgment of a received data message. The assignment of station addresses, and the resultant path of the token, are independent of the physical arrangement of stations on the cable, as illustrated in Figure 14.5.

In contrast to a CSMA/CD-type network, a token-passing network is constantly active. Even if no data are being transferred, the token is always whizzing around.

There's a small price to pay for the orderliness of the token-passing bus. When such a network commences operation, an initialization procedure must be carried out. This enables each station to determine the address of the next station in line, to which it must forward the token. Readers who have studied data structures will recognize this initialization as the establishment of a *singly linked circular list*. The list must be established dynamically, so that the network can operate with whatever stations happen to be on-line.

The initialization procedure, whose precise details depend on the token-bus design, is managed using time-outs. (Time-out schemes are immensely useful, and many networks, not just LANS, use them for various purposes.) When a new station comes on, it jams the network, destroying the current token and halting activity. A loss of activity is a very noticeable event in this kind of LAN, and all stations perceive it as an indication that the net must be reinitialized. By creating a new token, the new station takes charge of the reinitialization process whereby the list of stations is regenerated. Under normal circumstances, the process takes only a few milliseconds, does not interfere with network operation at the user level, and is not apparent to the users. However, where links are unreliable due to (say) electrical interference, as is sometimes the case in factory LAN installations, tokens may be obliterated for no apparent reason; if this happens frequently, token regeneration becomes all too obvious to the users.

When a station on a token bus is powered off, it is automatically dropped from the list of token receivers.

The protocol message that passes the token is very brief, and the time overhead for moving the token around is small—typically 2 percent or less. Equally important, this overhead is constant no matter how busy the network becomes.

The Token-Passing Ring

In a token-passing ring, stations may be cabled together in individual point-to-point links that form a physical ring. Figure 14.6 shows how the hubs in a string of stars effectively convert the topology into that of a physical ring for the token, whose passage is shown by arrows. Since signals are relayed from one station to the next, this arrangement, unlike the previously discussed ones, is not a broadcast system. The token is passed much as on the bus, but moves around the physical ring, as opposed to the logical ring of station addresses.

When a station with no data to send receives the token, it passes it on immediately. If the station does have a message to transmit, it replaces the token with the message. The message is then passed around the ring to its intended recipient, which reads and retransmits it after setting some acknowledgment bits. The modified message completes the circuit around the ring, landing back at its originator station. The setting of the acknowledgment bits tells the originator whether its message was received; a lack of acknowledgment normally means that the destination station is not active on the network. When its message is returned, acknowledged or not, the originating station replaces it with a token.

This token-passing procedure is somewhat more sophisticated in networks that allow stations to reserve the token in advance. In such systems, network software gives priority assignments to certain messages awaiting transmission. If a station that relays a message generated by another station has a message of its own to send, it may store its own address and message priority in a special field within the message being relayed, provided that no higher-priority reservation has already been made. (Typically, a station asserting priority may request any of several hierarchically organized priority levels.) Then, unless its reservation is subsequently overridden by another station with a message of higher priority, the relaying station is guaranteed first use of the regenerated token. All priority reservations are temporary in that they expire when used, but there's nothing to prevent a reservation

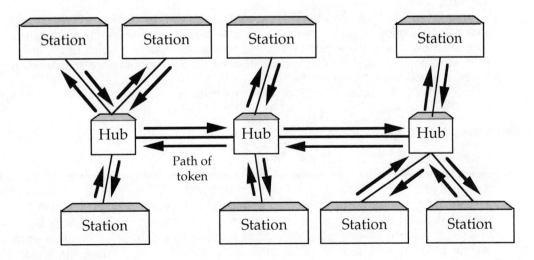

FIGURE 14.6: Token-Passing Ring

being reasserted by a station when it sends its next message. While almost universally implemented, priority assignment systems are not often used, for two reasons: they make it at least theoretically possible for a few stations to hog the network, and the token-passing ring does a pretty good job of distributing service to all stations without the use of priority anyway. Our description of the priority system is somewhat simplified; curious readers are directed to the IEEE 802.5 standard document for a thorough explanation.

Other MACs

Although CSMA/CD and token-passing are the predominant MACs in LANs, a few other systems are in use, including a variation of CSMA/CD called CSMA/CA. The "CA" stands for *collision avoidance*, a scheme to prevent collisions from happening in the first place. A combination of CSMA/CD and CSMA/CA has also been used.

LAN Standards

LAN standards are being prepared by several organizations, but the only ones in effect at this writing are the IEEE 802 standards adopted for the lower OSI layers we have been studying here. Four are relevant to PC LANs.

802.3 describes a CSMA/CD network based on Ethernet, with several extensions. The original Ethernet, and its early revisions, fall a little short of compliance with the standard; later Ethernets conform fully.

802.4 describes a type of token-passing bus system found in some factory automation LANS. ARCNET, the only token-passing bus LAN commonly used with PCs, differs considerably from this standard.

802.5 describes a token-passing ring running at 4 Mbps over twisted-pair cable. IBM's Token-Ring Network follows this standard.

802.2 describes a Logical Link Control (LLC). In LAN architecture, the OSI model's Data Link Layer, which delivers data packets across the link, is normally split into two sublayers. The lower sublayer is implemented by a MAC, as discussed above. The upper sublayer is implemented by a protocol like LLC, which strongly resembles HDLC and, consequently, the frame level of X.25.

In its frames, LLC carries addresses for both source and destination, with the destination address conditioned to permit multicasting (one-to-many transmission) and broadcasting (one-to-all transmission), in addition to one-to-one transmission. Since LLC can be used with any type of MAC, it forms a consistent low-level network interface and shields higher layers of network software from the MAC.

In addition to the formal IEEE 802 standards, there is one strong de facto LAN standard, ARCNET, discussed below in the section on LAN hardware products.

Which MAC Should You Choose?

When selecting a LAN, should you put your money on a CSMA/CD network, a token bus, or a token ring? The simple answer is that in most cases it doesn't matter. All the MACs described above are reliable and can perform well under average conditions. Conventional wisdom favors CSMA/CD for traffic that is "bursty" and token passing for settings in which network demand is very consistent. This makes sense in theory, and is valuable as a rule of thumb. In practice, however, traffic patterns rarely conform to such convenient extremes, and the choice of a MAC makes little difference in the long run. There are so many other, more important criteria for choosing one type of network over another that the type of MAC should be given little weight.

One exception to the above statement is vital: the MAC decidedly does matter for networks running real-time applications, those that must respond to events in real time lest something bad happen. "Something bad" could be a guided missile going off course, a $1,000,000 money transfer getting lost, or the death of a patient being monitored in a hospital. For such networks, token passing is likely to be fine, but CSMA/CD LANs should not be considered, because they don't impose a sufficiently strict limit on how long a station may have to wait before getting an opportunity to transmit. All stations are supposed to get fair and equal service, and they do—but only in a statistical sense. On a heavily loaded network with continual collisions, a station unlucky in generating random numbers could wait indefinitely for service. "Unlucky" means that, even if the station manages to generate the lowest random number in a group of colliding stations, another station does so, too. On a token-passing LAN, the token's orderly progression through the net and the strict limit on a station's "holding period" allow designers to state precisely the maximum time a station will have to wait for the token.

LAN HARDWARE PRODUCTS

The following are the preeminent hardware LAN products now available.

Ethernet

Ethernet was developed by XEROX® in the 1970s, initially alone and later in partnership with DEC and Intel™. The primary vendor of PC Ethernets is 3Com® Corporation, with other products offered by such companies as Excelan® and Torus Systems. Gordon Metcalfe, founder of 3Com®, was one of the inventors of Ethernet. As stated above, the 802.3 standard was based on Ethernet, but with a few extra features. Ethernet is considered the standard LAN in laboratory and research environments, and it is used in a fair number of PC-LAN installations.

Ethernet is a baseband CSMA/CD network operating at 10 Mbps over a maximum cable distance of 2,500 meters (approximately a mile and a half). It's one of the most flexible kinds of LAN, allowing a variety of cable types to be used for connections. The original design called for thick coaxial cable, but options now include thin coax, twisted pair, and optical fiber. Network construction is simplest if a single type is used throughout, but adapters such as 3Com's MultiConnect™ Repeater permit the use of any combination of the cable options. Although thin coax has traditionally been the most popular for PC use, it seems likely to give way to twisted pair.

Figure 14.7 is a diagram of a typical Ethernet, built from segments of coaxial cable interconnected in treelike fashion by repeaters. A repeater takes the signal off one cable segment and retransmits it on another. A network might, for example, have a separate cable segment on each floor of a building. In an Ethernet, an ordinary repeater interconnects two cable segments that are near each other, and a *remote repeater* is available to interconnect widely separated segments, perhaps in different buildings. One remote repeater is allowed per bus on the network, supporting a point-to-point link between segments up to 1,000 meters (0.62 miles) apart.

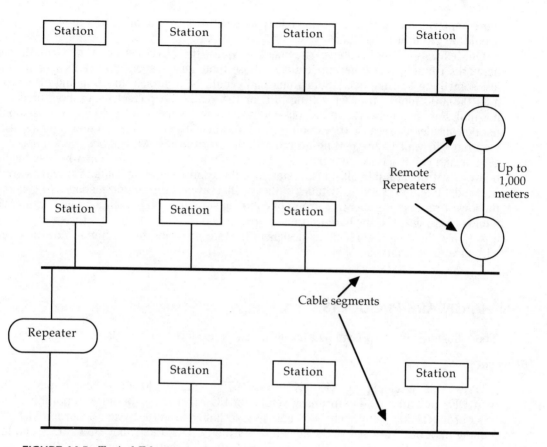

FIGURE 14.7: Typical Ethernet configuration

A few PC LANs that use CSMA/CD as their media access method are not Ethernet-compatible because they do not follow Ethernet's prescriptions for baseband operation, data rate, or cable type.

ARCNET

ARCNET was developed in the early days of LANs by Datapoint, a computer manufacturer. It was introduced in 1977 and has become one of the most widely installed LANs. Datapoint at first kept the ARCNET technology to itself, but in the early 1980s began licensing it to microcomputer vendors, including Radio Shack. Several companies sell ARCNET gear for PCs, chiefly Standard Microsystems (SMC®), manufacturer of the chip set used to construct the network interface.

ARCNET is a baseband network that accommodates up to 255 stations at distances of up to four miles, with a signaling speed of 2.5 Mbps. Its internal design (the specific details of its token-passing organization) is uncommonly simple, "elegant" in engineering terms.

Physically, an ARCNET is built around boxes called *hubs*, in a string of stars configuration. The hub's purpose is similar to that served by Ethernet's repeaters. Each station is connected to a nearby hub by its own private coaxial cable link; the hubs are hooked together with coax links, resulting in a treelike topology that often involves lots of branching. Hubs traditionally supported 4, 8, or 16 stations. In 1987, ARCNET adapters for PCs began appearing with built-in two-port hubs so that connected PCs formed "linear" networks, which might be viewed as having a simplified string of stars topology.

In addition to SMC, several other companies, including PureData, sell ARCNET products for PCs. An enhanced version of ARCNET developed by SMC and operating at 5 Mbps, twice the former speed, may prove popular in coming years.

The IBM Token-Ring Network

In 1984, IBM made known its intention of producing a token-ring–based LAN that would eventually interconnect all its major computer types. The first products, announced in late 1985, were for constructing PC networks, and mini and mainframe interfaces have followed. The PC Token-Ring is a baseband network operating at 4 Mbps over twisted pair or optical fiber cable. IBM has also recently announced Token-Ring products running at 16 Mbps over optical fiber. The largest current configuration accommodates a maximum of 260 stations.

The IBM Token-Ring Network employs a newer and more complex technology than Ethernet or ARCNET. It precisely follows IEEE 802.5, a standard to which IBM made a substantial contribution. Participation in the development of a formal standard, and subsequent adherence to that standard, are rather unusual for IBM. Because its Token-Ring follows an open standard, other companies are able to offer compatible products. At the heart of the Token-Ring adapter is a chip set known as TMS 380, manufactured by IBM for its own use and by licensee Texas Instruments®for sale to others. The set originally consisted of three microprocessors and two interface chips, all of which were recently redesigned into a single multifunction chip; a 16-Mbps version may be made available.

Physically, the IBM Token-Ring Network is constructed around wiring boxes called *multistation access units (MAUs)*. IBM's MAU has 10 connectors of the data connector type described for the IBM Cabling System. Each station is connected to a local MAU by an individual cable, which uses up 8 of the 10 connectors; the other 2 connectors are used to string MAUs together. The topology, then, is a string of stars, each of which has an MAU at the center. Other vendors offer MAUs in smaller sizes for wiring up fewer than eight stations. MAUs may be located in wiring closets, hidden under desks, or tucked in corners. The wiring distances permitted between MAU pairs, and between an MAU and a station, vary according to the type of cable used.

Token-Ring Networks can be assembled with any of the data cables described by the IBM Cabling System, including optical fibers. PCs may also be wired to MAUs by unshielded telephone-type cables; this will work satisfactorily in many environments, but the option should be considered with some caution. MAU-to-MAU connections must be made with shielded data cable.

IBM PC Network®

PC Network, introduced in late 1984, was IBM's first LAN product—first, that is, if you don't count the earlier PC Cluster, which had such feeble facilities (read-only file sharing, for example) that it was quickly abandoned. The original PC Network, co-designed by IBM and Sytek (a now-defunct company), used CSMA/CD at 2 Mbps on a broadband cable, and achieved limited success. Many observers thought it was doomed when IBM announced its Token-Ring products in late 1985, but IBM surprised the industry first by keeping the old PC Network alive, and again by introducing a revamped baseband version in 1987. IBM states that the Token-Ring is intended for large PC LANs, especially those requiring links to mainframes and other IBM systems, while the less expensive PC Network is appropriate for smaller LANs needing PC support alone. PC Network also supports, as a file server, an IBM Series/1 mini.

AT&T StarLAN™

StarLAN, another CSMA/CD network, was designed as a pared-down version of Ethernet suited to PCs, and has been adopted as part of the IEEE 802.3 standard. Because single-chip CSMA/CD controllers are available, and because StarLAN operates at a relatively slow 1 Mbps, it is one of the more economical networks available.

Other LANs

While neither a household name nor conforming to a network standard, Gateway Communications' G/Net™ is among the most successful PC LANs. G/Net uses a combination of CSMA/CD and Collision Avoidance on baseband RG-59 coax at 1.4 Mbps, supporting up to 100 PCs over 4,000 feet (about 1.2 kilometers). Although LANs that follow neither a formal nor a de facto standard must generally be recommended with caution, G/Net is rated very highly by many commentators. Gateway Communications is also known for its LAN-gateway and Ethernet products.

Token-passing LAN products predated IEEE 802.5 and IBM's Token-Ring. Proteon® has sold a proprietary high-performance 10-Mbps token-ring LAN for several years, and also makes a line of 802.5-compatible products.

Corvus was another early entrant in the microcomputer LAN market with Omninet™, which uses CSMA/CA at 1 Mbps twisted pair. Omninet is notable because it supports an amazing range of computers, including the Apple II and certain Commodore® and Atari® models.

HOW LAN SOFTWARE WORKS

LAN support software is known as the *network operating system*, here abbreviated "NOS" for convenience. We will emphasize networking in the DOS context. Our discussion of networking with OS/2 is limited: at this writing, many questions are still unanswered. IBM has announced the OS/2 LAN Server, but details of this product remain under wraps.

The IBM NETBIOS

IBM's PC Network has limited importance as a product per se, but it enjoys great historical significance, because it introduced the NETBIOS. Chapter 1 described the PC BIOS, which provides a set of standard functions for operating systems and other software to access standard PC devices. What the BIOS does for PCs, the NETBIOS does for PC LANs.

The IBM NETBIOS serves as a Session-Layer protocol, in OSI terms, allowing a pair of programs on the network to establish, use, and terminate a communications session. These programs use the session to pass back and forth messages of an Application-Layer protocol, the one that does the "real work." Several application protocols may be at work concurrently on the network for different purposes, but the most heavily used is generally the file service protocol. Although a majority of PC-LAN vendors have adopted NETBIOS, making it a de facto Layer 5 standard, many use their own proprietary file-serving protocols; IBM, for example, uses Server Message Block (SMB).

NETBIOS defines a set of 17 commands that programs may call to invoke network functions. A fundamental NETBIOS feature is the ADD NAME and DELETE NAME commands for registration of names identifying an entity on the network. Each active program in a PC can establish a unique network alias for itself; programs can then initiate NETBIOS sessions by "calling" one another by name. When a program attempts to register a new name, the NETBIOS searches through the LAN registry and halts the process if the name is already in use.

The CALL, LISTEN, and HANG UP commands enable pairs of programs to establish network sessions for the controlled exchange of data. Commands such as SEND and RECEIVE are used to transfer data messages between session participants. In addition, messages called *datagrams* may be sent outside of the session context, for example, for broadcast to all stations. Among other things, datagram broadcasts are used in the process of confirming the uniqueness of names submitted for registration.

The Redirector

In addition to NETBIOS, there is a second method by which application programs running under DOS may use a network. For network resources that are accessible exactly like local resources, such as reading and writing shared files on a network disk, the program simply employs DOS services. The pathname of a file betrays its local or network character, but the application program cannot tell the difference, since it knows only the file name furnished by the user. Suppose you instruct Excel™ to load a spreadsheet called "E:SALES." In this case, all Excel knows is that this name identifies a file and fits the syntax prescribed by the operating system.

Before being acted upon by DOS, all operating-system requests are filtered through a software routine that determines whether they refer to local or network resources. This routine can identify the volume cited in the example (the E in E:SALES) as a local or network disk. If the disk is local, the request is handed off to DOS for execution as usual. Otherwise, the request is passed across the network to the appropriate server. In IBM's NOS, the PC LAN Program, this filtering software is called the *Redirector*. When the network software is loaded, the Redirector becomes an integral part of DOS. Other NOS vendors provide Redirector emulators that similarly intercept DOS calls and perform necessary redirections. In either case, DOS itself remains ignorant of the network.

For multi-user application programs, the DOS services invoked include those added in version 3.0 for locking and unlocking file access. According to the parameters provided, this service either locks a contiguous range of bytes within a file or unlocks a range that was locked by a previous call. To lock an entire file, then, a program invokes a lock on the complete range of bytes contained in that file. Although standard database management practice would execute locking on a record-by-record basis, this more flexible mechanism permits the locking of a field, an item, or a single byte.

For distributed processing, the two programs running in different PCs communicate with each other by interfacing directly with, and through, the NETBIOS. However, this is possible only under DOS and certain DOS emulators, such as Microsoft's Windows/386. Programs tailored for OS/2 are physically prevented from calling either NETBIOS or PC BIOS functions directly. Microsoft's LAN Manager for OS/2 provides an alternative in the form of the *pipe*, introduced in Chapter 1. In this setting, a pipe is similar to a NETBIOS session, but it is accessed and named more like a file. The network software not only transmits, but also buffers data between the programs writing to and reading from the pipe. For full-duplex dialog, a pair of pipes is required, one for each direction.

OS/2 Networking via Named Pipes

Under OS/2, Microsoft's LAN Manager gives applications a single common interface to network services, in preference to the DOS method of requiring each application to provide its own interface to a specific network product via NETBIOS or an equivalent emulator. The interface provided by LAN Manager is at a fairly high level, typically lying between the application and the pipe mechanism. LAN Manager extends named pipes (Chapter 1) to make them visible, and thus accessible, to processes located not merely within one machine, but also in other machines on the network. From an application's viewpoint, the network is therefore transparent: the act of writing to a pipe that terminates in a local machine is indistinguishable from the act of writing to a pipe that flows to a remote machine. Just as importantly, applications need not become bogged down in network-related details, such as network addresses and boundaries, retransmission of lost packets, and so on. In this respect, the interface provided by the pipe mechanism is similar to the interface provided by the file system. In both cases, requests from applications are translated into low-level calls to (disk or network) device drivers, of which the applications themselves can remain ignorant. As we'll explain, DOS-based applications using NETBIOS find it far more difficult to ignore the network.

Within OS/2, named pipes are used primarily to create *server-requestor connections*, in which one process provides services in response to requests made by other processes. A simple example is a print spooler: when the requestor sends a stream of text to be printed, the server queues it up for printing. Here, the text stream itself constitutes part of the "request." The requestor process is then free to perform other activities, leaving the server to handle the mechanics of printing. Similarly, a file server, on receiving requests for files, responds by returning the requested data or, perhaps, annoying messages such as "file not found" or "permission denied."

APIs for OS/2 LANs

Whenever two or more processes communicate over named pipes, some sort of protocol is needed to facilitate their interaction. In this context, we will follow the IBM-Microsoft convention and refer to such a protocol as an API (Application Program Interface).

We first discussed APIs in the specialized context of 3270 emulation (Chapter 12), and will take a broader view of the subject in Chapter 16. For now, we'll make a few observations relevant to OS/2 networking. An API is a *software interface* that can help any two programs communicate with each other; here, as just noted, application programs use APIs to access named pipes for communication over the net. Such an API, as defined by IBM, actually has two components, an (upper) API and a (lower) protocol. The application sees only the API just below it; as long as it has a decent interface to the protocol below, it neither knows nor cares how the protocol operates. The protocol, of course, sets the rules for the communication. Again, we can view this arrangement as one that allows the application to issue comparatively high-level requests, which the API proper converts into "calls" to the protocol.

Two more facts are pertinent to our OS/2 discussion. First, these hybrid APIs are implemented by, and coexist at the same level with, LAN Manager, which means that they lie between the application and the pipe mechanism. Second, such APIs are often named for their protocol component. Below, we continue to use this terminology.

An OS/2 LAN File Server at Work

To see how a file-service API might work for both server and requestor, let's consider a simplified version of FTP, a file transfer protocol in the DDN protocol suite (Chapter 8), under OS/2. Assume that, on start-up, the server will create a named pipe called FILEMEAWAY, to which any requester may write. The requestor, which may be an application such as a word processor or spreadsheet program, connects to this pipe and begins writing its requests. By convention of our hypothetical API, a requestor about to use the file server must open a named pipe of its own to receive data. The new pipe's name consists of the username (here, let's suppose, belonging to the human user associated with the requestor) with "FTP" appended; thus, with user CARWASH, the requestor's pipe name will be CARWASHFTP. This suggests that the human user may be seen as part of the requestor process.

In the dialog below, the API commands shown are those sent down the pipe by server and requestor processes, denoted by S: and R:, respectively; we explain their meanings where not obvious. The numerical codes correspond to messages generated by the server.

Commands
USER - identifies a user for login
PASS - precedes the user's password
RETR - retrieve a file
QUIT - discontinue the file transfer session

S:	220 service ready	When the server is ready to work, it writes this command, which is therefore the first thing the requestor reads from the pipe
R:	USER CARWASH	The user "logs in" to the server
S:	331 user name ok, need password	
R:	PASS CHAMOIS	Password supplied
S:	230 user logged in	Acknowledging login complete
R:	RETR\BIGDISCUS\PRIVATE\MYOB.BUB	Asking to retrieve a file
S:	550 access denied	The particular file requested is one that the file server knows the user has no right to access
R:	RETR\BIGDISCUS\123\MYWRK.123	Requesting another file
S:	150 file status ok; opening data connection	At this point, the server begins writing data to the named pipe CARWASHFTP
S:	226 closing data connection; file transfer successful	
R:	RETR\BIGDISCUS\AUTOEXEC.BAT	
S:	150 file status ok; opening data connection	

R:	RETR\BIGDISCUS\CMD.EXE	Another file request made while the receiver is occupied
S:	425 can't open data connection	The assigned connection is being used to transfer AUTOEXEC-.BAT, and this API doesn't allow transfer of more than one file simultaneously
S:	226 closing data connection;	AUTOEXEC.BAT transfer complete
	file transfer successful	
R:	QUIT	Enough for now

This example of a simple API shows the kinds of messages a requestor application must send and be able to understand; perhaps this helps to explain IBM's use of the term *application program interface* in this setting. Note that the API determines the activities a user can perform. For example, since no command defined here allows the requestor to send a file to the server, the server essentially functions as a read-only device. A command could be added to permit the server to receive files from users; the server's functions might be further extended with commands to let users delete files, obtain lists of files, and abort transfers in progress. Like all APIs, this one also isolates its user (in the sense of "the program above it") from the underlying system; here, the human user's access to files in the directory \BIGDISKUS\PRIVATE is restricted, so the server doesn't allow certain files to be retrieved. Since the API is the only "language" the server understands, it can't be coerced or fooled into releasing files improperly.

Readers might have observed that many of these claims could equally well be made for DOS-based servers implemented without the benefit of OS/2, named pipes, or this API. True enough. The difference is that named pipes under OS/2 constitute a generic logical communications channel, allowing the programmer to implement an API and be done with it. Under DOS, on the other hand, he'd have to whip together something to interface directly with NETBIOS, creating a channel mechanism on which to operate the protocol. Because no two programmers think alike, each of these NETBIOS creations may be different from every other; getting both the API and the channel mechanism right can be very tiring for programmers who work with various applications and many different machines.

More Pipe Dreams

The named pipes facility can be used in concert with OS/2's multitasking facilities to allow workstations to perform "double duty" as nondedicated servers. Suppose that one LAN workstation has a large-capacity disk, on which a departmental database is stored. With the aid of a product like the 3Com LAN Manager, the workstation can be configured to come up as a server, that is, to start a server process automatically when it boots. A person using this station may access the same database and disk as other users, but need not even be aware that his or her machine is the LAN file server (except, perhaps, for all the activity going on in the busy drive). In addition, this user can access the database only through the API; because the API security "screen" cannot be penetrated, the user is prevented from tampering with database contents.

The flexibility of the named pipe as a generic interprocess communications facility, extended to be an intercomputer communications facility, makes it a simple building block out of which arbitrarily complex mechanisms can be constructed. Again, such generic interfaces allow the application programmer to focus on the task at hand, rather than on the foibles of the network hardware, confident that the developed API will run on all OS/2 machines. Many such APIs will also run on DOS 3.x computers. Further, since named pipes are a generic mechanism, they could, in principle, be implemented for any hardware, from Apple Macintoshes to IBM MVS™(Multiple Virtual Storage) systems.

Similar generic interfaces are becoming popular in other networking environments. For example, NFS™(Network File System), a product of Sun Microsystems®, is based on a named-pipe-like interface built into SunOS™, the operating system run on Sun Workstations. The Sun generic interface, known as Sockets, is not compatible with named pipes, but can be separately implemented on machines running OS/2.

In the same vein, APIs that incorporate various protocols are increasingly important for both DOS- and OS/2-based networking. APIs have been developed to transfer electronic mail (SMTP, MTP, and X.400), perform remote database queries (Sybase and CL/I®), and even support remote terminal sessions on other hosts, a form of "long-distance login" cited in Chapter 11 as being handled well by OS/2. For example, Telnet, an over-the-net terminal emulator protocol, allows an OS/2 machine to log into a computer running another type of operating system across a network; rlogin performs a similar function for two computers using a UNIX shell; and VTP supports remote login in a general ISO context.

Aspects of Network Operating Systems

What components make up an NOS such as the IBM PC LAN Program, Novell's NetWare®, or 3Com's 3+Plus™? We can first break down the NOS into five parts:

- Resident networking software for workstations
- User interface software for user PCs
- Software for file servers
- Software for print and other servers
- Network utilities

Workstation Software

The resident networking software that runs in each user PC consists of a NIC device driver, IBM's Redirector or an equivalent emulator for networks under DOS, and some low-level network protocol software. For a NETBIOS-compatible LAN, the low-level protocol will be either IBM's NETBIOS or a NETBIOS emulator; for an OS/2-type network, a named-pipes implementation is used. The NIC driver, the software that manages the network interface, is loaded as an extension of the operating system, as is any other driver for a nonstandard device. Loading is triggered by a command in the PC's CONFIG.SYS file. Under DOS, the Redirector and low-level protocol components are normally loaded into memory at boot-up by commands in an AUTOEXEC.BAT file, and remain memory-resident in order to be available to all programs that need them. In the case of IBM's PC Network (an Ethernet-type network), the NETBIOS is provided in read-only memory (ROM) on the NIC. This is a convenience in that it prevents the NETBIOS code, which occupies about 44 KB, from taking up valuable space in RAM. (Even though the NETBIOS is on a NIC chip in PC Network, the NETBIOS is executed by the PC's, not the NIC's, processor.) In other networks, including the IBM Token-Ring, the NETBIOS is provided as software with the NOS.

The User Interface to the LAN

The user interface software for user stations provides the facilities that the PC user requires in order for the station to play its role on the LAN. Network functions may be accessed via either menus or a set of DOS- or OS/2-level commands, often at the user's option. To give you a sense of the user interface facilities, here are some sample commands from IBM's PC LAN Program, which runs under DOS. Note that they all commence with "NET."

NET START RDR LOUISE

The NET START command brings up the PC as a network station, and is normally placed in the AUTOEXEC.BAT file so that the PC will automatically join the network when it's powered on. The first parameter indicates whether the PC is to take the role of a user or a server; here, RDR, for Redirector, means that the Redirector software alone is to be loaded, and implies that the PC will function as a user. (The use of SRV instead of RDR here would mean that the PC would come up as a network server.) The second parameter gives the PC its network name, "LOUISE." An error message will be returned if the name is not unique to the net as currently constituted.

NET SHARE BOOK = C:\TEXT

The NET SHARE command defines a shared resource. Printers and disk directories may be shared. The example declares the directory \TEXT on the local disk C: to be sharable, with the network name of "BOOK." For this command to take effect, the PC must have been booted as a server.

NET USE E: \\LOUISE\HUG

The NET USE command grants a user access to a shared resource, here the same resource as in the previous example, and would be given on another station. The effect is to associate the drive specifier E: with the directory HUG on the station named LOUISE. A resource must be NET SHAREd before it can be NET USEd.

To access a shared printer, a user would issue a command of the form:

NET USE LPT2: \\DAVID\CRUMPLE

where CRUMPLE has previously been defined as a shared printer on station DAVID. Once the association between the user and printer has been defined, files may be dispatched for printing by means of a NET PRINT command, such as:

NET PRINT DOCUMENT LPT2:

There are a few more commands in the NET set, but the average user could get by knowing only those just described. By making judicious use of batch files, a naive user could even deal with the network without knowing any specific NET commands.

Any NOS must provide, at minimum, the functions performed by the commands listed above. How the user accesses these functions varies considerably from one product to another.

File Server Design

A file server essentially emulates DOS or OS/2 I/O functions for shared files. Each workstation's Redirector relays PC application programs' requests to the server: open or close files, read or write data, lock or unlock records, and so on. The server acts on the requests and returns the results to the workstation. A state-of-the-art server program is, however, enormously complex, because it involves many embellishments. A properly designed server will perform efficiently, provide needed security, and supply suitable management and monitoring tools.

Dedication to Service

There's one radical design difference between file servers intended for dedicated and nondedicated use: a dedicated file server can run with its own operating system, independently of DOS or OS/2, whereas a nondedicated server must coexist with DOS or OS/2. This is especially significant in the case of DOS-based networks, since DOS is a single-task system ill-equipped to juggle numerous file-I/O requests piling up from a crowd of workstations. By definition, a DOS-based file server must be seriously limited in performance, although nondedicated servers for small networks can play a few tricks to speed up DOS and achieve a satisfactory compromise.

The strongest products for dedicated file serving in DOS-based networks, such as Advanced NetWare, 3+Share™, and VINES™(all discussed in the next section), either incorporate proprietary operating systems or depend on some version of the industry-standard multitasking system UNIX. Building a file server on a non-IBM operating system has both advantages and disadvantages. A principal advantage is that the operating system will almost certainly permit maintenance of disk volumes larger than 32 MB, which is the limit for both DOS and early editions of OS/2. One disadvantage is that, since the server file system is managed in a nonstandard way, booting DOS or OS/2 on the file server machine will not give the user access to the server file base. Many managers of such file servers find themselves wishing they could access server files via DOS for back-up and maintenance.

OS/2 promises to be a fine vehicle for either dedicated or nondedicated file servers. OS/2's multitasking facilities allow workstations to support user, file server, and print server processes; thus, the facilities usually added to other vendors' proprietary operating systems are built into OS/2. This "universal operating system" approach simplifies maintenance matters for network users and managers, who will not require familiarity with multiple operating systems in order to do their work.

Other Servers and Network Utilities

The last two NOS components on our list require little description. Print-serving software mirrors the file access functions of file servers for printing operations. In some LANs, the file server encompasses all serving functions. In others, print serving, communications serving, and other functions may be provided on any PCs, normally in a nondedicated manner.

Network utilities generally include an on-line help system, a tutorial for beginners, and an electronic mail service. Here are examples of some other utilities from Novell's NetWare:

SESSION provides information about various network resources. It can display a catalog of servers active on the net, a list of active users, a summary of a user's access rights in a given directory, or a table of his network drive mappings. It also allows users to send messages to one another.

SYSCON is the system administrator's tool for managing security and accounting. Among many other functions, this menu-oriented program facilitates the addition, modification, and deletion of user accounts and permissions.

QUEUE allows users to view and manipulate the queues of files spooled for network printing.

MENU allows users to customize menus for network functions they perform regularly.

LOCKTEST is provided for cleaning up locks on server files. This is useful because, if an application program crashes with a lock in place, the lock is not automatically removed.

Tracing a File I/O Request

To clarify the ideas presented in this section, let's follow the path of a request made by an application program in a user PC. Assume the program wants to read some data from a file on a server, and that the user PC is operating under DOS, while the server has its own operating system.

The program calls DOS with a request to read the next 40 bytes from a particular file, previously opened by the program. The arguments to the call (DOS function 3F hex) are the file identifier (called a *file handle*), the number of bytes to be read (40), and the address of the buffer to receive the bytes. Let's say the file handle is 6. The request, passed to DOS, is filtered through the Redirector, which checks its table of file handles to see whether 6 is a local or a remote file. In this case the file is remote, and the table entry indicates the network address of the station where the file is located. The Redirector then reformats the request (the buffer address need not be sent to the server, but must be recorded locally) and calls the appropriate NETBIOS service to transfer the request packet to the appropriate server. The server receives the packet and places it on a queue of pending requests. When it is the request's turn to be serviced, the server reads the appropriate data from disk (or retrieves it from the memory cache), formats them into a packet, and sends them back to the user PC. The user PC's Redirector gets the reply packet, copies the data into the user's workspace, and returns control to the application program.

This scenario has been slightly simplified, because some details of the procedure vary from one NOS to another.

NETWORK OPERATING SYSTEMS

In the following descriptions of the leading network operating systems, Novell's NetWare is given center stage, not because of its preeminence, but because it serves as a convenient representative of NOSs in general.

Novell NetWare

Novell's NetWare, dating from 1981, was an early entrant in the LAN software market, of which it has captured a large share. There is also widespread consensus that NetWare is the best NOS. A key factor in Novell's success was that it was established as a software company. Other early NOSs were developed by LAN hardware makers, who supplied operating systems more or less as an appendage to their primary product. Although Novell also sold some LAN hardware, it concentrated on software and pioneered many sophisticated and efficiency-enhancing NOS features. The company also benefited from foresight with its early development of software to accommodate a wide range of machines from many manufacturers, setting an example later followed by its competitors.

Novell markets everything needed to build networks, including assorted LAN hardware, fixed disks and controllers for PCs, and 80286- and 80386-based PC-compatibles intended for use as file servers. The company is still best known for its software, particularly the NetWare products.

The software for workstations, called the *NetWare shell*, is fairly uniform across the several versions of NetWare, but the file server software varies. Novell's primary focus is on centralized and dedicated servers for AT- and higher-class machines. These server implementations are founded on a proprietary operating system. For small installations, nondedicated, DOS-based versions of the NetWare server are available.

NetWare's outstanding virtues are its security, its efficiency, and its fault tolerance options.

NetWare's security, based on permissions, user groups, and trusteeship, is unsurpassed. An account with user identification and optional password must be set up on each server that a network user needs to access. A user must then log in to a server before being granted access to its resources; she may log in to as many as eight servers at a time. The system administrator can assign permissions to each user for each server directory, which, unless explicitly overridden, apply recursively to all its associated subdirectories. The permissions that may be granted are:

- To search the directory
- To execute files
- To read files
- To write to existing files
- To create and write new files
- To delete files
- To modify file attributes

In addition, a "parental" privilege allows a user to create and delete subdirectories and to grant access rights to other users.

The administration of security is simplified by the assignment of users to groups. Permissions can be set globally for all members of a *user group*. Furthermore, through the process called *trusteeship*, certain users may be given the right to alter permissions for users within their groups.

Security is further enhanced (or complicated, depending on your point of view) by the fact that rights are also associated with directories themselves. A directory might be established, for example, as read-only; its users are not allowed to write or delete files regardless of their own permissions. The effective access rights conferred upon a user within a directory are defined by the intersection of directory rights and user permissions.

Other security options may require users to change their passwords periodically, restrict the hours during which a user may log in, or automatically lock out an account-holder when an attempted intrusion is detected. Another valuable security feature is the ability to restrict the amount of disk space a user may occupy on a given server.

The once-legendary efficiency of Novell's networking system has kept the company in the vanguard, but its closest competitors, notably 3Com, have more or less caught up.

Here's a brief summary of some of NetWare's many other features:

- NetWare includes an electronic mail system that is impressively powerful, although perhaps not as easy to use as a beginner might wish.

- LANs operating under Advanced NetWare may be bridged irrespective of underlying hardware. Organizations stuck with several apparently incompatible LANs can unify them under the NetWare umbrella with suitable bridges.

- Often, the worst bottleneck affecting a server's performance is the path from the server to the network cable—that is, the NIC. Under Advanced NetWare, a server can be outfitted with two NICs per LAN to increase throughput. This feature, implemented via bridging software, may be thought of as a way to bridge the network to itself. For the modest cost of one extra NIC, system performance can sometimes be almost doubled.

- Novell supports an Asynchronous Communications Server (ACS) offering both dial-in and dial-out capabilities. A separate add-on product supports access to LAN services for remote PCs dialing into a LAN station.

- NetWare performs network accounting, a feature perhaps not widely in demand, but still a rarity in LANs.

- Last but not least, the deletion of files on a NetWare server is "soft": within a session, accidentally deleted files can be restored by means of a salvage command.

NetWare SFT™

Several LAN vendors offer fault tolerance options; Nestar, for example, does so in its PLAN series of products. Here again, though, Novell was a pioneer, having introduced a three-tiered scheme of fault tolerance in 1986. Novell calls its relevant products System Fault Tolerance (SFT). SFT has three levels.

SFT Level 1, involving software only, is designed to ensure the safety of data stored on a given disk. Among other things, Level 1 duplicates system tables and directories on different physical areas of the disk, and follows every write by a read operation to verify that the data can be retrieved.

Level 2 provides either *mirrored disk drives* or *duplexed disk drives*. Mirroring involves hooking two drives to a single disk controller; the drives are read and written identically. Duplexing uses two disks and two independent controllers, which not only offers the added protection of a redundant controller but also endows the server with an efficiency bonus: it can perform two distinct read operations, one per drive, almost simultaneously.

Level 3 uses two identically configured PCs with separate network attachments to operate as *duplexed servers*. This is the ultimate in redundancy: if any failure occurs in the "lead" server, the "hot" standby can take over. With the addition of automatic failure detection, the switchover can also be automatic, instantaneous, and transparent, in the sense that network users are not aware of it (although a network manager is, of course, alerted).

A separate fault-tolerance feature available with NetWare is the Transaction Tracking System (TTS). When implemented, TTS automatically tracks and logs database updates, generating an audit trail for reconstruction of a database after a catastrophic failure. In addition, incomplete or partial transactions, such as might occur when a workstation crashes while making an update, can be backed out of the database; we'll explain this procedure in Chapter 16.

3Com 3+Plus

3Com, the major supplier of Ethernet components for PCs, also markets Ethernet interfaces for Macintoshes, a proprietary file server called the 3Server, diskless PC workstations, and the 3+Plus NOS. The 3Server can connect to either an Ethernet or an 802.5 token-ring LAN. The diskless workstations, really bare-bones PCs, lack disk drives but have built-in network interfaces; they boot from a file server.

The 3+Plus system comprises several software components for various networking functions.

3+Share is the server software, which runs on an 80286- or 80386-based PC or a 3Server3®. The server, based on a proprietary operating system called Concurrent Input/Output System (CIOSYS™), incorporates file and print serving, dial-in workstations, and a network name service. 3+Share can operate as a nondedicated server by running a version of DOS as one of its tasks. A special version of this NOS, 3+TurboShare™, runs on a station equipped with extra RAM for caching.

The network name service built into 3+Share is particularly powerful. One server on a 3+® internet (a group of 3+LANs bridged together) is designated as a *name server*, to which users on all the nets can apply for information about network resources, individual users, and user groups.

Security is provided by both optional passwords assigned to resources (servers, directories, and printers) and access rights to files and directories. Under this scheme, a user's access to a server is managed independently of his access to files on that server.

The 3+Menus™ system provides customized menus for accessing network resources. By means of this tool, a system administrator can develop menus for each user providing access to all the network applications the user ever needs. The menus are linked to complete procedures; selection of a menu item invokes procedures for such purposes as finding the right version of an application program for the user's PC configuration, automatically routing output to an appropriate printer, and prompting the user for necessary passwords. The role of 3+Menus is much like that of a DOS shell, such as Magee Enterprises' Automenu® or the Norton Commander™, on a stand-alone PC.

3+NetConnect™ and 3+Route™ support local and remote bridging, respectively. Local bridges between Ethernet and/or Token-Ring LANs can be built at either a PC workstation or a 3Server. Each bridge connects one pair of networks; multiple bridges can create larger configurations. 3+Route supports full-function bridging over modem links between geographically separated networks. 3+Remote™ provides full network service to remote workstations that dial into a server. 3+3270™ is a standard 3270/SNA gateway.

A new 3+Plus product for OS/2, called 3+Plus LAN Manager, is not compatible with previous 3Com products, but does support an upgrade path for DOS machines. Under 3+Plus LAN Manager, OS/2 machines running Extended Edition are able to access the network facilities normally provided to NOS users, but the system does not use dedicated, proprietary servers. Instead, the server processes run on OS/2 workstations on the network. DOS machines are supported through software that implements named pipes on the DOS workstations. 3Com has announced plans to support named pipes on other computers, including the Apple Macintosh, to allow them to use file and printer services within OS/2 networks.

IBM PC LAN Program

The PC Network Program, designed by IBM as part of its PC Network product, was revamped with the introduction of IBM's Token-Ring so that it could be used with both types of network, and was renamed the PC LAN Program. With OS/2 now in the picture, IBM networking becomes more complicated, and involves three software products: the OS/2

LAN Server takes over server functions from DOS-based servers; user PCs under OS/2 must run the Extended Edition of OS/2, which includes user-networking capability; and user PCs under DOS run an updated version of the PC LAN Program. Thus, DOS-based users can access OS/2-based servers, but OS/2-based users cannot access DOS-based servers. Unlike the other NOSs discussed here, IBM's is intended for operation only with its own LAN hardware.

IBM's server, based on DOS, is necessarily limited in performance. (The announced IBM OS/2 server has not reached the market at this writing.) Nevertheless, it has the advantage of supporting servers equally well whether centralized or distributed, dedicated or nondedicated. (Despite this capability, the considerable amount of memory required by the server software tends to make a distributed network unattractive.) The PC LAN Program also permits temporary conversion of a workstation into a file server, a real boon to pairs of users who must occasionally or spontaneously share files.

Banyan™ VINES

Banyan Systems' VINES (Virtual Networking System) is intended for use with larger PC networks. The VINES server runs under the UNIX operating system. Although two versions, VINES/286™ and VINES/386™, are sold for 80286- and 80386-based PCs, respectively, most Banyan customers use networks that rely on Banyan's impressive proprietary servers. These servers incorporate fast 32-bit microprocessors, loads of memory, hundreds of megabytes of disk storage, and connections for several printers. The CNS™ (Corporate Network Server) model, for example, includes a 20-MHz 80386 processor, 4 MB of memory expandable to 24 MB, seven printer ports, up to 30 serial ports for dial-in workstations, and up to 2.5 GB of disk space. VINES also supports server functions on VAX/UNIX systems.

Banyan's proprietary file servers, like those of several other vendors, are PC-compatible in one crucial and clever respect: they include a PC bus with empty card slots. Since the server can thus take advantage of PC NICs, there's no need to use NICs specially engineered for the server. This feature also allows the server to accommodate many of the NICs available for PCs. You cannot slap just any old NIC into a Banyan server, because the server must include driver software specific to the particular NIC, but the selection is still fairly wide.

A VINES server can hold as many as four NICs and thus simultaneously serve four different LANs, which can be organized as independent entities sharing the hardware services of the joint server, but with separate file bases. Alternatively, files may be shared among all networks; the server then becomes a bridge enabling the four LANs to operate as a unit.

In addition, Banyan's proprietary servers include, as standard features, cartridge tape drives for disk back-up, and battery back-up as insurance against power supply maladies. VINES itself incorporates a sophisticated electronic mail system, a network manager, distributed print serving, full-service async dial-in, and powerful bridging options.

Torus

Torus of Great Britain has taken a different tack on network software. Instead of concentrating on communications and file-serving components, as other companies have, Torus has focused on the user interface. Its original product, Tapestry™, provided an icon-based full-screen user interface for networking. Tapestry was not NET-BIOS-compatible and achieved little success in the U.S. market, although there happens to be an installation in the Oval Office of the White House. In Europe and other parts of the world, where it proved very popular, Tapestry was marketed by both IBM and Torus. At this writing, Torus is introducing a successor to Tapestry that stands a good chance of being a hit in North America.

CHOOSING A LAN

The first question to ask when planning a LAN is whether a LAN is what you really need. Some companies have installed LANs because they thought they needed one or because it was the fashionable thing to do, only to discover that they did not require the full power of a LAN. In many cases, these organizations would have been better served by simpler and less expensive technology, such as data switches, RS-232-based networks, or multi-user computer systems. These and other possible LAN alternatives are surveyed in the next chapter.

The key usage factor calling for a LAN is the need to run multi-user applications in a PC environment. This is not the only justification for a LAN, but it is the overwhelmingly predominant one. If your needs are limited to printer sharing or to sharing files serially rather than simultaneously, consider other options first and LANs second.

Here are some tips for selecting LAN products.

Top-Down Purchase Decisions

The best order in which to buy networking components is from the top down. First, select the desired network application programs. Second, pick an NOS that will do a good job of supporting those applications. Third, choose LAN hardware that will allow the NOS to perform well. Advice from the vendors may be most valuable here.

Standards

Compliance with both software and hardware standards should be regarded as an important criterion. Since fairly strong standards are in effect—IEEE 802 standards, Ethernet, and ARCNET for hardware, NETBIOS and LAN Manager for software—it's wise to stick with them. (Additional software standards may emerge over the next few years.) There's little or no money to be saved by deviating from the standards and much risk in doing so, as nonstandard equipment makes it difficult to be sure of continued support as your network expands.

Hardware versus Software

Although NOSs tend to be costly, the bulk of a LAN investment is almost certain to be in network hardware, that is, NICs, cabling, and PCs for server duties. Picking a good LAN hardware product helps protect the investment. The best NICs for PCs already work about as well as such products are ever likely to, and there's no reason to expect them to require upgrading. (The same could not be said a few years ago.) Software is a different matter. Many organizations are now upgrading from DOS- to OS/2-based networks, and newer operating systems that take full advantage of the 80386 may eventually necessitate further major upgrades.

Performance

You should be concerned about network performance because any LAN will eventually "run out of steam," and the growth of most networks cannot be accurately predicted.

Unfortunately, the only performance-related numerical specification usually provided for a LAN is the raw signaling speed on the cable; this bears little relation to the overall performance observed in practice. A well-designed LAN rated at 2 Mbps can easily outperform a poorly designed one rated at 10 Mbps. Most of the design-related factors that do consistently affect network performance involve the NICs and the NOS.

The greatest variable is the use to which the LAN is put. IBM's PC Network installation in Boca Raton, Florida has more than 1000 PCs on it. This is staggeringly large for a PC LAN, yet performance is fine because the network is used primarily for file transfer and electronic mail, both very undemanding applications. The activity that puts the heaviest load on a LAN is file serving, but even its effect varies enormously with server types, distribution of traffic, brand of network software, and so on. For heavy file serving on a PC Network, five or ten stations may constitute a practical limit.

An organization planning a LAN should investigate LANs being used elsewhere to learn what works well for similar organizations, whose usage patterns are also likely to be similar. The prospective vendor is a source of references: both LAN administrators and users should be questioned about their experiences.

When LAN performance does begin to degrade, there may be several options. Better networking software is often available, and upgrades to faster-running servers may help (but beware of the performance limitations sometimes imposed by server NICs). If a LAN has become too big, it is often feasible to reorganize it, either by adding another server or by dividing the network into two parts, which are then bridged.

Security

Although competition is forcing many makers to provide higher levels of security, this is one area in which the traditionally considerable differences between networks persist. Security in NetWare products has always been outstanding.

Memory Requirements

NOSs vary widely in the amount of PC memory their workstations or nondedicated servers require. In a dedicated server, of course, it hardly matters how much RAM the network software occupies, because memory is not needed for anything else. A PC running OS/2 doesn't create a problem, either; at worst, you may have to buy some more memory. With a PC under DOS limited to 640 kB, however, careful planning is in order.

For example, some network software provides the option of setting up distributed networks with every PC sharing some of its files, but demands so much memory in exchange for the privilege that few customers faced with DOS limitations would choose such a configuration. The mere fact that a network is advertised as supporting a distributed organization does not justify the assumption that such use is practical. Even in a workstation, the memory-resident network software may restrict the use of certain very large application programs.

Special Considerations: IBM's Token-Ring

IBM introduced its Token-Ring as a PC product, but long ago made it clear that the network would eventually encompass all important IBM systems: PCs, minis, and mainframes. Token-Ring connections to mainframes, for example, may be made via either a 3174 control unit or a 3725 front-end. The 3174 and 3725 both require add-ons to support Token-Ring connections. Communication between PC and mainframe may be effected either by

3270 emulation or through APPC. Again, the Token-Ring is the connection of choice for supporting APPC.

For PC users who now want, or foresee wanting, to incorporate direct mainframe connection into a LAN, the Token-Ring is a very good network choice. In practice, most Token-Rings are, in fact, used primarily as SNA networks. It is doubtful that any vendor other than IBM could offer such a powerful solution for PC-to-mainframe communication. If, on the other hand, links to big IBM systems will never be needed, the Token-Ring still makes sense for PC networking, but other products may be even more attractive.

Fault Tolerance

Tandem Computers became a billion-dollar company by selling *fault-tolerant computers.* Such machines are constructed with redundant components, so if one component fails, another can immediately take over, with no disruption of operations. Processors, buses, disks, controllers, and just about every other important hardware subsystem can be duplicated in this manner. Fault-tolerant computers are indispensable for certain critical dedicated applications, where down-time due to hardware failures is simply unacceptable. One example is a complex security system. Here, a computer is hooked to check-stations that variously read security cards, accept security access-code input from keypads, open and close doors, and keep track of personnel movements. A loss of computing services in this context would mean a serious compromise in security. More often, fault-tolerant computers are used where the loss to be avoided is of an economic kind.

Fault tolerance options for PC LANs have already been described under the topic of NetWare.

Recommendations

Specific recommendations for LAN products are not particularly helpful because LANs are continually evolving. Especially with the twists and turns of the market impelled by the advent of OS/2, the relative fortunes of PC LAN products may change significantly. Precise recommendations are also unwise because needs differ so profoundly; no LAN can be best for everyone, perhaps not even for a majority.

Here is a checklist to consider when choosing a LAN:

- Does it fit your application requirements? This may seem obvious, but it's terribly important. To a degree, LANs tend to impose their vendors' views of how networking should be carried out, which may not be yours. Consider the application programs you will run, whether services are better centralized or distributed, the range of computers you may need to attach to the net, and so on.

- Are installation requirements easily met, especially for cabling?

- Will the LAN provide suitable performance?

- Is there adequate room for growth? For example, find out whether the cabling can be extended as far as you might need, whether new stations can be added easily, which upgrades to 80386-based or proprietary servers are available, how many megabytes of memory can be added for caching, and whether enough disk space can be attached to the server(s).

- Does the LAN support appropriate connectivity to other systems? What gateways are available? Are async dial-in and dial-out provided in a flexible manner?

- Some LAN idiosyncracies that at first seem of minor importance later turn out to be a real bother. Can shared printers be located conveniently, so that no user need take a ten-minute walk to get her printed output? Is the spooling of print files handled well? Does the LAN inform a user when printed output is ready? Find out how readily users (or the system administrator) can manage the print queues to delete files mistakenly sent for printing, or change the order in which file will be printed. Perhaps most important, how much delay is involved in starting and completing a print operation?

- Is there support for the sharing of needed devices, such as plotters, digitizers, and PC-based fax machines?

- Are suitable back-up devices available, and how flexible are they? For example, can a tape drive installed in one server be used to back up files from another server?

- Does the LAN software support standard locking operations, those defined by DOS 3.1? Some NOSs, such as NetWare, support extensions to these basic locking facilities, which some application programs may need.

- What are the options for monitoring network activity and tracking down problems? (Diagnostic and monitoring tools for LANs will be discussed in the next chapter.)

- Does the LAN provide adequate security? Generally, the NOS should discourage users from leaving passwords in batch and command files. Unless workstations are physically secure, the mechanism should require users to enter passwords from the keyboard each time they are needed. Can the LAN be set up with optical fiber (to make eavesdropping difficult) or devices that encrypt data in transit? Can security management be delegated in a suitable manner?

- What kind of electronic mail service do you need? For example, consider whether mail only within the LAN itself is sufficient, or whether you'll need to interface to public systems, such as MCI Mail. Perhaps, too, you'll need to exchange mail with a PROFS system on your IBM mainframe.

For many LANs, products are available to meet these various requirements.

15

LANS: ACCESSORIES AND ALTERNATIVES

In this chapter we describe some auxiliary products for LANs, survey products that may be seen as alternatives to LANs, investigate internetworking, and present a mixed bag of LAN-related questions and answers.

LAN ANALYZERS

A LAN analyzer is a tool that provides a window into LAN activity, enabling certain users to monitor and analyze network operations and to diagnose problems. A PC network analyzer may consist solely of software, to be run on a suitable network station, or may be sold as a complete package including both a computer (usually portable) and appropriate software. Network analyzers are thus a close relative of the Data Line Monitors (DLMs) mentioned in Chapter 9. Excelan, HP, Network General, and other companies offer many analyzers for Ethernets, but only a smattering have appeared for other LAN types. Although analyzers tend to be expensive, and are not needed for every LAN, organizations with large LANs, or many small ones of the same kind, should consider acquiring such a tool.

Analyzer Features

A good LAN analyzer should have at least the following features:

Capture Capability

LAN traffic is normally far too tumultuous to be monitored by a human observer in real time. Therefore, an analyzer should be able to capture a given period of traffic, store it in memory or on a disk, and allow it to be replayed in slow motion after the fact.

Filtering

Besides being able to capture all traffic on a net, an analyzer should be equipped to capture messages selectively on the basis of various criteria, so the user need not wade through masses of irrelevant material in the process of analyzing a problem. For example, the capture criterion may be "all messages with bad CRCs," messages sent by a particular station, broadcast messages, or invalid messages.

Triggering

Since LAN activity proceeds so quickly, an analyzer is programmed to initiate some action, such as capturing traffic, when it observes an event called a *trigger*, which can, in principle, be any recognizable network event. The best analyzers can be triggered by narrowly defined events, such as a particular kind of message being transmitted to or from a particular station. Similarly, triggers may serve to halt the capture process or to prompt the generation of test messages by the analyzer itself.

Protocol Interpreters

Because it must be equipped with a suitable interface to the network, an analyzer is necessarily limited to operation with a single type of LAN hardware, such as Ethernet or Token-Ring. At higher levels, the analyzer should be able to interpret messages created by various protocols, and display those messages in a readily understood form. Each field should be labeled, and the program should decode the message type and similar attributes.

Statistics Gathering and Display

The software should be equipped to perform statistical analysis of network activity, and display in real time such items as network load, error rates, and station activity.

The Sniffer™

An example of a good LAN analyzer is The Sniffer from Network General, sold in versions for several popular network types, including the 802.5 Token-Ring, Ethernet, ARCNET, and StarLAN. With the help of an outstanding menu-based user interface and excellent graphics, it can reveal nearly everything of interest that goes on inside a LAN. Not only can The Sniffer help track down network problems and determine usage patterns, it's also a tool for learning how the net functions.

Among other things, The Sniffer can help find bottlenecks in the system, reveal who makes the most use of the network, and determine whether two supposedly compatible components are really working together as they should. The Sniffer is a superb debugging aid for organizations developing their own programs to make use of network protocols.

Like many other analyzers, The Sniffer is not limited to monitoring, but can also be programmed to generate traffic. This capability may be used to test paths, verify protocol operation, simulate load conditions, and much more. A word of warning, however: the product's power also creates a potential for abuse, since it provides a view of any traffic passing on the network, and can even be used to generate messages that appear to originate at other stations.

INTERNETWORKING

Like all communications systems, LANS exist only to furnish services to their users. In fact, from the standpoint of the user, a LAN is not a communications system at all, but a service provider: it furnishes file sharing, printer sharing, electronic mail, and so on. Users may also want the services provided by other networks, access to which is essentially an additional service of the user's own LAN. Such access requires communication links between LANs and other networks—that is, *internetworking*.

We've already mentioned bridges and gateways, two crucial internetworking components. These components are studied in depth in this chapter.

The key to successful internetworking is *transparency*. Anne, a user on network A, should be able to access a service on network B virtually as if the service were on Anne's own network, even if networks A and B happen to be linked via networks X, Y, and Z. The same holds true for Bob on network B when it comes to accessing services on network A. Transparency is usually facilitated by establishing resource addresses that use universally known names. Imagine, for example, a company-wide electronic mail system that spans several networks in several locations. A user should be able to send a message to anyone on any of the networks, knowing only the recipient's name and (perhaps) department, but not his or her physical location, which, after all, may change. More importantly, the sender should not need to know any details of the communication path along which the message must travel.

Here's a sample list of networks, and associated services, to which a PC LAN user might want access:

Other PC LANs	file sharing, printer sharing, etc.
Non-PC LANs	file transfer, remote login, etc.
3270 nets	3270 terminal sessions with IBM mainframes
5250 nets	5250 terminal sessions with IBM System/3Xs
PSNs	ASCII terminal sessions with PSN hosts
Telex	telex messaging
Fax	transmission and reception of facsimiles
MCI Mail	electronic mail

Many network links are one-way affairs. A 3270 gateway, for instance, gives LAN users terminal access to IBM hosts on a given 3270 network, but does not provide the 3270 network users with access to the services of the LAN. Other network links are two-way. A LAN bridge, for example, normally extends the services of each LAN to users on all the other LANs connected by the bridge, thus creating a composite virtual network known as an *internet*, that is, a network of networks.

To understand the intricacies of network linking, we must delve more deeply into network protocols.

It is convenient to divide LANs into three functional layers, shown in Figure 15.1 with their relationship to the OSI Reference Model. At the bottom is the *medium access control layer,* which takes the form of CSMA/CD, token passing, or some other mechanism. This layer "gets the message onto the cable."

In the middle is the *subnet layer*, responsible for establishing sessions and transporting data between application programs. This layer's functions are implemented by different protocols on different LANs; the protocol used by a given LAN is part of its NOS, so the user generally hears little about it. In some cases, the subnet protocol is a standard, such as IBM's NETBIOS or the protocol pair called TCP/IP (to be described below). In other cases, it is proprietary to the vendor, as is IPX in Novell's NetWare.

At the top is the *service layer*. Several protocols may coexist at this level, one for each service provided by the network. On PC LANs, the most important is the client-to-server protocol used between workstations and file servers for file sharing. Examples of protocols at this layer include Novell's NetWare Core Protocol (NCP) and IBM's Server Message Block (SMB) and Enhanced Connectivity Facility/Server Request Protocol Interface (ECF/SRPI). Other service protocols may be used for e-mail, gateway access, etc. Users seldom need to think about the names and details of these behind-the-scenes protocols; indeed, very few people, mostly insiders, are familiar with them.

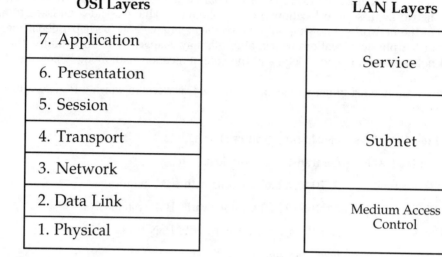

FIGURE 15.1: LAN protocol layers

Bridges

In Chapter 13, we somewhat simplistically stated that bridges join similar networks and that gateways connect dissimilar ones. To be more accurate, we should say that a bridge's usual function is to extend the distance covered by a LAN or LANs of a given type, connecting a pair of networks which may, in the case of a remote bridge, be physically separated by a great distance—for example, two Ethernets in San Francisco and Boston bridged via a T1 line. As discussed below, a bridge may also, in some circumstances, join dissimilar LANs with different MACs. For instance, an Ethernet and a Token-Ring may be bridged, provided that all network nodes actually communicating over the bridge are running some common higher-level protocol, such as TCP. While gateways can also connect dissimilar networks, a key distinction is that bridges, unlike gateways, do not perform protocol conversion.

A bridge typically joins two or more networks that use the same subnet and service protocols. Whether or not the bridged networks use the same MAC is irrelevant. When a message is to be sent from a station on LAN 1 to a station on LAN 2, LAN 1 routes the message to the gateway between them. The gateway relays the message at the subnet level to LAN 2. (We detail the function of gateways below.) Since the subnet messages encapsulate the service protocol messages, the bridged networks operate as a unit. Any service on any individual network is thus made equally accessible to users on all other such networks. Here is a summary of the tasks performed by each protocol in a bridging operation:

- The MAC carries a message from one LAN 1 station to another.

- The subnet protocol carries a message from one station to another station across an internet.

- The service protocol carries a message from one application program to a partner application program.

To be more concrete, let's say that a user should be able to sit down at any PC on the combined network, read her electronic mail, log into a file server, use a gateway to access another network, and so on, all without even having to know which LAN her PC-of-the-moment is physically attached to. All of this is true in principle; in practice, one factor, security, may prevent it. In some networks, it's possible to restrict the set of workstations a person may use for network access.

Bridges are usually sold by NOS vendors. Since a bridge interconnects LANs at a high level, typically involving proprietary protocols, it is hardly an appropriate arena for third-party involvement.

A *local bridge* interconnects LANs (typically two or four of them) in close proximity. It usually consists of one PC, an active member of all the LANs, that's equipped with some bridging software. With some products, this PC must be dedicated to bridging. A *remote bridge*, which joins a pair of distant LANs, involves two PCs, one per network, connected by a telecommunications link; both PCs must run bridging software. A LAN can normally be configured with any number of bridges, but the total number in an internet is restricted.

IBM offers a local bridge for a pair of Token-Ring Networks, and one for joining a Token-Ring to a PC Network. The former requires a dedicated AT; the latter operates on a dedicated XT or AT.

Novell's product line provides particularly strong support for bridging. Up to four Advanced NetWare LANs can be bridged locally via a single PC, no matter what form(s) of MAC the various LANs use. One limitation of this system is that two stations can communicate with each other only if no more than 15 bridges are interposed between them. Fortunately, this limit is not often exceeded in practice.

In order for bridging to work transparently, some mechanism, such as Simple Network Management Protocol (SNMP) or another suitable protocol, must be supplied to disseminate resource names across the web of bridged networks.

Gateways

A gateway interconnects two networks that have the same service protocol but different subnet protocols. Most gateways support a single service, such as terminal access or electronic mail. Generally, two or more gateways of the same or different types can coexist on a LAN.

3270 Gateways

The 3270 gateway, the type most in demand for PC LANs, provides a connection for 3270 terminal access to IBM hosts. In the normal configuration, a PC emulating a remote 3274 control unit functions as the gateway, and supports 8, 16, or 32 terminal and/or printer sessions, distributed according to demand among the workstations on the net. The high-speed link between gateway and workstations provides a very efficient form of 3270 emulation. It's often cost-effective, too, since the LAN cable serves both inter-PC networking and 3270 networking functions.

There are three subvarieties of 3270 gateway, distinguished by link protocol—the one each gateway uses for communication with the front-end processor of its IBM host. The most popular is SDLC. The alternatives are X.25 (used when the telecommunications link involves a PSN) and Bisync (for mainframe holdouts that still use the older protocol option). Typically, a vendor offering products for more than one of these protocols arranges to keep the hardware the same for all of them. The user can then reconfigure the product to accommodate another protocol simply by changing the software.

Most LAN NOS vendors sell SNA gateways; many excellent third-party products are also available, from such companies as Gateway Communications, INS, and Pathway Design.

X.25 Gateways

An X.25 gateway serves as a PAD (packet assembler/disassembler) enabling networked PCs to access PSNs. Alternatively, it can be used to support a direct multiplexed link between a LAN and an X.25 host. These two options are illustrated in Figure 15.2. Gateway Communications ranks high among vendors of these items.

Telex Gateways

Although they are not in great demand in North America, gateways to telex networks are important in many other parts of the world. A telex gateway ordinarily permits any PC to send, receive, and forward telex messages. This service is often implemented by sending telex messages through the LAN via an electronic mail system. LAN vendors offering telex gateways include Nestar and Torus.

Facsimile Gateways

Chapter 11 explored the rapidly growing market for facsimile machines, both stand-alone and PC-integrated. Since PC-based fax machines are fairly expensive and likely to be used only intermittently by any one user, they are good candidates for sharing on a LAN. A fax gateway, like the one sold by GMS, allows any workstation to generate, send, receive, display, and print Group III facsimiles. Scanning a document for fax transmission, however, calls for the use of the scanner on the gateway PC.

Mail Gateways

Mail gateways, sold by LAN vendors and others, permit users to send mail to and receive it from external mail services such as MCI Mail, EasyLink, and PROFS (IBM's PRofessional OFfice System).

Gateways to Non-PC LANs

As this book goes to press, the greatest internetworking challenge facing network vendors is the development of gateways between dissimilar LANs, especially between PC and non-PC LANs. The primary targets are gateways between PC LANs and the general-purpose LANs prevalent for UNIX-based systems. Secondary targets include Apple's AppleTalk®and DEC's DECnet. Unlike the other gateways we've discussed, which support a single service, this type ideally should support all the services available on both types of LANs, thus making it functionally similar to a bridge in creating an internet.

At present, such internetworking is rendered problematic by competing protocol standards. It may be that by the mid-1990s new higher-level ISO protocols will bring consistency to internetworking, but it could just as easily happen that other protocols, having gained an early tochold, will have become so entrenched as to thwart domination by the formal standards. At all events, the ISO offers protocols for the Transport and Session Layers, along with the following service protocols:

FTAM   File Transfer and Access Management

VTP   Virtual Terminal Protocol

X.400   Mail Protocol

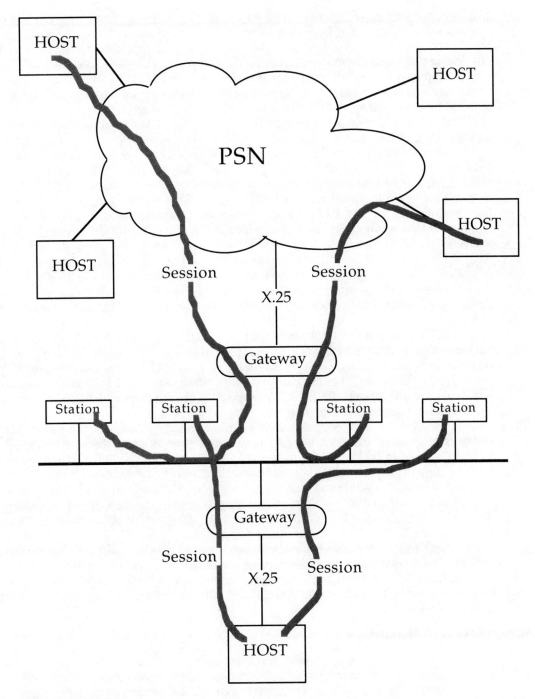

FIGURE 15.2: X.25 gateways

FTAM is a very sophisticated system for supporting access to remote files. It not only provides services for reading from, writing to, and otherwise manipulating a shared filebase, but also defines a virtual file format so that textual and numeric data can be presented to any system in a usable form.

VTP supports remote login for ASCII terminals. With VTP, it should be possible to start a terminal session with a host supporting dumb terminals without regard to the actual terminal types accommodated by that host.

X.400, already in widespread use, defines a standardized way of formatting, addressing, and routing mail messages.

While we're waiting for the ISO standards to take over, there are plenty of other protocols to be reckoned with. The LANs used in UNIX environments, while built by many different vendors, are fairly consistent: they are generally based on Ethernet and use TCP/IP (Transmission Control Protocol and Internet Protocol) as their internetworking protocols. TCP/IP was developed in the late 1970s by Jon Postel and others at the University of Southern California's Information Sciences Institute for the U.S. Department of Defense (DoD), and it enabled the Department to interconnect many networks falling under its jurisdiction. ARPANET, cited in Chapter 2 as the seminal PSN, supported a widely dispersed community of researchers, originally using some protocols of its own. In the late 1970s, many of the universities and research labs that used ARPANET were developing their own internal networks and wanted to tie these into ARPA. The appearance of TCP and IP allowed this to happen.

IP and TCP do not fit cleanly into the OSI model, but can be loosely identified with the Network and Transport Layers, respectively. Together, their job is to carry messages between users connected by a network or an internet. ARPANET was upgraded in 1982 to operate with TCP/IP and has since evolved into what is known as the ARPA Internet, or sometimes just *the* Internet. TCP/IP have supported growth from under 200 to more than 2,000 hosts, a phenomenal achievement.

TCP and IP have little competition as internetworking protocols in the United States, and constitute a DoD standard, but they have not become an international standard.

The first step in building links from PC LANs to other LANs, then, is implementing TCP/IP. Few PC LANs use TCP/IP as their native subnet protocols, but many PC implementations exist. TCP/IP-based LANs also tend to use standardized service protocols such as FTP (File Transfer Protocol), Telnet (a virtual terminal protocol), SMTP (Simple Mail Transfer Protocol), and a few others. There is no single standard protocol for file sharing, but Sun's NFS (Network File System) is very popular.

One day FTAM may bring all file servers under one roof; before then, we may see servers developed to support multiple file-service protocols. Indeed, network vendors are hard at work on them. PCs, Macintoshes, UNIX systems, and more will all be able to share the same files, with necessary data translation performed automatically according to an application program's needs.

Linking PCs with Macintoshes

In recent years, software vendors have developed increasingly sophisticated means of hooking together microcomputers from different manufacturers. Several have turned their attention to networking PCs with Macintoshes. TOPS®, the Transcendental Operating System, deserves special mention in this area. Sold by TOPS Systems, a division of Sun Microsystems, its most basic version uses AppleTalk® hardware, developed as a low-cost networking scheme and built into Macs from their inception. AppleTalk is a short-distance LAN designed to connect a small number of workstations in a restricted physical area. It operates at 230.4 kbps and uses several different types of cabling, including fiber optic. Other LAN options are available for newer Macs, such as the Macintosh II, that accommodate add-in cards. Ethernet, for example, can be used to tie such Macs to one another and to other Ethernet systems—including, of course, those made for PCs.

Since AppleTalk interfaces are stock equipment on Macs, the basic TOPS product for the Macintosh is inexpensive, consisting of software and documentation only; the Mac user provides suitable connectors and cables to complete the wiring. TOPS for the PC, which includes an AppleTalk-compatible NIC with appropriate software and documentation, is a bit more expensive. Options include two methods of obtaining speeds of 770 Kbps from a PC-Mac network; one of these entails a special TOPS enhancement to AppleTalk itself, while the other bypasses AppleTalk altogether.

TOPS may be used to give PCs access to Apple LaserWriter printers, or to allow PCs and Macs to share files. Although full file sharing is supported, the value of accessing PC files from Macs (or vice versa) is often substantially reduced by the two systems' use of different data formats. A few clever application programs, such as Microsoft's Excel, can access Mac and PC files equally well; in fact, Macintosh Excel can even read and write Lotus 1-2-3 spreadsheet files stored on a PC disk. Mac/PC file transfer is more generally useful, and TOPS supplies an excellent Mac-based utility program for translating files among many popular formats, especially those relied upon by word processing software.

TOPS offers a highly distributed approach to networking which, incidentally, sets it apart from Apple's own centralized networking software. To extend the size and range of the AppleTalk network, TOPS Repeaters are also available. Any station on a TOPS network can "publish" (that is, make available for sharing) any disk directories. Security is provided by passwords set on directories, and the memory overhead for sharing files is quite modest.

Among the other PC-Mac connection products are several less elaborate and even less expensive methods of sharing files. Traveling Software offers LAP-LINK™Mac, a simple serial-transfer approach that relies on a single cable between standard ports of the two machines and allows file transfer at 57.6 kbps. (The company also markets LAP-LINK PC for PC-to-PC transfers.) Another 57.6 kbps direct-connect product is MacLinkPlus/PC™from Dataviz, which includes more than 50 format translators for popular Macintosh and DOS word processors, spreadsheets, and other applications.

LAN ALTERNATIVES

For many requirements, there is simply no viable alternative to a PC LAN. A large number of products, however, claim to compete with LANs and, in certain circumstances, may be superior options. We'll survey the following alternatives:

- Multi-user computers (not PC-compatible)
- Multi-user PCs
- Host-based networks
- RS-232–based networks
- Data switches
- PBXs

Multi-User Computers

One of the traditional solutions for shared-use computing is that of a minicomputer hosting users at dumb terminals. Although possibly superior to PC LANs for certain applications, we have given the multi-user computer approach scant attention here, on the assumption that most readers have already invested in PCs and will not relish the prospect of replacing them with new hardware.

Among multi-user systems, we'll focus on minicomputers and supermicros running the UNIX operating system. Such machines are sold by AT&T, DEC, MIPS®, Pyramid, and Sequent, among many others. They have two potential advantages over PC LANs:

- Everything you need, except perhaps applications software, is easier to get from a single vendor.

- Security is simpler, since the users are furnished only with dumb terminals.

There are also two principal disadvantages:

- Only a minority of software vendors sell their packages for both PCs and UNIX systems. Software options for multi-user computers, while extensive, are not generally as numerous as those for PCs.

- Unless a fault-tolerant system is purchased, the multi-user computer represents a single point of failure. If it goes down, work stops, period. The same could be said of a centralized file server, but when a file server fails it may be possible to reconfigure another station to take over the job.

Cost comparisons between multi-user computers and PC LANs must be made on a product-by-product basis; "general" comparisons are generally meaningless. Still, a method of analysis dear to economists sheds some light on the matter. Consider the cost of putting the *next* new user on an existing system with a given number of users. This, the *marginal cost* of an additional user, is quite different for the two system types. Up to a point, it may be less expensive to add users to a multi-user system, since the only purchase required is a terminal for each. To complicate matters, though, such incremental cost increases are likely to be discontinuous: once the computer runs out of capacity, a high-cost step must be taken, such as upgrading the processor. In the long run, the average costs of adding users to the two systems probably balance out. The key factor is how close to saturation the system already is.

A multi-user computer may well outshine a PC network in circumstances calling for the exclusive use of a single application program. In an accounting department, for example, the cohesiveness of a minicomputer system is quite appealing.

Multi-User PCs

The distinction between a PC LAN and a multi-user computer is becoming progressively blurrier. A few companies sell hardware and/or software products that, in one way or another, permit a PC to be hooked to a number of terminals and used by several people simultaneously. Such products are all somewhat "kludgey" and out of the mainstream, but the best of them work well enough for certain applications.

The first hardware-based multi-user PC products provided "slave" cards, which were installed in a host PC and connected by RS-232 links to dumb terminals. Similar products, such as Alloy's PC-PLUS™, are still in use. Each slave is a bare-bones, diskless PC on a card, supporting a single user on its attached terminal. Kimtron and other companies sell PC-compatible terminals, with screens and keyboards that behave like those of a PC, ideal for use with these multi-user products. Software is included to allow the slaves to share the disks and printers of the host PC, which can itself continue to function as a workstation in the normal way. Products generally include record locking, but not always by standard (i.e., compatible with DOS 3.0 or later) means.

The second generation of such products is represented by ADC's PC II™and its successors, two-user slave cards installed in a host PC as discussed above. Each card houses a standard PC monochrome display adapter and keyboard interface for each user, who is thus supplied with a monochrome monitor and PC keyboard instead of an ASCII terminal. Resources are shared by means of a customized version of Novell's NetWare with the host PC acting as server. The result, which has been referred to as a "LAN in a box," is a hybrid of a traditional multi-user computer and a PC LAN, in which the bus of the host PC performs the functions usually assigned to a network cable. Its performance often compares favorably with that of a regular LAN.

Still other products consist of software alone and enable an AT-class machine to be operated in a multi-user mode, serving users at ASCII terminals. Since these users share the processor and memory of the host, performance is usually poor.

The attraction of the above multi-user PC products derives entirely from their low cost as compared to LANs. The facilities available to each user are inevitably limited. Although most application programs will work, including multi-user applications that support suitable locking, there's sure to be trouble in running certain memory-resident software, communications programs, and copy-protected programs. Individual workstations cannot be customized, and a user can't easily take advantage of any PC products, such as 3270 emulators, that require added hardware.

Host-Based Networks

Many of the services of PC LANs can be provided to PCs by software on hosts to which the PCs are connected. Most products supporting this approach work with PCs hooked to IBM mainframes as 3270 terminals, but options are also available for some other popular hosts, notably DEC VAXes running VMS™. In the next chapter we will meet Tempus-Share™, a product that provides the equivalent of file serving on an IBM mainframe.

The attractions of a host-based network are likely to be that it kills two birds with one stone, and that all shared resources remain the province of the host (and the data processing department). Its disadvantages are, however, significant: the host is a single point of failure; the requisite software is expensive; the method imposes a large additional load on the mainframe; and performance is limited by the terminal-style connections made to the PCs.

RS-232–Based Networks

For users who don't need the power of a full-scale LAN, a similar kind of network, based on RS-232 connections, may be just the ticket. Notable among the various products in this category is EasyLAN™from Server Technology. (It is open to debate whether such products should call themselves LANs; although they certainly are local area networks in a generic sense, they do not incorporate what is usually considered "LAN technology": a high-speed shared medium.)

Most RS-232 networks connect PCs in a star formation. A server PC sits at the center of the star, and workstations are connected to it by individual RS-232 links, ordinarily running at speeds between 19,200 and 115,200 bps. Some products allow a number of servers to be strung together, again by RS-232 links.

An RS-232 network may be the right choice when the network services you chiefly need are printer sharing, file transfer, and electronic mail. The capacity of such networks is insufficient to support any significant degree of file serving; indeed, only a few even include a file-serving option. Gateways, except for electronic mail, are simply out of the question.

RS-232 networks are very reasonably priced, perform quite adequately for their intended applications, and enable dialed connections to be integral links in the network. They are often found in law offices, where there is high demand for document sharing and e-mail.

Switches

If all you want to share in a PC environment is a couple of printers and a plotter, or some similar combination of devices, then even an RS-232 network may be inappropriate. Switches, both mechanical and electronic, facilitate the simple sharing of devices that communicate using an RS-232 or Centronics interface. Since switches support only point-to-point connections, they cannot possibly be used for file serving or multi-user applications. Their other major limitation is that, for the most part, they cannot be expanded easily.

For supporting connectivity in contexts where multi-user applications are not implemented, switches offer the following considerable advantages over LANs:

- They are usually cheaper than any kind of network, and vastly less expensive than a standard LAN.

- They require very little management.

- They are not restricted to PCs, but can connect almost anything to almost anything else.

Since some subtle differences distinguish the three common classes of switch—mechanical, printer-oriented electronic, and general-purpose electronic—we'll cover them separately.

Mechanical Switches

A mechanical switch is one with a knob that the user turns manually to make the required connection. It normally has one input and N outputs, and so is described as a *1-to-N* device. Such a switch can also be used for N inputs and one output. A three-way switch, for instance, can connect three PCs to one printer or three printers to one PC. An exception is the *cross-matrix* type, a 2-to-2 switch that alternates connections between two computers and two devices. A cross-matrix switch connecting two PCs to a printer and a modem, for example, would let one PC print while the other is telecommunicating.

A mechanical switch is a dumb passive device; all it does is switch. In fact, it's no more than a handy substitute for unplugging and reconnecting cables. This means, for example, that all inputs and outputs must have exactly matched speed and parity parameters. To their credit, mechanical switches are inexpensive, robust, and easy to use. Most are equipped with DB25 connectors and, if all 25 circuits are switched, can be used with RS-232, Centronics, and possibly other types of interface. When buying such units, check how many circuits are switched (some intended exclusively for RS-232 communication switch fewer than 25), and be sure that the connector genders are suitable for the application. Mechanical switches can be used for sharing modems, printers, plotters, host ports, and even for PC-to-PC links.

The two major limitations of mechanical switches are their 1-to-N or N-to-1 configurations (as opposed to the M-to-N capability offered by general-purpose electronic switches), and their size (most are made for switching four or fewer ports). An operational problem is *contact bounce*: when the knob is turned, there are a few milliseconds of "chatter" while the switch contacts settle into their new positions. The noise thus generated can result in such annoyances as a spurious character arriving at a printer.

Electronic Printer-Sharing Switches

A basic electronic switch designed for printer sharing is an automated, knobless version of the N-to-1 mechanical switch. When it detects the arrival of data on one of its N inputs, it connects that input to its output, manipulating its signal lines to refuse data from other sources. Different models are required for serial and parallel devices.

The more capable, buffered version of the electronic printer-sharing switch is vastly preferable because it can accept data on any or all inputs at the same time, spooling each file until an opportunity comes to send it to the printer. The switch can detect the end of a print file only by means of a time-out, that is, by noticing when data stop arriving for some short period. Therefore, the user must prevent spurious time-outs by ensuring that each print operation is uninterrupted at the computer. This may mean, for example, that it's not a good idea to print from within application programs.

When a switch is intelligent, as is needed for buffering, it can handle some other useful tasks as well. Most electronic switches, for example, accept input only on serial ports but give you the option of using serial or parallel ports on output. Implicit in the ability to buffer is speed matching; the input can be as fast as the switch allows, typically 19,200 bps, while the output can dawdle along at 1,200 bps or whatever the printer requires. In addition, most such switches can handle either software (XON/XOFF) or hardware (RTS/CTS) flow control.

When selecting an automatic printer switch, check such characteristics as the configurations (DTE or DCE) of the input and output ports, and be sure to obtain the appropriate cables (straight-through or crossover).

General-Purpose Electronic Switches

General-purpose electronic switches have multiple inputs and multiple outputs. Often called M-to-N or *many-to-many* switches, these devices might also be called data-only PBXs. They are switched by codes entered when a connection is to be made.

These switches do everything that the other electronic switches do, but also let you share any number of printers and other devices, connecting any input port to any output port on demand. Usually, some PC software is provided to assist with the switching. Thus, devices can be given names, so when you want to print something, you can simply run a utility that provides a menu of the names of available devices; once the device you select is free, the connection is made.

When suitably configured, these switches facilitate PC-to-PC communications for such purposes as file transfer, using standard communications packages on the PCs just as would serve for the same operation over a modem link. A disadvantage of switches for inter-PC communication is their data rate; the typical upper limit is 19,200 bps, much lower than LANs provide.

While remarkably inexpensive, these switches are actually quite complex, and may require extensive configuration upon installation. The configuration process usually involves plugging a PC into a master port of the switch and downloading a name and operating parameters for each port. The capabilities of fancier switches vary greatly from model to model. Some allow the user to configure any port for input or output; others come with a certain number of pre-established input and output ports. Almost all allow only serial input, but many support both serial and parallel output. The most popular size is an 8-port unit, while the biggest commonly found has 32 ports. Some vendors allow several of their switches to be strung together to increase the number of available ports, a method akin to bridging with LANs.

An illustrative example of such switches is the Commix™ 32 made by Infotron LAN Systems. Commix provides universal point-to-point connectivity for any and all devices capable of asynchronous RS-232 communication, including PCs, printers, plotters, host ports, modems, and terminals. Each port can be given a name, and group names serve resource groups such as host ports and modem pools. If you want a modem and the modem pool is busy, the switch can put you in a queue to wait for a free one. Commix comes with networking software for PCs and for Macintoshes. The PC version (for DOS) is memory-resident: it supports electronic mail, access to printers on the switch, and Kermit file transfer. The Kermit can act as either a user or a background server that allows file transfers to take place without disturbing the PC's other business. Basic security with passwords is incorporated.

The Commix can be configured with up to 32 ports by modular increments of four. Devices are connected to the switch via telephone cable and jacks. Each port can be set for operation in one of three modes. In the first mode, the user of one port is prompted to choose among the other ports for a desired connection. The second mode makes a port behave like a Hayes-compatible modem responding to "AT" commands; this is ideal for typical PC communications software. The third mode directs a port to manage a Hayes-compatible modem for dial-out use. Ports can also be configured for either fixed-speed operation or automatic speed recognition at rates up to 19,200 bps. Shared printers are supported by print buffer modules that plug into the switch in place of regular port modules. Each print buffer module contains a megabyte of memory for buffering output, and can drive two serial printers.

Up to 255 Commix switches can be bridged in a local area using Ethernet to supply a maximum of 8,160 ports. Remote bridging is also supported by means of point-to-point links between switches running at speeds up to 56 kbps.

Other features of Commix 32 include support for both software and hardware flow control, speed and character-format conversion, local echo at any port, a programmable inactivity time-out for breaking connections automatically, and diagnostic facilities.

PBXs

Private branch exchanges, first discussed in Chapter 2, also permit device sharing but, being limited to point-to-point and comparatively low-speed connections, are hardly competitive with LANs in any direct way. Many of our comments on general-purpose switches also apply to PBXs—indeed, the only major difference is that PBXs are assumed to be used on a wide scale (e.g., throughout an organization), while M-to-N switches are normally employed in limited areas, such as a single office.

Here are a few points of comparison between data PBXs and PC LANs.

- A PBX will usually guarantee a certain bandwidth to each connection, which many LANs do not. On the other hand, on average, a LAN will provide faster connections.

- It may be possible to use existing wiring with a PBX, although not as routinely as some PBX vendors claim.

- If rewiring for a PBX turns out to be necessary, then inexpensive, easily installed twisted pair will do. This is also true for many, but by no means all, LANs.

- With a PBX, it may be possible to use the same cables for both voice and data, thus saving considerably on total wiring requirements.

- PBXs provide only point-to-point connections, severely limiting opportunities for the concurrent sharing of resources. They can support file serving only if the file-serving function is incorporated into the PBX itself.

- Compared to PBXs, LANs can usually be expanded in smaller, less expensive increments.

- A well-planned LAN should require less cable, overall, than a PBX.

- Although both LAN and data-PBX technologies are fairly new, it's fair to say that LAN technology is more mature.

- In general, LAN throughput degrades smoothly and gradually as demand increases. PBX performance does not degrade with increasing demand, but eventually reaches a saturation point at which it will refuse new business.

- PBXs can and often do serve splendidly for bridging LANs.

LAN QUESTIONS AND ANSWERS

This section addresses an assortment of questions about LANs. Unfortunately, many common questions cannot be answered definitively because of the many differences between LANs.

Can I mix PC-family machines and PS/2s on a LAN? No problem, in principle, as long as you can buy NICs for each type of machine. But see the next question.

Can I mix DOS and OS/2 machines on a LAN? This depends on the LAN software you use, but generally you can. LAN software vendors moved quickly to support OS/2 not only because of presumed demand, but also because the multitasking features of the new operating system afforded them the opportunity to make their products more flexible.

Must all the NICs I use be made by the same manufacturer? No. As long as all NICs follow exactly the same signaling conventions, there should be no problem mixing products from different vendors. Many companies, for example, make NICs compatible with IBM's Token-Ring Network.

ZYX Corporation advertises that its RhuBarbNet cards are much more efficient than those sold by GHI, Inc. Can this be true? Yes, absolutely. The efficiency of a NIC depends, for the most part, on how slickly it moves data into and out of the PC in which it's operating, and has little to do with the type of MAC the NIC is designed to handle. Rather, it relates to such factors as the amount of memory on the board (explained below), the power of the NIC's processor, and the techniques used to copy data to and from PC memory.

Almost all NICs do their work by *staging* messages in their own memory buffers. That is, a message the PC wants to send on the LAN is first copied from PC memory to NIC memory and then transmitted. Likewise, a message received from the network is first stored in NIC memory and then copied to PC memory. It might seem that a one-step process, executing network I/O directly to and from PC memory, would be more efficient. On a different kind of computer, it might very well work out that way, but the architecture of the PC is such that the two-step arrangement is necessary for good performance.

The fact that all network messages must be buffered on the NIC means that the memory space available, and hence the number of messages that can be held at one time, is critical. The slowness of most very early LAN products was largely attributable to their meager complements of NIC memory. One notorious design had so little RAM that only a single message could be buffered in it. If an outgoing message were sitting in this NIC, poised for transmission, and a message arrived for the station, the NIC had to overwrite the waiting message with the one received. Later on, the outbound message would have to be recopied out of PC memory for another attempt at transmission. Would you buy a mailbox that was big enough to hold only a single letter?

Contemporary products, certainly the leading NICs, fare much better. Nevertheless, it should be clear that there is considerable room for performance variation.

How do I use a LAN remotely?   As mentioned earlier, it's possible to gain access to LAN facilities from a remote PC that dials up a PC attached to the net. Some LAN vendors offer their own software for this purpose, but standard remote packages such as Carbon Copy PLUS (discussed in Chapter 10) also do the job very well.

A dialed-in PC should be able to avail itself of all network services. The reverse is not true. It would be crazy, for instance, to try to use a remote PC at the end of a phone line as a file server (not only would it be ill-advised, but the network software would almost certainly not permit it). Dial-up use of LANs is handy for electronic mail and file transfer. Running application programs to access files on a network disk is possible but likely to be painfully slow.

Why have you said so little about LAN performance?   Because it's a very tricky matter. Perhaps you've heard horror stories about the performance of PC LANs. (Come to think of it, we just related one, and there are many more.) In times past, many organizations indeed found that, when they plugged more than four or five workstations into their single-server networks, the net turned into chilled molasses. It really was possible for a network to run beautifully with four PCs, and crawl with five. This is not likely to be true today. Since those Dark Ages (ca. 1984 A.D.), PCs, and thus PC-based servers, have become much more powerful; network software has made great strides in efficiency; and network hardware, mostly by virtue of vendors packing more and more oomph onto the NICs, has sped up as well.

Just what kind of performance can you expect from a LAN, then? Well, that question is impossible to answer in general. Far too many factors are involved: the network hardware, the network software, the PC operating system(s), the types of machine used as servers, the speed of shared disks, the amount of memory for caching, the multi-user applications, and, most variable of all, the patterns of usage.

What about a job server?   Good idea! If you have a spare PC on your network, why not press it into service as a batch processor? *Batch processing* here means executing a DOS batch file or OS/2 command file to run an application program, or sequence of programs, which can then zip along without supervision. The batch job should require either of two categories of keyboard input: none at all, or the kind that can be set up in advance on a file and provided as redirected input. Likewise, it should be sufficient to write any output to a file, by redirection if necessary, for inspection at a later time. One obvious application is program assembly or compilation, which is typically a time-consuming, thumb-twiddling activity for software developers. Many other types of PC users could undoubtedly find opportunities along the same lines.

PCnet™from Orchid Technology, a LAN that made its mark a few years back but has since faded into relative obscurity, sported such a feature, namely a remote command facility. This facility enabled a user to enter a DOS command for execution on any other PC on the net, which meant that he or she could be mischievous and puzzle other users by getting their PCs to do Strange Things without their bidding. We may see support for command serving introduced into more LANs in the future, but some people have discovered that they can create the same facilities for themselves by means of batch files.

With many LANs, remote command execution can be accomplished without special software. It is left to the reader's ingenuity to implement such a scheme if the idea seems valuable. Some measure of ingenuity is indeed called for. Some hints: Define a directory on a file server to act as a reservoir of jobs waiting to be run (a "job input queue," in batch-processing terms). Write a SUBMIT batch file that copies a job file into this directory. Arrange that the job server, when idle, constantly scans the job input directory; when it finds a file there, it downloads and runs it. All files needed by the job must be stored either on the job server itself, or on a file server where the job server can easily get at them.

How do LANs fit the OSI model?   The media access method (e.g., CSMA/CD or token passing) fits the lowest two slots of the OSI model, the Physical Layer and the Link Layer. Generally, LANs have no functions at the Network Layer because there's no connection switching or message routing to be done. The NETBIOS fits in at the Session Layer, and the NOS takes care of the Presentation and Application Layers.

Does this mean you can have distinct communities coexisting on the same LAN?   Yes, and this can be very significant. Suppose, for example, you want to set up an Ethernet to link a bunch of PCs, and you already have an Ethernet installed as a terminal network for some DEC hosts. You can plug the PCs into the existing Ethernet cable and have them operate as a network. The terminal network and the PC network may be incapable of meaningful communication with each other, but they can coexist without any interference. Each network will, of course, have a negative influence on the performance of the other, as stations in both communities compete for message slots on the cable.

Why would you want to combine two or more logical networks on one physical cable? Presumably in order to save the cost of installing separate cable for each. It is not unusual in large organizations to find Ethernets supporting five or six separate communities.

How do you network laptop PCs?   Laptop PCs present a networking problem because, with very few exceptions, they lack slots to accommodate standard PC-expansion cards, and therefore cannot be internally equipped with ordinary NICs. For most of the larger laptop models, expansion chassis and similar accessories enable them to work with standard add-on boards. Such devices, when available, are a fine solution as long as you're willing to sacrifice portability or tolerate some inconvenience. For example, you will be but slightly incommoded if you need to network your laptop only when it's sitting on your office desk. When you have to take it somewhere else, you disconnect it from the expansion box and from the LAN.

Many laptops do have space for one or two specially made add-in cards, usually to hold an internal modem or some extra RAM. The connector and interface for these cards are unique to each line of machines. For some of the most popular models, you can buy NICs that fit into these internal slots. Western Digital, for example, offers a StarLAN interface for the high-end models in Toshiba's laptop line, and PureData has ARCNET cards for Toshibas. When machine-specific NICs like these are available, they almost certainly represent the better choice, and should be cheaper than the expansion-chassis option (if you include the cost of the expansion device). An internal NIC maintains portability, a boon when an entire network is to be carried around. For demonstrations and hands-on seminars, for example, it may be necessary to transport LANs.

A third possibility is to connect a laptop via RS-232 as a remote workstation to the LAN. As already noted, most LANs offer support for PCs that dial in. A laptop can be connected locally via a modem eliminator, typically at 9,600 or 19,200 bps, and used in the same way.

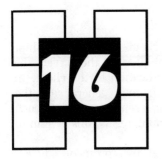

ADVANCED TOPICS

This final chapter is a catchall for topics of interest to the more technically inclined or just plain adventurous reader, who is rewarded (at last) with some troubleshooting tips.

DISTRIBUTED PROCESSING

In Chapter 1, we pointed out that many communication systems have been designed around old-fashioned notions of terminals and hosts. The watchword for the future is *peer-to-peer* communication, in which all partners have equal status. Easy interprogram communication facilitates the development of *distributed processing*, also called *cooperative processing*, in which the resources of two or more computers contribute to the performance of some task. Let's consider a few examples:

1. A system that allows users at two interconnected PCs to engage in a game of chess. The program running in each PC displays the chess board to its user, accepts moves entered at the keyboard, and relays them to the program in the other PC, which updates the partner's screen. This is not, perhaps, a very practical example of a distributed system, but it is one that's easily grasped. Note that the programs themselves are not playing chess, but merely automating and mediating a game between two human players.

2. A data entry application designed so that data are entered and validated on one PC, then used to update a database on another PC.

3. Maintenance of a distributed database whereby a company keeps its product orders on a mainframe at its headquarters while the inventory list is stored on a minicomputer at its warehouse.

4. A PC spreadsheet in which certain cells are defined to contain values actually stored in a mainframe database. Whenever the spreadsheet is recalculated, the spreadsheet program queries the mainframe for the necessary values.

5. File serving as used on PC LANs. File serving happens to be a prime example of *virtual service*, a particular subclass of distributed processing.

6. File transfer between computers. This is a somewhat trivial instance of cooperative processing.

In all these cases, and in distributed processing generally, two or more programs engage in what might be termed a dialogue, session, or conversation. Such behavior calls for a system of communication among the programs—in particular, a program-to-program protocol—that enables them to interact in a manner independent of both their relative locations and the details of the network that links them.

For the virtual service case, in which the programs have a client-server relationship, the required protocol is function-oriented. The client makes a request to the server; the server performs the requested action and returns some result indication to the client. In programming terms, this is akin to calling a library function. For the more general case, the appropriate protocol is send/receive-oriented. The partner programs send messages to each other with no coordination imposed by the network. In programming terms, this is akin to input and output.

IBM has designed (or "architected," in IBM's literary style) two protocols, ECF/-SRPI and APPC, to support distributed processing across all the company's computer systems. SRPI (Server-Requester Programming Interface), a part of IBM's Enhanced Connectivity Facilities (ECF), addresses the needs of virtual service systems. IBM uses ECF/-SRPI as a basis for providing file server facilities on their mainframes to PCs emulating 3270 terminals. APPC (Advanced Program-to-Program Communication) is IBM's primary tool for cooperative processing.

ECF/SRPI, a newer invention than APPC, has, at the start of 1989, yet to prove itself and become widely known. Therefore, we will not study it in detail. APPC, mentioned in Chapter 12 as a component of SNA, is widely accepted even by other computer makers. An overview of APPC is presented later in this chapter.

APIs Again

From the point of view of a program, a communication system such as ECF/SRPI or APPC appears as an Application Program Interface (API).

APIs were introduced in Chapter 12 as features of many 3270 emulators. In Chapter 14, we talked about another kind of API that was essential to a simple named-pipes interface. Here is a more general definition.

Recall that an interface is a point at which two independent systems meet and interact. We've seen many examples of hardware interfaces; an API is a *software interface*, a point at which two programs communicate with each other. It may also be thought of as a protocol, that is, a set of formal rules that two programs use in order to communicate with each other. Whether the two programs are co-resident (resident on the same computer) or are running on different machines connected by a communications link, if they wish to communicate with each other, they need an interface through which to do so. An ideal interface would serve equally well regardless of program locations. The highest layer of the OSI Reference Model, the Application Layer, is implemented by either a program (such as a file transfer utility) that performs a network service or an API, which an application program can call to get network service.

The most commonplace example of an API is the programmatic interface to a PC operating system. A user communicates with DOS or OS/2 by means of a command language, invoking such familiar services as FORMAT, COPY, and DIR. An application program communicates with DOS or OS/2 by requesting services such as *display output, get date, create a file, read from a file or device,* and *allocate memory.* This application interface is maintained uniformly across all versions of an operating system except that, as new versions appear, new services may be added. This explains why, although programs generally work equally well under any version of DOS, some programs require a certain minimum level (version) because they depend on services added or revised at that level.

Let's consider some other APIs. As we discussed in Chapter 12, it has become fashionable for vendors of 3270 emulators for PCs to incorporate an API in their products. This allows programmers to develop PC applications that can seize control of the emulated terminal and thereby communicate with a mainframe application program. Such an application may be developed in any programming language sanctioned by the API vendor; the programmer codes various calls to the emulator to request services such as emulating an input keystroke or reading a field from the display buffer. In essence, the application program replaces the human being as the operator of the emulated terminal. End users can take advantage of this scheme to arrange for PC programs to "talk" directly to mainframe application programs. Original equipment manufacturers (OEMs) can use 3270 APIs to interface data collection instruments, and other "foreign" equipment, to mainframe programs. Remember that this API is an interface between a PC application program and a terminal emulator in the PC, *not* between a PC program and a mainframe program. The mainframe program still "thinks" it's communicating with a terminal. A true program-to-program interface between PC and mainframe is another matter, as we'll see later in this chapter.

Incidentally, the interface between a mainframe application program and a 3270 terminal emulator is not an API but a terminal interface. The 3270-emulator communicates with the mainframe by pretending to be a terminal, a piece of hardware.

The trouble with 3270-emulator APIs is that there are several different and incompatible varieties: IBM's, DCA's, and others. It was primarily this mess of incompatible 3270 APIs that spurred IBM to develop ECF/SRPI.

The *RELAY Gold* API

APIs are generally associated with 3270 terminal emulators, and rarely appear in asynchronous communication packages. One of these rarities, a remarkable API, is incorporated into VM Personal Computing's RELAY Gold. RELAY Gold is a PC communications package heavily oriented toward asynchronous access to IBM mainframes, including direct "TTY mode" access to TSO or CMS, access via a 3270 protocol converter such as the IBM 7171, or access via VM Personal Computing's own RELAY/3270, a host-based 3270-conversion package for IBM's VM/CMS™operating system. RELAY Gold also has some unusual and appealing features for PC-to-PC communication.

As shown in Figure 16.1, RELAY Gold's API is really two interfaces in one: a general programmatic interface to the communications package itself, and an application-to-application program interface for PC-to-PC use. The RELAY Gold program must normally be installed in memory-resident mode (under DOS) for the API to be operative.

The first part of the API (Figure 16.1a) allows a PC application program to take control of the emulated terminal and thereby communicate with a host-based program. (Normally, terminal output goes to the PC screen. The API diverts these input and output channels to a specially designed application program.) This programmatic interface allows the PC applications programmer to code calls to certain functions within the communications package, the most important of which is a function to execute a command in RELAY Gold's powerful script language. The script command to be executed is passed as a string parameter. A succession of calls to this function could, for example, perform the script command sequence:

```
WAIT UNTIL 01:00
CALL NY_OFFICE EXECUTE NY_LOGIN
EXECUTE START_AP
```

The first command causes RELAY Gold to wait until one o'clock in the morning. The second initiates a connection to the host known as "NY_OFFICE," presumably defined in RELAY Gold's dialing directory. The application program must examine a return code from the CALL command to be sure the connection was established. Once this happens, the

PC Mainframe

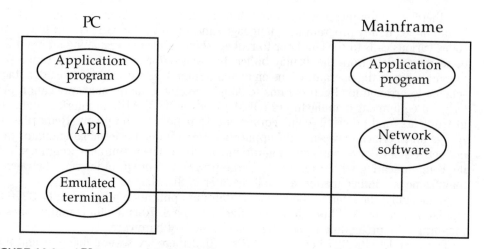

FIGURE 16.1a: API to an emulated terminal

PC PC

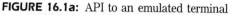

via RELAY protocol

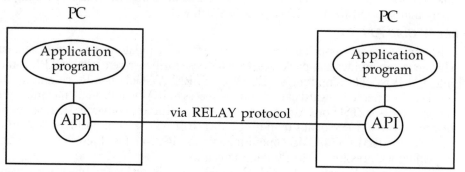

FIGURE 16.1b: API between two PC application programs

parameter "EXECUTE NY_LOGIN" comes into play; it calls for execution of the script file "NY_LOGIN," which contains additional script commands to handle the login procedure. Finally, if all goes well, the script file "START_AP" is executed. This, we'll suppose, takes care of starting up an application program on the NY machine with which the calling PC program is going to conduct a dialogue.

Once the two application programs are connected, the PC program calls other API functions to pass keystrokes to RELAY Gold for processing, and to obtain data returned from the host program. Keystrokes passed to RELAY Gold by the application program are handled exactly as if a user had typed them on the keyboard. Thus, if VT100 emulation is in effect and the VT100's PF1 key is assigned to the PC's Ctrl-F1 combination, a Ctrl-F1 code passed by the application program will be translated by RELAY Gold into the code a VT100 normally generates for PF1 (which happens to be the three-character sequence Escape-O-H). The API is designed for half-duplex operation in the sense that the PC application program sends a message to the host, waits for host output, and so on, in fairly strict alternation.

Here's a somewhat simplified summary of the functions available in this part of the API:

- Initializing and terminating the interface.
- Executing script commands. Two functions are offered; the difference between them relates to the time at which control is returned to the application program. This

is a significant issue for time-consuming actions, such as establishing a connection or transferring a file. Where the return is immediate, RELAY Gold will process the command in the background; alternatively, the return may be delayed until command processing is finished.

- Waiting. The application program invokes this function to wait until RELAY Gold has completed the execution of the active script command, if any.

- Checking RELAY Gold's status. The program can determine whether or not RELAY Gold is busy executing a script command.

- Passing keystrokes to RELAY Gold, as described above.

- Requesting information of several types from RELAY Gold. The most important information that can be retrieved is, of course, output sent by the host. The application program can also obtain almost every imaginable piece of status information about the connection, including such items as the line speed and the length of time the host connection has been open.

- Establishing a procedure within the application program to be called at approximately every clock tick, 18.2 times a second on most PCs. The application program could set up such a procedure for itself, but since doing so is tricky, the API function is a great convenience.

The API functions are well thought out and give the application program considerable power. In particular, the ability to have RELAY Gold process commands in the background gives an application program a great deal of control and leeway for efficient operation.

The second part of the API (Figure 16.1b) supports communication between application programs in two PCs connected physically by an async link and logically by RELAY Gold. RELAY Gold is one of very few products that facilitate program-to-program communication over async connections.

Before application-to-application communication starts, a RELAY Gold connection must be established between the two PCs, normally by means of a script file (a user can also do this manually). Once the two Relay GOLDs are talking to each other, the second part of the API comes into play, supporting full-duplex communication between the two application programs. A lower-level protocol, also called RELAY, ensures reliable data transfer between the PCs.

The functions provided by this part of the API can:

- Start and stop inter-application communication.

- Send a message to the remote application program.

- Receive a message from the remote application program.

- Query the status of messages in transit.

- Cancel messages in transit.

When an application program sends a message, control is returned to it immediately. The message is queued, and actual transmission may take place later in the background. Similarly, when an application program asks to receive a message, control will be returned immediately with whatever data is at hand.

ADVANCED PROGRAM-TO-PROGRAM COMMUNICATION (LU 6.2)

Imagine trying to communicate with a person incarcerated inside a terminal. That person's only sense organ is the keyboard, and his only mode of expression is to display characters on the screen. Communication is limited to messages representable in a small alphabet of characters that fit on a small screen; gestures, intonations, and nuances are impossible; interaction is slow and involves tedious typing. In fact, you probably could never be sure you were communicating with a human being, rather than a clever computer program emulating one. Liberate the prisoner from the terminal, meet him face to face, and that's peer-to-peer communication.

The hierarchical design of the original SNA reflected the asymmetric nature of terminal-to-application sessions. (Such a session is asymmetric in much the same sense that a dog leash is asymmetric.) In the early 1980s, IBM started adding some peer-to-peer capabilities for both programs and terminals, including LU session types 6.0 and 6.1. LU 6.2, the first to provide program-to-program communication in a completely general way, has now superseded types 6.0 and 6.1, and is on its way to becoming a standard for distributed processing.

With LU 6.2, programs residing on different computers in a network can converse as equals, using symmetric sessions. In fact, programs co-resident on the same computer also can, and very often do, communicate with each other via LU 6.2. These peer-to-peer communication capabilities should not be confused with the peer-to-peer protocol structure outlined in the section on SNA. Peer-to-peer protocols, designed into SNA from its inception, provide the network with an orderly *internal* structure. Peer-to-peer capability at the *user* level, facilitating sessions between equal partners, is a very different matter.

Advanced Program-to-Program Communication (APPC), strictly speaking, includes LU 6.2 and PU 2.1. An LU, remember, defines a user interface to SNA. LU 6.2, in particular, defines an API: a set of operations invoked by a program in order to engage another program in a conversation. PU 2.1 defines the requirements for the network communication functions underlying LU sessions of this type. It is common, however, for the terms "LU 6.2" and "APPC" to be used interchangeably. We haven't placed APPC under the rubric "Communicating with IBM Mainframes and Minis" because PC-based programs can, in principle, use it to communicate not only with programs running in larger IBM machines but also those on other PCs and, potentially, even non-IBM computers.

IBM was motivated to develop APPC partly by market pressures—its archrival DEC had taken an early lead in distributed processing—and partly by customer demand. APPC has been reasonably well received and is tightly meshed with IBM's strategic Systems Application Architecture (SAA). APPC is also the cleanest form of user-level communication in SNA, with a set of core functions that guarantees stable interconnection between two programs that invoke it.

An APPC for a DOS PC is a memory-resident program. It gives application programs access to relevant network services in the same manner that DOS gives programs access to local files. The Extended Edition of OS/2 incorporates LU 6.2, along with several other communication facilities, right in the middle of the operating system. This is significant because, in order for multiple application programs running under OS/2 simultaneously to use a communication facility, management of that facility must be centralized in the operating system.

We can think of APPC as a way of coupling two programs together so they can jointly perform some task. While LU 6.2 links programs in pairs, a program may have several such links active at any time. Multiple concurrent links are possible between a single pair of programs as well as among different programs. Thus, large numbers of distributed programs can converse as an intelligent community.

Although APPC is an exciting development for many PC users, it's not the sort of thing you can just go out and buy at ComputerVille, install in your PC, and boot up. Working with APPC is not like working with a 3270 emulator; it's more like getting involved with a programming language or an object library. To benefit from APPC, you must buy or develop application programs that employ it. IBM has developed several network service utilities for mainframes and System/3Xs that depend on APPC, including electronic mail and file archiving systems. Eventually, these utilities may extend to PCs. Many large IBM users will develop in-house application programs to take advantage of APPC, while, as is usually the case, commercial products will come from aftermarket developers.

While most early PC APPC implementations will probably serve to connect PC applications to mainframe programs, APPC is also capable of connecting application program pairs across the whole line of IBM's computers, including PC-to-PC links. In fact, APPC bids fair to become an industrywide standard, allowing programs to communicate irrespective of environment—that is, without concern for differences in processor, operating system, programming language, physical network type, and so on.

So, what will APPC do for you? If you're a user, it will open the door to a new breed of application program that takes advantage of APPC's seamless communication capability. PC spreadsheet programs can automatically access mainframe databases to pull out data; distributed database managers can handle a database that's either partitioned among a number of machines or perfectly replicated in each of several computers. If you are an application developer, APPC allows you to concentrate on writing exciting, powerful products that use cooperative processing without having to worry about how communication is to be accomplished.

It has been said that APPC does not actually permit anything new. In a limited sense, that's probably accurate. (Consider 3270 emulation, which has already had an amazing agglomeration of fancy and sophisticated capabilities heaped on top of it.) Applications that use distributed processing have been widely developed on IBM networks but, before APPC, always with ad-hoc interfaces requiring horrendous amounts of work. APPC provides program authors with an efficient, compact, standardized, and powerful interface to network communications. More to the point, APPC does offer one decidedly new capability: it allows peer-to-peer communication. All previous IBM communications methods, of which the most common is 3270 data stream (LU 2), followed the master-slave model; the terminal was a slave to the mainframe. APPC treats the PC and mainframe more or less as equals, each having a right to control communications. To appreciate what a tremendous advancement this represents, think about using a mainframe for file service or printing, and imagine how frustrating it would be if you had to wait for it to decide that it was in the mood to do what you wanted. While such a situation may sound intolerable, it is, in fact, an exaggerated but plausible description of the master-slave regime.

APPC also promises to render communications more efficient. For example, a 3270-based file transfer system puts an absurdly large load on a mainframe: a single PC uploading a medium-sized file can be more taxing than a large community of real terminals. APPC reduces mainframe load by facilitating the migration of applications, or portions of them, to PCs. Still, IBM needn't be too concerned about its market; a mainframe's burden may be reduced by each instance of distributed processing, but the growth in such developments will surely soak up any increased idle capacity. Most APPC applications will be newly developed. Distributed applications written for LU 6.1 can be converted to 6.2 with ease. Older applications built with proprietary interfaces will mostly be left as-is.

A Technical Overview

While IBM literature describes APPC as supporting distributed transaction processing, LU 6.2 will be valuable in other applications as well. Granted, APPC does have some special coordination features of prime importance to transaction processing, but it also stands as a general-purpose program-to-program interface.

For the purpose of this overview, keep in mind a classic case of distributed application: a funds transfer system operated between two computers. Here, a transaction consists of a debit to an account on one system and a credit (of equal amount, we trust) to an account on the other system. The difficult part is ensuring consistency in the event of an equipment-related failure, such as loss of communications between the two computers. Every effort must be made to avoid the possibility of a debit being entered without the corresponding credit, or vice versa.

Unlike much else in SNA, APPC is fairly simple. It defines an API consisting of a modest set of command "verbs." A program employing APPC uses these verbs to request network services and, thereby, to communicate with other programs. Each implementation may incorporate only a subset of all the available functions, if such a limitation suits its needs; to abide by the rules, however, it should be constrained to use one of several standardized subsets.

LU 6.2 further defines a fundamental unit of program interaction, called a *conversation*, consisting of a set of related transactions such as those required to complete a single payment transfer. Normal practice calls for a conversation to encompass a compound transaction that is either fully executed or backed-out if, for any reason, it cannot be completed. ("Backing out" a transaction means undoing any updates to data made as a result of that transaction.) In any event, the conversation is *never* to be left "dangling." Fortunately, such an outcome is rendered impossible by the very design of the conversation, as discussed below. The conversation defined here is known as an *atomic transaction*, which means what it sounds like—indivisible (no atom-splitting is allowed in this context).

The section on SNA in Chapter 12 indicated that the "6.2" in "LU 6.2" refers, properly speaking, to an SNA session type. APPC communication is accomplished, of course, via sessions of this type. A considerable amount of work is involved in establishing any kind of network session. This overhead is not significant for typical terminal sessions, which usually last for some time; but since most APPC transactions take place within a few seconds, setting up and taking down a session for each transaction would be quite burdensome. The conversation defined by APPC therefore serves as a new "sub-session" entity. Two APPC programs know nothing about sessions, but establish a conversation for each cooperative unit of work to be performed.

Behind the scenes, a conversation is allocated within an LU 6.2 session. When a conversation is complete, the session that hosted it is not discarded but kept around for possible reuse; normally, a session is indeed used for a succession of conversations, one at a time. When a program requests a conversation, the LU looks for a session with two attributes: it must be with the right partner (obviously) and must not already have a conversation assigned to it. If a suitable session is free, the LU assigns the conversation to it. Otherwise, the LU will open a new session, as long as the total number remains within allowable limits.

While the design of APPC is oriented to what are typically rather brief conversations, an application writer is free to use them without such constraints, and can, if need be, arrange for conversations that last for hours.

By definition, every APPC service, except those that create and terminate conversations, must pertain to a specific, active conversation. Communication can take place *only* within a conversation. Within each one, data transfer is strictly half-duplex, but data messages of arbitrary size and content may be transferred between partners.

A few LU 6.2 services address the synchronization needs of partners by, for example, allowing one program to signal its commitment to make permanent all changes made to databases and similar resources. Other partners respond either with confirmations of the changes or with error indications. Unless confirmations are forthcoming from all partners, the changes are retracted. Thus, in our funds transfer example, a single synchronization would probably be used at the end of each conversation, at which point each partner would log the changes made to its database and unlock the records affected.

Products

IBM has APPC implementations for its mainframes running Transaction Processing Facility (TPF) and CICS operating systems, its System/36, System/38, AS/400™, and ES/9370™ minicomputers, and PCs. (As a point of interest, TPF represents the cooperative engineering effort of IBM and several large U.S. corporations. This group modified an earlier IBM operating system expressly to allow use with LU 6.2.) The PC product is known as APPC/PC. In addition, IBM sells a few semi-intelligent devices, such as the 3820 laser graphics printer and the 8815 Scanmaster scanner, that communicate using APPC.

The Token-Ring Network is IBM's primary vehicle for supporting APPC connections to PCs. Such a LAN may interconnect multiple computers in a local area, including PCs, minicomputers, and mainframes (via 3174 control units or 3725 FEPs). Two programs wishing to communicate via LU 6.2 need not, of course, run on computers directly attached to the same LAN, but may reside anywhere on a given SNA network. They could be running on the same machine or thousands of miles apart.

APPC is one of two PC/Token-Ring software interfaces; the other is IBM's NETBIOS (Chapter 14), which is incompatible with LU 6.2.

Other computer manufacturers are jumping on the APPC bandwagon with products for many popular minicomputers.

Limitations

As explained above, LU 6.2 depends on PU 2.1 to support lower-level network communication functions. PU 2.1 functionality exceeds that of 3270 cluster controllers, rendering APPC incompatible with 3270-style network connections. On the other hand, ECF/S-RPI, mentioned in the previous section, is 3270-compatible and has been called a "poor man's APPC." It's considerably less powerful than APPC but serves the same purpose as an intended standard for distributed processing in the 3270 domain.

VIRTUAL DEVICES

Given the ability to connect one's PC to a host computer, one fairly drools to imagine taking advantage of the host's peripherals: fast line printers, huge disks, and industry-standard tape drives. File transfer is an important stepping-stone to such access, but wouldn't it be wonderful if PC applications could directly and transparently access host devices? Well, they can with *virtual devices*, of which the most useful and popular is the *virtual disk*.

Host-Based Virtual Disks

Almost all PC application programs work with files, usually disk files. In telling Lotus 1-2-3 to pull up a spreadsheet, you are actually telling it to read the file containing that spreadsheet. To tell WordPerfect to show you a certain document for editing, you must give it the name of the file containing that document. When you move data from one application program to another, you probably do so via a file. Files are the standardized, universal underpinning to PC productivity. No wonder files remain uniform between DOS and OS/2.

It's difficult to imagine life without the files to which we are so accustomed. Suppose every application program maintained its own files in unique formats guaranteed to be unusable by others. Or, suppose files had numbers instead of names. (It's been done in at least one system—in the name of security, believe it or not.)

Of course, PC files could be improved. We might, for example, have filenames longer than 11 characters or, better yet, be able to put a descriptive tag on each file—for example, "This is the version of the third-quarter sales spreadsheet I gave Marcia on November 9th." The File Info utility program, part of the Norton Utilities 4.0, provides this capability to some degree, but the function can be truly useful only if part of the operating system. Imagine a generational file system, like that found on DEC's VMS and a few other minicomputer systems, where several numbered versions of each file are maintained. When you change a file, a new generation is created, but older versions are not lost, and you can revert to a previous version if necessary. Again, something of the same ability is provided by a few PC add-on programs.

This digression was intended to help you appreciate the importance of the PC's file system. For programs to be able to read and write data other than on disks, the best approach is to provide one or more virtual disks, which logically appear and behave like disks but are not physical disk drives. A common example is the RAM disk that enables you to keep files in an area of memory and provides much faster access than any physical disk.

To introduce a disk, whether real or virtual, to your PC, the operating system must be provided with an appropriate driver. (DOS drivers were described in Chapter I.) When an application program asks the operating system for access to a file on disk D:, the operating system translates the access request into a request to the associated driver. It's entirely up to that driver where the data will come from and where it will be sent. The only requirement is that the data be organized into a series of numbered blocks, like sectors on a real disk.

So, with appropriate drivers, almost anything can be made to "look like" a PC disk: memory, as in a RAM disk; a real disk that happens to be connected to another PC, as with a shared disk on a LAN; or some storage medium on a host. A British communications expert known to the authors is fond of saying that he could make a PC believe a pile of spaghetti (organized into zeros and ones) was a PC disk, if he only had the right driver for it.

Of course, a prerequisite to host-based virtual disks is a suitable communication link between the PC and the host; this might be a terminal connection like that provided by a 3270-emulator for an IBM mainframe, but that's only one possibility. "Suitable" just means whatever is acceptable to the particular virtual-disk product. Many work on simple asynchronous lines.

Host-based virtual disks also require, at the PC end, a driver that communicates with the host via an API (this may necessitate running a terminal emulator in memory-resident mode) and, in the host, software that simulates a number of disks. A typical setup provides the PC with four *virtual diskette drives*, named with letters consecutive to those used for local disks. In addition to simulating the drives, the host software maintains libraries of *virtual diskettes*. The size of a virtual diskette can typically be anything from a few kilobytes up to 32 megabytes. Clearly, then, these are called virtual "diskettes" rather than "disks" not because they are low in capacity but because, like real diskettes, they are removable. (Virtual diskettes are unlike real diskettes, however, in that you can't very easily spill your coffee on them.) The virtual drives are managed by either DOS-level commands or menu selections that permit PC users to load and unload each virtual drive, query the status of drives, create and destroy virtual diskettes, and set passwords or permissions on the diskettes.

The ability to set permissions and passwords is very significant. Normally, one of the prime motivations for installing a virtual disk system is that it enables PCs to share files. The high cost of host software makes it unlikely that one would purchase a virtual disk system for a single PC. Such a system is most often set up for a community of users, which then shares access to virtual diskettes.

Virtual disks are enticing because they provide a transparent way for PC applications to use host storage. The single, and very great, drawback from the user's standpoint is *speed*. Accessing a virtual disk on a host (as distinct from, say, PC RAM disks) is inevitably much, much slower than accessing even a local floppy drive. It is impossible to give "typical" speeds, because transfer rates vary tremendously with the host's workload and the nature of the communication link. A "not-unusual worst-case" estimate, however, is that it will take about 20 to 30 minutes to transfer the contents of a 360K floppy.

If virtual disks are so slow, why does anyone use them? Because of the convenience. For certain applications, people will summon up amazing reserves of patience in order to acquire the benefits of such products. Let's look at some of the inviting aspects of virtual disk systems and more of the drawbacks.

- On a per-megabyte basis, host disks are cheaper than PC disks because they are much larger. The flip side of this is that PC virtual disks can fill up host disks in a hurry.
- Host storage is typically backed up to magnetic tape in a regular, reliable manner. PC virtual disks, being maintained as host files, will also be backed up. This may be an easy way of centralizing back-up for a community of PCs, but it rarely proves cost-effective.
- Uploading a file to a host can be as simple as, for example,

  COPY C: BLAH D:

  where D: is a virtual disk drive.
- PC files on virtual disks may reside on host storage but cannot be directly accessed by host application programs. The typical user of a virtual disk system will also use the host for other purposes, and will therefore have great interest in moving data between PC applications and host applications. The fact that the PC can immediately access data stored on the host's PC virtual disks goes a long way toward making such sharing possible, but two obstacles remain. First, special utilities must be used to copy data between regular host files and PC virtual files. Second, in many cases, format and character-set translations will be required.
- If a number of PCs already have host connections for other reasons, and the need arises for them to share data, virtual disks are a solution that calls for no additional communication channels. For intensive data-sharing, however, a host-based system is unlikely to prove satisfactory; a PC LAN promises to work much better.

Tempus-Link®, Tempus-Access®, and Tempus-Share

It is impractical to survey the entire range of virtual-disk products for PC users because there are so many for different sorts of host. (IBM has some ones for both its mainframe systems and System/3X minis.) Instead, we will illustrate by describing a single outstanding and mature product line provided for IBM mainframes by Micro Tempus. Although obviously a strong endorsement of the Tempus line, this choice should not be taken to mean that Micro's product is the only one worth considering.

Tempus-Link, the original product in what is now a trio, provides the PC user with up to eight virtual disk drives on the host. With local drives A, B, and C, for instance, the host-based drives would most likely be designated as D through K. Virtual disks may be created in sizes ranging from 32 kilobytes to 30 megabytes, and they are stored in "cases" holding as many as 255 disks each. The PC user has the choice of managing the virtual drives by either DOS-level commands or selections from pop-up menus. If a system administrator were to set up, in batch files, suitable Tempus-Link commands to establish the virtual disk environment, a naive PC user could use the virtual disks without knowing that the associated drives were being emulated by a mainframe.

Tempus-Link depends on some pre-established communication link between PC and host. It cannot function with just any old link, but does support an impressive range of connection options. Caching of virtual disk data at the PC is provided to boost performance.

Tempus-Access, added to Tempus-Link, enables the user to extract data from mainframe files and databases and to copy them to files on virtual diskettes. Certain types of data transformation may be incorporated into this extraction process. For example, text may be translated from EBCDIC to ASCII, and field-oriented data may be converted to the comma-separated variables (CSV) format readable by dBASE®and many other PC application programs. With a single command at the PC, a predefined set of data may be culled from not just one, but several, mainframe files and placed onto a virtual disk from which they can be immediately imported into, for example, a Lotus or Excel spreadsheet.

The sharing of data among PC users made possible by Tempus-Link is limited in one vital respect. Each PC has its own private, individual set of virtual drives. PCs cannot share concurrent access to a single virtual disk. Subject to appropriate permissions, any virtual disk may be loaded into any virtual drive but, as with physical disks, only one drive at a time. A virtual disk can be copied to facilitate shared read access to data, but there is no provision for shared write access.

Tempus-Share, taking advantage of facilities built for PC LANs, goes a step further to allow concurrent shared access to virtual drives. It makes possible the creation of any number of virtual drives of any size, bounded only by available mainframe storage, for simultaneous use by any number of users. This facility means that a mainframe can be used like a file server on a PC LAN to host, for example, multi-user data bases managed by network versions of PC products such as dBASE.

X.25 FRAME LEVEL

We introduced X.25 in Chapter 8. Here we provide a technical overview of X.25's Data Link Layer and, in the next section, its Network Layer. In describing the main points of LAPB operation, we will exclude many minor details in order to keep the discussion to a reasonable length. Let's start by reviewing the frame format, as illustrated in Figure 16.2.

When sending a frame, the DTE or DCE sets the A-field to one of two values, depending on whether the frame is a response to one received from the partner or is being originated for another reason. In other words, the value in the A-field distinguishes a "command" message from a "response" message—a vital bit of information, because there are several types of message that may function as either commands or responses in this sense. Thus,

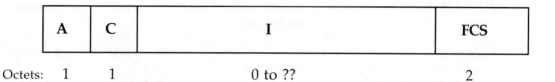

A	C	I	FCS

Octets: 1   1   0 to ??   2

A is an address
C is the control field
I is the information (i.e., data) field
FCS is the frame check sequence (16-bit CRC)

FIGURE 16.2: X.25 frame format

the A-field setting of a frame tells a receiving station whether it is appropriate to respond to the message, and prevents needless responses to responses.

The control field contains the frame type identifier and the *poll/final (P/F) bit,* used for synchronization (see below). Depending on the frame type, the field may also contain one or two sequence numbers to identify and/or acknowledge data. The exact coding of the C-field is intricate, so we'll leave you to refer to the standard for more information. The following types of frame are defined, divided into three categories: Information or I-frames, Supervisory or S-frames, and Unnumbered or U-frames. I-frames carry data. S-frames are used to acknowledge and otherwise manage the flow of I-frames. U-frames serve to manage the *state* of the DTE/DCE link.

	I-Frames		*U-Frames*
I	Information	SABM	Set Asynchronous Balanced Mode
	S-Frames	UA	Unnumbered Acknowledgment
RR	Receive Ready	DISC	DISConnect
RNR	Receive Not Ready	DM	Disconnect Mode
REJ	REJect	FRMR	FRaMe Reject

The I-field of an I-frame carries data on behalf of Layer 3 of the protocol. (The frame level itself acts simply as a carrier; the nature of the data is a matter of concern only for Layer 3.) A data packet is constrained to consist of an integral number of octets. FRMRs, while not data carriers in the above sense, do contain small amounts of diagnostic data for Layer 2. No other frame may contain data; thus, the I-field of any frame other than I or FRMR must be empty.

The X.25 standard sets no maximum limit on the length of an I-field, but any network using X.25 will dictate a limit, usually based on available buffer sizes. An I-frame, by the way, does not contain a count of its length. The receiving hardware can always determine the overall frame length by watching those ever-handy flags. The length of the I-field, in bits, is then determined by subtracting 32 (i.e., the fixed size of the A, C, and FCS fields combined) from the total frame length.

The Frame Check Sequence (FCS) contains a 16-bit Cyclic Redundancy Check (CRC) for detecting transmission errors. The FCS is normally tacked onto each transmitted frame by the I/O hardware; the same hardware checks the FCS of received frames. The receiver immediately discards any frame found to exhibit an FCS error; error recovery (the retransmission of bad frames) is driven purely by time-outs, rather than by negative acknowledgments of damaged messages. Any frame shorter than 32 bits is also discarded, which has the effect of eliminating most damaged flags from consideration as frames.

Under X.25, the DCE/DTE link can be in one of two states, also called *phases*: the *logically disconnected state* and the *link-established*, or *information transfer, state*. A virgin (newly created) link is always logically disconnected. The information transfer state is established when the DTE sends an SABM and the DCE acknowledges this by returning a UA. Note that, although the protocol is largely symmetrical, it is always the DTE's responsibility to establish the link.

I-frames may be sent only in the information transfer phase, as its name implies. Once the transfer state is established, it persists until either a serious error occurs or one end logically disconnects by sending a DISC, to which the appropriate response is, again, a UA. Note that *logical* disconnection has little to do with whether or not the link is *physically* disconnected.

I-frames are numbered in recurring cycles of zero through seven. This implies that, in principle, up to seven I-frames can be unacknowledged, or "outstanding," at any time. In practice, a network is likely to place a lower limit on the allowed number of unacknowledged I-frames, commonly two. Each station maintains two variables: the Send State Variable, $V(S)$, and the Receive State Variable, $V(R)$. Both are initialized to zero when the link is established. Whenever a new I-frame is sent, the sender sticks the current value of its $V(S)$ into the C-field of the I-frame as its sequence number, and then increments $V(S)$ modulo eight. Whenever a new I-frame is received, its sequence number should match the receiver's $V(R)$; if it does, the receiver increments its $V(R)$ and acknowledges the I-frame. Thus, $V(S)$ is the number of the next new I-frame a station will transmit, while $V(R)$ is the number of the I-frame it expects to receive next. When no transmitted frames are unacknowledged between a sender and receiver, the sender's $V(S)$ will match the receiver's $V(R)$.

Each station is required to acknowledge every I-frame upon receipt. First, however, the receiver must update its $V(R)$, assuming that the frame was received in order. A receiver may acknowledge by means of several frame types, each carrying (in the C-field) a copy of the receiver's current $V(R)$, according to the following priorities:

1. RNR, if the station is busy and wishes to receive no further I-frames for awhile, perhaps due to lack of buffer space. This says "I received that frame in fine spirits, but don't send any more until I give you the okay."

2. REJ, if the I-frame arrived out of order (i.e., its sequence number did not match the receiver's $V[R]$). This means "I received an I-frame, but not the one I was expecting; please send me the I-frame with this sequence number."

3. An I-frame, if the receiver has such a frame ready to send out, and has not exceeded the limit on unacknowledged frames. An I-frame can itself serve as an I-frame acknowledgment, since its C-field carries the sender's $V(R)$.

4. RR, if nothing else is appropriate. This says "I got that I-frame okay, and I'm ready for more." Thus, I-frame and RR acknowledgment types have the same meaning.

The above outlines the roles of the supervisory frames RR, RNR, and REJ in acknowledging data and managing flow control. After sending an RNR, a station will eventually (when it is no longer too busy) invite the other end to resume sending I-frames, normally by transmitting an REJ, which tells the partner specifically at which I-frame to resume. An RR will also serve to restart I-frame flow. A link reset (SABM/UA exchange) always clears a not-ready condition. Note that a station may continue to *send* I-frames after sending an RNR unless, of course, it has received an RNR from its partner.

What happens if a station sends a I-frame and receives no acknowledgment? This can occur for several reasons, of course, but most likely because the frame was damaged. Each time an I-frame is transmitted, the sender sets a timer (unless the timer is already running) for a period called T1. T1 is a *system parameter*: its value is defined by the implementation, which usually means by the particular network. Typical T1 values range between 100 ms and 10 seconds. When an acknowledgment for an I-frame arrives, the timer switch is *toggled*—that is, the timer is stopped if no further I-frames remain unacknowledged; otherwise, it is restarted. Should T1 elapse before an acknowledgment arrives, the sending station must determine what happened and retransmit the frame if necessary. The X.25 standard affords some latitude in how the sender may handle this: it may either simply retransmit the oldest unacknowledged I-frame or send an RR or RNR, as appropriate to its ability to receive I-frames, to determine which frame its partner is expecting. On retransmitting an I-frame, it will restart its T1 timer, repeating the process if T1 expires again. In case something is so wrong that an acknowledgment can never arrive, a station gives up after a number of retries defined by another system parameter, called N2. A typical N2 value is 20.

If, on an established link, a station receives a message with an invalid format, it should return FRMR. This is a diagnostic frame with a four-byte I-field containing data about the perceived error. (For the format of this particular I-field, please refer to the standard.) Some examples of invalid-format frames, whose receipt should provoke FRMRs, are those (other than I-frames or FRMRs) containing data, those with I-fields longer than the limit established by the network, and nonexistent frame types. On receiving an FRMR, a station should send an SABM to reset the link.

The P/F bit, found in the C-field of all frames, may be set on an outgoing frame to help the sender identify a subsequently received frame as a response to the one sent. When a station receives a frame with the P/F bit set, it should also set the bit on its reply frame. This usage implies that after sending one frame with P/F set, a station may not send another until it has either received a response to the first or timed-out waiting for it.

We have one last frame type to describe. The DM may be issued by a station in response to a frame received while the link is logically disconnected. This is particularly true of SABMs received at times when the responding station does not want to establish the link. DM thus says, "Look, buddy, we're closed." Some networks, such as Telenet, do not use DMs and do not require their DTEs to do so.

In the following examples of frame-level activity, the DTE is assumed to be a PC and the DCE a PSN node.

Example of normal frame-level activity

PC/DTE	DCE	Commentary	PC/DTE	DCE	Commentary
SABM		PC intitiates link setup		I: N0/R1	DCE sends its first I-frame, which acknowledges ("acks") the PC's first I-frame
	UA	Both stations enter information transfer phase			
I: N0/R0		PC sends the first I-frame			

Example of normal frame-level activity (continued)

PC/DTE	DCE	Commentary	PC/DTE	DCE	Commentary
RR 1		PC acks DCE's first I-frame	RR 4	I: N4/R3	DCE's fifth I-frame crosses with PC's ack of the fourth
I: N1/R1		PC sends its second I-frame	RR 5	I: N5/R3	
	I: N1/R2	DCE sends its second I-frame acking PC's second I-frame	RR 6	RR 3	PC acks DCE's fifth I-frame, and DCE leaves not-ready state
RR 2	I: N2/R2	PC's ack for DCE's second I-frame overlaps with DCE's third	I: N3/R6		PC sends its fourth I-frame
RR 3		PC acks DCE's third I-frame	I: N4/R6	RR 4	DCE acks the fourth, while PC sends its fifth I-frame
I: N2/R3		PC sends its third I-frame		RR 5	DCE acks the PC's fifth I-frame
	RNR 3	DCE acks and goes into busy state	DISC		PC initiates logical disconnect
	I: N3/R3	DCE sends its fourth I-frame		UA	Link is logically disconnected

Example of frame-level activity with transmission errors

PC/DTE	DCE	Commentary
SABM		
	UA	
I: N0/R0		
	I: N0/R1	
RR 1 (damaged)		
	...	DCE times out and repeats I-frames
	I: N0/R1	
RR 1		
	(damaged) I: N1/R1	
I: N1/R1	...	DCE times out again and repeats with new V(R)
	I: N1/R2	
RR 2		
I: N2/2		
	(damaged) RR 3	
...		DTE times out and polls with RR
RR 2(P)		
	RR 3(F)	DCE responds with final
I: N3/R2 (damaged)		
...		DTE times out again and polls
RR 2(P)		
	RR 3(F)	

Example of frame-level activity with transmission errors (continued)

PC/DTE	DCE	Commentary
I: N3/R2		DTE repeats I-frame
	RR 4	
I: N4/R2 (damaged)		
I: N5/R2		
	REJ 4	DCE did not see a frame 4
I: N4/R2		
I: N5/R2	RR 5	
	RR 6	
	DISC	
UA		

Example of frame-level activity with brain-damaged DTE

PC/DTE	DCE	Commentary
		Starts in disconnected state
I: N6/R5		DCE ignores
RR 5		DCE ignores
DISC		
	UA	
SABM		
	UA	Logical connection made
I: N6/R5		
	FRMR	
SABM		
	UA	
I: N0/R0		All okay for a while
	RR 1	
	I: N0/R1	
FRMR		No reason for this
	SABM	
UA		
I: N0/R1		
	FRMR	DCE objects to V(R) of 1
I: N0/R1		
	FRMR	
RR 1		

PC/DTE	DCE	Commentary
	FRMR	
	. . .	No activity from PC
	FRMR	DCE times out and repeats FRMR
SABM		PC finally catches on
	UA	
I: N0/R0		
	RNR 1	DCE goes busy
I: N1/R0		PC should not send data
I: N2/R0		No clear option for DCE
	REJ 1	DCE is compassionate
I: N1/R0		DTE responds correctly
	RR 2	
I: N2/R0	I: N0/R2	
I: N2/R0		
	RR 3	Repeat not called for but DCE cannot know this
	DISC	
	. . .	PC does not respond
	DISC	
	. . .	
	DISC	(DCE sends DISC N2 times, then gives up)

LAPB for Modems

In Chapter 8, we stated that LAPB is used as a protocol for error-correcting modems. It must be admitted that X.25 experts may question the protocol's aptitude for modem use because it does not include negative acknowledgments for damaged information frames, but rather relies on time-outs and REJect packets to trigger retransmissions. This suggests that, in the presence of persistent errors, performance may be relatively sluggish. In fact, the situation is not as bad as it looks.

The X.25 standard does not explicitly provide a means of expediting retransmission of damaged I-frames, but does leave LAPB sufficiently flexible to offer at least three opportunities for implementation in a manner that provides fine performance. For a start, the value for LAPB's T1 timer, the period during which a sender waits for an acknowledgment, can be set very low. Second, after the sender has completed an information frame, if the PC supplies no further data for transmission, the modem can transmit an RR (or RNR, when appropriate) with the P/F bit set; this should draw an immediate response indicating whether or not the previous I-frame was lost. Third, a modem, on receiving a frame long enough to be an I-frame but bearing a bad CRC, can assume the worst and dispatch an REJ requesting retransmission of the frame. This last option may entail some risk because, if the receiver mistakes a damaged frame of some other type for a damaged I-frame, it might return an REJ for a real I-frame that had already arrived intact and been acknowledged; this, in turn, might cause the other station to reset the link.

X.25 PACKET LEVEL

We'll now consider X.25's Network Layer, first examining the packet format, shown in Figure 16.3.

The GFI field always contains a value of binary 0001, except in Data packets or when the modulo-128 numbering scheme is used (see below). The combined contents of LCGN and LCN reflect the logical channel number appropriate to the packet, as dictated by network assignment.

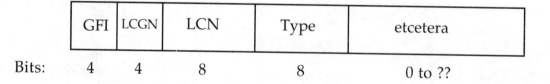

GFI is the general format identifier
LCGN is the logical channel group number
LCN is the logical channel number
Type is the packet type identifier
etcetera are anything else (packet-type dependent)

FIGURE 16.3: X.25 packet format

As the eight-bit size of the Type field implies, the total number of packet types could be fairly large. We are concerned here only with the general aspects of this field. The packet type, then, falls into one of five categories:

- *Restart*—for initializing or reinitializing the packet-level DTE/DCE interface
- *Call setup and clearing*—for establishing and terminating virtual calls
- *Data and interrupt*—for moving data
- *Flow control and reset*—to control the flow and acknowledgment of data
- *Diagnostic*—sent only by DCEs to complain about invalid DTE packets. Not all nets use diagnostic packets.

A virtual call consists of a sequence of three phases: *call setup, data transfer*, and *call clearing*. Call setup and call clearing may be initiated by either the DTE or the DCE. If the setup phase cannot be completed, the data transfer phase will not exist, and the call will be cleared. The setup and clear phases both involve the exchange of a pair of packets between DTE and DCE. Permanent virtual circuits are *always* in the data transfer phase.

Now let's consider the packet types used in this protocol:

Restarts.   When a station resumes operation after a crash or any other debilitating event, it starts the connection afresh by sending a restart. Either the DTE or the DCE may request a restart at any time. A restart clears any virtual calls and resets all PVCs. Any resetting of the link at Layer 2 (an SABM/UA exchange) will precipitate a packet-level restart exchange initiated by the DCE.

Note that the restart packets are "global" to the DTE/DCE link and contain a LCGN and LCN of zero. All other packets belong to a particular logical channel.

Diagnostics.   Some network DCEs may send a diagnostic packet to the DTE to indicate certain error conditions. Such a transmission is for informational purposes only; it does not change the state of the logical channel to which it pertains. This means that a DTE may safely, if not wisely, ignore diagnostic packets. Such diagnostic information is ultimately intended for the human DTE operators who may have a misbehaving X.25 implementation on their hands.

Call Setup.   The DTE initiates a virtual call by sending a Call Request packet to the DCE. This packet must contain the network address of the called (remote) DTE and may also identify the calling DTE, as prescribed by the network. (Optionally, the facilities fields described below may also appear in the Call Request packet.) The DTE selects a logical channel at the time of call request, properly taking the highest-numbered channel available. The DCE initiates a virtual call by sending the DTE an Incoming Call packet, and selects the lowest channel number available, minimizing the chances of a collision (in which the DTE and DCE simultaneously try to initiate a call on the same logical channel).

Call Clearing.   Either the DTE or DCE may clear a call—the DTE by sending a Clear Request packet, the DCE by sending a Clear Indication packet. In either case, the other station responds with a Clear Confirmation packet.

Each section in the following diagram illustrates a possible exchange in setting up a call on a given logical channel:

DTE	DCE	Commentary
1. Call Request		DTE places a virtual call
	Call connected	DCE completes
2.	Incoming Call	DTE is recipient of the call
Call Accepted		DTE completes
3. Call Request		DTE places a virtual call
	Clear Indication	Call fails
Clear Confirmation		DTE acknowledges the clear
4.	Incoming Call	DTE is recipient
Clear Request		but refuses it
	Clear Confirmation	DCE acknowledges the refusal
5. Call Request	Incoming Call	Collision!
	Call Connected	DCE defers to DTE

The Clear Request or Clear Indication packet will contain a code indicating the cause, such as, number busy, out of order, or access barred.

Data Transfer. Data transfer proceeds independently on each active logical channel. Normal network operation guarantees that all data pass unaltered through the network. This implies that no data are changed or lost, and that data packets are delivered in order, but allows for the possibility of the data being *repacketized*, that is, arriving in packets of sizes different from those in which they were dispatched. Repacketizing may occur for two reasons: networks may merge packets to improve efficiency or "fragment" them to pass data through nodes that restrict packet size.

Data packets that happen to be in transit when a call is cleared are discarded by the network.

The default maximum size for the user data field within a data packet is 128 octets. The protocol permits the maximum size to be established at other values on call setup: 16, 32, 64, 128, 256, 512, or 1024 octets. A ceiling, commonly 256, is also imposed by each network. The data field of any data packet may then contain any amount of information up to the agreed maximum.

To allow end-to-end transactions to consist of an arbitrarily large amount of data, a sequence of data packets may be bracketed together to form a "superpacket" called a *packet sequence*. The packet-sequence mechanism is complex, involving two control bits called D and M. X.25 guarantees that packet sequences will be kept intact, that is, that contiguous packets belonging to different sequences will not be merged. See the standard for details.

DTEs may distinguish two "levels" of data by setting or resetting a qualifier bit called Q in each data packet. The Q feature is apparently little used.

Interrupt Packets. An Interrupt packet is a special high-priority data packet typically used to get the attention of a host—for example, to send a Rubout, Break, or Control-C to a time-sharing system. The network should attempt to deliver an Interrupt as quickly as possible, unconstrained by flow control. Such a packet may thus overtake regular data packets in transit. In many applications, data sent before the Interrupt, but received after it, will be discarded upon receipt, but this is an application matter; the protocol continues to deliver all data as usual. Receipt of an Interrupt is acknowledged by an Interrupt Confirmation packet.

Flow Control.   Flow control mechanisms for Layer 3 data packets are very similar to those used for Layer 2. Packet sequence numbers, RRs, RNRs, and REJs do the job. Layer 3 flow control differs from Layer 2, however, in two vital ways. First, Layer 3 packet flow control is managed independently for each logical channel. Second, it operates on an end-to-end basis, that is, between DTE and DTE instead of between DTE and DCE as at the frame level.

Within each data stream (i.e., each direction of each logical channel) data packets are sequentially numbered, using a count that cycles between 0 and 7. (Networks may allow an extension to this scheme, with a count cycling between 0 and 127.) Each data packet contains a *packet send sequence number*, P(S), used to identify the packet. Data packets, RRs, RNRs, and REJs all contain a *packet receive sequence number*, P(R), used to acknowledge received packets. Many networks enforce a window size restricting the number of data packets simultaneously in transit in each direction of each logical channel to a value below the inherent maximum of 7 or 127. The standard window size is 2. REJ packets are optional at Layer 3, are not necessary on many networks, and often remain unsupported.

Note that Layer 3 has no error control of its own, but instead depends on the reliable transmission services provided by the frame level.

There are plenty of additional, complex details of data acknowledgment that we're avoiding going into here. Again, we refer the voraciously technical reader to the standard documentation. In addition to X.25-specific documents (See Appendix 1), some excellent IBM publications cover the closely related SDLC and HDLC protocols.

Facilities.   The packets used to initiate virtual calls may contain *facilities fields*. Facilities are used for specifying and negotiating various user options, such as nonstandard default packet and window sizes, reverse charging, and fast select. X.25 has twenty-odd standard facilities, to which network-specific ones are sometimes added. Generally, a DTE is free to refuse any option requested in a facilities field unless otherwise required by a particular network.

Some facilities, including fast select, are in the form of options ("Will you do this?"), which elicit yes-or-no responses. Others, like the nonstandard default packet size option, involve negotiation. A request might say, "Will you go for a default packet size of 256?" A proper response either accepts 256 or overrides it by choosing a smaller size. Such "negotiations" are barely worthy of the name: in the event of a conflict, the lower choice always prevails, and some networks place additional constraints on the process.

COMMUNICATIONS TROUBLESHOOTING

Now we leap from the abstract world of X.25 to the very practical matter of troubleshooting communications systems.

Checking a COM Port

Although COM ports tend to be fairly reliable, they may require testing occasionally. Here's a simple procedure.

Remove the cable from the connector of the suspect port. Start up your favorite terminal emulator, set it to use the port to be tested, and instruct it to put you on-line in direct-connect, full-duplex mode. Direct-connect is the mode used with a host to which you have a direct cable link; this should ensure that the communications software is not going to be looking for any modem control signals. The full-duplex setting is necessary to prevent the terminal emulator from performing local echoing of input.

Now type some characters on the PC keyboard. They should *not* appear on the screen because nothing should be echoing them there. If characters do appear on the screen, something is set incorrectly. Next, take a small screwdriver or similar metallic instrument— even a key will do—and hold it so that it touches both pins 2 and 3 of the connector. This shorts Transmit Data to Receive Data, creating a loopback (discussed below). Start typing again now; the characters should appear on the screen. When you remove the short, they should stop appearing. If this fails, either the software is expecting some control signals or the port is broken. You can exonerate your software by trying this test with another port, one you're sure is working properly. If you can arrange to check the software before you begin testing the suspect port, you'll have eliminated one possible source of the problem.

Of course, the above procedure tests only the data lines—the most important part of the port, but not all of it. If this test suggests that the port is working but the device to which it's connected isn't responding as it should, then replug the cable into the PC connector, remove its other end, and repeat the test there. This will tell you if the data lines in the cable are working properly.

If your communications package provides a screen display of the state of modem control lines, you can test them, too, but the procedure is a little trickier than dealing with the data lines. We won't go into all the details, which would be laborious. To check the modem control lines comprehensively, you'll need a device called a breakout box, introduced in Chapter 3.

If both port and cable appear to be working, perhaps the connected device is broken. If the device was just installed, however, first check that the right cable was used; it may be a crossover type when a straight-through type is called for, or it may lack a wire for a required line.

Loopback

When something goes wrong with a communication path, it may be difficult to determine which link in the chain of software, interfaces, cables, modems, phone lines, and other elements is causing the trouble. The best approach is to narrow down the position of the faulty component by a systematic trial-and-error method called *loopback*. Starting at one end of the path, the troubleshooter injects into the channel a continuous test signal from an appropriate source, and then checks how far down the line the signal reaches by "looping back" the signal path at each convenient test point. This creates a condition in which the signal source is talking to itself; if it can "hear" what it is "saying," then the tested channel portion is clear. By working progressively outward from the chosen point until the path is broken, the failing device can be isolated and identified.

Troubleshooting Modems and Phone Lines

To a large extent, loopback can be effected using plugs or adapters to bridge the two sides of a communications channel, but most PC modems have built-in loopback capabilities to make the job easier. The CCITT international standard V.54 describes four loopback procedures to be implemented in modems. These loopback types, called *local digital, local analog, remote analog*, and *remote digital*, are illustrated in Figure 16.4.

A modem in local digital loopback turns around the digital signal it receives from its DTE and sends it right back; in RS-232 terms, this means shorting TD to RD. Failure in a

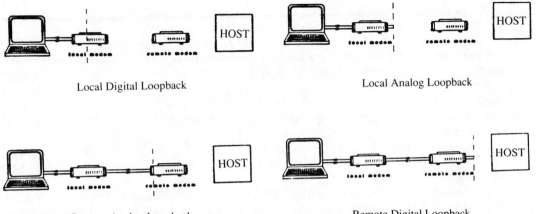

Local Digital Loopback   Local Analog Loopback

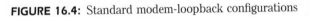

Remote Analog Loopback   Remote Digital Loopback

FIGURE 16.4: Standard modem-loopback configurations

local digital loopback test suggests a problem with the cable linking the DTE and modem. (The modem itself cannot be ruled out, but it's unlikely to be the culprit, since such a small part of it is operative in the test circuit.) A modem in local analog loopback diverts the signal it would transmit on the telephone line over to its receive circuitry. If a system passes the local digital but fails the local analog loopback test, the modem is definitely suspect.

Remote analog loopback effectively loops back the telephone line at the remote station. If a system passes the first two tests but fails with remote analog loopback, then the telephone line is probably the troublemaker but, again, either modem may be on the blink. As should be clear by now, if a system passes the first three tests and fails a remote digital loopback test, the remote modem is almost certainly broken.

It is sometimes fruitful to narrow down the list of suspects more precisely by performing the set of loopback tests first from one end of the link and then from the other.

Most PC modems offer some of these loopback options, but few offer all four. Hayes Smartmodems, for example, support both kinds of local loopback but not the remote kinds. Modems are typically placed into a loopback state by means of an internal switch, but some units can loop themselves back on command, rather like a trained seal. Beware of nonstandard loopback-test-mode nomenclature adopted by some vendors.

If your cables or modems are causing problems, you can try testing them individually, perhaps by replacing them. But what do you do if the trouble turns out to be coming from the phone line? (If you call the telephone company, they're likely to insist that their lines are impeccable and that the fault must lie with your modem. Then, when you're ready to hang up, they will brightly offer to install Call Waiting for you.) Fortunately, there are many ways and many instruments available to test a line. Phone connection testing will be of most interest to users of leased lines. We'll look at one diagnostic device: an Error Rate Tester.

When your phone line starts acting up, it's time to call in the services of a *bit error rate tester (BERT)*. You attach BERT to your local modem, put the remote modem into loopback, and push the BERT button. BERT sends bits around the loop, keeping track of the number damaged in transit. You might set it to test with, say, 1,000, 10,000, or 100,000 bits.

Suppose BERT says that 13 bits out of 10,000 are mangled. That's nice to know, but it's hardly the most complete diagnosis you could wish for. BERT can't tell you whether 13 consecutive bits were damaged or 13 separate, widely spaced bits were hit. If the bits were consecutive, the test result should be considered a single error that happened to be 13 bit-times long, while wide spacing would imply 13 distinct errors. The difference is highly significant, especially if you are using a protocol. To get more detailed information, you could summon BERT's big brother, the *block error rate tester (BLERT)*. BLERT allows you to select a block size to reflect the relevant protocol and sends a few thousand such blocks around the loop, counting the number damaged.

You may suspect that errors are occurring regularly, due, for example, to the clicking of some mechanical device. Some error rate testers can confirm such a conjecture by measuring the time distribution of errors.

Now when you have a problem with your line, you can call the phone company, tell them you did a BLERT test on it, and report that, at 1,200 bps, one 1,000-bit block is damaged out of every five, typically with an error burst lasting 10 milliseconds. They may actually sit up and take notice of such a statement—at least, if the company representative understands what you are talking about. By the way, it's not absolutely necessary to buy an Error Rate Test Set; just pick some good numbers and pretend that you did.

Error Rate Testers are available from Datacom Northwest, Black Box, and Kapusi Labs. A generic model is pictured in Figure 16.5.

Troubleshooting RS-232 Connections

In this section we examine several tools for diagnosing problems with RS-232 links.

Loopback Adapters. Loopback testing can profitably be applied to RS-232 links. A loopback adapter is a DB-25 connector with certain pins wired together. Normally, Transmit

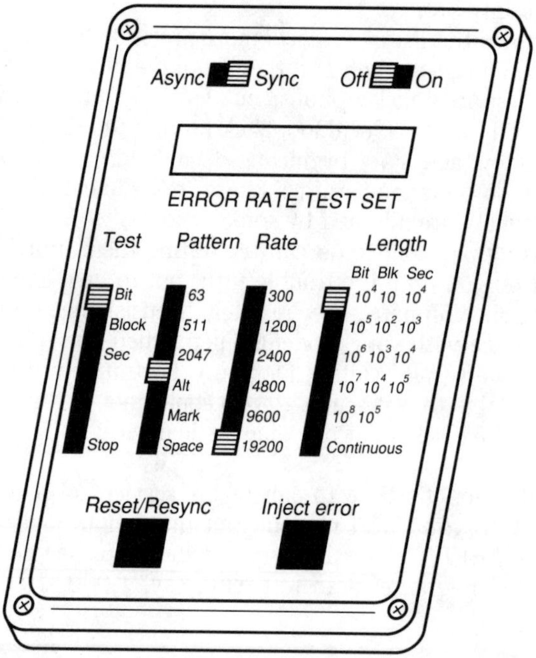

FIGURE 16.5: Error rate tester

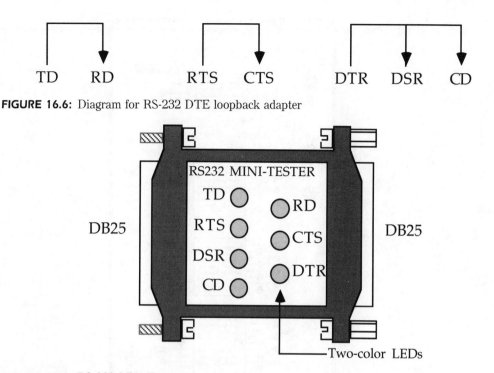

FIGURE 16.6: Diagram for RS-232 DTE loopback adapter

FIGURE 16.7: RS-232 Mini-Tester

Data is fed back to Receive Data, Request To Send gets cozy with Clear to Send, and Data Terminal Ready is wired to both Data Set Ready and Carrier Detect, as shown in Figure 16.6.

If you suspect that your serial port is misbehaving, plug in a loopback adapter and your PC will be talking to itself. It is possible to buy a loopback adapter for about $30, but we recommend that you make one yourself, perhaps by patching a breakout box (see below) to act appropriately.

Cable Testers. A cable tester is a little box for testing the continuity and cross-wiring of cables. You plug both ends of a cable into the tester, which is equipped with an LED for each pin. Using one end of the cable as a reference, the tester applies a voltage to each pin in turn, indicating on which other pin or pins (on either end) a voltage appears.

Mini-Testers. A mini-tester, illustrated in Figure 16.7, is a box with two DB-25s, wired straight through, and studded with two-color LEDs to indicate the status of certain circuits. An LED turns red or green when a voltage appears on its circuit. Unfortunately, no standard dictates which color is to represent what state (MARK or SPACE) on the line. The mini-tester shown sells for about $20.

Breakout Boxes. These are the most sophisticated tools for testing and patching RS-232 connections. One is diagrammed in Figure 16.8. RS-232 breakout boxes range in price from about $100 to $350. Breakout boxes are also available for other types of interface, including Centronics.

A breakout box serves both as a window into a connection and as a means of reconfiguring it. The unit illustrated is equipped with two-color LEDs on the most important circuits,

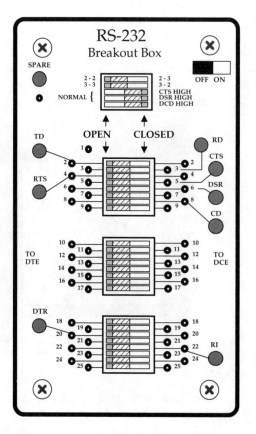

FIGURE 16.8: Breakout box

plus one spare LED, marked EIA TEST, which can be patched into any circuit. Each circuit is opened or closed by means of DIP switches. A patch pin on either side of every circuit, together with the patch cables in the lid, allow any combination of pins to be shorted together. The box can be patched, for example, to serve as a loopback adapter or modem eliminator. The top bank of DIP switches provides some shortcuts by crossing over the data lines or forcing on CTS, DSR, or CD.

A Case Study: The Missing Characters

A British communications expert known to the authors tells this story of data detective work:

"At a computer show a couple of years ago, I spotted a printer buffer selling at an enticingly low price. Since I needed some respite from the tedious waiting periods while my PC was busy feeding characters to my printer, I bought the buffer, took it home, and installed it according to the sketchy directions provided. It behaved well enough, except that once in every few lines of text, a single character was dropped.

"My printer, a Diablo®620, was connected at 1,200 bps via RS-232 to the buffer, which was configured as a DCE. I used hardware flow control; the printer raised DTR when it was ready to accept data and lowered DTR when it had had its fill. The buffer could stash an entire print file, up to 64 kbytes, and the printer would help itself to a few hundred characters at a time whenever its internal buffer got low.

"This problem turned out to be quite a challenge even for me. The first clue to the mystery was the spacing between the missing characters, fairly regular intervals of about 200 to 300. What could this mean? Evidently, it reflected the size of the internal buffer in the printer; perhaps one character was lost for each parcel of data accepted by the printer. I therefore deduced that the problem was related to the boundaries: a character was being lost at either the beginning or the end of each load. At first, I suspected that the buffer might be sending a character after the printer had dropped DTR, leaving the character orphaned in the pipeline because the buffer could not abort the transmission when DTR fell.

"I broke out my trusty breakout box and reduced the buffer-to-printer transmission speed to 110 bps so the winking LEDs would be easier to 'read.' I found no evidence to support my theory, but could not confidently discard it. I hoped I was wrong, for I saw no easy way either to confirm my suspicion or correct the problem if I turned out to be right. I decided to proceed by eliminating other, more easily tested possibilities.

"I noticed that the buffer kept DSR ON only while it was sending data, and the printer manual told me that the printer would accept data only when DSR was ON. A new hypothesis formed: perhaps the printer missed the first character of each bufferload because it was slow to recognize DSR. Fortunately, this was easy to check, because my breakout box provides a switch to hold DSR up all the time. My new hypothesis was soon confirmed.

"Providing a permanent fix was also tricky. Studying the buffer, I discovered that DSR behaved as it did because its state followed the state of DTR. In fact, the buffer immediately fed the printer's DTR back to DSR because of a jumper I had inserted, following the installation instructions for my equipment. The manual offered alternative means of managing the buffer's DSR output, but none of these promised to improve matters. It seemed that the best course was to keep DSR high all the time—but where could I find a high signal to feed it? A wistful glance at the breakout box revealed that the printer appeared to keep RTS up constantly, and the printer manual confirmed this. My solution was to insert a wire connecting RTS to DSR inside the buffer. This may not have been the only possible fix, but it certainly did the job. I cited it in my letter to the buffer vendor, suggesting a change in the manual."

APPENDIX A
THE RS-232 STANDARD

This appendix is a supplement to the description of RS-232 provided in Chapter 4. Aspects of RS-232 covered in that chapter are not repeated here.

Table A.1 summarizes the circuits defined by the EIA-232-D and CCITT V.24 recommendations.

A brief description follows of each interchange circuit which was not dealt with in Chapter 4. Since the circuits in question are generally not implemented in RS-232 ports for PCs, the descriptions are written with reference to a DTE and a DCE, as they are in the standard document.

Signal Quality Detector is a signal from the DCE indicating whether or not there are likely to be errors in the received data. The DCE keeps this circuit high (that is, ON) as long as it has no indication that an error has occurred. The EIA recommends that this circuit not be implemented in newly designed equipment.

The two circuits described next are relevant to an interface involving either a synchronous DCE capable of operating at two data rates, or an asynchronous DCE equipped for operation within two data-rate ranges.

Data Signal Rate Selector (DTE Source) is turned ON by the DTE to select operation at the higher speed or within the higher range of speeds.

Data Signal Rate Selector (DCE Source) is like the circuit previously described except that, in this case, the DCE is the source. With a dual-speed modem as DCE, this circuit might be employed to indicate the data rate of an incoming call, while Data Rate Selector (DTE Source) would be used to select the speed for an outgoing call.

The three circuits described next are relevant to synchronous operation of an interface.

Transmitter Signal Element Timing (DTE Source) is used to convey pulses for timing Transmitted Data in the case that the DTE houses the transmit clock.

Transmitter Signal Element Timing (DCE Source) is used to convey pulses for timing Transmitted Data when the DCE houses the transmit clock, as is more often the case.

Receiver Signal Element Timing carries pulses from DCE to DTE for timing Received Data.

The next three circuits relate to diagnostic modes of operation.

The DTE raises *Local Loopback* to put the DCE into a test mode in which the signal prepared for transmission on the communication line is looped back to the DCE's input circuitry. For a modem, this test mode would be local analog loopback.

The DTE asserts *Remote Loopback* to request the local DCE to establish a remote loopback condition in the remote DCE.

The DCE indicates that it is in a test state by turning *Test Mode* ON. Test Mode is actuated by the appearance of an ON condition on Local or Remote Loopback, or by any other event that places the DCE in a diagnostic mode of operation.

The last set of circuits provides a secondary data channel. Since these circuits have functions analogous to those of their counterparts in the primary data channel, they are not described individually here.

The secondary data channel comprises the five circuits: *Secondary Transmitted Data*, *Secondary Received Data*, *Secondary Request to Send*, *Secondary Clear to Send*, and *Secondary Received Line Signal Detector*.

TABLE A.1: **EIA-232-D/CCITT V.24 circuit designations**

DB25 Pin	EIA Circuit	CCITT Circuit	Source	Descriptive name
1	–	–	–	Shield
2	BA	103	DTE	Transmitted Date (TD)
3	BB	104	DCE	Received Data (RD)
4	CA	105	DTE	Request To Send (RTS)
5	CB	106	DCE	Clear To Send (CTS)
6	CC	107	DCE	DCE Ready (DSR)
7	AB	102	–	Signal Ground/Common Return
8	CF	109	DCE	Received Line Signal Detector (RSLD/CD)
9	–	–	–	(Reserved for testing)
10	–	–	–	(Reserved for testing)
11	–	–	–	(Unassigned)
12	SCF/CI	112/122	DCE	Secondary Received Line Signal Detector/Data Signal Rate Selector (DCE)
13	SCB	121	DCE	Secondary Clear To Send
14	SBA	118	DTE	Secondary Transmitted Data
15	DB	114	DCE	Transmitter Signal Element Timing (DCE Source)
16	SBB	119	DCE	Secondary Received Data
17	DD	115	DCE	Receiver Signal Element Timing (DCE Source)
18	LL	141	DTE	Local Loopback
19	SCA	120	DTE	Secondary Request to Send
20	CD	108.2	DTE	DTE Ready (DTR)
21	RL/CG	140/110	DCE	Remote Loopback/Signal Quality Detector
22	CE	125	DCE	Ring Indicator
23	CH/CI	111/112	Either	Data Signal Rate Selector (DTE/DCE)
24	DA	113	DTE	Transmitter Signal Element Timing (DTE Source)
25	TM	142	DTE	Test Mode

APPENDIX B
THE CENTRONICS PARALLEL INTERFACE

Parallel Interface (Centronics type)

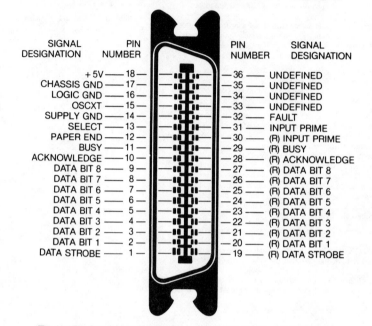

(R) INDICATES SIGNAL GROUND RETURN

FIGURE B.1: Centronic circuit assignments

APPENDIX C
HAYES MODEM STANDARDS

This appendix describes the AT modem-command language established by Hayes Microcomputer Products, and other aspects of Hayes modems imitated by other modem makers.

details. Many non-Hayes modems use certain Hayes commands, but in such a way that the commands operate differently or have a different effect than in Hayes units.

General Rules

Each command is denoted by either a single character or an ampersand followed by a letter. Most commands may be followed by parameters that generally take the form of decimal numbers; the dial command may be followed by a more complex argument. Many commands may be given in a single command line. Command lines are terminated by carriage returns except as otherwise noted.

All commands consisting of letters are listed here in uppercase. Lowercase letters are accepted by some modems, but to be safe it's wise to use capitals only.

A modem enters its default state on power-up or when given a reset command.

THE HAYES STANDARD
AT COMMAND SET

It's probably safe to say that no Hayes-compatible modem will follow these commands to the letter; indeed, even older Hayes modems do not. Many of the commands are irrelevant for modems that do not incorporate the particular features they address (synchronous operation, for instance). The documentation for any particular modem should provide a general idea of the commands it recognizes, but in some cases only experimentation can nail down the precise

Prefix, Repeat, and Escape

Normally, all command lines must commence with an **AT**, the attention prefix. The one exception is the **A/***repeat last command line* command. A command line may include any number of commands and is limited in length only by the modem's buffer size, which should be sufficient to hold at least 40, and often as many as 255, characters.

The **AT** prefix enables the modem to determine the data rate and character format used by the DTE. Specifically, the modem uses the **A** to detect the speed and the **T** to recognize the character size (seven or eight bits) and the parity, if any. Note that ASCII codes are such that **A** and **T** have different parity.

A Hayes modem interprets the **AT** characters on every command line, making it possible for each such line to be sent at a different speed or with a different character format. Some communication packages send commands at a uniform speed, regardless of modem-signaling speed, with the exception of a command line such as **ATO**, which puts the modem on-line and is sent at the modem's signaling speed. Some non-Hayes modems interpret the **AT** prefix only on the first command line following a power-up, reset, or escape from on-line, then assume that subsequent command lines will be sent with the same speed and format. Such a shortcut is safe with most software but may get you into trouble with, for example, Smartcom.

The command line **A/**, not followed by carriage return, tells the modem to repeat the last command line stored in its buffer.

The escape code, + + +, switches the modem from on-line state to command state. The escape code is not a command and is not preceded by **AT**; rather, it must be both preceded and followed by a period of idle time, normally one second. This time-bracketing of the escape code lessens the chance that a + + + character sequence within the outgoing data stream will be interpreted as an escape code. See the section below on states.

AT Command Summary

In this section, parameters that correspond to default modem settings are printed in *italics*. When a command that normally takes a parameter is given without one, a parameter value of 0 is assumed. The dial command is an exception to this rule.

A   puts the modem in *answer mode*. The modem goes off-hook and attempts to go on-line (establish a connection with a remote modem). This command is used to switch a voice call to data.

B   selects the signaling standard for 1,200-bps communication (the only rate at which there is normally a choice).

     B0   selects the CCITT V.22 standard.

     B1   selects the Bell 212A standard. (This is the default for North American modems only.)

D   puts the modem in *originate mode*. If this command is followed by a dialing string, the modem dials the given number and attempts to go on-line. If no dialing string is given, the modem immediately attempts to go on-line. Details of dialing strings are given below. This command serves to switch a voice call to data.

E   enables/disables echoing of modem commands. When command echoing is enabled, the modem echoes each character it receives while in command state.

     E0   disables echoing.

     E1   enables echoing.

H   operates the modem relay to go on-hook and off-hook.

     H0   makes the modem go on-hook, that is, hang up.

     H1   makes the modem go off-hook.

   H1 is akin to picking up the handset of a telephone, H0 to replacing it in the cradle.

I   interrogates the modem

     I0   returns the modem's identification code.

     I1   returns the checksum on the modem's program ROM.

     I2   performs a checksum on the modem's program ROM and returns an "OK" or "ERROR" response as appropriate.

On a typical Hayes Smartmodem 1200, for example, an ATI0 command elicits a response of "123." The "12" is Hayes' product code for the Smartmodem 1200; the "3" is the product revision level.

L   adjusts the volume of the signal sent to the modem's internal speaker.

     L0 or L1   selects low volume.

     L2   selects medium volume.

     L3   selects high volume.

Some modems are equipped with a potentiometer for controlling volume and do not support this command.

M   controls when the modem's speaker operates.

     M0   sets a mode in which the speaker is always off.

     M1   sets a mode in which the speaker is turned on for audible call-progress monitoring and then switched off when the modem goes on-line.

     M2   sets a mode in which the speaker is constantly on.

     M3   sets a mode similar to M1 except that the speaker is off during dialing.

O   returns the modem from command state to on-line state. This DTE sends this command after interrupting the on-line state in order to give the modem other commands.

     O0   simply returns the modem to on-line state.

     O1   returns the modem to on-line state and, at speeds of 2,400 bps and above, forces an equalizer retrain sequence to filter out noise.

P   selects pulse-mode, as opposed to Touch-Tone, dialing.

Q   determines whether the modem sends result codes in response to commands.

     Q0   directs the modem to return result codes for every command.

     Q1   directs the modem never to send result codes.

S   stores a value into a modem register or returns the value in such a register.

     $Sr = n$ sets the decimal value n in register number r.

     Sr?   directs the modem to return the value in register r.

Examples: S0 = 1 puts a 1 in register 0.

     S0?   returns the value in S0.

T   directs the modem to dial in Touch-Tone, as opposed to pulse, mode.

V   controls the form in which the modem returns result codes.

     V0   calls for result codes in numeric form.

     V1   calls for result codes in words.

When the modem is being used with a terminal, the user will likely prefer to see the result codes in words. Software will handle numeric codes more easily.

X   controls the set of features a modem may use in establishing connections. The selected features then define the range of result codes returned by the modem during connection establishment.

     X0   disables call-progress monitoring; the modem does not recognize dial tone and busy signals, but dials "blind." Only the most basic result codes, 0–4 (OK, CONNECT, RING, NO CARRIER, and ERROR), are returned.

X1   has the same effect as X0, except that the result code returned for a successful connection includes the line speed, e.g., "CONNECT 1200." The set of codes returned encompasses 0–5 and 10–14.

X2   instructs the modem to wait for a dial tone before dialing. The modem returns result codes 0–6 (adding NO DIALTONE) and 10–14.

X3   instructs the modem to dial "blind" but to recognize busy signals. Result codes enabled are 0–5, 7 (BUSY), and 10–14.

X4   allows the modem to use full call-progress monitoring, recognizing dial tone and busy. Result codes 0–7 and 10–14 are returned.

The X command is required to ensure compatibility with software equipped to handle only a subset of the possible result codes. A modem not equipped for call-progress monitoring, for example, would be capable of operating only at the X1 level.

Y   controls whether or not the modem disconnects on receiving a long SPACE. To be nice to some antiquated modems that do not readily accommodate abrupt losses of carrier, a modem may signal its intention to disconnect a call by sending a long period of SPACE. The MCI Mail network sends such long space disconnects before hanging up. (Note: A period of SPACE is used to convey a BREAK signal; here, we're speaking of much longer SPACEs).

   Y0   tells the modem to pay no special attention to a long SPACE.

   Y1   directs the modem to detect SPACE lasting longer than 1.6 seconds and to respond by transmitting SPACE for 4 seconds, then disconnecting.

Z   resets the modem. In most cases, the Z command simply returns a modem to its power-up state. The command is a bit more complicated with modems that can store user profiles, such as the Hayes V-series.

   Z0   resets the modem and recalls user profile number 0.

   Z1   resets the modem and recalls user profile number 1.

&C   controls the behavior of the RS-232 Carrier Detect (CD or DCD) line.

   &C0   designates that CD is to be kept on at all times, regardless of whether a carrier is being received from the remote modem. (This allows a terminal that refuses to transmit data when CD is off to send commands to the modem.)

   &C1   designates that the modem should follow RS-232 rules and set CD only when it detects a received carrier.

Irrespective of the state set by this command, CD gives a true indication of carrier detect when the modem is operating in synchronous mode.

&D   controls the modem's behavior in response to transitions on the RS-232 Data Terminal Ready (DTR) line.

   &D0   tells the modem to ignore DTR.

   &D1   tells the modem to assume command state when DTR goes off.

   &D2   tells the modem to hang up or disable auto-answer when DTR goes off. The modem then also assumes command state.

   &D3   tells the modem to reset itself when DTR goes off.

&F   completely reinstates factory settings as the modem's active configuration.

&G   selects a guard tone to be used by the modem.

   &G0   selects no guard tone.

   &G1   selects a 550-Hz guard tone.

   &G2   selects a 1,800-Hz guard tone.

&J   tells the modem what kind of jack is connecting it to the telephone line.

   &J0   denotes an RJ-11, RJ-41S, or RJ-45S type phone jack.

   &J1   denotes an RJ-12 or RJ-13 type jack.

&P   selects one of two modes of pulse dialing.

   &P0   selects a contact make/break ratio of 39:61.

   &P1   selects a contact make/break ratio of 33:67.

&Q   selects asynchronous operation, or one of four modes of synchronous operation. Multiple modes of synchronous operation are helpful because modems accept commands only when operating asynchronously.

   &Q0   selects asynchronous operation.

   &Q1   sets a mode in which the modem operates asynchronously during call setup and synchronously once a connection is established. This is the most convenient mode for DTEs that require a sync connection but are capable of async operation.

   &Q2   sets a synchronous-only mode of operation in which the modem dials a stored number when DTR is switched on.

   &Q3   sets a synchronous mode employed when manual dialing is used. After dialing the required number, the user raises DTR to get the modem to go off-hook.

   &Q4   sets a mode in which the Hayes Synchronous Interface is used.

&R   controls the modem's handling of the RS-232 Clear To Send (CTS) line to the DTE. The modem can either keep CTS high all the time it is on-line, or set CTS to follow the state of Request to Send (RTS) so that the modem can be used, in certain operating modes, with a DTE that expects to communicate with a half-duplex modem.

   &R0   sets CTS to follow RTS while the modem is on-line.

   &R1   sets CTS constantly on while the modem is on-line. The modem ignores RTS.

&S   determines the modem's manipulation of the RS-232 Data Set Ready line when operating in async mode.

   &S0   sets DSR constantly on.

   &S1   sets DSR to operate according to RS-232 specs. In *originate mode,* the modem raises DSR upon detecting an answer tone from a remote modem. In answer mode, the modem turns DSR on upon transmitting an answer tone. When operating synchronously, the modem always sets DSR according to RS-232 rules.

&T   initiates and terminates various test and loopback modes within the modem. This command is used, for example, to put the modem into local analog or any other loopback mode of which it is capable.

   &T0   terminates any test in progress.

   &T1   initiates local analog loopback.

   &T3   initiates local digital loopback.

   &T4   grants request from remote modem for remote digital loopback.

&T5   denies request from remote modem for remote digital loopback.

&T6   initiates remote digital loopback.

&T7   initiates remote digital loopback with self-test.

&T8   initiates local analog loopback with self-test.

&V   causes the modem to display stored information such as user profiles and phone numbers used for automatic connection in synchronous mode.

&W   prompts the modem to store user profiles.

     &W0   saves parameters for user profile 0.

     &W1   saves parameters for user profile 1.

&X   tells the modem the source of the transmit clock signal for synchronous operation.

     X0   indicates that the modem is to provide the transmit clock.

     X1   indicates that the DTE will provide the transmit clock.

     X2   indicates that the clock extracted by the modem from the received carrier is to be used as the transmit clock.

&Y   indicates which user profile is to become the default at modem power-up.

     &Y0   recalls user profile 0 on power-up.

     &Y1   recalls user profile 1 on power-up.

&Z   tells the modem to store a phone number.

     &Z$n = x$ tells the modem to store number x in location n.

Dial Modifiers

A dial command consists of a **D** followed by a string containing numbers to be dialed, punctuation of the kind normally written into telephone numbers (which the modem ignores), and dial modifiers from the following list:

0-9	digits to be dialed in pulse and Touch-Tone modes.
ABCD* and **#**	symbols to be dialed in Touch-Tone mode only.
P	Pulse dial
@	Wait for silence
T	Touch-Tone dial
,	Pause
!	Hookflash
W	Wait for second dial tone.
;	Return to command state.
R	Reverse mode.
S = *n*	dial stored number *n*.

DP9WT456-7890, for example, tells the modem to pulse-dial a 9 (perhaps to get an outside line through a Centrex system), wait for a second dial tone, and then dial 456-7890 using Touch-Tone.

A **P** or **T** command may be given outside of a Dial command to set the standard for subsequent dialing. For example, **ATP** tells the modem to use pulse dialing until overridden by another **P** or **T**, or until the modem is reset.

The **R** modifier allows a modem to place a call but then go on-line in *answer* rather than *originate* mode. This feature enables a modem to place a call to a modem equipped only for *originate-mode* operation.

Normally, upon completing a call, the modem goes into on-line state. This can be prevented by means of the **;** dial modifier, which directs the modem to remain in command state after dialing.

Most Touch-Tone telephones have 12 buttons for dialing (0 to 9, **#**, and *****), but AT&T's Touch-Tone standard includes 16 symbols, adding **A, B, C,** and **D** to the familiar set. These letters, used with certain PBXs for invoking PBX services, can be dialed by many newer modems.

A Brief History

Hayes introduced the **&** commands with the Smartmodem 2400. The **N, W,** and &K commands were added for the V-series Smartmodem 9600.

The Hayes Smartmodem 1200 and 1200B supported two commands not listed in the above summary (default settings are in italics):

     C   directs the modem to turn its transmit carrier on and off, overriding normal behavior. This allows a modem to receive data without asserting a transmit carrier.

         C0   turns off the modem's transmitter.

         C1   turns on the modem's transmitter.

Note: The C0 option is invalid with later-model Hayes modems.

     F   enables/disables modem echoing of transmitted data to the DTE.

         F0   sets "half-duplex" mode in which characters are echoed.

         F1   sets "full-duplex" mode in which characters are not echoed.

Note: the F0 option is invalid in later-model Hayes modems.

For backward compatibility with earlier models, the Hayes V-series modems offer partial support for the **C** and **F** commands. C1 and F1 are accepted, but C0 and F0 options have been eliminated, and these commands are treated as errors.

Result Codes

The basic set of result codes used by Hayes is shown below. Each code may be expressed by either a number or a word, as selected by the **V** command. The modem sends at least one result code per command line.

Number	Word	Meaning
0	OK	Command executed okay.
1	CONNECT	Connection established.
2	RING	Ring signal detected.
3	NO CARRIER	No carrier received, or carrier lost.
4	ERROR	Invalid command or other error in command line.
5	CONNECT 1200	Connection established at 1,200 bps.
6	NO DIALTONE	No dial tone detected.
7	BUSY	Busy signal detected.
8	NO ANSWER	
10	CONNECT 2400	Connection established at 2,400 bps.
11	CONNECT 4800	Connection established at 4,800 bps.
12	CONNECT 9600	Connection established at 9,600 bps.
14	CONNECT 19200	Connection established at 19,200 bps.

Note that numeric codes 9 and 13 are not used. Additional result codes are used by Hayes V-series modems.

COMMAND AND ON-LINE STATES

Since there is but one data path from the DTE to the modem, both modem commands and data to be transmitted travel the same road. To distinguish between the two, the modem has two operating states: *command state* and *on-line state.* Except for brief periods when it is occupied in such pursuits as dialing a call, the modem is always in one state or the other. In command state, it treats all data received from the DTE as commands; in on-line state, it transmits all data received from the DTE.

Transitions between the two states may be prompted by the following events:

- The modem's establishing a connection with a remote modem.
- The modem's loss of its connection with a remote modem.
- Commands entered by the user.
- Transitions on RS-232 control lines from the DTE.

The exact pattern of transitions varies according to the modem's configuration at any time. In a typical pattern of asynchronous operation, the modem goes into command state when first turned on. Once a connection is established with a remote modem, the modem goes into on-line state. The user may enter the escape code to interrupt on-line state and bring the modem back to command state. The escape code is normally + + + surrounded by a period of idle time, but may be changed to some degree by user commands, as explained above. The user directs the modem to return to on-line state by entering the O command. The modem reverts to command state when its connection with a remote modem is broken.

A modem can be in command state only while operating asynchronously. Because of this restriction, synchronous modems support several submodes of sync operation for the sake of user convenience.

MODEM S REGISTERS

There follows a summary of the S registers used by Hayes. The name of each register is followed by a range of values it may hold, the default (factory-set) value, and a description of the register's function.

TABLE C.1: Modem S Registers

S0	0 to 255	0	Defines number of rings after which the modem is to answer an incoming call. A zero value disables auto-answer.
S1	0 to 255	0	Used by the modem to count consecutive rings.
S2	0 to 255	43	ASCII value of the character (+ is the default), a sequence of three of which are recognized as an escape code. Valid settings for **S2** are 0 to 127; a setting of 128 to 255 disables escape-code recognition.
S3	0 to 127	13	ASCII value of the character (**CR** is the default) that the modem recognizes as the terminator for command lines and sends as the terminator of result codes. This is rarely changed from CR.
S4	0 to 127	10	ASCII value of the character (**LF** is the default) that the modem appends to an echoed command terminator or a result code terminator. This is rarely changes from LF.
S5	0 to 32, 127	8	ASCII value of the character (**BS** is the default) that the modem recognizes as a backspace character
S6	2 to 255	2	within command lines. This is normally set to the ASCII backspace character, control-H. The time period, in seconds, for which the modem waits between going off-hook and commencing dialing when dialing "blind." Normally two seconds, this wait allows time for a dial tone to be asserted by the exchange.
S7	1 to 255	30	Maximum time, in seconds, for which the modem waits for a received carrier after dialing.
S8	1 to 255	6	Duration, in tenths of a second, of the pause induced by the comma dial modifier.
S9	1 to 255	6	Time, in tenths of a second, for which the modem must recognize carrier before asserting Carrier Detect.
S10	1 to 255	14	Delay, in tenths of a second, between loss of carrier and disconnection by the modem. A value of 255 causes the modem to behave as if carrier were always present.
S11	50 to 255	95	Determines the tone duration, in milliseconds, and the gap between tones for Touch-Tone dialing.
S12	0 to 255	50	The guard time, in 20-millisecond units, that must precede and follow an escape code for the modem to recognize it as such. (The default setting represents one second.)
S25	0 to 255	5	Serves a dual purpose. First it defines a period, in seconds, following the establishment of a synchronous connection during which the modem will ignore DTR. This grace period allows a user to switch the modem from an asynchronous DTE (used to set up the connection) to a synchronous DTE (used for data transfer proper). Second, it defines a time, in hundredths of a second, marking the minimum period for which a change on DTR will be noticed by the modem while on-line.
S26	0 to 255	1	The delay, in hundredths of a second, between the modem's detection of an on-transition on RTS and its response, that is, turning on CTS. (Of course, this is relevant only to modes in which CTS tracks RTS.)

APPENDIX D
U.S. AND INTERNATIONAL MODEM STANDARDS

Bell Standards

Name	Speed in bps	Duplex	Sync or async	Line type	Comments
103	0–300	Full	Async	Dial-up	
212	1,200	Full	Both	Dial-up	incorporates 103
202	600/1,200	Half	Async	Dial-up	
201B	2,400	Either	Sync	Private	
208	4,800	Full	Sync	Private	
209	9,600	Full	Sync	Private	multiport type

CCITT Standards

Name	Speed in bps	Duplex	Sync or async	Line type
V.21	0–300	Full	Async	Dial-up
V.22	1,200	Full	Both	Dial-up
V.22 *bis*	2,400	Full	Async	Dial-up
V.23	600/1,200	Half	Async	Dial-up
	and 75/1,200	Split	Async	Dial-up
V.26	2,400	Either	Sync	Private
V.26 *bis*	1,200/2,400	Either	Sync	Dial-up
V.27	4,800	Full	Sync	Private
V.27 *bis*	4,800	Full	Sync	Private
V.27 *ter*	2,400/4,800	Full	Sync	Dial-up
V.29	9,600	Full	Sync	Private
V.32	9,600	Full	Sync	Either
V.33	14,400	Full	Sync	Private

APPENDIX E
THE PC CHARACTER SET

TABLE E.1: ASCII Control Characters

Dec-imal	Hex	ASCII name	PC[1]	Keyboard entry	ASCII Description	Control Class[2]
0	00	NUL		Ctrl-2[3]	Null	
1	01	SOH		Ctrl-A	Start of Heading	CC
2	01	STX		Ctrl-B	Start of Text	CC
3	03	ETX		Ctrl-C	End of Text	CC
4	04	EOT		Ctrl-D	End of Transmission	CC
5	05	ENQ		Ctrl-E	Enquiry	CC
6	06	ACK		Ctrl-F	Acknowledge	CC
7	07	BEL		Ctrl-G	Bell	
8	08	BS		Ctrl-H/left arrow	Backspace	FE
9	09	HT		Ctrl-I/tab	Horizontal Tabulation	FE
10	0A	LF		Ctrl-J	Line Feed	FE
11	0B	VT		Ctrl-K	Verical Tabulation	FE
12	0C	FF		Ctrl-L	Form Feed	FE
13	0D	CR		Ctrl-M or Enter	Carriage Return	FE
14	0E	SO		Ctrl-N	Shift Out	
15	0F	SI		Ctrl-O	Shift In	
16	10	DLE		Ctrl-P	Data Link Escape	CC
17	11	DC1		Ctrl-Q	Device Control 1	
18	12	DC2		Ctrl-R	Device Control 2	
19	13	DC3		Ctrl-S	Device Control 3	
20	14	DC4		Ctrl-T	Device Control 4	
21	15	NAK		Ctrl-U	Negative Acknowledge	CC
22	16	SYN		Ctrl-V	Synchronous Idle	CC
23	17	ETB		Ctrl-W	End of Transmission Block	CC
24	18	CAN		Ctrl-X	Cancel	
25	19	EM		Ctrl-Y	End of Medium	
26	1A	SUB		Ctrl-Z[4]	Substitute	
27	1B	ESC		Esc or Ctrl-[	Escape	
28	1C	FS		Ctrl-backslash	File Separator	IS
29	1D	GS		Ctrl-]	Group Separator	IS
30	1E	RS		Ctrl-6	Record Separator	IS
31	1F	US		Ctrl- -	Unit Separator	IS
127	7F	DEL		Del	Delete	

Note:

(1) Shows how the character is displayed on the PC screen. For Format Effectors, the character must be written in a special way for the given symbol to appear.

(2) CC: Communication Control; used in protocols.

   FE: Format Effector; control output formatting.

   IS: Information Separator.

(3) IBM defines Ctrl-2 as the approved method of entering a Null, but very few programs recognize it as such.

(4) DOS treats Ctrl-Z as an end-of-file for text files.

TABLE E.2: ASCII Printable Characters

Decimal	Hex	ASCII	PC symbol	Decimal	Hex	ASCII	PC symbol	Decimal	Hex	ASCII	PC symbol
32	20			64	40	@	@	96	60	`	`
33	21	!	!	65	41	A	A	97	61	a	a
34	22	"	"	66	42	B	B	98	62	b	b
35	23	#	#	67	43	C	C	99	63	c	c
36	24	$	$	68	44	D	D	100	64	d	d
37	25	%	%	69	45	E	E	101	65	e	e
38	26	&	&	70	46	F	F	102	66	f	f
39	27	'	'	71	47	G	G	103	67	g	g
40	28	(	(	72	48	H	H	104	68	h	h
41	29	)	)	73	49	I	I	105	69	i	i
42	2A	*	*	74	4A	J	J	106	6A	j	j
43	2B	+	+	75	4B	K	K	107	6B	k	k
44	2C	,	,	76	4C	L	L	108	6C	l	l
45	2D	-	-	77	4D	M	M	109	6D	m	m
46	2E	.	.	78	4E	N	N	110	6E	n	n
47	2F	/	/	79	4F	O	O	111	6F	o	o
48	30	0	0	80	50	P	P	112	70	p	p
49	31	1	1	81	51	Q	Q	113	71	q	q
50	32	2	2	82	52	R	R	114	72	r	r
51	33	3	3	83	53	S	S	115	73	s	s
52	34	4	4	84	54	T	T	116	74	t	t
53	35	5	5	85	55	U	U	117	75	u	u
54	36	6	6	86	56	V	V	118	76	v	v
55	37	7	7	87	57	W	W	119	77	w	w
56	38	8	8	88	58	X	X	120	78	x	x
57	39	9	9	89	59	Y	Y	121	79	y	y
58	3A	:	:	90	5A	Z	Z	122	7A	z	z
59	3B	;	;	91	5B	[	[	123	7B	{	{
60	3C	<	<	92	5C	\	\	124	7C	|	|
61	3D	=	=	93	5D	]	]	125	7D	}	}
62	3E	>	>	94	5E	^	^	126	7E	~	~
63	3F	?	?	95	5F	_	_	127	7F	(see list of control characters)	

TABLE E.3:   Non-ASCII Characters

Decimal	Hex	PC symbol	Decimal	Hex	PC symbol	Decimal	Hex	PC symbol
128	80	Ç	171	AB	½	214	D6	╥
129	81	ü	172	AC	¼	215	D7	╫
130	82	é	173	AD	¡	216	D8	╪
131	83	â	174	AE	«	217	D9	┘
132	84	ä	175	AF	»	218	DA	┌
133	85	à	176	B0	░	219	DB	█
134	86	å	177	B1	▒	220	DC	▄
135	87	ç	178	B2	▓	221	DD	▌
136	88	ê	179	B3	│	222	DE	▐
137	89	ë	180	B4	┤	223	DF	▀
138	8A	è	181	B5	╡	224	E0	α
139	8B	ï	182	B6	╢	225	E1	ß
140	8C	î	183	B7	╖	226	E2	Γ
141	8D	ì	184	B8	╕	227	E3	π
142	8E	Ä	185	B9	╣	228	E4	Σ
143	8F	Å	186	BA	║	229	E5	σ
144	90	É	187	BB	╗	230	E6	µ
145	91	æ	188	BC	╝	231	E7	τ
146	92	Æ	189	BD	╜	232	E8	Φ
147	93	ô	190	BE	╛	233	E9	Θ
148	94	ö	191	BF	┐	234	EA	Ω
149	95	ò	192	C0	└	235	EB	δ
150	96	û	193	C1	┴	236	EC	∞
151	97	ù	194	C2	┬	237	ED	ø
152	98	ÿ	195	C3	├	238	EE	ε
153	99	Ö	196	C4	─	239	EF	∩
154	9A	Ü	197	C5	┼	240	F0	≡
155	9B	¢	198	C6	╞	241	F1	±
156	9C	£	199	C7	╟	242	F2	≥
157	9D	¥	200	C8	╚	243	F3	≤
158	9E	₧	201	C9	╔	244	F4	⌠
159	9F	ƒ	202	CA	╩	245	F5	⌡
160	A0	á	203	CB	╦	246	F6	÷
161	A1	í	204	CC	╠	247	F7	≈
162	A2	ó	205	CD	═	248	F8	°
163	A3	ú	206	CE	╬	249	F9	∙
164	A4	ñ	207	CF	╧	250	FA	·
165	A5	Ñ	208	D0	╨	251	FB	√
166	A6	ª	209	D1	╤	252	FC	ⁿ
167	A7	º	210	D2	╥	253	FD	²
168	A8	¿	211	D3	╙	254	FE	■
169	A9	⌐	212	D4	╘	255	FF	(BLANK 'FF')
170	AA	¬	213	D5	╒			

APPENDIX F
GRAPHICS TERMINALS

As of 1987, the leading vendors of graphics terminals in the U.S. market were Tektronix (with 29%), IBM (27%), DEC (12%), and Hewlett-Packard (8%).

The VT125 is an older offering from DEC; newer products are the VT240 and VT 241. Tektronix's current series includes the 4205 and 4207. All of these terminals are capable of text-only operation in the manner of VT100s or similar models; a host sends the terminal a special escape sequence to switch it to graphics mode. The following summary of terminal models from Tektronix and DEC includes, for comparison, various graphics adapters offered by IBM for PCs.

Vendor	Model	Resolution	Displayable Colors	Palette Colors
DEC	VT125	768×240	(monochrome)	
	VT240	800×240	(monochrome)	
	VT241	800×2404	64	
Tektronix	4105	640×480	17	64
	4107	640×480	25	64

Vendor	Model	Resolution	Displayable Colors	Palette Colors
	4109	640×480	25	4,096
	4205	480×360	25	64
	4207	640×480	25	64
	4208	640×480	25	64
	4209	640×480	25	4,096
IBM	CGA	640×200	2	16
	or	320×200	4	16
	EGA	640×350	16	64
	VGA	640×480	16	256,000
	or	320×200	256	256,000

APPENDIX G
PAD PARAMETERS

This appendix describes the parameters, defined by the CCITT recommendation X.3, that control the operation of an X.25 packet assembler/disassembler (PAD) for character-mode terminals. Such PADs are discussed under PSNs in Chapter 2 and under X.25 in Chapter 8.

The parameters are numbered in decimal notation from 1 to 18. Each is described with respect to the values it may be assigned.

PARAMETER 1:

1 enables PAD recognition of an escape code, which the user can enter while connected to a network host in order to regain communication with the PAD. (This escape code is similar in principle to the + + + escape code implemented in Hayes-compatible modems.)

0 disables PAD recognition of the escape code. When escape-code recognition is disabled, the network connection can be broken only by the host (or, of course, by the PAD in the event the user disconnects from the PAD). Disabling the escape code may be prudent when binary information is being transmitted to the host, since the escape code may match a sequence of bytes in the transmitted data.

PARAMETER 2:

1 enables echoing. The PAD echoes each character typed by the user.
0 disables echoing by the PAD.

PARAMETER 3:

This parameter consists of a bit vector in which each bit identifies a certain class of characters the PAD recognizes as input-message terminators. In powers of two, the bits are defined as:

0 — any alphanumeric character (A–Z, a–z, and 0–9)

1 — carriage return

2 — the ASCII control characters: ESC, BEL, ENQ, and ACK

3 — the ASCII control characters: DEL, CAN, and DC2 (XON)

4 — the ASCII control characters: ETX and EOT

5 — the ASCII control characters: HT, LF, VT, and FF

6 — any ASCII control character

Bit 2^7 is unused. If no bits are set, packets will be dispatched only upon being filled or when a time-out occurs. For example, if Parameter 3 were set to a value of 18 decimal, input would be forwarded by the PAD on receipt of a CR, ETX, or EOT ($2^1 + 2^4 = 18$).

PARAMETER 4:

Establishes the time-out period for input dispatch. The value of this parameter is expressed in units of 20 milliseconds (0.02 seconds). Thus, if it were set to 25, the PAD would forward input to the host whenever half a second (25 × 0.02) passed without a character arriving from the terminal. A zero value may be set to inhibit input dispatch on time-out.

PARAMETER 5:

1 selects XON/XOFF flow control. If the PAD runs out of buffer space, it sends an XOFF to the terminal to suspend further input. Once buffer space is again available, the PAD sends an XON to restart the input flow.

0 disables flow control by the PAD. In this case, the PAD discards input for which it lacks buffer space, but warns the user by sending a BELL to the terminal.

It may be useful to turn flow control on when using a file transfer protocol with a large block size, assuming the protocol is one that will operate correctly on a flow-controlled channel.

PARAMETER 6:

1 allows the PAD to send messages to the terminal, when necessary, to notify the user of unusual events, such as network failures.
    0 suppresses such messages.

PARAMETER 7:

Defines the action to be taken by the PAD on receipt of a Break signal from the terminal:

    0—no action

    1—an X.25 Interrupt packet is sent to the host

    2—an X.25 reset packet is sent to the host

    5—an X.25 Interrupt packet and an "Indication of Break" message are sent to the host

    8—Break is treated like a PAD escape code, and the user is prompted for a command

Since an X.25 Interrupt packet may be expedited ahead of data packets in transit over the PSN, option 5 exists to alert the host to the occurrence of a Break signal as soon as possible, and to mark the position of that signal within the data stream.

PARAMETER 8:

1 causes the PAD to discard any data destined for the terminal.
    0 causes the PAD to promptly deliver all data for the terminal.
    A connection reset always causes this parameter to be set to 0.

PARAMETER 9:

Sets the number of padding characters the PAD sends to the terminal following each carriage return. This padding allows time for mechanical terminals to physically return the carriage or printhead to the left margin. For PCs and VDTs, this would normally be set to zero.

PARAMETER 10:

Enables the PAD to break output lines sent to the terminal. This capability prevents the disappearance of the ends of long lines off the right edge of the page/screen. The value defines the number of printable characters the terminal can display in a line, after which the PAD inserts a carriage return. A value of zero inhibits such action.

PARAMETER 11:

Encodes the terminal speed. A value of 3, for example, indicates 1,200 bps. It may be very useful for the host to determine the speed of the terminal, but, not surprisingly, this parameter may not be changed.

PARAMETER 12:

1 enables the PAD to respond to XON/XOFF flow control sent by the terminal.
    0 turns off such action.

PARAMETER 13:

Selects one of several ways the PAD may deal with line feeds following carriage returns. The PAD may be called upon to add line feeds after carriage returns on input, output, or both.

PARAMETER 14:

Much like Parameter 9, this selects the number of padding characters the PAD sends to the terminal following a line feed.

PARAMETERS 15, 16, 17, AND 18:

Configure the PAD for performing local editing of terminal input. If Parameter 15 is set to 1, the terminal user may edit data held in the PAD input buffer using: a backspace character set by Parameter 16; a delete-all-characters-in-buffer character set by Parameter 17; and a buffer-redisplay character set by Parameter 18. If Parameter 15 is set to zero, no local editing is possible.

TELENET

A Telenet node will inform you of its PAD parameters in response to the **par?** command. Here's an example (slightly edited for readability):

```
@par?
PAR1:1,2:1,3:2,4:80,5:0,6:1,7:0,8:0,9:0,10:80,
11:3,12:0,13:0,14:0,
15:0,16:127,17:24,18:18
```

We see that the time-out parameter (number 4) is set to 80, meaning that input will be forwarded after 1.6 seconds. The setting of Parameter 3 tells us that carriage return is the only input terminator recognized. Parameter 1 is set to 1, meaning that the PAD will respond if the user enters the Telenet escape code, which happens to be the three-character sequence: CR,@,CR. Since Parameter 15 is zero, local editing is off, but if it were on, the default editing characters would be DEL for backspace, CAN (Control-X) for buffer delete, and DC2 (Control-R) for buffer redisplay.

The user may change a parameter using the **set** command. An argument is the parameter number followed by a colon and value, as in the above display. Several parameters may be changed with a single set command; multiple arguments are separated by commas. The following example would turn on local editing and reduce the time-out period to one second:

```
@set 15:1,4:50
```

APPENDIX H
IBM PRODUCT IDENTIFIERS

Here's a handy list of many of the four-digit numbers IBM uses with such abandon to identify its products. Only current and recent models, plus a few of the more important older products, are included here. IBM lists all current products in its "Systems and Products Guide," available through dealers.

2770, 2780, 3780	Remote Job Entry (RJE) terminals (Bisync)
303X	A family of large System/370 processors
308X	A family of large System/370 processors
309X	A family of large System/370 processors
3101, 3161	ASCII terminals
3174, 3178, 3179, 3180	(See under 3270)
3270	Information Display System (a suite of terminals, printers, and auxiliary devices for mainframe access). Includes:
3174, 3271, 3272, 3274	Control Units (a.k.a. cluster controllers)
3178, 3179, 3180	Terminals
3262	Printer
3276	Integrated Control Unit and terminal
3278, 3279, 3290	Terminals
3287	Printer
3299	Multiplexer
3380	Disk drive
3480	Cartridge tape drive
3650	Retail Store System
3660	Supermarket System (a point-of-sale terminal)
3680	Programmable Store System (an "intelligent" cash register)
3705	Communications Controller (obsoleted by 3720/3725)
3708	Network Conversion Unit (SNA protocol converter)
3710	SNA protocol converter
3720	Communications Controller (low-capacity version of the 3725)
3725	Communications Controller (a.k.a. front-end processor)
3737	Channel-to-T1 adapter
3745	New-generation Communications Controller (intended to replace the 3705, 3720, 3725 units)
3770, 3780	Remote Job Entry (RJE) terminals
3812, 3820	Pageprinters

3848	Crytographic Unit (for link security in SNA networks)
3863, 3864, 3865, 3868	A line of intelligent modems
4210, 4214	(See under 5250)
43XX	A set of System/370 processors
4576, 4578, 4579	System/88 processors (457X family)
4680	Store System (a point-of-sale system)
4700	Finance Communication System for tellers and accountants
5250	Family of terminals for System/3Xs
4210, 4214	Printers
5224, 5225, 5256, 5262	Printers
5251	The original 5250 terminal
5291	Terminal
5292	Color terminal
5294	Terminal controller
53 XX	System/36 and System/38 processors
5500	Multistation (a PC with Japanese-language capability)
5811, 5812	Short-haul modems
5841	Modem
5865, 5866, 5868	Intelligent synchronous modems
6670	Laser printer
7171	ASCII Device Attachment Control Unit (3270 protocol converter)
7426	Terminal Interface Unit
8100	Information System
8232	Ethernet FEP for System/370s
8775	Display Terminal (an intelligent data-entry terminal)
8815	Scanmaster (a document scanner)
937X	Small System/370 processors (a.k.a Enterprise System/9370)
9404, 9406	AS/400 processor units

Below are expansions of some other common IBM abbreviations. Again, the emphasis is on terms likely to be important or confusing to readers of this book. Exhaustive and exhausting enumerations are to be found in literature available from IBM dealers.

ACF	Advanced Communications Facility. Family name for a group of enhanced communication products. ACF/TCAM (Telecommunications Access Method) runs on System/370 hosts. ACF/NCP (Network Control Program) runs on the 37X5 and 3745.

AIX	Advanced Interactive Executive. UNIX operating system for System/370 and PS/2 machines.
APPC	Advanced Program-to-Program Communication
BSC	Binary Synchronous Communications (a.k.a. Bisync)
BTAM	Basic Telecommunications Access Method. An older IBM network-interface software product; not SNA-compatible.
CICS	Customer Information Control System. A transaction-processing subsystem.
CMS	Conversational Monitor System. Interactive subsystem of VM.
DASD	Direct Access Storage Device. IBM's name for a disk.
DB/2	Database/2. A relational database.
DCA	Document Content Architecture
DDM	Distributed Data Management. A set of application-level SNA protocols that permit remote file access.
DIA	Document Interchange Architecture
DISOSS	Distributed Office Support System
EBCDIC	Extended Binary Coded Decimal Interchange Code
ECF	Enhanced Communications Facility
HLLAPI	High-Level Language Application Program Interface
IMS	Information Management System
ISPF	Interactive System Productivity Facility. Mainframe software that facilitates full-screen application programs with 3270-terminals.
JES	Job Entry Subsystem
MVS	Multiple Virtual Storage. A System/370 operating system.
NetView	Network management product
NCP	Network Control Program, a.k.a ACF/NCP. Front-end software for SNA.

NPSI	NCP Packet Switching Interface. Allows hosts to communicate via X.25 networks and to access host applications via 3270 devices on PADs.
NRF	Network Routing Facility. Routes SNA data between workstations, i.e., when a host is not involved.
NTO	Network Terminal Option. Front-end software for async terminal support.
OS/400	Operating System for AS/400 series processors
PROFS	Professional Office System
RJE	Remote Job Entry
RSCS	Remote Communication Spooling Subsystem. Enables hosts to manipulate batch jobs. Heir apparent to **RJE**.
SAA	Systems Application Architecture
SDLC	Synchronous Data Link Control. A data-link protocol.
SNA	Systems Network Architecture
SNADS	SNA Distribution Services (for documents)
SSCP	System Services Control Point. A focal point of SNA network management.
System/370	Architecture used in IBM mainframes, e.g., 3090, 4381, and 9370. Compare System/88, System/36, and AS/400, which are *not* System/370 machines.
TCAM	Telecommunications Access Method
TPF	Transaction Processing Facility. Message switching and processing system; commonly used in airline reservations systems, e.g., SAABRE.
TSO	Time Sharing Option. An MVS subsystem.
VM	Virtual Machine. A System/370 Operating system.
VTAM	Virtual Telecommunication Access Method. Mainframe SNA software.
XA	Extended Architecture. Adopted in the early 1980s; allows faster peripherals and processing for System/370 machines. Special versions of MVS (MVS/ESA) and VM (VM/XA) can exploit it.

APPENDIX I
RECOMMENDED READING

GENERAL DATA COMMUNICATIONS BOOKS

Data Communications, A User's Guide (Second Edition), Ken Sherman, Reston, 1985. This is one of the best-selling books ever on data communications. It is not oriented to PCs or any particular kind of computer, but is very general in scope and thorough in technical detail.

Technical Aspects of Data Communication, John E. McNamara, Digital Press, 1982. An earlier edition of this book formed the text for a university course on Data Communications taught by a colleague of the authors. He reports that it was excellent for the purpose and well liked by the students. McNamara's writing is very technical, good for reference, and somewhat minicomputer oriented.

Computer Networks, Andrew S. Tannenbaum, Prentice-Hall, 1981. Something of a classic.

Data Communications, Networks and Distributed Processing, Uyless Black, Reston Publishing, 1983.

BOOKS ON SPECIAL COMMUNICATIONS TOPICS

A Programmer's Guide to Video Display Terminals, David Stephens, Atlantis, 1985. Everything you always wanted to know about every VDT under the sun.

Packet Switching, Roy D. Rosner, Wadsworth, 1982.

KERMIT: A File Transfer Protocol, Frank da Cruz, Digital Press, 1986. (See comments in the text on Kermit.)

Data Compression (Techniques and Applications; Hardware and Software Considerations), Gilbert Held, John Wiley, 1983.

Modems and Communications on IBM PCs, W. David Schwaderer, Wiley Press, 1986. Somewhat mistitled, this book is mostly about programming in BASIC for communications on PCs. It will have a limited audience, but Schwaderer, an IBMer, does a thorough and excellent job of covering his subject.

Essential Guide to Bulletin Board Systems, Patrick R. Dewey, Meckler Publishing Corp., Westport, CT. Advice on setting up a BBS. (Unreviewed.)

X.25 Explained (Protocols for Packet Switching Networks (Second Edition), R. J. Deasington, Ellis Horwood Limited/Halsted Press, 1986. A short but illuminating treatise on X.25 and associated standards, including ISO Transport, and CCITT recommendations X.21, X.3, and X.29.

Modem Handbook for the Communications Professional, Cass Lewart, Elsevier Science, 1987. An easy-reading and technically thorough book on modem technology, applications, and products. The presentation is a little sloppy at times, but this is an invaluable text for nonengineers who seek deeper information about modems. Lewart gives considerable attention to PC modems.

The Elements of Networking Style, Michael A. Padlipski, Prentice-Hall, 1985. Another classic, feisty and informative.

SNA: Theory and Practice, Anura Guruge, Pergamon Infotech Ltd., 1984. A fine book covering details of SNA from soup to nuts. Does not discuss LU products or details, so information on LU 6.2 is lacking.

The SNA Handbook, Xephon Technology Transfer, Ltd., 1987. Good coverage of SNA and the products that implement it.

Handbook of Computer Communications Standards, Volume 1: The Open Systems Interconnection (OSI) Model and OSI-Related Standards, William Stallings, Sams, 1987; and *Volume 3: Department of Defense (DoD) Protocol Standards*, William Stallings, Paul Mockapetris, Sue McLeod and Tony Michael, Sams, 1988. Two good technical overviews of protocol stacks and associated standards. Neither covers technical details.

Inside OS/2, Gordon Letwin, Microsoft Press, 1988. A good general introduction to the workings of OS/2, written by the original chief architect of the system.

Internetworking with TCP/IP, Douglas Comer, Prentice-Hall, 1988. A detailed presentation of TCP/IP and the evolution of design choices in the system. Scant attention to the high-level protocols.

MAGAZINES AND PERIODICALS

Computer Communications Review is the quarterly publication of the ACM's Special Interest Group on Data Communication. It is oriented to academic research and likely to be of limited interest to the average professional working in the commercial world. It does, however, have good coverage of news on standards.

Data Communications is a technically-oriented monthly covering practical aspects of computer communications. The quality of articles varies, but the best are excellent. It is also a great source for news. The subscription rate is $30 per year from P.O. Box 1508, Neptune, NJ 07754-9977.

LAN is a monthly magazine oriented to PC local area networks. It is indispensable for anyone who needs to keep abreast of the subject and the PC LAN market. The subscription rate is $18 per year from 12 West 21 Street, New York, NY 10010.

LAN TIMES is a monthly paper published by Novell for its users. The free publication concentrates on Novell's own LAN products and offerings from its subsidiaries, such as PCOX. 122 East 1700 South, P.O. Box 5900, Provo, UT 84601.

Online Access Guide is a bimonthly for navigators of online databases, published by Online Access Publishing Group, Inc., 53 W. Jackson Blvd, Chicago, IL 60604.

PC Free reviews public domain and low-cost software. Subscriptions are $18 per year from Riverside Data Inc., Box 300, Harrods Creek, KY 40027. Phone: 502-228-3820.

Plumb is a newsletter devoted to BBS information. The source is the same as for PC Free above.

APPENDIX J
STANDARDS BODIES AND PUBLICATIONS

Standards bodies are listed in alphabetical order by their initials.

ANSI—THE AMERICAN NATIONAL STANDARDS INSTITUTE

An arm of the federal government established to create standards for commercial use in the United States. 1430 Broadway, New York, NY 10018. (212) 354-3471.

Some of ANSI's best known documents are:

X3.4	American Standard Code for Information Interchange (ASCII)
X3.15	ASCII bit sequencing for serial transmission
X3.16	ASCII character structure and parity sense for serial transmission
X3.41	ASCII code extension techniques
X3.64	Additional Controls for Use with ASCII
X3.100	CCITT X.25
X3.106	Data Encryption Standard (DES) modes of operation

CCITT—THE INTERNATIONAL TELEGRAPH AND TELEPHONE CONSULTATIVE COMMITTEE

General Secretariat, International Telecommunications Union, Place des Nations, 1211 Geneva 20, Switzerland.
  Standards may also be purchased from:
  United States Dept. of Commerce, National Technical Information Service, 5285 Port Royal Road, Springfield, VA 22161. (703) 487-4650
  and
  OMNICOM, Inc., 501 Church Street, N.E., Suite 304, Vienna, VA 22180. (800) OMNICOM or (701) 281-1135.

V.21	300-bps duplex modem for use on PSTN
V.22	1200-bps duplex modem for use on PSTN and leased circuits
V.24	List of definitions for DTE/DCE interchange circuits
X.25	DTE/DCE interface operating in the packet mode on PDNs
X.28	Start-Stop PAD
X.75	Gateway using international circuits between packet PDNs

EIA—THE ELECTRONIC INDUSTRIES ASSOCIATION

2001 Eye Street, Washington, DC 20006. (202) 457-4966.
  The EIA has published:

EIA-232-D	Interface Between DTE and DCE Employing Serial Binary Data Interchange
RS-449	General Purpose DTE/DCE Interface
RS-422	Electrical Characteristics of Balanced Voltage Digital Interface Circuits
RS-423	Electrical Characteristics of Unbalanced Voltage Digital Interface Circuits
EIA-530	High Speed 25-Position Interface for DTE and DCE

ISO—THE INTERNATIONAL ORGANIZATION FOR STANDARDIZATION

Also known as the International Standards Organization, **ISO** has about 90 member nations. It works closely with other standards groups, especially the CCITT, and draws support from many other organizations including computer makers and user groups. ANSI represents the U.S. at ISO deliberations, and other countries are similarly represented by their national standards bodies.
  Central Secretariat, 1 rue de Varembe, CH-1204 Geneva, Switzerland.
  ISO standards may also be purchased from ANSI and from OMNICOM (whose address is above).

ISO 646	7-bit character code—international version of ASCII
ISO 7942	Graphical Kernel System (GKS)

NBS—THE NATIONAL BUREAU OF STANDARDS

A branch of the U.S. Department of Commerce that adopts standards for use within the federal government.
  Gaithersburg, MD 20899.

INDEX